D1707943

# LE CORBUSIER'S FORMATIVE YEARS

H. Allen Brooks

# LE CORBUSIER'S FORMATIVE YEARS

*Charles-Edouard Jeanneret at La Chaux-de-Fonds*

**The University of Chicago Press** / *Chicago and London*

**H. Allen Brooks** is professor emeritus of art history at the University of Toronto and a past president of the Society of Architectural Historians. His earlier books include *The Prairie School: Frank Lloyd Wright and His Midwest Contemporaries* (1972); *Prairie School Architecture: Studies from "The Western Architect"* (1975); *Writings on Wright* (1981); and *Frank Lloyd Wright and the Prairie School* (1984). He served as editor of the thirty-two-volume set of Le Corbusier's drawings, *The Le Corbusier Archive* (the largest architectural publication ever undertaken, 1982–85), and of the one-volume anthology, *Le Corbusier* (1987), to which he was also a contributor.

The University of Chicago Press, Chicago 60637
The University of Chicago Press, Ltd., London
© 1997 by H. Allen Brooks
All works and texts by Le Corbusier © 1996 Fondation Le Corbusier (FLC), Paris / Artists Rights
    Society (ARS), New York.
All works by Peter Behrens © 1996 the estate of Peter Behrens / ARS
All works by Auguste Perret © 1996 the estate of Auguste Perret / ARS
All works by Frank Lloyd Wright © 1996 the Frank Lloyd Wright Foundation
All rights reserved. Published 1997
Printed in the United States of America

06 05 04 03 02 01 00 99 98 97   1 2 3 4 5
ISBN: 0-226-07579-6 cloth.

The University of Chicago Press gratefully acknowledges generous grants in support of the publication of this work from the Graham Foundation for Advanced Studies in the Fine Arts and from an anonymous donor.

Frontispiece: Charles-Edouard Jeanneret, self-portrait (for details, see page 472).

Library of Congress Cataloging-in-Publication Data
Brooks, H. Allen (Harold Allen), 1925–
    Le Corbusier's formative years : Charles-Edouard Jeanneret at La Chaux-de-Fonds / H. Allen
Brooks.
        p.   cm.
    Includes bibliographical references and index.
    ISBN 0-226-07579-6 (cloth)
    1. Le Corbusier, 1887–1965—Childhood and youth.   2. Architects—France—
Biography.   3. Architects—Switzerland—Biography.   I. Title.
NA1053.J4B76   1997
720′.92—dc20
[B]                                                                          96-22865

This book is printed on acid-free paper.

*I wish to dedicate this book to*

Gérard and Anne Prache of Paris
who opened the door of France to me
and made research for this book such a pleasure

*and to*

Wayland and Gwendolyn Drew of Bracebridge
for their wonderful friendship

# CONTENTS

# PREFACE

No individual since the Renaissance, it could well be argued, has influenced our built environment more profoundly than Le Corbusier. Whether as writer, urbanist, or architect, his ideas—although not always his architectural forms—have had a dramatic impact on the world in which we live.

This study, stemming from my interest in the origins of creative genius, focuses on Le Corbusier's formative years, those first thirty-three years that predate his acquiring his well-known pseudonym in 1920. During these years he evolved ideas and attitudes that guided him throughout life. And to better comprehend the man and his work, I have combined biography with the study of architecture, painting, and city planning, as well as the social and cultural environment in which he lived.

Concerning these early years, representing nearly half his life, Le Corbusier cultivated an image that led biographers astray. His seven-volume *Oeuvre Complète,* its title notwithstanding, excludes all buildings built during the first seventeen years of his architectural practice, an omission that allowed him to promote the impression of child prodigy. This study, on scores of historical and interpretive points, will endeavor to set the record straight.

Over 95 percent of the present book is based on primary, unpublished sources. The research has been an exhilarating experience; I have enjoyed a great privilege. I have seen and read vast quantities of material no eyes had seen since it was created in the earliest years of the twentieth century.

When I began my research, in 1973, amazingly little was known about Le Corbusier's early years—except what he himself had chosen to reveal. I was told that little more could be learned. Yet after nearly a decade of ardent effort, the contrary proved true; I unearthed so much that another decade was spent organizing and condensing the material into a book of reasonable length.

Among my happiest finds was discovering that his father kept a journal; eventually all the volumes were retrieved. What, after all, does a biographer say about a child, a youth? Yet these journals revealed much about the boy's character and personality, about his health, the developing eyesight problem that forced him to change his profession and ultimately resulted in the loss of vision in one eye. I also learned about his rapport with his parents and his brother, and about his evolving interests and activities. His father's account books offered further information.

Also recovered were the complete records of his schooling, as well as the minutes of the commission of the Ecole d'art detailing his activities there, first as a student but later as a teacher at the school. For later years there were thousands of pages of letters, hundreds of drawings and paintings, and several previously unknown sketchbooks recording his extensive travels. Concerning his professional career I retrieved the interrogatories of his lawsuit against Anatole Schwob; these completely revise our conception of the design process lying behind this famous villa. Likewise acquired were preliminary projects for all of his early villas, the villas Fallet, Stotzer, Jaquemet, Favre-Jacot, and Jeanneret. Yet perhaps most significant was finding the draft manuscript for his first, never-published, book, "La Construction des Villes" (The Building of Cities)—a study he labored on for several years.

Upon discovering new documentation in Switzerland, I deposited duplicate photocopies in the Bibliothèque de la Ville at La Chaux-de-Fonds whenever the originals could not be transferred. I realize I risked preemptive publication, yet I disapprove of scholars who hoard. Moreover, I believed that anyone utilizing this material would focus narrowly on the issues therein, which has proved true. My footnotes, therefore, do not necessarily acknowledge the precedence of articles based on documents I had gathered many years before—unless, of course, the writer drew significant insights from the information thus obtained.

I also taped oral histories with many of Jeanneret's closest friends and colleagues—all now dead. Léon Perrin (1886–1978), Jeanneret's schoolmate, traveling companion, and dearest friend, provided a wealth of information as well as guiding me through all the relevant local sites. Max Du Bois (1884–1989) revealed startling new facts about Jeanneret's early professional career which he substantiated with letters and documents. René Chapallaz (1881–1976), Jeanneret's first partner in the practice of architecture, provided further insights, as did his extensive archives. Others include Marcel Montandon, Jeanneret's chief draftsman at La Chaux-de-Fonds, Emile Biéri, builder of the Villa Schwob, Jean-Pierre de Montmollin, Jeanneret's lifelong confidant and banker, Mme Raphy Schwob, his client, Lucien Schwob, Maurice Ditisheim, Paulo Röthlisberger, and Hélène Stotzer. The one person I most regret missing (by eight years) was Le Corbusier himself.

I am most grateful for financial assistance I received as a Guggenheim Fellow in 1973–74 and subsequently for fellowships from the Canada Council and the Social Sciences and Humanities Research Council of Canada, both organizations providing supplementary grants as well. The University of Toronto helped with travel awards and allowed me several unpaid leaves of absence.

I also wish to thank numerous individuals who facilitated my research in essential ways, especially those who aided me in gaining access to private collections: Jacqueline Jeanneret, Fernand Donze, Mark Albert Emery, and Dr. Georges Zwahlen. The Bibliothèque de la Ville and the Fondation Le Corbusier opened their archives and generously provided help over a period of many years. Others who graciously assisted include Hélène Augsburger, Françoise Frey, Françoise de Franclieu, John Glover, Jacques Gubler, Pierre Hirsch, Isabelle Morillon, Francesco Passanti, Jean Petit, Elsa Scharbach, and Evelyne Trehin, in addition to those recognized in the footnotes. To all I am much indebted.

H. Allen Brooks
Sans Souci, Ontario
September 9, 1996

COLOR PLATES

**Plate I.** Villa Fallet, La Chaux-de-Fonds, 1906. View from southeast. Terrace extension in foreground is modern. (Photo by author)

**Plate II.** Or San Michele, Florence, Italy. Niche containing Donatello's statue of St. Mark. Painted October 9, 1907. Note that this watercolor is a study of the inlaid marble niche, not Donatello's sculpture. 31 × 15.5 cm. (Fondation Le Corbusier, hereafter FLC, 2162)

**Plate III.** Villa Stotzer, La Chaux-de-Fonds, 1908. As built. (Photo by author)

**Plate IV.**   Villa Jaquemet, La
Chaux-de-Fonds, 1908. White paint
is modern. (Photo by author)

**Plate V.** Villa Jeanneret-Perret, La Chaux-de-Fonds, 1912. The dormer is rebuilt, roof material changed, second storey fenestration modified, and mosaics around window added. (Photo by author)

**Plate VI.** Villa Favre-Jacob, Le
Locle, 1912. Entrance. Colors original. (Photo by author)

**Plate VII.** *Persistantes Souvenances du Bosphore,* 1913 (written in ink at bottom right). Gouache on paper. 55.7 × 57.5 cm. (FLC 4099)

**Plate VIII.**  Landscape, ca. 1913–
14. Note Jeanneret's typical lemon
yellow sky. Watercolor on paper. 19
× 28 cm. (Private collection)

**Plate IX.** Villa Schwob, La Chaux-de-Fonds, 1916. Street façade. (Photo by author)

**Plate XI.** *Whimsical Parisian Land scape,* 1917. Written on verso: "par un dimanche matin d'hiver, froid de canard! 20 rue Jacob, Paris 1917." Pencil and watercolor on paper. 47.8 × 63 cm. (FLC 4074)

**Plate XII.** *L'Italienne*. Postdated 1917 but more likely 1918. Watercolor on paper, 35.5 × 51 cm. (FLC 4504)

# I

## LA CHAUX-DE-FONDS

*1887–1907*

# 1

## CHILDHOOD AND EARLY SCHOOLING

### *1887–1902*

Charles-Edouard Jeanneret was born on October 6, 1887, in the Swiss watchmaking town of La Chaux-de-Fonds, high in the Jura mountains, a region of supreme beauty little known to the tourist who seeks the more sublime experience of the snow-capped Alps. The region lies just north of Neuchâtel, is almost crescent-shaped, and terminates near Geneva (to the southwest) and Basel (at the northeast). To the south it is bordered by Lakes Neuchâtel and Bienne, and to the north, although interrupted by the deep gorge of the river Doubs that creates a natural boundary between France and Switzerland, the Jura extends well into France—indeed as far as Besançon where the Doubs circles back in search of its rendezvous with the Saône. The French Jura, nearest Basel, is called Franche-Comté while in Switzerland the region is known as Franches Montagnes. South of the Jura lies the broad Plateau (Lausanne, Fribourg, Bern) that separates the Jura from the Alps.

The character of the Jura and its inhabitants profoundly influenced the future Le Corbusier, as anyone who has experienced the powerful visual imagery, the changing qualities of light, and the stern Calvinist nature of the people can well appreciate. Geographically speaking, the region was uplifted and then horizontally compressed thus bending the earth's surface into waves whose long valleys (now pasturelands) slope gently upward along their flanks to rounded, tree-capped summits: mountains by virtue of their height (the Chasseral is 1,607 meters or 5,273 feet) but with the appearance of

**Fig. 1.** La Chaux-de-Fonds, ca. 1900–1910. View toward the northwest. The hill in the background is the Pouillerel, on the lower slopes of which Jeanneret would build five houses between 1906 and 1916. (Bibliothèque de la Ville, hereafter BV)

well-groomed hills. The landscape is peaceful and majestic around La Chaux-de-Fonds and quite unlike the harsh, craggy Jura near Ornans that we know from Courbet's paintings. Except for the Doubs, no rivers gorge this setting, indicating much about its character and suggesting why La Chaux-de-Fonds was settled fairly late—a lack of running water (fig. 1).

The most distinctive feature in this landscape is the *sapin,* the French word for those majestically tall, straight, and symmetrical evergreen trees of the spruce or fir family, irrespective of their actual species. The spruce (*Picea*) predominates in the high Jura, and often attains heights of 140 feet or more with branches cascading ceremoniously to the ground. Each tree is so perfectly formed as to convey the impression that it was individually grown which, due to the Swiss system of reforestation, is virtually true. Free from neighbors, its branches develop fully and the lower trunk is never obscured by underbrush; closely grazed grass, lush and green due to the abundant rainfall, carpets the ground. Capability Brown would have been proud of this casually arranged land-scape, and it is understandable why Jeanneret's art school chose the stately *sapin* as the leitmotif for its regionalist style of design.

These isolated valleys were first settled by farmers, many of whom, like Jeanneret's ancestors, were escaping religious persecution in France. The remoteness of the high Jura, with its long, severe winter, afforded the protection they sought; yet in return it imposed a lonely, difficult life devoid of active communication or trade with the outside world. Home manufacture and self-sufficiency were the rule, and cheese, produced and stored at home or by a neighbor until weather permitted transport, provided the major item of trade until gradually superseded by watchmaking, which had its origins at the end of the seventeenth century. The latter, initially, was a family activity that kept other-wise idle hands busy during the long winter months when both the family and the herds were confined under the single farmhouse roof.

Many of these buildings still exist, continuing to serve the purpose for which they were built. Dates over doorways attest to the pattern of settlement. Passing along the valley road to La Sagne, where Jeanneret's mother was born, one reads on successive houses the following dates: 1661, 1721, 1734, 1683, 1692, 1682, 1726, 1687, 1711, 1833, 1762, 1675, 1790. Except for some modern conveniences, life therein has little changed.

Each region, often each valley, has its distinctive architectural type. Houses in the high Jura are characterized by their broad, low-pitched roofs, usually one storey above the ground. Le Corbusier, who nurtured a lifelong fascination for these forms, claimed they originated in the Languedoc and Armagnac regions of France, the region from which he also traced his ancestry. Built from the sixteenth till the early nineteenth century—a long period during which only minor stylistic change occurred[1]—their basic theme was that of protection against the winter cold.

Jeanneret was immensely fond of these Jura farms and, once his school days ended and his travels began, he would choose, each time he returned home, to abandon the comforts of his family domicile and spend the winter, often alone, in such a Jura farmhouse. Thereafter the symbolic significance of its unique central room (basically a giant chimney called "la chambre du tué") remained with him for life. In Chapter 6 we will discuss how this room-sized chimney found repeated expression in Le Corbusier's work, first in his project for a church at Tremblay, then the Assembly Chamber at Chandigarh (and by extension the General Assembly chamber of the United Nations in New York), and finally at the church in Firminy conceived near the end of his life.

Le Corbusier insisted that his ancestors arrived in the high Jura possibly as early as the mid-fourteenth century (when settlement first began) yet certainly by the 1600s when earlier records had been destroyed by fire. He was convinced that his family emigrated from former Albigenses territories in the Languedoc or Armagnac regions of France. Precise documentation is lacking, yet the significant fact is that he himself attached great importance to both the ancestral and architectural aspects of this story.[2] Later in life he relished the idea of tracing his lineage to southern France and thereby substantiating his claim to being (1) French rather than Swiss, (2) of Mediterranean origin, (3) and descended from the heretical Albigenses (since he considered himself to be a heretic). He also sought to associate Jura architecture, of which he was so fond,

1. A modest stylistic change occurred during the eighteenth century when the ends of the lateral walls, extending slightly forward (in antae) under the gable roof, assumed the character of classical pilasters; also the bargeboard of the gable was broadened and ornamentally treated with graceful curves. Previously such embellishments did not exist.

2. See Le Corbusier, *Croisade, ou le crépuscule des académies* (Paris, 1933), p. 33; Maximilien Gauthier, *Le Corbusier, ou l'architecture au service de l'homme* (Paris, 1944), p. 13; Le Corbusier, *Creation Is a Patient Search* (New York, 1960), p. 19; for the most carefully researched version, see Jean Petit, *Le Corbusier lui-même* (Geneva, 1970), p. 22. All these accounts vary somewhat in their dating.

with France. He recalled how three such farmhouses stood in an area designated "les Jeanneret" or "la Combe Jeanneret" on old maps and how one of these buildings—which he often visited in his youth before they were destroyed by fire—bore the Jeanneret name, coat of arms, and date of 1626.[3] "La Combe Jeanneret" is still found on maps, located a few kilometers from Le Locle on the road to La Chaux-du-Milieu. However, no habitation remains, just some scattered stones.

Place of family origin is significant to the Swiss. In times past, the amount and extent of social assistance to destitute families was paid by the town of origin and not by the community where they actually lived. Therefore for the Jeannerets, including Le Corbusier, Le Locle is their place of origin. It is an old town, settled in the fourteenth century and proud of the fact. To this day there exists a subtle rivalry, mingled with resentment, that the industrious watchmaking residents of Le Locle hold against the upstart—yet more prosperous—commune of La Chaux-de-Fonds, the sociological reasons for which will soon be discussed.

"La Chaz de fonz" is first mentioned in mid-fourteenth-century documents as a summer grazing ground used by inhabitants of a nearby valley (probably Fontaine-melon). The name is descriptive. *La Chaux,* which is derived from old French, may mean meadow, and therefore is a common prefix for names of Jura towns. *Fonds* means at the bottom or end of, so La Chaux-de-Fonds means the meadow or pasture at the end of the valley. At the opposite end of this valley lies Le Locle 7 kilometers away.

By 1523 La Chaux-de-Fonds had sufficient settlers (documents indicate thirty-five in 1531) to build a church, but a charter granting the status of commune (and separating it from Le Locle) was not forthcoming until 1656 by which time the population approached one thousand. In 1794 there were 4,392 inhabitants (Chaux-de-Fonniers) when, on May 5, fire destroyed more than fifty buildings and left 172 families homeless.[4] This date, 1794, remains central to the town's self-image. Statistics imply that much survived the flames, but local tradition vehemently maintains that the eighteenth-century town was utterly destroyed and that this explains La Chaux-de-Fonds' urban ugliness to this day.[5] The town was rebuilt on its existing street pattern, yet in 1835 a grid plan for future expansion was adopted.[6] This included an axial thoroughfare that ran along the valley floor where one might expect to find a river bed—except for the absence of natural water (rain must be trapped on roofs and stored in cisterns for public

3. See Le Corbusier, *Croisade,* p. 33, and Jean Petit, *Le Corbusier lui-même,* pp. 22–23, where Petit illustrates a sketch by Le Corbusier of the Jeanneret-Gris coat of arms of 1660.

4. *1944: La Chaux-de-Fonds, Documents nouveaux publiés à l'occasion du 150me anniversaire de l'incendie du 5 mai 1794* (La Chaux-de-Fonds, 1944), pp. 23–24, 27, 37–38.

5. Elsewhere in Switzerland La Chaux-de-Fonds is sometimes disparagingly called "la ville triste."

6. Jean Courvoisier, *Les Monuments d'art et d'histoire du Canton de Neuchâtel,* vol. 3, *Les Districts du . . . et de La Chaux-de-Fonds* (Basel, 1968), p. 334, This volume, essential to a study of this region's architecture, cites the little-known fact that Charles-Henri Junot prepared the plan (approved on January 10, 1835) that was actually executed. Courvoisier observes that local tradition falsely ascribes to Moïse Perret-Gentil the

use). This avenue, which points toward Le Locle, was later named after the neoclassical painter Léopold-Robert, whose birth occurred eight days after the great fire. Other street names are more characteristic of local values and concerns; these include rue du Commerce, de l'Égalité, de l'Industrie, de la Liberté, de la Paix, du Progrès, du Succès. Not honored among these names, however, was the commune's exceptional tolerance, codified into law, of minorities and political dissidents, a fact that ultimately contributed greatly to local prosperity in a nation where the rights to reside, to engage in commerce, and to own property were determined not by the central government but by the individual commune.

By 1888, some months after Jeanneret's birth, the town numbered 27,500 inhabitants, a figure that gradually increased (36,000 in 1900, 37,500 in 1910) until 1917, when he moved to Paris. That year the population stood at 40,640, but the influenza epidemic of 1918 and successive recessions in the watch industry halted future growth. By 1995 there were fewer inhabitants than in 1917: 37,669. Yet physically the town was expanding at almost an alarming rate. Translated into human needs, this meant greatly improved living standards where previously overcrowding was endemic. On visiting the three small rooms (plus minimal kitchen) inhabited by the Jeannerets at 8, rue Jacob-Brandt one realizes how terribly crowded these conditions were.

Jeanneret's parents were married on May 11, 1883, after a year's engagement.[7] His father, Georges Edouard Jeanneret-Gris (1855–1926), was the son of Edouard Jeanneret-Gris and Lise Rauss of Le Locle. An older, unmarried sister, Pauline Jeanneret, often shared the family home while a brother, Henri, lived in more comfortable circumstances at Soleure with his wife, née Chêtelain. The Jeanneret-Gris were a family of artisans for whom financial worries were not an uncommon concern.

An explanation of the hyphenated system for Swiss surnames is relevant here. Jeanneret-Gris is a family name, being one branch of the numerous Jeannerets (Jeanneret being the diminutive of Jean or, in English, John). Probably the Gris originates from a physical description—that branch of the family with a propensity for gray hair, just as Jeanneret-Gros refers to physique, etc. Yet this system is complicated by the fact that a married man has the option of adding, after his own name, the family name of his wife. Thus Le Corbusier's father usually signed his name "E. Jeanneret-Perret" though on legal documents the name Jeanneret-Gris would take precedence. As a schoolboy Le Corbusier was initially confused by this procedure, signing his work "Ed.

---

authorship of the present plan, yet the latter's post-fire plan, although approved, was never laid out.

Le Corbusier is among those who assumed Perret-Gentil's orthogonal plan of ca. 1796 was actually executed (see his letter to Fritz Jung dated January 16, 1956, and published in *L'Impartial* of October 4, 1965).

7. His parents, brother Albert (1886–1973), and aunt Pauline Jeanneret (1849–1933), are buried in the Protestant cemetery, called St. Martin, at Vevey. Le Corbusier is buried beside his wife, Yvonne, at Roquebrune/Cap-Martin on the French Riviera.

Jeanneret-Perret" which, though in imitation of his father, was quite wrong; his name, like all his male grandparents, was Jeanneret-Gris—this is why library card-catalogues list Le Corbusier not under Jeanneret or Jeanneret-Perret but under Jeanneret-Gris.

His mother, Marie-Charlotte-Amélie Perret, called Marie (1860–1960), was the daughter of Frédéric-Louis-Marie Perret and Amélie Pingeon of La Sagne. Apparently Amélie Pingeon was previously married to Jacot by whom she had three children, Louis Jacot, Mathilda Jacot, and Elise Jacot (who married Sully Guinand), and then to Perret by whom she gave birth to Charles Perret as well as Le Corbusier's mother, Marie-Charlotte-Amélie Perret. Thus Le Corbusier's given name, Charles-Edouard, combines that of his uncle (his mother's brother) and that of his father and grandfather. By family and friends he was called Edouard, not Charles-Edouard.

Uncle Charles Perret was widowed early but not before a namesake was born. Later, when the father left for South America to seek his fortune, young Charles was left behind and virtually abandoned, financially speaking. Thereafter relatives undertook his care and this became a serious bone of contention within the Jeanneret household. To make matters worse, Amélie, the matron of the family and mother and grandmother of the two Charles Perrets, also lacked support since neither the Jacot nor the Perret finances were very strong. She lived with the Guinand-Jacot's until their situation greatly worsened and then, from September 1901, she was largely dependent upon the Jeannerets until to her death in 1906.[8]

Most revealing is what Le Corbusier wrote, or failed to mention, about his ancestors. Specifically he refers to grandfather Jeanneret's participation (alongside patriot Fritz Courvoisier) in the march on Neuchâtel during the revolution of 1848 and to the death in prison of a grandparent Perret for his actions in the uprisings of 1831.[9] The revolutionary family spirit, not Swiss patriotism, is the element of self-identification here. Edouard was also proud of the bourgeois social status, as merchants, of his maternal forebears as opposed to the humbler Jeanneret background of artisans and farmers. He emphasized this point by referring to the ancestral portrait of Monsieur Lecorbesier of Brussels painted in 1841 by Victor Darjou, an artist who, with great pride, he said had also painted the Empress Eugénie.[10] Moreover (in 1920) he adopted the gentleman's name as a pseudonym, after modifying the spelling and dividing it into two words in order to imply certain overtones of nobility—Le Corbusier.[11] It was actually Caroline

8. These latter facts are derived from Mr. Jeanneret's "Comptes de famille" (family account book) where expenses are scrupulously recorded (collection of Bibliothèque de la Ville, La Chaux-de-Fonds, hereafter designated as BV).

A cousin of Le Corbusier's was the artist Louis Soutter (1871–1942) whose mother was Marie-Cécile Jeanneret-Piquet of Le Locle.

9. Le Corbusier, *Croisade*, p. 34, and reported by Maximilien Gauthier, *Le Corbusier*, p. 16.

10. Reported by Gauthier, *Le Corbusier*, p. 16.

11. Actually it was Amédée Ozenfant who first suggested this. Because Jeanneret and Ozenfant were

Marie Joséphine Lecorbesier who married into the Perret family. Her father's portrait always hung over the piano in the Jeanneret home (fig. 4).[12]

Le Corbusier never wrote a true autobiography. And what accounts he left are particularly selective with regard to his youth. This has led biographers to accept Jeanneret's version, if available, otherwise to skim over the voids with generalizations often based on hearsay. One of the fruits of my research was discovering that the architect's father carefully kept a journal, all four volumes of which I eventually recovered. Few documents have so enriched the present work, especially those pertaining to the early years, and I suspect historians in other fields (mountaineering, meteorology, watchmaking, social history, etc.) will some day rejoice in these journals too. I refer to them as journals (the journal of Edouard Jeanneret-Perret) in deference to the French word and also to dispel the English notion of a daily diary. The entries were written each week or so and frequently embraced a single subject—thus their special value.

Edouard Jeanneret-Perret was a meticulous man; his records add much to our knowledge of the family. From account books we learn of family income, expenditure, and savings, and a notebook marked "Inventaire" even includes the acquisition of children! This entry is worth quoting: "6 October 1887—Thursday: *Birth of the "Second"* [son], *Charles-Edouard*. During that day labor pains announced the imminent arrival of the expected child. Again Dr. Landry was put in charge of the undertaking while I went back to work. He anticipated the birth would be at 9 o'clock in the evening. As 9 sounded, the child was there, another boy, fine and healthy, bigger than the first. Mrs. Grattiker, the nurse, took charge of him. All went well, he was put immediately on cows' milk and he drinks his bottle like a man."[13]

An earlier page in the inventory announces the firstborn, Jacques-Henri Albert, on Sunday, February 7, 1886, some twenty months before his younger brother. And on March 22, 1892, a shorter note reveals that "Marie had a miscarriage of two months and was in bed for ten days." This, coupled with a worsening depression, terminated the family's growth. At Edouard's birth, his father was thirty-two and his mother twenty-seven.[14]

---

writing most of the articles for *L'Esprit Nouveau* it became necessary to conceal this fact by adopting a variety of pseudonyms. Ozenfant began using his mother's name and advised Jeanneret to do likewise. However, Perret was the name of Auguste Perret, the architect. So Ozenfant suggested going back further in the maternal line and Edouard mentioned Lecorbesier. For several years thereafter he used the name Jeanneret for what interested him most, that is, painting, and Le Corbusier for architecture.

12. The portrait is now at the Musée des Beaux-arts, La Chaux-de-Fonds, donated when the Jeannerets moved from La Chaux-de-Fonds in 1919.

13. This "Inventaire" is in the collection of the Bibliothèque de la Ville.

14. Born the same year as Edouard, nearby at 27, rue de la Paix, was Frédéric Louis Sauser, better known by his pseudonym as Blaise Cendrars. For a small provincial city, La Chaux-de-Fonds produced more than its share of notables: Cendrars, Le Corbusier, Léopold-Robert, and the man who became synonymous with the automotive industry in America—Louis Chevrolet.

Both boys were born at No. 38, rue de la Serre, a nondescript five-storey apartment building now bearing a commemorative plaque (fig. 2). At this address, on September 19, 1883, the parents first established residence in La Chaux-de-Fonds. Later, in June 1888, they moved to No. 17, Fritz-Courvoisier, and in December 1893 to a fifth-floor apartment, under the eaves and facing the narrow rue de l'Ouest (now renamed rue du Modulor), at No. 46, rue (now boulevard) Leopold-Robert,[15] where they remained during thirteen years of their children's youth (figs. 3–6).[16]

The boys' infancy was uneventful, their health being satisfactory in spite of Edouard's frail physique and the terrible cough he frequently had in winter. Notable was the time spent hiking and in the observation of nature. Mountaineering (climbing, not scaling) was their father's passion; he had joined the Neuchâtel Swiss Alpine Club in 1879, held the reins of its La Chaux-de-Fonds subsection when it was formed in 1884, and later served as president once the local club became independent in 1887; this post he reluctantly relinquished due to the depression of 1893.[17] From infancy his sons were taken on lengthy walks which proved immensely important to Le Corbusier's artistic development. Much later he would write: "From childhood my father took us on walks through the valleys and up the mountains, pointing out what he most admired: the diversity of contrasts, the staggering personality of objects, but also the unity of laws."[18]

Excerpts from the father's journal (now in the Bibliothèque de la Ville) will illuminate these early years:

> *December 25, 1889*—Decorated a small tree for our children who are a great joy. Albert plays with his toys. Doudou [age two years, two and a half months] is lost in contemplating a silver clad chocolate bar glittering on the tree.
>
> *October 6, 1890*—Our son Edouard having his third birthday and in perfect health, as is his brother Albert.
>
> *August 31, 1891*—Today our two sons begin school, at Miss Colin's [a private kindergarten using the Froebel method of instruction].
>
> *October 6, 1891*—Our little Edouard today reached his fourth birthday, in

**Fig. 2.** No. 38, rue de la Serre where the two Jeanneret boys were born. It, and its neighbors, are typical of the uniform, thin-skinned apartment blocks that dominate La Chaux-de-Fonds. (Photo by author)

**Fig. 3.** Jeanneret-Perret family portrait, December 1889. Charles-Edouard (on pedestal), Albert, and their parents. (FLC)

15. Changes of address were established from files at the Police des Habitants, Commune de La Chaux-de-Fonds.

16. "J'ai passé mon enfance au 46, de la Rue Léopold-Robert, à La Chaux-de-Fonds. Au quatrième étage nous dominions deux maisons de bardeaux, de style Sud-France, qui occupaient le milieu même de la rue Léopold-Robert . . ." Letter from Le Corbusier to Fritz Jung dated January 16, 1956, and published in *L'Impartial,* October 4, 1965.

These neighboring shingle homes were demolished about 1899 when the turreted, Victorian-style Banque Fédérale was constructed on the site.

17. Unable to afford the minor expense of his climbing trips any longer, he lovingly assembled a booklet comprising offprints of his annual reports as president, along with a newly printed title page: E. Jeanneret-Perret, *Mes vacances 1887 à 1892.* Neatly written inside the front cover is this dedication: "Mes chers enfants / C'est à vous que je destine ce petit volume . . . / Votre père / 26 mars 1892" (BV).

18. Le Corbusier, *Modulor 2* (Cambridge, Mass.: 1968), pp. 196–97.

**Fig. 4.** Living room at 46, rue Léopold-Robert showing Madame Jeanneret-Perret at her piano and the portrait of Monsieur Lecorbesier above. (Private Collection)

**Fig. 5.** Rue Léopold-Robert showing the shingle-roof houses that the Jeanneret-Perret family looked out upon from their fifth-floor apartment (under the jerkinhead roof) in the building beyond. This view predates the widening of the street into a boulevard. (BV)

District de
La Chaux-de-Fonds

**Fig. 6.** Boulevard Léopold-Robert, the main street in La Chaux-de-Fonds, shortly after it was widened. No. 46 is partway down on the right, the old Fleur de Lys hotel on the left. (BV)

good health except for a catarrh lasting several months and which we cannot cure.

*March 6, 1892*—Very fine weather, cold and wintry. Walked with Marie and the 2 children, Vue des Alpes and Hauts Geneveys. Left at 1:45, arrived Vue des Alpes 3:45. Left 4:15, arrived Hauts Geneveys 5 o'clock. Bad, snowy route, a little too difficult for the children and their mother. [At age four and a half Edouard had walked on a steep, snow covered mountain road for nearly three hours.] [In April, 1892, the boys had chicken pox and in August measles.]

*February 6, 1893*—Went yesterday with my two dear ones to Pouillerel [the gently sloping mountain between La Chaux-de-Fonds and the river Doubs]. Wonderful walk and beautiful view, but very cold. These two children hike well, are robust, especially Albert. Edouard, whose constitution is more frail, is rather thin, but these youngsters have survived the winter without coughs thanks to the cod-liver oil that we make them take.

*November 2, 1893*—[Albert] and his brother began taking piano lessons.[19]

*April 6, 1895*—Our Albert just passed his spring examinations with success, 110 out of 110—maximum. The boy gives us much pleasure. His brother is less conscientious.

19. During adult life Le Corbusier did not play a musical instrument, although from childhood onward his interest in music and rhythm remained constant and he devoted much thought and energy to finding ways to apply rhythm and numerical scale to architecture, culminating in the Modulor. See Luisa Martina Colli, "Musique," *Le Corbusier; une encyclopédie* (Paris: Centre George Pompidou, 1987), pp. 268–71.

*July 13, 1895*—Our two sons each took first prize in their class; this pleases us greatly. They leave at 3 o'clock to spend their vacation at Soleure with my brother. [As usual, much of their holiday was spent hiking, and on the nineteenth, from Fluelen, they mailed a postcard to "Ed. Jeanneret-Perret" with one of the signatories being "Edouard Jeannneret" (*sic,* misspelled with three n's).]

*January 26, 1896*—Edouard is in bed and once again coughs a great deal; the doctor says not to be alarmed, his lungs are still intact.

*August 1, 1896*—The children returned last night from their visit [with aunt Pauline for ten days] to Geneva and the Exhibition, enchanted, delighted, gay and in good health." [This was the Swiss National Exposition where the big attraction was the picturesque "Village suisse."][20]

Their mother's earlier trip to Geneva resulted in the earliest of Edouard's correspondence that I have found. The boys stayed home with aunt Pauline, who made sure they got to church, and papa took them on long walks. One of these letters, in a rather free translation, reads: "My dear mama I send you greetings, I miss you; we do our lessons well. I send you big kisses. We went to church. Mr. borel preached. We behaved well. Your little Edouard" (fig. 7).[21]

*February 6, 1899*—At home great undertakings: our Albert, who makes great progress in music, will play Wednesday in a concert with the Classical Choir at the Croix-Bleue: 2 solos and a trio by Mozart with his mother and his teacher. We have great hopes of success. This dear child gives us great pleasure, whether in his musical or his scholarly studies. He will be 13 tomorrow. His brother [i.e., Edouard, who is the black sheep of the family] is usually a good child, intelligent, but has a difficult character, susceptible, quick-tempered, and rebellious; at times he gives us reason for anxiety.

*September 19, 1899* [Edouard enters secondary school]—The musical studies of Albert continue regularly but there is so much to do, it is difficult. This is a major undertaking and let us hope that his mother was not misled in directing him into this career! [Unfortunately she was. Yet part of the fault lies with the instruction Albert received at La Chaux-de-Fonds where he was taught to force himself in the use of his fingers. Later, while at the conservatory in Berlin, his fingers cramped and he had to abandon the violin. As an alternative he turned to rhythmic dance and composing. His stuttering was perhaps a manifestation of these excessive pressures.]

20. Regarding the exhibition and Swiss village, see Jacques Gubler, *Nationalisme et Internationalisme dans l'Architecture moderne de la Suisse* (Lausanne, 1975), pp. 29–32.

21. Another letter reads: "Ma chère maman, Ton petit Edouard veux aussi t'écrire quelques lignes pour te demander si tu as du plaisir à Genève. On va aller promener au Doubs avec papa et nous deux. On t'en voié six bésé Edouard Jeanneret" (BV).

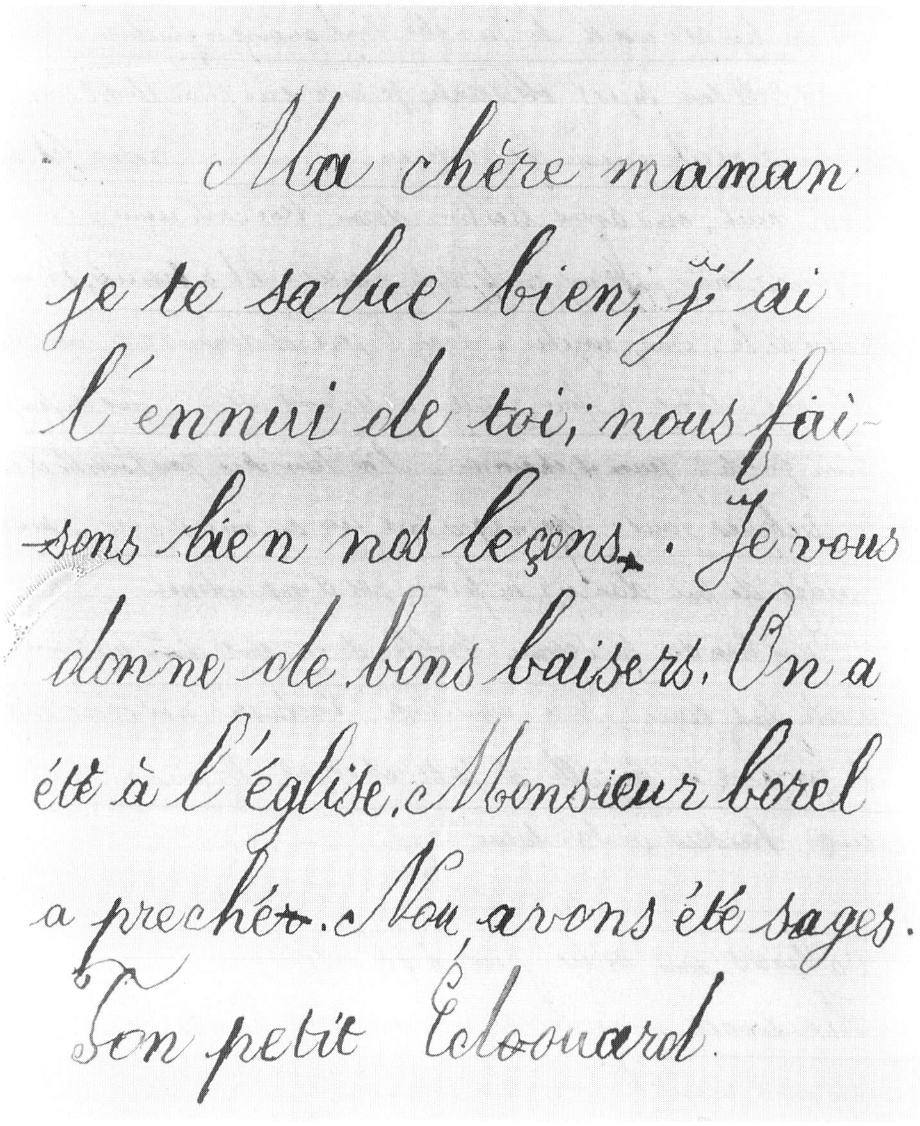

Fig. 7. Edouard's letter to his
mother, who was visiting Geneva.
(BV)

Ma chère maman
je te salue bien, j'ai
l'ennui de toi; nous fai-
sons bien nos leçons. Je vous
donne de bons baisers. On a
été à l'église. Monsieur borel
a prèché. Nou, avons été sages.
Ton petit Edouard.

*October 25, 1899*—The poor boy [Albert] stutters more and more and we are
greatly distressed. . . . His brother is well, but a bit frail.

*March 1, 1900*—Mama, Albert, and Edouard are spending their time partici-
pating in a fairy tale that the Classical Choir is playing at the theater: "Blanche-
Neige et Rose Rouge." Marie accompanies, Albert plays in the orchestra, Edouard is the gnome "Le Sarcasme." These episodes always disorganize the family;
everyone is up in the air.

*March 27, 1900*—Our Albert left school the first of March in order to devote
all his time to music . . . he is a tall and handsome boy who gives us great plea-

sure, unhappily he stutters and he is sometimes difficult to understand.

*April 10, 1900*—Edouard obtained a good third trimester report; 3rd among 35 students, and one of the youngest; his enjoyment in drawing increases, and he paints flowers very well; he has begun taking courses at the Ecole d'art.

*September 11, 1900*—Albert continues his musical studies and practices his violin 5 to 6 hours each day. . . . Edouard continues at school where his work goes well, with much less effort than his brother.

*December 27, 1900*—[Christmas gifts clearly indicate the children's interests.] Christmas day dazzling; we had a little family reunion at home in the evening— grandparents, aunts, and cousins. No tree. Peaceful evening that ended with tea and candies. The boys received many gifts: from us, music for Albert, drawing supplies for Edouard; aunt Pauline gave him a magnificent book and contributed 20 francs toward Albert's studies; from grandpapa 5 francs each, and music and paints from my brother at Soleure. Since the death of my brother-in-law Sully Guinand [in 1897] our celebrations have lost their animation; the children are getting older, ideas change, and the parents begin to settle down.

*April 19, 1902*—Albert successfully passed his entrance exams to the Conservatoire at Berlin . . . Edouard has also just been admitted to the Ecole d'art at La Chaux-de-Fonds. [Therefore, two years after taking his first art course, Edouard became a full-time student at the school—a logical moment to interrupt these excerpts from the father's journal.]

When reading these journals one develops a warmth and affection for this man who was Le Corbusier's father. His gentle, ever-present concern for loved ones is most touching, especially against the harsh background of adversities and worries he faced in business. At home he was a retiring man who sat in a corner and spoke when spoken to; often he was absent-minded and buried in his thoughts.[22] His real outlet for expression was the Alpine Club rather than his home where the dominant personality was his wife. She talked incessantly and had the unpleasant habit of contradicting others and ordering them around; she could be very possessive and brisk one moment, then very tender the next. She was of the people and exhibited a certain simplicity; her husband was more cultivated and more closed. Actually she was so dominating that throughout his life Le Corbusier remained a bit afraid of her in spite of his great respect and love.

---

22. During these years Mr. Jeanneret became disenchanted with the political party to which he initially adhered, the so-called "Parti Radical" which in Switzerland represented the middle-class establishment (right of center) as opposed to the socialists (left of center). One quote from his journal, written during the depths of the 1893 depression, will indicate his feelings: "Il y a des armées de gens sans travail dans les grandes cités. . . . Il y a aussi beaucoup de déperdition du sens moral, de la notion du bien chez les prolétaires, mais les revendications des masses sont légitimes, la séparation entre les deux castes est devenue trop grande, la classe moyenne (base d'un édifice solide) disparaissant rapidement" (January 7, 1893).

Everyone who knew the family can tell you about Madame; she left indelible impressions. Everyone speaks of her musical talents, yet in truth this seldom extended beyond childrens' piano lessons and occasionally collaborating with local instrumentalists. And all who know the family agree that Edouard was his mother's son, and that Albert was his father's.[23]

The journals, even these excerpts, make clear that Albert was the favourite son.[24] He seemed more gifted; his personality was exemplary. He was strong, healthy, and good-looking. And his mother had decreed that he, like herself, should be a musician. Architects who met her late in life (she lived until her hundredth year) have told me that when they complimented her on her talented son she thanked them for their kind remarks concerning Albert, never realizing that Edouard was her more gifted son.

The watchmaking industry, for which Edouard was initially trained, was introduced into the Jura late in the seventeenth century when Daniel Jean Richard (1672–1741), a locksmith from La Sagne, undertook to repair a traveler's English-made watch. Not only did he get it running, he copied the movement and, with his sons, began making watches. During the eighteenth and much of the nineteenth centuries watchmaking remained a home industry, ideally suited to snowbound families in winter. Specialization gradually increased. One person might be occupied with some aspect of the movement, another with the case. It was handicraft manufacture; each item was usually unique. Edouard's grandfather specialized in decorating watch faces, often with floral designs, while Edouard's father worked on something new: the perfection of watch faces of unblemished white enamel—thus reflecting the clients' desire for simplicity in a neoclassical age.[25] Edouard's own specialty was to be engraving designs on the backs of pocket watches; this is why he went to his hometown's industrial art school. The Jeannerets also sold watches, their name appearing on the face (see fig. 57). Thus they bought the movement from others, then designed and produced the case. One or two

23. For this résumé of the parents' personalities I am especially indebted to Mlle Lily Sémon, who lived in the apartment below the Jeannerets during their stay at No. 8 Jacob-Brandt from 1906 to 1912 and therefore saw them almost daily; she also studied piano with Madame Jeanneret. Likewise I am indebted to Mlle Hélène Stotzer (whose parents built the house designed by Edouard in 1908), Léon Perrin (Edouard's closest childhood friend), René Chapallaz (architect), and J. -P. de Montmollin of Neuchâtel, who later became Le Corbusier's most intimate and trusted friend.

24. Albert's studies at La Chaux-de-Fonds, Berlin, Geneva, and Hellerau were financed by his parents, the considerable disbursements being carefully recorded by his father. Edouard, by contrast, financed his own education. He did this by designing three houses, working for architects in Paris and Berlin, and receiving a grant for writing and research. He kept his money carefully in the savings bank, asking his father to make the withdrawals when funds were needed. And later in life he helped support his brother.

25. During the latter part of his life, with reminiscences of his youth growing ever stronger, Le Corbusier himself turned to enamelling as an art form. Ronchamp's great processional door is perhaps his most familiar example. Yet much earlier, during his 1909 stay in Paris, we find him sketching the small, late fifteenth-century Limoges enamel of Saint Christopher at the Louvre (Foundation Le Corbusier, hereafter designated as FLC, 1974).

employees assisted in the shop. Sales depended on orders, yet no one promoted sales.

By the turn of the century, however, the industry underwent a fundamental change. Consolidation took place. Home manufacture gave way to ateliers and these in turn were superseded by small factories that produced watches with interchangeable parts. Sales and promotion were soon professionalized. In all this the Jewish community played a leading part. In La Chaux-de-Fonds, unlike most Swiss towns, Jews, during the latter half of the nineteenth century, were gradually accorded such privileges as the right to settle, and later granted permission to engage in trade, and finally to own property, all of this occurring at La Chaux-de-Fonds long before it happened elsewhere. Thus, locally, the Jewish community was stronger and more numerous than in other towns (such as Le Locle) and they soon turned their talents to putting watchmaking on a modern, industrial basis and setting up a highly efficient system of promotion and sales. The financial benefits thus derived were twofold. On the one hand La Chaux-de-Fonds soon prospered more than many of its neighbors, a fact destined to lead to certain jealousies.[26] On the other hand the greatest economic rewards went to those who established these new industries. And because (initially) most of these entrepreneurs were Jews, this turn-of-the-century period witnessed undue anti-Semitism which over the decades would gradually dissipate as men of other persuasions learned to share the leadership.[27] But when Edouard entered architectural practice in La Chaux-de-Fonds in 1912 it was precisely this newly monied, highly cultured Jewish community that provided most of his clients, even though he, like so many of his contemporaries, was not fond of doing business with the Jews.

This revolution in the watchmaking industry affected directly the Jeanneret family because their artisan enterprise was already a thing of the past. The depression of 1891–94 hit them particularly hard, and psychologically papa never fully recovered. It prematurely aged him and increased his propensity for worry and his dread of change. Family initiatives invariably came from his wife; he was the moderating influence. And her piano lessons made the financial difference. She earned about 50 to 80 percent as much as he; between their marriage and 1895 his salary (while working for his father) remained at 3,000 Swiss francs per annum, then rapidly rose to 4,400 by May 1898, at which date he acquired the business—changing the name from E. Jeanneret-Rauss to

26. How this jealousy might manifest itself I can illustrate with a personal experience. During the 1970s I procured a photographer to record the blueprints of Jeanneret's buildings at La Chaux-de-Fonds (the negatives are now at the Bibliothèque de la Ville). Soon thereafter I located the blueprints for Jeanneret's Villa Favre-Jacot at the Le Locle town hall. I requested permission to have my photographer photograph them. Permission denied; the blueprints could not be photographed. Happily, a nonresident overheard the conversation and drew me aside. Upon returning to the authorities, I offered to hire a Le Locle photographer to do the job. Permission granted. The case was clear-cut. Permission was dependent upon keeping my money in the local economy and out of the hands of La Chaux-de-Fonds.

27. To Charles Thomann, historian, I am indebted for many instructive conversations about the history and social structure of La Chaux-de-Fonds.

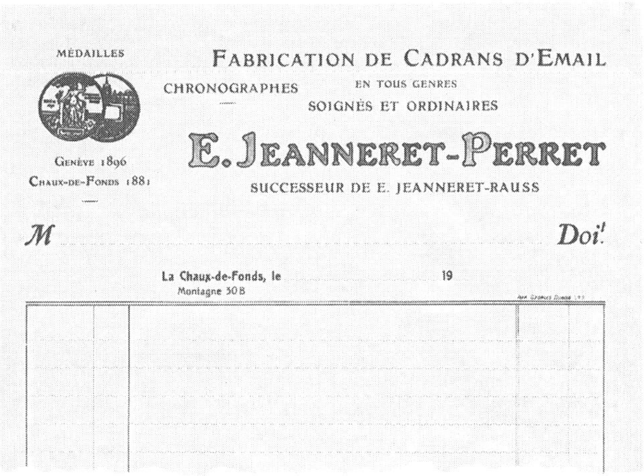

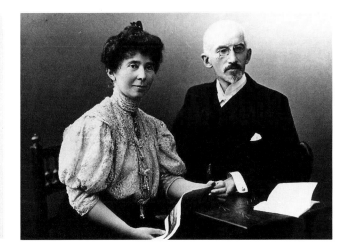

MÉDAILLES

FABRICATION DE CADRANS D'EMAIL

CHRONOGRAPHES EN TOUS GENRES

SOIGNÉS ET ORDINAIRES

E. JEANNERET-PERRET

SUCCESSEUR DE E. JEANNERET-RAUSS

GENÈVE 1896

CHAUX-DE-FONDS 1881

M Doit

La Chaux-de-Fonds, le 19

Montagne 30 B

E. Jeanneret-Perret (fig. 8). Meanwhile her income was 2,078 francs the year of their marriage, dropping off to 1,410 francs when Edouard was born and then rising to between 2,129 and 2,658 during the depression—after which it again declined. By May 1, 1900, their savings account contained 20,592.29 francs, up from 10,150.15 in 1894. Income from this fund paid for little luxuries such as summer holidays, trips to visit friends, and Christmas expenses; however, the principal was never touched.[28]

The depression began during the winter of 1890–91. It intensified without respite. Each month, each year, was worse than the one before. The journals of Jeanneret-Perret document it step by step. In 1892 he served as cashier for a committee to assist the unemployed. In December 1893 he declined the proffered presidency of the Alpine Club. His journal notes: "Little by little I retire from civic life in order to become more and more cloistered and ignored. Will I soon disappear completely!" By 1894, for financial reasons, he renounced his annual Alpine climb.[29] That autumn—suddenly—a dramatic change: a profusion of new orders. By 1898, the year of his father's retirement, he was much too encumbered with work to take his annual vacation or even a day of rest. New enemies had now appeared: competition from mass production and the introduction of new techniques, specifically photography and decalcomania—the process of transferring images from paper to other surfaces (such as watchfaces). Prices dropped enormously, and the skilled artisan was less and less in demand. He became ever more discouraged and depressed.[30] After 1900 he increasingly sold through Lon-

**Fig. 8.** Letterhead on invoice forms used by Edouard Jeanneret-Perret. (BV)

**Fig. 9.** Edouard's parents on their twenty-fifth wedding anniversary in 1908, with papa looking much older than his fifty-three years. (BV)

28. Financial data derived from the family account book (BV).

29. And of his work he wrote: "C'est fini, la fabrication des cadrans est flambée, il n'y a plus rien à en espérer" (July 10, 1894). And on August 1, 1894: ". . . nous sommes arrêtés à tous moments à l'atelier par défaut de commandes, et les prix sont tellement bas qu'on n'aurait pas osé même prévoir cela dans les deux mauvaises années de 92 et 93."

30. ". . . je ne réussis que médiocrement, j'ai beaucoup de peine, et des tourments sans nombre; l'année sous ce rapport [1900] a été des plus mauvaises, décourageante, et je suis bien souvent attristé du résultat de

gines, yet "Since I began working for Longines I have known anguish as never before; I have grown old. Their exigencies surpass what I can do and it is a constant battle to achieve the perfection they demand" (fig. 9).[31]

Why, at this gloomy moment, did Edouard's parents make the decision to apprentice their son to this frightful trade? This I cannot understand. Had the father not learned his lesson? Even though Edouard possessed skills at drawing, was this a reason to condemn him to a dying art? Alas, none of the documents contain an answer. True, La Chaux-de-Fonds was a one-industry town, but for Albert they had found another calling.

La Chaux-de-Fonds was and is the perfect example of a one-industry town. It exists to create clocks and watches and by 1914 controlled some 55 percent of the world's timepiece business.[32] Everyone works in the industry (horlogerie), or provides support services for those who do. There are some who gain more money and power than others, but that is the only real distinction. Absent is any social hierarchy based on institutions, such as a university, a military establishment, a seat of government, or an ecclesiastical center, because there are no such institutions in La Chaux-de-Fonds. Nor was there a nobility with its real, or figurative, social ranks.

Neuchâtel, though it lies but 29 kilometers away, possesses many institutions. It enjoys a long and illustrious history, had its princes, court, and nobility, has a fine university, a military establishment, and a governmental center as capital of the canton. In short, Neuchâtel had a social mix unknown at La Chaux-de-Fonds.

What La Chaux-de-Fonds possessed was its work ethic—combined with an abhorrence of conspicuous display. One lives to work, and the fruits of one's labor stay carefully cached away. No fine automobiles are seen at La Chaux-de-Fonds; if you have wealth, your car is no better than that of your neighbor, and the apartment block in which you live looks as ordinary as that of manual laborers. But once inside—once one penetrates within—one sees the comforts, the luxuries, and the fine collections that money can buy (and in the garage an expensive car used only for out-of-town trips where it will go unseen). Such attitudes, in origin, derive from religion, and anyone wishing to study the so-called Protestant work ethic might well begin at La Chaux-de-Fonds. Calvinism was strong in the region. The indefatigable reformer and orator Guillaume Farel (1489–1565) was pastor at Neuchâtel before going to Geneva where the young John Calvin became his assistant.

Le Corbusier, throughout his life, would remain a creature of his upbringing; he was

---

tant de persévérance et d'efforts. Pauvre métier et pauvre homme qui passe sa vie dans les inquiétudes, quelquefois imaginaires, le plus souvent réelles" (Journal, April 10, 1900).

31. Journal, November 7, 1900. He also suffered from rheumatism in both arms, and on his forty-fourth birthday (December 2, 1899) noted that "I am becoming old, and rapidly so." Then, to make matters worse, another recession began in 1901.

32. Jacques Gubler, "A l'heure des Horlogers jurassiens," *Revue Neuchâteloise,* 91 (Summer 1980), p. 7.

obsessed by the work ethic and by the belief that only through suffering and self-denial can one perform at one's best. He shunned luxury and conspicuous display, preferring, in Paris, to live under the roof in the Latin Quarter (20, rue Jacob) and to work in a cramped, clearly inadequate corridor at 35, rue de Sèvres (and for vacations built a small, flimsy wooden hut at Cap Martin).

The boys actually received their religious training from their aunt Pauline, their parents being less pious, often attending church only on religious holidays. They worshiped at the Independent Protestant Church, the word independent signifying that, in contrast to the National Church, no funding was received from the state. It was from Mr. Stammelbach at the "Temple Indépendant" that Edouard, during the summer of his sixteenth year, took the normal six weeks of formal religious instruction. Perhaps in later life he might be called agnostic, yet the Protestant faith had left a deep, indelible impression upon his mind.[33]

Concerning Edouard's academic education, my research uncovered all the records. They include each course he took, the grades he received, his examination marks, his relative standing among his classmates, the names of all his classmates, the number of times he was absent, and, for certain years, the reprimand or punishment if he misbehaved. The preservation of these records is a credit to the meticulous Swiss. Yet a detailed listing would be boring so I shall be brief.

Edouard began kindergarten on August 31, 1891 (at age three years eleven months) in Miss Colin's private Froebel class, continuing there through 1893–94 or the equivalent of his first year at primary school.[34] The second year (1894–95, called fifth grade in Switzerland where the numbering was from 6 to 1) he transferred to public school where he stood first in his class of 44 boys, 18 of whom were not promoted. These figures indicate why parents who could afford it sent their children elsewhere: classes were large (40 to 50), and the quality of the remaining students was low (18 out of 44 unable to pass their year). Edouard's first-place standing must be assessed in this light, yet throughout primary school he was always first, second, or third in his class.

After successfully completing six years of primary school, Edouard entered the Ecole Industrielle on April 25, 1899, the school being upgraded to the status of a gymnase during his three-year stay. He enrolled in the Section Réale, in which Latin was not

33. Jeanneret's creation, along with Amédée Ozenfant, of purism during the late teens and early twenties was certainly compatible with, and probably substantially influenced by, Jeanneret's Protestant upbringing.

34. The three years, at age four, five, and six, Edouard spent in Louise Colin's kindergarten class raises the question of whether her Froebel method of teaching influenced Le Corbusier as a designer. It seems highly probable. See Marc Solitaire, "Le Corbusier et l'urbain: la rectification du damier froebelien," *La Ville et l'Urbanisme après Le Corbusier,* Actes du colloque, 1987 (La Chaux-de-Fonds, Editions d'En Haut, 1993), pp. 93–117, as well as "Le Corbusier entre Raphael et Fröbel," *Journal d'histoire de l'architecture,* 1 (1988), pp. 9–25 (a publication of the Département d'Histoire, Ecole d'Architecture, Grenoble, France). Frank Lloyd Wright always acknowledged Froebel's influence, yet his introduction to the Froebel toys was in his ninth year, at which age the impact may have been more abiding.

required. His grades were less high and less consistent than in primary school where only in spelling, arithmetic, mental calculation (arithmetic), and gymnastics did he fail to receive top marks. In secondary school he often did best in languages (English, French, and German) as well as artistic design and music; he seldom received top grades in math. He took five years of German and three of English; French, of course, was taught each year. His most advanced math course was algebra (grade: 4 1/2 points out of a possible 6) taken during his penultimate year.[35]

During his last two years (six terms) his standing steadily declined. Ranked among 16 or 17 students, he placed as follows: 3d, 4th, 5th, 7th, 8th, 9th; thus by the final term he was in the *lower half* of his class—a dramatic change since primary school. Likewise, during these three post-primary school years, his absences increased: 0, 4, and 8. Reading between the lines, one assumes he was suffering from flagging interest, perhaps because since April 1900 he had also been taking courses at the Ecole d'art. A lack of commitment seems borne out by his "Carnet de Conduite et de Travail"[36] that his parents had to sign. Therein, on June 6, 1901, his algebra teacher wrote: "Student careless and negligent," and on September 25 his French teacher complained that he "talked with his neighbor while I was reciting the lesson," and on November 19 the same teacher imposed "1 h. of retention for letting something, I don't know what, fall which disturbed me." On December 18, 1901, his history teacher noted "Two hours of retention for punishment not fulfilled." This prompted the father to write, "I would appreciate knowing the reason for this punishment" and the following day the teacher answered: "During the last history lesson, Edouard left his seat in an unwarranted and noisy manner. His punishment was: to write three pages on the proper conduct of a student. The punishment having not been done, the Principal inflicted on the delinquent student two hours of retention. I hope in the future that Edouard's behavior will be faultless."

By the end of that school year (March 31, 1902), Edouard still needed two more years to complete the five-year program in order to graduate from the Gymnase. Instead, he transferred to the Ecole d'Art and began his training as a designer and engraver of watch cases. He was fourteen and a half years old.

35. It is informative to list his courses for a typical term, such as the first term (May–July 1900) in Classe IV of the 1900–1901 school year. The number following the course name is the grade, 6 being the highest grade possible. Spelling 5; French 5 1/2; Composition 4; German 6; English 6; Arithmetic 5; Accounting 3 1/2; Geometry 5; Design Tech. 4 1/2; Algebra 4 1/2; Surveying 6; Physics 5; Chemistry 5; Zoology 4 1/2; Botany 5; Geography 5 1/2; History 5 1/2; Writing 4: Artistic Design 6; Music 6; Gym 5; Conduct 5 1/2; total points 123; average 5.18; class standing, 3rd.

36. Private collection, Switzerland.

# 2

## L'ECOLE D'ART AND
## EARLIEST DESIGNS

### *1902–1907*

T he years spent at the Ecole d'art were crucial to Jeanneret's future. They witnessed a change in vocational orientation unimaginable except for the clear and decisive intervention of his strong-willed teacher, Charles L'Eplattenier. He and he alone determined that Jeanneret should become an architect, and with this decision the boy abided despite many misgivings about his mentor's choice.[1]

This five-year period represented the second stage of Jeanneret's education, embracing his fourteenth through nineteenth year. Thereafter a third phase, like a university education, would last four years. Largely self-directed, it combined extensive travel with two apprenticeships under well-known architects. Travel, then as now, was common among aspiring architects, and the absence of an architectural-school education was no hindrance in those days when no licensing exams set standards in the field. Finally, at the age of twenty-four in 1912, Jeanneret's student days would end and his professional career begin.

The Ecole d'art was not a place where one learned merely to paint and draw. It trained artisans who would contribute directly to the local economy. Through their

---

1. "il [L'Eplattenier] voulut faire de moi un architecte. J'avais horreur de l'architecture et des architectes" [mais] "j'acceptai le verdict et j'obéis; je m'engageai dans l'architecture" (quoted from Jean Petit, *Le Corbusier lui-même* [Geneva, 1970], pp. 25, 28). His letters, written while designing his early houses, express similar views.

artistic skill at ornamenting watches and other precious objects they would help maintain—and, it was hoped, increase—La Chaux-de-Fonds' share of the global market. Therefore the tuition-free school was financed and governed by the commune. Founded in 1870 by the Société des patrons graveurs, it was called L'Ecole d'art appliqué à l'industrie—an appellation akin to its objectives. Control then passed (1873) to the governing body of the town, the Conseil Communal, under whose authority, yet within the school itself, there was an elected commission headed by a president, and this commission elected a director to deal with day-to-day affairs. During Jeanneret's student days Henri Bopp-Boillot usually served as president and William Aubert as director, both men being staunch supporters of L'Eplattenier in subsequent periods of friction within the staff.

Knowledge of school affairs derives from the handwritten minutes of commission meetings, as well as their annual published reports. Jeanneret's father's journal provides additional information. The commission (and its executive committee, called bureau) met irregularly; they admitted new students, judged student design competitions, meted out discipline (both to students and to staff), settled disputes about salaries and teaching assignments, granted leaves of absence, and dealt with all policy changes within the school. Meanwhile the annual reports, entitled *Ecole d'art, La Chaux-de-Fonds: Rapport de la Commission* (followed by the year, and hereafter called *Rapport*), were intended for all those interested in the school. They summarized the year's activities (beginning in April and ending in March), sometimes contained excerpts from the inspector's report, often listed courses taught and the projects assigned therein, and always enumerated prizes and distinctions won by students.

Two divisions existed within the school, the "Classes professionnelles" for full-time, four-year contract students, and the "Classes du soir" for part-time students in the evening. The latter emphasized more general subjects such as "dessin artistique," "modelage," "dessin géométrique," and "perspective." Some of these courses were attended by Jeanneret during 1900–1902 while he was still in secondary school. In 1902, for example, there were only 60 full-time students among a total of 365 (334 boys and 31 girls) who took one or more courses at the school. No enrollment lists exist, thus making it is difficult to know which classes Jeanneret attended or which instructors he had each year.

One thing is certain however: L'Eplattenier was the predominant influence on Jeanneret and during the final two years was his sole instructor. Charles L'Eplattenier (1874–1946) was born at Neuchâtel yet raised in Les Geneveys-sur-Coffrane, a village in the Val-de-Ruz lying about midway between Neuchâtel and La Chaux-de-Fonds. His father died when he was twelve, and, having shown an early interest in the decorative arts and painting, he studied art briefly (1891–92) at Budapest while living with his aunt. Then, from 1893 to 1896, he went to Paris, first at the Ecole des Arts Décoratifs and later to the Ecole des Beaux Arts where his courses included painting and sculpture, as well as architecture. Following a sojourn at home, he then traveled in England, Belgium, Holland, and to Munich in Germany. He gained additional familiarity with England and her arts through an English friend, Clément Heaton II, who lived in Neuchâtel while executing decorations for the museum during the years after 1900. In 1898 L'Eplattenier received his appointment at the Ecole d'art, and during his holidays in 1900 and 1903 he visited Italy.[2]

Coincident with his appointment at the school, a dramatic increase in art journal subscriptions occurred that provides some index as to his interests. From a paltry two, both in French (*Gazette des Beaux Arts* and *Revue des Arts décoratifs*), subscriptions quadrupled to include three in German and two in English. Added were *Art et Décoration, Deutsche Kunst und Dekoration, Die Kunst, Berliner Architekturwelt, The Studio,* and *The Magazine of Art.* The latter, as well as the *Revue des Arts décoratifs,* were dropped in 1902 with *Innen-Dekoration* substituted in their place.[3] Understandably the decorative arts dominate the list, but remarkable is the emphasis given German publications in a French-speaking school. This German orientation would profoundly influence Jeanneret's future, including his studies, his travels, and the subject of his first published book: *Etude sur le mouvement d'art décoratif en Allemagne* (La Chaux-de-Fonds, 1912).

L'Eplattenier's usual courses were "dessin décoratif" and "composition décorative" (decorative design and ornamental composition), subjects basic to all areas of instruction within the school. This provided him with an omnipresence not shared by those who taught specialized subjects such as engraving, gem-setting, or enameling. The students, meanwhile, were expected to be proficient in both design *and* execution. To specialize in design only was not an option; the student who designed ornament must learn the technical and artistic skill to execute his or her own designs.

On April 15, 1902, the commission of the Ecole d'art met to admit new students into the various divisions of the four-year professional program. These included ornamental engraving (the mainstay of the school), jewelry, letter engraving, and painting on enamel (the latter was the specialty of Jeanneret's grandfather).[4] Each student's designs, previously judged and ranked by the teaching staff, were reviewed and ten of the seventeen candidates for the "Classe de gravure d'ornements" were admitted. "E. Jeanneret-

2. The best biographical source is the *Künstler Lexikon der Schweiz XX Jahrhundert* (Frauenfeld, 1958–67), pp. 571–72, although the romanticized biography by Maurice Jeanneret (*Charles L'Eplattenier* [Neuchâtel, 1933]) is also useful.

3. A list of library holdings was published in 1919: *Ecole d'art de la Chaux-de-Fonds, Catalogue de la Bibliothèque* (La Chaux-de-Fonds, 1919).

4. The *Rapport* of 1897–98 (p. 5) lists the revised program that became effective in 1898 and pertains to Jeanneret's course of studies.

> *Les classes du jour* ont 5 à 6 semaines de vacances par an; les élèves y sont admis dès l'âge de 14 ans après examens portant principalement sur le dessin.
>
> *En classe de gravure,* l'enseignement comprend: le dessin d'art, la composition décorative, le mod-

Perret 14 $\frac{1}{2}$ ans" was fourth on the nonalphabetic list of ten. Ages ranged from thirteen and a half to fourteen and a half so he was slightly *older* than the average.[5] The "Perret" was affixed to his name after another Edouard Jeanneret was admitted as number six. A Charles Jeanneret also studied at the school, Jeanneret being almost as common as Smith or Jones in Anglo-Saxon countries. To clarify matters, the administration began using his full Christian name, Charles-Edouard, on their records. Following enrollment, students were bound by contract to complete the four-year, tuition-free course of study.[6]

As we shall see, Jeanneret stood at the top of his (admittedly small) "Classe de gravure." He won first prize each of his first two years and the "Prix de distinction *Zélim Perret*" (open to students of any year) in his third.[7] Running second to Jeanneret each year was René Gigy (who designed the cover for the *Rapport* in 1903–4) while the other Edouard Jeanneret usually took third, fourth or fifth place. Competition, however, was rarely as severe as the commission wished; they openly complained that students showed greater interest in sports than in their studies, and the 1904–5 *Rapport* took the unprecedented step of publishing excerpts from the cantonal inspector's report that admonished

---

elage, la gravure practique. 10 heures de travail par jour avec obligation de suivre quelques cours du soir. La durée de l'apprentissage est de 4 ans.

The work load of well over sixty hours per week is most impressive, although the commission did complain that students were insufficiently conscientious about attending class. The commissioners themselves faced similar problems, and the *Rapport* of 1903–4 admonished their members who rarely, if ever, attended meetings.

5. This destroys the myth that Jeanneret was precociously young when entering the Ecole d'art, usually said to have occurred in 1900 at the age of thirteen. See Petit, *Le Corbusier,* p. 24, and Le Corbusier in *Creation Is a Patient Search,* p. 21, as well as the following footnote.

6. Full-time, or "interne" students (and probably their parents), were required to sign a contract guaranteeing completion of the four-year program. Le Corbusier implied, and sometimes specifically stated, that he broke the contract: "At thirteen [sic] I was put in art school; I had to sign a contract as an apprentice watchcase engraver; I broke [sic] the contract at seventeen. . . ." (Le Corbusier, *New World of Space* [New York & Boston, 1948], p. 10). His statement is dramatic but untrue. No supporting documentation exists in the minutes of the commission which judged such matters, and no mention appears in Mr. Jeanneret's journal or account books of paying the hefty 500 franc indemnity usually charged for a broken contract. Equally convincing is the fact that Edouard actually completed *five* years at the school (a detail completely overlooked by all his biographers) and therefore more than fulfilled his term of indenture. Thus the broken contract myth may be laid to rest along with many others intended to enhance his image as a precocious and rebellious youth.

Like many legends, this one is based on distorted fact. It *is* true that he failed to complete four years in the Classe de gravure, but that is because he switched into architecture and later into the Cours Supérieur, both changes being sanctioned by the school. And, concerning the previous footnote, it *is* true that he began taking "externe" courses in 1900, but he did not gain admission to the school until 1902.

7. He received prizes in specific courses as well. His first year, in the Classe de modelage, his "Tête de Lionne" received the Huguenin Virchaux award (the prize being a copy of Maxime Collignon's *Mythologie figurée de la Grèce*). In second year his "Modèle vivant (Académie)" received honorable mention, and in third year he tied for a third-place prize in the Classe de dessin artistique.

the fourth-year "Classe de gravure" for its abominable behavior (Jeanneret was then in third year).

Jeanneret stayed five years at the Ecole d'art, three years plus one term in the regular program followed by two years in the Cours Supérieur, the latter being founded under L'Eplattenier's direction in October 1905. Throughout this period his artistic development can be followed with precision, beginning in his first year (April 1902–April 1903) with exercises that encouraged general observation of nature as well as routine copying from books such as Owen Jones' *Grammar of Ornament.* By the second year Jeanneret was more carefully recording nature, not with photographic realism but rather abstracting and conventionalizing its most characteristic forms. Simultaneously the curving, unbroken line of the contemporary Art Nouveau became increasingly apparent in his work. By the third year the Art Nouveau thoroughly dominated his designs and a close stylistic comparison can be made with such French masters as René Lalique. This phase remained dominant even after his program was changed from engraving to the full-time study of architecture during his fourth year. This took place in June 1905, and briefly his building designs warrant comparison with the contemporary work of Antonio Gaudí in Spain or that of certain French architects.

A geometric style based on straight lines and right angles, which likewise had a basis in the observation of nature (rock strata, tree shapes, etc.), first appears in Jeanneret's projects in mid-1905, initially coexisting with, but later superseding, the curvilinear Art Nouveau. This stylistic change was perhaps encouraged by L'Eplattenier's ever increasing role in Jeanneret's education (in the Cours Supérieur, he was the only instructor). L'Eplattenier considered French art "frivolous," preferring the more disciplined art of Vienna. This tendency in Jeanneret's work was also fostered by the exigencies of architecture as well as his reading of Henry Provensal's *L'Art de demain* wherein an architectural style based on cubic shapes was advocated.

Jeanneret's initial year in the Cours Supérieur (October 1905–July 1906) saw him execute designs as well as conceiving them on paper. He designed and supervised the construction of the Villa Fallet as well as designing and engraving a watchcase that was exhibited in Milan in 1906. And along with others he participated in the design and execution of a music room at the Villa Matthey-Doret. During the second year in the Cours Supérieur (beginning September/October 1906) he and fellow students redesigned and constructed the interior of a small Protestant chapel at Cernier-Fontainemelon. Throughout this period geometric, crystalline forms almost completely supersede the Art Nouveau curve. Nature, however, remained the basis of his studies, with stone (the basic local building material) receiving more and more attention as Jeanneret sought to create columns, piers, and capitals whose forms and decorative qualities were derived from the characteristics of masonry rather than, as had been common throughout history, from living plant forms such as the lotus or acanthus.

A broad selection of Jeanneret's designs from this 1902–7 period exists, but their dating and chronology are not as simple and straightforward as the foregoing discussion might suggest.[8] The opposite, in fact, is true. Biographers have grouped his school drawings under a broad umbrella, such as "1902–6," without indicating any evolution throughout those years and often making no distinction between the drawings done during his student days and those created after 1912 when he became a teacher.

Assigning his drawings to a specific school year or actual date is aided—though sometimes hindered—by a variety of factors. These include an actual date (extremely rare), a signature the style and wording of which may be revealing, the size and kind of paper used, the subject matter, or a post-dating added by Le Corbusier much later in life (these, at best, are only approximations, yet the "L-C" accompanying such a date confirms the authenticity of the drawing). Ultimately, however, the essential factor in revealing the date is always the personal style of execution (connoisseurship, to use the art historian's term) and upon this I rely frequently in order to unravel the secret of the dating.

Turning from the general to the specific, each year will be discussed in succession, yet inevitably there will be some blurring at the edges in any attempt to assign each drawing or project to a specific moment in time.

## FIRST YEAR

On November 1, 1902, Jeanneret's progress at the Ecole d'art was noted by his father: "Edouard is making great progress at the school of art, he just finished two embossed and chiselled copper plaques with, to my eyes, splendid results: an architectural sculpture of a lion's head and a head of Calvin.[9] It is surprising that 6 months of schooling has brought such rapid results. His ornamental projects for watches are also interesting, several are remarkable. He is making some nice watercolor landscapes done out-of-doors; he is also attempting a little painting in oil."

8. Mary Patricia May Sekler's doctoral thesis *The Early Drawings of Charles-Edouard Jeanneret (Le Corbusier) 1902–1908* (Department of Fine Arts, Harvard University, 1973; later published by Garland Publishing, New York, 1977), is basic for the six-year period that it covers. In addition to the catalogue raisonné, the text discusses Jeanneret and L'Eplattenier's activities at the Ecole d'art and the dating of Jeanneret's drawings. However most of the classroom projects that I discuss and illustrate herein were unknown to Sekler; they are the fruit of my own research. Also unknown to her are many of the primary documents that I unearthed. These include the complete minutes of meetings of the commission (and its bureau) of the Ecole d'art, Mr. Jeanneret's journals, Edouard's letters to his parents, his primary and secondary school records, and scores of drawings (in addition to the school projects just mentioned) such as Jeanneret's various architectural studies for Beau-Site (1905) and for the Villas Stotzer and Jaquemet (1907–8). Obviously, therefore, my dating, which benefits from so much additional documentation, is sometimes at considerable variance with her's.

9. These plaques, or illustrations thereof, apparently have not survived, although the lion's head won a prize in the Classe de modelage.

One of these landscapes shows a typical Jura barn and is illustrated in figure 10. Dated "15 oct. 1902," it bears the monogram "E. Jt."[10] Edouard was fifteen and the watercolor is typical for a lad that age. Watercolor was also his medium when creating a gift for his father's forty-seventh birthday on December 2; the father's journal notes that "Edouard made me a nice painted frame for the photographs of my parents." The frame is a simple cardboard cut-out ornamented with painted scrolls.[11]

Other school exercises include copying artistic motifs from books, and one book superseded all others in importance. As Jeanneret himself recalled: "We had as our bible that large and magnificent folio by Owen Jones, *Grammaire de l'ornement,* a most splendid enumeration in color of the Egyptian, Asiatic, Greek, etc. styles . . . up to those of the middle ages."[12]

10. The date is on the verso and printed with the same orangish-brown watercolor as the monogram on the recto; surely it is integral with the original painting.

11. The frame is in the collection of the Bibliothèque de la Ville. Were we to believe Le Corbusier's exaggerated claims, he would, prior to this date, have already won a diploma of honor at the International Exposition at Turin, Italy, for his artistic skills. But more on this later.

12. Quoted by Jean Petit, *Le Corbusier lui-même,* p. 25. The French edition (1865) of Jones' 1856 book was used at the school. Le Corbusier also mentioned Jones in *L'Art décoratif d'aujourd'hui* (Paris, 1925), p. 135: "Ce livre était beau et vrai, car tout y était résumé de ce qui fut vrai, profondément *fait:* le décor du Sauvage, le décor de la Renaissance, du Gothique. . . . Avec ce livre, nous sentîmes que le problème se posait: L'homme crée une oeuvre qui l'émeut."

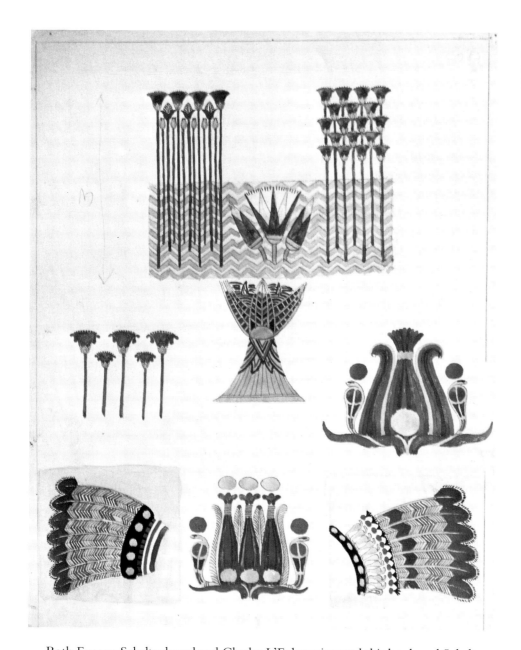

**Fig. 11.** Egyptian motifs copied from Owen Jones, *The Grammar of Ornament*. Watercolor, ca. 1902–3. 32.5 × 24.5 cm. (FLC 1779)

Both Eugene Schaltenbrand and Charles L'Eplattenier used this book and Schaltenbrand, before leaving the school in 1903, required that students in the engraving course copy motifs from Owen Jones (see *Rapport* 1901–2). Thus Jeanneret's copy-sheet, which is a composite of Egyptian motifs assembled from different plates, probably dates from this class (fig. 11).[13] The exercise elucidates one among Jones' numerous proposi-

13. Le Corbusier reproduced the topmost design from this sheet on p. 126 of *L'Art décoratif d'aujourd'hui* (Paris, 1925), thus explaining the publishers' notations (double arrow with number 3) to the left of the motif.

tions: "Flowers or other natural objects should not be used as ornaments, but [one should use] conventional representations founded upon them . . ." (no. 13). This statement summarizes a belief widely held by instructors at the school, that ornament should be based on natural things but conventionalized instead of rendered naturally; one should seek the essence of a thing rather than its visual reality.

Jones lists thirty-seven "Propositions," the first being that "The Decorative Arts arise from, and should properly be attendant on, Architecture." Another (no. 8) says that "All ornament should be based upon geometrical construction." A former student at the school, André Evard, reports that upon first meeting L'Eplattenier in 1905 he was handed Jones' book and instructed to copy the entire list of propositions.[14]

Concerning L'Eplattenier, his activities, and his position within the school, we learn much from the minutes of the commissioners' meetings. On July 4, 1902, for example, president Bopp-Boillot proposed that L'Eplattenier be sent as the school's representative to the International Exposition at Turin, Italy, because of all the staff "it is he who is the most able to profit from the visit and thereby profit the school." This was a nice vote of confidence. Then, during April 1903, four meetings were devoted primarily to his schedule. Due to the resignation of Schaltenbrand, who desired more time for private practice, L'Eplattenier was asked to take on several of his classes while retaining four hours of his own. Meantime rumors abounded that L'Eplattenier planned to resign and leave the community. In consequence thereof, he was invited to a special meeting called for the thirteenth at which he denied all rumors, observing that he had just (1902) built a house which should be proof enough of his intent to stay.[15] However, he requested a lighter, rather than heavier, teaching load because he needed time for his own work: "He wished to remain attached to the School by a minimum number of hours, with lessons given to the most advanced students."[16] (The latter remark holds premonitions of L'Eplattenier's more elitist "Cours Supérieur" established in 1905 and "Nouvelle Section" of 1912.) Concerning his own work we learn (December 3, 1903) that he requested a week's leave of absence in order to visit Paris concerning his commission from the commune to design an allegorical monument to the République Neuchâteloise, called "Hommage à la République" (which wasn't completed until 1910). This request was granted, as was one of March 1904 to spend five weeks in Paris. L'Eplattenier, unquestionably, was the most respected and prestigious teacher at the school.

14. Sekler, *The Early Drawings,* p. 101 n. 40, reports this from an interview with Evard.

15. The Police de Feu blueprints (no. 104) for the Villa L'Eplattenier are signed and dated "Ch. L'Eplattenier 24 juillet 1902." Yet it seems clear, as will be discussed later, that René Chapallaz played a role in preparing this design as well as that of the post office competition of January 1905. Still later, in 1916, he designed the "Projet de Transformation de l'Angle Sud-Est" (i.e., new lower-level entryway) at the Villa L'Eplattenier.

16. At the April 21, 1903, meeting it was agreed that L'Eplattenier would assume 17 class hours from Schaltenbrand and retain 4 of his former hours for a salary of 3,050 francs.

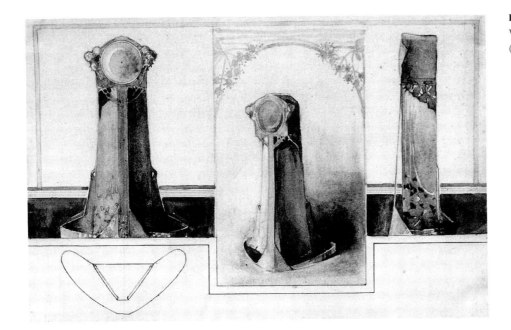

**Fig. 12.** Design for a table clock. Watercolor, 1903–4. 26.5 × 41 cm. (Private Swiss Collection)

## SECOND YEAR

Jeanneret's second year at the Ecole d'art began in April 1903.[17] This allows us to date his mantelpiece clock design that bears the signature "Ch.E. Jeanneret Perret 2e année" (fig. 12). The design represents a vine-covered tree stump with a flower stalk in front of it. The clock was later built and published along with a reviewer's comment: "The front has very stately lines, yet it is a varied piece of work with fretwork through which we see the beautiful colors of enamel. Discreet engraving and repoussé are among other qualities of this work."[18] Its form and silhouette probably derive from Edmond Becker's "pendulette" illustrated in the July 1903 issue of *Art et Décoration* (p. 232) to which the school subscribed. Jeanneret's design, however, substitutes Jura vegetation for the Parisian's roses, and eliminates the three legs while retaining the unusual triangular form.

17. The 1903–4 calendar was set forth in the *Rapport* of 1902–3 (pp. 13–14). Those sections pertaining to Jeanneret's second-year program are:

*Classe de gravure*
　　2me classe: Taille douce, raymolayé, ciselure, repoussé. Professeur: M. Lanz.
　　*Dessin artistique,* chaque classe 4 heures par semaine. Professeur: M. Aubert
　　*Composition décorative,* 18 heures par semaine. Professeurs: MM. Ingold et L'Eplattenier
　　*Modelage,* 4 heures par semaine. Professeurs: MM. Kaiser et Barbarier

In addition to the above, one was obliged to take several evening courses; the annual vacation that year was set for July 27–August 24.
　　18. *Revue internationale de l'Horlogerie,* 22, November 15, 1906, p. 1200. The published work is unattrib-

Two other watercolors can be assigned to this period due to their style and, as with the clock design, to their unusual signatures that incorrectly include Jeanneret's mother's name (Edouard was a Gris, not a Perret, as previously explained). One is an analytical, rather than pictorial, study of sapin branches and cones, exploring their structure and rhythms (fig. 13). Observe how the cone drawings (from right to left) examine the underlying geometrical pattern of the spiral grid, then the seemingly random outline of the scales and, finally, the naturalistic color study of the mature cone. A black and white illustration hardly does justice to this handsome work that combines outline, subtle washes, and areas of naturalistic color.

A third watercolor datable by its signature shows three pairs of watchcase designs; one pair is illustrated here (fig. 14). Perhaps each pair indicates exterior and interior designs for a single case. Stylized observable nature, rather than classical subjects as

uted yet sufficiently similar to Jeanneret's design to make attribution seem certain.

This design and its publication were previously unknown, therefore a brief history follows. In February 1903, before Jeanneret entered second year and produced the design, the school organized an exhibition of "cabinets de pendules" and invited the town fathers to attend. Impressed, the councilors asked (May 1903) that ten be selected and then (January 1904) authorized four of them to be built. No names were recorded in the commissioners' minutes, but at some point Jeanneret's design was apparently added to the group, because it was published along with the other four anonymous designs. All five demonstrate the domination of the French Art Nouveau tradition at the school, as opposed to the more stodgy, often geometric German clock designs being illustrated in *Dekorative Kunst,* 7, 1903, p. 114; 8, 1904, p. 65; 9, 1905, pp. 146–47.

**Fig. 14.** Designs for watchcases. Watercolor, signed on mounting "Ch. E. Jeanneret Perret," ca. 1903. 6.5 × 11 cm. (Private Swiss Collection)

**Fig. 15.** Four watchcase blanks engraved by Jeanneret, second and/or third year at Ecole d'art, 1903–5. (BV)

favored by many watchmakers at the time, recall the contemporary work of René Lalique and some of his French compatriots.

Jeanneret's earliest engraving exercises concerned technique, not originality, with designs copied from anonymous sources. Of five that I located (all five authenticated by a crudely engraved name or monogram on the back) one is on a thin, flat metal disk and is relatively uncomplicated in design; it probably dates from his first year at the school. The other four are on convex disks like true cases and have designs of much greater complexity; therefore they may date from his second and third year (fig. 15).

Other drawings attributable to 1903–4 include twelve nature studies glued to a large (35 × 65 cm.) sheet that is signed "Ch. Edouard Jeanneret." Two of these drawings are illustrated here (figs. 16,17). Observe the continuous outlines, including the frame, and the emphasis given to the curves, all of which fits the stylistic tradition at the turn of the century.[19]

On February 18, 1904, the commission met "to examine a small competition of report cards organized among the students of the school. Some 20 projects are exhibited. Chosen is the project (pen and ink drawing) of the student E. Jeanneret which is the best from the point of view of layout [*disposition*] as well as the quality of the design."[20] The card was lithographed and put to use (fig. 18). The landscape at the top (signed "Ch. Ed. Jeanneret") warrants comparison with those just discussed.

19. A preliminary study exists for figure 17, a pencil sketch mounted on the back of a watercolor that is postdated "1903 ou 1904" (FLC 2111).

20. Mr. Jeanneret learned of his son's achievement with the announcement of prizes in the spring: "Edouard vient d'obtenir une distinction en ce qu'il a été choisi dans un concours pour un projet de diplôme et une [sic] insigne pour le Club des Sports d'hiver" (Journal, June 12, 1904). Studies for the insigna I have seen, but not the finished work.

**Fig. 16.** Sketch of landscape. Pencil, ca. 1903–4. 12 × 9 cm. (Private Swiss Collection)

**Fig. 17.** Sketch of tree trunks, rocks, and leaves. Pencil with white highlights, ca. 1903–4. 9 × 7.5 cm. (Private Swiss Collection)

Unquestionably the finest work executed during his second year is a silver cane-handle presented to his father as a New Year's gift on January 1 1904 (fig. 19).[21] This skillfully tooled, highly professional design may have been prepared in L'Eplattenier's class since the latter was known to assign a "pommeau de canne" as a class exercise (see *Rapport,* 1901–2). Its whereabouts is today unknown but photographs of the original show a bird perched atop a spruce twig with its head bent down among the needles, thus creating a broad knob for one's palm while one's fingers would rest along the bird's back and tail.

From a comment in the father's journal of January 5, 1904, we learn that "Edouard has just made a gas chandelier of wrought iron for the dining room (he made the design for it) the manual work being executed by a local blacksmith. It is in the modern style. Mr. L'Eplattenier, his teacher, is very satisfied with this chandelier." No photograph, however, exists of this design.

On February 6 we see in the journal "Edouard at Bern to visit the exhibition of paintings by Segantini. What a lot of money we spend in our family, it's awful." And at

21. "Ed. m'a aussi monté [moulé?] et confectionné un très beau pommeau de canne en argent qui me fait le plus grand plaisir" (Journal, January 5, 1904). See *Dekorative Kunst,* 8, November 2, 1904, p. 86, for various German cane handles of this period.

year's end Jeanneret received the book, *Segantini,* by Marcel Montandon (Bielefeld and Leipzig, 1904) for winning first prize in his "Classe de graveur."[22]

The foregoing selection of projects, drawings, and executed works from Jeanneret's second year at the Ecole d'art clearly indicates the quality and occasional originality of his designs. Observable nature is, without exception, the source of inspiration, at times being studied with discerning care but frequently conventionalized into a more decorative scheme. His rendering style shows the influence of the Art Nouveau, and the work of those craftsmen was occasionally the source of his designs.

### THIRD YEAR

Jeanneret's third year at the Ecole d'art (April 1904–April 1905) saw the continued influence of the Art Nouveau. Likewise it witnessed increased awareness of an eyesight defect that eventually led to a reorientation of his life—and ultimately to a detached retina, the need for thick-lensed glasses, and exemption from military service. It also precluded continuance of such exacting work as engraving. Yet his fragile eyesight had existed *prior* to enrollment at the Ecole d'art; why, therefore, did his parents apprentice him to this visually demanding trade?[23] The first official hint of the problem is recorded on June 9, 1904 (soon after he began third year) when the commission considered the following petition from his father: "Read a letter from Mr. E. Jeanneret-Perret dating from 25 May, accompanied by a certificate from Dr. Speyr, physician–oculist, asking that his son Edouard, whose eyesight is delicate, be authorized to turn aside from [à se détourner de] engraving (several hours) in order to devote himself more especially to interior decoration and furniture. Agreed." A year later this reduction in engraving hours would be followed by its rejection, with architecture substituted in its place.

In spite of his reduced engraving load during 1904–5, Jeanneret ended the year by winning the "Prix de distinction" in the "Classe professionnelle de gravure." Jean Lanz was probably his principal instructor. He also participated in a student competition sponsored by the *Revue internationale de l'Horlogerie,* a trade journal based at La Chaux-de-Fonds. Announced on November 1, 1904, the regulations required projects to be submitted within thirty days and to include a design for two ladies' and one man's

**Fig. 18.** Report card for "Classe de peinture sur émail, Ecole d'art." Lithograph, 1904. 24 × 11 cm. (BV)

**Fig. 19.** Silver cane handle, 1903. (whereabouts unknown)

---

22. The dedication reads: "La Chaux-de-Fonds / 1904 / Ecole Spéciale d'Art Appliqué à l'industrie / Classe de gravure / 1er Prix Général / décerné à / Charles Edouard Jeanneret."

23. Albert, writing to his parents from Berlin (March 11–21, 1902), expressed concern that the required evening classes at the Ecole d'art might be "funestes à ses yeux déjà faibles." And again on May 6, 1902, he wrote: "Qu'Ed. ne se fatigue pas trop par ses cours du soir, il n'y a rien de plus mauvais pour les yeux." This same letter articulated another question insufficiently considered by the parents: "Pour ce qui concern Ed., j'espère bien qu'il deviendra autre chose qu'un graveur; son talent peut le mener plus haut." And three days later he again wrote his parents: "je trouve que de faire de lui un ouvrier graveur c'est le sacrifier; il peut arriver plus haut." L'Eplattenier and Albert recognized in Edouard qualities that the parents did not.

**Fig. 20.** Man's watchcase, entitled "Sapin." One of three designs that earned Jeanneret second place in the *Revue internationale de l'Horlogerie* competition of November 1, 1904. (*R.I.H.,* 1, 6e année, January 1, 1905, p. 20)

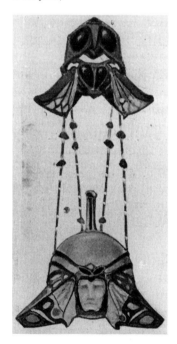

**Fig. 21.** "La Chrysalide," design for lady's pendant watchcase entered by Jeanneret in the *Revue internationale de l'Horlogerie* competition of November 1, 1904. (*R.I.H.,* 1, 6e année, January 1, 1905, p. 19)

watch. Jeanneret was awarded second place in a field of seventy; his prize was 50 francs.

Hitherto these designs were unknown—although they were actually published.[24] The man's watch, called Sapin, combined motifs from evergreen trees with the monogram CEJt (fig. 20), while the woman's pendant watch fused the pupa of a butterfly with a human face and was entitled Chrysalide (fig. 21). Louis Fallet, the Revue's specialist on ornament (and Jeanneret's future client), found the man's watch design too confused and reserved greater praise for La Chrysalide which he described as follows: "The head is of sculpted ivory and the wings are of turquoise and opal cloisonné enamel, as is the pin; the watchcase is of yellow gold." These pendants (see also fig. 22) appear strange to our eyes, yet perusal of contemporary German and French art magazines confirm that Jeanneret's designs are right in line with the times.

Three additional sheets of designs, each bearing the monogram E.Jt., may tentatively be dated 1904. One illustrates two pendants and two watchcases (the latter being glued to the larger sheet; fig. 22). Another depicts a richly ornamented lady's comb, its floral periphery enframing a pictorial landscape recalling the drawings in figures 16 and 17 (fig. 29, top left). The third is a handsome inlaid box rendered both in elevation and perspective (fig. 23). This design is more characteristic of German Jugendstil than French Art Nouveau, and its colors are predominantly olive green combined with yellow, orange, and accents of a lavender-red. It probably dates from the third year class in "Composition" because one project that year was "1 coffret bois incrusté" (see 1904–5 *Rapport*).

The most personal object designed and executed by Jeanneret while at school was a small, solid silver plaque combining his name ("Ch. Edouard Jt.") and the words "Ecole d'art" (fig. 24). Because this necessitated both the design and engraving of letters it probably was done in Albert Geel's class, "Graveur de lettre," which was required of all third-year students.

Extremely popular at this time was the type of metalwork known as repoussé wherein a thin sheet of metal (copper, brass, gold, etc.) is hammered from the back in order to raise a decorative pattern in relief. The technique was taught each year; we learned that Jeanneret in first year did a head of Calvin; in third year his "Model-age" class did a "Masque de Dante." Because no known likeness of Dante is known to exist, he was free to improvise. Figure 25, therefore, is probably Jeanneret's "Dante" although in actuality it is a portrait of Sigismondo Malatesta, another famous Italian, here wearing the laurel wreath that artists normally placed on Dante's head.[25] Perhaps it was because of this superb plaque that Jeanneret won the "Prix de distinction

24. *Revue internationale de l'Horlogerie,* no. 1, 6ème année (January 1, 1905), pp. 19–20, with the quotation from Louis Fallet (see below) being on p. 19. Other student designs were published in successive issues, perusal of which places Jeanneret's submission in better perspective.

25. On the back of this copper plate Le Corbusier wrote (in a black India ink that is rapidly becoming illegible) "gravé à l'âge de 16 ans par Ch. E. Jeanneret à l'Ecole d'art de La Chaux-de-Fonds," and on the

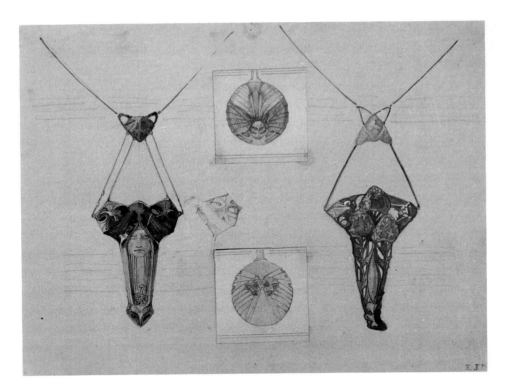

**Fig. 22.** Designs for pendants and watchcases. Pencil and watercolor on heavy paper (the two center designs are glued in place), signed "E. Jt," ca. 1904. 21 × 29 cm. (Private Swiss Collection)

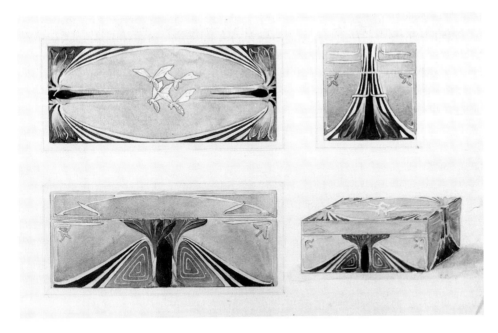

**Fig. 23.** Design for inlaid wooden box. Pencil and watercolor on heavy yellowed paper, signed "E. Jt.," ca. 1904. 32.5 × 52.5 cm. (Private Swiss Collection)

**Fig. 24.** Engraved silver plaque incorporating Jeanneret's monogram and the words "Ecole d'Art," ca. 1904–5. 6 × 4.1 cm. (Private collection)

**Fig. 25.** Embossed copper relief of Dante (actually Sigismondo Malatesta), ca. 1904–5. 14.8 × 10.5 cm. (FLC)

*Zélim Perret*" (the highest award, irrespective of year) at the conclusion of his third year at the school.

Before turning to Jeanneret's fourth and most momentous year at the Ecole d'art, we pause to mention family life as seen through his father's journal. The father remained grim concerning business, which continued its erratic pace. Long periods passed with insufficient work (especially in 1902, 1903, and the final months of 1904) interspersed

recto (almost invisible at lower right) the date "1905." Jeanneret turned sixteen in October 1903, so the dates fail to correspond.

The "Modelage" class was taught by either Edouard Kaiser or Armand Barbier, but most likely by the former. The "Masque du Dante" assignment is listed on page 14 of the 1904–5 *Rapport*.

To identify this figure, see illustrations accompanying the article "Le portrait de Sigismondo Malatesta par Piero della Francesca" by Michel Laclotte (*La Revue du Louvre,* 4 [1978], pp. 255–66; my thanks to Max Moulin for this reference). The exact source of Jeanneret's profile I have not found; perhaps it is a composite image.

with unusually large commissions as happened early in 1904 and then again from late 1905 through 1907. When times were good he would employ two or three helpers. Longines remained his most valued but exacting client and occasionally he suffered great difficulty in preparing the unblemished white watchface enamel for which his shop was known. Thus, when offered the presidency of the Swiss Federation of Watch-dial Manufacturers in 1907, he declined because of being overburdened with responsibilities.

Marie's earnings greatly augmented the family budget and made possible their modest life-style, yet her husband felt she failed to show sufficient prudence in how she spent it. In addition to teaching piano, she served as accompanist at various concerts. Her work required her to have full-time help (Christine left in June 1906 after seven-and-a-half years service), yet servants were not unusual then.

The family continued to live in their four-room walk-up apartment on the fifth floor at 46, rue Léopold-Robert until moving into a smaller, yet more modern, three-room flat at 8, rue Jacob-Brandt in October 1906. The move necessitated disposing of many of their former furnishings. Despite its size (hardly large enough for a single person by today's standards) the family of four plus servant welcomed this change and also the northerly view from the little iron balcony overlooking the railroad tracks, the center of town, and finally the slopes of the Pouillerel mountain beyond. Earlier that year, and prior to the move, grandmother Perret, the last of the grandparents, died of cancer after spending her final months living with the Jeannerets. Meanwhile the divisive situation regarding her son and grandson (Marie's brother and nephew), both named Charles Perret, had, by 1902, resolved itself when Mr. Perret took his son to Buenos Aires—yet the Jeannerets never received reimbursement for the 1,750 francs they advanced for the boy's support.[26] Close harmony existed only with three relatives: Pauline Jeanneret (now living in a flat of her own), Henri Jeanneret and his family, with whom New Year's was normally spent at Soleure, and Elisa Guinand née Jacot, Marie's step-sister (whose husband was now deceased), with whom they often celebrated Christmas.

Holidays and summer vacations were the highlight of every year, and these were financed with the interest from the family's retirement savings fund. In the summer of 1902, Edouard's first at the Ecole, he and his parents (Albert then studying at the conservatory in Berlin) visited Champex in the Valais where they climbed and hiked, the father staying two weeks, the others three (cost, 400 francs). Unfortunately Mr. Jeanneret contracted a cold which after five years he still could not dispel and had to learn to live with. In 1903 they had their twentieth wedding anniversary, yet no vaca-

26. The Perret family tombstone, sculpted by Léon Perrin and located in the La Chaux-de-Fonds cemetery, shows that Edouard's uncle and first cousin, Charles Perret (1859–1935) and his son Charles (1889–1935), died the same year. Two other sons died in infancy: Paul Perret (1894–94) and Emile Perret (1896–97).

tion was planned because of the recession; however, the two boys did spend four wet August days climbing in the Oberland. New Year's with Henri Jeanneret at Soleure was also canceled in order to reduce expenses. By early 1904 business improved, but during this mini-boom Mr. Jeanneret contracted pneumonia, after which he and his wife sojourned thirteen days at Clarens (270 francs). Then, in the summer, they rented an unfurnished two-room cottage, west of town and above the church at Eplatures, at Les Endroits. Edouard and his father walked the forty minutes to town each day. That summer he undertook his six weeks of religious instruction (as Albert had done in 1900) with Mr. Paul Stammelbach of the Eglise Protestante Indépendante; confirmation occurred on August 28. In December, at the annual banquet of the Alpine Club (with 160 in attendance and Albert providing the musical entertainment), Mr. Jeanneret received an engraved ice-axe in recognition of his twenty-five years of service—the longest of any living member. He used the occasion to announce his retirement from the committee over which he had presided for so many years. The club was his sole non-family interest throughout his life and their intermittent Sunday climbs (cost about 2.25 francs) were among his greatest personal pleasures.

In April 1905, as Edouard began his fourth year at the Ecole d'art, his parents traveled ten days in the lake country and in northern Italy, mainly Venice and Milan (530 francs). In July the boys were dispatched (with 200 francs) to Pralong in the Valais for two or three weeks of climbing. And in December Mr. Jeanneret celebrated his semicentennial; an event which caused some reflection:

> On the 2nd, I reached my 50th birthday! Is it possible, 50 years, with my hair entirely gray for so long, so long since I have appeared young; but one develops illusions every now and then; yet the rheumatic pain, my eternal cold (3½ years it has lasted), these weeks on end without the sense of taste or smell; meanwhile the boys are growing whiskers—all this is a warning of passing years.
>
> My dear wife is always energetic, although often spiritually and physically fatigued. Our Albert, soon to be 20, has not met the expectations we had of him at the age of 12—from the musical standpoint, which after all is his vocation; that is to say he works like a Trojan but lacks both subtlety and technical ease. The dear child, so good, upright, and honest, is an arduous worker, knowing no compromise when it comes to duty, occupied from morning till night with his studies. He is giving lessons to defray the cost of his violin, he drudges steadily but finds it difficult. Much taste and understanding, [yet] he doesn't attain the expression that he wants or should obtain. I don't believe he has enough companionship with his contemporaries; he is too serious and our milieu too dull to stimulate him. We wish he would return to a metropolitan center to complete his studies, where he would find an atmosphere compatible with his vocation. From our point of view he has stayed here too long with his teacher Pantillon, convinced that he could not obtain better teaching; yet he needs other things,

musicians for comrades and some contact with the outside world. All this is greatly disquieting for us. He played last night in a benefit at the theater, the Légende de Vimawski; it was well done, but imperfect because it lacked conviction, enthusiasm, spirit, and always certain lapses in technique.

Edouard, after his successful studies at the Ecole d'art, now jumps into architecture with great enthusiasm and dogged perseverance; he is a real slugger. But is he doing the right thing? Won't this new undertaking bring on its own frustrations?

None of these questions are intended to cheer our lives.

How clear it is from these words—as all others in the journal—that Albert is the more precious son, the one whose every success or setback is carefully watched, interpreted, and measured against the future, the boy in whom the family invests its pride, as well as its finances.[27] He is understood—analyzed in depth and with affection— while Edouard, in spite of his success at school, is relegated to the role of an enthusiastic slugger, somewhat frail of health, on whom less family effort is expended in trying to assess, comprehend, and guide him. At age fourteen and a half he was committed to the laborious task of becoming an engraver, this in spite of the fact that his eyesight was probably too fragile to withstand the rigors of the trade.[28] However there was no lack of love for him, and both sons gave their parents a tremendous amount of pleasure.

As previously noted, Albert left school in 1900 to devote full time to music. The next two years he spent in Berlin (Königliche Hochschule für Musik in the class of A. Moser) and following a summer at home (1903) he and his mother visited Henri Marteau at the conservatory at Geneva with the result that "it was decided that Albert will not return to Berlin, that he will spend the winter here while continuing his studies with Mr. Pantillon, yet this will be intercalated with a lesson from time to time with Marteau at Geneva, and that next year he will enter Marteau's most advanced class" (Journal, September 17, 1903). When the year was over, however, Albert had qualms about the plan and it was not until September 1906 that he finally left for Geneva. In the meantime he continued to make progress, especially after purchasing a new violin in 1905 that he financed by giving lessons, as well as by earning money from some local recitals that he gave.[29] He obtained exemption from the Swiss universal military service

27. Albert's room, board, and tuition at the conservatory in Berlin cost the family over 500 francs each trimester, yet, as previously noted, when Edouard took a day trip to nearby Bern to visit the Segantini exhibition his father observed: "Que d'argent on dépense chez nous, c'est effrayant." Similar remarks were never made when dispensing major sums for Albert.

28. See note 23 concerning Edouard's eyesight and misjudged talent.

29. In order to buy the 1,800-franc violin in August 1905, Albert borrowed 700 francs from his father who was happily surprised upon being repaid in full in March 1906.

due to a slight heart condition (a surprise to his parents) and a "faiblesse générale," and by 1906 we learn that he was studying dance—which very shortly became the major preoccupation of his life. That year cramps in his wrist gave him increasing trouble and by September, just prior to his oft-postponed departure for Geneva, his practice time with the violin was reduced to one hour per day. The severity of the problem just prior to resuming his studies implies that it was psychosomatic, a hypothesis confirmed by Marteau who, in answer to a worried parent, wrote "that this malady is in great part imaginary" (February 25, 1907). Albert's lack of self-confidence was part of the reason why he eventually remained a second year before completing his studies which, incidentally, were then costing his parents some 400 francs a semester for tuition and board.[30]

## FOURTH YEAR

Edouard, meanwhile, continued with his reduced program in engraving when the new school year began in April 1905, and on June fifth the commission received another request from his father: "that his son Edouard, student in fourth year, be exempted completely from engraving because of his desire to dedicate himself completely to architecture. After certain explanations given by the Director, this request was granted." The concerned father made further comments in his journal on June 12:

> Edouard has just completely renounced engraving despite the fact that he was the best student at the school in this field; he is about to begin architecture, pushed by his teacher L'Eplattenier who speaks glowingly of him and guarantees his success!?
>
> As a result of these ideas Edouard is urging us to buy land to build a house in the outskirts; his mother enthusiastically supports him without taking into account the disastrous consequences for me and for her of such an out-of-town location—deplorable for the practice of our professions. Nor do they consider the problems and anguish of loans, of mortgages, and of amortizations inherent in such undertakings. This unhappy idea has already been, and will again be, the cause of regrettable conflict between us. [N.B. The house was eventually built, but not until 1912.]

Thus it was L'Eplattenier—not Jeanneret's own initiative or questions of eyesight—who launched Jeanneret into architecture, a decision, incidentally, that aided and abet-

---

30. His 1906–7 report card, signed by Marteau, states: "Une connaissance approfondie de la technique du violon, et un très bon sentiment musical, telles sont les qualités principales de cet élève auquel il manque une certaine confiance en soi-même. Celle-ci et la maturité de l'âge apporteront ce je ne sais quoi qu'il lui manque encore. Joue le quatuor en artiste et compose très joliment" (BV).

ted L'Eplattenier's own interests at the school.[31]

L'Eplattenier's interest in architecture was demonstrably increasing; he had built his house in 1902 and had entered a design competition for the local post office during the winter of 1904–5. However, his real ambition was to establish a "Cours Supérieur d'art et décoration" open to both advanced and former students as well as those from outside the school. Likewise he wished to offer a "Cours de Conseil" for those seeking advice on matters of design or any of the professions related to the arts. He hoped thereby to raise the artistic level of the community and encourage others to enter the fine as well as the industrial arts (as was then occurring in Austria and Germany). All this we glean from the commission's meeting of April 13, 1905, where L'Eplattenier presented his proposal. In addition we learn from the 1904–5 *Rapport* that the students would be trained as artists, architects, painters, sculptors, industrial designers, etc., and that a maximum of fifteen would be accepted each year. The program was actually launched in October 1905.[32]

L'Eplattenier's course description gives additional evidence of his artistic attitudes.[33] He never speaks of training "designers" or making "designs" but rather of training "decorators" and "ornamentalists" and of studying "ornament" to be "applied to objects." His primary concern, like that of Ruskin, is with what is added to the surface of a thing rather than the thing itself. His approach, therefore, is typical of the nineteenth century. Years later Jeanneret would rebel against the "ornamentalist" side of L'Eplattenier's teaching as his diatribe in *L'Art décoratif d'aujourd'hui* (1925) makes clear. Another aspect of L'Eplattenier's teaching, however, remained forever an essential part of Jeanneret's method of design and that is his mentor's emphasis upon synthesis—the need to synthesize a vast amount of knowledge in order to produce an original design.

31. L'Eplattenier was a power to be reckoned with. He had enough clout, for instance, to ask for a reduced work load and simultaneous increase in salary—and get both. That was in April 1905. The previous year he got the administration to pay for the construction of a large mahogany sideboard that he designed. The commission, however, which was not informed, was very annoyed to learn of this project through the local press, then stunned to receive a bill for 2,400 francs—an amount almost equal to two-thirds of L'Eplattenier's annual salary! Yet L'Eplattenier emerged unscathed. Today this handsome but rather ponderous piece, with all its carved and hand-forged Jura motifs, languishes in a basement storeroom at the school.

32. The commission, after unanimously voting to accept the "Cours Supérieur," undertook necessary adjustments to the staff. In place of L'Eplattenier, Paul-Emile Ingold would teach ornamental design to the "Classe de Gravure," and the latter course would be reduced from three to two sections and taught by Jean Lanz and Albert Geel.

33. "C'est en ayant pour but de faire de vrais décorateurs que la plus grande partie du temps a été consacrée à l'étude de l'ornement. Suivant l'exemple des artistes d'autrefois, l'inspiration a été puisée dans la nature environnante; le sapin, la neige, ont été les principales sources d'inspiration, et ont donné des motifs qui resteront comme des types de la décoration du pays. Ces motifs ont été appliqués aux objets les plus divers correspondant pour chaque élève à la branche à laquelle il se consacrera (architecture, meuble, bijou ou décoration de la montre, etc.). . . . Le domaine de la décoration étant des plus vastes, il faut aux élèves un temps assez long pour devenir des ornementistes accomplis" (*Rapport*, 1905–6, pp. 14–15).

In directing Jeanneret toward architecture L'Eplattenier knew full well that the "Cours Supérieur" soon would be a reality. Likewise he knew that if Jeanneret left the "Classe de gravure" he would become L'Eplattenier's full-time protégé, a worthwhile objective since the boy was clearly the most gifted student in the school. Therefore events moved rapidly for Jeanneret as 1905 progressed. In June he substituted architecture for engraving, and by July was working on designs for Beau-Site. October saw him enroll in L'Eplattenier's "Cours Supérieur" and in November, when the commission decided to enter a watchcase exhibit at the 1906 international exposition in Milan, Jeanneret contributed. And before year's end he obtained his first architectural commission—the design of the Villa Fallet. Meanwhile he read widely on his own and this helped formulate, and confirm, ideas and values that he retained throughout his life.

On October 2, 1905, Jeanneret and fourteen others were admitted to the "Cours Supérieur d'art et décoration" as the inaugural class.[34] Thus he became a full-time student of L'Eplattenier's. Unfortunately, however, the annual *Rapport* does not list courses, projects, or prizes for the "Cours Supérieur," and Jeanneret less frequently signed and dated his work at this time. Therefore it becomes increasingly difficult to date his designs. Stylistically, however, the trend is away from more plastic, swelling, Art Nouveau forms toward tighter, more disciplined shapes that are more adaptable to construction. Drawings from these years include buildings, columns and capitals, nature studies, decorative patterns, and even watchcases. All are stylistically interrelated but we will begin with architecture because within days of changing his course of study from engraving to architecture L'Eplattenier came up with a new proposal; this was to allow the boy to participate in an architectural design project that was already underway. The story is complex, yet briefly told is this.

The Union Chrétienne de Jeunes Gens (analogous to the YMCA) was adding a building to its property at Beau-Site. L'Eplattenier had been a member of the jury that selected Robert Convert, an architect from Neuchâtel, requiring only that he make certain modifications to his competition design. With this, L'Eplattenier's official role had ended, yet the following year he urged Jeanneret and Léon Perrin to seek permission to see the plans and, because Perrin was a member of the Union, the secretary acquiesced.[35] Thereby L'Eplattenier obtained the revised plans and requested permis-

34. Of the 19 candidates presented for admission 10 were accepted outright and 5 conditionally. Among the former were René Gigy, Léon Perrin, Jeanneret, and Georges Aubert, who was the son of the school's director. Octave Matthey was admitted conditionally and André Evard refused.

35. Léon Perrin (1886–1978) was ten and a half months Jeanneret's senior yet two years ahead of him at the Ecole d'art where he won many prizes. His family, like Edouard's, came from Le Locle. His life was devoted to sculpture and his work may be seen in various parks and cemeteries around La Chaux-de-Fonds and Le Locle as well as at the museum in Château de Môtiers. He traveled (1907–9) with Jeanneret in Italy, Austria, and France and both taught together at the Ecole d'art beginning in 1912. Twice, in 1912 and 1916, he executed architectural sculpture for Jeanneret's early houses. I am much indebted to his friendship and many kindnesses; this book owes much to his personal knowledge of the events recounted herein.

sion of the building committee to make suggestions. This he did on June 14, 1905 (a mere seven days after Jeanneret's course was switched to architecture), presenting an oral critique while simultaneously stating that his visual ideas could better be demonstrated by his students who, therefore, were invited to submit designs.

The student drawings were ready by July 14 and a delegation was sent to see them. Being impressed, the entire council convened on the nineteenth at which time Perrin's north (principal) facade was accorded special praise. The minutes inform us that it "gives the building a more modest character than the facade of Mr. Convert"; elsewhere it is described as "picturesque." "Jeanneret's project, though very original, would be, from first impressions, very expensive if we execute it as it is; moreover his west facade recalls a little too much that of a Protestant church or chapel."

On July 21 the official architect was invited to inspect the plans: "Mr. Convert delivers a critique of the two projects which he insists are the work of decorators rather than of architects; he recognizes however that certain of the ideas are good and since most of the committee prefers the picturesque facade of Mr. Perrin he is willingly disposed to make a study along these lines." In a subsequent discussion (July 28) we learn something of Convert's original design: "He conceived of a monumental building in the classical style, now we propose to him an architecture of more modern taste in the villa style." And on August 7 Convert finally rebelled: "Mr. Convert believes that the influence of Mr. L'Eplattenier and his students is complicating the situation; he asks the committee to be sole judge of the designs that he will present, and states that the projects submitted by L'Eplattenier's students could not be carried out in an actual building."

When ground was broken on August 14, 1905, the plans were still unfinished; however, both the design and its style had undergone a complete change since their inception. The working drawings, which called for extensive use of reinforced concrete (Hennebique system), were finally submitted in November. But not until June 1907 did the inauguration take place.[36]

Neither Convert's nor Perrin's proposals for the Union Chrétienne have survived; the verbal description is all we have. Jeanneret's drawings were also presumed lost, yet fortunately I recovered and identified several of them. Attribution hinges upon three factors: the verbal descriptions quoted above; old photographs made prior to subsequent modifications in the dormer windows (fig. 26); and a small perspective drawing with "Ch. E. Jeanneret" carefully printed along one side and the date, written in longhand, "Juillet 1905" (fig. 30). This was mounted on a cardboard sheet carrying the subsequent notation: "Projet pour le bâtiment de l'Union Chrétienne de Jeunes Gens / Mai, Juin, Juillet 1905."

36. The full text of the relevant minutes of the Conseil de l'Union Chrétienne and of the Commission de Construction de l'Union Chrétienne is conveniently transcribed as Appendix I, pp. 346–54, in Sekler, *The Early Drawings*.

Fig. 26. Union Chrétienne de Jeunes Gens, Beau-Site, La Chaux-de-Fonds, 1905. Robert Convert, architect. The west, or entrance, facade is not visible here, only the north (attached to the old building) and east elevations. This photo predates the remodeling of the picturesque dormer windows of the central hall. (BV)

**Fig. 27.** Jeanneret's projects for the Union Chrétienne de Jeunes Gens, June–July, 1905. Pencil and watercolor on tracing paper. Sketch at upper left shows his earliest scheme while the watercolors relate to his final proposal for the west and east facades. 25 × 32 cm. (Private Swiss Collection)

One might assume this was the drawing presented on July 19 except that the west facade (left) does not recall, as the minutes indicate, "a Protestant church or chapel." Nevertheless another study of this west elevation (as well as the east elevation, both in watercolor on tracing paper) shows at the upper left a small pencil sketch of a "church" and this "church" presumably represents Jeanneret's original project (fig. 27). On the basis of this visual evidence two other sketches can be identified. One is in India ink on tracing paper superimposed over several pencil drawings that are difficult to discern. Apparently this is the rear view of the building looking toward the tower (fig. 28). Yet the most carefully drawn and shaded perspective representing this project is the one published in 1914 along with various (unidentified) student designs, the entire page being reproduced here because it shows typical examples of work done at the Ecole d'art (fig. 29).[37] The lady's comb at the upper left is also one of Jeanneret's designs.[38]

The published perspective is probably the one exhibited by Jeanneret on July 19, 1905, its symbolic reference to a church recalling the origins of the Union Chrétienne. Its plastic, sculptural forms (compare with Ronchamp) generally defy the nature of materials and confirm the statement of a design "very original" but "very expensive"

37. *L'Education en Suisse,* 10ième année (Geneva, 1914), p. 389. I am indebted to Jacques Gubler for discovering this published source.

38. Identification is possible because the original signed watercolor exists in a private Swiss collection.

and, according to Convert, "unrealizable." Its style is reminiscent of the Art Nouveau and thus suggests why Le Corbusier was fond of the architecture of Antonio Gaudí.

Of these two projects the one containing Jeanneret's name and date (fig. 30) is stylistically closer to the verbal description of Perrin's project as well as to the executed building (fig. 26). Therefore it was probably influenced by Perrin's design. But whether Convert's final scheme took ideas directly from Perrin's project or from Jeanneret's reinterpretation thereof cannot be known without knowledge of Perrin's lost designs (when I visited Beau-Site with Léon Perrin in 1974 I had not yet located these drawings by Jeanneret, and Perrin had no record of his lost designs). Many characteristics and motifs found in Jeanneret's Beau-Site designs reappear in other work, whether watch-case designs or villas. These include a predilection for symmetry, emphasis on geometric shapes (especially the equilateral triangle), and use of stylized, symbolic forms derived from the Jura. Note for example the equilateral triangles of the dormer windows (a motif derived from the sapin), the Y-shaped window mullions that recall tree branches, and the T-shaped foundation masonry that suggests the underlying crystalline structure of bedrock. Meanwhile the heavy trim, especially of the west facade, perhaps owes something to L'Eplattenier's post-office project from earlier that same year (fig. 40).

**Fig. 28.** Early studies for the Union Chrétienne looking from the rear toward the tower, June–July 1905. India ink and pencil on tracing paper. 27 × 23 cm. (Private Swiss Collection)

**Fig. 29.** Published designs by students at the Ecole d'art, La Chaux-de-Fonds. Jeanneret's first project for the Union Chrétienne is at lower left, a comb he designed at upper left. (*L'Education en Suisse,* Geneva, 1914)

**Fig. 30.** Second project: Union Chrétienne de Jeunes Gens, Beau-Site, signed and dated Ch. E. Jeanneret, July 1905. Ink and pencil on heavy paper. 16 × 25 cm. (Private Swiss Collection)

In analyzing Jeanneret's thought process it is useful to study his preliminary projects for Beau-Site, many of which are executed on the same squared notebook paper with a soft pencil and occasional highlights of watercolor. The sketch at the top left of figure 31 relates to Jeanneret's final project (see fig. 30), while the more rectangular classical temple form at lower right may be a variation on Convert's initial scheme. All the triangular shapes symbolize either rows of sapins (cf. figure 54) or even mountain peaks (fig. 32). The small plan (lower left) shows a central hall that could alternately serve as gymnasium or auditorium. The sketches in figure 33 (with one exception) are more compact, solid, and geometricized. A single triangular mass dominates the center of each design while stepped angular forms project symmetrically from either side. The monumentality achieved in these designs is very striking. All three of these sheets exhibit a quick, assertive drawing style showing none of the timidity or lack of self-confidence that one might expect of a seventeen-year-old making his first architectural design.

A variety of other architectural studies assignable to 1905–6 also exist, and some may be for Beau-Site. Those shown in figures 34 and 35 were once on a single sheet now torn in half (the tear marks fit exactly) and the paper is the same as for figures 31, 32,

and 33 (projects for Beau-Site) so their dates are probably the second half of 1905. Figure 34 may well be another study for the Union Chrétienne except for the heavily wooded site. Noteworthy is the monumentality of the design, the rigid symmetry of the entrance doors (compare with the Villa Schwob, 1916), and the corbeled motif over the doors. The triangular "sapin" dominates throughout.

The designs in figure 35 are square in plan though turned 45 degrees to the hillside; the elevations are emphatically vertical. This may be a preliminary idea for the Villa Fallet (the site is right) despite its excessive monumentality. Also extant are two water-color studies of this same design as well as a badly out-of-focus photograph showing three clay models, the one at the left being similar to figure 35 and the one to the right close to the executed design of the soon to be discussed Villa Fallet; in the background a third model is difficult to discern but located on a site similar to that of the Villa Fallet (fig. 36). The date is therefore autumn 1905 or the early months of 1906.

Other drawings, because of their identical size, paper, style, and other factors, can be assigned to the second half of 1905, and these provide additional insight into Jeanneret's interests and attitudes (figs. 37, 38, 39). Fondation Le Corbusier sheet no. 2461 was removed from a sketchbook consisting of long sheets stapled at the center, and there-

**Fig. 31.** Studies for Union Chrétienne, July 1905. Pencil and watercolor on ruled notebook paper. 22 × 18 cm. (Private Swiss Collection)

**Fig. 32.** Studies for Union Chrétienne, July 1905. Pencil and watercolor on ruled notebook paper. 22 × 18 cm. (Private Swiss Collection)

**Fig. 33.** Studies for Union Chrétienne, July 1905. Pencil and watercolor on ruled notebook paper. 22 × 18 cm. (Private Swiss Collection)

**Fig. 34.** Project, unidentified, ca. late 1905. Pencil and watercolor on squared notebook paper. 22 × 17 cm. (Private Swiss Collection)

fore, after being torn out, the two half-sheets constitute four sides. One side bears the stamp "Douane Centrale/Exportation Paris," implying that it was exhibited, plus the words "La Chaux-de-Fonds 1904 L-C." Such postdatings by Le Corbusier are always approximations; most factors favor the following year. Figure 37 is the recto of this sheet with the two chimney designs at upper right repeating motifs sketched on the adjoining page.[39] There are various drawings for buildings (two look like double houses except for the tower set between them) as well as numerous details (plans, doorways, stairways). In addition to the swelling, sculptural, Art Nouveau forms one is struck by the creator's passion for symmetry. Each drawing is a romantic conception, yet the designer's predilection for balance and order betrays a fundamental classical sensibility which, as we shall see, is found consistently in Jeanneret's work.

The fourth side of FLC 2461 illustrates facades, sections, and plans for an auditorium that could be a study for Beau-Site (fig. 38). This hypothesis gains both credence and doubt from additional drawings that, on one sheet, have sketches for the Beau-Site

39. The inspiration for this series of chimney designs is perhaps the same *Moderne Bauformen* source that inspired Henri Sauvage to undertake similar studies about 1903. See Robert Delevoy, Maurice Culot, et al., *Henri Sauvage* (Brussels: Archives d'Architecture Moderne, 1978), p. 96.

**Fig. 35.** Project, unidentified, ca. late 1905. Pencil on squared note-book paper. 22 × 17 cm. (Private Swiss Collection)

**Fig. 36.** Three clay (?) models, probably projects for the Villa Fallet. That at left is similar to figure 35, that on right corresponds to the villa as built. Winter, 1905–6. Old, out-of-focus photograph. (FLC)

**Fig. 37.** Architectural studies, unidentified, second half of 1905. Pencil on heavy tan colored paper. 18 × 25 cm. (FLC 2461)

**Fig. 38.** Architectural studies, unidentified, second half of 1905. Pencil on heavy tan colored sketchbook paper. 18 × 25 cm. (FLC 2461)

Fig. 39. Architectural studies, un-identified, but probably for the post office, La Chaux-de-Fonds, 1905. Pencil on heavy tan colored note-book paper. 18 × 24.3 cm. (Private Swiss Collection)

Fig. 40. Charles L'Eplattenier's competition designs for the new post office, La Chaux de-Fonds, submit-ted January 1905. 26.8 × 55 cm. (BV)

church tower *and* three versions of facades for the building shown in our figure, two of which have written over the doorway in barely legible letters "FLEUR LYS" and "HO-TEL FLUR [?] LYS" respectively. There was an Hôtel Fleur de Lys in La Chaux-de-Fonds but the connection here eludes me. More important are the drawings themselves—the conviction with which they are sketched, their originality, and their consistency of style. Right angles and geometric shapes are effaced in favor of soft, rounded corners and fin-de-siècle heart-shaped windows. Perhaps certain germinal ideas for Jeanneret's La Scala cinema of 1916 already exist here (see figs. 347–49).

Figure 39 is detached from the same sketchbook as FLC 2461. The highly original yet fanciful left-hand design shows freestanding piers with corbeled arches creating covered walkways with bay windows above; angular forms (sapin and rock strata) predominate throughout.[40] The right-hand project divides the building into broad bays of differing design, those at the center recalling the narrow, multi-storeyed arched windows seen in figure 35.[41] The setting is evident from the tree-lined mall, the three-sided exposure of the building, and the streetcar stop in the foreground; it is the site, as seen from the railroad station, of the new post office for which an inconclusive design competition had been held in January 1905. L'Eplattenier participated, his design paying far less attention to Jura regionalism than one might expect (fig. 40). The corbeled arches used over doors and windows probably encouraged Jeanneret's use of this motif and also the curious little spire set between corner gables on the roof (compare figure 35).

At the bottom right of Jeanneret's sketch are tentative studies for terminating the end of such a building, usually with a hexagon. This problem he investigates further in a pen and ink and pencil vignette at the upper left of figure 41, a sheet taken from the same sketchbook and containing a variety of sketches including gateways that look like the entrance to a castle; there are also window designs derived from, and placed beside, the outline of an evergreen tree.

Figure 42 (FLC 2157) is from the same sketchbook and contains a variety of studies for buildings and plans plus a pen and ink and pencil perspective of a house situated on sharply sloping ground with its entry to the left. Both the design and the site suggest this is a study for the Villa Fallet, yet the intended purpose of the other designs, which seem to have interior courtyards, is unclear.

Also unidentified is an ink drawing on tracing paper (fig. 43), for which a preliminary

40. There is a certain affinity between these upper bay windows supported by central piers and the arrangement of the metal and glass facade at 124, rue Réaumur, Paris, of 1904–5. Whether Jeanneret knew of this design so soon after its construction is doubtful; what is certain, however, is that he visited, admired, and photographed the building during his 1908–9 sojourn in Paris.

41. Verticality takes precedence in a manner similar to Alfred Messel's Wertheim Department Store, Berlin, of 1896–99, yet I am not proposing an influence here.

**Fig. 41.** Architectural studies, unidentified, late 1905. Pencil and pen and ink on heavy tan paper. 18 × 25 cm. (FLC 2155)

**Fig. 42.** Architectural studies, unidentified, late 1905 or early 1906. Upper left sketch is probably a study for the Villa Fallet. Pencil and India ink on heavy tan paper. 17 × 26 cm. (FLC 2157)

sketch exists. The size, massing, and generous fenestration suggest an artist's studio. If it were not so small, it might be a project for René Chapallaz's atelier at Tavanne. Yet as a design, this one-room masonry structure is quite intriguing.

The buildings thus far discussed were all drawn in perspective rather than as two-dimensional elevations. Jeanneret was therefore concerned with mass and not merely decorative surface as might have resulted from L'Eplattenier's teaching. This is to his credit. One exception, however, is figure 44, where his principal concern *is* the flat, decorative effects of "sapin" and rock motifs on a facade. Yet the consequence is rather overbearing.[42]

Jeanneret most often used motifs derived from trees for the wooden portions of his buildings, and motifs derived from rock stratum or crystals for the masonry parts—such as foundations, piers and capitals, lintels over doors and windows, and wherever else stone might be used in the construction. This is consistent with his attempt to create a regional style. His reading (ca. 1905–6) of Henry Provensal's *L'Art de demain* influenced him in this direction since the latter makes a clear connection between the use of crystallized mineral forms and architecture: "Through its crystallizations the mineral world offers us . . . examples from which the architect can derive inspiration. . . . More-

42. Le Corbusier published this drawing in *L'Architecture d'aujourd'hui* (19e année, avril 1948) on a page dated "1907" along with a caption reading: "recherches d'une ornementation dictée par la nature ambiante (enseignement L'Eplattenier)." Another drawing of the same facade is FLC 5812 which is postdated "1904 L-C." His dates differ by three years.

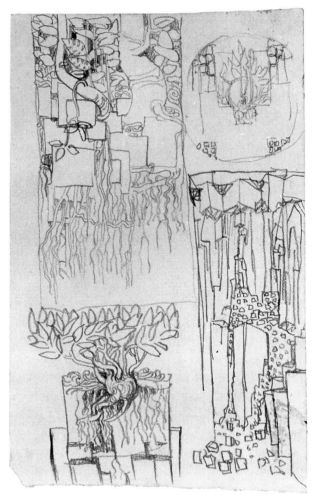

over these geological formations can prompt the artist to make adaptations, to make architectonic models capable of being realized in space."[43] This is precisely what Jeanneret did. He didn't think of the entire building in these terms, only the elements of support—in the same sense that rock formations in the earth's crust support organic growth above (see figs. 44–46). These forms have a visual kinship with the limestone substructure of the Jura mountains.

The four sketches in figure 45 provide a key to many of his column and capital designs, as well as to interpreting much of Jeanneret's decorative work from this period. That at lower right shows upraised and striated limestone fracturing into smaller stones while still supporting an upper surface. The two left-hand sketches are still more decorative and stylized in their representation of roots penetrating into the earth's rocky

43. Henri Provensal, *L'Art de demain* (Paris, 1904), p. 162. However this was not one of the four passages that Jeanneret bracketed in the book.

**Fig. 44.** Decorative designs for facades, ca. 1906. Pencil on heavy paper. 18.5 × 12 cm. (FLC 2533)

**Fig. 45.** Four designs based on rock, earth, and plant forms, ca. 1906. Pencil on heavy paper. 18.5 × 12 cm. (FLC 2518)

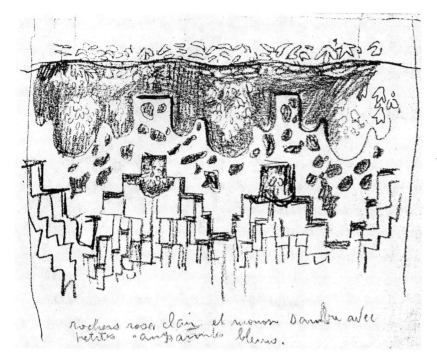

rochers rose clair et mousse sombre avec
petites campanules bleus.

**Fig. 46.** Stylized cross section of the earth's crust: bed rock, earth, and plants, ca. 1906. Pencil on paper. 12 × 18.5 cm. (FLC 5811)

**Fig. 47.** Three studies for piers, columns, and capitals, 1905–6. Pencil on heavy paper. 18.5 × 12 cm. (FLC 1997)

crust while supporting tuberous or tree-like growth above. These stylizations become even more abstract at the upper right where the tuber becomes a disk located at the center with crystallized rocks, as cubes, symmetrically disposed within a still larger circle that certainly represents a watchcase. Thus this single sheet records a progression from nature studies to an ornamented object.

Figure 46 is still more explicit in creating a stylization of the earth's crust; it creates a horizontal repeat pattern that shows cubic rock formations below, then smaller stones, above which is soil, and finally the campanula or blue-bells growing in the ground.[44] The crow step, ziggurat, or corbelled silhouette pattern, or its inverse, that Jeanneret emphasizes in this drawing, was, from 1905 through 1908, one of his favorite motifs; it finds repetition in almost everything he designed, be it watchcases, furniture, or buildings.

The correlation between rock sketches and architectural studies for capitals and columns is manifestly clear in figure 47 where, nevertheless, the crystallized elements are more carefully ordered and regularized. There are numerous such studies among Jeanneret's drawings.

Tree motifs were also employed in the design of columns and capitals (presumably for those to be constructed of wood). The earliest of these show the influence of

44. Written below is "rochers rose clair et mousse sombre avec petites campanules bleues" and in the margin "1904 L-C."

**Fig. 48.** Studies for columns and capitals, 1905–6. Pencil on heavy paper. 15 × 22.5 cm. (FLC 2002)

Jeanneret's school studies from Owen Jones wherein the long-stemmed Egyptian lotus flower was transformed into column shafts and capitals; simultaneously one senses the continuing influence of the sinuous Art Nouveau. The latter is much diminished in our figure 48 yet is still evident in the "root" formations at the base of each column shaft. The triangular sapin or evergreen tree forms the capital.

Figure 49 shows a more contained and disciplined pier at the upper left that combines stylizations of both trees and rocks, each having become so abstract as to be virtually unrecognizable except through our preceding discussion. The other two sketches illustrate columns with composite shafts composed of clustered tree trunks with the "eyes" of their detached branches becoming the principal motif for the surface decoration. Note also the diagonal grid at the upper right that contains a repetitive pattern of sapin trees; such grids later became the basis of many ornamental designs.

At this point in time, in the life of forms, a fascinating parallel exists between the work of Frank Lloyd Wright and Charles-Edouard Jeanneret, both men working independently thousands of miles apart. Regard figure 50 and especially the little perspective drawing at the center right. I feel confident I could pass this sketch off as one of Jeanneret's pier and capital studies dating from 1905–6. True, the drawing *does* date from the winter of 1905–6 but it is a study by Frank Lloyd Wright for the exterior piers at Unity Temple in Oak Park, Illinois. There can be no question of influence here; rather we have a perfect example of the simultaneous manifestation of similar

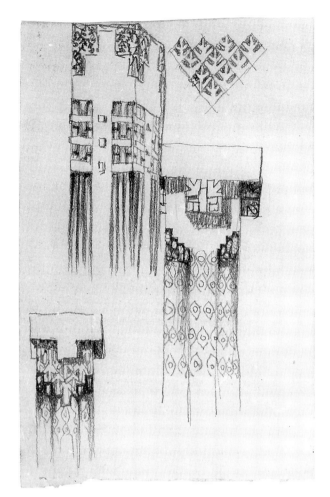

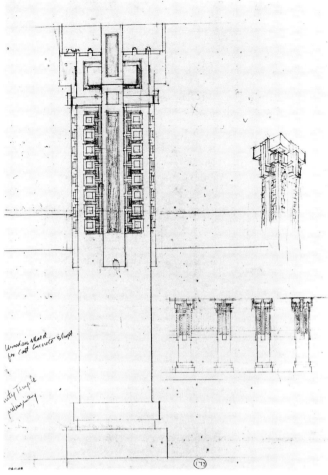

**Fig. 49.** Studies for piers, columns, and capitals, 1905–6. Pencil on heavy paper. 18.5 × 12 cm. (FLC 2006)

**Fig. 50.** Frank Lloyd Wright. Studies for the piers and capitals at Unity Temple, Oak Park, Illinois, 1905–6. (*Frank Lloyd Wright Disegni 1887–1959* [Florence, 1976], fig. 23)

forms (or ideas) occurring among original thinkers, at a given moment, in different parts of the world.

Particularly fascinating is a sketch showing the metamorphosis of a tree, not merely into a decorative detail for a building, but into the building itself (fig. 51). Whether this is intended as a house, church, Beau-Site or something else is inconsequential compared to the intellectual statement made here; also astounding is the bravura of a teenager who single-handedly would endeavor to create an architectural style that had no historical precedent. Audacity aside, such an act sets Jeanneret apart from others, be they peers or patriarchs. And it is precisely this intellectual process that he would employ again during the 1920s when machine-age forms, whether ocean liners or mass-produced factory products, served as his point of departure rather than the forms of nature.

A rather undistinguished drawing showing tree branches spreading from the trunk might pass unnoticed except for the fact that Le Corbusier selected it as his initial

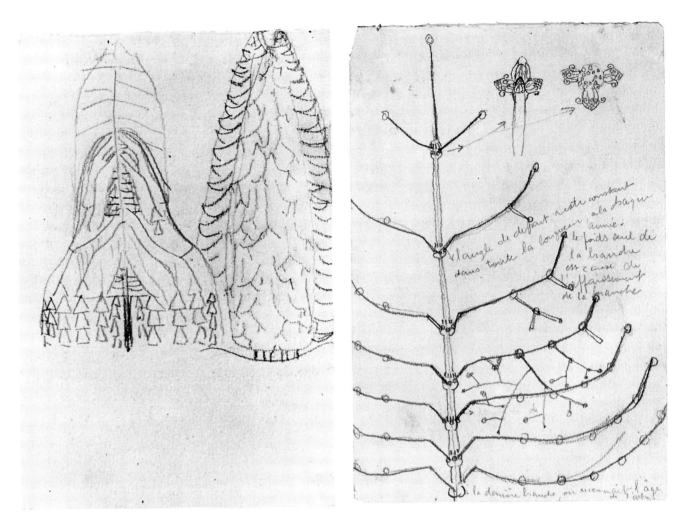

illustration in *Le Modulor* to demonstrate his early interest in visual or harmonic measure (fig. 52). There, however, as when published elsewhere, he deleted the handwriting which failed to correspond with what he wished to prove—a not uncommon custom. The excised text explains how the angle at which a branch grows from the trunk remains constant over the years with subsequent sagging caused only to its weight; also that the age of the tree can be determined by the nodes on its lowest branch.[45] Its date seems to be 1906 judging from various drawings on identical sketchbook sheets. The

**Fig. 51.** Tree (Sapin) metamorphosed into a building, 1905–6. Pencil on heavy paper. 14 × 9.5 cm. (FLC 2527)

**Fig. 52.** Study of tree growth, 1906–7. Pencil on heavy paper. 18 × 12 cm. (FLC 2517)

45. Jeanneret's lack of comprehension concerning annual tree growth is rather shocking. First of all, the original bottom branch is almost never extant after the first few years, therefore to judge age from the lowest existing branch gives a totally false conclusion; one should assess age from the nodes on the trunk, not on a branch. Jeanneret's sketch shows eight years of the tree's growth. His second error is in indicating a consistent increase in growth rate with each passing year; this is not true (unless for eight consecutive years weather conditions improved). When publishing this drawing in *Le Modulor* in 1948 (p. 25) he added a

idea for this sketch apparently derives from Ruskin's *The Seven Lamps of Architecture* ("The Lamp of Life," plate XII, fig. 5) which, however, varies in several respects.[46]

Jeanneret's designs that are purely decorative, rather than related to architecture, are more difficult to arrange chronologically during this period from 1905 to 1907. To complicate matters further, there is often no clear stylistic break between these drawings and those done from 1912 to 1914 when he himself was a teacher at the school. Their impetus comes from L'Eplattenier's instruction in "dessin décoratif" and "composition décorative," yet none have contemporary signatures or dates. When Le Corbusier (probably during the late 1940s) postdated many of these drawings, he gave most of them 1904 or 1905 dates with a few assigned to 1912–14.

I feel that a significant number belong to the later period despite the lack of documented evidence. The evolution of Jeanneret's drawing technique is toward increasingly disciplined and abstract forms that eventually are controlled by an underlying unit system (circles, triangles, etc.) that is consistent throughout a given design. Figures 286–87 and 289–91 are certainly from the 1912–14 period, yet figures 54 and 55, while tending in this direction, are more questionable but perhaps still predate the four-year hiatus caused by Jeanneret's absence from La Chaux-de-Fonds.

Imaginary landscapes, such as seen in figures 16, 17, and 18 from the period 1903–4, do not fit our description although figure 46, with its continually repeating pattern (as in wallpaper), comes somewhat closer. So does the small diamond-shaped motif at the upper right of figure 49. Initial experiments at a "composition décorative" are seen in figure 53 which, with its flat, two-dimensional repetitive pattern of evergreen trees moving across the page, is characteristic[47]—as is his more precisely delineated sgraffito decoration at the Villa Fallet (fig. 72). Figure 289, by contrast, although its subject is also rows of evergreen trees, is more disciplined, and the design is controlled by an underlying pattern of regulating lines. Therefore it certainly dates from the later period.

---

footnote claiming the reductions were due to the size of the paper, an excuse abrogated by the fact that the space between each node is *progressively,* not arbitrarily, different. He also published this drawing, minus the handwriting, in *L'Architecture d'aujourd'hui,* 19e année, avril 1948, numéro hors série "Le Corbusier," p. 109, where the caption reads, "C'est à ces croquis d'arbres, faits en 1905, que s'attachent les premières idées de mesures harmoniques qui devaient conduire au "Modulor" quarante années plus tard." In his "autobiography," *Creation Is a Patient Search,* it appears on p. 23.

46. For a discussion of Ruskin's influence on this and possibly other drawings, see Patricia May Sekler, *The Early Drawings,* pp. 85–88, as well as her "Le Corbusier, Ruskin, the Tree, and the Open Hand" in *The Open Hand,* edited by Russell Walden (Cambridge: MIT Press, 1977), pp. 42–95, which is an expanded version of Chapter 4 of her dissertation.

I also wish to thank Christopher Thomas for observations concerning Ruskin's influence, and Ivan Franko for views on dating Jeanneret's drawings. Bill McDonough aided me by taking photographs.

47. Le Corbusier published this and other drawings under the relatively late date of 1907 in *L'Architecture d'aujourd'hui* (19e année [April 1948]) along with the caption "D'après nature: racines, rochers recherches d'une ornementation dictée par la nature ambiante (enseignement L'Eplattenier)."

**Fig. 53.** Decorative composition of evergreen trees covered with snow, ca. 1906–7. Pencil and India ink. 15 × 17 cm. (FLC 2520)

Individual trees are also the theme of decorative designs, the drawing becoming increasingly abstract until the tree itself is almost unrecognizable after being dissected into all the geometric shapes of which Jeanneret was so fond (fig. 54). Even an imaginary valley landscape with storm clouds is analyzed in terms of its intersecting diagonals (fig. 55). However, the three-stage development of this design suggests that it might be a demonstration prepared by Jeanneret for his students after 1912 rather than an exercise he formulated for himself. Emphasis given to an underlying structure based on straight lines, whether horizontals, verticals, or diagonals, has a certain affinity with drawings he made in Rome in October 1911 (see Chapter 8) and therefore lends weight to a later dating.

Although Jeanneret designed many watchcases while at the Ecole d'art, he engraved but one, and it bears the manufacturer's name, Jeanneret-Perret, on its pure white enamel face (figs. 56, 57). Justly proud, he often spoke of it, claiming to have designed it in 1902 at the age of fifteen. Also, he declared that it had won the Diplôme d'honneur at the International Exposition at Turin in 1902.[48] These assertions are all false; they were merely invented to enhance his myth as child prodigy.

48. In *Creation Is a Patient Search* (p. 23) Le Corbusier illustrated the watchcase with the caption "A watch chased in silver, steel, copper, gold, etc. by Charles-Edouard Jeanneret at the age of fifteen . . . won

**Fig. 54.** The "sapin" transformed into a decorative design, ca. 1907(?). Pencil on coarse paper. Detail from 14 × 30.5 cm. sheet. (FLC 2511)

It is unimaginable that Jeanneret could have prepared this highly sophisticated design within the first days of entering the Ecole d'art in April 1902; one need only compare his stylistic development to recognize the impossibility of this claim. Furthermore there is no documentary evidence to support it. However, four years later, on November 2, 1905, the commission of the Ecole d'art did decide to enter a watch exhibit at the 1906 International Exhibition in *Milan,* and instructed Mr. Geel's "Classe de gravure" to devote maximum effort to these preparations. By June 15, 1906, the watches were in Milan after previously being exhibited at the Ecole d'art. Also, the *Revue internationale de l'Horlogerie* published a selection of these watches beginning in mid-July, with Jeanneret's design among those illustrated in August 1906 (p. 808).

Prior to the closing of the exhibition, the school received word that "un diplôme d'honneur était décerné à l'Ecole d'art de La Chaux-de-Fonds" (*Rapport,* 1906–7, p. 4), thus the award went to the school's exhibit of 108 watches, not specifically to Jeanneret as he claimed. The Diplôme d'honneur was second only to the Grand prix in a category of six. Various publications reported the event, noting that nature played a leading role among the student designs.[49]

Stylistic analysis also confirms the later date even though, officially, Jeanneret had

the Diploma of Honour at the International Exposition of Decorative Arts at Turin, 1902." On the facing page he published the drawing which is our figure 45. Sekler, *The Early Drawings,* p. 99, was the first to note the discrepancy between Le Corbusier's dating of Turin 1902 and that of Milan 1906.

49. See, for example, the article by Georges Hantz published in *Journal de Genève* and reprinted in *Journal Suisse d'Horlogerie,* 31st année, no. 11, (May 1907).

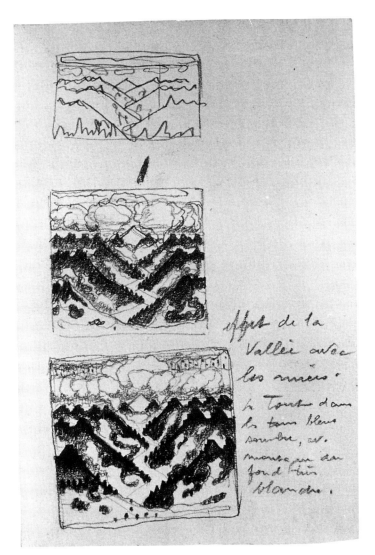

Fig. 55. Analysis of an imaginary valley landscape that may be a demonstration Jeanneret prepared for his students in 1912–13, the date therefore being either ca. 1907 or more likely 1912–13. Pencil on sketchbook paper. 18 × 12 cm. (FLC 1748)

dropped engraving from his program in June 1905. Comparison with his November 1904 submission to the *Revue internationale de l'Horlogerie* competition (figs. 20, 21) bears this out; his watch must postdate that year yet predate the June 1906 opening of the exhibition. The same conclusion is deduced from his ornamental studies, already discussed, plus the fact that a similar watchcase design (FLC 1745) appears on the back of a Villa Fallet sketch that apparently dates from the early months of 1906.

Le Corbusier's most lengthy description of the design reads: "1902–1903 Watch by my father; case of silver inlaid with steel, copper, brass, and yellow gold, all cut with burin and chisel. Small diamonds encrusted. Executed entirely by Le Corbusier.

**Fig. 56.** *(Opposite top)* Watchcase designed and executed by Jeanneret, 1906. Materials: diamonds, gold, silver, copper, and steel. (FLC)

**Fig. 57.** *(Opposite bottom)* Face of the same watch. Although it bears the manufacturer's name, Jeanneret-Perret, only the white enamel face would have been by Monsieur Jeanneret. The hour hand seems to be broken. (FLC)

Theme: rocks and moss with a fly and drops of dew."[50] Meanwhile a reviewer wrote: "a stone covered with moss yet without any intention of rendering the rock as it would be in reality but rather as seen in different planes; a conventional manner is used in representing the moss on the top of the stone where a fly is searching for drops of dew, the fly being of yellow gold, the moss of red gold, copper, or steel, and the dew-drops are diamonds."[51]

I, however, wish to propose a new, symbolic interpretation for this design, one that involves two distinct levels of meaning. The first is the literal one, mentioned above, that incorporates observable, yet stylized, Jura motifs (compare with figure 45). The second is a symbolic metaphor for La Chaux-de-Fonds—as epitomized by its coat of arms (fig. 58). The latter's heraldic emblem consists of three horizontal bands comprising, from top to bottom, three stars, a gold-colored hive surrounded by bees, and a checker-board of alternately blue and silver squares. All these elements are present in Jeanneret's design. The three glittering diamonds symbolize the three stars. The insect, executed in real gold, represents the yellow bees and gold-colored hive.[52] The rows of squares or rectangles, executed in real silver, exemplify the silver and blue squares at the bottom of the coat of arms.[53] Thus, through synthesis, Jeanneret created a work of art that is far more sophisticated and complex than we hitherto imagined, and one that does him great honor. Already apparent are the powers that characterize the mature work of Le Corbusier.

Jeanneret possessed remarkable talent and determination yet often lacked the confidence of his own convictions. He might waver in direction and, upon seeing his goal, be unsure how to get there. L'Eplattenier became his initial mentor, leading him into

50. This is a handwritten note by Le Corbusier published by Jean Petit (*Le Corbusier lui-même*, p. 27) beside an illustration of the watch. I have translated "mouche" in its literal sense of "fly" although the related compound word "mouche à miel" means "honey bee." In French, therefore, unlike in English, the words fly and bee are not totally dissimilar.

51. *Revue internationale de l'Horlogerie*, 7th year, no. 15 (August 1906), p. 808, perhaps paraphrased from a description provided by Jeanneret.

52. I am assured by Professor A. G. Knerer of the Zoology Department, University of Toronto, that this insect, while sufficiently abstract to make positive identification impossible, is probably studied from a squashed and dead house fly. The limp position of the wings indicates death, and the right wing is damaged. Slight indications of a second pair of wings are the only grounds for identifying this insect as a bee. My thanks to Professor Knerer.

Thus Jeanneret studied a real insect, and although the evidence favoring my analysis would be enhanced had the insect been a bee, it was, for Jeanneret, certainly easier to find a dead house fly in winter than to find a bee. And most people, including myself, would hardly notice the difference.

53. These overlapping rectangles undoubtedly derive from Eugène Grasset, *Méthode de composition ornem-*

architecture and, after 1910, into urbanism. He also encouraged his power of synthesis. But methodology and goals were not enough; the boy must test his thoughts against those of others. He also required a rationale larger than Jura regionalism. Reading offered him the means; its influence upon his creative and intellectual formation proved profound. Fortunately it is possible to reconstruct much of what he read, as well as when he read it, and sometimes—thanks to marginal notes and underscoring—which passages in these books most attracted him.[54]

School reading, by his own account, emphasized Owen Jones, Eugène Grasset, and John Ruskin.[55] Jones and Grasset were primarily concerned with analysis and the stylized or conventionalized treatment of natural forms,[56] while Ruskin was mainly re-

**Fig. 58.** The coat of arms of La Chaux-de-Fonds.

*entale,* fig. 129 (compare with our figure 45). My thanks to Christopher Thomas for this observation. The design of this watchcase, but not its symbolic significance, is also discussed by Paul Turner (see the following footnote) and by Jacques Gubler, "A l'heure des Horlogers jurassiens," *Revue Neuchâteloise,* no. 91 (Summer 1980), pp. 17, 19.

54. For a comprehensive analysis of Jeanneret's reading prior to 1920, see Paul Venable Turner's Harvard dissertation of 1971, *The Education of Le Corbusier,* published by Garland Publishing, New York, 1977. This has since been republished in French, with updated footnotes, as *La Formation de Le Corbusier* (Paris: Éditions Macula, 1987). It is unquestionably the most authoritative study of Jeanneret's intellectual formation yet published.

To Turner's "Before 1908" list (p. 240) I can add the following books: Charles Blanc, *Grammaire des arts du dessin* (Paris, 1867); Pierre Gusman, *Venise* (Paris, 1904), bearing the stamp "Ch. E. Jeanneret/Rue Léopold-Robert 46"—his address until October 1906; John Ruskin's *Sesame and Lilies* (translated by Marcel Proust, 1906) and *Stones of Venice* (French edition, 1906); Edouard Schuré's *Sanctuaires d'Orient* (Paris, 1898); and Mathias Duval, *Précis d'anatomie à l'usage des artistes* (Paris, n.d.; first published 1881, subsequent editions 1900, etc.), signed "Ch. E. Jeanneret/La Chaux-de-Fonds." There is no internal evidence that Jeanneret used the latter book, unlike an identical copy signed by his friend "C. Humbert, Noël 1906" which is well worn and includes sketches and underscorings (BV).

55. The best autobiographical account of his reading appears in *L'Art décoratif d'aujourd'hui* (Paris, 1925), pp. 134–37. In addition to the three authors mentioned, he repeatedly speaks of the French Art Nouveau designer Emile Gallé: "La vie de Gallé est belle, partagée entre l'étude directe de la nature et les caprices du feu de ses fours. Gallé laisse des objets qui sont de belles oeuvres, plastiques et sensibles" (p. 136).

His reading of Blanc's *Grammaire des arts du dessin* is revealed in a letter to his parents written from Florence on October 8, 1907: "Il y a trois ans, quand je lisais la première ligne de la Grammaire des Arts: L'Architecture est le premier des Arts, je ne comprenais pas et n'étais point d'accord. Un voyage en Italie me fait aimer mon métier." Only a few statements in this long (691-page) book seem significant for Jeanneret: that beauty depends on laws of order, proportion, and harmony (p. 6), and ideas applicable to Jeanneret's teaching during 1912–14 (pp. 88–89).

Charles Blanc (1813–82), like Jeanneret, began his career as an engraver. He later became Directeur des Beaux-Arts in Paris and founded (1859) the *Gazette des Beaux-Arts.* His *Grammaire des arts décoratifs* was perhaps also known to Jeanneret.

56. Le Corbusier recalled that "Grasset fut le géomètre et l'algébriste des fleurs. Il fallut avec lui admirer jusque dans le secret de leur structure toutes les fleurs, les aimer tant, qu'il était de rigueur de les disperser sur toutes les oeuvres que nous aurions aimé entreprendre," and a few sentences later on he says, "Ruskin questionnait les chapiteaux fleuris du Palais Ducal et parcourait dans ses portiques et ses stalles, la 'Bible

68    **La Chaux-de-Fonds**

membered as the moral or spiritual guide of the day.[57] Ruskin, passionately read by all those at the school, was then enjoying a revival that saw several of his most significant works translated into French between 1900 and 1906. Jeanneret was familiar with an impressive number of these including *The Seven Lamps of Architecture* (translated 1900),[58] *The Bible of Amiens* (1904), *Sesame and Lilies* (1906—the latter two translated, with notes and introduction, by Marcel Proust), *Mornings in Florence* (1906), *The Stones of Venice* (1906), and excerpts from *Lectures on Architecture and Painting* (available in French only after 1910).

No wonder L'Eplattenier and his circle were so enthusiastic about Ruskin. With infectious intensity he declared his love of nature, reveled in the splendors of mountain flora, and spoke poetically of the Jura landscape. He championed the Gothic style for its truth to nature, and conversely disparaged Classic. He championed the study of nature, insisted that nature was based upon natural laws that must be pursued by the artist, and urged artists to draw analytically while endeavoring to isolate and synthesize these fundamental laws. Good art, for Ruskin, represented a storehouse of natural truth. He also exalted the skill of the artisan and craftsman against the impersonality of the machine. In short, his ideals conformed perfectly with those of the Ecole d'art, and theirs with his.

Jeanneret's own choice of extracurricular reading (though often proposed by L'Eplattenier) looms with equal importance. An early instance is Henry Provensal, *L'Art de demain,* published in Paris in 1904 and bearing Jeanneret's pre–October 1906 address. Expressed therein are many of his lifelong beliefs concerning art and the artist's role in society, ideas that his subsequent reading explored more deeply. The text insists that the artist is a superior being, a member of the elite, one who has a capacity for synthesis

---

d'Amiens,' tandis que Grasset établissait, une fleur à la main, et le scalpel du chirurgien botaniste à portée, la *Grammaire de l'ornement* [*sic*]" (*L'Art décoratif d'aujourd'hui,* pp. 134–35); Le Corbusier has erred by quoting Owen Jones' book title rather than Grasset's *La Plante et ses applications ornementales* (Paris, n.d. [ca. 1896–97]). He also knew Grasset's two-volume study: "Eugène Grasset . . . a été . . . l'un des plus lucides théoriciens du modernisme. Il avait publié, en 1905, une importante *Méthode de composition ornementale,* aussitôt adoptée par l'Ecole d'art de La Chaux-de-Fonds" (Gauthier, *Le Corbusier,* p. 27).

Christopher Dresser, *The Art of Decorative Design* (1862) may also have been known to Jeanneret, judging by stylistic comparisons, yet I have no factual evidence to support this observation.

57. Of Ruskin, Le Corbusier recalled in 1925: "Notre enfance fut exhortée par Ruskin. Apôtre touffu, complexe, contradictoire, paradoxal. Les temps étaient unsupportables: cela ne pouvait durer; c'était d'un bourgeoisisme écrasant, bête, noyé dans le matérialisme, enguirlandé dans le décor idiot et tout mécanique, décor fabriqué par la machine qui, sans qu'on sût le lui interdire, produisait, pour les jubilations d'Homais, le carton-pâte et les rinceaux en fonte de fer. C'est de spiritualité que parla Ruskin. Dans ses *Sept Lampes de l'Architecture,* brillaient la Lampe de Sacrifice, la Lampe de Vérité, la Lampe d'Humilité" [*sic;* there is no such chapter] (*L'Art décoratif d'aujourd'hui,* p. 134).

58. This French edition of *Seven Lamps* included three lectures that Ruskin published under the title *The Crown of Wild Olive* (*La Couronne d'olivier sauvage*).

and original invention and who possesses a strong sense of mission. Provensal also emphasized that art was governed by eternal laws that the artist must reveal if he is to succeed in his search for unity, harmony, and truth.

Jeanneret bracketed four passages in this book. The first appears on page 87 and is part of a long quotation from the blatantly elitist Max Nordau, who classified the general public as inferior beings incapable of thinking about the original ideas that are proposed by others; these others—"apostles of truth," as he calls them—the public will endeavor to destroy but finally will come to honor and accept.[59] The second section bracketed by Jeanneret (p. 89) embraces Provensal's conclusions—drawn from Nordau—that the artist must sow his seeds among the elite for they alone have the intellectual capacity to cope with originality and with truth. This is pretty strong stuff for the seventeen- or eighteen-year-old boy to embrace, yet it clearly explains why, during 1907–8, Jeanneret would delve so deeply into both Schuré and Nietzsche's discussions of prophets and how prophets conduct themselves. Jeanneret, among other things, was seeking lessons in how to comport himself.

Two additional paragraphs were bracketed on pages 143–44, the first asserting that most artists, as well as their teachers, are incapable of analyzing a problem—and therefore are unable to achieve the synthesis that is essential to a work of art. And the following paragraph (the only one with double brackets in the margin) states that whereas a superior sense of instinct is valuable for a creative person, science must ultimately be brought to the aid of instinct in order for the creative mind to achieve truly harmonious results. Here, perhaps, is the origin of Le Corbusier's lifelong search, aided first by the *tracés régulateurs* and then by the Modulor, to isolate a scientific means by which to refine and perfect the artistic achievements of the human mind.

The fourth and final passage bracketed by Jeanneret in Provensal is: "Le beau, c'est la splendeur du vrai, a dit Platon.—C'est la qualité de l'idée se reproduisant sous une forme symbolique (Plotin)" (p. 145). Although only these sections in *L'Art de demain* were marked by Jeanneret, many others correspond to his future thinking. For example: "The work of art is primarily a creation of the spirit which, governed by an ideal, helps to develop and formulate human thought" (p. 143); "The artist is primarily a thinker who juggles sounds, cubes, colors, and words in order to obtain a harmonious expression [unité] of the idea" (p. 128); and Provensal's own definition of architecture as "*the harmonious, three-dimensional* [cubique] *expression of thought, according to certain laws of equilibrium, statics, cohesion, and strength*" (emphasis in the original, p. 158). Also recall our previous quotation from Provensal (p. 162; see p. 57–58 above) about how nature's crystallized forms can serve as architectonic models.

In addition to these theoretical considerations, Provensal devotes much space to his-

59. Max Nordau was a physician as well as a prolific and controversial writer whose greatest success was *The Conventional Lies of Our Civilization* (1883; English translation 1884) which went into an impressive seventy-three editions in various languages.

tory. However, instead of commencing his discussion thereof with the customary stylistic concerns he analyses the cultural conditions that he sees as the generative force behind the evolution of these architectural ideas. Jeanneret would adopt this same method in 1910 when outlining what he intended to be his first book, "La Construction des Villes."

Returning to our discussion of Jeanneret's first year in the Cours Supérieur (October 1905–July 1906), one is inevitably impressed by L'Eplattenier's emphasis upon learning by doing and by his ability to obtain actual work for his inexperienced students. For Jeanneret, this began with a commission to design and build a house for Louis Fallet.[60]

Louis Fallet designed and fabricated jewelry, wrote about ornament, served on the *Revue internationale de l'Horlogerie* jury that in 1904 awarded Jeanneret second place in a design competition, and was a member of the commission of the Ecole d'art. Fallet certainly showed great courage—and the power of L'Eplattenier's persuasion—in allowing a student who knew absolutely nothing about construction to design and build his house. To overcome this deficiency L'Eplattenier telephoned a friend, the architect René Chapallaz at Tavannes, saying "I have a young man here who has a house to build. He has ideas, but he doesn't know how to realize them. Can you take him in hand?" To this Chapallaz agreed, and "with my employees, we put his plans in order. I lent him an assistant who went to La Chaux-de-Fonds to stake out the house, his first to be built on the rue de la Montagne."[61]

This transpired during the winter of 1905–6 although the first firm date we have is June 17, 1906, when the following note appeared in the father's journal: "Edouard has just broken ground for the house he is building for Mr. Fallet, for which he made the plans."[62] Characteristically, Jeanneret senior made no mention of the original commis-

60. Louis Edouard Fallet; born March, 23, 1879, La Chaux-de-Fonds; religion, Protestant; profession, engraver, chaser; moved to 1, Chemin de Pouillerel (Villa Fallet) August 9, 1907; married Clothilde Schriffmann 1910, four children born between 1911 and 1917, three of whom died by 1918; moved out of Villa Fallet June 9, 1921; died September 17, 1956, at La Chaux-de-Fonds (Police des habitants).

61. These quotations are from a letter to Professor von Senger dated February 6, 1961; they correspond perfectly to what Chapallaz told me in 1974. He did the work gratis, but perhaps his draftsman was paid.

René Chapallaz (1881–1976) did not study architecture at school but at age sixteen apprenticed for three years with Pfleghard & Häfeli in Zurich before moving to Geneva and then, in July 1902, to La Chaux-de-Fonds where he worked with Piquet & Ritter before establishing his own practice at Tavannes (1906) and later (1908) La Chaux-de-Fonds. He was Jeanneret's senior by only six years. See Marc Albert Emery, "Chapallaz *versus* Jeanneret," *Archithese*, 2–83 (March/April 1983), pp. 23–28.

62. The blueprints (scale 1:50) are undated, and those in Chapallaz's file are signed both by "Louis Fallet" and "Ch. E. Jeanneret" (no title after his name); Chapallaz's name appears nowhere. The set of plans registered with Travaux Publics are signed only by Fallet and is no. 62 among 145 plans deposited in 1906, thereby implying that it was deposited well after the beginning of the year.

sion but once something tangible existed he maintained a running account. On September 11 the roof was raised and by December 2 "Edouard has many worries about the house; costs exceed estimates; the boy has undertaken a task in excess of his means." On December 16 "The house that Edouard is constructing has taken a turn for the better, he has installed some nice windows, it is on the interior that they are now working." And on April 19, 1907, "Son Edouard has a cold, he works extremely, indeed excessively hard finishing the Fallet house, directing the restoration of a chapel at Cernier, and arranging a studio for Mr. Gallet.[63] He intends to leave us end of May to travel in northern Italy and then go to Vienna. Vast projects, indeed."

Work dragged on and Edouard was unable to leave in May; by June 18 the house was still unfinished: "Edouard is almost finished with the Fallet house which is very good-looking and original. This undertaking has been for him an invaluable school of practical experience. He emerged victorious from this test, much to his honor. His plans for departure remain indefinite." Finally, on August 5, 1907, the father noted that the house was finished. Four days later Fallet moved in, an incredibly long fourteen months after construction began.

Since no mention of the Villa Fallet appears in Chapallaz's Copie de lettres (letter copybook) he probably played no major role in its supervision; Edouard, as his father's account implies, shouldered this responsibility. Other students in the Cours Supérieur, however, participated in executing both the exterior and interior decoration, and there is a marvelous photograph taken by André Evard showing Jeanneret (with glasses) and Louis Houriet (right), both in their working clothes, being interrupted by the well-dressed Octave Matthey as they complete (in the best Ruskinian tradition of craftsmanship) the sgraffito on the southeast facade of the Villa Fallet (fig. 73). To evoke Ruskin's name is not fortuitous since Jeanneret presented a dedicated copy of Sesame and Lilies to Evard in appreciation of his helping hand.[64]

The Villa Fallet overlooks La Chaux-de-Fonds from the southeastern slopes of Mount Pouillerel, the last high barrier before the river Doubs and France. The house was, and still is, on the outskirts of town where geography defied the engineers' attempts to implant a grid system on the streets. A plot plan of circa 1907 shows this neighborhood where Jeanneret built four houses and where two others exist in which

63. This was probably Louis Gallet, sculptor, who lived at 55, rue David-Pierre Bourquin in a house designed by Chapallaz in 1904. The ornament is imbued with the Jura spirit yet is not characteristic of L'Eplattenier's students; Jeanneret was apparently concerned with emplacement, not design.

64. John Ruskin, Sésame et les Lys: des trésors des rois; des jardins des reines, traduction, notes et préface par Marcel Proust (Paris, 1906). The dedication reads: "A mon bon compagnon d'études et ami, Monsieur A. Evard,—modeste merci d'un fameux coup de main. / Ch. E. Jeanneret / Août 1907." And printed with a ball-point pen in the shaky hand of an elderly man (Evard) are the words "Villa Fallet" (BV).

Other photos document various stages of construction and show some six to eleven employees on the job. Léon Perrin, with whom I visited the Villa Fallet on October 24, 1973, informed me that he took no part in the work.

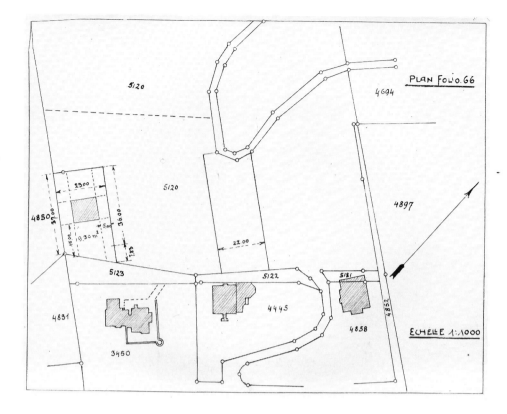

he worked (fig. 59). Across the plan from lower left to right are the Villas Matthey-Doret, L'Eplattenier, and Fallet, and just above (lot 5120) is the measured layout for the Villa Stotzer and beside it (the lot 22 meters wide) for the Villa Jaquemet, both designed by Jeanneret in 1908. The director of the Ecole d'art, William Aubert, later built his house on lot 4694 (upper right), and directly across the street (still blank on the map) Jeanneret would build his parents' house in 1912. The road that curves between L'Eplattenier's property and that of Fallet (later renamed Chemin de Pouillerel with the Villa Fallet being no. 1) was soon linked up with the Rue de la Montagne above.

I encourage all who visit the site to allow time to climb the road (Route de Chappel) at the top left of the plan. It cuts through a dense, tranquil wood and emerges on a noble, pastoral Jura landscape filled with monumental fir and spruce, a setting which seems centuries removed from our own. But *walk, don't drive,* and if you have a generous hour this route will gradually lead you back to town; in the meantime you will learn more about Jeanneret than you would in twice the time spent on his buildings or this book.[65]

65. The high Jura abounds in some of the most splendid and unspoiled scenery in all the world. Life is too short to pass it by. Don't expect the awesome snow-capped Alps; this is an idyllic, monumental landscape where the quiet nobility of each tree, pasture, or farmhouse contrasts with the fragile delicacy of the alpine

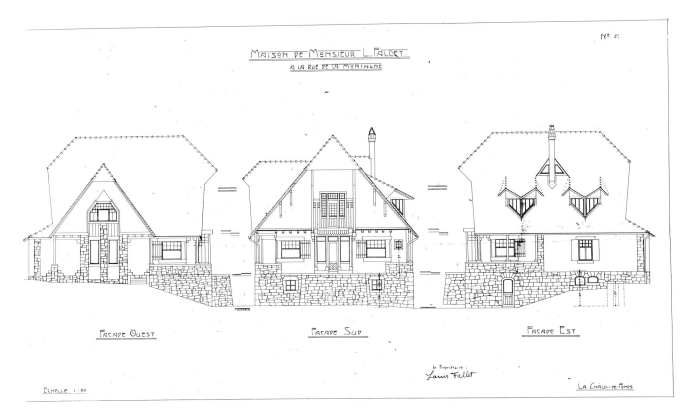

MAISON DE MONSIEUR L. FALLET
A LA RUE DE LA MONTAGNE

N° 5.

FAÇADE OUEST

FAÇADE SUD

FAÇADE EST

le Propriétaire :
Louis Fallet

ECHELLE 1:50

LA CHAUX-DE-FONDS

The Villa Fallet, like many of Jeanneret's buildings, was built on terraced land that largely negates its site yet does enhance the view (figs. 60–63, color plate I). Limestone blocks, cut stone, timber, and stucco were his materials.[66] To perfect the design he

**Fig. 60.** Villa Fallet, La Chaux-de-Fonds, 1906. Elevations from original blueprint. The "Façade Sud" actually faces southeast, see map. (BV)

flora (remember, even in the valleys you're about 3,500 feet high). In the springtime whole hillsides are lavender or white with wild crocuses, while the valleys are carpeted with millions of yellow daffodils.

Should you make the pilgrimage to see Jeanneret's buildings at La Chaux-de-Fonds, add a day for landscape. The time will be well spent. Take the trolley-train from La Chaux-de-Fonds to Saignelégier for lunch (a horsey, equestrian town well stocked with hotels and restaurants), and if you're driving, go and return by different routes. Also, just beyond the outskirts of La Chaux-de-Fonds (road to Saignelégier) there is the hamlet of Le Bas Monsieur (I enjoy the name) with its eighteenth-century farmhouse where one may eat or drink (preferably out-of-doors) before hiking north along the lane that cuts through a little valley and then up the hill. Or drive the ten minutes to Valanvron where, after a fondu at the local farmhouse, a stroll beside the pastures at sunset—or by the light of the moon with all its marvelous sounds of night— will long be remembered. And perhaps some morning, with the sun in the eastern sky, take a one-to-two hour drive down the valley of La Sagne (the town where Jeanneret's mother was born) traveling slowly to observe each farmhouse with its seventeenth-, eighteenth-, or nineteenth-century date cut into the stone lintel over the door; return either by the same route or pass over the "mountain" between Les Ponts-de-Martel and Le Locle; while descending the far slope you will pass through the now extinct hamlet of "Les Jeannerets."

66. Metal I-beams were also used to span the basement ceiling.

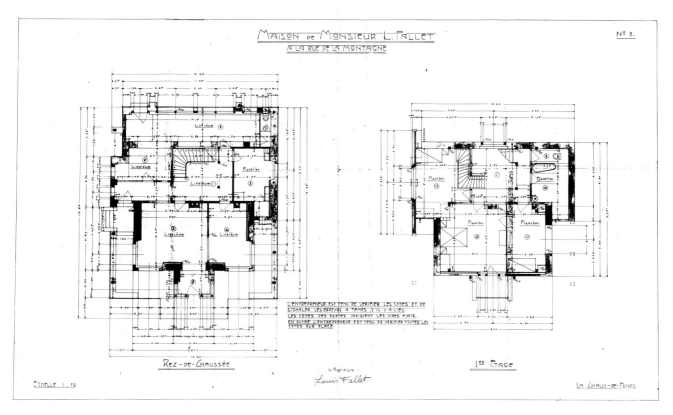

Rez-de-Chaussée

1ᵉʳ Étage

L'ENTREPRENEUR EST TENU DE VERIFIER LES COTES ET DE
SIGNALER LES ERREURS A TEMPS S'IL Y A LIEU.
LES COTES DES PORTES INDIQUENT LES VIDES FINIS.
EN OUTRE L'ENTREPRENEUR EST TENU DE VERIFIER TOUTES LES
COTES SUR PLACE

Echelle 1 : 50

Le Propriétaire :
Louis Fallet

La Chaux-de-Fonds

**Fig. 61.** Villa Fallet, plans from original blueprints. (BV)

studied it sculpturally in a series of clay models known to us through photographs, a process that contributed to the harmonious proportions he achieved (fig. 36).

The design incorporates various influences including medieval, Swiss châlet, and turn-of-the-century vernacular. Stanislaus von Moos correctly observed that the steep roof, hipped gables, and general massing owe much to the medieval revival, and when one compares Jeanneret's sketches made two years later of Gothic houses at Rouen the point is well taken.[67] Elements of the proverbial Swiss châlet (whose origins are medieval) are also prominent as, for example, the unconcealed structural members (which are decoratively carved) and the generous roof overhangs that protect balconies underneath. The iron, wood, and sgraffito ornament, however, has more in common with the art of circa 1900. Conspicuously absent is any real indebtedness to typical Jura buildings.

The massing is compact and each facade is completely different. A bay window overlooks the view; it is topped by a balcony and surrounded by a terrace.[68] The broad

67. Stanislaus von Moos, *Le Corbusier, Elements of a Synthesis* (Cambridge, Mass., and London, 1979), p. 7.

68. Subsequent owners squared off the south corner of this U-shaped terrace to provide enough width for table and chairs. This was done with unusual sympathy by reusing the original masonry and ironwork, thereby causing a minimum of visual harm. Another external change involved walling up a door and several windows at the back of the house where Mr. Fallet's atelier had been.

hipped-gable roof offers shelter underneath.[69] This area is richly ornamented. A cross-gable shields the off-center entrance while the lean-to at the rear shelters the atelier of Mr. Fallet—over which a large clerestorey window illuminates the central hall (figs. 64, 65). The fourth side, opposite the entrance and dominated by triangular dormer windows, is invisible due to the steep terrain.

The interior rooms are small and rather cramped except for the well-lit, two-storey hall, two sides of which are surrounded by a gallery at the upper level; a mirror conforming to the underside of the stairway adds to the sense of space (figs. 66–68). Above the hall is the third-floor children's room that is the real fun-room of the house.

Extensive use of light-colored natural wood imparts great warmth to the interior, and throughout Jeanneret has incorporated his favorite Jura motifs. Compare the pattern of the hallway ceiling with the lower portion of Jeanneret's watchcase, observe the incised green triangle (symbol of a sapin) at the top of each door and along the walls, or the wrought-iron door latches in the form of salamanders that crawl up each door (fig. 69), and the inverted corbiesteps found under the posts of the gallery—a motif previously observed in Jeanneret's work that also appears in Owen Jones and in Persian architecture.

No trace of the original living-dining room remains since it was later merged into the adjacent bedroom, thereby giving the bay window a central position within the

**Fig. 62.** Villa Fallet, La Chaux-de-Fonds, 1906. Early photograph taken by Jeanneret. (BV)

**Fig. 63.** Villa Fallet, view from the south prior to terrace modifications. (Photo courtesy of Fernand Perret)

69. This type of gable, hipped only for part of its height, is called a jerkinhead ("pignon en demi-croupe," in French) and for centuries was common in Switzerland and eastern France (especially Alsace).

**Fig. 64.** Villa Fallet. Sketch by Jeanneret showing roof decoration as seen from the west, 1906. The one-storey lean-to (at left) is Fallet's ate-lier and above it the window that illuminates the stair hall. Pencil on yellowish paper. Detail from 18.5 × 12 cm. sheet. (FLC 2064)

**Fig. 65.** Villa Fallet, seen from the west. (Photo by author)

Fig. 66. Villa Fallet. Central hall with staircase. (Photo by author)

**Fig. 67.** Villa Fallet. View from the central hall into the entrance hall with the opened front door at the end. Thus one sees the "sapin" decorative design on the *exterior* of the front door. (Photo by author)

enlarged space. An old photograph, taken from where the partition wall once stood, reveals the small, multipurpose room (fig. 70). An unexecuted sketch, showing a more elaborate sideboard at this location (FLC 1749), is clearly by Jeanneret's hand, thus confirming that the erected cabinet, with its numerous Jura motifs, is also from his design. The chairs and table are certainly his as well; note his favorite corbiestep motif on the chairback rail as well as above the table legs. This unique old photograph preserves for us the only known record of Jeanneret/Le Corbusier's earliest designs for furniture. Unfortunately the whereabouts of these several pieces is unknown today.

The wall frieze over the cabinet is ornamented with (barely visible) butterflies seen in silhouette against a somewhat darker background. The shiny floor is linoleum, as was true for all ground-floor rooms except the kitchen. Jeanneret always specified linoleum for his floors; at the Stotzer house (1908) I discovered some still in situ. It was a mottled gray or grayish-green in color (gray, the color of a dense Jura fog, was Jeanneret/Le Corbusier's favorite color).

**Fig. 68.** Villa Fallet. Upper level of hall showing a portion of the ceiling with its decorative pattern of boards. (Photo by author)

**Fig. 69.** Villa Fallet. Every door latch throughout the house is in the form of a salamander, an animal that Jeanneret particularly liked to sketch. (Photo by author)

**Fig. 70.** Villa Fallet. Original dining-living room with table, chairs, and sideboard all designed by Jeanneret. Old photograph. (BV)

**Fig. 71.** Villa Fallet. Rejected study for sgraffito design on southeast facade. Pencil and watercolor on tinted paper. Sheet size 17.3 × 23; drawing size 13 × 14.5 cm. (Private Swiss Collection)

The exterior ornament is far richer and more intricate than is generally realized. It is so well integrated that it is not obtrusive. All the materials—wood, stone, stucco, iron—display the symbols of Jura regionalism with the sapin being most prevalent. This is observed in the metal triangles on the terrace railing,[70] the wood brackets supporting the overhanging roof, and especially the sgraffito work where some five different, often superimposed, sapin motifs appear (figs. 71–73). Meanwhile the wood, glass, and metal strapping on the front door represents a single tree, showing its branches, trunk, and roots (fig. 67), while all window mullions in the house portray trees and branches (the source perhaps being Emile André's Art Nouveau buildings at Nancy, France, although Jeanneret has suppressed the gentle curves and made the branches straight.)[71] The metal-work on the balcony illustrates a natural scene in silhouette—a row of stylized sapin

70. These nature forms, which are cut in metal, recall the Jugendstil railing design at Joseph Maria Olbrich's own house in Darmstadt of 1901.

71. See especially André's Villa Huot, quai Claude-le-Lorrain, of 1903, or his apartment building on the Avenue Foch, both in Nancy.

**Fig. 72.** Villa Fallet. Sgraffito decoration on southeast facade. (Photo by author)

**Fig. 73.** Octave Matthey, Edouard Jeanneret, and Louis Houriet executing the sgraffito decoration on the Villa Fallet, 1907. (André Evard photo, BV)

with billowing clouds behind[72]—while the corbeled, layered stonework at the corner evokes stratifications of Jura rock, recalling motifs used on Jeanneret's watchcase and in many of his drawings (fig. 74).

Fortunately, except for the living-dining room, the house (as I write) is still in mint condition with not even the delicate sgraffito work needing restoration. Therefore, before someone decides to "improve" the building, it should be acquired and preserved as a house museum—it is one of the very few houses by Le Corbusier that subsequent owners have not found it necessary to remodel.

Few preparatory drawings for the Villa Fallet exist other than the bird's-eye view from the west,[73] the tentative projects previously discussed, and the clay models known from an early photograph (figs. 35, 36, 42, 64). There is also a color study (in pottery red, orange, with some blue, black, and white) for the sgraffito on the garden facade, yet this design differs from the executed one; its decor seems to emerge from the upstairs bedroom window and conform to the shape of the roof rather than being a regimented repeat pattern as was actually used (fig. 71). Note also the branched window mullions on the lower level. Another pencil and watercolor sketch exists on the back

72. The image of clouds seems strange without reading Jeanneret's own description as paraphrased in 1944 by Maximilien Gauthier (*Le Corbusier,* p. 20) concerning the ornament at the Villa Fallet: "ses façades étaient recouvertes d'une abondante ornementation dont le sapin, le nuage et le corbeau firent les frais, tandis que les revêtements intérieurs figuraient des forêts à flanc de montagne et que le couronnement des meubles ambitionnait d'évoquer la majesté et le mystère des horizons alpestres."

73. I am uncertain whether the patterned arrangement of roof tiles seen in figure 64 was actually executed. Although I have found no original photographs that might show them, one old timer told me that the present roof is not authentic. Many old roofs in Tavannes have such roof patterns.

**Fig. 74.** Villa Fallet. Detail from south showing bay window, masonry, wood timbers, sgraffito, and balcony railing. (Photo by author)

of this sheet which shows trees with long trunks and billowing clouds above; its 1 meter 40 cm. width suggests it is a gate, but not the one constructed.

Obviously the ornamental scheme for the Villa Fallet was not entirely envisioned from the start. For one thing the blueprints indicate an entirely different fenestration (double-hung windows with shutters) although other decorative details would not normally be recorded on the blueprints.

In conclusion, we cannot look at the Villa Fallet without admiring its unity, coherence, and pleasant proportions. By any standard it is an admirable work, a credit to its architect. And being Jeanneret's first endeavor makes it even more remarkable, raising the question of what role others may have played in its design. The answer, I believe, is virtually none. L'Eplattenier would be a possible choice yet Léon Perrin assured me that L'Eplattenier provided no help, except as friend and critic, and this seems substantiated by comparison with the latter's roughly contemporary post-office design (fig. 40) plus the fact that Jeanneret was actually designing certain (albeit minor) changes within L'Eplattenier's house at this time.[74] Chapallaz is another possibility, yet we have already

74. These modifications were in the south corner of the basement and consisted chiefly in adding windows. The blueprints are entitled "Réparations dans la maison de Monsieur L'Eplattenier" and are signed and dated "La Chaux-de-Fonds / Le 20 sept. 1906 / Ch. E. Jeanneret."

**Fig. 75.** René Chapallaz's office building (including small apartment on second floor), 9 Chemin des Rochettes, Tavannes, 1906–7. South facade with its row of drafting room windows. Did Jeanneret participate in its design? (René Chapallaz photo, BV)

read his disclaimer. Also, having studied many of Chapallaz's villa designs from 1904 to 1907, I doubt that his talents were involved; his designs have a different sense of proportions and not the same degree of harmony, clarity, and consistency as found at the Villa Fallet.

At an early stage of my research I found among Jeanneret's memorabilia an unidentified photograph (fig. 75) that I assumed was a building he admired and might have used as a design source for the Villa Fallet. Later, however, I learned that it was the south elevation of Chapallaz's 1906–7 office building at Tavannes which postdates the Villa Fallet by several months.[75] It is remarkably consistent with Jeanneret's work, and al-

75. The blueprints for Chapallaz's atelier are dated from October to early November, 1906, with the south elevation being dated October 31. By this date the Villa Fallet was already under roof. Construction of the atelier, located at 9, Chemain des Rochettes, Tavannes, occurred between November 1906 and April 1907. My source for these dates is *Schweizerische Bauzeitung,* 52, no. 7 (August 15, 1908), pp. 88–91, wherein the south elevation is illustrated. Its stylistic affinity to Jeanneret's work was unintentionally attested to by Stanislaus von Moos (*Le Corbusier,* p. 332 n. 19) who mistakenly identified this photograph of Chapallaz's atelier as the Villa Stotzer by Jeanneret.

I am much indebted to Marc Albert Emery and Mme Vera Baumgartner for making the Chapallaz archives (subsequently transferred to the Bibliothèque de la Ville) available to me following Chapallaz's death in 1976.

**Fig. 76.** Music room, Villa Matthey-Doret, La Chaux-de-Fonds, 1906. Demolished. Designed and executed by students in L'Eplattenier's "Cours Supérieur d'art et décoration." (Russell Walden, ed., *The Open Hand: Essays on Le Corbusier,* [Cambridge: MIT Press, 1977] p. 46)

though the only evidence I can offer is stylistic comparison, I cannot help but wonder whether Jeanneret had some hand in its design.[76]

Another project arranged by L'Eplattenier for his Cours Supérieur was to decorate a music room being added to the Albert Matthey-Doret house (fig. 76). Chapallaz was the architect and his letter-copy book abounds with correspondence to the client between December 1905 and February 1906 when the plans were finished. Subsequently, throughout the summer and into the autumn, the students—including Jeanneret, Léon Perrin, Maurice Perrenoud, and Octave Matthey (no direct relation)[77]—were busy executing the ornament that covered virtually every inch of wall and ceiling and included the furnishings as well. Perrin, who sculpted the exterior stone capitals (birds and plants) as well as the bronze fireplace screen, recalled that Jeanneret designed the actual fireplace (just barely visible in old family snapshots) that had a mantle consisting of overlapping horizontal slabs reminiscent of the brackets at the Villa Fallet.[78]

76. That Le Corbusier never mentioned the atelier as one of his works is inconsequential since *none* of his built buildings prior to 1923 are mentioned or illustrated in his so-called *Oeuvre Complète.* Nor is the absence of drawings any proof since we have none by his hand for the Villa Matthey-Doret, only one from the chapel at Cernier-Fontainemelon, and a mere half dozen or so for the Villa Fallet.

77. The participation of Matthey and Perrenoud is recorded in the October 15, 1906, minutes of the commission because they misbehaved while working at Matthey-Doret's and were suspended from school for fifteen days. Matthey-Doret himself was nominated to the commission in December.

78. My information was obtained from Léon Perrin in 1974 when we visited the site together and studied old photographs in the collection of the owner. Perrin could contribute no other details.

The entire house was demolished in 1963 to make way for a new one, but the ceiling of the music room, with its diagonal geometric patterns in wood, was saved for reuse in the dining room of the new home. The furniture was dispersed. The chairs, seen in old photographs, are comparable to those at the Villa Fallet except they are less elaborate (no carved terminals or corbie motifs cut into the backs). The bowed slates, however, are similar, their curves imparting a degree of elegance not found in the angular vernacular pieces that probably was their source. The original room terminated in a picture window at one end (compare Jeanneret's Villa Favre-Jacot dining room of 1912) while a piano and organ flanked the entrance doorway opposite.

## FIFTH YEAR

The second year of the "Cours Supérieur d'art et décoration," with L'Eplattenier as director and sole professor, commenced in the autumn of 1906 after the annual entrance examination which saw Jeanneret, Perrin, Matthey, Evard, Houriet, and Aubert among some twenty candidates admitted.[79] By this time Jeanneret had spent nearly four and a half years at the Ecole d'art. According to the *Rapport* (p. 23), "Lessons are held Thursday, Friday, and Saturdays from 8 until 12 on the ground floor of the old hospital." This schedule left large blocks of time for learn-by-doing projects. In addition to finishing the Villa Fallet and the Matthey-Doret music room, L'Eplattenier arranged to redecorate an entire chapel in Cernier-Fontainemelon as well as embellish a sun porch for a new house in La Chaux-de-Fonds.[80]

The success of these projects, within a few years, netted a tidy profit of 24,000 Swiss francs. The commission, obviously, was delighted and decided (September 17, 1908) to employ these funds in constructing a much-needed new school which, however, was never built (although Jeanneret did prepare schematic designs for it in 1910). Meanwhile the students also decorated the interior of the Villa Henri Sandoz (Chapallaz's father-in-law) at Tavannes (1907–8), the new crematorium at La Chaux-de-Fonds (both interior and exterior, 1909), the great hall of the new post office (1910), the foyer of the observatory at Neuchâtel (1911), and several smaller projects. It was a fantastic achievement as well as a splendid exercise in learning—all combined with much camaraderie and a jocular good time.

By the spring of 1907 the Cours Supérieur had largely completed redecorating the Chapelle Indépendante, which was originally built in 1876, and which lies on the

79. Jeanneret was among seven admitted "conditionnellement," four others were admitted "provisoirement," but the significance of these terms is unclear; perhaps these students had not completed their work from the previous year (see minutes of Séance du Bureau, September 1, 1906).

80. The veranda, so-called, was on the garden side of a house for Isaac Schwob, 129, rue du Progrès, Léon Boillot, architect. The blueprints are dated March 1907. In local dialect "veranda" implies a glazed sun porch.

**Fig. 77.** Chapelle Indépendante, Cernier–Fontainemelon, 1907. Interior (demolished). Ornament designed and executed by students in L'Eplattenier's "Cours Supérieur d'art et décoration." (L' Eplattenier Collection, BV)

**Fig. 78.** Unfinished sketch by Jeanneret. Apparently a preliminary study for wall frescoes at the Chapelle Indépendante, Cernier-Fontainemelon, of 1907 (now destroyed). Pencil and watercolor on heavy paper. 14 × 18 cm. (Private Swiss Collection)

line between Cernier and Fontainemelon in the Val-de-Ruz en route to Neuchâtel. Everything therein—wall paintings, woodwork, leaded-glass windows, ceramics, metalwork, sculpture (stone and wood), light fixtures—was created by L'Eplattenier's students with the windows signed and dated (1907) by Jules Courvoisier and the communion table sculpted and signed by Perrin. Jeanneret's role is uncertain. He apparently supervised when L'Eplattenier wasn't present, but more importantly probably designed the wall frescoes which are a major feature of the design. Compare figure 77 (a poor-quality photograph yet contemporary with the interior) with figure 78 which seems to be one of Jeanneret's preliminary studies for these frescoes. The motif, as well as the three-one-three repetition of vertical elements, is strikingly similar in both. Also, Jeanneret's great interest in fresco decoration was already demonstrated at the Villa Fallet.

Mr. Jeanneret's journal says (April 19, 1907) that Edouard is "directing the restoration of a chapel at Cernier" yet after visiting it uses the word "collaborate" to describe his son's participation, concluding that "It is very beautiful and a great success for these youngsters" (May 14, 1907). Léon Perrin, with whom I visited the chapel (and whom I subsequently questioned on the subject over a four-year period) was unable to designate individual contributors, perhaps because his own work had not been executed in situ.

Of L'Eplattenier's role he would only say "il dirige"—employing the same verb that Mr. Jeanneret had used concerning his son.

A delegation from the commission of the Ecole d'art inspected the completed chapel in September 1907 and their published report provides a contemporary interpretation of the ornamental scheme. "The ensemble, in clear and warm tones, contains the entire spectrum of yellows, blues, greens, and browns. The light, filtered by predominantly yellow stained-glass windows, diffuses a golden ambiance throughout that is truly impressive. The fundamental idea . . . of the decoration was this: In the midst of a forest all is calm and silent; one sees the sky only when lifting the eyes; all around, the sapin and its branches form a tapestry rich in design and color which is linked to the ground by columns—the verticals of tree trunks; lower still the flowers of various plants form a most agreeable carpet. The calm is complete; involuntarily one's sight is drawn by the radiance in the sky where The Cross appears, resplendent in light."[81]

Unfortunately this unique and remarkably complete example of Swiss cultural heritage was ruthlessly destroyed when the chapel was remodeled into a house late in the 1970s. Neither cantonal nor federal authorities mustered enough interest to take documentary photographs or arrange for examples of the decorative work to be saved; Perrin's stone communion table was saved because it was needed in a nearby church, and some of the glass was reused in the house. The previous decade had already seen the destructive remodeling of the great hall at the La Chaux-de-Fonds post office (1910), and as I write there is talk of destroying the splendid foyer (1911) of the Neuchâtel observatory (once the "Greenwich" of Swiss timekeeping). One thing is absolutely certain: once most traces of this highly inventive episode in Swiss cultural history have vanished, those responsible for the "beaux arts" in Switzerland will belatedly open the public purse and acquire at greatly inflated prices a few remaining bits and pieces.

Locally this movement is so little known that it has never acquired a name; if it is mentioned at all, people will say "work done by the students of L'Eplattenier." A fitting designation, it seems to me, would be the Ecole du Jura (the Jura School), taking a cue from the Ecole de Nancy with which it had so much in common.

81. *Rapport*, 1907–8, p. 8. The description continues: "Le plafond, de sapin naturel, est percé de quelques ouvertures de ventilation, recouvertes par des grilles de cuivre découpé où sont suspendus des lustres de même genre destinés à un éclairage électrique. Les lambris sont agrémentés de quelques losanges de métal brillant. . . . La frise sombre du soubassement est éclaircie par quelques fleurs ou insectes en métal repoussé; par de petits carrés en faïence émaillée de diverses couleurs. Les vitraux représentent des plantes du Jura stylisées se découpant sur des silhouettes de montagnes font l'effet d'échappées sur des parties de nos pâturages ou de nos prairies." The possibility of a Ruskinian literary influence on the ornamental design is discussed by Sekler in *The Open Hand*, pp. 57–61.

Jeanneret and Perrin each received 20 francs for working at the chapel (see Perrin letter to L'Eplattenier dated November 23, 1907) which implies that students were given token payment, with most of the income going into the common fund.

**Fig. 79.** Charles-Edouard Jeanneret, August 1907, just prior to his departure for Italy. Compare this self-assured young man with later photographs. (BV)

During the years of Jeanneret's preoccupation with the Cours Supérieur, family life continued pretty much as usual. The two brothers visited Basel in February 1906, and in March and April the father reported "Edouard not too plucky" and that he was taking treatment for albuminuria. The summer holidays saw the family, minus Edouard, who was too busy, depart on July 22 for Gruben, Canton Valais, in the high Alps. Although mother and elder son remained three weeks (500 francs), the father stayed only ten days due to the pressure of work back home. Watchmaking again was thriving, even expanding, yet new problems beset Mr. Jeanneret's endless endeavors to produce the pure enamel his watchfaces required. At year's end, with his brother absent from Soleure, the family remained at La Chaux-de-Fonds where "Edouard, all occupied with dancing and with girls, has just bought a pair of skis. He doesn't appear too healthy, this boy" (Journal, January 5, 1907). Snow was abundant that year with 1.2 meters (4 feet) falling in a single storm, thus requiring a team of eight horses to pull the ploughs. Snow and inflation marked the beginning of 1907, and the head of the household became increasingly distraught at his inability to consistently create the white enamel needed for his bountiful orders from Longines. Both morally and financially he was being ruined, and he suffered additionally because of his family's inability to comprehend his problems. When August arrived he renounced his cherished Alpine climb in order to work at his enamels; meanwhile the others visited Gruben again, staying a little over two weeks (cost 450 francs). Albert was back from the conservatory at Geneva, strong and in the best of health, his wrist problems being much improved. Of Edouard, who had visited Fribourg in June,[82] his father noted on September 3, 1907: "Edouard left us this morning on his big trip to Italy to last 3 months and then goes to Vienna in order to complete his knowledge and education. He left full of courage and determination [see fig. 79]. Voilà—taken from us for one or several years. God be with him!"

82. Several sketches of Fribourg sculpture and architecture exist, one of which (FLC 2056) says "sculp. en bois musée Marcello, Fribourg juin 1907," thus providing the date of this trip. As at Basel the previous year, late medieval work is what appealed to him—a stylistic preference he would maintain in Italy. In January 1907 he had also visited Thur (Thoune) and Bern.

# II

## TRAVELS AND APPRENTICESHIPS
*1907–1911*

"Today I am accused of being a revolutionary, yet I confess to having had only one master: the past; and only one discipline: the study of the past."

Le Corbusier (1930)

# 3

## TRAVELS IN NORTHERN ITALY
### *1907*

Early Tuesday morning, September 3, 1907, Charles-Edouard Jeanneret departed from La Chaux-de-Fonds on what would become a four-year period of travel and apprenticeship. In certain respects this was the nineteen-year-old's university education; at its conclusion he returned home to begin a career of teaching and the practice of architecture.

This four-year period encompassed six clearly distinct episodes, each lasting a different length of time. His travels, as was traditional among architects, commenced in Italy. He then went to Vienna (4 months), Paris (21 months), had two sojourns at home during 1910 (totalling 4 1/2 months), followed by Germany (12 months) and finally a "Voyage d'orient" (7 months in the Balkans, Turkey, Greece, and central Italy). The pattern was consistent: winters in cities—Vienna, Paris, La Chaux-de-Fonds, and Berlin—and summers of random travel, often with a friend. Only the first few months were preplanned; thereafter chance and Jeanneret's changing values played the decisive role.

Previously these years were known only through Le Corbusier's own recollections, yet now they are documented by hundreds of letters written to family and to such friends as Charles L'Eplattenier and (after 1910) William Ritter and Max Du Bois. In addition, there are numerous, still unpublished, sketchbooks and drawings. He also amassed a large collection of postcards and scores of photographs taken with one of his two cameras (one required glass plates and the other roll film).[1] These resources permit an amazingly precise reconstruction of his travels and his ever-changing attitudes and values. Therefore the problem is not to embellish but rather to condense, organize, and analyze this overwhelming abundance of documentation.[2]

Before immersing ourselves in the details of his daily itinerary, we should make some broad observations about Jeanneret's interests and attitudes which, surprisingly, underwent very little change during his two and a half months in Italy. Firstly, his taste was not characteristic of the early twentieth century but rather that of the 1860s and the Gothic Revival. John Ruskin, Owen Jones, Charles Blanc, and Hippolyte Taine were the authors he identified with in spite of having read in Henry Provensal's *L'Art de demain* that artists should be ahead of their time and must set standards for the future. When confronted by the avant-garde, as he was in Vienna, he rejected it completely.[3]

His preference in Italy was the architecture of the 1300s (and earlier) and his favorite buildings were the cathedrals of Pisa and Milan, the Doges' Palace and St. Mark's in Venice, and the Palazzo Vecchio, Or San Michele, and the Bargello courtyard in Florence. Concurrently, Europe and America were experiencing a resurgence of classical values, yet Jeanneret arrived in Italy with eyes unable to observe the Renaissance. The architecture of Alberti, Bramante, Brunelleschi, Michelozzo, Palladio, concerned him not at all (not even enough to express a reaction against it) and, with but one exception, no building by these men received comment in his extensive correspondence.

Secondly, Jeanneret lacked the concerns basic to an architect. Mass, volume, space, materials, construction, as well as plans of buildings and urban spaces passed largely unnoticed. By contrast, such painterly considerations as color, light, pattern, and surface decoration dominated his attention. Naïvely he wrote his teacher from Florence on September 21: "The city appears to me *not rich* in architecture, isn't that true?" (emphasis in original). What a thing to believe! Clearly Jeanneret's thoughts were less on three-dimensional architecture than on two-dimensional surface and how best it might be decorated.

1. By 1910 photography became very important to Jeanneret, probably under the influence of René Chapallaz. The occasional photographs that exist from northern Italy and France may have been taken after 1910. He often developed, and usually printed, his own films, the prints frequently being of atrocious quality. The negative sizes are 8.25 × 8.25 cm and 5.75 × 8.25 cm and one of these cameras, a Cupido 80, remains in the collection of the FLC.

2. Jean Petit, *Le Corbusier, lui-même* (Geneva, 1970), also quotes autobiographical writings by Le Corbusier for which he never reveals the source. These were probably prepared in the early 1960s specifically for Petit's use; if so, they are not contemporary with the events.

3. A belated appreciation of an artist, or art form, was characteristic of Jeanneret's personality. He was inevitably *retardataire* rather than avant-garde; during his Vienna stay he consistently disparaged Hoffmann and the Secession yet later he cultivated the (totally false) impression that he had admired Hoffmann's work and had apprenticed in Hoffmann's office. Actually, it was not until a decade later that he embraced the avant-garde. Jeanneret's gradual closing of this time and culture gap is really the story of this book.

It was painting and the decorative arts, not architecture, that pleased him most and it was the late Middle Ages, with their stylistic continuance into the fifteenth century, that he especially admired. Giotto, Gozzoli, Orcagna, and Fra Angelico were his favorites. He did admire Renaissance portraits, especially those in silhouette that had neutral backgrounds. In the decorative arts color and rich materials impressed him most, with his preference running to inlaid marbles and mosaics.

The majority of his watercolors and sketches were of mural decorations, wall frescoes, mosaics, and inlaid marble pavements—things that were applied to construction rather than construction itself. Easel paintings, as seen in museums, he rarely sketched yet often praised in his correspondence. Therefore he apparently considered mural decoration within the purview of the architect (recall his sgraffito work at the Villa Fallet), but easel paintings, which could not be applied to buildings, were not.

The breadth of knowledge required of an architect greatly troubled him; of this he wrote to his parents on October 8. He contrasted his position with that of his traveling companion, Léon Perrin: "He concentrates on sculpture and somewhat on fresco, whereas I am obliged to be interested in all things, architecture embracing absolutely all, leaving its mark on everything. When, three years ago, I read the first [sic] line of the *Grammaire des arts* [*du dessin*, by Charles Blanc of 1867, p. 64]: Architecture is the first of the Arts, I did not understand and was certainly not in agreement."

Sculpture, however, received less attention from Jeanneret than the other visual arts (perhaps because he thought it less germane to architecture) yet curiously enough it alone was the domain wherein his preference ran to Renaissance rather than Gothic forms. Donatello and early Michelangelo were his favorites, apparently because he saw naturalism in their works—something he also praised in Gozzoli.

When making sketches Jeanneret favored pencil (which became blunter and softer as the years went by) often combined with ink (or perhaps ink alone). This he frequently overlay with a watercolor wash through which the underlying drawing could be seen. The result was a strong, assertive statement unburdened by precise detail. The color, texture, size, and thickness of his paper often varied, yet normally it was in the 16 to 20 cm range except when he was drawing entire buildings where he liked to include details on the same sheet, which might be 25 × 32 cm in size. The principal purpose of such drawings was as an aid to memory, yet he was duly proud of them and occasionally exhibited them—usually under the rubric Langage de Pierre.[4] Clearly a historian at heart, he identified the subject of these renderings by name, place, date, and then added a few descriptive words before signing and dating the completed work. During October his watercolor technique reached a perfection he was never to surpass.

Jeanneret augmented this visual documentation with numerous picture postcards. These confirm what we learn from his renderings and correspondence—that he liked thin, linear, quiet, and often sentimental art rather than plastic, dynamic, and forceful

4. This title perhaps defers to Ruskin's *Stones of Venice*.

things. His subsequent fondness for the paintings of Puvis de Chavannes is therefore easy to understand; so are certain parallels with his architecture of the 1920s. The largest group of cards is of Benozzo Gozzoli's frescoes at Pisa and Florence, but there is also Giotto, Cimabue, Fra Angelico, Uccello, Ghirlandaio, early Botticelli, Mantegna, Bellini, and a few early Raphaels. There is little sculpture except for Donatello's *David* and *Gattamelata*. Architecture, surprisingly, represents considerably less than half of the collection and (except for Ravenna) tends to duplicate the buildings he chose to sketch.

In Italy, three books served as guides: Baedeker, Ruskin, and Taine. Baedeker was "a lucky find" (letter to parents, September 14) and therefore was probably a recent acquisition. The others are signed "Ch. E. Jeanneret/La Chaux-de-Fonds" and thus purchased prior to his departure. John Ruskin's *Les Matins à Florence* (Paris, 1906; although the first English edition dates from 1875) was extraordinarily important in guiding his steps, his eyes, and his mind; prior to leaving Florence he executed more than a dozen watercolors based on Ruskin's six different itineraries. His taste closely paralleled that of Ruskin except for his admiration of a few early paintings by Raphael and others whom Ruskin rejected. Therein Jeanneret demonstrated some independence, or more correctly a concurrence with certain ideas of Taine. Ruskin's *The Stones of Venice* (1851–53) was, of course, also well known to Jeanneret.

Hippolyte Taine's *Voyage en Italie* was written as a travelogue, enumerating the writer's reactions to what he saw. It provides a sense of déjà vu. Yet being a Frenchman, writing in the 1860s, his orientation was understandably more classical than that of his English contemporary. This caused Jeanneret considerable discomfort when, for example, at Pisa Taine praised the whiteness of the marble facades and Jeanneret saw only rich colors and ever-changing hues at different times of day. Taine lavished praise on the Renaissance, and perhaps it is due to this, in spite of Ruskin, that Jeanneret found beauty in selected works by Raphael, Titian, and Tintoretto, and certain other sixteenth-century masters.

The chatty and familiar style exemplified by these books, including Ruskin's format of "letters to a friend" and Taine's title (*Voyage en . . .*), as well as his "en route" presentation, would all find parallels in Jeanneret's *Voyage d'orient* written toward the end of his own European travels in 1911.

These travels, which began September 3, 1907, took Jeanneret via Bern on an eight-day train trip to Florence. Using second- or third-class rail, he favored early departures or late arrivals so as to keep the bulk of the day free, yet once installed in some town he wanted nine or more hours of sleep (9 till 6 or 10 till 7). At Bern he visited the museum, admiring the work of Böcklin and Hodler of whom he remarked to L'Eplattenier (September 19): "Hodler invented nothing. . . . His techniques are those of the [Italian] painters of the fourteenth century."

Continuing that same afternoon, he crossed the St. Gotthard Pass and arrived late at Lugano where the next morning—with fine weather and after walking to the Belvedere—he bid farewell to Switzerland. By two he was in front of the cathedral at Milan. Tremendously impressed by its grandeur and enormity, he likened its interior to the "mystery of the forest." Of the Monumental Cemetery, starred by Baedeker, he had no words of praise but did find "the exterior of the Sforza Palace very beautiful, simple, [with] sgraffito in the manner of Fallet" (to L'Eplattenier, September 19). Of works by Bramante and Leonardo da Vinci he made no mention.

He did visit the chartreuse, or Carthusian monastery, at Pavia and there rhapsodized over the "splendid stalls of marquetry, what beautiful work, same for the altars of precious stones encrusted in white marble, fabulous!" (L'Eplattenier, September 19). His fascination with things precious and richly ornamented characterized his sensibility; he was certainly a decorator at heart. He also remarked (à la Baedeker) on the terra-cotta work at the cloisters, but nowhere mentioned the twenty-four "maisonettes" of which he may not have seen the inside.

Next he stopped at Genoa, arriving at 1 a.m. on Friday the sixth. Up early, he walked the entire length of the quay; this was the first seaport he had ever seen. He also visited a Lombard church, looked up a family friend, and departed by second-class train along the Riviera di Levante (too often obscured by its 67 tunnels) to Pisa where, by three o'clock, he was at the Duomo and Campo Santo. Stupefied by the beauty of the ornamental details, he remained nearly four days in their presence, contemplating and sketching, and straying merely long enough to visit the civic museum. In contrast to Taine, who praised the white marble and solid, geometric architectural forms that underlay the decoration, Jeanneret saw only the surface ornament and coloristic effects without noticing the geometric shapes or the spatial relationships between them. At the Campo Santo frescoes, especially the *Triumph of Death* and the *Last Judgment* (then still attributed to Andrea Orcagna), and also the Old Testament scenes by Benozzo Gozzoli, Jeanneret found much to praise and sketched various details. Later, when writing L'Eplattenier of his six most positive impressions of Italy, the Pisa cathedral and Orcagna frescoes were, along with the Milan cathedral, rated among the best.

Following Baedeker's itinerary, Jeanneret intended to visit Lucca but inadvertently passed through it on the train and continued to Pistoia (of little interest) and Prato (the interior of the cathedral he found "délicieux"), arriving in Florence at eight o'clock that evening (Tuesday, September 10). There he met Léon Perrin, his schoolmate, with whom he shared a room at 5, Piazza della Signoria (2 Swiss francs per day including dinner). He described the city as noisy and full of mosquitoes, flies, cats, and degenerate Italians. And soon thereafter he depicted Perrin as moody, dull-witted, and incompatible as a roommate. Writing by lamplight, he frequently complained of eye fatigue.

Once in Florence, we might expect him to discover the Renaissance, but this was not the case. Giotto, Fra Angelico, Gozzoli, and Orcagna were his favorite artists, with the Palazzo Vecchio (fig. 80), Bargello courtyard, and Or San Michele his favorite buildings. Thus it was the 1300s, including its stylistic persistence into the fifteenth century,

Fig. 80. Palazzo Vecchio, Florence. On September 16, 1907, Jeanneret wrote his parents: "Cet après-midi dessiné le Palais-Vieux; c'est la grande merveille." Pencil and ink on gray fibrous paper. 36 × 25 cm. (FLC 2173)

that caught his fancy; these works he praised as simple, strong, and robust. Elimination was also among his complimentary words, used in the context of omitting that which was secondary (such as the background in a painting). In an apparent contradiction, however, he loved scrumptious, small-scale ornaments such as delicate inlays of colorful marble, rich mosaics, and intricate wood marquetry.

Incredible as it may seem, Jeanneret was unsure of how to study architecture—or even what he should be looking at. Eleven days after arriving in Florence he wrote L'Eplattenier: "The city appears to me *not rich* in architecture, isn't that so? or are my eyes still dazzled by Pisa? As I told you, the Palazzo Vecchio is a great marvel but it is difficult to study, it's an abstract power, isn't it? Mustn't I *look primarily* at painting and sculpture (useless, it seems to me, to copy Raphael or Botticelli) or am I doing the wrong thing and must I sketch the various palazzi? A word from you will help me greatly" (September 21; emphasis in original). Incidentally, he did not sketch the various palazzi, nor Raphael and Botticelli.

That Jeanneret believed the study of painting and sculpture was fundamental to the study of architecture certainly merits further comment. First of all it conforms to L'Eplattenier's concern for decorated surfaces as well as Ruskin's belief that architecture consists of that which is added to a building. Secondly, this attitude of Jeanneret's—that the key to architecture was to be found in painting—remained basic in his thinking throughout his life. "The secret of my quest must be sought in my painting," Le Corbusier observed.[5] Thus it is no coincidence that the best part of every day, the mornings, he devoted to painting and only went to his architectural office in the afternoon. Painting might adorn a wall (as at the Villa Fallet or as did Giotto's frescoes) but most importantly it instilled basic principles of design—concerning form, color, and the relationship of part to part.

It is not surprising, therefore, that Ruskin's *Mornings in Florence* was Jeanneret's valued companion; this book "teaches how to see" (to L'Eplattenier, September 19). The two men's taste diverged but rarely. One instance is Jeanneret's fondness for the work of Gozzoli, whom Ruskin ignored, another is Ruskin's denunciation of the interior of Santa Croce for its lack of vaulting—protesting that it has "the roof of a farmhouse barn" (p. 14)—yet this is precisely what attracted Jeanneret and it was one of the rare instances during his Italian stay that he manifested an interest in construction (fig. 81). Normally he sought only such painterly features as color, texture, and the shadow effects of sculpted ornament (as at the Palazzo Vecchio) or such compositional considerations as size and arrangement of windows, proportions, and the placement of sculptural enrichment. Thus his analysis of Or San Michele shows only details of the plastic embellishment; the entire facade he does not bother to record (fig. 82).

Another of the detailed studies from Or San Michele is among Jeanneret's most

5. Le Corbusier, *Modulor* 2 (1958), p. 296.

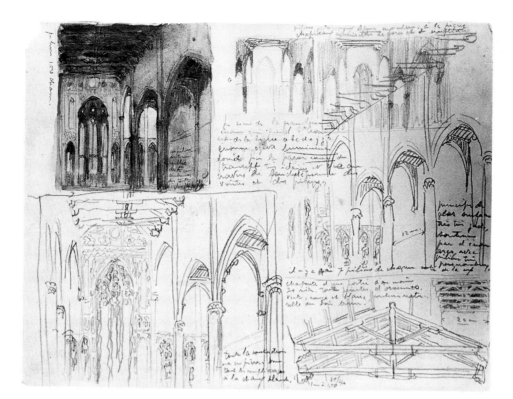

**Fig. 81.** Santa Croce, Florence, interior. Pencil and watercolor on ivory paper. 24.5 × 32.3 cm. (FLC 2175)

subtle and lovely Florentine watercolors; his medium consists of brown washes over pencil, all set off against white paper with tiny accents of blue and green (fig. 83, color plate II). The caption reads "Florence 1413 Niche of Donatello at Or San Michele. White marble inlaid with black marble. October 1907 Ch. E. Jeanneret." These words confirm what the painting itself reveals: Jeanneret is not recording Donatello's statue of St. Mark but rather the encrusted marble niche in which it is placed. On October 9 he wrote his parents: "This morning spent 6 hours sketching one of the delightful niches that decorate Or San Michele."

The embellishment of architecture—niches, towers, windows, balconies, cornices—was what Jeanneret studied rather than the monument itself—its massing, shape, and structure. This generalization applies as well to sculpture. Inside Or San Michele, for example, he made a hasty pencil sketch of Orcagna's tabernacle. Yet on another sheet, subsequently mounted and exhibited, he painstakingly drew and painted a small detail of this tabernacle—the area where a richly inlaid miniature pier meets the horizontal frieze (fig. 84).[6] In similar manner he recorded Donatello's choir gallery at San Lorenzo,

6. To his parents he wrote: "Fait une étude ce matin [Tuesday, September 24] du Tabernacle d'Orcagna à Or San Michele. Vous ne pouvez pas vous faire une idée, vous ne pouvez croire que le centième de ce qui est. La richesse fabuleuse accumulée en cet[te] châsse de marbre par un génie tel qu'Orcagna dépasse l'imagination, il faut le voir, le palper, caresser ces marbres polis et devenus transparents à force de finesse,

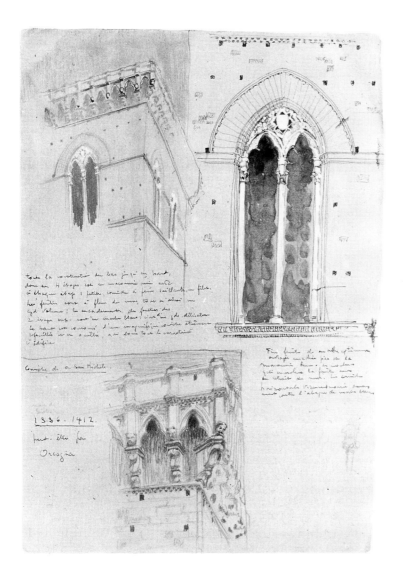

**Fig. 82.** Or San Michele, Florence. Details of the exterior. Pencil, ink, and watercolor on tan-colored paper. 36 × 25 cm. (FLC 2082)

**Fig. 83.** Or San Michele, niche containing Donatello's statue of St. Mark. Painted on October 9, 1907. Pencil and watercolor on ivory paper. 31 × 15.5 cm. (FLC 2162)

carefully detailing a single console while (on the same sheet) making a smaller, more impressionistic sketch of the entire cantoria (fig. 85). His notations establish that it was the "unprecedented richness" of the carving that caught his eye.[7]

When studying frescoes Jeanneret was less concerned with details, inevitably captur-

il faut fouiller avec la jumelle les recoins les plus sombres. . . ." This rhapsody continues for another full page.

7. Meanwhile Pisano and Ghiberti's baptistry doors receive only passing reference in his correspondence and no sketch of them (if made) survives.

For many more illustrations of his Italian paintings, all reproduced in color, see Le Corbusier, *Il viaggio in Tuscana (1907)* (Venice, Cataloghi Marsilio: 1987), with texts by Giuliano Gresleri, Grazia Gobbi, and Paolo Sica.

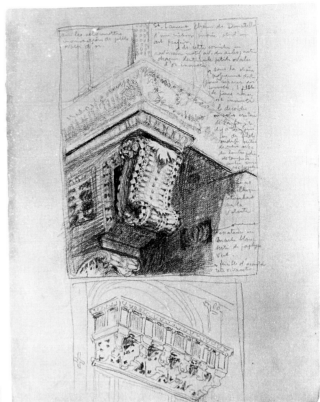

ing the entire panel with quick pencil strokes which he then overlaid with watercolor. The technique was amazingly effective. Typical are his paintings of Giotto's *Saints Joachim and Anna at the Golden Gate* (specifically recommended by Ruskin; fig. 86), and the *Procession to Calvary* which he captioned "Fresque de S. Memmi aux Espagnols" that includes the out-of-date attribution to Memmi found in Ruskin's thirty-year-old text. The exterior of this chapel, dating from the mid-fourteenth century, was also praised by Ruskin, who specifically mentioned the "two windows with traceries opening into the cloister" (see "The Fourth Morning"). Jeanneret recorded this, adding the caption "1355 Fenêtre de la Chapelle des Espagnols St. M. Novella Florence oct. 1907" (fig. 87). Although this watercolor dates from October, he initially visited the Spanish Chapel (letter to his parents) on his second day in Florence.[8]

Fra Angelico and Gozzoli frescoes, though greatly admired, were less often copied. He observed that certain Fra Angelico paintings "made 500 years ago seem to date from

8. Jeanneret likewise studied the Gothic wall-tombs outside of Santa Maria Novella of which Ruskin said ("The Fifth Morning") he "would fair have painted, stone by stone" except for the street urchins who threw pebbles at him. Jeanneret's persistence, during three hours from 11 till 2, was rewarded with a severe sunburn (letter to parents, October 8).

**Fig. 84.** Tabernacle (detail) by Andrea Orcagna at Or San Michele. Caption reads: "Tabernacle, Orcagna 1359." Pencil, watercolor, and perhaps gouache on paper. 14.5 × 12 cm. (FLC 1983)

**Fig. 85.** Cantoria (choir gallery) at San Lorenzo, Florence, by Donatello. Detail and full view. Pencil with charcoal on paper. 34.5 × 25.5 cm. (FLC 1978)

**Fig. 86.** Giotto, *Meeting of Saints Joachim and Anna at the Golden Gate,* Santa Maria Novella, Florence. Pencil and watercolor. 16.5 × 16.5 cm. (FLC 2264)

**Fig. 87.** Spanish Chapel (detail), Santa Maria Novella. Caption reads: "1355 Fenêtre de la Chapelle des Espagnols, St. M. Novella, Florence. oct 1907." Pencil and watercolor on paper. 23.5 × 23.5 cm. (FLC 2037)

tomorrow" (to parents, September 23), thereby implying how painting might look in the future. Botticelli, praised by Ruskin, also was included on Jeanneret's list.

Portraits by Raphael, Titian, and Velazquez were also praised. The inclusion of these sixteenth- and seventeenth-century works at first seems to contradict Jeanneret's characteristic taste, yet such was not the case. Simply put, these *portraits* (unlike other subject matter) manifest the clear outline and neutral backgrounds that Jeanneret admired, for example, in Fra Angelico's *Crucifixion* which was one of his favorite paintings. The most striking inconsistency in Jeanneret's stylistic bias was his ardent enthusiasm for Michelangelo's *Day* at the Medici tombs, the twisted, muscular back of this female figure receiving much praise despite the fact that Michelangelo's work was usually considered too tormented.[9]

On Sunday, September 15, after first visiting the Medici tombs, the Medici chapel (Gozzoli frescoes), and San Marco (Fra Angelico), Jeanneret spent the afternoon at the Chartreuse de Galluzzo (fig. 88)[10] where he underwent the most profound architectural experience of his life. By his own admission, ideas derived therefrom formed the basis

9. "Je trouve M-A beau, très grand, mais il me paraît bien tourmenté, j'admire beaucoup plus tel torse grec en pierre verte aux Offices" (to L'Eplattenier, September 19, 1907).

10. The Carthusian order was founded in 1084 by Saint Bruno, who established the motherhouse in the rugged Chartreuse Mountains just north of Grenoble, France. This monastery assumed the name Grande-Chartreuse, with auxiliary charterhouses carrying the name "chartreuse" plus a nearby town. Thus the name Chartreuse de Galluzzo (or of Florence which is 6 km away but better known). Both Baedeker and Ruskin, in common with other guidebooks of the period, spoke of the "Chartreuse du Val d'Ema," the Ema being

**Fig. 88.** Chartreuse d'Ema (Certosa del Galluzzo), general view. (© 1996 Marconi Ediz Ris)

for his immeuble-villas of 1922, Pavillon de l'Esprit Nouveau of 1925, and the numerous Unités d'habitation built in France and Germany after World War II. And just as important as the architectural experience was the revelation that individuality and community life could coexist—and in fact strengthen one another in the process. "From this moment on I saw the two terms, *individual and collectivity,* as inseparable," he would write.[11]

Carthusian monasteries are unlike all others since each monk lives not in a narrow, ill-lit, one-room cell but in a modest house of several rooms with fireplace, cellar, attic, terrace, and a small private garden with flowers, vegetables, and fruit trees. A bridge-like walkway (the origin of Le Corbusier's "architectural promenade") connects the house to the cloister's outer wall which, in turn, is pierced by an unglazed window through which one may contemplate the distant view (cf. the window in the wall at Le Corbusier's Villa Savoye, Poissy, of 1929, or his parents' house at Corseaux-Vevey on Lake Geneva, 1923). During the week the monk lived alone in these pleasant surroundings that were intended to nurture contemplation and reflection, his meals being brought to him each day. Only on Sundays or feast days did he speak with his brethren, joining them for services, then a refectory meal, and finally conversation during a long stroll in the countryside.

This existence, in such a setting, became Jeanneret's dream of the ideal life; much that he designed and built in future years would reflect his love affair with the Chartreuse d'Ema.[12] Yet his letters make no mention of revisiting the chartreuse during his

---

a tributary of the Arno River. Jeanneret, however, chose to omit the word "valley," thereby creating the misnomer Chartreuse d'Ema which he popularized throughout his writings and which, for the sake of consistency, will often be used here.

11. *Unité d'habitation de Marseilles* (Paris: Edition Le Point), November 1950, p. 35.

12. "Je voudrais toute ma vie habiter ce qu'ils appellent leurs cellules. C'est la solution de la maison type unique ou plutôt du paradis terrestre" (to L'Eplattenier, September 19). See also Peter Serenyi, "Le Corbusier, Fourier and the Monastery of Ema," *Art Bulletin,* 49, no. 4 (December 1967), pp. 277–86.

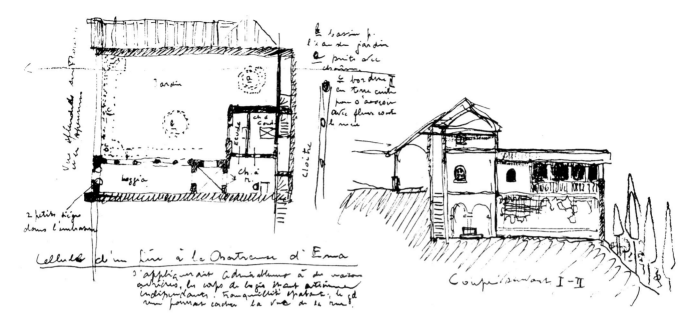

**Fig. 89.** Plan and cross section by Jeanneret of "Cellule d'un père à la Chartreuse d'Ema," drawn September 1907. (Lost original is reproduced from Jean Petit, *Le Corbusier lui-même*, p. 43)

remaining weeks in Florence, nor is there more than a single sketch (a cross section and plan, fig. 89) that exists from this initial visit. Thus it was the idea, rather than specific forms, that primarily impressed him. However, he vowed to return to the chartreuse before terminating his European travels and this he did four years later, in October 1911, just prior to his return to La Chaux-de-Fonds.

Jeanneret and Perrin interrupted their Florentine stay long enough to spend the week of September 29–October 5 in Siena, staying at the Albergo della Scala (recommended in Baedeker; 2 francs per day) facing the baptistry of San Giovanni (fig. 90) where the tranquillity, after the noise of Florence, allowed them to get to sleep by eight. Jeanneret was delighted with Siena, its picturesqueness, its rich colors (especially the warm red brick), and the greenery of its many trees. "The cathedral is a jewel, a thing unique in the world, so interesting that the days slipped by without our being aware of it" (to parents, October 8). He also praised, and sketched, the Piazza del Campo in a rare acknowledgment of urban space; not until 1910, and then only at L'Eplattenier's command, did Jeanneret show an interest in urban planning.

His most moving experience in Siena was witnessing the strange, luminous after-effects of a violent, early evening thunderstorm that distorted and intensified colors into something quite unreal. He recorded these impressions in a small watercolor by using—as a fauve painter might do—relatively unmodulated areas of strong color—black for the vanishing thunder clouds and dark green or white for the remainder of the sky; below were the rich, warm colors of the Palazzo Pubblico (fig. 91). Jeanneret was obviously proud of this painting, *Après l'orage,* which he mounted on black paper and included in his Langage de Pierre exhibit; later he defended it against L'Eplattenier's

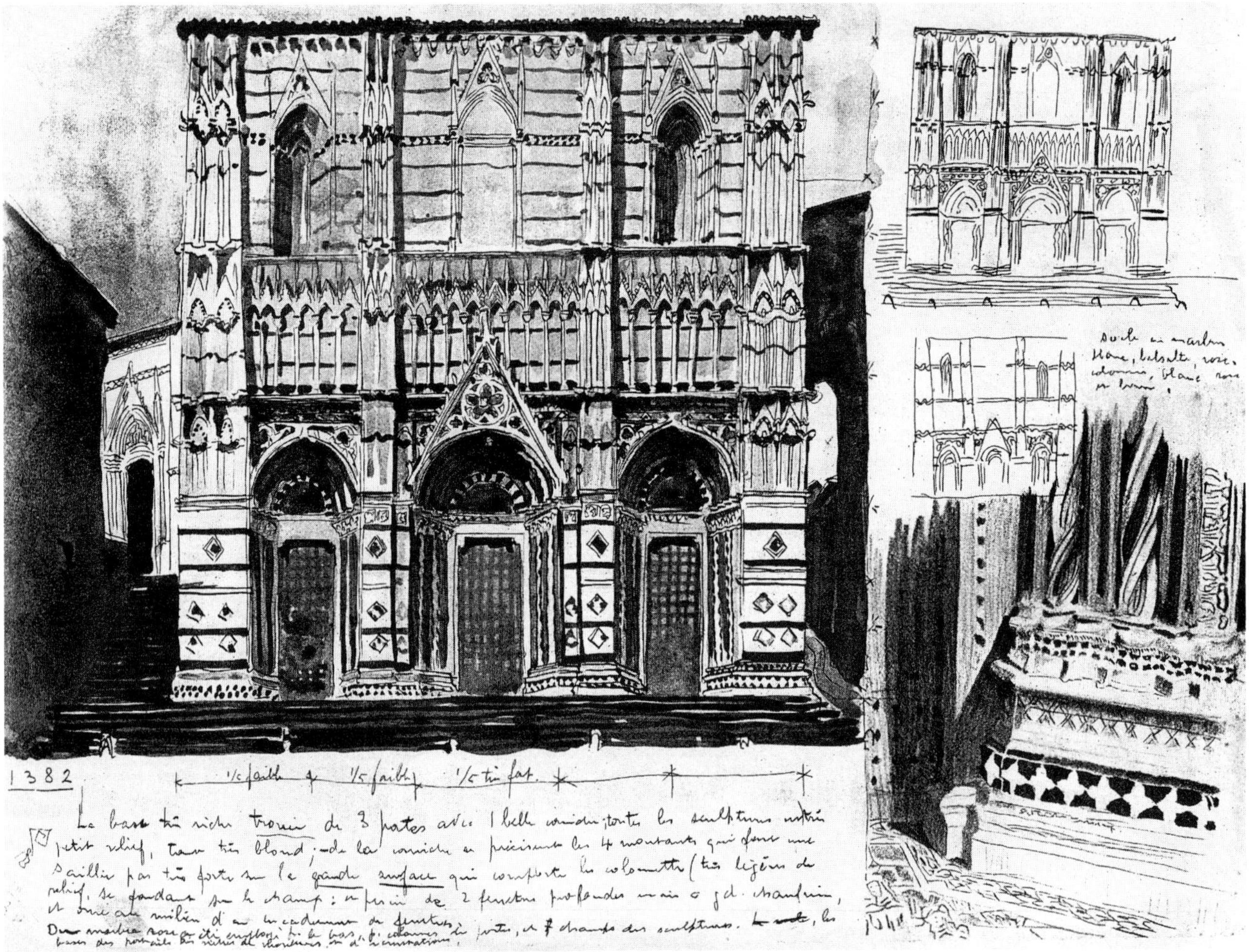


**Fig. 90.** Baptistry, Siena, 1382. Pencil, ink, and watercolor on paper. 24.6 × 32.4 cm. (FLC 1791)

criticisms (in an undated letter from Paris the following year). On certain occasions thereafter, as when in Germany in 1910, he would again execute such expressionistic/fauvist paintings.

Saturday evening the boys returned to Florence. The next day, Jeanneret's twentieth birthday (October 6), he revisited Florence with intensified pleasure thanks to his stay in Siena; he began the morning with Michelangelo's Medici tombs. His continuing exposure to Florence commenced to have an effect; the Renaissance with its classical ideals started, though tentatively, to catch his attention. Perhaps Ruskin set the door ajar when he said "all Florentine work of the finest kind . . . is absolutely pure Etruscan" and that "Giotto was a pure Etruscan-Greek of the thirteenth century" or "that painting a Gothic chapel rightly is just the same as painting a Greek vase rightly."[13] Jeanneret

13. Ruskin, *Mornings in Florence* (New York, 1891), pp. 61 and 60.

**Fig. 91.** *After the Storm,* Palazzo Pubblico (dated "1289–1305") on the Piazza dei Campo, Siena. Signed and dated "1[?] October 1907." The sky is rendered in black, green, and with areas of white unpainted paper. Watercolor on paper. 18.5 × 15.8 cm. (FLC 2852)

**Fig. 92.** San Martino, Lucca. "Lucques. 1204 Colonnes sculptées ou incrustées de la cathédrale. Marbre blanc. oct 1907. Ch. E. Jeanneret." Pencil and watercolor on paper. 24.5 × 20.5 cm. (FLC 2464)

visited the Archaeological Museum where he greatly admired the Greek black-figure vases, statuettes, and Etruscan tomb paintings. He raved to his parents and to L'Eplattenier about these works of art.[14] And in the letter to his mentor he rescinded his previous judgment of Masaccio, now praising "these eternal frescoes" at Santa Maria del Carmine that some years later, in the early teens, he would paint from memory while recalling his visit to Florence.

Renaissance architecture also saw a modest reappraisal, yet only for a single structure—Brunelleschi's cathedral dome. Not until his penultimate evening in Florence did he write to his parents that the great dome "has finally revealed itself to me after four weeks of indifference" and that the next day, his last in Florence, he intended to climb it. Some hours later he continued: "[I] descended stupefied by its grandeur; I retract all the foolish things I thought and perhaps wrote concerning this genius [Brunelleschi] who daringly constructed a thing that is so colossal and so strong."[15] Henceforth he

14. To L'Eplattenier on September 19 and to parents on September 23 where half a page is devoted to this subject, beginning "Je suis allé verser mes larmes dans les vases grecs du musée archéologique . . . larmes d'admiration et de béatitude."

15. Letter to parents of October 8–10, 1907. Jeanneret's chief impressions of Florence merit full quotation: "Je trouve Florence magnifique, je la revois encore avec plus de plaisir après Sienne; l'élimination devient formidable, il ne reste plus que Giotto, le plus grand de tous les peintres décorateurs, Sta. Croce

would marvel at this imposing form that so proudly dominated Florence; he was thrilled upon seeing it four times from the train on the following day. During his early visits to Fiesole and San Miniato, which overlook Florence, Brunelleschi's masterpiece had left him cold. Nevertheless, it was only the splendor, the nobility, and the size of the dome that now touched Jeanneret's soul, not the other qualities we associate with Renaissance design.

By contrast, Brunelleschi's small-scale work, even though starred in Baedeker, never received a passing reference in Jeanneret's letters. He never mentioned the Pazzi Chapel at Santa Croce, the interiors of San Lorenzo (though he sketched Donatello's cantoria therein and repeatedly visited the Medici tombs), or Santo Spirito, or the Spedale degli Innocenti, all major works by Brunelleschi. Nor did he have eyes for Alberti (Palazzo Rucellai) or Michelozzo (Palazzo Medici). Therefore what Jeanneret failed to "see" in Florence is, for us, far more revealing than what he chose to notice ("Eyes That Do Not See" is a chapter heading in his book *Vers une architecture* [Paris, 1923] wherein he castigates others, and perhaps secretly admonishes himself, for what people fail to see).

His final morning in Florence being devoted to Brunelleschi's dome, Jeanneret reserved the afternoon to revisit old favorites, first the Palazzo Vecchio, where he climbed to the top of the 94-meter tower, and thereafter the "magnificent" Gozzoli frescoes in the Medici-Riccardi chapel. Thus ended his twenty-third day in Florence.

At six the following morning they left for Lucca which Jeanneret had missed en route to Florence. There he executed a watercolor illustrating two arches from the marble-encrusted cathedral facade (fig. 92).[16] Generally, however, he was unimpressed with Lucca and reported to L'Eplattenier (November 1): "If the visit didn't yield very much, at least it permitted me to see Brunelleschi's dome [from the train] four times instead of once."

The next day, Saturday the twelfth, after an overnight in Florence, they left for Ravenna where they intended to stay a week before continuing on to Ferrara, Bologna, Modena, Mantua, Verona, Vicenza, Padua, and Venice. However, they gave less time to Ravenna than originally planned.

In Ravenna, without Ruskin, Jeanneret relied on Baedeker and Taine as his guides and this rekindled his one-sided debate with Taine, whose artistic judgment he had

---

(église) chef-d'oeuvre de force, le Palais Vieux, vieux rébarbatif, Or San Michele, la merveille du génie *fort et robuste* faisant des délicatesses et de la *beauté*. Le coupole du dôme, qui s'est enfin révélé après 4 semaines d'indifférence, la Chapelle des Espagnols [et] . . . la Chapelle des Médicis où Michel-Ange vous fait presque pleurer."

16. This Romanesque detail from the facade of San Martino (1204) is curious because neither the sequence of these three columns nor the spandrel ornament above correspond to the present building. Did Jeanneret rearrange these elements for his own purposes or did this occur during a restoration? This painting was included in his series, Langage de Pierre.

**Fig. 93.** San Vitale, Ravenna. "VI siècle. Ravenne St Vidale Colonnes en porphyre. Chapiteaux sculptés et dorés. Voûtes en stuc modelées. Le reste en mosaïque. oct 1907 *Ch. E. Jeanneret.*" Pencil, ink, watercolor (and gouache?) on paper. 20 × 19 cm. (FLC 1970)

criticized at Pisa. Visibly moved by the splendid mosaics at Ravenna, Jeanneret fumed because they were "so stupidly disparaged by Taine," whom he called "a perfect imbecile, and I'd be ready to say it to his face" (to parents, October 24). Nevertheless Jeanneret admitted that Taine had greatly helped him appreciate Florence, as well as Siena and Pisa, and therefore to better enjoy his trip.

During five days, while well housed and enjoying excellent dinners (3 francs per day), Jeanneret acquired numerous postcards of the buildings while concentrating his own efforts on producing watercolor studies of the mosaics and architectural decoration. Within San Vitale he executed a beautiful study, full of vibrancy and color, of two of the sixth-century capitals (fig. 93) as well as the panel of Theodora and her attendants. At Sant'Apollinare in Classe he rendered the apse (with both a full view and a detail on a single sheet), at Sant'Apollinare Nuovo four figures from the procession of virgins, and at the baptistry beside the cathedral a watercolor plus a pencil sketch showing portions of the dome.

Leaving Ravenna on Friday morning the eighteenth, on a seven-day rail pass, they went to Ferrara where Jeanneret praised the beautiful and stately cathedral yet left us no known sketch. By late afternoon they were in Bologna where they spent two days and three nights. The stellar attraction was Raphael's *St. Cecilia* yet Jeanneret was likewise impressed by the odd grouping of buildings called Santo Stefano and by an unnamed palace of brick with windows of white marble.

Although not explicitly stated in his letters, one senses that the boys were wearied by so much art. This is apparent by their actions. There are no extant sketches by Jeanneret from Ferrara, Bologna, Mantua, Verona, or Padua, and very few from their lengthly stay in Venice. They also altered their itinerary, selecting picturesque scenery instead of works of art. Saturday night in Bologna, for example, the youths opted for such unconventional excitement as entraining for the Apennine Mountains to observe the sunset, returning by the light of the moon. And upon leaving Bologna on Monday morning, they bypassed Modena because "we lacked spirit and our dear Baedeker indicated nothing [of great importance there]" (to L'Eplattenier, November 1).

Therefore they went directly to Mantua, city of history and art, where only Mantegna's frescoes were mentioned. Jeanneret was greatly impressed but bought postcards rather than making drawings or watercolors himself. Unbelievable, however, is the fact that he made no reference to Alberti's greatest work, the church of Sant'Andrea, or of Giulio Romano's masterpiece, the Palazzo del Tè. Yet Jeanneret, as already noted, had eyes that did not see; he not only failed to see Renaissance architecture but also that of the sixteenth and seventeenth centuries—Mannerism and Baroque. And when given the choice, he looked at paintings instead of buildings.

Rather than studying Mantuan architecture he enjoyed "dozing on a bench in the sun" (L'Eplattenier, November 1) and had the spur-of-the-moment idea of visiting Lake Garda rather than Verona. So off they went. Within hours they were enjoying a "succulent" dinner under a pergola at Gargnano with the waters of beautiful Lake Garda at their feet. Jeanneret began a postcard to his parents, then finished it by moonlight as they rowed over the tranquil waters of the lake.

Next morning they strolled for an hour through olive groves and cypresses before taking the nine o'clock steamer up the lake to Riva in the Austrian Tyrol. There they arrived at noon and briefly went ashore, then continued for another five hours down the opposite shore to Desenzano where they caught the evening express train to Verona.[17]

17. Apparently they changed trains at Brescia because Jeanneret bought some postcards there, and because he advised his parents that neither Brescia nor Verona were worth the trouble of a visit.

Jeanneret's letters, both to his parents and L'Eplattenier, were ecstatic; this was a high point of their trip, far surpassing even the beauty of Lake Lugano. He urged his parents to vacation there, insisting, however, that they not waste time at the various cities en route.

At Verona they detrained in thick haze and a wintry chill that terminated the seven-week spell of mild, sunny weather they had enjoyed thus far. This put Jeanneret in a negative mood. To his parents he wrote (October 24): "Verona, dreary impression, because I saw it too rapidly in the haze," a poor excuse since his twenty-four hours there equalled the time spent in many other cities. And to L'Eplattenier he begrudgingly explained how he wasted an entrance fee on the Scaliger tombs (fourteenth century) which were under restoration and difficult to see. He did mention the "very beautiful [Romanesque] church of San Zeno with a fine Mantegna," but nothing else. No reference to the famous Roman ruins which included a splendid Arena, nor of Sanmicheli's major architectural works from the sixteenth century. These were all starred in Baedeker, as were the magnificent Giusti gardens.

Their next omission was far more serious. Their intended itinerary was Verona, Vicenza, Padua, Venice. However they skipped Vicenza, passing through it without bothering to get off the train! No explanation is given in their letters. Modena they missed, saying that Baedeker indicated nothing of great importance there, yet Vicenza was the home of Palladio, the "last great architect of the Renaissance" according to Baedeker, who starred and listed Palladio's works and also gave explicit directions for visiting the nearby (a half-hour trip) Villa Rotunda. In truth, Jeanneret had no interest in Palladio as is confirmed by his ensuing neglect of Palladio's Venetian churches.

At Padua they stayed two days and nights, arriving on the evening of the twenty-third. Here Jeanneret's enthusiasm waxed once more, especially over Donatello's *Gattamelata* (he bought postcards) and high altar at San Antonio, as well as Mantegna's frescoes at the Eremitani. On the second morning they visited the Arena chapel, Jeanneret praising Giotto's frescoes with somewhat less emotion than before. And at five o'clock they were off to Venice.

Jeanneret commenced, in Padua, a long letter to his parents from which we learn that the frescoes *inside* the Villa Fallet had crumbled into dust (Jeanneret was arranging compensation) and that—as mentioned in other letters as well—he was thinking about the design for the villas of Messrs. Stotzer and Jaquemet which he would begin work on in Vienna (thus we know these commissions were received before he left La Chaux-de-Fonds).

His letter includes a list of items to be shipped to Vienna. In addition to clothing, "all the books that I had prepared, above all the Musée d'art, Cordova and Granada, Cairo, Michelangelo, Rodin (from *Deutsche Kunst*), Duval's Anatomy, booklet of logarithms of Vega, others also, the Ruskins if I have any more of them."[18] Already he had one book in hand that L'Eplattenier, in a rather revealing yet unlikely going-away present, had sent to him in Florence: Edouard Schuré's *Les Grands Initiés*—the lives of many of the world's great prophets. L'Eplattenier, as it proved, had a deep understanding of Jeanneret's personality.

Plagued by bad weather and flagging interest, their stay in Venice exhibited little of the enthusiasm or productivity that characterized their earlier travels. Jeanneret admitted to his parents that "during your 2 day visit to this city you saw more of it than we in 15. We have blissfully enjoyed ourselves, carefully leaving Baedeker behind and imagining that there was only San Marco and the Piazzetta in Venice. Here we have not worked; in total I made two sketches. But at San Marco we have heard marvelous masses, extraordinary sensations of beatitude, almost of ecstacy, emotions quiet and profound" (to parents, November 17). The letter, after effusively praising the beauty of St. Mark's and especially the sound of music therein, concludes with a short list of other things seen in Venice: the Frari (Santa Maria Gloriosa dei Frari) and Santi Giovanni e Paolo (both being Gothic churches of the fourteenth century), Verrocchio's equestrian statue of *Colleoni* (judged much inferior to *Gattamelata*), the Academy and Civic museums, and a day's excursion to the Lido and another to the port city of Chioggia just south of Venice. To L'Eplattenier (November 1) Jeanneret made brief allusions to architecture, reporting that the Doges' Palace, St. Mark's, and the Ca d'Oro were the "pearls" of the city. No Venetian building after the 1300s was ever mentioned—assuming we discount the reference to a splendid sunset that occurred over the dome of Santa Maria della Salute.

Jeanneret acknowledged making two drawings. One was of several pointed arches at the Doges' Palace wherein the masonry joints are delineated in a manner similar to Ruskin's in *The Stones of Venice* (fig. 94), while another, as Patricia Sekler first observed, is the same archivolt that Ruskin illustrates from the facade of St. Mark's.[19] He also obtained about a dozen postcards of painting, sculpture, and architecture while in Venice.

18. To parents, October 24–25, 1907. This is a curious list. It shows great breadth but raises more questions than it answers. Why did he need books on Cairo, Cordova, and Granada when he wasn't going there? Did he think they might provide source material for the Villas Stotzer and Jaquemet? And Duval's anatomy book plus Rodin and Michelangelo; had he already anticipated studying the human figure while in Vienna? And on November 2 he restated most of this list with one important addition that he carefully underscored—Charles Blanc: "Comme livres: Le Musée d'art, *la Grammaire des Arts de Charles Blanc,* Cordoue et Grenade, Le Caire, Logarithmes, Anatomie Duval, Michel-Ange (en allemand) *me sont nécessaires.*"

19. See Sekler, *The Early Drawings,* p. 463, and figures 182, 183. Ruskin's drawing appears in volume 2, plate 6, of *The Stones of Venice.* Jeanneret owned, but did not take to Italy, Pierre Gusman, *Venise* (Paris, 1904), wherein is printed "Ch. E. Jeanneret, Rue Léopold-Robert 46," an address his family left in October 1906. In Venice they stayed at the Albergo Antica Busa (3 francs, including dinner) with which they were highly pleased.

**Fig. 94.** Doges' Palace, Venice. Detail of gallery in the manner of John Ruskin, *The Stones of Venice.* Pencil and ink on paper. 24.5 × 32 cm. (FLC 2176)

In his letter to L'Eplattenier Jeanneret lavished more attention on painting than on architecture. In part, this was because the youths stumbled across the seventh biennial international art exhibition that was due to close in late October. He obviously enjoyed discussing the various artists, thereby giving the impression of great familiarity with the world of art. He admired the Belgium exhibit most, largely due to its unity of expression, while the Russian, French, and Austrian rooms were merely "interesting"; he was disappointed in Rodin's *Thinker,* which he called a "butcher" because the proportions lacked the refinement of Michelangelo's *Day.* He singled out Carl Larsen in Sweden, Franz von Stück in Germany, and Walter Crane in England as "courageous" men, and condemned the Italian galleries because they offered "nothing but nothing at all."

Their next destination, Budapest, was ordained by L'Eplattenier, who briefly lived and studied there as a youth. Therefore at 8:00 P.M. on November 7, Jeanneret and Perrin embarked on their maiden sea voyage, crossing the Adriatic to Fiume (now Rijeka). Thus ended Jeanneret's sixty-fifth day in Italy; however, he would return four years later at the conclusion of his European travels.

At Fiume, after twelve hours at sea, they entrained and slowly ascended the mountains of Dalmatia, crossed Croatia and Hungary and arrived that evening at Budapest. Jeanneret immediately disliked the city, calling it noisy, unsympathetic, and dominated by huge architectural and sculptural monuments of ugly proportions. He praised only the museum of modern art where, as he authoritatively assured his parents, French art could be studied just as well as if in Paris. After three nights in dirty hotels they departed on Monday morning the eleventh, arriving at three o'clock in Vienna where they would spend the next four months.

Italy had been a joy and a revelation. Yet it revealed how inflexible and out-of-date were Jeanneret's ideas on art. He lived in the world of the Gothic Revival and the mid-nineteenth century—in spite of the fact that this was the twentieth century and an era of neoclassicism. He rejected the values of the Renaissance and ignored the most important architectural creations for which Italy was justly famous.

Equally revealing was his preference for painting over architecture, and his unorthodox assumption that the study of painting was essential to the study of architecture. This belief he maintained throughout his life.

As for contemporary art, whether painting or architecture, he had no sympathy, and his first close encounter with it, in Vienna, proved such a disillusionment that he abandoned the Austrian capital at the first convenient moment.

# 4

## VIENNA AND
## TWO VILLA DESIGNS
### *Winter 1907–1908*

Jeanneret was in Vienna for a very specific purpose—to study contemporary design. He was in precisely the right place at the right time. The creative impulse which successively dominated several European cities was now centered in Vienna. Earlier the focus had been on England and the Arts and Crafts movement, then on Belgium with the Art Nouveau, and subsequently on Nancy and Barcelona. Glasgow, with the work of Charles Rennie Mackintosh, would, however, have the strongest impact on Vienna, where Mackintosh not only participated at the eighth annual Secessionist Exhibition in 1900 but also built a widely acclaimed music room.

Of all of these turn-of-the-century developments, the most enduring proved to be that which transpired in Vienna where, as Jeanneret arrived in November 1907, many of the most significant architectural and design achievements were already in place. Yet he totally rejected them.

The avant-garde in Vienna was represented by Otto Wagner (1844–1918) and various younger men, many his former students. His own architecture had gradually evolved from neo-Renaissance which, however, was far less heavy and ponderous than most Viennese architecture of that day; it was thinner, less plastic, and the surface treatment just prior to 1900 was often decorated with rich, two-dimensional floral motifs in the Art Nouveau style—such as the Majolika Haus of 1898–99. In the new century he abandoned this rich overlay in favor of expressing certain structural characteristics such as seen at the 1904–6 Postal Savings Bank or the contemporary Steinhof church where a decorative pattern was created with aluminum bolts that ostensibly fasten the square marble plaques to the facade.

The Wiener Sezession, born out of conflict with officialdom, gave its name to this art movement as well as to the exhibition hall built for the presentation of their work. Joseph Olbrich (1867–1908), co-founder of the Secession and former student of Wagner's, designed the gallery (1898–99) that marked, stylistically, a transitional phase in which the sculptural heaviness of traditional Viennese Renaissance or Baroque design was modified by areas of flat, unadorned surfaces and highlighted (as around the entrance and in the perforated dome) with Art Nouveau ornament. After its completion, however, Olbrich moved to Darmstadt, Germany, to become director of the art colony where he remained until his untimely death in 1908.

Adolph Loos (1870–1933), who spent the years 1893–97 in the United States, completed the Karntner Bar, renowned for its mirrors and polished marbles, in downtown Vienna in 1907, just prior to Jeanneret's arrival. Yet some of his later residences, such as the Steiner and Scheu houses of 1910–12, postdate Jeanneret's sojourn.

The dominant personality on the architectural scene, however, was Josef Hoffmann (1870–1956), Loos' exact contemporary and former student of Wagner's at the Academy. He had participated in founding the Secession and was co-founder—along with the interior designer Koloman Moser (1868–1918)—of the Wiener Werkstätte, an arts and crafts center that he directed for some thirty years. He also taught at the Kunstgewerbeschule (School of Applied Arts). Thus Hoffmann, in common with so many designers of his age, placed almost equal emphasis on the decorative arts as on architecture. His Purkersdorf Convalescent Home, with its proto-International Style geometric clarity and plain white stucco walls, was completed in 1903–4, while the Stochlet Palace, his masterpiece of monumental elegance, was, from 1905, under construction in more distant Brussels. Meanwhile his famous Cabaret Fledermaus, located in downtown Vienna, opened a mere three weeks prior to Jeanneret's arrival while the remodelling for the Wiener Werkstätte sales shop on the Graben was completed the same month that Jeanneret came—November 1907. Therefore several of Hoffmann's major works were available for Jeanneret to see but, due to his strong aversion, he deliberately ignored them.

Gustav Klimt (1862–1918), another founding member of the Secession, was, by 1907, at the height of his creative powers. Flat, decorative patterns typified his contemporary portraits such as *The Kiss* of 1907–8 which is probably his best-known work. Soon thereafter he designed the mosaics for the Stochlet Palace. Meanwhile Jeanneret's contemporary, Osker Kokoschka (1886–1980), was on the verge of asserting his presence on the artistic scene. Thus, with so much activity in the visual arts, there is no doubt that Jeanneret was in the right place at the right time, having been allured there by the widely published work of these designers.

Upon arriving in Vienna Jeanneret intended to register at an art or architectural school while simultaneously seeking part-time employment with an architect. Two names mentioned in this latter connection were Hoffmann and the sculptor Franz Metzner (1870–1919). Yet no preliminary enquiries had been made and he was annoyed to learn that late registrations at school were unwelcome, that school transcripts from home were necessary, and that he was not cordially received when appearing at someone's door without first making an appointment (eventually he learned the importance of an introduction). He wasted days discovering that Hoffmann taught at the Kunstgewerbeschule and not at the Academy, that Metzner was also there, or rather had been until 1906 when he moved to Leipzig; also that Koloman was not a surname but rather the first name of Koloman Moser, who taught at the same school as Hoffmann (whose name Jeanneret misspelled). In short, this naive lad from the provinces was in such confusion that he resolved it by the simplest expedient of all—that of renouncing the idea of school altogether. This decision, made in early December, required numerous pacifying letters to parents and teachers back home, coupled with an unequivocal denunciation of Hoffmann and Moser as viable designers or potential teachers.[1]

He was fully aware that his education was entirely artistic and totally devoid of technical knowledge, a fact emphasized as work on his designs for the villas Stotzer and Jaquemet progressed. The resolution of this problem dominated more and more of his thinking as the winter advanced, yet he never considered commencing engineering studies while in Vienna. Stubbornly he resisted making whatever personal commitments this might involve, such as spending from a few months to two years in school as well as perfecting his German in order to study at Zurich where, as a Swiss, he was being advised to go. Also, he disliked mathematics, a subject he did not excel in while at school. His ideal, therefore, was to find some architect willing to take him under his wing and, in addition to paying him, to simultaneously train him in the technical skills he needed—all, of course, to be done in French, not German.

As for secessionist architecture in Vienna, he had eyes that did not see. Instinctively he disliked the purified, refined, and often elegant designs that he denounced as "sanitary architecture" or ridiculed as being in the genre of "toilets" or "Dutch-kitchens." He made no serious effort to study these buildings during more than four months in Vienna and made no known sketches or watercolors of what little he may have seen. He did see Wagner's Postal Savings Bank, which he didn't like; neither did he like the art gallery that he later learned was the famous Sezession gallery designed by Olbrich. And we have no evidence that he went to Loos' Karntner Bar and to either Hoffmann's

1. "J'ai renoncé tout à fait à l'idée d'entrer dans une école. Les professeurs viennent rarement, je ne me soucie pas d'apprendre à composer à la Hoffmann ou à la Moser. Ce que je veux, c'est trouver un architecte très capable, entrer chez lui comme employé salarié si possible, mais en tous cas me l'intéresser. C'est lui qui me guidera alors, me dira quelles mathématiques je dois faire" (to parents, December 5, 1907).

Purkersdorf Convalescent Home or—until invited there in March—his Cabaret Fledermaus.[2]

To his parents and L'Eplattenier he attempted to excuse his lack of interest by informing them that most of the buildings were in the suburbs and too hard to find. Only when L'Eplattenier *ordered* him to visit the Steinhof church did he see Wagner's most recent work (letter received January 13). This, as the bank, he denounced as unworthy of an architect's attention; he mocked it as commendable only for the eyes of some gasometer builder or structural engineer.[3] And when further pressed by L'Eplattenier, he hastily visited (without appointments or letters of introduction) six architectural offices on a single Saturday afternoon (February 29) including Wagner's, Hoffmann's, Deininger's and Prutscher's, but found no one in—because it was Saturday afternoon! Jeanneret outdid himself to avoid contemporary architecture and its architects, and he succeeded very well. And what slight effort he made was only at the conclusion of his stay.

Rather than architecture, he decided to study the human figure, his parents having

2. That he knew the Cabaret Fledermaus existed is confirmed in a note to his parents (January 27): "Dire à P. Guchenète qu'il y a un nouveau cabaret à la Kärtnerstrasse: la Fledermaus," which, however, does not imply he visited it.

3. Concerning these buildings he wrote to L'Eplattenier on February 26, 1908:

Tout ça est bâti en ciment et en fer blanc et où il n'y a pas eu d'argent, c'est revêtu de placages de marbre boulonnés, telles les feuilles d'acier d'un pont ou de la coque d'un cuirassé. Ces placages c'est là, la grande, l'unique trouvaille—et la suprème étincelle géniale ce sont les boulons apparents qui les fixent dans la brique et qui apportent certainement, par leur effet décoratif beaucoup de joie aux ingénieurs des ponts et chaussés, aux constructeurs des gazomètres et autres engins sympathiques. A l'intérieur, ce sont les mêmes placages avec des boulons, qui au lieu d'être en aluminium, comme à l'extérieur, sont dorés à la pile—ou alors, ce sont des catelles de format carré exigé, bleu-noir avec bordure blanc de neige, parois et plafond gypsés blanc cru, des portes à vitrages biseautés, des lustres sous forme de caisses carrées, en verre avec plaques laiton poli.—Impression générale: une cuisine hollandaise ou un WC modèle. (Je parle tout spécialement de l'intérieur de l'église Steinhof, de la poste et du hall Deininger [l'académie du Commerce]).

Tout cela très intéressant toutefois, prouvant beaucoup de sincérité, *un culot formidable,* peu d'invention ou peut-être point du tout. L'art et l'émotion de ces oeuvres ne se révèlent hélas point encore aux imbéciles qui ont trouvé beau St Marc ou Or San Michele. Oui, certainement, il y a là un mouvement très fort et qui prend beaucoup; Wagner est en tête et il est grand seigneur à l'académie; ce style tout de froideur, de propreté reluisante a produit deux ravissants magasins qui sont gais à cause des fleurs qu'on y vend. Il déroute (ce style), il hypnotise et attire beaucoup de jeunes, car au fond il est la b a ba du goût et il permet à Wagner de faire de faux frontons, de supprimer les toits [as Jeanneret would begin doing in 1914], les montants et les couvertes des fenêtres, de dédaigner complètement l'appel de la nature. Il permet de produire des oeuvres on ne peut plus (actuellement) originales, nouvelles (dans 10 ans, rasantes). Ça durera juste autant que Wagner et ça mourra après avoir empoisonné Darmstadt, Düsseldorf, Berlin, et Dresde."

In reading these lines one must recall that Jeanneret was defending his decision to leave both Vienna and Germany behind in order to move, against L'Eplattenier's will, to Paris.

forwarded his books on anatomy and sculpture to Vienna. Meanwhile Léon Perrin discovered that Franz Metzner no longer lived in Vienna, so he began, in November, private lessons with a relatively obscure sculptor who had studied at the Academy, Karl Stemolak (1875–?). Jeanneret soon joined him. Both boys found Stemolak immensely likable and described him as another L'Eplattenier—young, enthusiastic, talented, and with similar theories.[4] Jeanneret began to study drawing with Stemolak on December 23. He went mornings from nine till noon, paying forty francs per month plus model fees; he intended to stay about two months.[5] His enthusiasm was unbounded and upon Stemolak he bestowed the same praise he had conferred upon Ruskin while in Florence: "from Stemolak I learn to see" (to parents, January 7).

One is struck by Jeanneret's unorthodox pursuit of an architectural education. He rejected formal schooling, either in architecture or engineering, and rather than seeking an apprenticeship in an architect's office he spent both time and money on a sculptor for private lessons on how to draw the human figure. This seems incongruous. Yet it is consistent with what Le Corbusier believed throughout his life—that the act of creating architecture was a long, patient search in the study of form. Concerning the education of an architect, his letters home consistently emphasize two essentials: the study of nature and the study of form, with the latter best epitomized in works of art exhibited in museums.

Museums were often part of his Sunday schedule yet—as in Italy—he never sketched paintings by the masters; what he recorded were usually furnishings, the decorative arts, or works produced by distant cultures. A few months later, in Paris, this trend would intensify. On December 8, for instance, they visited the Hof-Museum where he insisted the Egyptian collection was superior to that at Florence (and sketched several examples of Egyptian furniture as well as sculpture), and on February 9 they went to the Kunsthistorisches Museum where he commented on the superb *Madonna* by Perugino which evoked sweet memories of Italy—yet simultaneously complained about the cold, pompous, overscaled architecture of official Vienna. His relatively few museum sketches (about a dozen) date from late February–early March and these include three of an Arabian room and five of Gothic interiors and furniture—mostly chests and beds (figs. 95 and 96). On March 2 he wrote of these to L'Eplattenier,

4. "Perrin, très content, travaille toute la journée chez Stemolak, mais vous n'êtes pas au courant. Stemolak, un sculpteur très calé, genre L'Ep[lattenier], théories les mêmes, chic type, jeune, enthousiaste chercheur, inconnu encore du grand monde. Perrin est son unique élève, il l'aide même à tailler ses marbres, a de la chance" (to parents, December 5, 1907).

5. And after beginning his studies with Stemolak, Jeanneret wrote his parents on December 27: "je vais tous les matins de 9 heures à 12½ chez le sculpteur Stemolak pour dessiner. Je suis seul avec Perrin, j'ai commencé lundi dernier, je sens que j'apprends énormément. C'est une chance extraordinaire, car c'est un homme de tout grand talent. Même générosité que M. L'Ep[lattenier]; une moins grande envolée dans les idées; mais il nous tient bien, et comme je dois faire du dessin, je suis très heureux d'avoir trouvé un si bon maître."

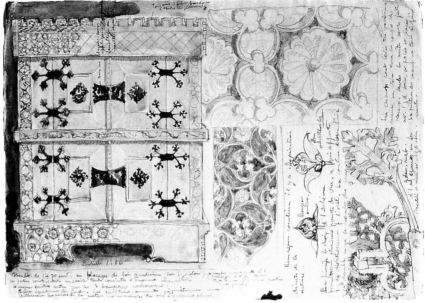

praising Gothic furniture for its grace and rigorous logic of construction, while extolling the Moorish room for its ingenious plan, comfort, and lighting.

Art galleries apparently got short shrift, judging by his letters. The first week he visited two, reacted negatively to what he saw, and never mentioned contemporary painting again. On February 26 he sent L'Eplattenier a watercolor sketch of some modern furniture displayed at the J. & J. Kohn showrooms, a store selling works by Moser and Hoffmann, and he derided these table and chair designs as dubious "novelties" that served only to prove that Viennese design had nothing of worth to offer.

Jeanneret's first priority in Vienna was getting settled. This he quickly achieved, finding a comfortable room at Kaiserstrasse 8, Wien VI (4ème étage, 28 francs) just southwest of the Ring.[6] He ridiculed his landlords, however, as being bourgeois and uncongenial. Perrin found lodging a block away at Bernardgasse 8; he was much happier with his landlady but unable to take possession until December 1.

Once installed, Jeanneret reported his daily routine to his parents (December 5): up at 7:30 or 8, café au lait and two rolls provided by "la bourgeoise," work on his villa designs till 12:30, dress in respectable clothes, go to restaurant (1.10 to 1.50 francs), go to a bakery to buy a sweet (20 centimes) and some bread and rolls (20 to 40 centimes), return to room at 1:30, put bread and other goodies in bureau drawer, continue work on villa design until 7 or 8, relax, extract delectable treasurers from bureau drawer, heat

Fig. 95. Arabian room (details thereof including lamps and stools), formerly in Kunstgewerbemuseum, Vienna. Pencil, ink, and watercolor on paper. 34 × 24.5 cm. (FLC 2081)

Fig. 96. Gothic chest (ca. 1470) with details of its ornament, Osterreichische Museum für Kunst und Industrie, Vienna. Pencil, ink, and watercolor on tan paper. 25 × 36 cm. (FLC 1989)

6. Jeanneret was quite comfortable there, calling it "une jolie chambre" (to parents, November [?], 1907). Yet to Maximilien Gautier in 1944 (*Le Corbusier,* p. 23) he referred to it as "une chambre sans confort," a misrepresentation that added to his martyr image.

milk and add some cocoa, eat abundantly but saving something for next day, read or write letters, and then, about 10 when all are asleep, do Müller exercises (sometimes repeated in the morning). He decorated his room with photographs of home and family, his Italian drawings, a view of the Villa L'Eplattenier, and he purchased a photograph of Ruskin ("Quelle tête, quelle noblesse, quelle probité" (to parents, November 17) that he placed at the head of his table.

Jeanneret cherished his evenings most of all, huddled under a lamp with his books and correspondence. Social life was viewed as an intrusion. And girls, he admitted, he never really looked at before arriving in Vienna.[7] Perrin he saw regularly, especially at Stemolak's and on Sundays, yet their friendship was without great warmth. By contrast, Jeanneret met a young painter from Geneva, Fernand Blondin, during the first week in Vienna and quickly there developed a strong bond, Blondin being extravagantly praised in each successive letter. When he departed just before Christmas, Jeanneret was much grieved, having lost not only a congenial friend but also an intellectual companion with whom he enjoyed exchanging ideas.

Reading was an evening occupation that extended his education. In November he reread Charles Blanc's *Grammaire des arts du dessin* which he thought about while in Italy and which, at his request, his parents had sent from home. Concurrently he read L'Eplattenier's parting gift, *Les Grands Initiés* by Edouard Schuré, and early in January he commented on *La Glu* by Jean Richepin which he had bought in Pisa, saying it was a book that was "not ideal, often unwholesome, that I have never reread" (to parents, January 7). He also read a book by Ruskin (unidentified) that he had exchanged with his aunt Pauline, and while on the tram read the libretto of the operas *Carmen* and *Siegfried*. By mid-January he had finished the nearly 600 pages of *Les Grands Initiés* and began Schuré's less philosophical *Sanctuaires d'orient*.

What questions Jeanneret grappled with while reading *Les Grands Initiés* are revealed in his January 31 letter to his parents. He commented that his own innate ideas, reaffirmed by his contemplation of Nature, failed to coincide with the rationalism that he encountered in actual life and that even his superficial, schoolboy's knowledge of science strongly confirmed. He had often struggled to reconcile these differences, yet Schuré taught him that this was not necessary; the two positions could coexist. This was a revelation to Jeanneret. It freed him from his dilemma; unburdened, he was filled with happiness. Yet the solution to his problem (not elucidated) still eluded him, and he hoped that some day it could be resolved.[8]

7. "... depuis que je suis à Vienne je commence à voir ce qu'est la femme.... J'ai passé toute ma jeunesse sans jamais avoir regardé une fille. Maintenant c'est une douce musique qui me pénètre . . ."—specifically referring to a "jolie harpiste . . . Elle a 20 ans et des yeux!" that he saw at Stemolak's (to parents, January 7, 1908).

8. His remarks about Schuré deserve quotation: "Ce Schuré m'a révélé des horizons qui m'ont comblé de bonheur. Je pressentais cela, non c'est trop dire; plus justement, mes luttes entre le rationalisme, que la

Historians and critics have long been troubled by the dualism often found in Le Corbusier's life and work, and here perhaps is an explanation of how he could maintain seemingly contradictory positions simultaneously.[9] His own answer seems to be that from Schuré he learned that reconciliation was unnecessary; moreover that it was perfectly natural to sustain conflicting positions concurrently. And the implicit struggle between these contradictions soon became the essence of his life.

A less intellectual pastime was his passion for music, his devotion to which exceeded even that anticipated for the son of a piano teacher and brother of a violinist. His first day in Vienna he found time for a Bach mass and he soon became an habitué at the philharmonic concerts given Sunday afternoon, which were often conducted by Richard Strauss. There he heard music by Beethoven, Spohr, Mendelssohn, Chopin, Wagner, Lalo, Brahms, Saint-Saens, Tchaikovsky, Dvorak, Richard Strauss, and Debussy whose *Prélude à l'après-midi d'un faune* was the work he singled out for particular praise. Chamber music he almost never mentioned. Opera, however, was a revelation. Whereas he said (to Albert, February 2), "music is the most beautiful of the arts," he reserved for opera the remark that "it is perfection in music." Bizet's *Carmen* was perhaps his favorite, with much praise reserved for Puccini, whose *La Bohème, Madame Butterfly,* and *Manon Lescaut* he also saw. Wagner both fascinated and troubled him; it was the clarity and force that attracted him. He heard *Siegfried* on December 4 and then

---

*vie réelle* active, que les petits bouts de science emmagasinée au gymnase, avaient établi fortement en moi, et d'autre part l'idée innée, intuitive d'un Etre suprême, que la contemplation de la Nature me révélait à chaque pas, cette lutte avait préparé le terrain à recevoir cette noble semence dont ce bouquin de 600 pages est rempli. Je suis maintenant plus à l'aise, je suis plus heureux, il me manque toutefois la solution, et j'espère bien un jour l'apercevoir afin de me lancer à sa conquête. Ce bouquin-là est superbe." (to parents, January 31, 1908).

*Les Grands Initiés,* first published in 1889, is still in print. Each chapter is devoted to the life of a different prophet: Rama, Krishna, Hermes, Moses, Orpheus, Pythagoras, Plato, Jesus. Prior to each biography there is a short introduction in which Schuré invariably mentions the dualities found in the life and theories of the prophets.

9. For a cogent discussion of the "dualistic pattern in Le Corbusier's work and thought" see Paul Turner, "Romanticism, Rationalism, and the Domino System," in *The Open Hand,* edited by Russell Walden (Cambridge, Mass.: MIT Press, 1977), pp. 15–41. Turner, on p. 18, observes that "these two conceptions, the romantic or idealistic and the rationalist [have] their specific sources . . . in Charles L'Eplattenier and Auguste Perret." However, Jeanneret's letter of January 1908 demonstrates that he was well aware of rationalism long before meeting Perret. He himself lists his sources as daily experience combined with bits of science accumulated while at school. Blanc, like other authors read by Jeanneret, emphasized the dual role of the architect as a logical constructor and one in search of beauty.

Another writer admired by Jeanneret, whose biographers insist his life and work were marked by duality, was Edgar Allan Poe. Is it possible, therefore, that Le Corbusier's stylized sketch of a raven, which he often used to sign his personal correspondence, was a self-sought identification with Poe—thus making sort of a pun on the French word "le corbeau," the raven?

the entire Ring Cycle (*Das Rheingold, Die Walküre, Siegfried,* and *Götterdämmerung*) during the first week of February. He also heard *Der Fliegende Holländer, Die Meistersinger von Nürnberg,* and *Tristan und Isolde* for an amazingly complete Wagnerian education. Beethoven's *Fidelio* was conducted by Weingartner, his only mention of a conductor.[10] Indeed, after seeing *Carmen* on January 6, he vowed to attend the opera at least once a week, a frequency that he far exceeded.

Attending opera meant leaving his room at 4:45, forty-five minutes en route, an hour's queue to obtain good standing room in the parterre opposite the stage (2 francs), four and a half hours standing during the performance, then home, for a total of seven and a half hours on his feet. Of this he never complained—except that Wagner was a bit too long. By contrast, he had neither the time nor the patience to spend a few hours looking at modern architecture. Yet he would brag about attending four operas plus one concert in a single week!

All this transpired as Albert experienced renewed setbacks in his musical education. The report covering his first quarter at the Conservatoire in Geneva, in spite of some encouraging comments from Henri Marteau, plunged mother into tears and papa into depression, confirming his worst fears of Albert's weakness in musical interpretation. Edouard rushed off a long, bracing letter to his brother and an equally long letter to his parents beseeching them to have confidence in Albert and imploring them never to express their doubts. A few days later (February 19) Marteau played in Vienna thus permitting Edouard to fabricate the tale that Marteau was a "man of marble" and try to shift the blame for Albert's problems to his teacher. At month's end however, the devastated father—still convinced his son's life had miscarried—dutifully dispatched 250 francs for Albert's second-quarter studies.

Meanwhile the younger son continued to live off his own earnings. Edouard's one mild extravagance was photography. On January 10 he and Perrin developed their Italian photographs with good results. Yet he confessed to his brother that he rarely looked at his photos, preferring to relive his Italian trip through his drawings. Nonetheless he invested (letter to parents, February 11) 30 francs purchasing the developing apparatus he hankered for plus a stand and two lenses for 15 francs. Placed in the perspective of his other expenses—28 francs per month for his room and breakfast, 40 francs a month for his half-day tutorials with Stemolak, 2 francs to attend an opera, or 700 francs for his entire sojourn in Italy—this 45 franc expenditure was slightly out of line.

10. To his biographer Maximilien Gauthier (p. 23) Le Corbusier mentioned that either Gustav Mahler or Weingartner was on the podium. However his letters make no mention of Mahler (either as conductor or composer) who in fact was director of the Vienna Court Opera only from 1897 to 1907, with Weingartner taking the baton in 1907. Gauthier also reports that it was *La Bohème* that turned Jeanneret's thoughts toward Paris, but at the time (January 1908) this is a subject he would not have mentioned in letters home.

Jeanneret's time was mostly spent doing what he could better have done at home—designing two houses for La Chaux-de-Fonds. L'Eplattenier had promoted the idea which Jeanneret, due to his impending trip, was hesitant to accept. Yet it speaks well for Louis Fallet's satisfaction with his recently completed home that he encouraged his brothers-in-law to hire Jeanneret as their architect.

Albert Stotzer (1872–1939) married Berthe Fallet in 1899 and their three daughters were born by 1906. He taught mechanics at the Ecole d'horlogerie. Jules Jaquemet (1873–1942) married Jeanne Fallet in 1903 and their two children were born in 1904 and 1908. He was employed in the watch industry in a variety of jobs including polisher of watchcases.[11] The two families were of limited financial means which caused them to devote the second floor of each house to rental accommodation and led Jaquemet to sell his home in 1923. Members of the Stotzer family remained in residence until the 1980s and this resulted in their house being maintained in its original condition. The Jaquemet house, however, was converted into a single-family home by its new owners who, fortunately, made only minor exterior changes (such as enlarging the ground floor terrace, which was sympathetically done, and changing the color scheme).

Both houses are located a bit further up the slope from the line formed by the villas Matthey-Doret, L'Eplattenier, and Fallet, and at a point where the ground slants toward the southeast (see fig. 59). The facades overlook the view with entrances at the rear. Originally the houses were adjacent but much later a small house was erected in between. Their address, after the renaming of the street, is Chemin de Pouillerel 6 (Stotzer) and 8 (Jaquemet).

Jeanneret was officially the designer of the Villa Fallet despite receiving much technical assistance from Chapallaz's office. The situation with the Stotzer and Jaquemet houses, however, was quite different due to the existence of a partnership, "Chapallaz and Jeanneret, Architects." Thus Chapallaz deserves to be listed as co-architect. Recently discovered correspondence confirms that Jeanneret was the designing partner although he constantly sought comments and advise from Chapallaz and L'Eplattenier.

This arrangement is verified by Chapallaz's proposed division of their 7.5 percent commission (a percentage fixed by code for Swiss architects) wherein Jeanneret alone is credited with preparing both the preliminary and the final designs with both men sharing equally in the execution of plans and working drawings. Chapallaz also took responsibility for all paper work (including some fourteen contracts with the various contractors) and the supervision of construction. The final cost of the two houses was approximately 30,000 and 32,000 Swiss francs, respectively, and therefore Jeanneret's

11. Biographical data from the Police des Habitants, La Chaux-de-Fonds. Miss Hélène Stotzer kindly provided me with much information pertaining to the houses and their occupants.

3.3 percent honorarium was just over 2,000 francs—an amount he could live on for quite some time.[12]

To put these money matters into better perspective we should note that Chapallaz employed, in September 1908, a technician whose wages were 150 francs for each of the first two months and 170 thereafter. Thus he would require over a year to earn the equivalent of Jeanneret's commission. And still more startling were the working hours: 7 to 12 and 1:30 to 8:30 for a total of 12 hours per day or 72 hours in the six-day week. Today, as these words are being written, the workweek in La Chaux-de-Fonds is 40 hours, that in France is 36 (with over six weeks of paid vacation each year).

The drawings and correspondence concerning the Stotzer and Jaquemet houses were found in Chapallaz's attic following his death in 1976. These completely revise our previous assumption that both houses, as built, pretty much represent Jeanneret's desires concerning their design.[13] The houses have frequently been praised for their simplicity, sobriety, and clarity of form, yet suddenly we learn that these characteristics were not originally intended by Jeanneret—they were imposed upon him by his money-conscious clients.[14]

For each house there are two sets of designs—the initial one (which subsequently had to be greatly modified) and the executed design. Their chronology can be established with precision. After much forethought, Jeanneret commenced the Stotzer design immediately after his November 11 arrival in Vienna. It was completed on November 26 and mailed (along with, apparently, a clay model) on the twenty-ninth. The Jaquemet drawings were finished and mailed on December 11—thus each design took about two weeks. A few days thereafter, on December 15, Perrin wrote L'Eplattenier saying that he and Edouard were so disappointed with Vienna they were thinking of moving on; he asked for information concerning schools for himself and, on behalf of Jeanneret, a list of architects in Munich, Dresden, Düsseldorf, and Berlin. This theme

12. By letter of April 2, 1908, Chapallaz proposed the following division of their 7.5 percent commission.

| Votre part | | Ma part | |
|---|---|---|---|
| Esquisse et avant-projet | 1. | Plans et détails d'exécution | 1.1 |
| Projet définitif | 1.2 | Devis | 0.7 |
| Plans et détails d'exécution | 1.1 | Direction et surveillance | 1.9 |
| | | Vérification des mémoires | 0.5 |
| | 3.3 | | 4.2 |

13. The René Chapallaz archives are now housed at the Bibliothèque de la Ville, La Chaux-de-Fonds. I am much indebted to Mrs. Vera Baumeister and Marc Albert Emery for making them available to me at an earlier stage.

14. As an analogy, one is reminded of the much-praised simplicity of Chicago's early skyscrapers, such as the Monadnock, which we subsequently learned was a condition imposed upon the architects by dollar-conscious clients.

was repeated in subsequent letters, with Dresden becoming the top contender as a place to go, with departure dependent upon Jeanneret first finishing the two house designs.

Once Jeanneret's plans were mailed on December 11, he remarked that he was out of work. He might have used the time to study Viennese architecture or seek employment with an architect. Not so, however. Instead, he visited Stemolak and arranged for tutorials to begin on Monday the twenty-third. He also spent much time with his friend Blondin. Likewise he caught up on correspondence. And in a letter to Albert he spoke of L'Eplattenier: "Mr. L'Ep. knew how to develop within us a broad outlook. Therefore we are qualified to judge most of the developments in art, and we have a solid and healthy knowledge of the History of Art which allows us to benefit from the great laws that guided the masters. Finally, at home [La Chaux-de-Fonds] the ornamental side is highly developed, here they have never looked at a flower." He then observed that L'Eplattenier "I take for an extraordinarily gifted and profound intellect. In theory he already surpasses, and in a few years he will also do so in practice, most modern artists. For me, he is my second father, and he treats me as a son" (to Albert, December 15, 1907).

Jeanneret's self-imposed vacation ended abruptly on December 21 when Stotzer returned his plans. Both he and L'Eplattenier were generally content (except for the probable cost) yet Stotzer insisted on greater simplicity.[15] Suddenly, Jeanneret lost confidence in himself;[16] he became so confused that he lost the Stotzer plans somewhere on the street, never to be refound. Finally, after spending Christmas Day with Perrin visiting the Schönbrunn Palace (about which he made no comment) and the zoological gardens (described as wonderful), his world utterly collapsed when news arrived on the twenty-seventh that Jaquemet was not happy with his design and wanted something more like L'Eplattenier's house.

Jeanneret wrote home for photos of the villas L'Eplattenier and Fallet. After two weeks of preparing a revised design, the Stotzer plans were sent off on January 6. On these the cost estimates were 3,600 francs over the 22,000 construction budget (about 14 percent too high), yet the villa was built substantially according to this new design.

Another week passed while Jeanneret awaited return of the unsatisfactory Jaquemet plans, a week during which he heard three concerts, including Beethoven's Ninth Symphony, and the opera *Carmen*. Finally the plans with comments were returned by L'Eplattenier on January 13, and Jeanneret spent the next five and a half weeks reworking them and preparing new elevations, sections, and construction details. On February 20 they were finally finished, having taken almost as much time as all his previous work on both designs.

15. Whatever was written to Jeanneret we know only through what he wrote to others. This is because he never saved the letters he received.

16. "Je travaille à mes plans dans une incertitude de moi-même qui me fait peur" (to parents, December 27).

**Fig. 97.** Villa L'Eplattenier, 1902. (Chapallaz archives, BV, courtesy of Marc A. Emery)

Before discussing the two designs we should examine L'Eplattenier's home since Messrs. Stotzer and Jaquemet both asked that it serve as Jeanneret's model—rather than specifying a building similar to the Villa Fallet.[17] L'Eplattenier, it seems, had largely contrived his own design, making watercolor renderings of all four facades and signing, on July 24, 1902, the official set of plans that were registered with the commune. In all likelihood, however, he received generous advice as well as technical and drafting assistance from René Chapallaz who had recently moved to La Chaux-de-Fonds and was working in the office of Piquet and Ritter.[18] One recalls, in this respect, the arrangement of Jeanneret and Chapallaz at the Villa Fallet, except in that instance Jeanneret did his own drafting.

For a family of four the Villa L'Eplattenier was very small. Only the ground floor (some 11 by 13 meters including terrace) was reserved for daily living while the storey and a half above was L'Eplattenier's spacious studio. Several features—but not the steep roof and open balcony—derive from local eighteenth-century farm houses, notably the extended, in antas, side walls and the kidney-shaped curve under the gable. Chapallaz's photograph, figure 97, clearly shows the 1902 design.

Two years later a two-and-a-half storey studio was annexed toward the rear and the former studio converted into more generous living quarters; an entrance pavilion was then added at the corner. Also, in 1906, Jeanneret undertook "Réparations dans la maison de Monsieur L'Eplattenier," the blueprint being signed "La Chaux-de-Fonds,

17. According to the original blueprints, L'Eplattenier's residence was called a "chalet," and those of Fallet, Stotzer, and Jaquemet "maisons." Customarily all of Jeanneret's houses in the Jura are called villas, even though that conforms more to British than to American usage.

18. For more on this question, see Marc Albert Emery, "Chapallaz *versus* Jeanneret," *Archithese,* 2–83 (March/April, 1983), pp. 23–28, where the writer gives Chapallaz complete credit for the design of the Villa L'Eplattenier—an assertion that I do not accept.

**Fig. 98.** Project for a schoolhouse in the Jura style. Maurice Braillard, architect. Dated November 2, 1907. (*Architektur des XX Jahrhunderts,* 8 [1908], plate 30)

ECOLE
DANS LE
JURA

M. BRAILLARD
2.11.07.

Le 20 septembre 1906, Ch.E. Jenneret" (while he was constructing the Villa Fallet). This minor work consisted of adding three basement windows along the south wall with the overhead masonry (in addition to a stone lintel) being carried on *three* metal I-beams placed side by side. L'Eplattenier's house was not generously supplied with windows.

Also worth comparing with Stotzer/Jaquemet is a project by Maurice Braillard dated November 2, 1907, in the so-called Jura style (fig. 98). The affinity is striking in numerous respects including windows, arched entrance way, use of masonry in combination with stucco, and the gambrel roof; compare especially with the second project for the Stotzer house. Could Jeanneret have known this or a similar design?[19]

The first Stotzer project (fig. 99)—like that for Jaquemet—strikes us as extremely rich and elaborate after recalling Jeanneret's praise of elimination as an important quality of Florentine art, or even by comparison with the Villa Fallet. Decorated surface remains uppermost in his mind; his rendering shows great activity and richness over the entire facade and includes scenes of men, women, and animals to be executed in fresco or sgraffito under the arched gable of the roof. Only the sense of solidity and permanence might recall trecento Italy.

Interestingly enough, the vertical sequence of decorative motifs for the Stotzer facade follows closely that of certain nature studies made by Jeanneret while at school (see figs. 45, 46). Near the bottom of each we observe subsurface rock formations (represented by the Stotzer masonry wall); above this is depicted the ground level with flowers and trees growing from the soil (as shown across the balcony, as well as by live potted shrubs placed on the terrace and balcony walls), then a pair of sculpted birds nesting atop the lateral in antas piers of the house and, finally, a mural under the arched gable roof showing both animals and people (at left a man working with outstretched arms—Mr. Stotzer?—and at right a woman—Mrs. Stotzer?—beside a table, with a bird roosting in the rafters overhead). To dismiss this as pure romanticism would be a mistake; Jeanneret is still searching, à la L'Eplattenier, for an ideal, presumably a Jura style to rival that of his European contemporaries.[20]

The pointed (Gothic) arch of the roof is entirely unexpected; it lacks precedence among Jeanneret's self-proclaimed sources as well as in vernacular design. Its shape recalls the *interior* of the chapel at Cernier that Jeanneret and friends decorated earlier that year (fig. 77). Its chief asset would be to provide additional space under the (expensive to build) roof, yet the fenestration indicates a room of little importance. Also out of context are the two tracery-filled round-arch windows (shades of Italy?) that, incom-

19. Influence is not impossible here, yet in the days before photocopies and fax the means of communication is dubious. True, the drawing, dated November 2, 1907, is by the Genevese architect Maurice Braillard with whom Chapallaz worked prior to moving to La Chaux-de-Fonds in 1902, but would Chapallaz have seen the perspective and been able to obtain a copy to send to Vienna? It was published in *Architektur des XX Jahrhunderts,* 8 (1908), but that postdates Jeanneret's project by several months. Nevertheless Chapallaz might have furnished Jeanneret with other, not dissimilar, drawings by his former employer.

20. Concerning the Stotzer design he wrote his parents on November 18: "Travaillé de rage jusqu'à maintenant à mes plans; je ne trouve pas la solution, l'idéal est de nouveau à une terrible distance de la main. Que faire sinon s'obstiner." And again on December 5: "Papa a mal compris ma pensée quand je disais avoir de la peine pour les plans de ces deux petites maisons. La question technique pour de pareilles peccadilles ne me tracasse point. C'est l'*idée* qui est dure à venir. . . . La maison Stotzer est composée et les plans envoyés; qu'en pensera M. L'Ep.? C'est là l'épée de Damoclès. Je l'ai composée dans le type Fallet et L'Ep. et ai obtenu assez d'unité me semble-t-il." On December 11 he received word of L'Eplattenier's approval.

**Fig. 99.** Preliminary project: Villa Stotzer, November 1907. Pencil and watercolor on tracing paper. 15 × 21 cm. (Private collection)

**Fig. 100.** Project: Villa Stotzer, November 1907. Blueprint made from a lost drawing. 17.5 × 17 cm. (BV)

patibly, fail to repeat the pointed arch of the roof above. And, in common with the L'Eplattenier house, this early pencil and watercolor sketch shows no projecting bays at either side.

The blueprint version of this elevation, with fanciful chimneys and symmetrical projecting bays, is hardly more restrained (fig. 100). A small arcade (such as one might see in Italy) appears below the balcony, and a corbelling motif—similar to what Jeanneret used at Beau-Site and the Villa Fallet—finds liberal expression, especially over windows, on other elevations (fig. 101). These multiple facades on a single sheet, signed "Vienne—novembre 1907," defy tradition by representing each elevation as a separate house placed in a pictorial landscape with a continuous ground line, thereby giving the blueprint some of the qualities of a presentation drawing.

The plan is quite similar to L'Eplattenier's except for the communal stairway and the light-seeking, triangular bay windows that convert it into a stunted "T" (fig. 102). As a two-family house, both floors have identical plans consisting of three bedrooms and a combination living-dining room; the Stotzers intended to live on the ground floor. Only one usable room, plus storage, existed under the roof.

Three weeks after these designs were submitted (shipment of the clay model was apparently thwarted), they were returned with comments and suggestions by Stotzer and L'Eplattenier. Jeanneret immediately set about simplifying the design and coping with such problems as roof shape, gallery supports, and stairs. Unfortunately his preliminary sketches for this revised project have not survived, only the final elevations, plans, and sections dated January 1908 and signed by Chapallaz, Jeanneret, and Stotzer (figs. 103–5). The degree to which the house was redesigned is quite dramatic. Basic massing and floor plan remained much the same, yet the bays are no longer pointed and offer a bit more glazing. Curved forms, except the round chimneys, are replaced by strong, often continuous, horizontals.[21] A gambrel roof supplants the pointed arch, the roof projecting a full meter forward from the house. Meanwhile the lateral bays are more pronounced and dominated by a hooded or cowl-like jerkinhead roof. Greater restraint is exercised throughout the design with the facade more reminiscent of the Villa L'Eplattenier—except for the overall proportions that are less broad because of the additional floor. Jeanneret's design is more distinguished than his mentor's, being stronger and more sophisticated. To use his term, it is well "composed." It indicates a maturity well in advance of his twenty years (figs. 106, 107 and color plate III).

On April 2, 1908, a cost estimate was presented to Stotzer in the amount of 27,960.55 Swiss francs including the architects' 7.5 percent fee of 1,950.75 francs. This was about 18 percent over the proposed budget. The size of the house was given as 1,170 cubic meters (102.60 square meters) at an approximate cost of 23.80 francs per meter. A contract between "Chapallaz et Jeanneret, Architectes" and Albert Stotzer

21. "Mon principe a été de faire dominer toutes les horizontales" (to L'Eplattenier, January 6, 1908).

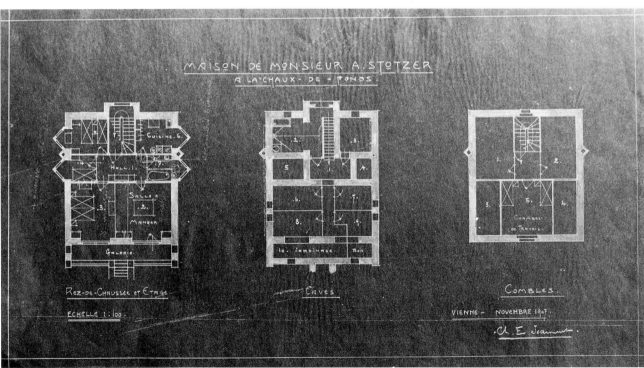

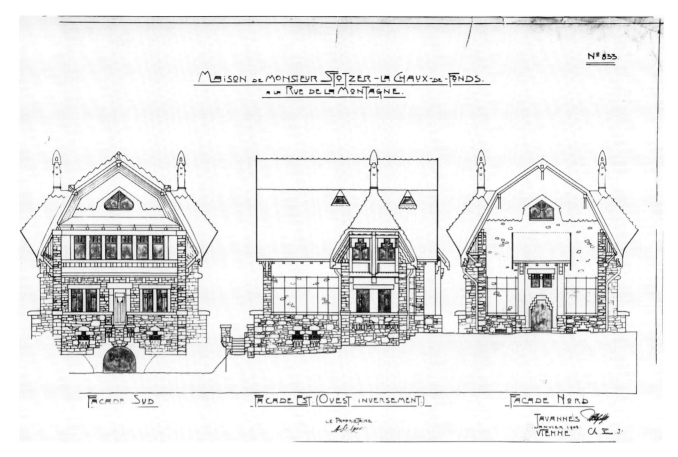

MAISON DE MONSIEUR STOTZER – LA CHAUX-DE-FONDS.
À LA RUE DE LA MONTAGNE.

FAÇADE SUD — FAÇADE EST (OUEST INVERSEMENT) — FAÇADE NORD

LE PROPRIÉTAIRE.
A.B.Styer

TAVANNES
JANVIER 1908.
VIENNE. Ch. E. J.

**Fig. 101.** *(Opposite top)* Villa Stotzer. Project that was rejected by the client. "Vienne—Novembre 1907/Ch. E. Jeanneret." Blueprint. 28.8 × 58.2 cm. (BV)

**Fig. 102.** *(Opposite bottom)* Villa Stotzer. Plans for the first project; the first two floors are identical. Blueprint signed and dated November, 1907. (BV)

**Fig. 103.** Villa Stotzer, elevations, dated January 1908. 61 × 92 cm. (BV)

was signed on April 13 and on October 30 the Stotzers moved into their new home (the Jaquemets moved into theirs, which cost 32,500 francs, on December 31). On December 22 Chapallaz rendered the final account indicating costs, including architects' fees, as 29,815 against the April estimate of 27,960. A separate bill indicates that the architects' commission was based on the April estimate (no honorarium paid on the overrun) plus a fee of 148.85 francs on certain extras requested by the client. Thus the total commission earned by the architects amounted to 2,099.60 Swiss francs.

Construction was not undertaken by a prime contractor and various subcontractors but rather through a series of some fourteen contracts coordinated under the direction of Chapallaz, each contract being signed by both client and architect and, in most instances, covering both houses. One of these, dated May 25, was with W. Hilliger & Company of Neuchâtel for reinforced concrete floors, system Hennebique. Earlier, Chapallaz had suggested using concrete to speed the process of construction, yet this is nowhere indicated on Jeanneret's initial plans. At this time concrete floor slabs were not uncommon in La Chaux-de-Fonds. At the Stotzer and Jaquemet houses they are supported on masonry walls a half-meter thick.

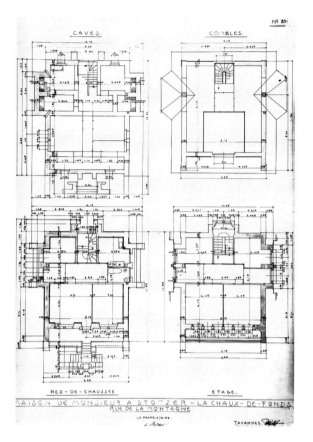

**Fig. 104.** Villa Stotzer, plans of the two apartments. (BV)

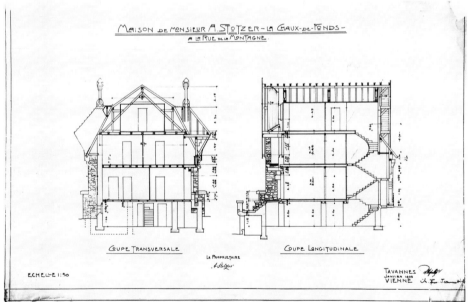

**Fig. 105.** Villa Stotzer, sections. (BV)

**Fig. 106.** Villa Stotzer seen from the southeast. Chapallaz photo, winter of 1908–9. The two-tone decoration around the attic window, delineated on the elevation drawing and clearly visible at the site, is hardly discernable in this photo. (BV)

**Fig. 107.** Villa Stotzer, west side. Note that the window muntins take the form of a leafless tree, thus recalling those at the Villa Fallet. The roof is tiled. Chapallaz photo, 1908. (BV)

The preliminary Jaquemet project is documented in three distinct ways. First as a pencil and watercolor rendering, then as two clay models known through Jeanneret's photographs thereof, and finally the verbal revelation of his thought process, written to L'Eplattenier, while creating the design. The latter, indeed, is a unique document.

Two things, among many, catch our eye when reading Jeanneret's thoughts while designing this house for Jules Jaquemet. "For this devil of a house with its irregular site, I have finally created a facade inspired by the building site itself rather than trying to apply, on this terrain, facades invented in the mind." His attitude is consistent; inspiration should come from the topography itself and from local materials, be they mineral or vegetable. Simultaneously, he endeavors to incorporate design principles learned during his travels, with memories of Florence often cited as justification for what he has done, as, for example: "I observed in all Florentine art this principle of . . ."[22]

The clay models tell more about his process of design. One shows the entire house, the massing being the object of his study, while the other, somewhat larger, analyses the plastic qualities of the facade (fig. 108). He exhibits great interest in the three-dimensional character of his forms, seeing the building as a sculptural entity rather than as four facades. When we remember his fondness for surface decoration, demonstrated in Italy, it is heartening to see such emphasis given to the sculptural quality of buildings (one might have expected the contrary).

22. A partial, though lengthy, excerpt from Jeanneret's letter to L'Eplattenier of December 11, 1907, is quoted here:

Cette maison Jaquemet m'a donné du mal. J'ai compris la valeur du type créé; on trouve déjà des difficultés à la varier. Mais quand on se pose le problème sur d'autres bases, tout est "inconnus" et "imprévus." Pour cette diable de maison avec son terrain biscornu, je me suis enfin mis à créer la façade d'après le terrain et non pas à chercher à appliquer des façades d'imagination à ce terrain-là. Pour cela, j'ai commencé par le fameux trou, puis ai tourné par des croquis d'angle, sur la façade nord-ouest et enfin sud, et le reste ne pouvait se tenir. En même temps, je raisonnais le plan comme indiqué dans la lettre à M. Jaquemet et j'en suis arrivé à trouver cette solution qui me paraît presque unique. Avant, j'avais fait une vue d'ensemble de votre maison, de celle de Fallet, à Stotzer et cherché les lignes qui arriveraient à se soutenir à côté de ce trou, entre votre maison solidement assise et celle de Fallet qui danse un pas de polka. J'ai vu que de grandes lignes sont urgentes et qu'il est inutile de fignoler, d'accuser des piles et des contreforts afin que la maison si désavantageusement située, n'ait pas l'air de dégringoler. Naturellement que j'en ai trop mis au début, les vices enracinés ne s'effacent pas si vite. Pour finir, il n'y a plus que la construction nécessaire et tout le reste a été mis de côté. J'ai abîmé le rendu des 4 façades, étant encore sous l'influence de mes ribotes quand je l'ai fait. Elles ont l'air lamentable, comme je l'étais moi-même ce jour-là. Il y manque ce tracé d'ombre qui est toute la vie de cette bicoque, puisque j'ai de grandes surfaces pleines. Enfin, tant pis.

I. En façade sud, point de terrasse au bas et point de nivellement. Au contraire, un fouillis d'arbustes, dissimulant la base horizontale et amenant la chute dans le grand abîme à droite, un mur pour retenir les déblais et l'oeil à droite avec pile. Trois grands montants de moëllons soutenant le fronton

Fig. 108. Clay models used to ana-
lyze the design of the Villa Jaquemet.
Sculpted and photographed by
Jeanneret, December 1907. (BV)

et encadrant 2 groupes de fenêtres, reliés au bas par une horizontale en forte saillie servant de base à des caisses à fleurs. Les deux fenêtres cintrées avec leurs encadrements roc et moëllons noyés dans le crépi et la corniche, à peu près sur le même plan que les piles. Les fenêtres elles-mêmes très peu enfoncées, de manière à obtenir un *plein* tenant tout le rez-de-chaussée tout autour de la maison. A l'étage 2 espèces de loggias, porte-balcons soutenues par six montants en roc avec base de l'encorbel-lement en saillie, (extrémité de la traverse de pierre reliant le mur du fond au mur extérieur). Encor-bellement en briques crépis, le tout abrité sous avant-toit de verre. J'ai longtemps essayé un toit de tuile qui n'allait pas du tout. Ma maquette exigeait là une horizontale et je crois que ce verre donnera une note originale. Ai-je eu tort de profiler les plaques de verre; aurais-je dû garder une horizontale rigide comme sur le croquis en couleurs? Les trois supports en fer sont à étudier. J'ai remarqué dans toutes les belles constructions florentines sévères, l'effet très fort du tirant de fer et autres appliques. (Bargello, Palais Vieux). Ces deux cornes de chaque côté sont nécessaires, elles m'ont été imposées par la maquette, elles sont, je crois le point de vue de l'affaire. Je les ai faites en moëllons, n'ayant point d'autre idée. C'est derrière ces deux cornes en surplomb que se donne la retombée du toit. J'ai remarqué dans tout l'art florentin ce principe de surplomb qui est si vigoureux et qui est directe-ment inspiré du rocher. (Badia, Bargello, Palais Vieux). Le pignon avec faible saillie du toit (un chevron supporté par cinq corbeaux de pierre) est en crépi grossier avec des moëllons noyés par-ci par-là. C'est ce qui donne tant d'attrait à tous ces murs en Italie, c'est d'un travail encore plus simple que le mur ordinaire et c'est beaucoup plus beau.

His pencil and watercolor sketch is similar in design to that of the clay models yet as a two-dimensional medium is unable to convey the rich plasticity of the facade (fig. 109). This is especially obvious in the columns on the second storey that divide the windows into a 1:2:2:1 rhythm, as well as in the degree to which the shelf roof projects above the terrace. The band of ornament over these windows is deeply incised on the model; perhaps this suggests that sgraffito rather than fresco was intended. The colors throughout the sketch are rich earth tones with neither white nor bright colors included.

Jeanneret prepared, as he did for the Stotzer house, a drawing with all three Jaquemet elevations set side by side and in a landscape setting (figs. 110, 111). Here the garden facade, compared to the watercolor, has been simplified: the columns on the second floor have lost their entasis as well as their block-like capitals and become cylinders, the ground-floor windows have lost their curved form, and the stylized band of "sapin" trees below the attic is less lively and closer to the sgraffito design at the Villa Fallet.[23]

Superficially, except for their roof shapes, the side elevations seem similar to those at the Villa Stotzer. However, the street, or north, facade is more complex and places greater emphasis on the horizontal. But after the discovery that the topographical calculations were wrong, the position of the front door had to be raised and a new, less well integrated, entrance pavilion designed.[24]

The final set of plans, elevations, and sections—from which the house was built— is dated February 1908 and signed by the two architects and the client (fig. 112). The massing and ancillary elevations were only imperceptibly altered, yet the south facade underwent dramatic change—a transformation just as spectacular as that at the Villa Stotzer which it now quite closely resembled, except for the shape of the roof. Rounded and curved forms were excised in favor of straight lines and the only vestige of the original second-storey design is that the windows are grouped in pairs rather than, as chez Stotzer, a continuous horizontal band.

The plans of the two superimposed apartments are not identical because the bay windows of the ground floor are merely open balconies on the floor above. Thus the

23.  Also observable below the south elevation is a faint sketch that shows, in plan, a short section of the second-storey wall that indicates, as does the dotted line on the shelf roof of the elevation, the possibility of having the wall curve in and out in order to create small bay windows. The rooms behind are labelled "ch. à manger" and "ch. à coucher" with a party wall between. This complex design would inevitably have been quite expensive.

24.  A troubling matter concerning these elevations is a hastily written note in the upper right corner which says: "Wien le 19 [the 9 was then changed to 0] fevrier 19../ChE Jeanneret." Was this added later? The designs are certainly those of circa December 10 rather than February 10; remember that the preliminary designs for the Villa Jaquemet were mailed to L'Eplattenier on December 11 and the final, revised design was finished on February 20. Did Jeanneret confuse the two dates—or the two sets of drawings— when adding this longhand note? I expect so.

**Fig. 109.** Preliminary project for Villa Jaquemet, December 1907. Pencil, charcoal (?), and watercolor on tracing paper. 52 × 31.8 cm. (BV)

**Fig. 110.** Project: Villa Jaquemet, detail of south or garden facade that also appears on the sheet of three elevation drawings. December 1907 (?). Pencil and charcoal. (BV)

adjoining rooms are reduced in size and the bathroom is too small even for a tub (fig. 113). Meanwhile the cross section shows the front door prior to its being raised (fig. 114)—compare this with Chapallaz's photo of the completed house (fig. 115).[25]

Construction materials for the two houses are identical—quarry-faced ashlar stone for foundations, corner piers, and facing for the ground floor of the south facade. The ashlar on the side elevations of each house rises to a different height, with cement plaster above. At the Stotzer house this stucco surface begins at a lower level and is enlivened by the placement of random stones. The two-tone decoration under the Stotzer gable—so clearly visible in color photographs or at the site—is distinctive since none exists on the Jaquemet facade, now repainted stark white (figs. 116, 117 and color plate IV). Both houses are beautifully roofed with dark red tiles; these add texture that is consummate with the design.

25. Whether these drawings, from which the blueprints were made, are by Jeanneret's hand or were redrawn in Chapallaz's office is difficult to ascertain, yet I believe they were done in Chapallaz's office.

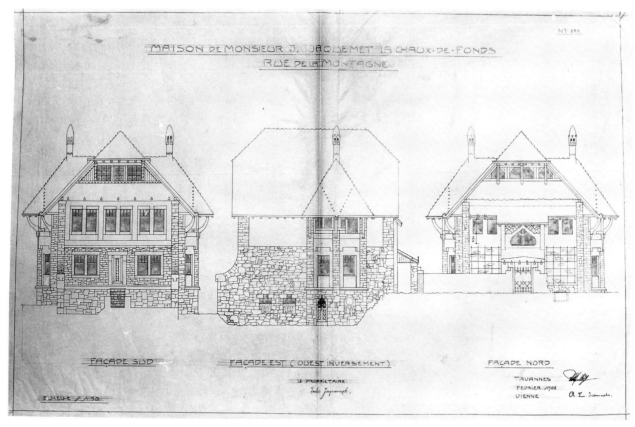

**Fig. 111.** (*Opposite*) Project: Villa Jaquemet. This proposal was rejected by the client. Pencil and charcoal. 38 × 91.3 cm. (BV)

**Fig. 112.** (*Opposite*) Villa Jaquemet. Final elevations. Signed and dated February 1908. Ink on tracing paper. 60 × 93 cm. (BV)

**Fig. 113.** Villa Jaquemet. Plans. (BV)

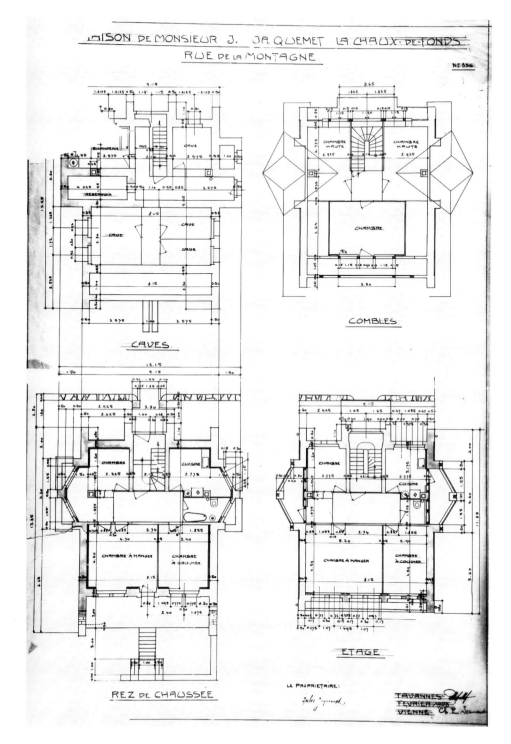

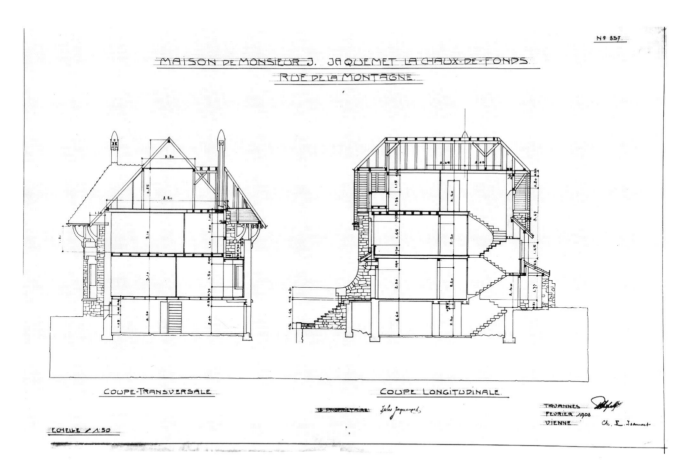

MAISON DE MONSIEUR J. JAQUEMET LA CHAUX-DE-FONDS
RUE DE LA MONTAGNE

COUPE TRANSVERSALE                    COUPE LONGITUDINALE

LE PROPRIETAIRE: *Jules Jaquemet,*

TAVANNES
FEVRIER 1908
VIENNE          *Ch. E. Jeanneret*

ECHELLE ⁄ 1.50

**Fig. 114.** Villa Jaquemet. Cross sections. (BV)

The proportions are carefully considered. There are few willful acts. Every aspect of the design is related to the overall scheme. Horizontals line up to create unity and restfulness rather than agitation or tension.

In addition to these houses on the slopes of Mount Pouillerel, Jeanneret had prospects of designing two more—as well as an addition to the Villa Fallet. All this, however, came to nought.[26]

Meanwhile, at home, Jeanneret's schoolmates were actively sculpting wood and metal ornament for the Villa Sandoz at Tavannes; Chapallaz was supervising construction although he was not the designing architect. L'Eplattenier had also obtained, for his Cours Supérieur, an appropriation to design and construct a model dining room for

26. "Dire à l'occasion à M. Fallet que j'ai des idées déjà bien précises sur son annexe; de même j'ai déjà quelques idées sur les deux bicoques en dessus de votre terrain. Je m'amuserai une fois à faire un rendu général des six maisons" (to L'Eplattenier, December 11, 1907).

**Fig. 115.** Villa Jaquemet as seen from the northeast. Photo by René Chapallaz. (BV)

**Fig. 116.** Villa Jaquemet seen from the southwest. Chapallaz photo, ca. December 1908. (BV)

**Fig. 117.** Villa Jaquemet. Note that, over the years, the south terrace has been extended outward, new chimneys installed, and the plaster walls painted white. (Photo by author)

the international exhibition to be held at Nancy in 1909.[27] We also learn that "the Commune has commissioned the Ecole d'art to specify and select its site for a future school-building"; Jeanneret, two years later, would propose a design for this site.

After spending five and a half weeks redesigning the Villa Jaquemet (finished February 20), Jeanneret and Perrin's post-Vienna agenda was still uncertain. They had spoken of Munich, Dresden, Dusseldorf, or Berlin in mid-December but by early January the choice seemed to favor Dresden. Then it became Paris, the news being withheld due to L'Eplattenier's edict against their going to France.

Meanwhile Jeanneret's parents so persistently pressed him for news of his plans that he became extremely annoyed, answering curtly on January 21 that (1) he never had budged an inch in order to see an architect in Vienna; (2) he had no intention of frivolously traveling without clear objectives and did seriously want to apprentice six months to a year with an architect; (3) he rejected the idea of attending architectural school; (4) if the architect he worked for did not help him with mathematics and engineering he would spend a year, in about a year's time, at Zurich; (5) he would then go to Berlin to work as a well-qualified employee in a large office; (6) finally, after another year, he would stop work and travel in a carefree manner in Belgium, France, and

27. ". . . la commune a alloué un crédit de 10,000 f. au cours supérieur pour la construction d'une salle à manger pour l'exposition internationale de Nancy 1909" (Jeanneret to parents, January 31, 1908). Apparently it was never built.

England; (7) and then he would return home.[28] He concluded by restating his annoyance at both his parents' and teacher's failure to comprehend how much effort and intellectual input had been spent in designing the two houses, time he considered lost relative to his formal training. However it did provide him with his financial independence.

On February 26, with the Jaquemet plans in the mail, both Jeanneret and Perrin penned long letters to L'Eplattenier. They informed him of their impending trip to Paris and gave reasons for their decision. Jeanneret stressed his need for technical training while reiterating his objections to German art, his arguments being augmented by page-by-page references to *Dresdener Kunstler* (Heft 2 and 3, 1906) wherein the work of Lossow, director of the Dresden Kunstgewerbeschule, as well as his colleagues, was illustrated. He said it would be a lesser evil to study under Wagner. He then compared "the German movement" and "the Latin movement," a theme that virtually became an obsession in the years to come and ultimately became the topic for an intended book. In this initial reference he merely stated that "The German movement seeks the utmost in originality, being concerned with neither construction, nor logic, nor beauty. There is no point of rapport with nature." Of the Latin movement, by contrast, he said it concerns itself with the great works of the past—"Gothic (and Louis XV and Louis XVI for furniture design) *is founded upon nature, upon basic laws* of construction that seek beauty above all else." He asserted that contemporary French art was not, as L'Eplattenier insisted, frivolous; rather it was based, as L'Eplattenier's own teaching, upon nature—just as the design of the Matthey-Doret music room—which was the direction Jeanneret wished to follow.

Unwittingly, however, Perrin had previously written to his parents about Paris. Therefore, well before L'Eplattenier received their lengthy explanations, they received from him a letter that, in Jeanneret's words, treated them "like ten-year-old children." Jeanneret endeavored to soothe matters by writing on the twenty-ninth and again on March 2, and finally he received L'Eplattenier's forgiveness and apparently even his blessing for the trip to Paris. Tensions, however, remained high, so to avoid confrontation the boys bypassed La Chaux-de-Fonds en route to Paris, asking Chapallaz to meet them in Munich to discuss the villa plans. *Four months* elapsed before Jeanneret would again write to L'Eplattenier.

On the first of March they filed their two-week departure notice with their respective landlords; Jeanneret then attended a concert and occupied himself with writing letters (he was still pressing Chapallaz on how best to obtain a technical education). On

28. Except for minor modifications, Jeanneret adhered quite closely to this program. He did work for an architect (Perret) who assisted him with engineering (but he stayed 17 rather than 6 to 12 months), he then went to Berlin to work in a large office (Behrens'), then traveled in a carefree manner (to the Balkans, Turkey, and Greece rather than to France, Belgium, and England which he had partially seen), and then returned home.

Saturday afternoon he visited six architects' offices and of course found no one in. Feeling sheepishly guilty, he belatedly—during the week of March ninth[29]—located Hoffmann. After Jeanneret showed him his Italian drawings, Hoffmann apparently offered him a job. Presumably Jeanneret was not interested, but in any case it was too late to accept as their departure date was already fixed for less than a week away. Years later, after becoming an admirer of Hoffmann's work and being impressed by his international fame, Jeanneret regretted the opportunity he had lost and falsely implied that he had worked in Hoffmann's office—an assertion grossly exaggerated by several biographers.[30]

Hoffmann also invited him to his Cabaret Fledermaus which evidently Jeanneret had never seen. Years later he claimed to have been introduced there to Koloman Moser and Gustav Klimt.[31] More consequential, however, this meeting of important people was apparently the opening wedge in Jeanneret's tardy appreciation of Hoffmann and the Secession—and it occurred only three or four days before he left Vienna. A month later, in Paris, he would carefully draw to scale the plans and elevations of the Cabaret Fledermaus, including elaborate notes about the materials, colors, and the lighting which he particularly admired (fig. 118).[32] This, in fact, is Jeanneret's *only* known drawing of Viennese architecture, and it was made when Vienna was but a memory.

On Sunday, March 15, the boys relinquished their rooms and boarded the evening train to Munich where they arrived at 6:30 the following morning. Disappointed because it wasn't grander, they nevertheless were impressed by its museums. Chapallaz, for whom Jeanneret had great affection, arrived Tuesday morning and the three had a hilarious time together. Then, on Thursday evening, they set off for Nuremberg where Jeanneret was ecstatic over the Gothic architecture, especially the fortifications but also

29. When writing to his parents on Sunday, March 8, he makes no mention of seeing Hoffmann. Therefore the meeting must have occurred the following week.

30. Jeanneret, in his *Etude sur le mouvement d'art décoratif en Allemagne* (La Chaux-de-Fonds, 1912) said on page 5, "j'avais été engagé à Vienne . . . par Joseph Hoffmann" and on page 40, "ayant été engagé . . .," both of which imply that he worked for Hoffmann without actually saying that he did. There is no published statement by Le Corbusier that unequivocally asserts that he worked in Hoffmann's office. Even Maximilien Gauthier (*Le Corbusier* [Paris, 1944], p. 24) merely says: "Hoffmann lui offre une place dans ses ateliers—une place payée! Pris au dépourvu, Jeanneret n'ose pas dire qu'il a cédé, déjà, à l'attraction de Paris." Yet several biographers including Maurice Besset (*Qui était Le Corbusier* (Geneva: Skira, 1968, p. 198) would claim: "il passe six mois chez Josef Hoffmann."

31. This is known only from Le Corbusier's report to his biographer, Maximilien Gauthier, *Le Corbusier,* p. 24: "Invité au cabaret Fledermaus, la plus récente création de la Wienerwerkstätte, il y est présenté, avec éloge, aux artistes les plus marquants, de Koloman [sic] à Klint [sic]." By Koloman he means Moser and Klimt is misspelled. Jean Petit (p. 28) repeats these identical errors, so he presumably used Gauthier as his source.

32. A small notebook sheet exists at the Fondation Le Corbusier on which he describes the interior in greater detail and includes a plan of the gallery. These notes, entitled only "Le Cabaret," were probably penned soon after his visit.

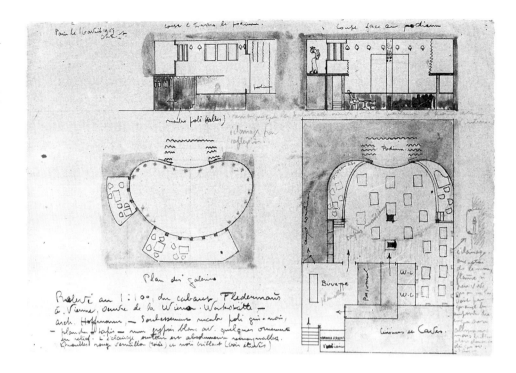

**Fig. 118.** Die Fledermaus Cabaret, Vienna, 1907. Josef Hoffmann, architect. Jeanneret's drawing dated "Paris le 16 avril 1907 [*sic;* the year was 1908]" Pencil, India ink, and red and green watercolor wash on heavy gray paper. 25 × 36 cm. (FLC 2466)

the medieval buildings. These had more in common with his recently designed villas than anything he had seen in Vienna. He made countless drawings, as well as photographs, and sketched Gothic furniture in the various museums (fig. 119). On Saturday he wrote a jubilant postcard to his parents, the tone of which was more upbeat than anything since Italy. From Nuremberg Chapallaz returned to La Chaux-de-Fonds and the boys went on to Paris.[33]

Was Jeanneret's four-month sojourn in Vienna the almost total loss to his educational development that his letters imply? Certainly not. The aftereffect of what he had seen left an indelible impression on his mind. And whereas he did not like what he had seen, it did make him start thinking and as time passed this meant that his values changed. Even before the year was out he admitted that "Vienna killed my purely plastic conception of architecture (the research only for forms)."[34] And in subsequent years he slyly

33. Jeanneret's March 8 letter to his parents says, "Je pars pour Munich dimanche soir et y resterai trois ou quatre jours, puis à Nuremberg, pour y dessiner deux ou trois jours, puis à Paris." His March 21 postcard from Nuremberg gives Paris as his next mail address. His father's journal notes that as of April 2 two postcards had been received from Paris where Edouard had arrived the week before. Therefore it seems unlikely that any important sightseeing was done between Nuremberg and Paris. When I asked Léon Perrin whether they had visited Strasbourg and/or Nancy en route he wasn't sure. Significantly there are no sketches from either place in Jeanneret's collection (later he visited both cities). One thing is certain however: Jeanneret did not go to Paris via Lyon and meet Tony Garnier as stated by Jean Petit (p. 28) and others.

34. Letter to L'Eplattenier, November 22, 1908.

**Fig. 119.** Medieval fortifications and watchtowers at Nuremberg, Germany. Pencil and ink on sketchbook paper. 20 × 12 cm. (FLC 2158)

encouraged people to think he had apprenticed under Hoffmann. And still later, in the days of *L'Esprit Nouveau,* he proved himself to be an admirer and supporter of Adolf Loos. The "sanitary architecture" that he ridiculed while in Vienna would become even more stripped, pure, and evocative of industrial process in his own architecture of the 1920s.

Nor can we overlook his remark that "from Stemolak I learn to see." He highly valued his weeks of study under this Viennese sculptor and when we consider the emphasis he placed, throughout his life, on spending part of every day on painting and sculpture as preparation for designing buildings, the lessons with Stemolak were hardly a waste of time.

Designing two houses was also a splendid educational experience, especially because he was not at La Chaux-de-Fonds where L'Eplattenier, Chapallaz, and others could offer constant support and advice. The responsibility rested largely on his own shoulders and this helped develop within the twenty-year-old an early independence, requiring him to think things through on his own. This was important. So was the fact that his work provided financial security, thus assuring that his studies could go on.

Actually, he did admit to learning one thing in Vienna, and that was to look at girls!

# 5

## PARIS

*Auguste Perret and the Search for an Ideal*
*1908–1909*

Jeanneret arrived in Paris determined "to know," to delve into the innermost depths of architecture and to gain insight into the phenomenon we call design, insights that would crystallize for him his own "ideal" of just what contemporary architecture should be. This was a tall order, especially for a lad of twenty, yet he was prepared to accept professional martyrdom, if necessary, in pursuit of his cause. He was, in short, an idealist in search of an ideal. With envy he looked upon L'Eplattenier and others who apparently possessed an ideal, failing to realize that what he sought lay within himself; he must build faith in his own convictions—once he understood what these might be. At the outset he directed his research through books, devoting weeks and months to this endeavor before concluding that books too often contained fundamental flaws; museums, by contrast, provided the unblemished truth: the work of art faithfully answered the questions that he posed.[1]

---

1. "Recherche de la vérité dans les Bibliothèques. Les livres. Les livres sont innombrables; où est le commencement? Ces heures de bibliothèques où l'on poursuit dans les livres, la vérité! Et l'on tombe tout à coup dans un trou. Il fait nuit, on ne comprend plus rien.

"Les musées m'ont fourni les certitudes sans trous, sans embûches. Les oeuvres sont là comme des entiers, et la conversation est sans fard, le tête-à-tête est à [la] merci de celui qui questionne; l'oeuvre répond toujours aux questions qu'on lui pose. Ce sont de bonnes écoles que les oeuvres des musées" (*L'Art décoratif d'aujourd'hui* [Paris, 1925], pp. 201–2).

The family was overawed at the intellectual development of their son, his father noting in his journal (September 16, 1908): "Received from Ed. a 30 or 40 page letter which has created quite a stir within our family and has given rise to profound discussions and emotions. He is entirely carried away with idealistic ideas." And Albert, who long cast Edouard in the "little brother" role, gradually recognized his brother's superiority[2] and his letters began to change in tone, sometimes agreeing with his parents' assessments but more often defending Edouard (and himself) for having ideas different from their own. However, he concurred with them that his brother was "always analyzing himself . . . [which is] a defect that I also find in Ed; he envisions life too much as a struggle, a fight, finds battles at every turn" (February 12, 1908). As 1908 slipped by, Albert increasingly became the intermediary, trying not to explain Edouard but to seek his parents' patience: "didn't you love Edouard when he made you stop before each flower, each different texture, each tint, when he said something of which you didn't yet understand the meaning" (November 24, 1908). And Edouard, who occasionally felt slighted when his parents found communication difficult with him, was comforted by big brother: "If the parents write less often to you than to me it is because they consider you a "self made man" [English in the original], the robust type, he who stands on his own; one considers me the convalescent in the family" (October 21[, 1909), a statement not entirely true but nevertheless reassuring.

Writing to L'Eplattenier on July 3, 1908,[3] Jeanneret is tormented by his need for an idea or ideal, words he repeats no less than a dozen times. He remarks how "Life, at this period of my existence, is a rough battle," then praises the solid principles of L'Eplattenier's teaching which, nevertheless, has created in him an insatiable desire for his own ideal, the identification of which he fears may be beyond his ability to discover.[4] He entreats his mentor to remember that it is not easy to find oneself, and speaks with satisfaction of his own isolation in Paris where, away from influences of home and school, he has the freedom to think out his problems on his own.

Then, after a four-month silence and on the eve of his first face-to-face meeting with L'Eplattenier in nearly a year and a half, Jeanneret wrote his teacher a remarkable

2. Albert to his parents on August 2, 1908: "et quand je réfléchis qu'il [Edouard] a commencé son travail d'affranchissement il y a des années . . . il a une grande avance sur moi."

3. The full text of this letter, as well as that of November 22, 1908, are published in Jean Petit, *Le Corbusier, lui-méme* (Geneva, 1970), pp. 31–36. This July 3 letter is apparently Jeanneret's first since leaving Vienna.

4. ". . . je me trouve avoir des besoins d'idéal tellement au-dessus de mes forces." And speaking of men like Eugène Grasset: "Ces hommes-là ont la foi déjà idéalisée, déjà paradisiaque de ses [ces?] initiés qui ont vu et savent que c'est vrai. . . . Vous êtes aussi une de ses [ces?] âmes nobles . . . qui recherche[nt?] l'idéal pur, abstrait, l'idéal qui vit dans l'âme . . ." (to L'Eplattenier, July 3, 1908). It seems that he believed, at this time, that an idea or ideal was unique to the individual, rather than universal, and to share another person's idea or ideal was to be a follower, an imitator, rather than an innovator.

letter on November 22, 1908. It was profound, full of introspection, and intended to explain "what I am, in order that our reunion will be filled with joy and—from you—encouragement, and not one of misunderstanding." He told how his endless quest for an ideal had led first to the question "What is architecture?" and that Vienna had taught him that it was not merely a search for forms. But what was it? For the answer he turned to the art of former times: "I chose the most *zealous* fighters for a cause, those to whom we, we of the twentieth century, are now ready to become the equals: the early Medieval architects. And during three months I studied Romanesque architecture evenings at the library.[5] And I went to Notre-Dame, and I listened to lectures on Gothic architecture by Magne at the Ecole des Beaux-arts—and I understood. . . . I realized, by the study of Romanesque, that architecture was not a question of proportion and harmony of form but something else, but what? I still didn't know. And so I studied mechanics, then statics . . . strength of materials. It's difficult, but it's beautiful, these mathematics—so logical, so perfect! Meanwhile Magne offered a course on the Italian Renaissance and, by negation, I learned what architecture was. Boennelwald gave a course on Romanesque and Gothic architecture and that also clarified what architecture is. Meanwhile with Perret I learned about reinforced concrete and the revolutionary forms that it requires. These eight months in Paris cry out to me: Logic, truth, honesty . . . 'Burn what you have loved, love what you have burned.'

"You, Grasset, Sauvage, Jourdain, Paquet and others, you are all deceitful—Grasset, a model of truth, deceitful, because you do not really know what architecture is all about. . . . •

"The architect must be a man with a logical mind, the enemy of love of plastic, sculptural effects, a man of science yet with a heart, an artist and a scholar. I know it now—yet none of you told me: fortunately our ancestors know how to speak to those who are willing to consult them.

"One speaks of the art of tomorrow. This art *will be*. Because mankind has changed his lifestyle, his way of thinking. The program is new. It is new in a new context . . . of iron . . . of reinforced concrete."

Then, three days later, Jeanneret continued his letter, focusing on L'Eplattenier's teaching which he criticizes as endeavoring to create competent artists from unthinking youths of twenty who do nothing but follow the example of their masters. He concludes that L'Eplattenier's attempt to establish a new art movement was begun too soon, is built upon sand, that this is because his recruits have never thought for themselves, and because the art of tomorrow will be an art *based on thought* (a phrase highly reminiscent of Provensal). "My quarrel against you, my master whom I love, will be against this error: dazzled and overwhelmed by your own internal strength, which is extraordinary, you believe that you see similar strength everywhere. You believe [that your

5. He is referring to Corroyer's *L'Architecture romane,* soon to be discussed.

young, enthusiastic students] are already mature, already victorious. . . . [Similarly] my struggle will be against these, my friends, against their ignorance: not that I know something, but *because I know* that I know nothing."

The letter concludes with a reaffirmation of Jeanneret's fondness and respect for his teacher: "Never doubt me, I am too attached to you to forget you for a single moment. I am too much in love with your splendid work not to wish other than to desire with all my strength that *we,* in whom you have placed your confidence, will be worthy of that task, and prepared at the decisive moment. I say to you au revoir, but only briefly, because soon I will have the joy of being able to speak with you, so I sign / Your very affectionate student / Ch. E. Jeanneret"

This incredible letter, composed by someone quite out of the ordinary, records Jeanneret's sentiments during the height of his infatuation with rationalism, mathematics, and engineering, so much of which he would soon set aside, just as his outspoken rejection of proportion and harmony of form is totally contrary to what he learned two years later in the office of Peter Behrens which resulted in his life-long fascination with *tracés régulateurs* and the Modulor.

Ultimately, however, the contradictions are not what is significant but rather Jeanneret's alert, inquiring mind and his preparedness, indeed willingness, to defend his beliefs even at the expense of what, and whom, he holds most dear. One contradiction, we shall see, was his rejection of L'Eplattenier's art movement as something premature, built upon sand, and supported by a brigade of phantom soldiers who knew not what they were doing because they had not begun to think for themselves. "I am through with childish dreams of a success similar to those of one or two schools in Germany—Vienna, Darmstadt. That's too easy; I want to do combat with truth itself." Yet precisely one year later he returned home in order to join, work, and live among L'Eplattenier's soldiers, to be reinspired by his teacher, and blindly to set forth on a new campaign of conquest—to write a book on what was for him the unknown subject of urbanism! He soon would eat his words about being "through with childish dreams of a success similar to those of one or two schools in Germany" when he agreed to do research on the teaching at these same German schools, research which resulted in the first book he ever published. And three years later he curtailed his Mediterranean travels in order to hurry home and assume a teaching post at the Ecole d'Art, *under L'Eplattenier's direction,* in order to train still more soldiers (to build more earthworks out of sand?). No, in sum, this November 1908 letter is a marvelous document, but it is not a forecast of the future either in terms of Jeanneret's conception of architecture or his acceptance/rejection of L'Eplattenier's ideas.

Although Jeanneret criticized L'Eplattenier for being selective by informing students of certain things to the exclusion of others (such as emphasizing design and decoration to the neglect of materials and engineering), Jeanneret himself was equally guilty of being biased and selective. From books he extracted thoughts that reinforced his own

**Fig. 120.** Edouard Jeanneret photographed in May 1908 in front of
his window at 9, rue des Ecoles,
Paris. Note the view of rooftops with
Notre-Dame in the background, a
view identical to that recorded in several of his paintings (compare the following illustration). (FLC)

**Fig. 121.** Watercolor by Jeanneret
showing skyline of Paris with Notre-
Dame in the distance. Painted from
his window at 9, rue des Ecoles in
July 1908. Watercolor. 26 × 20 cm.
(FLC 1924)

ideas while frequently overlooking the author's central theme. And although he was—
even if he didn't realize it—a child of the classical tradition, he scorned classicism while
retaining his myopic devotion to the Middle Ages.

Concerning his vehement rejection of classicism and fervent love for medieval, he
later told the following story on himself: "I spent entire weeks exploring the mysteries
of Notre-Dame while in possession of the Ministry's keys. Auguste Perret was astonished by this research into distant history. 'You know Versailles?'—'No'—'Oh, you
must go there!' and later: 'Versailles—you went there?'—'No.' And still later: 'You
went to Versailles?'—'No, I won't go there.' 'Oh, and why not?'—'Because Versailles
and the classical period represent decadence'—Boom! That was too much! He really
bent my ears! In short, not until a year after my arrival in Paris did I discover Versailles,
during one sparkling morning in May."[6] Apparently this was the morning he took his
parents there, having never visited it on his own.

After Jeanneret and Perrin arrived at Paris on or about the twenty-fifth of March,
1908, Edouard initially lodged with an old school friend (Charles Schneider?) at 41,
rue Charlot before taking a top-floor room at the Hôtel d'Orient, 9, rue des Ecoles,
not far from the Sorbonne (fig. 120). The panorama, with its view toward the towers
of Notre-Dame, was one he often painted (fig. 121), and the photo of himself standing

6. Le Corbusier, "Perret," *L'Architecture d'aujourd'hui,* 7 (October 1932), p. 7.

there makes a revealing comparison with the far more self-assured young man who left home eight months before. In August he moved still closer to his beloved cathedral, taking lodgings diagonally across the Seine from Notre-Dame at 3, quai St. Michel where, under the mansard, he would spend the remaining fifteen months of his Paris stay.

His arrival in Paris was even more ill-prepared than in Vienna—if that is possible. He had no list of architects with whom he wished to work, and no information about registration dates at schools. He was, as it transpired, three weeks late for the spring term entrance exams at the Ecole des arts décoratifs,[7] yet when he did take the exam in September he ranked a remarkable sixth among 230 candidates[8]—but failed to register. Why, after constantly criticizing L'Eplattenier for emphasizing the decorative arts to the neglect of engineering, and after months of bitterly complaining that he lacked the fundamentals of an architectural education, did he endeavor to enter a school of decorative arts rather than a school of architecture or engineering? There is no logical, or even reasonable, answer to this question other than that contradictions and complexities were a constituent part of Jeanneret's thinking.

He soon buried himself in the Bibliothèque Sainte-Geneviève, not far from his hotel, and spent *three months* devouring Edouard Corroyer's *L'Architecture romane* while simultaneously filling two notebooks with an extensive résumé of the text and sketches of the illustrations.[9] He did inquire about lecture courses at the Ecole des Beaux-Arts (the school of architecture), making a list of six—mathematics, descriptive geometry, stereotomy, construction, history of architecture, and theory of architecture—and eventually he audited (rather than enrolling in) a history course offered by Lucien Magne and one on construction by Paul-Louis Monduit.[10] Significantly his list *excluded* all studio

7. "Reçu 2 cartes d'Edouard depuis Paris où il [est] bien arrivé il y a 8 jours. La première était optimiste, les démarches qu'il avait faites semblaient avoir fait apprécier ses aptitudes. La seconde en rabat; arrivé 3 semaines après l'examen d'entrée aux Arts décoratifs; la crise sévit à Paris" (father's journal, April 2, 1908).

This indirect method of reporting on Edouard's correspondence is necessary because his mother forwarded the Paris letters to Albert in Geneva, and although she asked for their return, Albert apparently threw them out. Only after Albert's visit to Paris in July 1909 is the French correspondence relatively intact.

8. "Ed. me dit qu'il est reçu aux Arts décoratifs 6 sur 230!" (postcard from Albert to his mother, October 13, 1908).

9. "Et pendant 3 mois j'étudiai les Romans, le soir à la Bibliothèque" (to L'Eplattenier, November 22, 1908). On the cover of the first notebook Le Corbusier subsequently wrote: "étude faite à Paris à mon arrivée printemps 1908 à la Bibliothèque Ste. Geneviève d'après Corroyer." Notations on the back cover referring to Perrin and Perrochet clearly confirm this 1908 date, while notes about interest payments (on his savings account?) dated 1920 and 1921 imply that he was rereading these notebooks at the time he was writing his *L'Esprit Nouveau* articles.

10. These courses, which had begun the previous October, are listed on the back of a sketch made at Nuremburg (FLC 2219). The theory of architecture course was offered by Julien Guadet, who died on May 17, 1908. Of the construction course, Le Corbusier recalled in 1932: "Monsieur Monduit [?] sévissait à l'amphithéâtre de 'Construction' avec des kilomètres de formules de haute mathématique: un cours à la

courses or those concerned with architectural design, nor did he attempt to register at the school. Meanwhile Léon Perrin obtained employment with Hector Guimard, the famous Art Nouveau architect of Paris' métro stations; Perrin also took courses at the Ecole des Arts Décoratifs.

Jeanneret's quest for work depended on referral from person to person rather than the usual method of liking the built work of a certain architect and seeking apprenticeship in his office. Had Jeanneret responded to his own preferences he might have looked up the designer of the rue Cassini studio-houses that he liked and wherein he sensed the glimmer of an "idea." That at 3 bis, rue Cassini had an expressed concrete frame infilled with brick and a flat roof; that at No. 5 was far more traditional (fig. 122).[11] Other Paris buildings that caught his attention were at No. 124, rue Réaumur, remarkable for its exterior metal frame that he photographed (fig. 123), and No. 1, rue Danton, which is the earliest example (1899–1900), not of concrete frame, but of a building actually *cast* in reinforced concrete—even though its exterior was [as it is today] covered with a very thin coating of cement. The engineer, owner, and principal occupant was François Hennebique. Otherwise, Jeanneret found little of interest in contemporary Paris architecture; he never mentioned the still popular Art Nouveau, nor the recently completed Garage Ponthieu by Auguste Perret which was constructed of exposed reinforced concrete. Other avant-garde works, such as Frantz Jourdain's Samaritaine Department Store or Anatole de Baudot's church of Saint-Jean de Montmartre, he merely mocked.[12]

_____

mitrailleuse pour têtes fortes; un tir de barrage, un tornade. Personne n'y comprenait rien et nous sentions que cet abrutissement pèserait sur toute notre vie" (Le Corbusier, "Perret," *L'Architecture d'aujourd'hui,* 7 [October 1932], p. 7).

To understand these mathematical formulas Jeanneret needed additional training which, beginning in July 1909, he obtained from an engineer named Pagès with whom he tutored two hours each Monday evening during the final months of his stay in France. He also studied mathematics for its own sake; he recounts: "Auguste Perret s'étonnait de me voir ainsi aimer les musées: 'Si j'avais le temps, disait-il, je ferais des mathématiques, elles forment l'esprit.' Je fis des mathématiques qui, pratiquement, ne me serviront jamais à rien dans la suite. Mais peut-être m'ont-elles formé l'esprit" (*L'Art décoratif d'aujourd'hui,* "Confessions" [Paris, 1925], p. 206).

11. On July 3, 1908, he wrote L'Eplattenier about these "deux maisons délicieuses où je vais souvent le soir, en pèlerinage, entraînant soit Perrin, soit Perrochet, soit Georges [Aubert] pour partager mon enthousiasme. C'est encore bien peu de chose, mais c'est déjà tout en idée. L'une [No. 5] en briques rouges doit être celle de J. P. Laurens; l'autre [No. 3 bis, for Lucien Simon] en beton armé celle d'un autre peintre." The architect was long thought to be François Le Coeur but more recent research attributes these houses (No. 7, 1903; No. 5, 1905; No. 3 bis, 1906) to Louis Süe. At No. 3 bis the raw concrete is not visible. It seems to be covered with a very thin coat of cement (almost as at No. 1, rue Danton) and then painted a light cream color which harmonizes with the yellow-brown bricks. In terms of structural expression, it recalls No. 25 bis, rue Franklin.

12. "When I first came to Paris in 1908 Frantz Jourdain's Samaritaine was already built. We got a lot of fun out of laughing at the decorative fretwork of his metal domes and quite overlooked the fact that his

Jeanneret's search for work, as recounted by Gauthier,[13] led from Frantz Jourdain, to Charles Plumet, to Henri Sauvage. His visit to Jourdain was motivated less by architecture than by Jourdain's position within the profession and his post as president of the Salon d'automne where Jeanneret apparently hoped to exhibit. Jeanneret arrived with his portfolio in hand and Jourdain was duly impressed, providing a letter of reference to the vice-president of the Salon, Charles Plumet. But the latter had no job to offer and sent Jeanneret to the Salon's sectional president for architecture, Henri Sauvage, who did offer him some minor work designing a decorative frieze—which Jeanneret understandably declined.

By chance, in the telephone book, Jeanneret saw the name Eugène Grasset whose books on ornament and design he knew from the Ecole d'art. So, with drawings in hand, he went off to meet Grasset with whom he spent two memorable hours: "he spoke to me with the grandeur of a prophet."[14] Yet Grasset merely confirmed what

**Fig. 122.** Louis Süe, studio-houses at Nos. 3 bis (left) and 5 (right), rue Cassini, Paris, 1906 and 1905 respectively. Jeanneret often came here to see and admire these buildings. (Photo by author)

**Fig. 123.** Jeanneret's photo of 124, rue Réaumur, Paris (1903–5), another building wherein he appreciated the rational expression of structure and use of new materials. (BV)

---

lateral facades are formed of unbroken expanses of glass"; "we thought de Baudot's church of Saint-Jean de Montmartre appalling" (*Oeuvre Complète,* vol. 1, pp. 12, 13).

    13. Gauthier, *Le Corbusier,* pp. 26–27, where the story of his meeting with Grasset is also told.

    14. Quoted in an undated letter from Albert to his parents probably written in April 1908.

L'Eplattenier had already said—that Parisian architecture represented decadence, and that the great hope generated by the new materials of the nineteenth century had been lost. Grasset then recalled the Perret brothers who built in reinforced concrete, so, with drawings in hand and a letter of introduction, Jeanneret went to 25 bis, rue Franklin where he obtained an apprenticeship that fulfilled his fondest dreams. Working part-time, usually mornings, with the remainder of the day free for his own pursuits, he was engaged for the first of July although he actually undertook his negotiations with Perret in April. It was somewhat before July 1, however, that he began work,[15] some three months after arriving in Paris.

Auguste Perret soon became a father figure, more a friend and counselor than a "boss" (very unlike Peter Behrens two years later). Jeanneret recalled that Perret carried his head high, caressed his well-trimmed beard, dressed discriminatingly, and kept his worktable impeccably arranged; he admired perfection in everything, whether it be cleanliness, a skillfully made object, but most of all a well-constructed building. He was also superb with clients.[16]

Despite Jeanneret's expectations, so often expressed in letters from Vienna, that his employer would provide instruction in mathematics, strength of materials, and engineering, this was never realized; Perret only urged him to acquire these skills elsewhere. Meanwhile the one thing he might have absorbed from this office experience—a profound respect for the principles of classicism—left only a cursory, though ultimately important, impression in his mind. And rationalism—that attitude or philosophical approach based on logic and reason rather than the romanticism that Jeanneret had grappled with in Vienna—did receive an important boost from his Paris experience, yet never did he accept it completely. When he wrote L'Eplattenier that Paris cried out "logic, truth, honesty," there was perhaps more Ruskinian morality than French rationalism mingled with these words.

Because he failed, for the moment at least, to embrace either classicism or rationalism, then what did he extricate from his office experience? In short it was an idea or ideal that he matured in future years about all these things—taking something from structures, techniques, materials, and methods and something from classical proportions, scale, harmony, and order—but never strictly practicing in one camp or the other and never, as Perret did, quite synthesizing the two. In this respect Jeanneret and Auguste Perret were very different men.[17]

Perret Frères, as the firm was called, included Auguste, Gustave, and Claude Perret.

15. His father's journal of June 14, 1908, states that "Il est engagé pour le 1 Juillet chez l'architecte Perret à Paris," yet by June 28 the family received word that Edouard was already at work.

16. Le Corbusier, "Perret," *L'Architecture d'aujourd'hui*, 7 (October 1932), p. 8.

17. They were different and yet too much the same. This largely accounts for the love/hate relationship that Jeanneret developed toward Auguste Perret during the twenties, the basis of which, more than anything else, was professional jealousy.

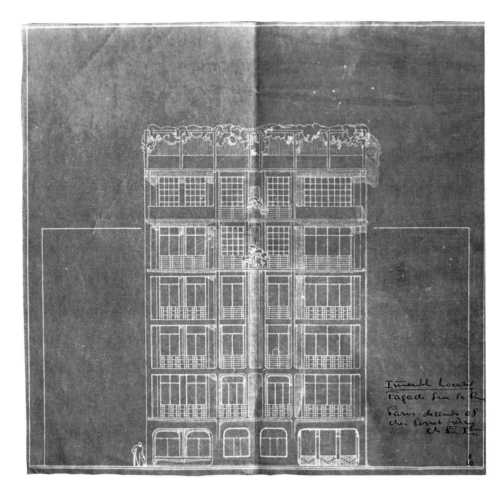

**Fig. 124.** Project for an unidentified building, 1908. Blueprint. Inscribed in ink (lower right) "Immeuble Locatif / Façade sur la Rue / Paris décembre 08 / chez Perret frères / Ch E Jt." This design was probably prepared by Jeanneret under Auguste Perret's direction. (FLC)

Usually Auguste did the designing. But this was an atypical organization because it was an architect's office *and* a construction firm. Therefore they might design and construct a building, or merely execute the designs of others, using their expertise in reinforced concrete. The major work in progress during Jeanneret's tenure was the cathedral at Oran, Algeria, designed by the architect Albert Ballu but engineered by the Perrets, whose ingenious reinforced concrete structure made the spacious interior possible. Unfortunately, however, Ballu faced the building with brick and mosaics thus camouflaging the structural system. Jeanneret assisted with the blueprints for the cathedral, as well as helping with other drafting where his participation was also anonymous.[18]

The only drafting attributable to him directly consists of several blueprints he wrote upon and saved throughout his life. Three are floor plans, two being for one site and

18. Jean Petit (p. 30) notes that Le Corbusier said he also worked on a two-hundred-bed hotel for Rio de Janeiro, some houses at Dakar, and modifications to the French legation at Brussels.

**Fig. 125.** La Saulot, Salbris, Loire-et-Cher, 1908. Perret Frères, architects. (Photo by author)

the third for a totally different location. They are identified neither by captions nor by the existence of similar drawings in Perret's archives; nor were they built.[19] For the single plan there is a corresponding elevation that shows a seven-storey apartment block upon which, in black ink, is written: "Immeuble Locatif / Façade sur la Rue / Paris décembre 08 / chez Perret frères / Ch.E.Jt." (fig. 124). This raises the question of whether the design was actually prepared by Jeanneret under Perret's direction, as would seem to be the case. The cantilevered balconies on the top floors imply the use of reinforced concrete and the roof garden is a feature used by Perret atop 25 bis, rue Franklin. The alternate plans for a different site have similar identifications (written in India ink) except for being dated "février 1909." Their arrangement of rooms shows an openness similar to that at 25 bis, rue Franklin.

Another blueprint refers to Salbris, a town south of Orléans in the Sologne region of France that is famous for "la chasse." There the Perrets designed a hunting lodge in 1908 for Maurice Lange called La Saulot (figs. 125, 126), but the building was assumed destroyed at some date after its construction notice appeared in *L'Architecte* in 1909. I, however, through my research, discovered the lodge, which was in mint condition, and subsequent efforts resulted in its being "inscrit sur la liste supplémentaire" by the

19. When Perret Frères moved from 25 bis, rue Franklin they destroyed most of their architectural drawings except for the buildings they actually owned or particularly liked (such as the Garage Ponthieu). The remaining material is preserved in the Fonds Perret at the Conservatoire National des Arts et Métiers in Paris.

ARCHITECTE_1909

FF P PERRET ARCH

**Fig. 126.** La Saulot, color plate with plans as published in *L'Architecte,* July, 1909. The original watercolor may be attributed to Jeanneret. Due to the angular view, the symmetry of the design is not apparent. (*L' Architecte*)

government but denied the highest preservation designation of "classe." The result was that the French Ministry of Culture permitted an autoroute to be constructed quite literally through the front yard and within a few feet of the house—a dreadful fate for one of the finest, yet least known, Perret buildings still extant in France.

Jeanneret's participation at La Saulot is documented by drawings and a much later remark: "J'entrai chez [Perret] et fis la cheminée de Salbris, l'aquarelle de Salbris, les lambris de Salbris. Puis la 'maison bouteille' (une maison c'est une bouteille, est un mot de Perret, pas de moi)."[20] The word "fis" (*faire* = to make) is intentionally ambiguous, leaving unclear whether he drew, designed, or executed the works in question; obviously he wished to imply a maximum rather than minimum participation, otherwise his words would have been chosen with more precision.

20. Jean Petit, ed., *Le Corbusier Parle* (Geneva, 1967), pp. 46–47. The "bottle" remark will be discussed later.

**Fig. 127.** La Saulot, view of free-standing fireplace as seen from living room while looking toward small salon. Blueprint of perspective which was perhaps traced from a photograph by Jeanneret in 1909. At lower left is a sketch-plan with brief description in German and at bottom right, in India ink, "Cheminée de Salbris / Paris juin 1909 / chez Perret Frères / Ch. E. Jt." (FLC)

**Fig. 128.** La Saulot, view of fireplace. (Photo by author)

Each claim will be discussed in sequence. The first, "la cheminée" or fireplace, is represented in three identical perspective views, each in a different medium. They show the free-standing, hooded fireplace in the context of the room. Everything is exactly as built, therefore they are not preliminary studies but probably, from the precision of the perspective, tracings from a photograph.[21]

One sketch is quickly done in pen and ink and an ink wash on tracing paper (FLC 1995), another is the carefully prepared drawing published in *L'Architecte* in July 1909 for which the original is now lost, and the third is a blueprint of the lost original that Jeanneret made as a keepsake and to which he attached a small sketch-plan and description in German as well as this note: "Cheminée de Salbris / Paris juin 1909 / chez Perret Frères / Ch. E. Jt." (figs. 127, 128). Therefore the drawing/tracing is probably by his hand but not the design of the actual fireplace.[22]

21. This process of tracing photographs recalls an unprecedented discovery I made back in the 1960s that many of Frank Lloyd Wright's architectural perspectives were actually traced from photographs rather than being, as was then thought, original presentation drawings made prior to construction of the building. See H. Allen Brooks, "Frank Lloyd Wright and the Wasmuth Drawings," *Art Bulletin,* 48 (June 1966), pp. 193–202.

22. The style of rendering the overstuffed chair, windows, and perhaps the foliage on the mantelpiece

The fireplace is most unusual due to its open firebox, sloping sheet-metal hood, decorative band of bronze repoussé, and finally the curious wooden structure that is articulated with thin wood slats and stands on the mantelpiece (or hangs from the ceiling) and looks less like a chimney than a piece of furniture that should be standing on the floor. Although the repoussé of the fireplace hood recalls work done at La Chaux-de-Fonds, it was also a favorite form of decoration with the Perrets, who chose the same stone pine motif for their repoussé work at 119 Avenue de Wagram of 1902.[23]

As for Jeanneret's remark concerning "l'aquarelle de Salbris," it assumes considerable validity thanks to a tear-sheet of color plate 37 from L'Architecte of July 1909, which is still preserved in his archives (see fig. 126). This perspective includes three plans and, added to the lower left in Jeanneret's hand, "Fait chez Perret en 1908." Obviously this refers to the watercolor and not the building itself. Happily I located the original; it is quite large, 28 by 87 cm, of which 12 cm at the extreme left were not reproduced in the color plate. No signature identifies authorship, yet attribution to Jeanneret seems safe especially since in 1908 he wrote L'Eplattenier (undated but probably July 31) that: "je passais mon temps chez Perret à faire de l'aquarelle. Voilà 2 semaines que c'est fini . . ."

Jeanneret's third statement concerns "les lambris de Salbris." This assertion is the most difficult to establish since no documentation exists except a passing remark to L'Eplattenier about making, at the time of the aquarelle, "des boiseries." Could this woodwork be the handsome high wainscotting still extant at La Saulot? (visible in figures 127 and 128). Probably so. And probably it means he was doing the detail drawings for its execution rather than the conceptual design. Stylistically there are overtones of medieval forms, as in the hunting lodge itself. Actually these Tudor revival aspects of the building's design would be more at home in Deauville, on the channel coast, than at Salbris, Loir-et-Cher. The woodwork, however, has absolutely no resemblance to any designed by Jeanneret at La Chaux-de-Fonds.

La Saulot is a most impressive building, especially for its strong pyramidal form and remarkably harmonious proportions. Its style recalls the half-timbering so in vogue in Normandy where the interval between exposed timbers was, as in England, whitewashed stucco rather than brick infill as was traditional in Sologne. Very uncharacteristic

---

suggests they were drawn by Jeanneret. The original drawing, now lost, was published in L'Architecte (quatrième année) (July 1909), pp. 55–56, along with two construction photos, a brief statement concerning the plan and materials used, and the color plate discussed below. The name given, La Sauleau, is phonetic but incorrectly spelled. Among the blueprints extant at La Saulot are the ground floor, dated February 26, 1908, and the basement, dated March 11, 1908. These predate Jeanneret's employment by four months, thus making it impossible, as some have claimed, that he contributed to the conception of the design.

23.  Over the years I have enjoyed many a happy weekend in front of this marvelous fire yet surprisingly it is among the most inefficient, in terms of the amount of wood consumed vs. heat given, that I have ever known. It also takes one day to sufficiently heat the chimney so that it won't smoke.

is the absence of windows in the front of the second storey. This increases the sense of scale, as the windows are at the sides, and the height of the living room finds expression in the row of windows above the French doors. Meanwhile a series of thin brick arches—recalling the substructure of some bridge—create a smooth visual transition between the covered veranda and the inner window-wall. Construction is of reinforced concrete—floor slabs, ceiling beams, and vertical walls—though only on the verandas and in the basement can raw concrete be seen.[24]

The V-shaped, bilaterally symmetrical plan extends toward the rear at forty-five degrees from the octagonal "Grande Salle"; at one side the free-standing fireplace spatially separates the more intimate "Salon" (see plans, fig. 126). In 1920, however, Perret Frères enlarged the building along both these axes, adding a dining room, guest suite, and extensive service areas, all on the ground floor and under a flat roof. These additions are remarkably unobtrusive and do not destroy the central pyramidal form.[25]

Contemporary with La Saulot, and referred to by Jeanneret in the same quotation, was the "Maison bouteille"—"a house is a bottle, this is an expression of Perret's, not of mine." I would never have identified this project except that Le Corbusier later published one elevation along with the following statement: "Draftsman 10 years ago for Auguste Perret, whom he holds in high regard, he had the opportunity to draw, on his instructions, a project for a villa that originated with the shrewd initiatives of this fine builder that Auguste Perret is but who sacrificed the style of the day to the 'expression of construction.'"[26]

This convoluted sentence seems to divide credit for the idea between Perret and Jeanneret. Jeanneret's contribution relates primarily to the style of the building, which owes much to the Art Nouveau and recalls aspects of several previous designs including his early, unexecuted projects for the villas Stotzer and Jaquemet. The design is devoid of any "expression of construction." It is on the interior plan that Perret's influence is primarily perceived.

Four different elevations exist for the principal facades; three (one in watercolor) are

24. The phrase "une piscine en béton armé" in *L'Architecte* (p. 56) has led some writers to claim that La Saulot has an indoor swimming pool. What actually exists is a tile-lined bathtub recessed in the concrete floor.

25. The various farm buildings, mostly designed by Perret, are contemporary with the house. The central feature is a large hall with a free-standing fireplace at the center. It is intended for donning and storing clothing, and for warming-up during and after the hunt. Crops raised on the cultivated fields (located near the center of the estate) are intended to attract wild game. Two artificial lakes entice ducks and provide for fishing. The estate consists of 285 hectares (705 acres) with the main house located near the center.

26. This statement continues: "En 1916 un client de Le Corbusier feuilletant un portefeuille dans son atelier tombe en arrêt devant le dessin reproduit ci-dessus et dit: 'Faites-moi quelque chose de semblable.' Le Corbusier est très heureux de mêler à son oeuvre le souvenir de son ancien maître Auguste Perret" (*L'Esprit nouveau*, 6, p. 704). This note, accompanied by a small-scale reproduction of figure 130, was published at the end of an article about the Villa Schwob.

**Fig. 129.** Project: "Maison Bouteille," designed by Jeanneret, 1909. Clay models showing both the entrance facade and the side elevation. Photograph by Jeanneret. Negative 8 × 7.7 cm. (BV)

for the entrance facade, and one for the nearly similar garden facade. The plan shows that the entrance projects forward and contains a staircase on the inside corner, therefore the side elevation reflects this fact. In addition to these elevations there are transverse and longitudinal sections, first- and second-floor plans, a plot plan, and two clay models known through photographs—making an exceptionally complete documentation (figs. 129–33, 358). All the drawings are small (about 15 × 18 cm.), freehand, and not to-scale. An actual site probably existed for this intriguing "bagatelle" as there is a plot plan as well as the note, "vue sur Paris," on the garden side.

Of exceptional importance are the plans, for here Perret's ideas found expression in their openness and the use of octagonal forms. The ground floor resembles an elongated octagon unencumbered by partitions; it rises two storeys at the center with great window-walls facing both directions. At the upper level this space is overlooked by a transverse gallery that connects two lateral bedrooms at either end. All these features of the plan (except the half-octagons that become half-circles) reappear eight years later at the Villa Schwob, thus confirming Jeanneret's statement that the plan of the Villa Schwob was based on the "Maison bouteille" and owed a great deal to the inspiration of Auguste Perret.[27]

27.  For further discussion of "Maison bouteille" as well as La Saulot, see H. Allen Brooks, "L'évolution de la conception de l'espace . . . de Charles-Edouard Jeanneret à La Chaux-de-Fonds," *La Ville et l'Urbanisme après Le Corbusier, Actes du colloque: 1987* (La Chaux-de-Fonds: Editions d'En Haut, 1993), pp. 13–31.

**Fig. 130.** Project: "Maison Bouteille," front façade, 1909. Blueprint.
This is the elevation that Le Corbusier published in *L'Esprit Nouveau*,
no. 6, in 1921. (FLC)

Thus far we have discussed work-in-progress but equally important is Jeanneret's knowledge of Perret's earlier designs. The 1902 apartment building, constructed of masonry and load-bearing walls, at 119 Avenue de Wagram sufficiently interested him to photograph it as well as save (after first making pencil notations thereupon) the published illustrations thereof. The refined elegance of its entrance-way, including its oval windows, is perhaps later recalled at the Villa Schwob.

The following year, 1903, the Perrets designed and built (for their own account) 25 bis, rue Franklin wherein their office was located on the ground floor and Auguste Perret occupied the penthouse apartment (fig. 134). This was the first of their concrete-frame buildings although this material, both for aesthetic and technical reasons, was sheathed with ceramic tile, smooth tiles being used to express the structural elements and foliated ones filling the areas in between. However, the most prophetic aspect of the structural system was the introduction, on the interior, of point-supports of reinforced concrete in place of load-bearing walls—as can clearly be seen on the original plans. Such point-supports, or pilotis (which are even more dramatically expressed in Perret's Théâtre des Champs-Elysées of 1911–13) later became one of Le Corbusier's five points

**Fig. 131.** Project: "Maison Bouteille," side elevation. Pencil and watercolors (black, blue, red, green, and white) on tracing paper. Picture 17.6 × 24 cm. (FLC)

— COUPE LONGITUDINALE

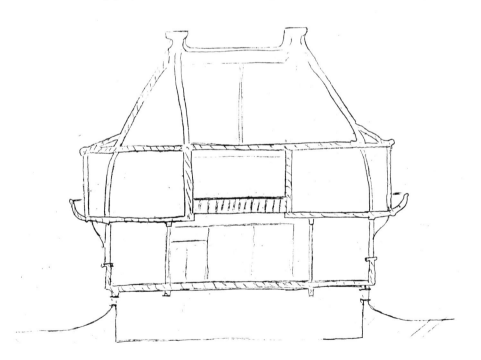

**Fig. 132.** Project: "Maison Bouteille," cross section (retraced by author). (FLC)

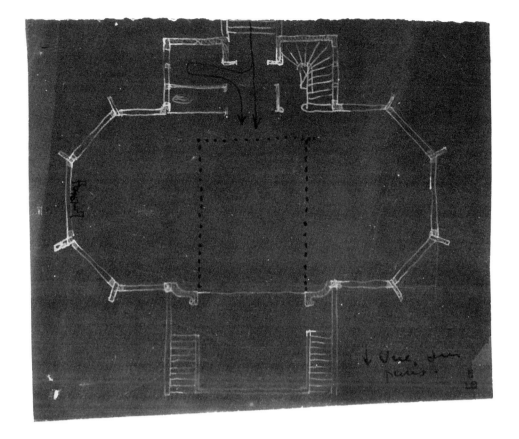

**Fig. 133.** Project: "Maison Bouteille." Blueprint of ground-floor plan. Jeanneret has added, in black ink, dotted lines indicating the central two-storey space; also added is "Vue sur Paris" and an arrow, thus implying that an actual site existed. Approx. 15 × 18.4 cm. (FLC)

of architecture—after he first disengaged the nonstructural walls from the vertical supports.[28]

The Garage Ponthieu in Paris, where Perret first exposed raw concrete to view, represents a different story. Le Corbusier later praised it with virtually every mention of Perret, and since then historians have assumed it was his favorite Perret building while he was working in Perret's office. Such, however, was not the case. During Jeanneret's Paris stay the Garage Ponthieu never once was mentioned in his letters, nor did he sketch it, photograph it, save published illustrations of it, or bother to conserve blueprints from the office. In truth, this most recent (1907) work by the Perrets was much too stark and utilitarian for Jeanneret's taste.[29] In 1908–9 his preference was for

28. See Peter Collins, *Concrete: The Vision of a New Architecture* (London, 1959), pp. 183 and 200, concerning the point-supports at 25 bis, rue Franklin. And for an astute comparison between Perret and Le Corbusier's use of interior columns, see pp. 200–201 and especially 233–34.

29. The executed Garage Ponthieu design dates from January 12, 1907, although the building is traditionally misdated 1905–6 due to the existence of an earlier project which had an exterior of brick, ceramic tile, and glass block, and where the concrete frame was not visible. See L. Citti, J.-B. Ache, P. Collins, H. Poupée et al., *A. et G. Perret* (Paris: Conservatoire Nationale des Arts et Métiers), n.d. [1976], p. 42.

**Fig. 134.** Auguste Perret, 25 bis, rue Franklin, Paris, 1903. Published magazine illustration upon which Jeanneret has noted on the plans, in pencil, the dimensions of all the rooms as well as the furniture layout in Perret Frères' ground-floor office where he worked. (FLC)

the earlier Perret designs that had a lingering kinship with the Art Nouveau or the historical styles. The Garage Ponthieu, as with the work of Wagner or Hoffmann in Vienna, was much too avant-garde for his taste. Not until 1916 did he sketch the Garage Ponthieu (Sketchbook A2) at which time it perhaps influenced the design of the Villa Schwob (see Chapter 10 and figs. 379, 396).

Upon receiving his first month's pay, and probably on the recommendation of Auguste Perret, Jeanneret purchased Eugène-Emmanuel Viollet-le-Duc's ten-volume *Dictionnaire raisonné de l'architecture française du XIe au XVIe siècle* (1854–68) in which he wrote "I bought this work August 1, 1908, with the money from my first payment from Messrs. Perret. I bought it in order *to learn,* because, *knowing* I will then be able to create." And to L'Eplattenier he wrote, "I am reading Viollet-le-Duc, this man so wise, so logical, so clear, and so precise in his observations. I have Viollet-le-Duc and I have Notre-Dame which serves as my laboratory so to speak. In this marvelous old ramshackle building I verify the words of Viollet-le-Duc and formulate my own observations. It is there that I also undertake my design sessions 'after the antique'!"

These design sessions produced many fine watercolors and drawings, plus a sketchbook devoted entirely to Notre-Dame (figs. 135–37).[30] This sketchbook, the earliest of Jeanneret's to survive intact, is not at all concerned with structural questions but focuses on visual effects and decoration; it analyzes the different stained-glass windows, the painting thereupon, and the methods by which the glass was affixed to the windows, the windows to the walls, and how the glass-filtered light animates the masonry. Other pages, in profile and elevation, show how column clusters are set against the piers. Extensive annotations accompany most drawings, with color a recurrent theme. From one of these texts we learn that Jeanneret is seeking, among other things, to learn how art forms represent or embody a dominant idea: "this subjective *impression, rendered* by the idea. . . ." Evidently he is endeavoring to deduce from medieval art its controlling idea in order to apply a similar methodology to his own, present-day search for an ideal.

Jeanneret's reading of Viollet-le-Duc's *Dictionnaire,* in spite of what he believed at the time, had less influence on his future than we might assume. It did give him greater insight into medieval structure, but what he learned about rationalist theory he might equally well have absorbed from Perret and other contemporary sources. Meanwhile the more theoretical of Viollet-le-Duc's books, *Entretiens sur l'architecture,* which deals specifically with problems of architectural forms evolved through a rational expression of construction and the utilization of modern technology and materials (principles that could be distilled from Gothic architecture), went unmentioned by Jeanneret nor did he acquire it for his library.

Jeanneret, and even more so Le Corbusier, was interested in structural systems, new

30. This sketchbook is discussed by Anne Prache, "Le Corbusiers Begegnung mit Notre-Dame in Paris," *Bau-und Bildkunst im Spiegel internationaler Forschung, Festschrift zum 80 Geburtstag von Prof.-Dr. Edgar Lehmann* (Berlin, 1989), pp. 276–79.

materials, and programmatic ("compositional") requirements, yet to place him squarely in the rationalist camp, as did a generation of historians culminating with Sigfried Giedion, is to deny a fundamental truth: whereas Le Corbusier was interested in rationalism in all its aspects, he nevertheless remained steadfastly an idealist in temperament and at heart. He strove for the universal. His personal brand of rationalism remained subservient to, and tempered by, his overriding idealism that exercised veto power over too strict an adherence to rationalist doctrine; for Jeanneret, the artist's creative genius must prevail as final arbiter in all matters of design. Therefore I agree with Paul Turner's conclusion that "these new principles of rationalism seem to have been grafted onto, or laid over, Jeanneret's existing idealism, rather than replacing or modifying it" (p. 52). Provensal, not Viollet-le-Duc, remained closer to Jeanneret's thinking.

**Fig. 135.** Notre-Dame, Paris. Two heads from the south transept rose window. This is the first page from Jeanneret's 1908 sketchbook which is devoted entirely to Notre-Dame. Ink and ink wash. (Private collection)

Prior to purchasing Viollet-le-Duc's *Dictionnaire,* Jeanneret spent months reading and outlining Edouard Corroyer's *L'Architecture romane* (Paris, 1888), a book that treats history as a rational evolution modified by local influences, materials, and building techniques. The scope of the book is far broader than its title suggests since it begins in Roman times and traces the history of ecclesiastical architecture through the mid-twelfth century. Yet Corroyer's second volume, *L'Architecture gothique* (Paris, 1891), was apparently not read—which seems curious—but in December 1909, after leaving Perret and on the eve of his departure from France, he bought and very carefully read (judging from internal markings) J. -K. Huysmans' popular novel *La Cathédrale* (29th edition, Paris, 1908). Nevertheless these extensive readings on medieval architecture did not, in the long run, have an influence commensurate with the effort he gave them, a fact undoubtedly explained by his conversion, within a year, to classicism.

More decisive was his reading about prophets, not because he had any interest in religion, but because he sought parallels with himself; he was also seeking insight into how others established an ideal. Having read Schuré's two books in Vienna, he purchased in Paris Ernest Renan's enormously popular *Vie de Jésus* which, when published in 1863, scandalized the established church because of its portrayal of Jesus as a human being whose birth, life, and work involved no miracles and who did not miraculously rise from the dead. Extensive marginal marks indicate Jeanneret's great interest in the suggestion that Jesus possessed no unnatural powers but rather derived his strength from an ideal; also that Jesus' family and background had close parallels with his own. In short, this reading indicated to Jeanneret that he too—once in possession of an ideal— could achieve in his own field exactly what Jesus had done in his.

Paraphrasing nearly half the passages marked by Jeanneret will demonstrate what attracted him to Renan's book. And while reading these lines we should substitute the name Jeanneret/Le Corbusier for that of Jesus Christ: Jesus was trained as an artisan in his father's trade (p. 75); his family were simple, everyday people, not among the highly educated or the professions (132); he renounced politics (123); he was indifferent to worldly things (175) and not desirous of power or riches (132), occasionally contenting

**Fig. 136.** Notre-Dame, Paris. Gallery below south rose window. Detail showing bays 2, 3, and 4 from right. Pencil, ink, and watercolor. 50 × 35 cm. (Private collection)

**Fig. 137.** Notre-Dame, Paris. Pinnacle receiving a flying buttress, being one of the three located at the southeast above the ambulatory chapels. Note, at right, the small elevation sketch shows how each block of masonry relates to the sculpture thereon. Dated 25 June 1908. Ink, ink wash, and watercolor on heavy paper. 50 × 35 cm. (Private collection)

himself to meditate in the mountains or some other solitary place (91); while in the mountains he lived alone (124). Jesus was a man who sought perfection (86) and truth, for truth is the equivalent of freedom (126). He was the perfect idealist (132), having faith in the reality of an ideal (296) and wishing to establish on earth the ideal that he had conceived (120). His idea was the most revolutionary ever hatched in the mind of man (129), and his success in uniting two completely opposed conditions, that of the ideal and that of reality, was a singular achievement (130–31).[31]

31. Jeanneret's markings, and therefore these paraphrases, derive primarily from chapters concerned with Jesus' ideas, i.e., "Premiers aphorismes de Jésus—Ses idées d'un Dieu père . . ." (chap. 5); "Développement des idées de Jésus" (chap. 7); "Forme définitive des idées de Jésus sur le royaume de Dieu" (chap. 17). At page 301 in Chapter 17 of *Vie de Jésus* the markings stop, indicating that he read no further, having satisfied his needs. Jeanneret's copy of Schuré, *Les Grands Initiés,* was also in Paris with him since the half-title page is inscribed "Ch-E. Jeanneret / 9 rue des Ecoles / Paris."

These lines resemble a capsule biography for Le Corbusier's life; it is uncanny, perhaps frightening, to observe the parallels that Jeanneret drew. And if we recall his quandary in Vienna, when reading Schuré, concerning the validity of idealism and whether or not it could coexist with rationalism, Renan's book provided the affirmative answer that he sought.

Friedrich Nietzsche's *Ainsi parlait Zarathoustra* (translated by Henri Albert, 15th edition, Paris, 1908) was purchased at approximately the same time as *Vie de Jésus* as both books bear the signature "Ch.E. Jeanneret / 3 quai St. Michel." Yet Nietzsche's philosophy held comparatively little interest for Jeanneret who—except for reading the Prologue where he made his usual marginal marks—made no attempt to delve into the main text of this hefty 476-page book. It was Renan's *Vie de Jésus,* not *Zarathoustra,* that held his attention. Nor is there evidence that he read other works by Nietzsche.

Therefore to claim, as some have, that Le Corbusier's personality and outlook were formulated by his youthful study of Nietzsche is quite absurd. What is true, however, is that Jeanneret's personality, reinforced by his diverse reading, exhibited certain points in common with Nietzschean thought. But this does not mean that he comprehended, or was influenced by, the Nietzschean vision as a whole. Furthermore, all of these so-called Nietzschean characteristics were a basic part of Jeanneret's personality long before he ever read Nietzsche.[32]

What actually caught Jeanneret's eye when reading the Prologue of *Zarathoustra* is well recorded because, as with *Vie de Jésus,* he marked the passages that interested him most. These are few in number so the majority are quoted here, though not always in their entirety: "I love mankind"; "*I am about to* bestow on mankind a gift" (page 9; emphasis by Jeanneret); "*remain faithful to the earth*" (12); "What does it matter, my reason? . . . my justice! . . . my compassion!" (13); "That which is great about man is that he *is a bridge* and not a goal" (14); "I love . . . those who *sacrifice themselves to the earth* in order that one day the earth will belong to the superman" (15); "I love those who live *in order to know*" (15); "[the people] laugh, they don't understand me, I am not the mouth necessary for their ears" (17); "Behold the good and the just! Who is it they hate most? He who breaks their code of values, the destroyer, the criminal:—yet it is he who is the creator" (26); "The creator seeks other creators like himself, those to

---

32. In 1961 Le Corbusier reread *Zarathoustra,* writing on the half-title page: "Cap Martin, 1 août 1961. je n'ai pas lu ce livre depuis 1908 (Quai St. Michel Paris) = 51 ans = ma vie d'homme. Aujourd'hui ayant butiné ces pages je devine des situations, des faits, des décisions, des destinations qui sont des faits d'homme. Je décide d'en noter les pages." Fortunately the 1908 markings, as was characteristic, are in pencil, those of 1961 in ink, therefore they can be told apart. In ink he wrote "La main ouverte" on page 8 opposite the sentence "Je voudrais donner et distribuer, jusqu'à ce que les sages parmi les hommes soient devenus joyeux de leur folies, et les pauvres, heureux de leur richesse."

**Fig. 138.** Japanese mountain deity Zaô-gongen, taken as a representation of the Buddha Sâkyamuni, Japan, late nineteenth century (although thought to be antique at the time Jeanneret made this sketch). Wood painted black. Height 1 m. Guimet Museum, Paris. Pencil on the back of old blueprint paper, 1909. 27 × 19.5 cm. (FLC 2246)

inscribe new values on new codes of value" (27); "I will join up with other creators, to *those who* reap a harvest and rest" (27); "Zarathoustra *follows dangerous paths*" (28); "To gain the right to create new values—that is the most terrible of conquests for a patient and respectful person" (35).[33]

Thus the few pages of Nietzsche actually read by Jeanneret merely confirmed, and perhaps expanded, the views he instinctively already held. For him to probe further into the complicated, often repetitive text, was not necessary.

Jeanneret's reading typically covered much more than architecture and religion. By listing his books bought in Paris, then inscribed and kept throughout his life, we can sample some of these concerns. They include J. -J. Rousseau, *Les Confessions* (2 vols.); J. Laforgue, *Moralités légendaires;* Ch. Baudelaire,[34] *Les fleurs du mal;* G. Flaubert, *Salammbô;* Homer, *Odyssée;* and three books concerning the orient, G. Le Bon, *Les Civilisations de l'Inde;* P. Claudel, *Connaissance de l'Est;* and L. Ménard, *Histoire des anciens peuples de l'Orient*—all, without exception, inscribed in 1909 and several containing passages that are marked or underlined.[35]

Noteworthy is the absence of technical books on construction, materials, mathematics, or engineering. Apparently he did not consider such books worth owning or, for that matter, worth reading. The only mention of such a book is when Jeanneret reported to his parents (August 9, 1909) that Max Du Bois—a Swiss childhood friend who had just translated E. Mörsch, *Le Béton armé* from the original German—had lent him a copy that he thumbed through, thought might be useful, but had not read. However, he never acquired a copy of his own.

He later recalled that museums proved more reliable, as teachers, than books. He specifically mentioned the Cluny Museum for tapestries, miniatures, and Persian ceramics, the Guimet for Asiatic art in bronze, wood and stone (fig. 138), the Pottier gallery for Greek and Etruscan art, the Trocadero for casts of French cathedral portals and the ethnographic art from Mexico, Peru (fig. 139), and Africa, the Museum of Decorative Arts (Pavillon de Marsan) for its Persian watercolors, rugs, and brocade, and also certain more secluded parts of the Louvre where he could study undisturbed (fig.

33. These texts I have translated directly from Jeanneret's French edition because it gives a somewhat different flavor than do English texts translated from the German.

34. A wonderful quote that might well serve as Le Corbusier's motto I discovered written in his hand on a drawing (FLC 1765) that he postdated 1911: "L'inspiration est la récompense de l'exercice quotidien. Ch. B." I am indebted to Professor David Smith, French Department, University of Toronto, for confirming my suspicion that Ch. B. was indeed Baudelaire; the quote is derived from a book review of 1861; from what source Jeanneret found the passage is unknown.

35. Turner (pp. 208–9), on the evidence of signatures, suggests adding the following: Dostoievsky, *L'idiot,* Byron, *Don Juan,* and Homer, *Iliade.*

**Fig. 139.** Peruvian vases at the Ethnology Museum (Trocadero), Paris. Jeanneret's text describes how the fired clay vases are made in two molds, their suture following the meridian line. Pencil, ink, and watercolor on yellowish paper and dated July 1909. 25.7 × 36 cm. (FLC 1984)

140).[36] Yet—unless many of his sketches are lost to us—his productivity in Paris cannot compare with his much shorter stay in Italy.[37]

Contemporary art is another topic not found among Jeanneret's collection of books and catalogues, nor is it discussed in letters to L'Eplattenier. From his postcard collection we learn that Puvis de Chavannes—hardly a contemporary since he was born in 1834—was his favorite nineteenth-century French painter, and Rodin soon became his favorite sculptor.[38] Otherwise he was remarkably silent on the subject of painting and

36. See note 1 above and *L'art décoratif d'aujourd'hui* (Paris, 1925), pp. 201–3. He also visited the museum at Chantilly where his watercolor of the château is dated 1908 (FLC 4061).

37. Jeanneret's July 1908 correspondence with L'Eplattenier concerns plans for an exhibition at Basel. Jeanneret showed little interest and therefore proposed that L'Eplattenier choose the travel drawings he preferred, yet suggested they include St. Vitale as well as the Memmi fresco at the Spanish chapel in Florence which, therefore, must have been among Jeanneret's favorites. Sekler, p. 362, has identified the exhibition as the Pie IX Nazionale Kunst-Ausstellung der Schweiz held from August 6 to September 27, 1908, at the Kunsthalle and the Stadtkasino.

Meanwhile, in France, Jeanneret resumed his study of flora and fauna, his sketches so much in the style of the Ecole d'art that they are associated with Paris only by an occasional date such as "2 avril 09" on a sketch of sprouting plants, or "Paris, mai 08" on a study of salamanders.

38. Jeanneret owned seven postcards of Puvis de Chavannes' "Vie Pastorale de Sainte Geneviève" at the Pantheon. These are badly faded with thumb-tack holes at the corners since they formed part of the decor of his room. Initially he did not like Rodin, whose work he had seen in Venice, yet gradually he changed his mind; subsequently Aristide Maillol became his great favorite. When Léon Perrin left Paris,

sculpture. From Albert, while visiting Paris, we learn that "Ed. demolishes the moderns, and I joined him, to please him, but also by conviction" (to parents, August 9, 1909).

Considering his interest in art, and especially his enthusiasm for Gothic architecture, nothing is so surprising as his apathy toward visiting the great cathedrals of northern France—Chartres, Amiens, Reims, Beauvais, Soissons, Sens, Laon, Noyon—all easily

---

Jeanneret's parting gift was *Auguste Rodin et son oeuvre* (Paris, 1900) which he inscribed "Témoignage d'amitié à l'ami Perrin / Ch.E.Jeanneret / Paris 1908 juin."

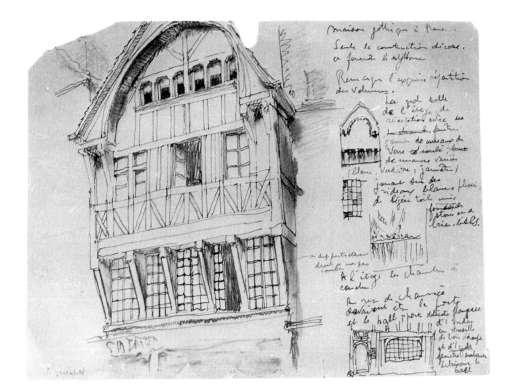

**Fig. 141.** Gothic house at Rouen. Pencil and ink, dated July 1908. 24 × 31 cm. (FLC 2019)

accessible by train from Paris.[39] In Italy he often whistle-stopped through two or three towns in a single day, but never in France.

He did take one trip which proved unexpectedly eventful. During the Bastille Day holidays he and other students of L'Eplattenier—Perrin, Perrochet, and Aubert—went to Le Havre by way of Rouen where Jeanneret quickly made two sketches of Gothic houses (fig. 141). However this was a pleasure trip and Jeanneret was in a very jovial mood. He always loved to clown around, be photographed in silly poses, and joke in his cards and letters—which often irritated his serious-minded brother.[40] From Le Havre he sent a battleship card to L'Eplattenier—signed by the other three—also a card to Chapallaz (a masonry farmhouse at Sainte-Adresse), and cards to his parents and cousin Marguerite at Soleure. The latter's card, as reported by his father, said: "Assez de tourments! Assez lutté! Je suis terrassé! La vie est sans répit! Le 18eme La Lorraine [a transatlantic liner] m'arrachera à tout ce que j'aime pour m'emporter dans les vastes solitudes de l'Amérique. A toi, ma chère cousine, un dernier adieu!"

Marguerite, most upset, showed the card to her father who, excited, dispatched a

39. Nevertheless he purchased postcards of cathedrals located throughout France, as well as those of Notre Dame in Paris. (This postcard collection is partly at the FLC, partly at the BV.)

40. As early as 1901 we find Albert commenting negatively upon Edouard's propensity for clowning: "J'aimerais qu'il perde sa mauvaise habitude de faire le clown" (to parents, October 29, 1901), and the next week (November 6) refers to his brother as "ce clown d'Ed."

telegram to his brother and took the next train to La Chaux-de-Fonds where he arrived at noon and pressed the distraught father to go to Le Havre. The parents had already received their "normal" (father's term) card from Rouen yet, unconvinced, had telegraphed Paris only to learn that Edouard was not there. Meanwhile the Swiss emigration bureau confirmed a sailing on the eighteenth but advised that it was the Touraine, not Lorraine. Papa then telegraphed the steamship line asking whether his son was booked and, if so, not to permit his departure. At 4:30 a cable arrived from Le Havre: "Rien délivré à E. Jeanneret." Much relieved, his uncle caught the 7 p.m. train back to Soleure and at 8:20 a second telegram arrived from the hotel in Paris: "Jeanneret rentré mercredi soir." What a relief; but what embarrassment for the family! Papa's entry in his journal concludes: "the day of the 17th of July will always remain in our minds as one of the most painful that we have ever experienced." And then there is one final note: 10 francs were spent on telegrams!

That same month, the twenty-first to be exact, Edouard and friends visited the park at St. Cloud and did some painting, returning that evening by boat. These were immensely happy days for him and he regaled in the comradery of old school chums—Aubert, Perrochet, Puvis, and Perrin.[41]

He also enjoyed his work at Perret's which provided the freedom to spend afternoons, evenings, and weekends as he liked, perhaps in museums, at Notre-Dame, in libraries, or simply reveling in his detachment from such hometown influences as family, school, and the strong personality of his much-respected mentor. His self-questioning, his desire to know, and his search for an ideal, remained incessant, and he thrived on the masochistic torment that he caused himself. "Life, at this period of my existence, is a rough battle," he had written to L'Eplattenier on July 3. And obsessed with the need for an ideal, it is understandable that he underscored such thoughts while reading *Vie de Jésus*.[42]

At home, meanwhile, the realities of life prevailed. The Stotzer and Jaquemet houses

41. Jeanneret, whose warm friendship with Léon Perrin was reestablished after a certain strain in Vienna, wrote L'Eplattenier on July 3 that Perrin had learned all he could from Hector Guimard and intended to leave; by month's end Perrin was back in La Chaux-de-Fonds. Another friend to whom Jeanneret drew particularly close during 1909 was the young sculptor (in wrought iron) Hermann Jeanneret from Le Locle whom Edouard referred to as Hagen. Léon Perrin informed me that he and Edouard met Hermann shortly after their arrival in Paris; he was hungry and without a place to stay so Edouard offered to share his room with him since he was from their part of Switzerland. On May 11, 1910, the minutes of the commission of the Ecole d'art record that Hermann Jeanneret was examined and admitted to L'Eplattenier's Cours Supérieur.

42. Music provided fewer distractions in Paris than in Vienna. Yet on May 27, 1908, he apparently attended the "Festival Gabriel Fauré" at the Salle Gaveau where Pablo Casals played in duet with Fauré, the program for which is in Jeanneret's copy of Ruskin's *Les Matins à Florence* marking pp. 82–83 (so he was rereading Ruskin!). And a letter from Albert to his parents (December 23, 1908) notes that Edouard had recently heard Marteau and Beethoven's Ninth on successive Sundays.

were under construction, and although Jeanneret stayed aloof he tapped another 580-franc honorarium in September, depositing it in his savings account. Earlier, in May, his parents celebrated their twenty-fifth wedding anniversary and the following week Marie was off to Geneva to visit Albert; her husband followed a few days later, stopping en route at Neuchâtel to hear the Berlin Philharmonic conducted by Richard Strauss. By the end of June, as Edouard commenced work with Perret, came the welcome but overdue news that Albert had received his "diplôme de virtuosité" from the conservatory at Geneva.

Nevertheless, instead of returning home, Albert vanished into the mountains to live alone, writing his parents a twenty- or thirty-page letter which revealed his altered attitudes and left his family not knowing what to think. Eventually, on August 2–3, papa went to him and was much relieved to find him "normal"; Albert then joined his parents later in the month for their vacation at Grachen in the Valais.

Then, following twelve days at home, Albert returned to Geneva to begin his professional career. He also gave concerts at La Chaux-de-Fonds on October 26, performed as soloist with orchestra on November 15, and gave an audition the following month. His father had certain, albeit mild, reservations about the initial concert but thereafter pronounced his son, at long last, a true and splendid artist. Imagine, therefore, the terrible shock the parents endured when Albert announced, in March (1909), that due to the condition of his arm he would abandon the violin for a year or so! Nine years of great expense, and all for naught! Albert now had no livelihood. Meanwhile his father's business was in the clutches of yet another depression; therefore it was Marie's piano lessons that must pay for her elder son's support.

Brighter events cheered the family during the departing months of 1908. Edouard was thriving in Paris and his nearly completed houses at home were drawing favorable comment and even some acclaim. By late November his parents made a day's trip to Basel to hear the Marteau quartet and see Böcklin and Holbein paintings, also finding time to dine with friends. Christmas was spent quietly without the usual family reunion and on Christmas day the parents took a long hike to Vue des Alpes, the boys being expected the following week—sixteen months after Edouard had last been seen! And after his January 9 departure his father would write: "We have, as we wished, seen him again and, although possessing a rather 'arty' air, he was well-mannered, agreeably talkative and with solid morals and opinions (notwithstanding a complete modification of his beliefs and his religious faith), tall, with a new reddish-blond beard (fig. 142); always confident of the future, energetic, and in good health. The times of real intimacy were less frequent than we might have wished, Edouard being monopolized and laid claim to by all his former friends."

New Year's eve was spent at the Hôtel de Paris, a group of thirteen family and friends including the Henri Jeannerets from Soleure. Albert departed on the third, his brother following him to Geneva a week later, remaining three days before going on to Paris.

**Fig. 142.** Edouard with his parents at La Chaux-de-Fonds. January 1, 1909. His father described Edouard as having "a new reddish-blond beard." (BV)

At Paris he resumed his work at Perret's, continued his research in museums, and studies of Notre-Dame.

In March he heard his first aircraft and instantly became infatuated with flight, swarming with 300,000 (so he said) other riotous, destructive Parisians to the airport to watch an exhibition that never happened.[43] Several days later he returned to the site where, while awaiting an abatement in the wind so that the flight could take place, he penned a postcard (of a Latham airplane) to Chapallaz describing the event.

In May his parents, who had spent Easter at Bern where they had heard Wagner's *Tristan and Isolde,* came to Paris, the visit being succinctly described in the father's journal: "From May 8th to 17th we *went to Paris* to see our son Edouard and enjoy that

43. See his book entitled *Aircraft* (London and New York, 1935), pp. 6–7, where he describes his introduction to flight.

magnificent city. The weather was *superb,* our pleasure uninterrupted, and we returned home enthusiastic. Spent 600 francs—interest on our savings. Very good accommodations in L'Hôtel du Quai Voltaire 19, opposite the Louvre (price 8 frs.), room with 2 beds—visited the Louvre, Luxembourg, Cluny, Trocadéro, Notre-Dame, Opéra Comique (*Orphée* by Glück), Sarah Bernhard (Russian concert), Parisiana (glorified obscenities), an entire day at Versailles, a half day at St. Cloud—Bois de Boulogne. Our son knew his city like a native and we took great comfort and interest in his knowledge in art, his good judgement, his amiability, his politeness—in spite of his being garbed like an art student."

There is nothing remarkable about this itinerary except for Edouard's belated discovery of Versailles which he soon revisited in order to make watercolors and sketches, especially of the orangerie which particularly impressed him by its proportions, charm, and more human scale, but also of the Petit and Grand Trianon.

Late that May L'Eplattenier arrived in Paris and together they set off for London, L'Eplattenier apparently seeking technical information for the casting of his sculpture. Yet of their activities and itinerary little is known except that Jeanneret was much impressed with London, the South Kensington museum (Victoria and Albert), and Benin art at the British Museum.[44]

Albert was next to arrive in Paris, coming before mid-July and staying six weeks. The boys spent much time together, often attending concerts at the Tuileries or the Palais Royal, or going to the Opéra; meanwhile the museums mentioned in Albert's correspondence were the Trocadéro (for its Hindu, Assyrian, Egyptian, and Gothic art), and the Marsan Pavilion at the Louvre for Persian watercolors. Thus, as in London, it was mainly non-European or medieval art that attracted Jeanneret's attention, a fact corroborated by his dated watercolors and sketches. The brothers also visited Ablon-sur-Seine, just south of Paris, and once again Versailles, where Albert was properly impressed. Meanwhile Edouard was continuing his weekly mathematics lessons for which he did have to do some homework.

Therefore Edouard, who cherished seclusion yet enjoyed his friends, had little private time during the spring and summer months of 1909. And with the arrival of autumn his Paris sojourn was drawing to a close; he already had announced he would be home for Christmas.[45] In a long letter of November 8, 1909, we learn of his well-

44. The L'Eplattenier correspondence is obviously incomplete because there are no letters preparatory to this trip. Jeanneret senior's journal (June 7, 1909) merely says "Reçu 2 cartes de Londres d'Edouard qui est en Angleterre depuis quelques jours, avec son ancien professeur L'Eplattenier." And Albert wrote to his parents on June 12: "Ed. de retour à Paris est emballé de London." And in Jeanneret's "Confession" (*L'Art décoratif d'aujourd'hui* [Paris, 1925], pp. 203–4) he mentions: "A Londres, le South-Kensington est l'éblouissement des bayadères. L'art du Bénin au British."

45. At home tragedy struck when Edouard's first cousin, young Henri Jeanneret, was shot and killed in a military training accident. And later that summer his parents, their vacation money already spent on Paris,

formed future plans. Already he had left his quai St. Michel room which overlooked the Seine and was sharing space with Puvis at 8, rue Descartes. The next day, November 9, was to be his last with Auguste Perret (with whom he had been some sixteen months) and he expected to spend the next month or so doing intensive study in museums before leaving Paris.

Once at home he wished to stay with his parents during the holidays, maybe a total of two weeks (eventually he spent four), and thereafter find a room in a farmhouse near the one rented by his Ecole d'art comrades with whom he wished to spend much time, but not to share a room.[46] After three months he would depart for Germany to seek employment, but if appropriate accommodation in a farmhouse could not be found he would leave for Germany much sooner. He entreated his father's aid in locating a room, perhaps the one they had rented in September, except that it was much too near the farmer's noisy workshop.

In short, Jeanneret was planning to throw himself, heart and soul, into L'Eplattenier's activities as well as those of the past and present students of the Cours Supérieur—at least for a period of three months. The misgivings expressed the previous year (letter to L'Eplattenier of November 22, 1908) had apparently been set aside; Jeanneret could not resist the temptation of returning to his professor's friendly nest (as, indeed, he would do again two years later). His last postcard from Paris was dispatched on November 27 saying he was leaving on Monday the sixth and, after perhaps stopping at Sens, Dijon, and Beaune en route, he would arrive home before the weekend. Thus his stay in Paris had lasted twenty and a half months. And on December 15, 1909, his father wrote, "Edouard arrived last week [apparently on December 10] from Paris, cheerful and in good health, a big fellow decked out with a wide-crowned top-hat [tromblon] and a huge military coat. We took great pleasure in seeing our son back home."

---

rented a room in a farmhouse near the top of Mont Cornu where Albert joined them after his visit to Paris and prior to returning to Geneva to try his hand at musical composition—with his parents still paying for his support.

46. He was quite explicit in not seeking total isolation but rather the close companionship of his friends: "Et papa qui me dit qu'on me cherche une chambre loin de la ferme de mes copains! Ce serait aller contre tout ce que je souhaitais. Si je veux rester au pays quelque temps ce n'est pas pour revivre en sauvage comme ici mais pour vivre et travailler avec les camarades, plus spécialement avec Perrin qui est mon ami. Il est naturel que si on me flanque à $\frac{1}{2}$ heure de toute compagnie, je n'irai pas m'enterrer ainsi, et, bien déçu je partirai de suite pour l'Allemagne. . . . D'autre part je ne voudrais pas partager une chambre avec quelqu'un parce que je suis horriblement jaloux de ma liberté, et j'adore la solitude (la solitude à volonté)" (to parents, November 8, 1909).

# 6

## SWISS INTERLUDE

*Jeanneret's Sojourn at Home*
*1910*

After rather uneventful holidays—Christmas spent at Elisa Guinand's and New Year's with family and friends at home—Albert returned to Geneva, and the next day, January 6, 1910, Edouard moved into his rented farmhouse on the slopes of Mont Cornu from which he overlooked La Chaux-de-Fonds from a vantage point some three kilometers southeast of town. Mont Cornu, in the region known as Les Petites Crosettes and presently crowned by a huge television antenna, imparts its name to a steep road terminating near the summit and along which there were four typical Jura farmhouses. Detective work, based on fragmentary clues, was necessary to locate this particular area, and specifically the building wherein Jeanneret spent the winter of 1910,[1] the photographing and measuring of which I accomplished only months prior to its being entirely rebuilt and enlarged beyond all recognition.

The Jura farmhouse would become one of Le Corbusier's favorite—though unacknowledged—metaphorical images, its symbolism finding expression in several of his best-known works. Thus this obscure vernacular type requires our close attention. Not only did he winter in such a farmhouse in 1910, but the following summer he made photographs and watercolors of several of them, and again in 1912, after returning from

---

1. I am much indebted to Héleǹe Augsburger and the brothers Léon and James Perrin for their collective assistance in helping me establish the location and identity of these buildings.

four years of travels and upon opening his architectural office, he again chose to live in such a farmhouse, this one called *Le Couvent* and located on the outskirts of town. His romantic attraction to this indigenous Jura type was shared by his schoolmates; it brought them close to nature.

The farmhouse in which Jeanneret installed himself in January 1910 was the quintessence of the High Jura type. Its broad, low-pitched, single roof was designed to protect both man and beast while sheltering all their needs by way of nourishment, equipment, and productive means during the long winter months—a veritable *unité d'habitation* for several generations of a given family (figs. 143, 144).

Winter survival determined the design of a Jura farmhouse where, when it was exceptionally cold, a hapless inhabitant might freeze to death while asleep at night. Every aspect of the plan helped ward off cold and conserve heat. Overhead the low-pitched roof retained its thick blanket of protective snow while under it the loft was full of insulating hay. Below, at ground level, the outer walls were usually assigned to animals—cow stalls along one wall (often the south), horse stables and pig pens against other walls—their body heat providing a first line of protection for the human inhabitants gathered inside.

Near the center of the building was "la chambre du tué" or kitchen with its masonry walls supporting a huge, room-sized chimney that might be fifteen or more feet square. Pyramidal in shape, and constructed of hewn timbers, this chimney rose through the roof where its truncated form was cut off diagonally and capped by a hinged and often weighted shutter. This was controlled by a long cord within that allowed the inhabitants

**Fig. 143.** Farmhouse, Mont Cornu, near La Chaux-de-Fonds. Jeanneret lived here, all alone, during the winter of January–April 1910. Note the chimney with its sloping top, the cover of which tilts open to admit light and emit smoke. (Photo by author)

**Fig. 144.** Closeup of chimney showing its sloping walls and diagonally severed flue, the aperture of which is protected by a hinged cover controlled by a long cord from the room below. (Photo by author)

to regulate how much smoke and heat they wished to escape and, inversely, how much light, precipitation, and cold air might enter. The actual "tué" was located at the base of this timber chimney, where it rested on the head-height masonry walls, and there were hung the meat, vegetables, and herbs that were being smoked and dried. Milk was preserved by being turned into cheese that could be aged until weather permitted transport (figs. 145–47; see also fig. 272 in Chapter 9).[2]

The dark, soot-blackened "tué," with its cheerful fire burning against one wall, was reached by a corridor leading directly from the entrance; it was, after all, the heart and soul and communal gathering place within a Jura farmhouse. Alongside this hallway was a well-lit room variously serving as parlor, bedroom, and workshop. Often it shared one wall with the kitchen, from which it received some heat and from which its masonry "poêle" or stove was fed. In such rooms the home industry of watchmaking was practiced during the long winter months. More prosperous farms might have additional rooms both on the ground floor and on the floor above.

These buildings were usually placed against a hillside to facilitate access, by means of an earthen ramp, to the hayloft and storage above. Therefore they occupy the uphill side of the road, facing the broad valley floor below. When enlargement was necessary,

2. Although not mentioned in literature on the subject, my own observations indicate a clear nationalistic distinction between chimney shutters in the Swiss, as opposed to the French, Jura. Those in Franche-Comté have a pair of flaps which, when closed, form a gable; one or both can be opened, presumably in response to the direction of the wind. The single shutter in Switzerland imitates the slope of the roof. Le Corbusier, without exception, always used this single slope shutter in his designs.

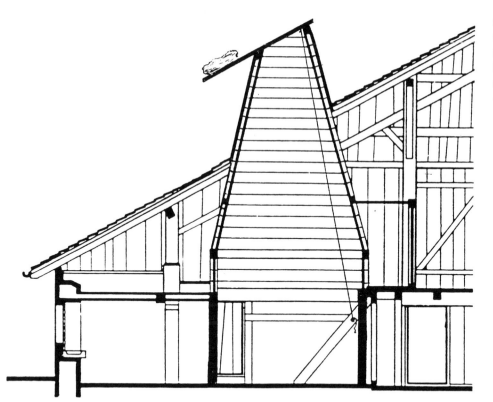

**Fig. 145.** Transverse section of a typical Jura chimney which rises from the masonry walls of the kitchen or tué below. (Jean Courvoisier, *Les Monuments d'art et d'histoire du Canton de Neuchâtel,* vol. 3 [Basel, 1968], p. 121, modified by author)

**Fig. 146.** Pyramidal Jura chimney constructed of squared timbers and set on the masonry walls of the kitchen below. The floor seen here is that of the hayloft, the living quarters are below. This is the Grand-Cachot-de-Vent farmhouse at Val-de-Travers, dating from the sixteenth century onward, and photographed during restoration. (André Tissot and Léon Perrin, *Autour de la ferme du Grand-Cachot-de-Vent,* La Chaux-de-Fonds [1968], p. 41)

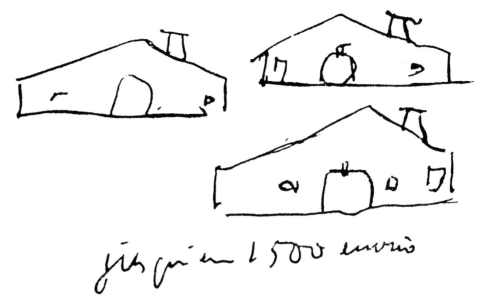

the entire roof was often raised or rebuilt so that the rectilinearity of the single-gable silhouette remained unchanged. An add-on process of expansion—so common in New England—was virtually unknown.[3]

The traditional form of "la chambre du tué," with its symbolic reference to gatherings and relationships, and to a sense of security, unity, cooperation, and family well-being, finds repeated expression in Le Corbusier's designs that are intended for the assembly of human beings. The first instance is perhaps his church project for Tremblay of 1929 which is essentially a giant "tué" minus its surrounding farmhouse. Like the "tué," it is square in plan, the altar positioned against one wall where one might expect to see the farmhouse fire. The walls, however, rise straight up rather than creating a pyramidal form.

Another example of the "tué" type is the Assembly Chamber at the legislature building in Chandigarh where the earliest sketches (I am informed by Olek Kujawski, who worked in Le Corbusier's office at the time) specified a square plan. This was subsequently modified to a circular plan at the explicit request of Prime Minister Nehru. Thereafter the walls were given a subtle parabolic curve more reminiscent of local industrial cooling towers. However, unlike machine-age cooling towers (which serve as steam stacks rather than smoke stacks), the top was severed diagonally and covered with a shutter that clearly recalls the flap atop a Jura chimney; also the manner in which this "chimney" projects through the building's roof is reminiscent of its Jura prototype (fig. 148). Therefore the final design at Chandigarh synthesizes two diverse images, one derived from modern industrial forms, the other from the more private, but more

3. Curiously enough, Jura farmhouses were usually enlarged in breadth, not depth, perhaps because they were often hemmed in between the hillside and the street.

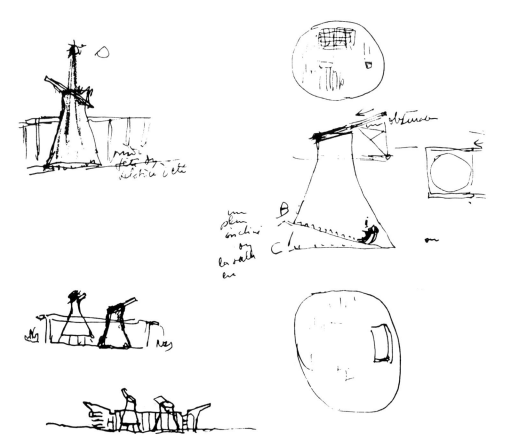

Fig. 148. Le Corbusier. Early studies for the Assembly Chamber, Chandigarh, India, dated December, 1954. (Le Corbusier, *Creation Is a Patient Search* [New York: Praeger, 1960], p. 210)

appropriate (symbolically speaking), connotation of the family "tué." This same form, yet without projecting through the roof, would reappear in the General Assembly chamber at the United Nations in New York.

Subsequently Le Corbusier abandoned the industrial imagery of the cooling tower when he created the purest "tué" of his career. This was the church at Firminy, France, where, although he initially envisioned a conical shape, its final form was close to the very distinctive conception found in a Jura farmhouse (fig. 149).[4]

Concerning the farmhouse where Jeanneret lived in 1910, the "chambre du tué" measured some eleven feet square, and two rooms (the first windowless) distanced it from the south facade facing the street; the remainder of the building served as a barn. The doorway lintel was undated yet the building's style was that of the late 1500s or early 1600s; it is (or was) the first building on the left (called No. 34) when one is mounting Mont Cornu. Léon Perrin and Octave Matthey were then living at No. 36 (the last on the left) which carries the date 1645. Whether other students were simulta-

4. Le Corbusier's interest, late in life, in High Jura farmhouses is further confirmed in his correspondence with Fritz Jung, historian from La Chaux-de-Fonds (partly published in *L'Impartial,* October 4, 1965, p. 11) as well as his discussion of the subject in his 1960 "autobiography," *Creation Is a Patient Search,* pp. 18–19.

**Fig. 149.** Le Corbusier. Conceptual sketch, dated June 9, 1961, for the church at Firminy, France. Its silhouette is basically that of a giant Jura chimney without a farmhouse around it. (FLC 16542)

neously in residence I was unable to ascertain. The latter farmhouse is where the senior Jeannerets rented a room on the second floor during September 1909, with the Perrins lodging on the floor below.[5]

Jeanneret set three objectives for himself during these long winter months on Mont Cornu, the first being to live with nature, the second to study, and the third to enjoy the comradeship of his friends, most especially Léon Perrin. Of his studies we know little since no books bear this date and no hard evidence exists that he continued, as intended, his inquiry into mathematics and reinforced concrete. Our scant knowledge results from the scarcity of correspondence because, being at home, he had little need to write.

Nevertheless he did correspond with Max Du Bois, a childhood acquaintance whose friendship he had renewed in Paris and who, as we previously noted, had lent Jeanneret *Le Béton armé* by Emil Mörsch, which Du Bois had translated in 1909 from the German (*Eisenbeton Bau*). With Du Bois, Jeanneret resurrected the subject he had debated with

5. Information obtained (June 25, 1979) from James Perrin, who recalled Mr. Jeanneret coming downstairs with shoes in hand each morning at 5 A.M. on his way to work.

Chapallaz and L'Eplattenier from Vienna—his desire and need to apprentice with an engineer. Obviously he believed that his sixteen and a half months with Perret, plus several months of private tutorials and of auditing courses in Paris, left him inadequately prepared to cope with the engineering requirements of an architect. Therefore he asked Du Bois to arrange an apprenticeship for him with Mörsch (whom he was willing to visit for an interview) or, failing that, to furnish letters of recommendation and perhaps even go so far as to intercede on Jeanneret's behalf with other German engineers; Jeanneret specified, however, that these engineers must be of the caliber of François Hennebique, the great French specialist in reinforced concrete.[6] Such inquiries, if ever made, came to naught.

These letters to Du Bois also show the depth of his need to repose in nature, and how he was beginning to "sense my concept of life, the reason for my efforts; my objective becomes more and more clear" (to Du Bois, February 1, 1910). Likewise he mentions going cross-country skiing with L'Eplattenier and friends, going to the oculist, attending a concert, and how he and his mentor are dreaming up grandiose schemes that they fully intend to realize.[7]

L'Eplattenier, as usual, was supercharged with new projects and ideas and Jeanneret became so captivated and excited that he devoted most the next seven months—and much of the next four years—to collaborating with L'Eplattenier toward the realization of these objectives. It is hard to believe that this is the same Jeanneret who, on November 22, 1908, had written that severe, highly critical letter admonishing L'Eplattenier for his methods and his goals. Could it be that Jeanneret had abandoned his search for an ideal, or had he done another about-face and come to identify L'Eplattenier's goals with his own, believing that his teacher's route would satisfy the professional life toward which he was striving?

Much had happened during the twenty-seven months of Jeanneret's absence from La Chaux-de-Fonds. The Cours Supérieur was thriving and L'Eplattenier was proposing its separation from the Ecole d'art, himself to be appointed director. Success could be measured by the practical work completed by his students, beginning with the Matthey-Doret music room, the chapel at Cernier-Fontainemelon and the Villa Fallet. By September 1908 24,500 francs had been earned.[8] Work done since Jeanneret's de-

6. Why, then, didn't Jeanneret seek employment with Hennebique and return to France? He must have felt committed (to L'Eplattenier?) to study in Germany.

7. From his father's journal we learn that Edouard spent two days at home in early February and on March 6 both boys came home for three days. But on the first day their father was struck by a bobsled that broke his right ankle, and at month's end (when Edouard left for Germany) his father was still unable to walk. Each Monday he had to be carried to his atelier, and returned home on Saturday evening. Fortunately his sister Pauline's flat was in the same building as the atelier so he stayed with her throughout the week.

8. *Procès-verbal* of the commission of the Ecole d'art, September 17, 1908.

parture included the interior decoration at the Villa Sandoz at Tavannes (1907–8), sculpted stonework for the sun porch at 129, rue de Progrès for Isaac Schwob (1908),[9] and, most important of all, completing the entire ornamental scheme for a new crematorium, decorating the great hall of the post office, and designing and decorating the entrance pavilion at the observatory at Neuchâtel in 1911.[10]

The crematorium for the Cimetière de la Charrière at La Chaux-de-Fonds, along with the observatory at Neuchâtel, is the finest and most complete of extant examples of work by L'Eplattenier and his students (figs. 150, 151). The plans, by the architects Belli and Robert, are dated 1908 with revisions through September 1909, the year in which the cornerstone was laid and the first cremation (November 11, 1909) took place. The official inauguration was not until June 27, 1910.

Above its entrance rises a gilded statue, *Vers l'idéal,* sculpted by L'Eplattenier, for which René Chapallaz served as model.[11] The archway, with its decoration combining both the sapin and flames, was carved by Léon Perrin and inside everything was executed by students from the Cours Supérieur or by their professor. This includes the floor mosaics, the walls sheathed in repoussé metalwork with painted murals above,[12] and a frescoed ceiling—as well as the catafalque, lamps, and benches. Fire is the motif of the interior decoration, the flames sometimes being metamorphosed into spruce trees or their cones. The effect is stunning, rich, and almost overpowering, especially

9. Léon Perrin informed the author (May 20, 1977) that he executed the sculpture in stone; the fireplace decoration was executed at the same time.

10. The Hirsch Pavilion at the Neuchâtel observatory (which, like Greenwich, England, marks the point from which Swiss time is measured) was decorated inside and out by Les Ateliers d'art réunis during the summer of 1911. The sixteen-foot-square entrance lobby is sheathed in polished black marble with three symmetrical copper repoussé doors (most of them are fake) on each side, the signs of the zodiac being embossed on each of the twelve doors. The overhead skylight incorporates lightning, birds, and clouds in its repoussé ornament. The total effect of black and gold is dignified and quiet, its impressiveness transcending its actual size. The source for the design would seem to be Bruno Paul's vestibule at the Arts and Crafts Exhibition in Brussels of 1910 (see Robert Breuer, *German Arts and Crafts at the Brussels Exhibition of 1910* (Stuttgart, n.d.), pp. 20–21). Currently the pavilion is threatened with demolition; it must be saved.

With Léon Perrin I visited the building in 1974; he said that under L'Eplattenier's supervision he executed the stone sculpture above the exterior door and did some of the signs of the zodiac, that Houriet and Harder did most of the repoussé, while Matthey worked on the mosaic floor. The bust of Hirsch, set on a black marble pedestal, is signed and dated 1911 by L'Eplattenier.

For a more complete list of the Atelier's executed works, see *Ecole d'Art, La Chaux-de-Fonds, 1910–1911, Rapport de la Commission,* pp. 17–18.

11. Chapallaz confirmed for me that he indeed had modelled for this statue, yet modestly added "only from the waist up" (the figure being in the nude).

12. The oil paintings across the upper part of each of the four walls are signed and dated by L'Eplattenier in 1912, the one above the catafalque (see fig. 151) being entitled *La Mort, la Douleur et la Paix.* L'Eplattenier also executed the two large mosaics on the lateral exterior walls in 1926.

**Fig. 150.** Crematorium, La Chaux-de-Fonds, 1909. Relief sculpture at entrance by Léon Perrin, statue above entrance and mosaics on the side walls (1926), by Charles L'Eplattenier. (Photo by author)

**Fig. 151.** Crematorium, interior. Decoration designed and executed by students from the Cours Supérieur, Ecole d'art, except for the (1912) paintings on the upper walls by L'Eplattenier. (Photo by author)

during the ceremony when the catafalque mysteriously sinks through the massive floor and into the consuming flames below.[13]

The construction of the Hôtel des Postes—the Central Post Office—was a much more protracted process. A design competition was held in 1904 which closed on January 31, 1905, with the winning architects being from Geneva. L'Eplattenier was one of the competitors (see Chapter 2, fig. 40). Yet delays in financing and construction retarded the opening until December 1910 when work was still in process. L'Eplattenier—as with the crematorium—obtained for his students the commission to ornament the great hall and by early 1909 they were busy preparing the designs.[14] According to Perrin neither he nor Jeanneret worked there, but Matthey, Houriet, and Harder did.[15]

As at the crematorium, much of the decoration was in low relief, or "cuivre repoussé," which is thin sheets of copper alloy containing small amounts of zinc and tin and having the color of brass or bronze. Repoussé was very popular at that time; we previously observed that the Perret brothers used it in France. Eventually, however, it went out of fashion and during the 1960s the repoussé was removed from the post office in an attempt to "modernize" the building.

Only one of these student commissions was undertaken during Jeanneret's 1910 sojourn at La Chaux-de-Fonds. That was 30 bis Grenier where he, along with Georges Aubert, Hermann Jeanneret, and Eric de Coulon, participated in the work.[16] The project consisted of remodeling an existing living room (some 14 by 24 feet) which they sheathed with vertical unpainted pine paneling topped by a carved wood frieze representing conventionalized pine cones or sapin set against a dark green background. Jeanneret was responsible for the general layout of the room and its woodwork, and the decoration of the paneling and frieze could well be his although Eric de Coulon was involved as well. The door carries the date and monogram of the owners, "EM 1910 HM"—Emile and Hélène Moser. Hermann Jeanneret executed the ornamental ironwork over the street door that consists of simulated stalks of grain crowned by the words "Le Grenier."

13. During the 1970s there was pressure to enlarge the crematorium but happily a public outcry averted this disaster and instead a low, unobtrusive annex was added at the rear. The crematorium deserves historic classification to preserve it for posterity.

14. Minutes of the commission of the Ecole d'art, April 8, 1909.

15. In conversation with Léon Perrin, July 11, 1974. According to Lucien Schwob (October 1973) Harder also did much of the repoussé at the crematorium. The names of others I have been unable to discover.

16. Léon Perrin (June 30, 1974), although he did not assist with this project, was absolutely certain that Edouard Jeanneret worked on the design for the room at 30 bis Grenier; also that Georges Aubert designed a table and chairs and that Hermann Jeanneret (whom he and Edouard had met in Paris) did the exterior ironwork. However, Willy Moser, son of the owners, believes that Eric de Coulon designed and executed the sapin frieze; de Coulon studied architecture at the E.T.H., Zurich, 1908–10, then, 1910–12, studied under L'Eplattenier before moving to Paris as a poster designer.

When one considers the success of L'Eplattenier's loose collection of past and present students, it is surprising that it was not until March 15, 1910, that they banded together into a formal organization—called Les Ateliers d'art réunis. Jeanneret was active in its formation and during several years prior to its dissolution in 1916 served as executive secretary. The first and ongoing president was Léon Perrin and initially Georges Aubert served as secretary-treasurer. Their office was in the same building as the Cours Supérieur, that is, the former hospital at 54 Numa-Droz. Their objective was "the development of art in all areas of public and private life,"[17] but more specifically L'Eplattenier envisioned it as the sequel to his Cours Supérieur that would provide employment for students he had trained.

As early as September 17, 1908, L'Eplattenier had proposed to the commission of the Ecole d'art "the creation of workshops grouped around a common studio" with artist/teachers in charge of each apprenticeship section and with a paid *chef d'atelier* (L'Eplattenier?) supervising the operation. Although direct commissions would be sought, noncommissioned work would be sold at a salesroom with the monies raised being used to pay the rent and provide a livelihood for the artists.[18] The commission reacted favorably to this proposal, hesitating only because of the costs involved. There was also the matter of priorities since the Ecole d'art had long hoped to construct its own building, thereby gathering its disparate activities under a single roof. The question arose as to whether to include the studios and workshops that L'Eplattenier envisioned in the same structure as the school itself or, if not, then which building should be built first. William Aubert, director of the school, generously proposed (October 1, 1908) that the ateliers be constructed first. A search for an appropriate site was already underway.

When Jeanneret returned to La Chaux-de-Fonds in December 1909 these issues remained very much alive (see *Rapport,* 1909–10, pp. 10–11). But the matter was further complicated by L'Eplattenier's subsequent request to sever the Cours Supérieur from the Ecole d'art (approved in principle by the commission on March 23, 1910, and

17. The founding of the society is reported in the *Feuille d'avis,* May 28, 1910.

18. L'Eplattenier's recommendation to the commission was summarized in the minutes of September 17, 1908: "Il nous est donné connaissance des articles proposés établissant la création d'ateliers pratiques groupés autour d'un atelier commun. Ces ateliers seraient ouverts suivant les besoins, patronnés par des chefs d'atelier responsables, qui eux-mêmes seraient placés sous le contrôle de la commission. Des ouvriers et apprentis seraient admis et le chef d'atelier indemnisé par apprenti formé. Les autorités seront indemnisées par compensation des frais de construction et d'installation. Une salle de vente sera créée et un voyageur sera spécialement désigné pour chercher les commandes et s'occuper d'une partie administrative. Pour éviter toute concurrence aux ateliers de la ville les travaux seront essentiellement artistiques. Une grande unité dans l'exécution des travaux d'ensemble sera observée et un pour-cent sera prélevé sur ces travaux. Les premiers ateliers à fonder seront ceux de la sculpture en pierre, la sculpture sur bois, les meubles d'art, la fonte, les travaux sur métal (ciselure et orfèvrerie), enfin la céramique, plus tard les émaux, la mosaïque, le vitrail, la peinture décorative, la cuiroplastie, la broderie et le fer forgé."

afterwards referred to the commune for authorization). This raised the additional question of whether the Cours Supérieur should have its own building or, if not, with whom it could share space.

Jeanneret must have been delighted at the prospect of these new constructions (although none actually materialized) and for the Ateliers d'art he proposed a design dated January 24, 1910. It demonstrates his growing power of synthesis. It is both fascinating and provocative; likewise it holds the honor of being the earliest work that Le Corbusier considered acceptable to include in his so-called *Oeuvre Complète* (fig. 152).[19]

The first key to unlocking the sophisticated synthesis of this design is, in my opinion, the architecture of Peter Behrens. Recall Jeanneret's letter to L'Eplattenier of two years before (February 29, 1908): "Frankly, what would you say if some day I worked in the style of Kreis or Behrens (remembering, I beg you, the pavilions that he built at the Düsseldorf exposition)."[20] These comments were in reaction to L'Eplattenier's remarks about Behrens, and although Jeanneret's words were intended in the negative sense, that detail is less significant than the fact that he had fixed in his own mind the idea of some day preparing a design for L'Eplattenier based on the Behrens exhibition building. And the comparison is so striking as scarcely to require comment (fig. 153).

In addition, the Behrens building embodies Henry Provensal's clarion call in *L'Art de demain* for cubic forms in architecture, insisting that they are the most perfect and universal, and the most expressive of an ideal reality. Provensal also asserted that visual effects should be created, not by decoration or detail, but by the judicious play of volume and void, of light and shade.

A third component in Jeanneret's design was the Chartreuse d'Ema where each unit was separated from its neighbor by a private garden which established an alternating sequence of volume and void arranged around the perimeter of the cloister (see Chapter 3, fig. 88). In Jeanneret's scheme, however, this central common space was covered rather than being open to the sky, yet it did serve a communal function. Nevertheless the actual architectural forms—a central pavilion topped by a pyramid and surrounded by symmetrically placed cubic volumes—are clearly derived from Behrens.

A fourth element, perhaps less obvious, is the Turkish mosque where curved, not cubic, forms progressively build toward the central dome, and where minarets rise at the corners of the precinct. Jeanneret greatly admired these Byzantine buildings which the following year he would sketch, photograph, and write about while visiting Istanbul (see Chapter 8, fig. 191). Their massing provided confirmation for his own more complex, post-Behrens design in which the minarets served as smokestacks for the forges of the metalworking shops.

19. The only record of this seminal design are the two illustrations published in *Oeuvre Complète;* the originals are apparently lost and no preliminary sketches seem to exist.

20. There is a minor discrepancy here since Jeanneret apparently confused what Behrens built at Oldenburg with Düsseldorf.

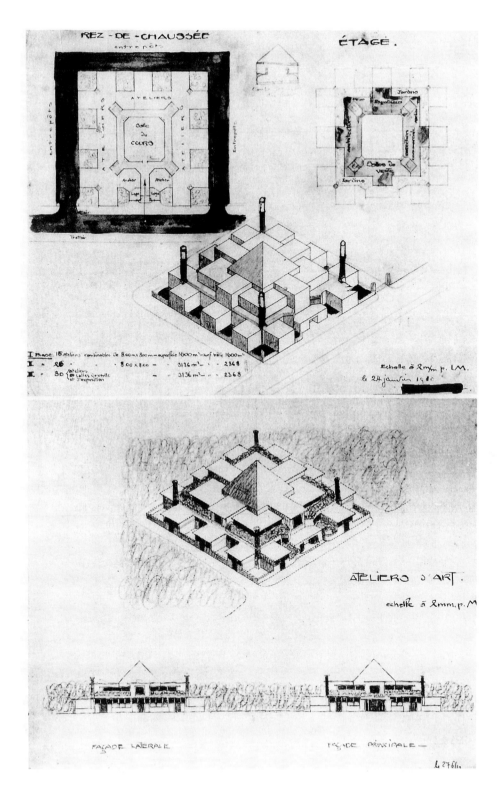

Finally we must ask how sincere Jeanneret was in preparing this design (which he did *not* present to the commission of the Ecole d'art). When writing his letter to L'Eplattenier in February 1908, I suspect he was genuinely anti-Behrens. However, as time passed and he learned more about (to paraphrase his words) "what architecture was, and what it was not" I am sure he perceived certain real values in Behrens' work that had previously eluded him. And by the time he thought of designing the Ateliers d'art he was certainly more favorably inclined toward Behrens but still was intent on presenting L'Eplattenier with an architectural joke—based on Behrens. And the more he ruminated about the design, and before the final synthesis took place, he may have—in a flash of insight—truly perceived the full value of his design. It was a worthy premonition of Le Corbusier and (in the same context) a logical first project for him to include in the *Oeuvre Complète*.[21] However, the classical values so implicit in this design were entirely out of context with Jeanneret's still current medievalist frame of mind.

Jeanneret's schematic plan for the Atelier follows carefully L'Eplattenier's behest for

21. In terms of premonitions of the future, I see the 1910 Ateliers d'art project as occupying a similar seminal position as Frank Lloyd Wright's project for the Cooper House, La Grange, Illinois, of ca. 1887. Jeanneret was twenty-two when he created his design, Wright was twenty, and for both men almost exactly thirteen years would pass before they arrived at their mature style; also both designs were a synthesis of several of the most vital ideas around. These parallels are incredibly striking. For an illustration of Wright's project, see H. Allen Brooks, *Frank Lloyd Wright and the Prairie School* (New York, 1984, plate 2), but for a detailed discussion and analysis with comparative illustrations of the designs upon which Wright based his synthesis, see H. Allen Brooks, "Frank Lloyd Wright—Towards a Maturity of Style," *A.A. Files: Annals of the Architectural Association School of Architecture,* I, no. 2 (July 1982), pp. 44–49.

"workshops grouped around a common studio." On the ground floor there are eleven ateliers at the perimeter,[22] a corridor, and at the center a large lecture hall (square, like a cloister). The upper level (not carefully articulated) would contain space for offices, a salesroom, exhibition areas, architects' drafting tables, additional ateliers, and access to the balcony above the lecture hall. A roof garden would surround this upper level. The small scale of these drawings, combined with the fact that they are primarily volumetric studies, unfortunately gives no indication as to what decoration may have been intended.

Such cubic, flat-roofed forms did not reappear in Jeanneret's work for another four years—until his Dom-ino projects of 1914–15. And during the next two years he created no new architectural designs whatsoever because his interests were directed elsewhere.

During his four-month sojourn at La Chaux-de-Fonds Jeanneret was introduced to yet another field of inquiry. It would become one of the passions of his life and the domain in which his international influence remained supreme throughout most of the twentieth century. This was urban design, although that term had scarcely been coined by 1910.

Why urbanism? Purely a matter of chance. The chance being L'Eplattenier's agreement to present a paper on "L'esthétique des villes" at the general assembly of the Union des Villes Suisses to be held at La Chaux-de-Fonds in September 1910. He transmitted his enthusiasm to his student, including the proposal that Jeanneret research the subject and that together they produce a book. L'Eplattenier had already discovered "le beau livre de Camillo Sitte sur *L'Art de bâtir les villes*" in its French edition (1902) as translated by their countryman Camille Martin. The translator, however, had added a new chapter on "streets" that did not appear in *Der Städtebau* when the book was originally published in Vienna in 1889. Jeanneret immediately became, and remained for the next five years, a devoted disciple of Sitte on all matters pertaining to urban design. This is quite understandable since both Sitte and Jeanneret were ardent medievalists (in spite of the latter's recent design for the Ateliers d'art).

Planned cities have existed since ancient times, yet as a modern professional discipline the subject made its debut late in the nineteenth century. It was at that time that Sitte proposed his piecemeal beautification of cities (designing individual elements therein) and soon others—led by Ebenezar Howard, Barry Parker, and Sir Raymond Unwin in England and Georges Benoit-Lévy in France—focused attention on so-called garden cities (be they self-sufficient entities or city extensions). Yet no one (short of Daniel Burnham in his remarkable 1907–9 plan for Chicago) thought of remaking the entire core of existing cities as Le Corbusier would eventually do.

22. Jeanneret's notation on the plan specifies that Phase I would contain fifteen ateliers. Thus the four second-floor cubes must also be ateliers (11 + 4 = 15) although this is not evident from the plan. He states that Phase II would contain additional ateliers, yet there is no indication as to how he would expand the plan.

Jeanneret's research and writing coincided with numerous other activities and a great deal of moving about—several months in Munich, visits to Berlin and other German cities, and a second sojourn at La Chaux-de-Fonds during the summer of 1910. On June 29 he wrote to his parents that soon he would be home for the holidays, and of his research and writing he said: "This study will be published as a book, the importance of which surpasses my expectations. . . . It will be signed by L'Eplattenier and by me, and will have a greater than local interest. . . . Today it is almost ready. But it is written in such abominable French that I count on the quiet of the countryside to give me a chance to improve it."[23] Such optimism proved unwarranted because on November 1, when beginning his apprenticeship with Peter Behrens, the manuscript was far from finished; he would resume the project in 1915 and once again during 1922–25 before the totally recast book was published as *Urbanisme* in 1925. But to avoid fragmenting our discussion throughout the remainder of this book, I shall treat the subject as a single unit here, concluding with certain remarks about the published work of 1925.

The 1910 manuscript is entitled "La Construction des Villes" and consists of two or three outlines, several chapters comprising nearly 135 pages, several alternate drafts, various notes, and more than 150 drawings in addition to many postcards and photographs intended for use as illustrations. So formidable was the task of reconstructing this book, and then analyzing its contents, that initially I published my findings as "Jeanneret and Sitte: Le Corbusier's Earliest Ideas on Urban Design," then reduced those seven thousand words to the more manageable length that appears below.[24]

Jeanneret modeled his book closely on that of Camillo Sitte. Their titles are similar (*Der Städtebau / La Construction des Villes*), and their division into two major parts is identical—the first a historical, analytical analysis of medieval towns, the second a specific case study (Vienna in Sitte's book, La Chaux-de-Fonds in Jeanneret's). Also, both books devote principal chapters to streets and squares, with Jeanneret copying many of Sitte's illustrations. What Jeanneret contributed on his own were certain creative aspects, that

23. "J'ai une peine épouvantable à l'écrire en français," he had written to L'Eplattenier on June 2. The fact that he could not write well, or even correctly, was noted by parents and friends and soon became a matter of acute embarrassment. Later, by the early twenties, he surmounted this problem by adopting a telegraphic style. In spite of various references to L'Eplattenier as coauthor of the book, there is no evidence that the latter contributed more than editorial advice. No portion of the text was allocated to him nor does his handwriting appear in the existing manuscript.

24. See H. Allen Brooks, "Jeanneret and Sitte: Le Corbusier's Earliest Ideas on Urban Design," *In Search of Modern Architecture: A Tribute to Henry-Russell Hitchcock,* edited by Helen Searing (New York and Cambridge, Mass., 1982), pp. 278–97. With additional illustrations, this article was republished in Italian in *Casabella,* no. 514 (1985), pp. 40–51, and in an abridged form it appeared twice in German, as "Jeannerets Auseinandersetzung mit Sitte" in *Archithese,* 2 (1983), pp. 29–32, as well as in the exhibition catalogue *La Chaux-de-Fonds und Jeanneret* (Niederteufen, 1983), pp. 29–32. Following upon my research, Mark Albert Emery has since published the manuscript (Charles-Edouard Jeanneret/Le Corbusier, *La Construction des Villes* [Lausanne: L'Age d'Homme, 1992]) but I do not always concur with his remarks or his arrangement of the various texts.

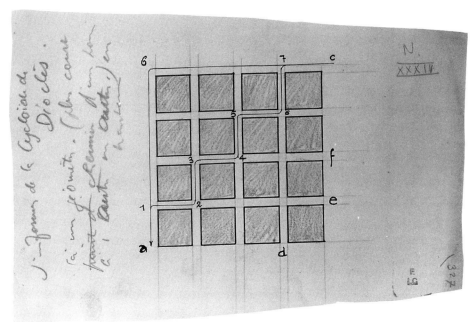

**Fig. 154.** "La Construction des Villes." Illustration by Jeanneret demonstrating the absurdity of designing streets on the grid system because there is no reasonable way to get from point c to point a. 1910. Pencil and ink on tracing paper. Approx. 14 × 22 cm. (FLC)

**Fig. 155.** "La Construction des Villes." Bird's-eye view of medieval Weissenburg. Jeanneret argues that "An occasional straight street, which is short and closed at both ends, is permissible, but long straight streets without a nearby visual terminus are deplorable." Of Weissenburg, which demonstrates this proposition, he also notes that "the town hall (far left) was not placed on axis with the street because two important buildings standing at two extremities of a straight street create a trite impression." 1910. Ink on tracing paper. Approx. 16 × 19.5 cm. (FLC)

is visual demonstrations, often abstract in nature, showing how—and how not—to design streets and squares and how to enrich them by the artistic placement of buildings, monuments, and trees. A precedent, in part, for this is due to the journal *Der Städtebau* (also founded by Sitte) which Jeanneret singled out for special praise, yet he showed much greater interest in translating the analysis of old towns into specific "rules" (illustrated by diagrams) that might be applied to new designs.

His chapter on streets (*Des Rues*) he called the most important in his book; it also is the most carefully considered and well written. He declares that all streets should be curved, their width and slope should vary, that views along them must be closed, and that symmetrical or geometric layouts must be avoided. He states specifically that "The lesson of the donkey should be retained" ("La leçon de l'âne est à retenir") and asserts that planners must learn from donkeys how to design streets that respect and enhance the landscape, and that vary in their slope.

Jeanneret ridicules the grid system for failing to respect the gradations of nature and

**Fig. 156.** "La Construction des Villes." Neuhauserstrasse, Munich. The dotted lines indicate how the horizontal views are closed yet the splendid vista toward the towers of the Frauenkirche is retained. 1910. Ink on tracing paper. Approx. 7.5 × 20 cm. (FLC)

**Fig. 157.** "La Construction des Villes." Theoretical analysis of street patterns. Of 'a' (which recalls Neuhauserstrasse in Munich) and 'b' Jeanneret says, "The beauty of this solution surpasses the need for commentary" while 'c' is not recommended because of its symmetry, yet may be greatly improved by the modifications shown in 'd'. 1910. Ink on tracing paper. 18.5 × 25 cm. (FLC)

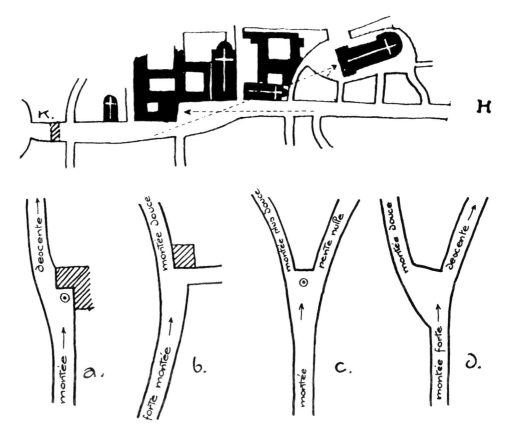

for creating an absurd situation when trying to get from point c to point a by either the route c-b-a or c-7–6-5–4-3–2-1-a (top right to bottom left in fig. 154). Although he praises the right angle ("L'angle droit est le plus beau, le plus monumental") he observes that "the straight line, the most noble line in Nature, is justifiably the rarest of all!" and therefore should be used very sparingly in planning cities. "An occasional straight street, which is short and closed at both ends, is permissible, but long straight streets without a nearby visual terminus are deplorable." He cites Weissenburg (fig. 155) as a positive demonstration of this, as well as the Champs-Elysées in Paris.

Invariably taking his lessons from the past, Jeanneret sketched Neuhauserstrasse in Munich and indicates, with dotted lines, the idyllic closed view in both directions (fig. 156). With this in mind he drew the analytical diagram in figure 157 where, in a and b, "The beauty of this solution surpasses the need for commentary" while c is "*froid*" (cold) due to its symmetry—yet it may be improved by the modifications shown in d. From modern times he cites Hampstead Garden Suburb in England as exemplifying these same laws (fig. 158). Hampstead, along with Bournville and Hellerau, are also praised in the short chapter entitled *Des Chéseaux* (the layout of building lots) as a excellent demonstration of how this should be done.

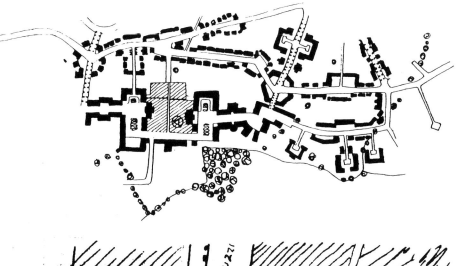

**Fig. 158.** "La Construction des Villes." Hampstead Garden Suburb, London, England. Plan traced by Jeanneret who praises it for embodying the laws that he is endeavoring to promulgate. 1910. Ink and pencil on tracing paper. Approx. 28 × 17 cm. (FLC)

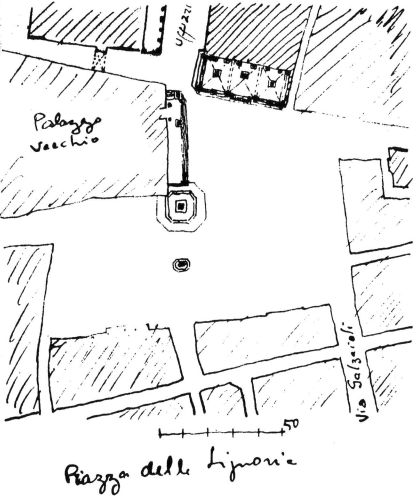

**Fig. 159.** "La Construction des Villes." Piazza della Signoria, Florence, Italy, as sketched by Jeanneret to demonstrate that squares should be closed to prevent looking out, and to illustrate how major buildings should be part of the surrounding fabric rather than standing in isolation. 1910. Ink on tracing paper. Approx. 15 × 19.3 cm. (FLC)

Another chapter in this opening section on *Des Eléments Constructifs de la Ville* is entitled *Des Places*—open squares and plazas—and here Jeanneret insists that plazas should be closed with streets entering only at an angle, or be curved so as to prevent one looking beyond the central space. Also—and contrary to the nineteenth-century preference for geometrical squares in which major buildings are isolated—Jeanneret reiterates Sitte's argument that buildings should be imbedded in the surrounding fabric; his drawing of the Piazza della Signoria, Florence, makes this point (fig. 159).

A short fourth chapter discusses enclosing walls (*Des Murs de Clôture*) and here Jeanneret extols the wall at the Hôtel de Cluny in Paris:"The court behind this wall, under its great chestnut tree, is an oasis of tranquil refreshment that visitors to the museum may well enjoy." He contends that the more important the space, the higher the wall should be; metal grills are only for the parvenu.[25]

Unfortunately these chapters terminate on the same negative note that permeates the entire book—a constant harangue against civic leaders, administrators, and bureaucrats who, according to Jeanneret, have no respect for art, or for the landscape, and who tear down handsome old buildings on the grounds that what is new is better. So saying, he alienates precisely those people whose sympathy he is trying to win. Similarly he rails against architectural competitions and the juries that judge them.

Part II of the book, *Application critique: La Chaux-de-Fonds,* begins its heavily edited and obviously unfinished pages on a similar negative note—by lambasting "les géomètres" which is Jeanneret's euphemism for administrators who create gridiron plans. Of his home town he has no praise: "Nowhere in the plan of La Chaux-de-Fonds does one find a single layout that creates a pleasant view," and "There is not a single public or private building in the town that is favorably situated in the manner proposed in Part I." Only late in this chapter does his criticism become constructive; he proposes creating several closed, intimate views and developing focal points within them. Roughly sketched on a single sheet (fig. 160) are two plans, a section, and a perspective view of how he might modify the terminus of Avenue Léopold-Robert by throwing a visual barrier, penetrated by two traffic lanes, across the boulevard (where Léon Perrin's allegorical statue dedicated to Léopold Robert now stands) in order to create a more enclosed space around the fountain and better show off the twin buildings that lie behind; another proposal was to modify the market square. Later he also produced a design for the Place de la Gare.[26]

With this chapter on La Chaux-de-Fonds Jeanneret concludes "La Construction des

25. During the summer of 1910 L'Eplattenier asked Jeanneret to expand his study to include chapters on bridges, trees, gardens and parks, cemeteries, and garden cities. Upon returning to Münich in September, Jeanneret began to research these topics but never wrote of them.

26. The plan for the Place de la Gare is discussed in the following chapter since it was conceived for the emplacement of L'Eplattenier's newly commissioned sculptural work dedicated to Numa Droz (see fig. 172).

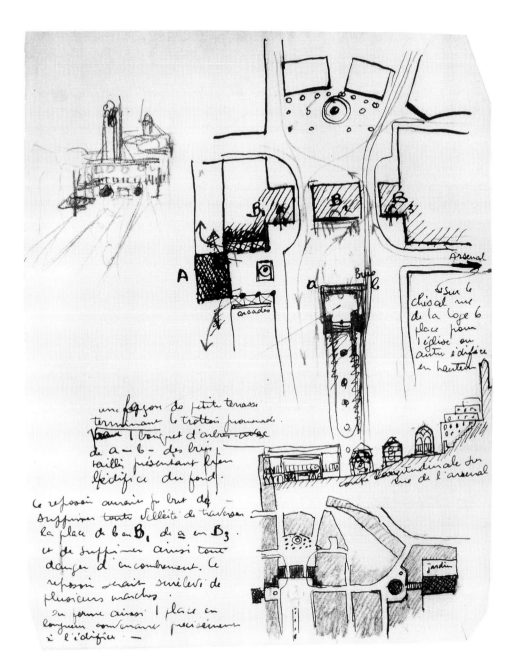

**Fig. 160.** "La Construction des Villes." Jeanneret's sketches showing how he would modify the terminus of Avenue Léopold-Robert, La Chaux-de-Fonds. 1910. Pencil and ink on writing paper. 30 × 21 cm. (Private collection)

Villes," a text that, although heavily dependent upon Camillo Sitte, offers much more by way of theoretical analysis. It also proposes a series of descriptive diagrams for application in actual situations. These, in turn, were then translated into specific "rules" to serve the architect/urbanist in his work. This interest in establishing rules, or laws, would become an earmark of Jeanneret/Le Corbusier throughout his life (recall his

Five Points of Architecture). Unfortunately, however, Jeanneret's text is severely marred by his incessant condemnation of municipal authorities. For a young man of twenty-two writing his first book he imparts far too much self-righteous indignation.

After a hiatus of over five years, Jeanneret resumed work on "La Construction des Villes" in 1915. This time he conducted research at the Bibliothèque Nationale in Paris (see Chapter 10 and figs. 333–35) where he became fascinated with classical principles of town planning. This, in turn, required him to completely rethink the basic thesis of his book. But in spite of carrying out extensive research, and preparing new outlines, no significant rewriting occurred at this time.

Once again in 1922–25 he revived the project, totally rewriting the text but retaining his structural organization from 1910. This time the manuscript did get published but under a new title: *Urbanisme* (1925). It became one of the most influential books he ever wrote. Yet before I discovered the manuscript "La Construction des Villes," *Urbanisme* was, of necessity, viewed entirely out of context.

Both the 1910 and 1925 books are similar in organization but not in interpretation. Each begins with introductory remarks followed by two major parts, one devoted to a theoretical analysis of city plans, the other to the case study of a particular town. In the 1925 book, however, Le Corbusier substituted, in Part II, Paris in place of La Chaux-de-Fonds, and rather than selecting medieval towns for his analysis in Part I he discussed his own "Contemporary City for Three Million Inhabitants" (designed for the Salon d'Automne in 1922). The similarities, however, end there. "La Construction des Villes" is predicated on *pedestrians*—how people see, enjoy, and move through a city—whereas *Urbanisme* is predicated on the *automobile,* and how to move vehicles rapidly through the city (thereby rationalizing the disappearance of the traditional street).

Also, rather slyly, Le Corbusier built his various themes in *Urbanisme* upon the destruction of those in "La Construction des Villes," as if by so doing he could achieve some kind of personal catharsis. Therefore he entitled the first chapter of *Urbanisme* "Le Chemin des ânes, le chemin des hommes" ("The Donkey's Way and Man's Way"), and devoted an extravagant amount of time to demolishing his earlier dictum that "The lesson of the donkey should be retained." In like manner Chapter 2 assumes the title "Order," with geometry now elevated from devil to deity. Interestingly enough, however, many of the illustrations prepared for the 1910 manuscript were published in 1925, but in a textual context that gave them exactly the opposite meaning.

An obvious comparison with "La Construction des Villes" is L'Eplattenier's paper on "L'esthétique des villes" presented at the Union des Villes Suisses on September 24, 1910.[27] His theme is based on the theory that old cities—their roads, squares, and buildings—were designed with an eye to beauty and thus we should study their aesthetic principles and adopt them as our own. After praising Sitte's book he discussed

27. Charles L'Eplattenier, "L'esthétique des villes," *Compte-Rendu des Délibérations de l'Assemblée Générale des Délégués de l'Union des Villes Suisses* (Zurich, 1910), pp. 24–31.

streets and squares, citing examples in old Swiss towns. Often his topics and arguments are similar to Jeanneret's as both men were influenced by Sitte. The principal difference in their texts is L'Eplattenier's positive and constructive attitude. From the outset he lauds efforts already made, and praises civic authorities for their deep concern over the quality of our cities. He also presents a series of practical proposals: (1) that municipalities should enact regulations relating to land development, speculation, and the preservation and creation of beauty within their city; (2) that a massive campaign, enlisting the help of journalists and schoolteachers, should be launched to educate the public as to the importance of beautiful cities; and (3) that schools which train artists and artisans should offer instruction in this field, as well as leadership in the crusade.

Reading this report gives much insight into L'Eplattenier's personal magnetism and power of persuasion. First he stirs one to the point of action, then explains how results may best be obtained.

L'Eplattenier also published, during Jeanneret's stay at home, an article on the "Renouveau d'Art" (*L'Abeille: Supplément du National Suisse,* February 20, 1910, p. 1) which, among other things, insists that art must acknowledge the strides made by science and find therein "the elements for the style of the future." A decade later Jeanneret would implement these words in his architecture.

When Jeanneret departed for Germany on April 7, 1910, L'Eplattenier's influence was firmly reestablished and the breach that began in Vienna and widened in Paris seemed entirely healed. Not only did Jeanneret, as urged by L'Eplattenier, go to Germany but he returned to La Chaux-de-Fonds in order to honor L'Eplattenier during the dedication of his *Monument de la République.* And while in Germany he largely worked on projects assigned to him by L'Eplattenier—"La Construction des Villes" and the preparation of a report on the decorative arts in Germany.[28] In addition he was probably aware that L'Eplattenier, once the Cours Supérieur was separated from the Ecole d'art, would call him back to join the staff. So, in spite of Jeanneret's making certain resolutions about not returning home again, his brother remarked (to parents, April 6, 1910) "It seems to me that this time his parting is no more irrevocable than it was in Paris; perhaps even sooner than he believes he will come back and establish his abode in our town."

28. Of the thirteen and a half months Jeanneret devoted to Germany, five were spent with Peter Behrens and the remainder devoted to L'Eplattenier's projects.

# 7

## GERMANY AND
## JEANNERET'S AWAKENING

*Peter Behrens and the Deutscher Werkbund*

*1910–1911*

Throughout adult life Le Corbusier was remarkably silent about the year he spent in Germany, and what little he revealed was negative and derogatory. Yet his experience there was of decisive importance to his development because in Germany he established many of the views and values that he nurtured throughout his life.

Indeed, before terminating his protracted stay in Germany in May 1911, Jeanneret was converted from a medievalist to a classicist; was infused with a deep concern for harmonious proportions (leading to Les tracés régulateurs); was persuaded that white was the only proper color for buildings; embraced the idea that standardization and industrialization held the key to the future of architecture; underwent his first intellectual challenge to ideas based on Camille Sitte; discovered and acclaimed the merits of European folk art; and, thanks in part to his contact with German new towns such as Hellerau, began espousing socialist views concerning land use and its capital appreciation that he would later champion in the 1920s. In short, his German experience brought about a complete revolution in Jeanneret's thinking.

Germany confronted him with his own immaturity, and from Munich he wrote his parents: "I have never, during my short life, spent such enriching months as these . . ." (June 29, 1910). His coming of age, so to speak, during these early months in Munich, was nurtured by Theodor Fischer—whose name would seldom appear in Le Corbusier's writings.

To atone for his "lost" years while admiring medieval art—for his "eyes which do not see" (the admonition he so often evoked against others)—Jeanneret soon set his sights on Rome; he renounced his earlier intention of undertaking three successive apprenticeships in Germany in favor of studying folk art and the origins of the classical tradition. A reformed person is often the most adamant and Jeanneret's conversion (or "evolution" as he preferred to call it) from gothicist to classicist evoked in him an extraordinary zeal. Yet Jeanneret, as a Francophile and Germanaphobe, was in no way prepared to give credit where credit was due. Therefore, for the sake of posterity, he subsequently invented the more romantic image of undergoing a sudden conversion to classicism at the foot of the Acropolis, thereby avoiding mention of the arduous and often painful evolution that ultimately made him receptive to what he saw in Greece.

Whereas Le Corbusier slighted Germany in his autobiographical accounts, the available documentation on his time there is amazingly complete. We have his letters to his parents, to L'Eplattenier, the beginnings of a voluminous correspondence with William Ritter, as well as occasional letters to August Klipstein, Léon Perrin, Karl-Ernst Osthaus, and Auguste Perret. Then too there is his book *Etude sur le movement d'art décoratif en Allemagne,* published in 1912, that details one aspect of his German research, as well as "La Construction des Villes" that treats another; he also published one article in the hometown press. And of upmost importance is his series of sketchbooks that record, in words and images, his extensive German travels.[1] In addition, there are numerous loose drawings and watercolors, a rich collection of postcards (many annotated), as well as his own photographs. In sum, the documentation is overwhelming and poses a challenge for the biographer who must condense it into a single chapter.

1. There are at least six sketchbooks—Carnets as Jeanneret called them—pertaining to Germany. Three of these (two of which he called Carnet II and Carnet III plus the Green Carnet) I unearthed in the early 1970s and prepared duplicate photocopies of each, retaining one set for my use while depositing the others at the Bibliothèque de la Ville in La Chaux-de-Fonds so that all researchers, without restriction, might use them. Electa in Italy and Monacelli in the United States have now published two of these plus two others: Ch.-E. Jeanneret/Le Corbusier, *Les voyages d'Allemagne Carnets* (New York: Monacelli and Fondation Le Corbusier, 1995), these four (renumbered by the publisher in Arabic numerals 1–4) being reproduced in facsimile and matching in design the *Voyage d'Orient Sketchbooks* published in 1987. The latter set began with one which Jeanneret called Carnet V but the publisher renumbered as Carnet 1; its first 36 pages concern his days in Germany. Thus one of the German sketchbooks still remains unpublished, the one I call the Green Carnet because of the color of its cover; Jeanneret gave it no name. It is larger (21.5 × 13.5 cm) than those he called I-V and truly is a sketchbook, being predominantly drawings rather than written notes. The few internal dates therein are from October 1910. Other sketchbooks that I discovered and that still remain unpublished are one captioned "Paris Automne 1913" (discussed in Chapter 9) and "Voyages d'études" (discussed in Chapter 5) devoted to Notre-Dame in Paris.

All of Jeanneret's reasons for sojourning in Germany in 1910 relate, in one way or another, to L'Eplattenier. First, he was paying off an old debt to his teacher who, back in 1908, insisted he study in Germany (rather than France), and now, two years later, he was fulfilling this obligation. Second, his immediate priority was to continue work on their book "La Construction des Villes," although obviously the library research could better be done in a country where Jeanneret was fluent in the language. And finally, L'Eplattenier arranged a grant from the Ecole d'art that helped keep Jeanneret in Germany while simultaneously requiring him to do extensive traveling, this in sharp contrast to his sojourns in Austria and France when he rarely left either Vienna or Paris.

Although L'Eplattenier carefully planned and organized for the future, Jeanneret did not. He arrived in Germany, as in Vienna and in Paris, without making the most basic of prior arrangements—yet he expected everything to fall neatly into place. When they did not, others were blamed for the consequences of his lack of forethought. He was certainly not interested in attending architectural or technical school, especially now that he put "Architect" after his name.

He had come to Germany to study town planning, learn the language, and earn both money and experience while working under one of the more progressive architects of the day. Yet he was dismayed, after installing himself in Munich, to find that most German architects lived in Berlin. Characteristically he had written no one in advance, and did not know with whom he wished to work. Whereas in France three months had passed before he began to work, in Germany it took *seven*. And five months thereafter he restlessly quit the one and only full-time job he ever held (with the Perrets he had worked only half-time).

Jeanneret's route to Munich was via Karlsruhe, Stuttgart, and Ulm, making one-day stops at each and purchasing postcards of medieval streets and squares. To these he often added notes and sketches relating to Sitte's themes (fig. 161). In Karlsruhe he found the interior of Curjel and Moser's Lutheran church "très, très beau; c'est vraiment bien," while in the next two cities the work of Theodor Fischer really caught his eye. In Stuttgart Fischer's Heusteigstrasse school, Church of the Redeemer, and Gustav Siegle house, and in Ulm the nearly completed Garrison Church, were the only contemporary works that he singled out for mention. The Garrison Church won particular praise as exemplifying Jeanneret's ideal of combining medieval historicism with the use of modern techniques and materials, especially reinforced concrete (fig. 162). He made one small sketch, in section, showing the church's concrete frame, and this is one of the exceedingly rare instances when he recorded anything related to a building's structure.

In Munich, where Jeanneret had spent four days in 1908 and where the imprint of nineteenth-century classicism is so strong, he was disappointed by comparison with what he had just seen. He liked Fischer's early (1899–1901) Redeemer church and German Bestelmeyer's more Romanesque, recently completed (1908), University of

Stuttgart-Altstadt.    Geiss-Strasse.

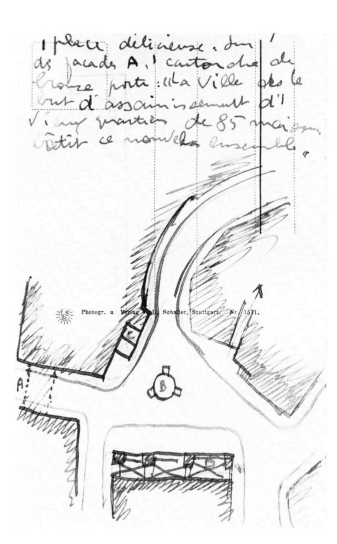

Fig. 161.   Postcard of Geiss-strasse, Stuttgart, with sketch and notes by Jeanneret on the back, April 1910. (BV)

Munich addition, but the broad, straight Ludwigstrasse lined with famous buildings left him cold (April 16 letter to L'Eplattenier). What he most enjoyed and often sketched were the twin towers of the Frauenkirche that were darkly silhouetted above the medieval quarter of the town.

What Jeanneret praised, or failed to mention, provides a barometer of his aesthetic stance. For him, "progressive" meant designs dependent upon tradition yet utilizing contemporary materials and techniques. Although he conceded that historical references made buildings less "modern" and therefore less daring, yet to his mind this was a positive quality of great merit. And for this reason he preferred contemporary German work to what he had seen in Vienna. However, combined with his wish for some historicism he also sought sobriety, austerity, and severity, three words he repeated often

**Fig. 162.** Garrison Church, Ulm, 1908–10, Theodor Fischer, architect. (Winfried Nerdinger, *Theodor Fischer* [Berlin, 1988], p. 107)

and qualities which, minus the historicism, would be demanded, after the war, by German municipal authorities for low-cost housing.

In this connection it is worth noting which of Munich's historic buildings Jeanneret apparently liked most, judging by his postcards, paintings, and drawings. The answer, perhaps unexpectedly, is the restrained, block-like, early eighteenth-century Nymphenburg Palace (fig. 163) which possesses qualities that can be compared with the Villa Jeanneret-Perret that he built for his parents in 1912.

The week of Jeanneret's arrival in Munich was a busy one. First he looked up his schoolmate Octave Matthey, then found a comfortable if not always quiet room chez Frau Vogt (Lotzbeckstrasse 3, III Stock), and then, on the strength of what he'd seen in Stuttgart and Ulm, presented himself at Professor Fischer's office with portfolio in hand. His drawings included studies from nature, architectural projects, and designs for ornament which, according to Jeanneret, duly impressed Fischer who, however, expressed the opinion that seeking inspiration from the character of the countryside (landscape) was preferable to using the motif of a single flower or tree.

Concerning employment, Fischer was apologetic because—as Jeanneret could well see—there was no space to seat another draftsman, but perhaps in about four weeks there might be an opening. In parting, he cordially invited the young Swiss to visit his home the following afternoon (Sunday) where Jeanneret had such a splendid time that he lacked superlatives to describe it. He was tremendously impressed by Fischer's hospitality, by his wife, his children, the various guests, the music, the intellectual ambiance, and the quality of the house. All was so right and proper, so sane, tranquil, serene, and restrained. And Fischer even proffered the use of his tennis court whenever Jeanneret might wish to play! (letters of April 16–17 to L'Eplattenier and April 18 to his parents).

Distraught at not obtaining work in Fischer's office (an architect, he admitted to L'Eplattenier, he had never thought of before), Jeanneret thumbed through issues of *Deutsche Kunst* in search of names and thereby learned that the majority of German architects were located in Berlin. This, of course, he could have learned while in La Chaux-de-Fonds.

A logical solution to Jeanneret's problems would have been to study under Professor Fischer at the Technische Hochschule, but it is doubtful that this thought ever crossed his mind. Yet nothing was more reasonable. It would offer such fringe benefits as meeting other students, the opportunity to speak German, having an entrée into the artistic life of the community, and being able to take courses in engineering—all of which he wanted but knew not how to bring about. Instead he remained in near total isolation in his secluded room while eating solitary restaurant meals because he lacked the wisdom to take meals at a pensione where he might have practiced German.

Fischer, who was professor of city planning, was a devoted Sitte follower. He had incorporated Sitte's ideas in the plans for expanding Munich that he had supervised

**Fig. 163.** Nymphenburg Palace, Munich, eighteenth century. Watercolor by Jeanneret of the Kronprinzen Traukt wing. 17.4 × 24.8 cm. (FLC 2053)

since 1893 and which, in turn, had earned him a nice citation in the 1902 edition of Sitte's book. He was also a founding member and first president of the Deutscher Werkbund (1907) as well as one who subscribed to August Thiersch's theories concerning the use of regulating lines as an aid to creating harmonious proportions in buildings—all reasons that would have struck a sympathetic response in Jeanneret.

Erich Mendelsohn and Edouard Jeanneret make an interesting comparison at this time. Both were born the same year and came to Munich in 1910. Yet Mendelsohn chose to study with Theodor Fischer at the Technische Hochschule, and to help support himself he sold his own paintings and did commercial art work, soon making contact with members of the Neue Künstlervereinigung (founded 1909) and its splinter group, Der Blaue Reiter, whose expressionist paintings were first exhibited in 1911.[2] These artists included Wassily Kandinsky, Franz Marc, August Mache, and Paul Klee.

What an exciting moment to be in Munich! Yet Jeanneret chose isolation and remained unaware of what was going on. Meeting these younger men might have jolted him out of his provincial conservatism long before it actually happened—which belat-

2. Notable is the fact that Mendelsohn's first expressionist architectural work was the Einstein Tower of 1919–21, whereas Le Corbusier's might be considered to be Ronchamp in 1950–55. Other architects who chose to study under Fischer include Bruno Taut and J. J. P. Oud.

edly occurred after encountering Amédée Ozenfant in Paris in 1918. But for Jeanneret, in 1910, contemporary painting was epitomized by all that he disliked in the Neue Pinakothek, which was his least favorite of museums. He complained to his parents (April 18) that he had wasted $7\frac{1}{2}$ *minutes* by going there, having already oversaturated himself in 1908 during a visit of 25 minutes. The Alte Pinakothek, however, was a different story. It spoke to him. He mentioned only two painters by name, Rubens and Rembrandt, but this provides an index to his evolving taste. Two and a half years earlier, in Italy, he sought out pre-Renaissance masters from Giotto to Fra Angelico, but now he was tuning into the seventeenth century. Nevertheless his truly favorite Munich museum was the Bavarian National Museum with its fine collection of applied arts beginning in the Middle Ages.

As the weeks passed, Jeanneret halfheartedly sought employment (never mentioning where) and typically found time for music (though outraged at the price of standing room). Operas, alone, received mention including an extraordinary *Elektra* by Strauss, Wagner's *Tristan und Isolde,* some of the *Ring of the Nibelung,* and a misconceived *Orphée et Eurydice* by Gluck which, contrary to the general rule, he thought had been better done in Paris. Praise was never bestowed on German cuisine. Meanwhile pleasurable reading took less time than usual, undoubtedly because of his strenuous library research. He did acquire *Du vrai, du beau et du bien* by Victor Cousin but left many of its pages uncut.

Concerning Jeanneret's political posture we learn more at this time. An April letter to his parents says that Carlo Picard, a family friend and outspoken socialist, is regularly sending him *La Sentinelle,* the hometown socialist newspaper, which Jeanneret discusses at length and recommends to his father over the more conservative *National Suisse,* also of La Chaux-de-Fonds. However it was the latter that printed Jeanneret's first published work, an article entitled "L'Art et Utilité publique," on page 1 of its May 15 Sunday supplement.

Written in a grandiose and florid style, the article describes a new housing project˙ in Stuttgart sponsored by the Society for the Well-being of the Working Class. The author employs all the appropriate socialist phrases like "the working class," "proletarian milieu," "the people," and insists that "Art must become social and then it will live." Also, in the first tentative outline for "La Construction des Villes" sent by Jeanneret to L'Eplattenier on April 16, he proposes a section on "common people and aristocrats; crisis—then nineteenth-century industrialism to excess; social crisis; disequilibrium." Thus, by 1910, the basis for Le Corbusier's outspoken socialist and syndicalist views of the 1920s and 1930s was already well established; it had no need to await his arrival in France and his ensuing friendships there.

Jeanneret's letters from Munich are optimistic, buoyant, jocular, and enthusiastic. He is riding the crest of a wave. He is confident and assured, his only complaint being slow progress with conversational German—because it impedes his research and postpones his plans to travel. For a brief time he exchanges conversation with a German student for four hours each day. Yet his linguistic difficulties appear exaggerated when we recall that he wrote two long letters to his parents entirely in German (admittedly not good grammatically) and also had a five-year German background, with good grades, in school. And the Sunday he visited the Fischers he conversed in German all day.

His correspondence with L'Eplattenier, meanwhile, dotes on matters concerning "La Construction des Villes": problems of obtaining illustrations, retrieving lost photographs, whether he should prepare careful drawings or merely schematic ones, and his fruitless efforts to find a French edition of Sitte's book (would L'Eplattenier please lend him his?). Curiously enough, there is never any intellectual discussion of the contents of the intended book. Meanwhile each successive card or letter announces the imminent completion of the manuscript—but finally he admits that book writing is far more difficult than anticipated and that he awaits his return to La Chaux-de-Fonds so that, together, they can rework the poorly written text. Until then his research continues, mainly at the Bavarian State Library.

Jeanneret, rather childishly, kept the book a secret from his parents but in June they learned of his deception and were understandably hurt, having believed their son was in Munich to seek employment. He justified himself, in two long letters, by maintaining the book was so important, and would be so controversial because of its negative stance concerning La Chaux-de-Fonds, that absolute secrecy was essential. He seemed to believe that this was the biggest event of his life and was quite certain it would secure his future reputation.

Meanwhile he had not forgotten the Ateliers d'art réunis. On their behalf he penetrated the bureaucracy of a Munich sales organization and met Baron von Pechmann, endeavoring to convince him to buy from the Ateliers just as he bought from the Deutsche Vereinigte Werkstätten. And because Jeanneret needed samples, he sent Léon Perrin an urgent letter (April 28) but nothing ever materialized from this project.

May witnessed two events of great significance for Jeanneret. The first was making the acquaintance of William Ritter, the second was obtaining a grant from the Ecole d'art to study the decorative arts in Germany—how they were being taught and how the resulting designs were fabricated and sold. A final remark in the authorization for the grant suggested that notes on beautifying the city and its architectural embellishment could also be included.[3] Every word was obviously selected by L'Eplattenier to create a unique program to fulfill the multiple objectives of requiring Jeanneret to

3. The authorization stipulated that "Vous auriez à fournir un rapport sur tout ce qui intéresse l'enseignement professionel, l'organization des métiers d'art, la création, la fabrication et la vente des productions artistiques; vous pourrier joindre des notes sur tout ce qui concerne l'art dans la ville et dans l'architecture,— en résumé, sur tout ce qui pourrait favoriser le développement de l'art et de la beauté chez nous" (*Etude*, p. 5).

remain in Germany, of helping finance his stay and his travels while there, of partly subsidizing work on "La Construction des Villes," of creating a report on the decorative arts that would strengthen L'Eplattenier's own hand in establishing a Nouvelle Section within the Ecole d'art (which occurred in 1912), and of giving Jeanneret experience that would help lead to his appointment within the school. All these diverse objectives were eventually achieved, and the report, *Etude sur le mouvement d'art décoratif en Allemagne,* was so well received that it was published in 1912 as Jeanneret's first book.

William Ritter was Jeanneret's senior by twenty years yet Jeanneret quickly developed a profound and deeply dependent friendship for the older man who soon became the second great mentor in his life. But Ritter never completely supplanted L'Eplattenier because each filled very different roles. Jeanneret leaned for guidance on L'Eplattenier in matters pertaining to his actions, his immediate objectives, his attitudes—how he should think about external things.

To Ritter, by contrast, he confided his doubts and opened up his soul—the man to whom he later paid this tribute: "I met a friend much older than myself in whom I could confide my doubts and incredulities because he welcomed them. . . . Together we wandered across those wide regions of lakeside, uplands, and Alps that are pregnant with historical significance. And little by little *I gradually began to find myself, and to discover that all one can count on in life is one's own strength*" (emphasis mine).[4]

William Ritter (1867–1955) came from a large Neuchâtel family whose engineer father had successfully brought running water to La Chaux-de-Fonds in 1887. William's education was broad and international with periods of study in Neuchâtel, Fribourg, Dole, Prague, Vienna, and Florence. By 1901 he had settled in Munich as music and art critic for various, but mainly Swiss, periodicals. He was an early admirer of Gustav Mahler, yet only recently have historians recognized that his writings rank among the most sensitive and prophetic concerning this Austrian composer. In the visual arts, however, his taste was exceptionally conservative and be it Cézanne or Picasso he had no use for either. He himself was a watercolorist and fond of painting landscapes. He was a man of the world and in the highly cultured milieu of Munich, Prague, and Vienna he held an exalted place, enjoying all the proper contacts; his Sunday afternoon salon in Munich attracted many admirers.

Ritter was also a biographer and prolific novelist. His literary style emphasized colorful, flowing sentences rich in verbal pictures. Plots were merely vehicles for vivid descriptions of peasant peoples, their arts, the landscape, with the settings usually being in Slavic countries. *L'Entêtement slovaque* (Paris, 1910, with a copy dedicated to Jeanneret

---

4. *Oeuvre Complète,* vol. 1, p. 12. The geographic setting described herein is Landeron above Lake Biel in Switzerland where Ritter moved after the outbreak of war in 1914. Max Du Bois, in April 1974, described Ritter to me as "Very polite, calm, reserved, and quiet. A perfect gentleman. Totally different from Jeanneret, who was a volcano; Ritter served as a brake."

on July 16, 1910) is typical. His enthusiasm for peasant life (see also *Fillette slovaque*) clearly influenced Jeanneret's decision to visit this region in 1911. More important, however, was Jeanneret's admiration for Ritter's writing style and his wish to emulate it; even as late as 1917–18 he is sending manuscripts to Ritter for critical analysis and appraisal. Yet Jeanneret never attained his goal of composing clear, flowing, uncomplicated sentences and finally, therefore, performed one of his characteristic turnabouts and adopted, in 1920, the brief, telegraphic style for which he soon became well known (*Vers une architecture* for example).

Jeanneret, in letters and actions, was exceedingly deferential to Ritter and treated him with great respect. He considered him a great man, sought his counsel, yet never was submissive, preferring to think for himself. And toward Ritter he was eternally grateful for his friendship and advice.

Jeanneret was an optimist, a cheerful person who loved to joke and clown, yet he had his ups and downs; he was on a high while in Munich but down while in Berlin. He was a workaholic and happiest when driving himself very hard. He was sensitive, intense, and cherished his privacy because he liked to be alone so that he could think. He was remarkably loyal to his friends, for whom he always found time, and consistently generous to those in need. However, after he left the Ecole d'art, new friends his own age became quite rare. None from the two years he lived in Vienna and Paris (incredible that he made none in France other than his employer and a fellow Swiss), and only one life-long friend from his year in Germany—August Klipstein. His new friendships and loyalties were usually with older men, as with Auguste Perret or William Ritter.

Jeanneret met Ritter at the end of May, obtaining his address from Charles L'Eplattenier, and during his initial visit learned that a vast city planning and building exhibition, and concurrent congress, was about to open in Berlin; it would close on June 15. His ignorance of this momentous event testifies to the isolation in which he lived, yet equally amazing was his reluctance to attend an affair so central to his task in Germany. As late as June 2 and again June 7 he wrote L'Eplattenier of his indecision whether to attend (on the sixth he had revisited Fischer's office and learned that no job was in the offing). Surprisingly, therefore, at 10 p.m. on the night of June 8 he departed for Berlin, stopping twenty-four hours en route at Nuremberg.

"Nuremberg le 9 juin 1910" are the opening words on an unfinished, loose manuscript page that would be incomprehensible without its date and the authenticity of its handwriting. Except for the picturesque layout of streets, he was far less enthusiastic about the medieval city than during his visit of 1908. More significant is the objective of this curious document which, in style, tries self-consciously to be beautiful prose. I suspect, therefore, that it is an exercise in writing, an early attempt to begin a journal, perhaps at the suggestion of William Ritter.

Jeanneret's arrival in Berlin coincided with the opening of the third annual

Deutscher Werkbund congress on Friday, June 10,[5] and he immediately participated in a tour of the AEG (Allgemeine Elektrizitäts Gesellschaft) buildings and a presentation of their products, an experience that filled ten enthusiastic pages of his Carnet I including its share of praise for Peter Behrens as architect and designer. He then visited, apparently as part of the program, a villa by Bruno Paul which he found "admirable in every respect," and that evening sought out Charles Schneider, an old school friend studying organ in Berlin, whom he resaw several times the next few days.

Saturday he spent the day, ten till five, at the Städtebau Ausstellung where he was delighted to discover how strong Sitte's ideas were among German city planners. The experience proved a confirmation rather than a revelation, and although he was much impressed by the strides being made on the German front he considered them primarily reformist when compared to those in America where he thought "a more formidable exploitation of their builders' genius" was evident in spite of his strong regret that "American cities persist in their geometric layouts."[6]

That evening he visited the Rheingold restaurant designed (1906–7) by Bruno Schmitz, for which he had very mixed, often negative, reactions, yet it held a fascination that brought him back several times. Much of his concern resulted from the decor by Franz Metzner and his students, which he found too heavy and overdone.

However the Ton-Zement-und Kalkindustrie Ausstellung, organized by Peter Behrens, which Jeanneret visited on Sunday, truly captured his imagination and provided lasting food for thought. It focused on the relation between building materials—clay/ceramics, cement/concrete, lime/plaster—and style and stimulated a lively exchange of ideas among architects, engineers, and industrialists concerning future transformations of architectural forms due to the introduction of new materials and techniques. Compared to traditional materials, Jeanneret observed, these were often more economic and perhaps more beautiful if rationally applied (*Etude,* p. 37). And four days later he revisited the exhibit, remarking how "it creates an entirely new basis for exterior and interior construction. These new materials demand both new forms and a new decoration" (Carnet II, p. 99).

He was particularly impressed by the various uses of plaster or roughcast which, as a material, is "very beautiful, very durable, colored in many ways, and lends itself to flawless execution" (II, p. 99). Likewise he was fascinated by an exhibit of artificial

5. Jeanneret claimed that "Me rendant à Berlin, j'eus l'occasion de faire voyage avec M. le baron Gunther von Pechmann," who invited him to attend the Werkbund congress (*Etude,* p. 19). Jeanneret, a notorious name-dropper, is certainly exaggerating since it is doubtful that he and the baron traveled in the same coach class; besides, Jeanneret had boarded the train in Nuremberg at midnight. More likely they met on the platform. Yet if he needed an invitation, why didn't he obtain it from Fischer before leaving Munich?

6. Quotes from *Etude,* p. 35, and June 21 letter to Ritter. On Monday he would visit the Gross-Berlin exhibition where the various competition entries for Berlin's expansion were on display, and, at Ritter's request, he obtained this and the Städtebau catalogues, annotated them, and mailed them off to Munich.

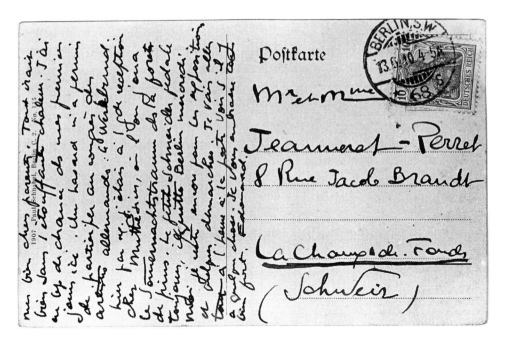

**Fig. 164.** Postcard written by Jeanneret to his parents from Berlin, postmarked June 13, 1910. This typical card mentions his attendance at the Werkbund congress and participation at a reception in the home of Hermann Muthesius. (BV)

stone made from a mixture of cement, pebbles, and sand pressed into a mold, the result being "très beau." Such remarks clearly presage the future, whether it be Jeanneret's subsequent attempts to manufacture cement blocks at Alfortville, his unfortunate experiments with cement guns at Pessac, or his enduring preference for plaster surfaces, often tinted.

Jeanneret also attended certain secessions of the Werkbund congress. His notes, however, include few names, implying an unawareness of who most of the speakers and interlocutors were. Apparently he heard part of a debate between Hermann Muthesius, who was advocating a machine style, standardization, and an acceptance of new materials, and the various adherents of Henry van de Velde, who favored the handicraft tradition of individual artisans. Jeanneret's stance was rapidly advancing toward that of Muthesius.

To terminate the congress, Muthesius held a reception at his home in Nikolassee that Jeanneret attended (fig. 164), Berlin having provided the opportunity to meet, among others, Peter Behrens, Bruno Paul, Hermann Janson, and Wolf Dohrn, the latter being the current director of the Werkbund whom Jeanneret interviewed to obtain (mainly factual) material needed for his *Etude*. Subsequently Jeanneret wrote L'Eplattenier (June 27) that he wished to work for Behrens, Paul (calling his interior designs "of great beauty"), and Janson—the city planner who had won the Gross-Berlin competition and whom Fischer had been most generous in recommending. Jeanneret then made a most revealing comment: "Would you believe that no one, anywhere, willingly believes that I am an architect; they all attribute to me the qualities of a painter." Painting, of course, lay very close to Jeanneret's heart and he noted with great satisfaction that both Behrens and Paul began their careers as painters.

During the following week Jeanneret revisited all the exhibitions, sought out various architects,[7] went to museums, and continued his study of the newer suburbs. Nikolassee, Zehlendorf, and Neu-Babelsberg received special attention and praise. He sketched (Carnet II) their curved streets, the implantation of trees, and made watercolors of two houses that showed direct British influence, one of which was the Georg Schinkedanz house (1909) in Zehlendorf by Ino A. Campbell, an architect of Scottish extraction (fig. 165).[8] Likewise he remarked that "chimneys à la Mackintosh are to be admired." And to Ritter (June 21) he mentioned Hampstead, Bourneville, and Port Sunlight—thus revealing his keen interest in, and considerable familiarity with, the British scene. He also noted how these garden cities, as he called them, radiated out from Berlin like peddles on a flower, with forest areas in between, this in contrast to Paris which had grown in concentric circles. Berlin proper he curtly dismissed as being as monstrous as London yet newer and richer than Munich; of its monumental buildings he made no mention.

Jeanneret also visited numerous museums. At the Kaiser Friedrich he commented favorably on della Robbia's terra-cottas, several Renaissance medallions, and Rembrandt, yet at the National Gallery, where the collections emphasized German nineteenth-century painting, he was disappointed; even the old Flemish, Gothic, and fifteenth/sixteenth-century religious paintings aroused no particular emotion. By contrast, at the spring Berlin Secession exhibition he found much to praise (to Ritter, June 21, 1910) including Matisse for his color, a "très chic" Van Dongen (whose work he had already admired in Paris), Zorn, and Hodler. Three of Cézanne's works particularly enchanted him plus a marvelous but less powerful Renoir. And quite characteristically he remarked that French painting impressed him more than German; in fact, Die Brücke exhibitions are never mentioned. Finally, at the Vereinigte Werkstätten exhibition he found "rien de tout frappant" but did sketch a postcard display-stand that he thought ingenious. Not alluded to is anything to do with Classical art, or the famed Pergamom Museum.

7. Jeanneret listed his schedule for each day and pasted it inside Carnet I. That for June 18 leaves unanswered questions. It reads: "*Samedi* jusqu'à 10 heures mise au net notes. 11 heures Behrens, 2 heures Muthésius, 4 puis 8 heures de nouveau Muthesius. entre temps visite de 2 colonies-jardins." This perhaps implies that he did see Behrens (about a job?) and that he was extremely anxious to see Muthesius (why?) but whether he found him in at 8 p.m. we do not know. Thursday the 16th at 11 a.m. he was "chez Bruno Paul" and presumably found him in.

8. Julius Posener kindly researched for me the identity of these houses. He discovered that the Schinkedanz house still stands at Klopstockstrasse 19 in Berlin-Zehlendorf and was designed in 1909 by Ino A. Campbell, who built numerous houses in greater Berlin prior to the 1914 war. The other house he was unable to locate or identify.

**Fig. 165.** Georg Schinkedanz house, Berlin Zehlendorf, 1909, by Ino A. Campbell, architect, as sketched by Jeanneret in June 1910. Pen and ink and watercolor. 17.2 × 10.7 cm. (Private collection)

A commercial display of extreme interest was that of the furniture buyer and manufacturer Keller und Reiner on Potzdamer Strasse. Nothing previously seen in Berlin, even the Städtebau exhibition, filled so many pages of his Carnet as did this presentation of furniture and furnishings, with some of these sketches being strikingly close to furniture designs executed for the Ditisheims as well as his parents once he returned to La Chaux-de-Fonds.

Monday, June 20, was his last day in Berlin. After packing and visiting the Vereinigte Werkstätten (not particularly impressed), he was off to Potsdam at three o'clock where he remained until 11 p.m., being enraptured by the palace of Sanssouci. It is hard to believe that only the year before, in Paris, Auguste Perret had had such difficulty persuading him to visit Versailles, which Jeanneret had always considered decadent. Now he marveled at the beauty of Louis XV and claimed it to be almost modernistic.[9] He made photographs and sketched the axial plan of the reflecting pool, grand staircase, and palace (of which he painted a watercolor upon his return to Berlin that autumn), he made measured drawings of the arbors as well as profiles of eighteenth-century table legs, and he raved about the palace plan, the dining room, the gallery, the perfect proportions of the library, and especially the orangery (apparently not realizing that this was a nineteenth-century addition).[10]

On Tuesday morning, after eleven days in Berlin, Jeanneret set forth on a whistle-stop tour of medieval towns. At ten he was in Wittenberg, at one in Halle, at four in Naumburg, and at nine o'clock in Weimar where he spent the night. At each stop he bought postcards (2, 5, 10, and 14 respectively),[11] took photos, and made notes concerning the old streets and squares. Jeanneret no longer sketched medieval *buildings,* as in his 1908 visit to Nuremberg, only medieval urban plans—à la Sitte (fig. 166). His infatuation with Gothic architecture—the medieval phase of his formative years—was nearly over and he was already entering his classical phase, having entered through the seventeenth and eighteenth centuries, as we saw at Potsdam. At Wittenberg, for instance, he reserved his praise for "2 maisons en superbe baroque" (II, p. 139).

At Naumburg he spoke of the unity achieved when street facades were of a single material: colored plaster—some ochre, others cobalt green, white, or a diluted emerald green, each being a soft pastel color. In Berlin he had observed the appeal of colored plaster, and soon he would paint a watercolor of a similar street at Mittenwald (July 24, FLC 1760).

Wednesday, June 22, he visited the Art School at Weimar and learned that its director, Henry van de Velde, was in Paris. Nevertheless he took extensive notes and these he edited only slightly before publication in the *Etude* (pp. 68–69). He observed with displeasure that students were not permitted to study nature and that the use of machines was not taught, everything being made by hand. He did find the quality of their work very high, yet thought it lacked much by way of character.

That afternoon he continued on to Jena, where he was much impressed by the new (1905–8) university buildings, filling pages of Carnet II with notes and drawings; likewise he cited them in his *Etude* (p. 52).

9. "Hier je m'emballai à tous crins à Potsdam qui est une pure merveille, évoquant le souvenir de Versailles dans un rococo exquis. Des jardins merveilleux" (to parents, June 21, 1910). The previous evening he wrote to Ritter: "J'ai passé une superbe journée à Sans-Souci, à l'Orangerie, au Belvédère. Le Louis XV y est convainquant de beauté large et moderniste presqu'encore."

10. A selection of his photographs from Potsdam and the ensuing trip are published in *Le Corbusier Viaggio in Oriente,* with introduction and footnotes by Giuliano Gresleri (Venice and Paris: Marsilio Editori and Fondation Le Corbusier, 1984), pp. 113–28.

11. The cards from his trip were discovered in his parents' home at Vevey and are now at the Bibliothèque de la Ville, La Chaux-de-Fonds. Each has a stamp in green ink on the back: "Ch. E. Jeanneret/ Architect/La Chaux-de-Fonds," thus providing a terminal date for its acquisition.

**Fig. 166.** Jeanneret's postcard of Halle showing penciled notes and a sketch of the marketplace on the back, June 1910. (BV)

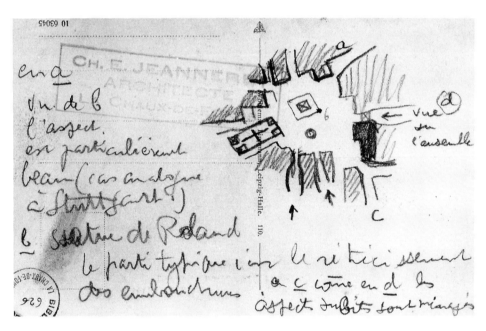

What particularly impressed him was the picturesque harmony achieved between asymmetrical buildings, townscape, and the surrounding hills, and this he contrasted with the more severe sobriety of Bestelmeyer's university buildings at Munich which of necessity conformed to the formalism of Ludwigstrasse. He applauded the effect of the scraped concrete walls, yet perceived that the quality of the design was actually

**Fig. 167.** Charles-Edouard Jeanneret, self-portrait included as part of a letter to William Ritter, dated Munich, June 29, 1910. (National Library, Bern)

dependent upon its proportions—something that could be achieved by the most economic of means. He thought the buildings were much in the spirit of Theodor Fischer and, upon inquiry, learned that Fischer was indeed the architect. So once again he complimented Fischer on being essentially an architect—more so, he believed, than either Behrens or Paul.

At Coburg he spent the night and the following morning, then went on to Lichenfels where he photographed and sketched, both in plan and perspective, the curved approach to the cathedral square before continuing to Bamberg for the afternoon. Würzburg, where he arrived at 8 p.m. and then walked the streets till 10, held far greater attraction; he bought 24 postcards. The highlight, of course, was Balthusar Neumann's eighteenth-century Residenz (and the Sittesque approach to it) with many notes devoted to the decor and painted plaster walls. Then on to Rothenburg to spend the night and following morning before continuing to Augsburg (14 and 10 cards respectively), which was his final stop before arriving at Munich at 9:30 on the evening of Saturday the twenty-fifth of June.

After his eighteen-day trip Jeanneret was exhausted and looked emaciated (fig. 167). Nevertheless, except for certain exhibitions, his interview with Wolf Dohrn, and the visit to the Weimar Art School, he had devoted almost all his energies to research on "La Construction des Villes" rather than the decorative arts in Germany.

His mail, always of primary importance, brought unwanted news; the inauguration of L'Eplattenier's monument, *Hommage à la République,* was being postponed until September. However he decided to return home as planned, toward the end of July, and use the time to improve the "abominable French" of his manuscript; he again conceded how incredibly difficult it was to write a book. Problems of illustrations also plagued him; although twenty photographs from the recent trip were satisfactory, those he requested from municipal authorities in Switzerland were not.

To his parents he wrote (June 29) enthusiastically about his trip; he believed the past three months to be the most fulfilling of his life; at last he was "merveilleusement orienté" toward the future (but within a few months his orientation again would change). He also endeavored to justify his prolonged secrecy about the "La Construction des Villes" while boasting that he and L'Eplattenier had additional plans for the future that could not be divulged.

Another topic was that of his brother Albert who, after fifteen years of expensive tutoring at home and abroad, announced his intention to abandon the violin. His parents were devastated. Edouard, already aware of the decision, leapt to his brother's defense and in page after page of reasoning listed all the positive advantages for Albert's future. Emile Jaques-Dalcroze, the Swiss musician and composer who originated eurythmics and founded the school of eurythmics at Hellerau in 1910, had invited Albert to become his pupil (later, during the 1920s, Albert would teach eurythmics in Paris). Edouard portrayed this as a great opportunity, opening new horizons for Albert and freeing him from a modest career as violin teacher now that it was evident he wouldn't be a virtuoso.

Edouard then applied similar reasoning to himself (his parents often viewing his actions with skepticism) by saying it would be ten times easier to get an architect's diploma at a polytechnic than not to do so. In short, it was better for Albert, and for himself, to struggle like the simple, good-natured men Zarathustra preached about.[12]

This letter also reveals that Jeanneret had met an interesting and well-traveled art history student with whom to resume his German conversation. It was August Klipstein (1885–1951), whose query on a university bulletin board prompted Jeanneret's reply. Their first encounter was at the Staatsbibliothek on June 28 and there began a lasting friendship that drastically modified Jeanneret's future plans. Rather than seeking employment from several German architects, as he had intended, he eventually left Germany the following spring in order to join Klipstein on his travels.

In early July Jeanneret was busily attending exhibitions,[13] taking extensive notes on both furnishings and fabrics (he was always fascinated by fabrics, their colors, and how they were made into window curtains, lamp shades, bed spreads, etc.—his sketch books conclusively demonstrate that he was more interested in interior decoration than in architecture).

He was particularly taken by the décor at the Brakl gallery on Goethestrasse and when he discovered the Brakl house on Lessingstrasse by architect Emanuel von Seidl he thought it truly remarkable, especially for its proportions (fig. 168). He wrote to Ritter (July 8), who had recommended the villa to him, asking whether a visit might be arranged. It was, but not until October when Jeanneret was equally ecstatic about its interior design and decoration (fig. 173). For him it was an ideal example of "modern" (his word) architecture and therefore it provides a precise index to Jeanneret's taste in mid-1910.

Jeanneret saw much of Octave Matthey while in Munich; he also kept L'Eplattenier informed on the progress of the painter's work. On July 21 the two left to go hiking in the Tirol, taking the train to Garmisch and spending the night at a Wiener Neustadt cabin. They then passed the Zugspitze to Rainthal and finally on to Mittenwald, spending each night with peasants. From Mittenwald (July 24) Matthey returned to Munich while Jeanneret stayed on to make a series of watercolors. These included a chapel (fig. 169—observe his choice of classical architecture)[14] as well as a street scene (FLC 1760, as mentioned above) showing uniform house facades of tinted plaster in a variety of soft

12. "Et que, en quelque sorte nous avons un peu de la couleur des cheveux du bonhomme que prêche Zarathoustra" (to parents, June 29, 1910).

13. An exhibition of Mohammedan art at the Munich fair particularly impressed him. He described and sketched vases and other items in Carnet II, pp. 179ff. and enthusiastically commented on the exhibit in the *Étude* p. 33.

14. The verso of this watercolor (FLC 1759) records the dates and itinerary of their trip.

**Fig. 168.** Franz Joseph Brakl house, Munich, ca. 1908. Emanuel von Seidl, architect. Jeanneret considered this a truly remarkable design, perhaps the finest in Munich. (*Die Kunst,* 13 [March 1910], p. 359)

**Fig. 169.** Chapel, Mittenwald, pencil and watercolor sketch by Jeanneret dated July 24, 1910. 26.5 × 20 cm. (FLC 1759)

pastel colors such as he had previously admired in Germany. At 5 o'clock he left for Seefeld on foot, arriving at 8 and staying the night before continuing on to Innsbruck— although not without stopping en route to make another painting (FLC 2199). A rendezvous with Klipstein at Innsbruck had been envisioned but may not have transpired.

By month's end Jeanneret was at home after a four-month absence, arriving some weeks after Albert's return from the conservatory at Geneva. Already the family was installed at Les Endroits where they had summered the previous year, but the weather was so frightfully wet and stormy (as throughout Europe, which was suffering from a cholera epidemic) that papa often spent the night in town. Sundays, however, frequently proved sufficiently pleasant for the family to take their customary all-day hikes.

Edouard's fascination with Jura farmhouses continued unabated, following on his experience of the previous winter. To Ritter he wrote (September 6) that "Since the time of the old eighteenth-century farmhouses we have lacked a true tradition in art. However, these sweet, splendid old houses provide me with a gauge of what we can do if we want." Meanwhile he made watercolors and photographs of many old farms along the valley of La Sagne from La Corbatière to Les Ponts-de-Martel where I counted more than twenty houses bearing lintel dates between 1670 and 1762. His choice of view usually included the chimney or *tué* penetrating through the roof, as at the 1693 farmhouse at Les Coeudres (fig. 170; this house, although not its chimney, still stands). Likewise he made photos and watercolors of where he and his parents spent the summer at 149 and 150 Boulevard des Endroits.

**Fig. 170.** Farmhouse, dated 1693, at Les Coeudres near La Chaux-de-Fonds, as photographed by Jeanneret in September 1910. Note that his choice of viewpoint includes the chimney projecting through the roof. (FLC)

In addition to seeing old school friends, rereading two of Ritter's books (*L'Entêtement slovaque* and *Leurs lys et leurs roses*), and working on "La Construction des Villes" (his mother assisted by neatly transcribing several chapters),[15] Edouard's principal occupation was helping to prepare the festivities surrounding the September 4 inauguration of Charles L'Eplattenier's monument, *Hommage à la République*. Eight years in the making, it stands at the center of an intersection facing the Hôtel de Ville. The four-sided bronze allegorically treats major events in the establishment of Neuchâtel as a canton within the Swiss Confederation, the first of which, in 1831, resulted in the death of one of Edouard's maternal grandparents and the second, the revolution of 1848, saw his grandfather participate in the historic march on Neuchâtel.

The magnitude of these celebrations was overwhelming. In addition to local inhabitants, 15,000 people arrived by train, including the president of Switzerland; the resulting crowd at the inauguration was incredible (fig. 171). And at the Parc des Sports, 5,000 paid to attend a series of presentations, with all the newspapers agreeing that the highlight was "The Dead Merovingian King Brought Back from the War" with music specially composed and directed by Albert Jeanneret and with sets and costumes designed by his brother Edouard.[16]

Although the press was overwhelmed by the festivities, their praise was more muted concerning the sculpture that was the raison d'être for the whole affair. Even Edouard, in his letter to William Ritter, was reserved in his assessment of its artistic merit.[17]

Nevertheless this letter reaffirms Jeanneret's affection for L'Eplattenier ("L'Eplattenier . . . me plaît toujours plus") and thrice restates his attachment to his homeland ("dans ce pays que j'aime toujours plus").[18] Therefore his interest in creating a regional style

15. Jeanneret's difficulty with expressing himself in writing was reiterated in his letter to Ritter of September 6:" Je m'étais fourré dans la tête de terminer mon étude sur la construction des villes. Hélas, hélas! de quoi me suis-je mêlé? Vous ne sauriez croire la difficulté que j'ai de m'exprimer en français; j'ânonne des heures sur une page et rien ne se fait."

16. "Nous avions monté, mon frère et moi, pour la représentation populaire en plein air . . . une scènerie mimée avec musique (orchestre et choeur) qui laissa la foule parfaitement indifférente" (letter to Ritter, September 6, 1910).

17. Jeanneret merely called it "un monument qui, s'il n'est pas un chef-d'oeuvre, marque dans l'histoire de la sculpture contemporaine une belle étape."

18. This entire paragraph of September 6, 1910, is worth quoting: "Pour nous, nous aimons toujours plus notre pays, et, à cause de son caractère puissant nous pensons devoir le doter d'un art autochtone. Comment y réussirons-nous? Certes il nous fait beaucoup étudier les mouvements d'art des pays voisins et peu à peu y découvrir la marque de notre époque. La Chaux-de-Fonds est une tache lépreuse. Vous avez

**Fig. 171.** Charles L'Eplattenier's monument, *Hommage à la République,* with the massive crowd attending its dedication on September 4, 1910. This event brought Jeanneret back from Germany during the summer of 1910. (BV)

of art and architecture remained very much alive and we can easily comprehend why he returned to La Chaux-de-Fonds, and to L'Eplattenier, at the end of the following year.

On September 17 he left for Germany intent upon obtaining employment with Peter Behrens, in spite of some foreboding about living in Berlin.[19] Likewise he would continue work on "La Construction des Villes" for which L'Eplattenier had suggested new topics, hoping to give greater breadth to the book; these were cemeteries, parks, gardens, garden cities, and bridges. His research was fruitful, except concerning bridges, which he acknowledged he had never even looked at before. He visited cemeteries, parks, and gardens as his sketchbooks attest. Obviously he enjoyed research, but not writing, and now, several months down the line, his enthusiasm was muted by the magnitude of the task still before him.[20] Meanwhile he ultimately postponed work on *Etude sur le mouvement d'art décoratif en Allemagne,* for which he had received his grant, until April of the following year.

---

vraiment trouvé le terme qui caractérise cette agglomération incohérente de laideurs. Mais il y souffle un vent d'idéalisme vivant qui est très remarquable et qui nous donne plein espoir. Nous n'avons depuis les vieilles fermes du XVIII siècle plus aucune tradition d'art. Mais ces vieilles et splendides maisons me donnent justement la mesure de ce que nous pourrons faire si nous voulons. Il est étonnant aussi de voir le nombre de jeunes gens, qui dans tous les domaines, cherchent chez nous, à se rallier pour former un bloc efficace."

19. Obviously he wanted a job with Behrens very much. Otherwise he simultaneously might have been seeking employment with Fischer, Paul, or Jansen, all of whom were on his list.

20. Letters of September 30 to Klipstein and October 1 to L'Eplattenier. It's curious that Jeanneret didn't remain at home an additional week in order to attend the Union des Villes Suisses conference at which L'Eplattenier read his paper on "L'esthétique des villes."

He returned to Munich via Zurich in order to attend an exhibition (presumably that at the Gewerbeschule) that he recommended to L'Eplattenier both for its displays as well as for some of its furnishings that seemed particularly appropriate for the new post office at La Chaux-de-Fonds. He also visited the Musée National as well as a new (1908) church by Karl Moser, St. Anton's, where he was deeply impressed by its stripped Romanesque forms.

Once back in Munich, at Lotzbeckstrasse, Jeanneret penned a long, chatty letter to L'Eplattenier concerning the latter's newest commission, a commemorative statue of the local patriot Numa Droz to be placed beside the small park just south of the railroad station (but not executed until 1914–17). Jeanneret commiserated over the problem of obtaining, in the current day and age, a suitable "ambiance of beauty" for works of art, and forthwith proposed a design for a plaza in front of the station (fig. 172). It is a striking scheme wherein he successfully synthesized both classical and romantic elements into a single plan, one aspect being formal, symmetrical, and strongly axial, the other picturesque with an unfolding series of intimate, closed, and ever-changing views—à la Sitte. The Numa Droz statue is shown on axis with the station, yet in front of a semicircular setting labeled CC. The dotted line represents the route of a meandering pedestrian passing along the Boulevard Léopold Robert but taking a short detour past the station.[21]

From a letter of September 30 to August Klipstein, declining the latter's kind invitation to visit the family home at Laubach, we learn that Jeanneret was seriously considering a relaxing sojourn in Rome, including leisurely walks in parks and gardens and studying the work of Bramante (sic!). Rome, not Athens, would remain his priority even after they agreed to travel together. In February Jeanneret still argued in favor of Rome, yet consented to go by way of Constantinople; in March, when he first men-

21. Jeanneret's description of the plan is worth quoting:

La rue Léop. Robert me plait même passablement lors qu'on la regarde de la gare vers la [church] tour. Elle a même du caractère, mais du côté du Locle [right on the plan], c'est une souffrance. . . . Mon croquis montre une chose ramenée à une bonne unité. Deux fers à cheval se fermant sur la gare, formés de maisons à un étage à toiture tranquille, bordés à rez-de-chaussée d'arcades ou de boutiques, plein-cintres s'accordant, en leur laissant leur valeur, aux trois grandes baies de la gare et aux baies de la [bureau de] poste [to the left of A]. En A un grand bâtiment de cube analogue à celui de la poste par, peut-être une banque ou d'autre administration permettant des rez-de-chaussée surélevés. . . . De cette place de la gare on sortirait dans une autre plus petite bordée par l'edifice B, jeté au travers du "podium." Les deux petites maison CC subsisteraient mais seraient modifiées dans leur couleur et peut-être leur toiture. Un fer à cheval les relieraient. Les arbres seraient enlevés devant la poste. Un édicule (bureau de renseignements ou baraque à fruit, à journaux, etc) E nuirait[?] fictivement notre petite place ECBA dont tout le cadre, hormis la poste pourrait être fait en architecture harmonisée. Alors là, le monument N.D. [Numa Droz]. . . . Et La Chaux-de-Fonds aurait une plus digne entrée (letter to L'Eplattenier, October 1, 1910).

**Fig. 172.** Jeanneret's proposal for modifying the Place de la Gare at La Chaux-de-Fonds and thereby creating an appropriate setting for L'Eplattenier's statue of Numa Droz. Late September 1910. Ink and watercolor. 10.3 × 12 cm. (FLC)

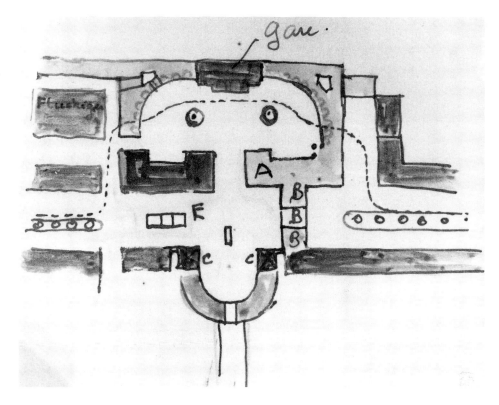

tioned the subject to his parents, he signified that his destination would be Rome.[22]

On October 4, Jeanneret's wish to visit the Franz Joseph Brakl house by Emanuel von Seidl was fulfilled. Accompanied by William Ritter, Janko Cádra, and Marcel Montandon, he had plenty of time to fill eight pages of Carnet III with notes and sketches as well as watercolors of two of the rooms—the living room and the great stair hall (fig. 173).[23] His notations, as seen in our illustration and transcribed in the

22. To Klipstein he wrote on February 13, 1911: "Je quitte Behrens le 1er avril et ai décidé de finir mes études—dans le rêve. J'avais pour cela songé à Rome. Je maintien à Rome, mais serais d'accord d'y aller par Constantinople."

And on March 6 Jeanneret senior wrote in his journal: "Edouard va 'requitter' Berlin et l'architecte Behrens pour entreprendre dès le 1r avril un grand voyage en Allemagne et peut-être à Rome!!" As things evolved, Edouard visited Rome alone, Klipstein returning home before the two reached Italy.

23. A transcription of Jeanneret's text on these two pages follows:

portes de la salle de réception. Un tapis fourrure noire brillante s'étale au travers de la pièce. (splendide) des canapés fixes à chaque bout avec 3 et 4 coussins ensemble. plafond blanc. Les 4 panneaux de Fritz Erler les 4 éléments ornent largement, dans leurs larges cadre argent-or. (faisant la tonalité d'un tronc de Bouleau) ces cadres à mouluration ample et visqueuse—Les 2 grande portes qui donnent dans le hall sont alors plaquées en brun et noir (ce noir est plutôt du chêne fumé très sombre)—damier [and on p. 29] la couverte n'est qu'une planche noire dont on ne voit que la

footnote, are typical, being characteristic of an interior decorator rather than an architect. Nowhere does he discuss interior space or the arrangement of rooms but only fabrics, furniture, picture frames, carpets, and especially colors—of which his fondness for black and white is evident.[24] He is tremendously impressed, saying that few things he has ever seen have given him such pleasure.[25]

Carnet III records several things that interest Jeanneret, including the sunken garden at the Military Museum, the new Waldfriedhof cemetery, views of the Englischer Garten, a marionette theater, and a long discussion of the Künstler Theater by Max Littmann with its simplified stage arrangement where Fritz Erler designed the current production of Hamlet. However the adjacent Theater Café, as well as the theater building itself, left him relatively unimpressed, and he concluded that "In sum the Fledermaus cabaret at Vienna was incomparably better, much better from the point of view of the architecture and materials employed."[26] And his final sketchbook entry prior to moving to Berlin were several pages devoted to German Bestelmeyer's 1908 University of Munich building (especially its interiors) that Jeanneret had particularly admired, and bought numerous interior postcards of, earlier that year.[27]

Jeanneret was becoming increasingly impatient with the lack of response from Behrens, so impulsively he left Munich on October 17, stopping ten hours at Regensburg where he sketched St. Emmeram's both inside and out, then spent an uncomfortable night in a third-class railway coach while continuing to Berlin. Upon arrival he was in no mood to learn that Behrens was absent, yet an appointment was arranged for Friday (it then being Tuesday) which was subsequently canceled due to the death of Behrens' mother-in-law and the grave illness of his wife. Not withstanding such valid reasons,

---

tranche moulures négatives en faisceau—Ce Hall tout blanc tout en forms gauches blanches avec seule la balustrade, mais par le limon, sombre (chêne sombre poli).

For excellent photos of the house, see "Das Haus Brakl in München," *Die Kunst*, 13 (March 1910), pp. 358ff.

24. In his ongoing fascination with the color white, he notes on page 25 of Carnet III, "Il faudrait, dans chacune de mes maisons, ménager une fosse à chaux blanche afin que soit incité le propriétaire à retaper chaque année ses façades."

25. "C'est une des choses vues qui m'a fait le plus plaisir. Il n'y a pas le comfort anglais (préraphaélite) de Muthesius. Il y a moins d'éclate que Bruno Paul. Mais il y a de l'ampleur beaucoup" (Carnet III, p. 33).

26. Note this belated appreciation of Josef Hoffmann, whose architecture Jeanneret had rejected while in Vienna in 1908.

Perhaps his sudden interest in theater design relates to a project undertaken by the Atelier at La Chaux-de-Fonds since his Künstler Theater discussion ends with this sentence: "Il y aurait dans *notre* [emphasis mine] petit théâtre des choses à essayer, mais je préférerais disposer de 10 ou 15 mètres de scène" (Carnet III, p. 8).

27. Concurrent with Carnet III, which served more as a journal or notebook, Jeanneret was using his larger Green Carnet wherein he made sketches at Westerndorf, Freising, Regensburg, Donaustauf, Dresden, and elsewhere. Therein is also a brief quote from Marc-Antoine Laugier, whose *Essai sur l'architecture* was published in 1753. Thus, by October 1910 if not before, Jeanneret was reading Laugier.

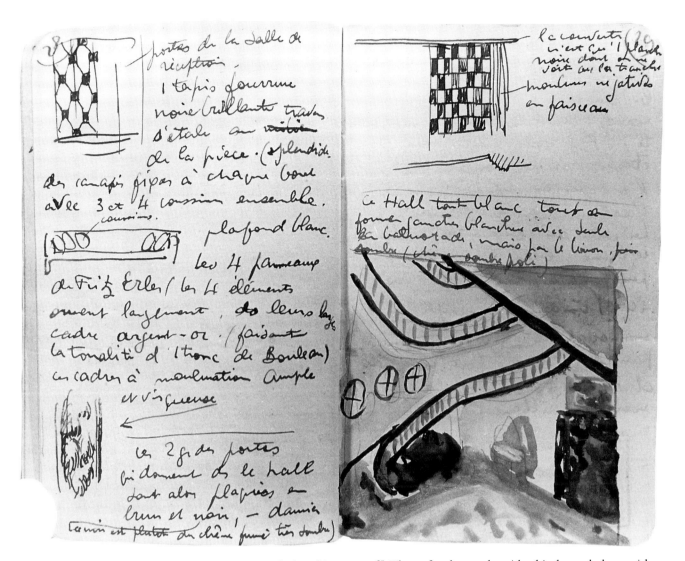

**Fig. 173.** Franz Joseph Brakl house, Munich. Facing pages of Carnet III showing Jeanneret's verbal and pictorial notes made during visit to this house on October 4, 1910. Pen and ink and watercolor. Each sheet 17 × 10 cm. (Private collection)

Jeanneret utterly lost his temper.[28] Thereafter he rarely said a kind word about either Behrens or Berlin and gradually his dislike embraced most things German—irrespective of how much he was favorably influenced by them.

Jeanneret always polarized his emotions; it was love or hate with little in between. The polarity for Behrens and Berlin was now set. This was confirmed when Jeanneret learned, once he began working, that Behrens was really a boss and not a father figure

28. That night (October 20) he wrote his parents: "Berlin ne me conquiert pas, et dès que l'on sort des immenses avenues, c'est de l'écoeurement, de l'horreur. Je passe par toutes sortes d'états d'esprit; aujourd'-hui, alors que je pensais dans une heure être face à face avec le monstre [Behrens], j'étais persuadé qu'il ne [illegible words in original] être autrement que de la réussite. Aller dans les musées me dégoûte d'avance. Le mal a pris chez moi une tournure pathologique."

like Perret. And to make matters worse, Jeanneret, for the first time in his life, was holding down a full-time job (with Perret he had worked half days). For someone accustomed to being carefree and independent, coming and going as he pleased, this was a new and very demanding situation. And contrary to Vienna, Paris, and Munich, Berlin was the first city where none of Jeanneret's school chums were present for companionship when it was needed (Schneider having left in August).[29] Nor did the people speak French. On the one hand Jeanneret prized his independence, yet on the other he needed assurance and support. He routinely had trouble making friends with those his own age, due partly to social ineptitude but largely to his sense of insecurity which he dared not reveal among his peers (only to older men). Of these concerns, however, he was free when among his friends from the Ecole d'art where his stature was secure.

Jeanneret's almost pathological dislike of Behrens stemmed from his damaged pride at Behrens' failure to immediately offer him a job, and these feelings intensified when the most famous and busiest architect of the day found neither the time nor inclination to single out his newest employee and offer help, friendship, and even a little affection.[30] Only a person like Jeanneret would have had the audacity to assume that such special attention was his due! Behrens was probably the first important person who failed to treat him with deference, and this Jeanneret would not excuse.

Jeanneret freely admitted to being a masochist, and to intensify his suffering he denied himself many of his former pleasures. He virtually stopped attending concerts and the opera,[31] he stopped going to museums, he nearly stopped visiting or sketching architecture, he stopped making paintings, he stopped (with one known exception) reading books, he moved from a comfortable room into a less comfortable mansard, he largely abandoned work on "La Construction des Villes" and research for his *Etude*. He became a recluse and, in short, did everything possible to fuel his hatred of Behrens and Berlin.[32] By mid-winter, however, he would begin to mellow. Meanwhile, briefly

29. Feeling particularly lonely, he complained bitterly to L'Eplattenier that except for Hagen none of his friends bothered to see him off during his recent departure from La Chaux-de-Fonds, nor did they ever write.

30. "Et puis Behrens lui, ne sait que nous terroriser; nous ne trouvons là aucune sollicitude, aucune affection" (to Ritter, December 14, 1910).

31. Ritter, through friends, arranged for Jeanneret to review concerts and operas in Berlin for the musical journal *S.I.M.,* thereby receiving excellent reserved seats for free. After much back-and-forth, Jeanneret declined, making the lame excuse of pressure of work and the cost of an 80 pfennig train ticket. Thereafter, for five months, he heard almost no music in Berlin—unlike in Vienna, Paris, and Munich where he regularly paid the price of admission. The idea of comfortable reserved seats in the best part of the house was not to his liking.

32. Jeanneret always acknowledged that he loved what he lost and lost what he loved, and within a year he would write Ritter (November 25, 1911) that the time had already come when Germany was beginning to benefit from his tender feelings and that "Je verse des larmes sur Munich et presque sur Behrens."

fleeing Berlin was his one great pleasure, and this he did with an occasional visit to his brother.

Albert had moved to Dresden early in October to study eurythmics under Emile Jaques-Dalcroze and therefore it was to Dresden that Jeanneret fled on October 21.[33] But first he visited Zehlendorf (which he had admired in June) where he interviewed the developers, then lavished praise (Carnet III) on Alfred Messel's Wertheim department store as well as on the displays and products available therein; most especially it was the folk arts that particularly impressed him (see *Etude* pp. 38–39).

On Saturday the twenty-second the brothers toured Dresden; Jeanneret was reasonably impressed by the baroque/rococo architecture that he saw. Sunday and Monday they spent at Hellerau, where they went on a tour of the Vereinigte Deutsche Werkstätten factory, a detailed description of which filled twelve pages of Carnet II. He showed particular interest in both the quality and efficiency of the machinery (some imported from America), the cleanliness of the shops (he was fascinated by the built-in vacuum-cleaner system), the white walls, and the natural pine furniture. Apprenticeships, he noted, lasted three years and cost 800 marks, the day was eight-and-a-half hours long, and although well-known artists provided their designs for free they received a royalty on the sales. Jeanneret liked the factory's architectural style with its steep gabled roofs but was less impressed by Richard Riemerschmid's house designs than by those of Fischer, Baillie Scott, and Muthesius. Two furnished houses were on display and both received Jeanneret's enthusiastic praise, especially for their furnishings. He made no mention, however, of Ebenezer Howard's having influenced the plan of Hellerau which, along with Riemerschmid's house designs, would influence his 1914 project for Arnold Beck at La Chaux-de-Fonds.[34]

Returning to Berlin on the Tuesday morning express, Jeanneret was welcomed with the news of his employment with Peter Behrens which would begin November 1—

33. He might profitably have used this time to visit the great Brussels international exhibition of April–November 1910 that was being reviewed in all the periodicals. The German presentation was especially impressive and included works by all those whom Jeanneret most admired. "Emanuel von Seidl exemplifies the solid Munich style, Bruno Paul the elegance of Berlin, Peter Behrens typifies the iron vigor of industrialism, and Kreis manifests the mysterious pathos of the thoughtful man," wrote Robert Breuer in *German Arts and Crafts at the Brussels Exhibition of 1910* (Stuttgart: Julius Hoffman, n.d., n.p.). Von Seidl designed both the main and the flanking buildings, the restaurant and the beer garden, Behrens did the Railway Hall and the Engineering Hall, while the fine arts rooms were by Bruno Paul, whose vestibule, as previously noted, was probably the source for L'Eplattenier's vestibule at the Neuchâtel observatory of 1911. Jeanneret knew of the exhibition from publications (he refers to it in a letter to L'Eplattenier of January 16, 1911) and von Seidl's German pavilion perhaps influenced his entranceway at the Villa Favre-Jacot of 1912. Why Jeanneret missed this important event that was so central to his *Etude* is difficult to understand.

34. In his *Etude*, pp. 49–50, Jeanneret restates many of his notes from Carnet III and adds a section on the financial arrangements for home ownership as well as a discussion of Jaques-Dalcroze's Institute.

exactly one year after leaving Auguste Perret. Hours were 8:30 till 1 and 2 till 6, and Saturday 8:30 till 1. Wages to be determined at month's end; by March he was earning a tidy 180 marks. Immediately he took a room bei Frau Folk, 83 Stahnsdorferstrasse, Neubabelsberg, near the office (a one-storey building in the garden of Behrens' home) and near where four other of Behrens' thirteen (later he said twenty-three) draftsmen (age twenty-three to twenty-seven) lived. He described his room as very large and comfortable, and what with balcony, central heating, and breakfast he paid 28 marks; a good dinner at noon, eaten with his fellow draftsmen (excellent opportunity for German conversation), cost one mark while his light supper he prepared in his room. His neighbors he found very musical and noisy, however, and the comfort of his room conflicted with his implicit need to suffer, so at month's end he moved into a mansard next door at No. 81 bei Riedel (fig. 174).

He referred to Neubabelsberg as a garden city twenty-five minutes by train from Berlin's center and five minutes from Potsdam where, with his new-found respect for rococo architecture, he visited Sanssouci on October 28 and again on Saturday afternoon November 5 when he made a watercolor of the palace from the reflecting pool (FLC 2857). He probably also saw Schinkel's Potsdam buildings at this time.

During his days prior to commencing work, Jeanneret attended the Joseph Olbrich retrospective at the Akademie der Künste where he found the drawings finicky and dry: "One does not have the impression of being in front of a great man, a thinker" (Carnet III, p. 65). Later, upon reflection, he acknowledged Olbrich's historic contribution yet remained unimpressed by his dry and thin (sèche et mince) decoration. Another exhibit, organized by the Deutsches Museum at Hagen and subsequently discussed in his *Etude* (p. 27), focused on packaging (wrapping papers, box design). He was particularly impressed by various Wiener Werkstätte and Künstgewerbeschule designs and made several sketches in his notebook. However, shortly after October 27, there is a lapse in Carnet III until February 11, and thereafter the entries are far less revealing except for the frequent and enthusiastic references to furnishings in black and white.

On October 28 he wrote his parents, L'Eplattenier, and Ritter announcing his new job and new address, reassuring his parents (in an act of self-justification) that none of the draftsmen in Behrens' office had degrees or were intending to get them, musing to Ritter how wonderful Munich and Paris seemed now that he had left them, and complaining to L'Eplattenier that his school friends never wrote. Obviously he was very lonely.

Ritter, meanwhile, recommended that he read *Les Entretiens de la villa du Rovet; essais dialogués sur les arts plastiques en Suisse romande* by Alexandre Cingria-Vaneyre (Geneva, 1908), a book that, in addition to confirming many views that Jeanneret already held, influenced him profoundly. Perhaps nothing since Provensal's *L'Art de demain* had such an impact. In addition to marginal brackets he wrote comments such as that on the final page (p. 383) "Fini de lire le 22 nov 1910 à Neu-Babelsberg" which continued by expressing his complete agreement with the "inspired" text that would allow him to reorientate himself and "unlock for me the German vice. In a year, at Rome, I will reread it, and, in my sketches, lay the foundations for my own Jura, Neuchâtelois discipline."

Cingria-Vaneyre's thesis was that the Suisse romande (French-speaking Switzerland) was unique within the Swiss confederation for the purity of its racial stock which, unlike in other cantons, was not diluted by German or Italian influences. Rather its peoples were of Greco-Latin stock that had survived since Roman times in remote Jura valleys and the mountains around Geneva—mountains, incidently, that he compared sympathetically to those in Greece. Meanwhile the popular or folk art of these isolated enclaves had preserved ancient classical values that, according to the author, must be reintroduced into the region's architecture. He is never specific about how this new architecture should look, except to say that it must not imitate classical building types, such as temples, but should be "of regular features and calm" and have a "geometric treatment" (p. 262)—opposite which, in the margin, Jeanneret wrote "Des idées . . . absolument positive au Haut Jura."

These elitist and often racist themes draw heavily on a rather warped interpretation of the Comte de Gobineau's *Essai sur l'inégalité des races humains* (1853–55), which is quoted at length and serves as a kind of model.[35] Yet for Jeanneret Cingria-Vaneyre resolved certain problems that had plagued him since Paris when his quest for an ideal began. L'Eplattenier's call for a Jura style was now accorded renewed validity as well as a rationale.[36] Also accommodated was Jeanneret's more recent wish to learn from the lesson of Rome.[37] Likewise it helped justify his growing resentment toward Germany. "A remarkable book, written *for us*" he wrote to L'Eplattenier, and henceforth he had even better reasons for returning to La Chaux-de-Fonds to help originate a Jura style.[38]

One of Jeanneret's inner thoughts is revealed by his marking in Cingria-Vaneyre of this passage in the précis of Chapter 2: "An individual's influence on the artistic destiny of a people" and the subsequent marking in the text (p. 98) of the relevant statement: "man more often transforms the country where he lives than the earth influences the people who inhabit it." Thus Jeanneret senses that he has a preordained role on earth, just as he did while learning of the world's great prophets in books by Renan and Schuré.[39]

Once in the Behrens office Jeanneret wrote (as at Perret's) much about the man but little about his own activities there. The "bear" ("l'ours"), as he called Behrens, was repeatedly referred to as autocratic, tyrannical, and a brute who terrorized the office staff. As an architect he was severely criticized for having excessive concern for form and for taking inspiration from the Doric and Empire styles. But most of all he was

35. Gobineau is discussed at length in Jeanneret's January 16, 1911, letter to L'Eplattenier wherein, because Cingria-Vaneyre asserted that Gobineau said German influence had a negative effect, Jeanneret concluded that Gobineau's prediction had failed to foresee how formidable Germany would become.

36. Cingria-Vaneyre concurred with L'Eplattenier's thoughts on the decorative arts, saying of nature "Il fournit les motifs . . . de sa flore ou de sa faune aux styles décoratifs" (p. 144). He also evoked such Jeanneret favorites as Ruskin, Corroyer, and Sitte, the latter's medieval romanticizing being reinterpreted as possessing certain Greco-Latin values and ideals.

37. This phrase, "La Leçon de Rome," would become a chapter heading in his 1923 book, *Vers une architecture*.

38. It is a notable coincidence that Jeanneret's reading of Cingria-Vaneyre occurred just two years after his oft-published letter to L'Eplattenier of November 1908 that biographers repeatedly cite as "proof" of Jeanneret's permanent rupture with L'Eplattenier, an assumption that left inexplicable his return to La Chaux-de-Fonds in 1912. However, throughout this and the previous chapter I have, I believe, made clear that, for the time being at least—and despite his ever-changing moods—Jeanneret's loyalty to L'Eplattenier and his cause continued as the dominant influence in his life.

39. Jeanneret's on-going interest in Cingria-Vaneyre is confirmed by his December (25?), 1913, statement to Ritter: "La Cingria-Vaneyre lu en 1909 [1910, actually] me reste toujours présent à la mémoire, il exprimait trop clairement beaucoup de ce que je sentais." By 1916 the two had met, and during several years a correspondence ensued. Another book purchased in November 1910, was Dante, *La Divine Comédie*, which, except for a signature and date, gives no real indication of being read.

condemned for a lack of honesty because he was interested in the flesh of a building rather than—as with Perret—the bones.[40] Nevertheless, as years passed, Jeanneret/Le Corbusier would embrace all of these characteristics that Behrens was condemned for.

Deep down, Jeanneret had great respect for Behrens, but this caused a certain inner conflict. During five months in the office Jeanneret learned more about architecture than he had ever learned before. "Chez Behrens, the shock has been brutal" he wrote L'Eplattenier on January 16, "I arrived at Behrens' knowing almost nothing about what was a style, and totally ignorant of the art of profiles and their harmonious relation. I assure you it isn't easy. And yet it is these relationships that give rise to harmonious form. . . . Behrens rigidly insists upon rhythm and subtle proportions and so many other things that were entirely unknown to me."[41] And two days earlier he had confided to Ritter: "I like Behrens so much as a man, as a male, that to maintain any admiration I have decided that he is ill." And in this same letter Jeanneret defines an architect: "I consider that an architect must, above all, be a thinker. His art, which consists of harmonious abstractions, lacks the possibility to describe or to depict except by symbol."

Of others in the Behrens office Jeanneret was not specific, saying merely that "Among my many colleagues I cannot even make an acquaintance, let alone a real friend" (to Ritter, December 12, 1910). Simultaneously he acknowledged that they were nice, courteous, polite, and refrained from hazing the newcomer. This seems to reflect his usual social ineptitude. And as usual he was greatly concerned about his clothing, noting that his fellow workers were better and more fashionably dressed than he.

Whereas history records that Walter Gropius and Ludwig Mies van der Rohe were in the Behrens office in 1910, both left earlier that year and Gropius, with Adolf Meyer, was then designing the famous Fagus Factory at Alfeld-an-der-Leine. Mies' stay spanned almost the same period, late 1907 to 1910, but in 1911 (the year he designed the Perls house in Zehlendorf) he returned to Behrens to supervise the ill-fated Kröller project at The Hague in Holland, at which time (spring 1911) he was briefly introduced

40. By January 4, 1911, Jeanneret already began to question whether Behrens, rather than Perret, wasn't right: "Chez Behrens on n'y fait pas de pure architecture. C'est de la façade. Les hérésies constructives abondent. D'architecture moderniste on n'en fait pas. *Peut-être est-ce plus sage—plus sage que les élucubrations peu classiques des Perret frères* [emphasis mine]. Perret frères avaient l'avantage de chercher beaucoup avec les matériaux nouveaux. Behrens lui, serait un protestataire." (Quoted from Jean Petit, *Le Corbusier lui-même,* p. 38; Petit gives no source for this quotation.)

41. It is clear from these remarks that Jeanneret was more than one who traced construction drawings but was, by mid-January, involved in making decisions as to where these lines should be drawn. It is also clear that he was learning ways of achieving harmonious proportions, a subject then so central to the practice of architecture in Germany and Holland. When he subsequently implied (in *Vers une architecture,* etc.) to have originated the *tracé régulateur* it is merely another instance of his refusal to acknowledge his debt to Germany.

to Jeanneret.[42] Mies was just eighteen months older than Jeanneret yet obviously more precocious.

In 1910 Peter Behrens (1868–1940) was preeminent in the profession and at the height of his creative powers. Rarely in modern times has an architect enjoyed such diverse and prestigious patronage ranging from commissions for embassies and private homes to total artistic control over all that was needed or produced by such a powerful conglomerate as AEG—German General Electric. For this industrial giant Behrens designed everything from stationery to factories as well as many of the products produced therein, whether street lights or electric fans. His most famous work, the AEG Turbine Factory, had just been completed; in various stages of design or construction were his Small Motors Factory (construction began late in 1910), the High Tension Factory, the Hennigsdorf Workers Housing (mentioned by Jeanneret in his *Etude*, p. 44), and the boathouse Elektra, all for AEG. Also, he began making designs for the Wiegand house in Dahlem. And by January 1911 he began working on the five-storey head office for the Mannesmann-Röhrenwerke at Düsseldorf, a stone-clad steel frame building, and later that year started work on the Goedeche house at Eppenhauser, the Assembly Hall (Montagehall) for AEG, and the German Embassy at St. Petersburg, Russia. All this with perhaps twenty draftsmen in the office! Initially Jeanneret was assigned to the Bootshaus Elektra drawings yet complained to his parents of the relaxed work pace when Behrens was absent and that he himself had no significant responsibilities.[43]

The design of the Elektra boathouse (fig. 175) is characteristic of Behrens's smaller buildings, that is, a rigid geometric shape enlivened by simplified classical elements that are linear and geometric, whereas his larger buildings—whether factories or an embassy—have heavier, more sculptured forms and an even greater emphasis on massiveness. It is this thinner, more delicate rendering of simplified classical forms, owing much to Schinkel, that finds expression in Jeanneret's own work, as at the Villa Favre-Jacot of 1912 where the circular stairway is perhaps indebted to the Behrens Cuno

**Fig. 175.** Elektra boathouse, Berlin, 1910, Peter Behrens, architect. River facade. See figure 398 for the street facade. (Fritz Hoeber, *Peter Behrens* [Munich, 1913], p. 159)

42. Based on a letter received from Mies van der Rohe, Stanislaus von Moos reports (*Le Corbusier: Elements of a Synthesis* [Cambridge & London, 1979], p. 12) that Mies "recalled having met a certain Jeanneret on the doorsteps of Behrens' office." In 1907 Mies had built the Riehl house in Neubabelsberg after apprenticing for two years with Bruno Paul; Behrens, upon seeing the house, had immediately hired Mies.

43. As this is the only time that Jeanneret discussed his work, I quote the entire passage: "Pour moi, je me désole d'être constamment sans ouvrage, car je suis habitué, même chez Perret où j'avais en somme une responsabilité, à débrancher. Tandis qu'autour de moi on chôme, on chante, on dit des farces etc. Mentalité de ces compagnons? J'en reparlerai dans quelques mois. Ce que je fais? Pour le moment une grande bicoque, 'Bootshaus Elektra,' espèce de cercle-club pour les ouvriers de l'A.E.G." (to parents, November 12, 1910). Thus it is understandable why Behrens "terrorized" the office when he was there as no one took work very seriously while he was away. Also the letter refutes what others have claimed, that Jeanneret *designed* the boathouse Elektra.

house of 1909–10 at Eppenhausen near Hagen. Also the cornice of this house, synthesized with certain Jura prototypes, would reappear at Jeanneret's 1916 Villa Schwob while his parents' house of 1912 owes something to the Schröder house and gazebo of 1908–9 which originally stood beside the Cuno residence. Of almost similar date is the Catholic Community House at Neuss am Rhein which, as other Behrens buildings of the period, has a precisely cut arcade, lacking both moldings or imposts, and this motif is repeated on the garden facade of Jeanneret's Villa Favre-Jacot. All of these Behrens designs were of course available to Jeanneret at the office and most of them he actually visited.

Previously unknown is the possibility that Jeanneret assisted with drawings for the Wiegand house at Dahlem, a suburb of Berlin. The evidence consists of two documents, one being a blueprint of the garden layout on which, in black ink on the dark blue paper (and therefore not visible in our illustration), Jeanneret wrote "Peter Behrens/Neu-Babelsberg." The blueprint itself is dated "Okt. 1910," the month prior to his arrival (fig. 176). Jeanneret, we may recall, had also saved prints from Perret's office, adding similar notations in ink. The second is a sketch by Jeanneret of the plan of the house with the following notation: "See on another sheet the garden plan," which apparently refers to the blueprint (fig. 177). This interesting sketch does not precisely correspond to the house as built (fig. 178), nor to the outline of the house on the blueprint. The variations are small yet significant. They occur in the relationship of the peristyle to the street and to the depth of the setback of the house at the right side behind the peristyle. Jeanneret's sketch, like the final plan but unlike the blueprint, aligns the peristyle (which is not yet partly open to the sky) to the sidewalk, but the setback of the house remains three bays rather than one in depth. The subsequent reduction to one bay increases the volume of the house and permits the introduction of a large entrance hall.

Where in the evolution of the Wiegand plan does Jeanneret's sketch fit in? Did he trace it from an existing plan, or was he proposing this to Behrens? The answer is perhaps less significant than his interest in the garden layout and the plan itself (which recalls the Cuno house with its U-shaped configuration of major rooms). Noteworthy is the absence of any elevation drawings that show how the house would look, the design of which is more in the spirit of Schinkel than either the Cuno or the Schröder house. The peristyle is especially appropriate for Theodor Wiegand, the archaeologist who excavated at Didyma, Samos, and Miletus and was then serving as director of antiquities for the Royal Prussian Museums. An open peristyle would later appear in Jeanneret's 1915 house project called Le Moulinet (fig. 336) but otherwise the Wiegand design left a less significant legacy to Jeanneret than the designs already discussed.

What other works Jeanneret assisted with are unknown, but his concurrent exposure, in actuality or through magazines, to German furniture design and interior decoration was of great and lasting significance. It is especially amazing to observe, after his studied

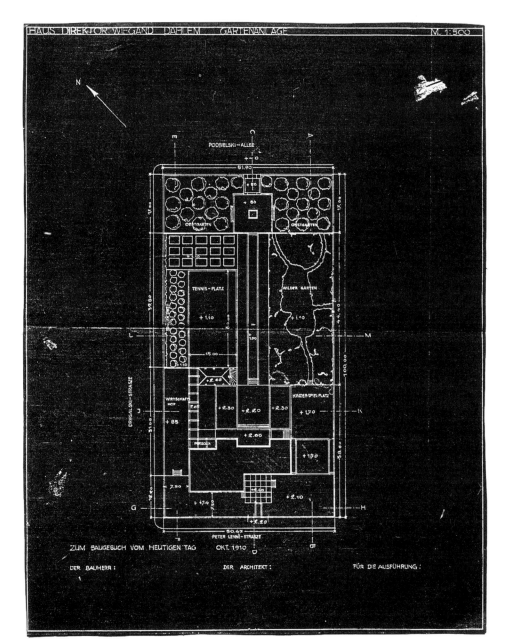

**Fig. 176.** Theodor Wiegand house, Dahlem, 1910–12, Peter Behrens, architect. Blueprint of garden plan, including layout of house, dated October 1910. 35 × 27 cm. (BV)

neglect of Josef Hoffmann during his sojourn in Vienna, that the Austrian's chairs from this period would directly influence such famous 1920s designs by Charlotte Perriand and Le Corbusier as the Siège grand confort.[44] More immediate, however, was the

44. See for example Hoffmann's armchairs published in March 1910 by *Deutsche Kunst und Dekoration,* vol. 15, p. 409; compare with Le Corbusier, *Oeuvre complète,* vol. 3 (1929–34), p. 44.

**Fig. 177.** Wiegand house plan. Sketch by Jeanneret. Black ink on tracing paper. Approx. 22 × 37 cm. (BV)

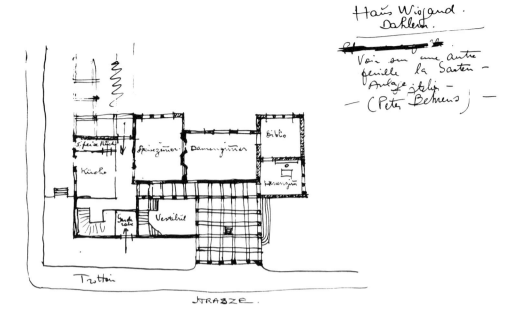

**Fig. 178.** Theodor Wiegand house, Peter Behrens, architect. Ground plan as built, 1911–12. (Julius Posener, *Berlin* [Munich, 1979], p. 170)

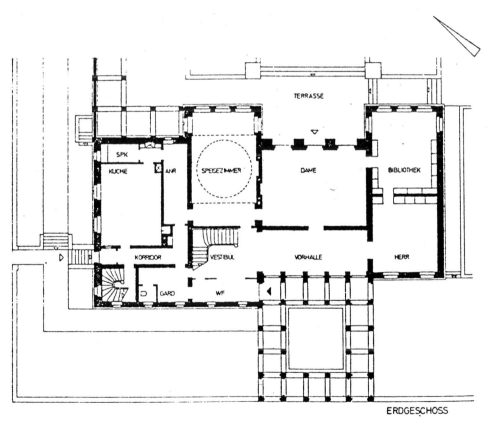

influence of men like Karl Bertsch and Bruno Paul whose chairs, desks, cabinets, lamp shades, and wallpaper would have a direct impact upon Jeanneret's designs of the 1910s at La Chaux-de-Fonds.

At midpoint during his five months with Behrens Jeanneret wrote an extremely long, some 3,500-word letter to L'Eplattenier that is really a "position paper" setting forth his stance on various issues at this juncture in his development. Much, perhaps half of the letter (completed on January 16, 1911) represents a dry run for his *Etude sur le mouvement d'art décoratif en Allemagne,* or at least the "Considérations Générales" that introduce and conclude the book. The letter, because it is written in an intimate, conversational style, more accurately reflects Jeanneret's true feelings, and a comparison between it and the book will be made later.

The crux of the letter concerns questions of design and the historical styles, including lengthy comparisons between France and Germany. Gothic is completely dethroned ("folies de gothique décadente," "leur démon moyen-âgeux"), classicism is ennobled, and Louis XVI is crowned. Poetically Jeanneret describes his tardy visit—grudgingly undertaken at the behest of Perret—to Versailles in the spring of 1909 when he saw "spread before my eyes the unforeseen and colossal spectacle of Versailles. It was the downfall of my gloomy [medieval] mythology, this radiant classic clarity. Even so, it took time before I could annul so many little pettinesses that I saw in art, very petty. And now, at present, I have much enthusiasm for Greece and for Rome, and only an eclectic interest in those arts which make me feel uneasy—northern Gothic, Russian barbarisms, German torments.

"This, then, is my evolution. I have before me, and I regard them often, some sixty interiors of Versailles, of Compiègne, of Fontainebleau. What lessons can be learned! I also have a splendid book of Doric, of Ionian, of Corinthian, of Roman art constructed of colossal vaults and great solid walls. . . . Oh, dear friend, the verification of my happy aesthetic evolution is the only thing that keeps me still alive." And after leaving Germany he says, "I will go collect my thoughts. Where! to Rome. Then afterwards, if you still want me. . . . !" (and twice thereafter, in the letter, he speaks of his future as being "chez nous").

An interesting statement is his early phrasing of what later became Le Corbusier's personal definition of architecture, here, however, made not in reference to architecture but to sculpture: "to create *volumes which play under the light* in rhythms based on geometrical shapes; joy of form rediscovered for a feast of the eyes" (emphasis in the original).

Also mentioned in this letter is Karl Friedrich Schinkel ("One of their greatest geniuses, the architect Schinkel expresses concretely in splendid buildings this archaeological desire for things Hellenic") as well as other architects including Messel, Bruno Paul, Schmitz, Paul Schultze-Naumburg, and, as often in Jeanneret's letters, the painter whom he greatly admires, Arnold Böcklin. Gobineau's racial theories, which Jeanneret apparently learned of through Cingria-Vaneyre rather than the original, are discussed with Jeanneret concluding that within Germany the German racial qualities of logic, method, and discipline have had a formidable and positive result. Yet her creative genius is mediocre at best and therefore in the end "France will subjugate Germany." Then, because his parents sent him four photographs of L'Eplattenier's *Monument to the Republic,* Jeanneret launches into a laudatory analysis of its design.

A month prior to composing his epistle to L'Eplattenier, Jeanneret dispatched a postcard (Puis de Chavannes, one of his favorite artists) to William Ritter that, contrary to earlier statements, said he was terribly overworked and left the office each night too exhausted to write letters, attend concerts, or even read. There is also this revealing remark: "I have been through a crisis of profound anxiety. The sky is now clearing. To what to attribute this terrible disenchantment? I must examine myself to find out" (December 14, 1910). Apparently he is referring to his deep psychological depression of the past several weeks, a crisis engendered by his agonizing conversion to classicism that required overthrowing most of the values that he previously held dear. Once the conversion became an accomplished fact, however, his spirits perk up, and his letters again become jocose and full of fun—although "the bear" is never praised.

Christmas holidays were spent at Dresden, with Albert, and proved a very social time.[45] Yet Albert remarked to his parents that Edouard lived too much alone, never developing a circle of friends and always being rather lonely. Very rarely in Jeanneret's abundant correspondence does he mention women, though occasionally he might comment on the way they dressed.

While in Dresden and nearby Hellerau (where a collective party was held on Christmas day) Jeanneret met Heinrich Tessenow (1876–1950), architect-to-be of Jaques-Dalcroze's Festival Hall. Jeanneret was offered a job to help with the plans and, though tempted, he set the condition that his role be truly significant—which Tessenow naturally declined (to Ritter, January 14, 1911). When completed, the hall and school, like many of Tessenow's designs, was somewhat dry and of unusual proportions; perhaps Jeanneret might have produced less stark forms.

After mid-January Jeanneret's known correspondence slackens.[46] His work, and the learning process, were taking most of his time.[47] The one new topic was future plans. A

45. At home their parents followed the usual routine, Christmas eve dinner with relatives and New Year's at Soleure with the Henri Jeannerets. On December 3, at the annual banquet of the Swiss Alpine Club, Jeanneret senior received a great honor and surprise. He was presented with a bronze bust of himself executed by L'Eplattenier; he had posed for it under the false impression that L'Eplattenier was in need of a model. Today it is at the Musée des Beaux-Arts, La Chaux-de-Fonds. Meanwhile the father's work, mainly for Longines, remained abundant.

46. Partly, but not entirely, this is because some letters to his parents are missing and known only through references in his father's journal of February 2, March 6 and 19, April 4, and May 18.

47. The 1911 Werkbund congress, at which Muthesius gave his famous speech "Wo stehen wir?" (Where do we stand?), was held in Dresden in February. There is no indication that Jeanneret attended. Why he missed this major event is just as baffling as why he missed the Brussels fair, especially with his

letter of February 12 from Klipstein proposed visiting Constantinople, an idea Jeanneret accepted as he had sometimes dreamed of going there (perhaps in part because Cingria-Vaneyre praised it so), and thereafter they could go to Rome; he said he had given Behrens notice effective April 1.

On March 10 Jeanneret made more detailed proposals, to wit that they depart May 15 from Dresden, visit Prague, hike through rural parts of Bohemia (this on Ritter's recommendation), see Vienna,[48] Budapest, and Bucharest, where Ritter could arrange an introduction at the royal palace to see several El Grecos (El Greco being Klipstein's doctoral dissertation topic). Jeanneret already had bought a Baedeker of the region as well as a new, more sophisticated camera, and was wondering about obtaining letters of introduction. He accepted Klipstein's renewed invitation to visit Laubach, proposing the end of April because he would be seeing his brother in Dresden April 3–7 and Ritter in Munich April 7–14 (he actually stayed twelve days),[49] then Stuttgart, Karlsruhe, the Rhine, Hamburg, Berlin, and back to Dresden again. To Ritter he remarked that Klipstein, age twenty-six, was the exact opposite of himself, being quiet, composed, and having little ambition, hoping merely to be a librarian.[50]

Jeanneret's brief apprenticeship ended unceremoniously on April 1. A few days earlier Albert visited him, the two attending *Oedipe,* Voltaire's early tragedy, with Jeanneret sketching the set as well as the seating arrangement. Soon thereafter he followed his brother to Dresden Alt-Stadt (Töpferstrasse 1), spending a few days there before continuing on to Munich on April 7.

Jeanneret's inability to define, and stick with, what he believed in is chronic during his years of continued immaturity. Some of this, of course, is typical of human nature, but in Jeanneret's case his vacillations are carried to such extremes as to be almost comical. Munich architecture, except for the rare building, he had thoroughly disliked when there five months ago. Now, suddenly, Munich was filled with beautiful buildings! He has nothing but praise for nineteenth-century classicism and the splendid structures lining Ludwigstrasse, and even observes that the seventeenth-century "Theatinerkirke is one of the most beautiful things I know" (to Ritter, May 4–8, 1911). But what of his former favorite, the medieval Frauenkirche? And what of Theodor Fischer's work! Can this be the same Jeanneret that we knew a few months before? No, certainly not.

---

brother then living in Dresden. However, upon his return to La Chaux-de-Fonds, he ordered the 1911 Werkbund yearbook.

48. ". . . to re-see Vienna—and this time to like it," he commented to Ritter on March first.

49. With his time so flexible, why no plan to visit his parents while in southwestern Germany? It was seven months since he had been home and would be another seven before he would return.

50. Actually Klipstein eventually moved to Switzerland, founding in Bern the highly respected Kornfeld und Klipstein fine arts auction house which is active to this day. Mrs. Regula Bandi-Klipstein has kindly made this correspondence available to me.

It is a malleable young man who has just spent five months under the spell of Peter Behrens. His debt was so great, indeed so profound, that Le Corbusier thought it best that it should be left unknown.

In Munich Jeanneret really began serious research on his *Etude* with a visit to the school of applied art directed by Wilhelm von Debschitz where he recorded his usual statistics about subjects being taught, teaching methods, the number of students and instructors, fees charged, etc. (see Carnet IV, 4–7, *Etude,* 60–61). He also met the directors of the Deutsche Werkstätten and the Vereinigte Werkstätten seeking details of their operations, and compiled information concerning exhibitions and artistic events seen during the past year. Then on April 12 he visited the villa of Franz von Stuck of which he acquired postcards.

While at a library he discovered C. A. Drach's book on architectural proportions, *Hütten-Geheimniss vom gerechten Steinmetzen-Grund* (Marburg: N. G. Elwert, 1897), the result being that he filled numerous pages of Carnet IV with lists of numerical proportions, the golden section, and diagrams of the proportional systems used for the Egyptian pyramids. Further on in this notebook he devotes five pages to studies of optical illusions, ideas that might be applicable to street layouts and decorative designs.

Leaving Munich on April 19, five days later than planned, Jeanneret set forth to gather material for his *Etude.*[51] First stop was Stuttgart where Bernhard Pankok, director of the Werkstätte, took him through the school with its four sections (woodworking, ceramics, metalworking, and bookbinding) and some eighty students.[52] He then went to Karlsruhe, being much impressed by the pyramid that stands at the center of the town, before continuing via Heidelberg to Darmstadt with its artists' colony of which he had heard so much. His reactions to Olbrich's work were mixed but definitely on the negative side and his final conclusion was similar to that on seeing the Olbrich exhibition in Berlin: "An agreeable renderer, but never an architect" (IV, p. 46). He

51. At the Fondation Le Corbusier there exist many individual sheets from a now mutilated sketchbook. Their size is consistent (12.5 × 19.6 cm), they were removed along identical perforations, and the paper quality, color, and thickness is identical. At Le Corbusier's death many of these sheets were still stacked together and therefore were given nearly similar inventory numbers in the 2000 range. For example 2030 shows the Odeonplatz at Munich, 2092 a metal bridge at Stuttgart, 2098 two villas sketched during his trip down the Rhine, 2089 passengers on the Rhine steamer, 2091 classical details of the arsenal at Cologne, 2096 street fronts at Cologne, 2032 a cemetery at Hagen, and 2094 a cemetery at Hamburg. It should, therefore, be quite easy to reconstruct this sketchbook that Jeanneret used during April/May, 1911. Carnet IV, which begins on April 3, covers virtually the same itinerary yet consists almost exclusively of text. And since this text forms the basis for much that is in the *Étude,* the latter two notebooks are often redundant. Incidentally, it should also be possible to reconstruct one or more of Jeanneret's Italian sketchbooks.

52. Pankok's studio building is certainly a precursor, and perhaps the source, for the wall and window treatment found in Le Corbusier's studio designs of the 1920s (Ozenfant, Jeanneret, Lipchitz, Pavillon de l'Esprit Nouveau, etc.). See *Deutsche Kunst und Dekoration,* 20 (1907), pp. 120–21.

detected certain details that had influenced Behrens but he made no specific comment concerning Behrens' former house, actually the first architectural work of his recent employer.

At Frankfort he was enraptured by the cathedral as, shortly after, he would be at Cologne and, in 1914, upon visiting the cathedral at Strasbourg. Therefore the cathedral, not as inspiration for contemporary design but as a work of art and spatial marvel, retained its elevated rank in his mind even though he was now a classicist. He devoted page after page of Carnet IV to the building and its contents and executed a watercolor showing the old city with the cathedral in the background (FLC 2855). On the verso he later wrote: "Exhibité à Munich 1911, Neuchâtel 1912, Paris Salon d'Autonne 1913, Zurich 1913"; this, then, was one of the series called Langage de Pierre. From Frankfort he took side trips to Wiesbaden, Offenbach, and Hanau, visiting, at the latter, the important jewelry school of the Zeichen Akademie, but finding the instruction conventional and academic and seeing nothing of particular note.

That evening, April 24, he arrived at Laubach, staying with Klipstein's brother, Felix, and Felix's wife, Editha. He enjoyed himself so thoroughly that he remained twelve days. Their home was literally an old Gothic tower consisting of one room on each of its four floors. Felix was a painter whose work Jeanneret much admired, and whose studio was a half hour's walk away. For the studio Jeanneret designed an addition.[53] And for Felix's wife, who made magnificent puppets, Jeanneret built a marionette theater. Three years later, he would design a house for them.

On Friday May 5 Jeanneret left Laubach via Frankfort for Mainz where the following morning he took a Rhine steamer to Cologne. The Rhine journey, as he wrote L'Eplattenier, was a superb experience for those whose souls were warmed by Gothic stones but "You know that I have evolved." Nevertheless he enjoyed the trip.[54]

The school of applied arts, or Kunstgewerbeschule, at Düsseldorf impressed Jeanneret as one of the best in Germany. He observed that the top students were offered classes in both architecture and landscape architecture, yet it was in book and fabric design, as well as weaving, that he thought the best instruction took place. The director of the school, Wilhelm Kreis, was his guide, saying that the élan evident at the school was the happy legacy of Peter Behrens, who had been director from 1903 until called

53. I visited the studio with the family in March 1978 and, although the structure makes no pretense at sophistication, I do believe that some details, such as the design of the large front window, recall subsequent work by Jeanneret, and that therefore his hand was involved in the design.

54. In this same letter of May 4–7 Jeanneret discusses finances, saying that his reserves are down to 900 or 1,000 francs, and asks that the remainder of his 1,200 franc research grant (of which he apparently spent 300 in June) be transferred into his account. The current trip, thus far, had been financed with his own funds; he emphasized that no grant money would be used for Constantinople. Later in May (apparently the twenty-third), he asked his father to arrange letters of credit through the Riechel bank for Vienna, Bucharest, Philippopoli (now called Plovdiv), Constantinople (Istanbul), Athens, Naples, Rome, and Florence. Thus his itinerary was well established.

to Berlin in 1907 as design consultant for the AEG. Such praise for Behrens was probably not anticipated.

Hagen was the next stop. There, on May 9, he met Karl Ernst Osthaus, proprietor of the Folkwang Museum (painting and sculpture) who was likewise a moving force behind having the Werkbund create the Deutsches Museum für Kunst im Handel und Gewerbe (German Museum for Art in Commerce and Industry). The latter sponsored traveling exhibitions such as "Art in the Service of the Merchant" (wrapping paper, packaging, etc.) that so impressed Jeanneret when he saw it in Berlin. Osthaus' own house of 1907–8 was designed by Henry van de Velde and Jeanneret inspected it thoroughly, providing lengthly descriptions but without appraisal. Osthaus was warmly receptive to Jeanneret's visit and subsequently a limited correspondence, though always initiated by Jeanneret, ensued.

Jeanneret also visited, but without much comment, the nearby buildings by Peter Behrens, that is, the Schröder and Cuno houses and the Crematorium, all of 1906–10. He remarked (IV, p. 75) how the pillars on the front of the Crematorium created a noble effect, especially when contrasted against the rural countryside, and that this idea might look well at "la petite maison." Thus the design of his parents' house, built a year later, was already on his mind.

Jeanneret's route took him next to Bremen, Hamburg, Lübeck, Lüneburg, and Berlin where he arrived on Saturday evening the thirteenth of May, having spent fourteen days, excluding the Klipstein visit, en route since Munich. At Hamburg he again saw the traveling exhibition Bemalte Wohnräume, which was in Munich the previous year, yet here he found the installation far superior thanks, he thought, to the influence of Richard Meyer, who was also director of the Staatliche Kunstgewerbeschule at Hamburg. This school received special accolades, perhaps because of its similarities with that at La Chaux-de-Fonds. Its program took three to four years with most students coming directly from primary school—unlike Düsseldorf where the average age was twenty-three to twenty-six. Particularly impressive, thought Jeanneret, was the treatment of the youngsters as adults, giving them complete liberty in choosing their projects as well as their courses. The architecture section was taught by Richard Schmidt. While in Hamburg Jeanneret also visited the botanical gardens with which he was much impressed.[55]

55. The first 36 pages of Carnet V (published as Carnet 1 in *Voyage d'Orient Sketchbooks* (New York: Electa/Rizzoli, 1987), see note number 1 above), are not entirely consistent chronological. They open with "Suite de la visite de l'Ecole de Hamburg," a visit that occurred on May 11, 1911, followed by a sketch of the proposed Villa Favre-Jacob of 1912, then discuss other material before returning to 1911. Page 36, "Le 23 visite école Dresden," I believe refers to May 23, 1911 (see letter from Dresden to parents of Tuesday (23?), with postscript on Wednesday, about his visit to the school and of Klipstein's impatience to depart). Giuliano Gresleri, who wrote the introduction and notes in *Voyage d'Orient Sketchbooks,* assigns an October 23, 1910, date to the Dresden visit, and a May 8, 1911, date to the following page (p. 37) that begins "Prague." This is an incorrect date since Jeanneret wrote L'Eplattenier from Berlin on May 16 (confirmed

Awaiting Jeanneret in Berlin was L'Eplattenier's alarmed response to his May 4–7 letter from Cologne that announced Jeanneret's proposed trip, not just to Rome but also to the Orient. He had kept his eastern itinerary secret from L'Eplattenier and his parents for fear of their negative reaction, perhaps even interdiction, remembering full well how L'Eplattenier had forbade him to go to Paris in 1908 and probably would argue that he was too young to benefit fully from such an extended trip. As for completing the *Etude,* Jeanneret wrote that his grant stipulated no deadline; of the unfinished manuscript for "La Construction des Villes" he was conspicuously silent.

Now that the Voyage d'Orient, as he called it, was open knowledge, Jeanneret felt free to inform his mentor that he wished to write a serialized account of his travels for one of the hometown newspapers, hopefully being paid for this endeavor. Obviously L'Eplattenier was being asked to negotiate the arrangements, and this he did through the family friend Georges Dubois at the *Feuille d'Avis.*

While in Berlin for the third and final time, Jeanneret frantically visited exhibitions, bookstores, home furnishing displays, and print dealers (suddenly he was fascinated by Piranesi) as we learn from Carnet V. He also inspected the art school at the Royal Arts and Crafts Museum, meeting its director, Bruno Paul. This visit, and the one shortly thereafter at the Kunstgewerbeschule in Dresden—both of which might better have been undertaken several months before—concluded research for his *Etude sur le mouvement d'art décoratif en Allemagne.*

Discounting the days he spent with the Klipsteins, journeying down the Rhine, and studying medieval towns, the time he devoted to inspecting schools of applied art and attending relevant exhibitions during June 1910 and April–May 1911 amounted to perhaps thirty days. Subsequently his writing of the *Etude* progressed slowly because of his travels but accelerated once he returned home. By January 1912 the manuscript was complete, and when read to the commission of the Ecole d'art it was so well received that publication was authorized; thus it became Jeanneret's first published book.

Its seventy-four pages consist of two parts with the bulk of the text (pp. 17–70) being a clear, straightforward description of organizations and institutions.[56] The Werkbund naturally leads the list, followed by its offshoot, the Deutsches Museum, then other exhibitors and exhibits of decorative arts. The commercial side is emphasized by discussion of various sales outlets (specialty shops, large department stores) as well as job-creating production units such as Werkstätten factories and the AEG. The pitch is obvious: well-designed objects create a market and markets create employment. And to

---

by the postmark). I believe they left Dresden and arrived in Prague on or about May 24, 1911, or seventeen days later than Gresleri's chronology. On June 4 they arrived in Budapest where Jeanneret posted a card. This would mean they were in Prague and Vienna for ten days.

56.  The book is available in a Da Capo Press (New York, 1968) reprint that I proposed to the publisher while also arranging for the republication of the twenty-eight numbers of *L'Esprit Nouveau* by Da Capo in 1968–69.

provide skilled designers there must be schools, like the various Kunstgewerbeschulen Jeanneret visited during April and May (only the Weimar school, where van de Velde was director, did he visit in June 1910). Here the unspoken theme is also clear: the Ecole d'art at La Chaux-de-Fonds must broaden its program and encompass a greater range of decorative arts, including architecture and landscape design, and give special attention to promotion and sales.[57]

Although the core of the book is strictly objective, the opening and closing chapters are highly subjective. Entitled "Considérations Générales" and "Considérations Finales," and encompassing only ten pages, they present Jeanneret's own garbled and biased version of art history as it relates to Germany and France. The gist of his theme is stated in the final paragraph: "Whereas Paris is the home of art, Germany remains the great center of production." To reach this point, however, he discusses the social classes, their ever-changing roles in defining taste, the various styles, and the idea that styles in France result from progressive evolution but in Germany from revolution. Then he debates the greater hierarchical importance of the metaphysical arts of painting and sculpture that are produced by individuals of genius in France in contrast to Germany, where the applied arts dominate due to the German corporate genius for organization and production that creates a supremacy for the applied arts and leads to the diminished role of Art, with Art subsequently becoming a pretext, a means, rather than the underlying motive power as it is in France. Jeanneret pointedly excludes discussion of folk or peasant art, saying that "the popular arts, above all, are humane, therefore international" (p. 12), an idea that encouraged Le Corbusier to seek inspiration from the popular arts by the 1920s.

Jeanneret's January 16, 1911, letter to L'Eplattenier was basically a dry run for these chapters in his *Etude,* with many of the same thoughts, even phrases, first appearing here. Yet the privacy of a letter gives greater freedom to be outspoken ("France subjugue l'Allemagne. Et l'Allemagne s'incline.") as well as to discuss sensitive topics like Gobineau's thesis of the inequality of human races. And Jeanneret, whose admiration for the beauty of machines and the creations of engineers was already a reality, observed that in Germany "architecture derived from the industrial arts," an idea that Le Corbusier would soon implement.

No period during Le Corbusier's formative years, no matter how long, matched in significance the twelve months he spent in Germany. It is impossible to imagine the direction his career would have taken if deprived of this fruitful experience and its

57. It is from the intentionally misleading and sometimes downright false statements in this book that biographers have incorrectly concluded that Jeanneret worked for Josef Hoffmann while in Vienna. For example (pp. 5–6), "En 1908, j'avais été engagé à Vienne, sur présentation de mes dessins, par Joseph Hoffmann, aux Wiener Werkstätte; cet engagement devait m'être d'une utilité constante en Allemagne." And again on page 40, "Je connais fort bien les rouages de la Wiener Werkstätte ayant été engagé dans le bureau de Joseph Hoffmann."

consequences. Only one thing seems certain: his work would have oriented itself differently, and proceeded at a different pace.

Much that he himself claimed, or implied, was the consequence of his own original thinking, or which he ascribed to non-German sources, was actually the direct result of what he learned in Germany. Recall his confession to L'Eplattenier that "I arrived at Behrens' knowing almost nothing about what was a style, and totally ignorant of the art of profiles and their harmonious relation. I assure you it isn't easy. . . . Behrens rigidly insists upon rhythm and subtle proportions and so many other things that were unknown to me." Yet his statement only touches the surface in its references to harmonious proportions (*tracés régulateurs*), style, and rhythm. Form, and especially its essence as a severe, spartan, Werkbund type of classical form, was one of the legacies of the Behrens office where Jeanneret came to appreciate and praise pure geometric shapes, such as he would come to recognize in Cézanne, but which he would later attribute to none other than "The Lesson of Rome."

His repeated condemnation of Behrens as the image maker, as one dishonestly preoccupied with the skin of a building rather than the bones, eventually softened into acceptance with the result that Jeanneret's own concern for his lack of engineering skills was heard no more. He was well aware that Behrens, like himself, began life as an artist and that without any formal academic training in either architecture or engineering had become the foremost architect of his day. "Architecture," in Germany, "derived from the industrial arts" he had observed, and to express this utilitarian aesthetic of machines and engineers, as well as the standardized products of the production line, would, a decade later, become an underlying expression of his architecture. We should recall that it was Le Corbusier who coined the famous phrase, "A house is a machine for living in."

Jeanneret, since about 1908, had searched for an ideal. He sought it through reading, visiting museums, studying Gothic cathedrals, and in the practice of architecture. Although he admired the architecture of Perret, Fischer, von Seidl, and Behrens, none of these fulfilled the idealistic goal that he was seeking. A decade of thought and reflection would pass before the objective, the components of which were already in place by 1911, fully clarified itself in his mind. And that goal was to create a synthesis between the most positive artistic qualities that each of these two nations had to offer—the creative talent of the individual French artist united with German organizational genius and standardization in the production of the industrial arts. The genes representing these two cultures must somehow be crossed within a single person, French artistic creativity being combined with Germany machine aesthetics.

Jeanneret often made a practice of spelling Art with a capital A when referring to French painters of individual genius who, by what he called the sublime abstractions of their work, were pushing back the frontiers of aesthetic knowledge. Similar artistic creativity or originality he failed to find in a Germany that, though dependent upon the artistic motive power of French evolutionary invention, nonetheless managed to

252    **Travels and Apprenticeships**

produce decorative arts and even architecture superior to that of France. Therefore Le Corbusier, for nearly forty years, devoted the best part of each day to painting, going to his architectural office only in the afternoon, and always insisting that to comprehend his architecture one must seek the answer in his painting. In his own life, therefore, he ceaselessly tried to combine these two roles, that of the French painter who generated the creative motive power for the architect, and that of the architect who in turn used standardized machine-made products and industrial processes, as well as their images, to create architecture. This helps explain the otherwise inexplicable attraction Le Corbusier felt for his own manufacturing endeavors such as producing standardized concrete blocks at Alfortville or using a mechanical cement gun at Pessac. But as an industrialist determined to create standardized products, he was no match for the Germans.

Despite his criticism of Germany and praise for France one fact remains: he praised, and sought employment from, only *one* architect in France—Auguste Perret. In Germany, by contrast, he admired a whole galaxy of architects and planners, at least five of whom he wished to work for—Fischer, Behrens, Jansen, Paul, and Tessenow—not to mention having falsely implied that he had actually worked for Josef Hoffmann.

In Germany Jeanneret had redefined his loyalties. In April 1910 he arrived a medievalist, in May 1911 he departed a classicist. Schinkel rather than Fischer received his praise, and white became his color of choice. After undergoing this 180-degree turn, he was now anxious to visit Constantinople, Greece, and Rome. And thanks to Germany he had come to know Ritter, Cingria-Vaneyre, and Klipstein. Ritter became a dominant influence during these formative years, Cingria-Vaneyre provided him with the rationale to exploit classicism upon his return to La Chaux-de-Fonds (and reinforced his motivation for returning thereto), and without Klipstein he would not have traveled to Constantinople or Athens before going to Rome.

Dresden, with its pleasant memories, was the point of departure for the east—the Voyage d'Orient. Klipstein joined the brothers there and in a last letter home of May 23[58] Edouard said that while Klip (as he called him) was agitating to get underway, he still needed more material for his *Etude* and would, that very day, go to the Königliches Sächsische Kunstgewerbeschule which he'd failed to visit during previous trips to Dresden. The school, however, left him unimpressed.

Two remarks in this letter indicate how Jeanneret's values have changed. He reported that during the past week, while in Berlin, he found the city very agreeable and truly pretty. Also that he had purchased a Louis XV armchair that he was shipping home![59]

58. This undated letter begins "Ce mardi matin, Albert se rasant" and continues by stating his intention to visit the Dresden Kunstgewerbeschule that day. Carnet V, page 36, begins "Le 23 visité école Dresden." May 23, 1911, was a Tuesday so the dates correspond; the previous week Jeanneret was still in Berlin.

59. This chapter has gained much from research done by my graduate students over the years, of whom I especially wish to thank Catherine Bull, Hélène Jobidon, Richard Joncas, Claudia Mandler, and Lauren Weingarden.

# 8

## VOYAGE D'ORIENT

### *1911*

Jeanneret's Voyage d'Orient—his five-month trip to southeastern Europe—was truly a rite of passage. From it he would emerge more confident and mature both as a man and as a designer. It was a time of enlightenment when much of his past fell into place and assumed a relatedness that hitherto had escaped him.

The pieces fit together nicely. He recalled from his early reading of Henry Provensal's *L'Art de demain* the dictum that architecture must adhere to eternal *laws,* including those of number, unity, and harmony, that cubic forms best expressed an ideal, and that architecture must be based upon an idea. Eugène Grasset's *Méthode de Composition Ornemental* had taught the use of abstract, geometric shapes and forms, while Cézanne, whose work Jeanneret so admired, spoke of the cylinder, sphere, and cone. More recently Peter Behrens impressed upon him the significance of harmony and proportions, including the use of regulating lines, while in architecture Behrens made extensive use of geometric forms both in the shapes he gave his buildings and in his architectural decoration. Geometric abstraction was likewise found in the art of ancient peoples; Jeanneret had learned this at school while copying illustrations from Owen Jones, *A Grammar of Ornament,* and from hours of sketching ethnographic art in the museums of Paris. Still more recently folk art caught his attention, whether peasant farmhouses in the Jura or wonderful shapes and patterns found in the pots and carpets that Ritter recommended he admire and collect while in the Balkans. Nor was Cingria-Vaneyre forgotten in crediting peasants of the Swiss Jura with preserving the ancient, classical heritage of Jeanneret's homeland, a tradition upon which the young architect hoped to build. Thus, during his trip, Jeanneret was well prepared to observe and honor objects as diverse as Serbian pots and the Parthenon and to recognize in them a set of universal values that until recently he would not have been able to discern.

In short, an *ideal* (such as Jeanneret had sought since his days in Paris) was beginning to take shape in his mind. He increasingly recognized certain universal, abstract geometric principles in much of the art that he admired. A hitherto unsuspected catalyst may have been the writings of Wilhelm Worringer. The latter's *Abstraktion und Einfühlung* of 1908 (English edition, *Abstraction and Empathy* [New York, 1953]) may have accompanied Klipstein, a Worringer protégé, on the trip since a direct quote therefrom appears in his journal, and Jeanneret mentions Worringer both in his notebook and his letters. The quotation from page 44 reads: "The primal artistic impulse has nothing to do with the rendering of nature. It seeks after pure abstraction as the only possibility of repose within the confusion and obscurity of the world-picture, and creates out of itself, with instinctive necessity, geometric abstraction."

One may imagine that Jeanneret and Klipstein discussed Worringer at length because even this passage provides a lively topic for debate—which may explain why Klipstein recorded it. Here Worringer rejects "the rendering of nature" except perhaps as a "geometric abstraction" (recall L'Eplattenier), believing that "the primal artistic impulse . . . seeks after pure abstraction." This "urge to abstraction," as he repeatedly describes it, is equally manifest in cultures at their highest levels of development; Jeanneret, apparently, started to see a connection, an underlying unity or universal relation, between the geometric abstraction of peasant art and that found in the most brilliant achievements of Greek and Byzantine art. This "ideal" that he started to formulate required him to abandon many of his previous idols. It is entirely understandable, therefore, why the trip retained such a vividness in both his mind and his future writings; it became one of the most publicized episodes in the first half of his life. In virtually every book he wrote he made references to the trip such as those in *Vers une architecture* (1923), or the autobiographical "Confession" in *L'Art décoratif d'aujourd'hui* of 1925—by which date, however, the five-month trip had become so magnified in his mind that it lasted "près d'un an" (p. 212). And in *Oeuvre Complète* (1929) he published forty-two sketches from this one trip—while totally ignoring all his previous travels.

Equally important were the serialized articles published in *Feuille d'Avis* in 1911; their publication, however, was never completed. "Les Mosquées" was the final chapter to appear in the hometown press (November 22, 1911) although half again as many articles had been written. Their cessation was caused by lack of readership. The rhapsodic, flowery, often convoluted text was written for effect, and being preoccupied with style it was sometimes hard to follow. Their interest lies chiefly in the man who wrote them. Even Edouard's parents were among his critics.

The author tried too hard to be a stylist; he sought to imitate others instead of being himself. Other than Ritter, major models include Pierre Loti (1850–1923), whose works Jeanneret then was reading and whose name repeatedly appears in sketchbooks and in correspondence,[1] and Claude Farrère (1876–1957), whose name is also often mentioned; both used Constantinople as settings for their novels. Jeanneret absorbed from each specific descriptive topics as well as phraseology, which suggests that copies of their books were close at hand.[2] Nor was Hippolyte Taine forgotten, whether for the title of his book, *Voyage en Italie,* or the often colorful, sometimes startling use of words.[3] Yet Taine's word-pictures are inevitably more vivid and historically informed. Jeanneret showed little concern for history and was amazingly oblivious to the nationalistic political strife then fermenting in this region, strife that within a year would erupt into the sequence of the two Balkan Wars of 1912 and 1913, and the year thereafter lead to World War I.

Three years passed before Jeanneret completed his articles (or chapters), and the sequence of writing is not easy to reconstruct. Few were produced in situ, yet all but two (and the dedication to his brother) were completed sometime between June and October, 1911, while he was still on the trip.[4] The longest, and two final, chapters— "L'Athos" and "Le Parthenon"—were written in 1914 from hindsight and without notes. At that time, with international attention focused on the Balkans, Jeanneret unsuccessfully hoped to publish the articles as a book. "L'Athos," which was completed

1. Jeanneret was currently reading Loti's *La Mort de Philae* (1909). Ritter, who had published *Pierre Loti aux Lieux-Saints* in 1895, probably introduced Jeanneret to Loti's writings.

2. On Jeanneret's use of passages from Farrère, see Tim Benton, *Le Corbusier Architect of the Century* (London: Arts Council of Great Britain, 1987), p. 56. For calling my attention to the significance of Loti, my thanks to Eva Hoepfner; other students who contributed to this chapter were J. Andrew Church, Greta Moray, and Sylvia Osterbind.

3. *Voyage en Orient,* by Gérard de Nerval, is noted on page 120 of Carnet 2, the title being even closer to that of Jeanneret's book. Yet when Jeanneret's articles first appeared in 1911 the title was "En Orient" (n.b.: When a carnet is designated by an Arabic numeral it refers to the *Voyage d'Orient Sketchbooks,* and when in Roman numerals it means the German carnets (see Chapter 7, notes 1 and 55).

4. The first article, "Quelques Impressions," Jeanneret signed and dated "ce 6 juin 1911" yet on June 22 he wrote Ritter "je n'ai encore rien envoyé [to the newspaper] donc rien encore n'a été imprimé. Je mettrai mes notes en ordre à Constantinople"; these "notes" are in his Carnet 2. The second article, "Lettre aux Amis . . . ," was apparently written in Hungary (judging from internal evidence), with the next five ("Vienne" through "Sur Terre Turque") probably written in Constantinople. However of the nine articles relating to Constantinople ("Constantinople" through "Pêle-Mêle, Retours et Regrets") only "Le Désastre de Stamboul" is dated, i.e., "Pera, ce lundi 24 juillet 1911," which is one day after the great conflagration of July 23. From internal remarks, it appears that "Constantinople" was being written on shipboard while Jeanneret was headed toward Brindisi, "Les Sepultures" in an Athens café, "Elles et Eux" in the train between Brindisi and Naples, "Deux Féeries, une Réalité" just after he left Naples, and "Pêle-Mêle . . ." sometime after he left Turkey; the intervening articles carry no suggestion of date. The unedited manuscript for the final chapter, "En Occident," appears in Carnet 4, pp. 67–70 where it is dated "ce 10 oct," but only about half the text was subsequently printed. The initial nine articles, through "Les Mosquées," were published serially in nineteen parts in *Feuille d'Avis* from July 20 through November 22, 1911; Jeanneret had returned to La Chaux-de-Fonds on November 1st.

"ce 24 juin 1914," and "Le Parthenon" were submitted to Ritter for a critique; Jeanneret's writing style, by this date, was already much improved.[5] He was learning from his critics.

*Voyage d'Orient* (Forces Vives, 1966), as we know it, appeared posthumously under the aegis of Jean Petit. Nevertheless, Le Corbusier read and arranged the text, added additional footnotes, and did minor editing the month before his death. At the conclusion he wrote: "Relu le 17 juillet 1965, 24 Nungesser et Coli [his Paris street address], par Le Corbusier." Petit, notorious for avoiding scholarly documentation, provides little enlightenment although one assumes that he, not Le Corbusier, wrote the unsigned, untitled, one-page introduction on page five. Subsequent Italian and English editions, edited by others, have added illustrations, as well as much by way of documentation, to this text.[6]

The most useful publication, however, is a superb facsimile reproduction of the *Voyage d'Orient Sketchbooks* by Electa/Rizzoli (1988). This boxed set includes all six carnets used by Jeanneret during the trip; the publisher has numbered them in Arabic numerals 1–6, and I shall follow suit. Seeing and handling these gems is almost like owning the originals. And a supplementary volume contains text transcriptions along with detailed notes.

As a result of these, and other, publications, Le Corbusier's "voyage" has become one of the best-known and best-documented periods of his life. For him, this apparently was important. It focused attention on the "revelation" of the Acropolis and thereby distracted attention from the really significant influences that so directly impinged on both his artistry and his intellect as a result of his recent year in Germany; therefore Germany no longer seemed to offer a threat to his implied claims of inherent originality.

In addition, the "voyage" is the only time for which his parents letters are preserved. This adds richly to our story; likewise it offers insights into their personalities. Another

5. Initially sent to Ritter for a critique and later presented to him as a gift, these two chapters were briefly borrowed back in 1925 when Jeanneret published excerpts from "Les Mosquées," "Le Parthenon" (retitled "Sur l'Acrople" perhaps in imitation of Ernest Renan's *Pierre sur l'Acrople:* see below), and the one-page "En Occident" in *Almanach d'Architecture Moderne,* Collection de "L'Esprit Nouveau" (Paris: n.d.), pp. 55–71. The original longhand versions of the two chapters are now deposited at the Bibliothèque de la Ville (dossier MS 122–1 and 2). Deleted from the Athos chapter in the published version is a long, three-page quotation from Elisée Reclus, *Nouvelle géographie universelle* about Mount Athos. The 1914 attempt to have the entire book published by Mercure de France came to naught.

6. There are two related Italian editions: Charles-Edouard Jeanneret, *Le Corbusier Il Viaggio d'Oriente* (Faenza, 1974) and *Le Corbusier Viaggio in Oriente,* with introduction by Giuliano Gresleri (Venice and Paris: Marsilio Editori and Fondation Le Corbusier, 1984). The latter contains a magnificent collection of Jeanneret's photographs taken during his trip; also many of his drawings, as well as much footnoted documentation. The English edition is: Le Corbusier, *Journey to the East,* edited and annotated by Ivan Žaknić (Cambridge and London: MIT Press, 1987. This version has much less by way of documentation yet illustrates some eighty of Jeanneret's drawings. Notwithstanding the existence of this English edition, however, I found it preferable to use my own translations when quoting Jeanneret's text.

useful source is August Klipstein's unpublished "Orient-Reise 1911."[7] All these items corroborate one another very nicely; we even find passages from letters reappearing almost verbatim in Jeanneret's book. However, concerning substantiation, there remains one notable exception and that involves Mount Athos, for which Jeanneret had little or any praise in 1911 but completely reversed himself when writing of it in 1914.

On May 25 (or perhaps the evening before) Jeanneret and Klipstein left Dresden for Prague where they spent nearly three thoroughly enjoyable days. Jeanneret's new Cupido 80 camera recorded the usual attractions as well as views recalling "La Construction des Villes" such as enclosing walls, plazas, and squares. Increasingly the camera supplanted postcards as his means of visual documentation. Also the speed of their travels allowed less time for watercolors than he would have liked. However, as a gift for William Ritter—who had urged them to visit Prague as well as the rural countryside (recall Ritter's *L'Entêtement slovaque* published the previous year)—he made four sketches of the Royal Palace and its approaches (fig. 179).

A broad, monumental staircase, such as seen in this drawing, became one of his favorite themes for photographs and drawings. Another popular subject was the enclosed courtyard. Carnet 1 (p. 37) speaks rapturously of one in Prague and includes a sketch-plan showing its vaulted entrance at one corner of an adjacent courtyard (where there is an off-center group of trees) while the passageway to the contiguous courtyard is not, as anticipated, on axis but rather diagonally across the square; this sequence of spaces he also recorded on film.[8]

From Prague the youths left for Vienna, arriving Saturday evening May 27. They stayed nearly a week. Jeanneret's attitude, surprisingly, had little changed during the three years since 1907–8. He remained uninspired by most of what he saw. What particularly impressed him, he wrote Ritter, were the parks at Schönbrunn Palace, the Belvedere (both designed in the French manner), and the paintings of Pieter Bruegel.

Rather than architecture, it was interior decoration that especially attracted him with work by the Wiener Werkstätte, as seen in their sales shop on the Graben, holding top spot. He made numerous sketches of designs for lamp shades, light fixtures, ceiling lights, wall and ceiling coverings (of linen and muslin), stools, display cases, devices for hanging pictures, methods for erecting temporary partition walls, and even made measured drawings of a Louis XV sofa and chair. The interior of the salesroom itself, by Josef Hoffmann, also fascinated him and he sketched the room in plan, elevation, and

7. I am indebted to Klipstein's daughter, Mrs. Regula Bandi-Klipstein for providing copies of Jeanneret's correspondence as well as the fifty-three-page typescript of "Orient-Reise 1911."

8. This photo is reproduced in *Le Corbusier Viaggio in Oriente,* p. 140. It is described in Carnet 1, p. 37: "Prague. J'ai pris des photos d'une cour exquise qui n'est qu'une répétition du très excellent principe noté à Karlsruhe et à Lubeck."

**Fig. 179.** Prague, Royal Palace. Pencil and watercolor wash, late May 1911. 21.3 × 26.4 cm. (BV)

perspective in order to show its glazed display cases lining the walls (fig. 180). But the exterior of this building he neither sketched nor photographed, a building which, incidently, existed during his earlier sojourn in Vienna yet had failed to attract his attention. His Vienna sketchbook, rather amazingly, includes only one exterior and that is the nearby Knize Shop, also on the Graben. His full page description of the design lists no architect and apparently he was unaware that the designer was Adolph Loos (fig. 181).

Except for these few shops, Jeanneret's remarks about Viennese architecture were far from complimentary. And what comments he made appear mostly in his *Voyage* manuscript (p. 28) where he mentions "the bad taste that inundates the boulevards with parvenu and grandiloquent architecture" from which one can find some solace in the "recent architectural creations of the younger school: works full of good sense, but at the same time a bit mad." During his brief stay in Vienna he did write Hoffmann requesting an interview (mentioned in an undated postcard to his parents), but this belated, half-hearted attempt produced no results.[9] He did, nevertheless, spend an eve-

9. It was quite out of character for Jeanneret to write for an interview rather than knocking on a person's door as, in fact, he had done with Hoffmann in 1908.

**Fig. 180.** Vienna, Wiener Werkstätte salesroom, 1907. Josef Hoffmann, architect. Pencil sketch, Carnet 1, p. 52, ca. June 1, 1911. Note:
all the Voyage d'Orient sketchbooks
at the Fondation Le Corbusier are
approx. 17 × 9.5 cm. in size.

ning with Karl Stemolak, the sculptor with whom he had studied life-drawing in 1908.[10]

Jeanneret spent more time in galleries and museums than in searching for buildings, yet these also disappointed him and rarely did he mention the pictures on the walls. At the Liechtenstein, famous for its paintings by Rubens and Van Dyck, he sketched Louis XV furniture and listed items that were for sale, but made no reference to the paintings. He also visited the Secession, Hagenbund, Künstlerhaus, Miethke (the gallery designed by Hoffmann and Kolo Moser), and Kunsthistorisches Hofmuseum, but his search for interesting pictures was "a useless effort—banality is everywhere, mediocrity triumphs" (*Voyage,* p. 67). What he and Klipstein especially sought, but found little of, were paintings by Hodler, Cézanne, Van Gogh, Gauguin, and Matisse.

Instead of discussing the art world with his newspaper readers Jeanneret spoke of life in the streets, crowded as they were in springtime. He contrasted the elegant rich with the "sordid" and "grubby" poor in a rather elitist and offensive manner that was not appropriate considering his hometown audience. To make matters worse he opened his "Vienna" article (p. 23) with: "The rich, by helping the poor, amuse themselves." Then, after continuing in this vein for a couple of paragraphs, he quipped "May my friends at *La Sentinelle* pardon these rapid and superficial impressions." Jeanneret's hu-

10. The future design for his parents house was also on his mind. His father's June 6 letter mentions that "mama" was saving for "la petite maison," and Carnet 1, p. 44, says "Pour la petite maison des parents consulter le tableau de Bellini aux Offices [i.e., Uffizi] (la conversation Heilige)." Jeanneret's eyesight is also a recurring subject at this time: "mes yeux de myope derrière mes lunettes, ces tristes lunettes qui confèrent l'air doctoral ou clergyman" (*Voyage,* p. 11).

**Fig. 181.** Vienna, Knize Gentlemen's Outfitters, the Graben, 1909–13. Adolf Loos, architect. Pencil and colored pencil in Carnet 1, p. 57, ca. June 1, 1911.

mor at the expense of the socialists was hardly very funny. Certainly L'Eplattenier did not think so; he caused quite a fracas.[11]

11. L'Eplattenier had to maintain peace with the socialists if he hoped to establish his Nouvelle Section at the Ecole d'art as well as secure a post therein for Jeanneret. The commotion is reported in Jeanneret senior's card of July 27 with its long paragraph of constructive criticism concerning how Edouard could improve not merely writing style but the presentation of his ideas: "tes phrases sont . . . *trop touffues, trop longues;* on s'y perd un peu, encore que les idées si nombreuses ne soient pas admissibles par chacun, par beaucoup même. Des idées je n'en puis discuter en général quoique certaines me paraissent un peu outrées en avant, et en arrière. Ce sont ces *idées* qui ont mis en ébullition Mr. L'Eplattenier qui a même telephoné à Mr. Dubois [the editor] aujourd'hui pour lui demander la suspension des articles jusqu'à nouvel ordre; il y voit pour toi une menace de perte des soutiens que tu peux avoir dans son entourage. . . . C'est un conseil paternal que je te donne." It would be another decade before Edouard followed this advice.

After six days the youths left Vienna without regret. On Friday evening, June 2, they boarded a Danube steamer, sleeping on a bench (to avoid the cost of another night at the Goldener Pelikan Hotel) while awaiting the early morning sailing. Jeanneret became fascinated by every aspect of their river trip, beginning with the view of Esztergom which he both sketched and photographed from on deck while remarking in his Carnet (1, pp. 54, 58) the wish to obtain photos of its cloister. They debarked at Vác, where the Danube bends south to Budapest, and the following morning (Sunday, June 4) Jeanneret penned an enthusiastic card to his parents praising not only the river trip but also the typical Hungarian town where he purchased three ceramic pots of which he was most proud. That afternoon they took the local train to Budapest.

Of Budapest, where Jeanneret had briefly stopped in November 1907, he only said "I neither understood nor liked her. To me she seemed like leprosy on the body of a goddess" (*Voyage,* p. 35). Their only enjoyment was the central market where they purchased two pots while deciding against a stunning Czech shawl. L'Eplattenier had requested they lay flowers on Emma L'Eplattenier's grave, which they did—while Jeanneret concurrently sketched the monument in its dreary setting. His reply to L'Eplattenier was written over several days and finally posted from Belgrade on June 9. From it we learn that Léon Perrin had just been appointed at the Ecole d'art (to Edouard's delight) and that Jeanneret is up for nomination. This brought home to him that his youthful wanderings were quickly drawing to a close and that a new phase of his life would soon begin. He pleaded with L'Eplattenier not to burden him with work until his feet were firmly on the ground. He also observed that "I, myself, feel that it is good for me to return," this in response to a suggestion from L'Eplattenier that the time was right to settle down, and that this should be done at home.[12]

Concurrently he wrote Ritter about exploring the rural countryside in search of pots (some, he believed, as fine as those in Ritter's collection) and apologizing for breaking his promise about sending an ongoing journal-account of the trip, proposing instead to transmit the articles when published (thereby avoiding editorial advice). This, actually, was his first letter to Ritter since Cologne, when he was sailing down the Rhine.

The Budapest-Belgrade trip, which commenced at nightfall June 6, was soon interrupted because the captain, during a midnight chat with Jeanneret (who had mastered

12. Meanwhile Ritter was urging Jeanneret to abandon both La Chaux-de-Fonds and L'Eplattenier and to seek broader, more challenging horizons. Jeanneret, however, was insufficiently sure of himself to do so, and gradually became annoyed at Ritter's insistence, stating emphatically (undated card to Ritter postmarked Athens) that one cannot serve two masters and that L'Eplattenier was his choice. When he initially informed Ritter of his appointment at the school (undated letter from Istanbul) he said he had no (*sic*) foreknowledge of this event, which, nevertheless, would give his father great satisfaction; thus he treated the whole matter rather lightly. And once again he expressed concern over his lack of readiness: "Vraiment, je vous jure, je ne suis pas fort. Tout le métier [of architecture] me manque."

the trick of traveling first class on a second class ticket), advised them to disembark at the market town of Baja—which they did at dawn. This resulted in the extraordinary pottery expedition discussed in chapter two ("Lettre aux Amis . . .") of *Voyage d'Orient* (pp. 13–22; fig. 182).[13] Also described therein are the dress and appearance of peasants and the high-walled courtyards with arcaded verandas of these whitewashed rural homes (fig. 183). Such courtyards, called by Jeanneret summer rooms (chambre d'été), reminded him of the Chartreuse d'Ema and, combined with the little viewing "windows" found in cemetery walls (see fig. 193), this concept would reappear at his parents' home near Vevey when it was designed in 1923. From Baja they crossed the Danube and spent the night at Mohács,[14] continuing to Belgrade by boat the following day (June 8).

Belgrade was another disappointment. "A ridiculous capital; worse: a dishonest, dirty, disorganized city" (*Voyage,* p. 39). Only the ethnographic museum received praise and that for its carpets, clothing, beautiful Serbian pots, and collection of decorated eggs (he remarked that perhaps his Atelier d'art friends should ornament eggs at Easter [Carnet 1, p. 60]).

Here they decided to prolong their stay by traveling (by rail and foot) into the Serbian highlands. They proceeded as far south as Niš before working their way back (exact route unknown) to the Danube and Negotin (*Voyage,* pp. 40–44), then continuing to Bucharest where they arrived Friday evening June 16 and stayed until the twenty-second. The excursion netted many photographs and increased their stock of pots.[15]

Bucharest was the first capital since Prague for which Jeanneret had real praise. "Bucharest is full of Paris; there is even more" (*Voyage,* p. 49); then he discussed everything from paltry examples of Beaux-Arts architecture to beautiful women decked out in the latest Parisian fashions. Ritter's friends, and others, added greatly to the warmth to his impressions. The youths lived well, being received by the former metropolitan primate, His Eminence Ghénadie, in the monastery at Caldarushani where they dined like kings (menu in Carnet 2, p. 24); a car provided by the minister of public works took them to monasteries and cemeteries of the region. The Chapel of Paradise left a most profound impression. They also enjoyed entrée at the royal palace where Klipstein wanted to study the El Grecos in Carman Sylva's collection. This adventure, and Jeanneret's scorn-

**Fig. 182.** Serbian pot purchased at Baja which was still in the Jeanneret house near Vevey at the time of Le Corbusier's death. His photograph, published in *L'Art décoratif d'aujourd'-hui,* page 34, serves as our illustration.

13. Chronologically his chapter should have followed, rather than preceded, the one on Vienna. It was published in three parts on July 25, August 3 and 8, 1911, in *Feuille d'Avis* whereas "Vienne" appeared on August 18 and 25.

14. This stop, recorded both in Carnet 2, p. 127, and in the above-mentioned letter to Ritter, is not listed in the *Voyage* itinerary of p. 8.

15. Jeanneret's long and varied list of purchases, with costs, is recorded at the back of Carnet 1, pp. 124ff. He shipped some items periodically, but the majority were packed and sent from Turkey. He also carried the heavy and fragile 9 × 12 cm glass negatives for his Cupido camera which, considering the number of pictures taken, was quite a burden.

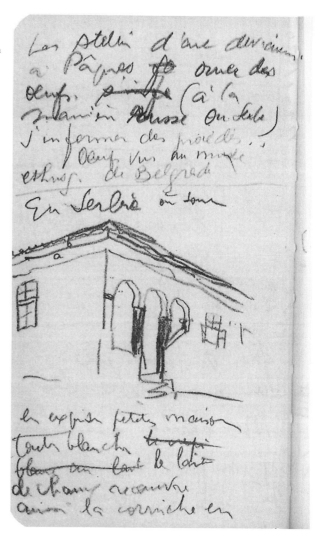

**Fig. 183.** "In Serbia there are exquisite little houses, all white," is the penciled caption under this sketch in Carnet 1, p. 60, of June 1911.

ful reaction to the queen's bad taste, filled his "Bucharest" chapter in *Voyage d'Orient* (fig. 184).

Leaving Romania and the Danube they traveled by various means—train, horseback, wagon, and on foot—southward across Bulgaria. They began on the main rail line from Ruse to the ancient capital of Tŭrnovo (today Veliko Tŭrnovo), a picturesque city built on near-vertical cliffs 800 feet above the Yantra River.[16] Jeanneret was fasci-

16. "Tirnovo" is the chapter in *Voyage d'Orient,* written in early September, covering the trip across Bulgaria. Jeanneret's style is showing steady improvement; it has become more coherent and flowing and much less fractured. A footnote, added later, observes that Bulgarian door and window frames are painted blue; is this why he painted the front door of his parents' home blue in 1912?

**Fig. 184.** Romania, an "Romanian type house" is Jeanneret's caption on this pencil sketch in Carnet 1, p. 64, of June 1911.

nated by the site, sketching and photographing it from different angles (fig. 185). He also sketched the interior of a house with its "fenêtre en longueur," this being among the earliest travel sketches subsequently included in his *Oeuvre Complète* (fig. 186).

From Tŭrnovo they proceeded to Gabrovo. There Jeanneret did a watercolor of the church looked at from below a monumental flight of steps, a painting later included in his "Langage de Pierre" exhibit (fig. 187).

The Balkan Mountains between Gabrovo and Kazanlŭk were the ruggedest part of this trip, and animals provided transport over the Shipka Pass. And sure enough, once on the southern slopes, Turkish influence became evident both in the buildings and

**Fig. 185.** Bulgaria, view of Tŭrnovo. Pencil on paper, June 1911.
12.5 × 20 cm. (FLC 2496)

**Fig. 186.** Bulgaria, interior of
house at Tŭrnovo with its "fenêtre
en longueur." Pencil on paper, June
1911. (*Oeuvre Complète,* vol. 1)

peasant dress. Jeanneret recorded them with many sketches and photographs (fig. 188).
Klipstein and Jeanneret began a search for icons. Cemeteries and tombstones remained
an obsession.[17] Then, from Kazanlŭk they proceeded to Stara Zagora and on to Turkish soil.

17. I have no explanation for Jeanneret's fascination for cemeteries and tombstones, or why so many of

**Fig. 187.** Bulgaria, monastery church at Gabrovo. Pencil and water-colors on heavy paper, June 1911. This painting was included in Jeanneret's Langage de Pierre exhibition. 30.5 × 39.5 cm. (FLC 2853)

**Fig. 188.** Bulgaria, house with courtyard at Kazanlŭk. Notation (upper left) reads: "La fontaine est du marbre blanc. Le crépi blanc." Pencil and ink, June 1911. 29 × 39 cm. (FLC 1793)

**Fig. 189.** Adrianople (Edirne), Turkey, Eski Djami Mosque, 1403–14. Plan and section. Pencil and blue pencil, Carnet 2, p. 56, ca. July 1, 1911.

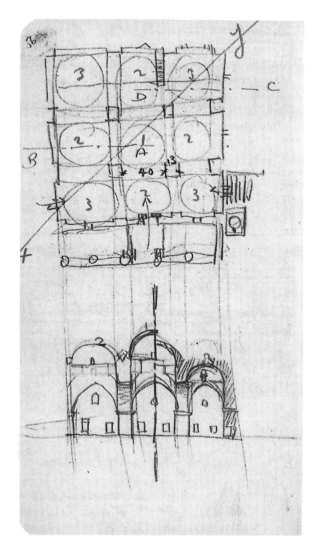

Eight days after Bucharest they arrived at Adrianople (today Edirne), enjoying three or four days in the ancient capital while exploring and photographing its famous Selimiye Cami (Mosque of Sultan Selim II) built by the celebrated Ottoman architect Sinan. Still more impressive to Jeanneret, however, were the plan and visual effects of the interior of Eski Djami built for the Emir Suleiman early in the early fifteenth century (fig. 189).

Wishing to arrive at Constantinople in the traditional manner, by ship, the youths took the train to Muratli (July 4) and then proceeded by auto to the picturesque port

his sketches, postcards, and particularly photographs are of them. His notes and letters frequently speak of them. See letter of July 18 to L'Eplattenier wherein he mentions how Léon Perrin will find this documentation interesting, but this hardly explains the vast amount of time and energy Jeanneret devoted to them.

**Fig. 190.** Constantinople (Istanbul), Turkish house. Pencil and watercolor. July-August 1911. 11.3 × 19.2 cm. (FLC 6111)

**Fig. 191.** Constantinople, Süleymaniye mosque, 1550–57. Sinan, architect. Pencil on sketchbook paper. 12.3 × 20 cm. (FLC)

of Rodosto (today Tekirdag) where Jeanneret completed several sketches before being invited to dine with some local merchants with whom they passed a most agreeable evening (see "Sur Terre Turque" in *Voyage*). The following day they spent thirteen miserable hours braving rough seas in a small, overcrowded boat, the views from which were entirely unworthy of the sickening trip.

Jeanneret's initial reaction to Constantinople (later named Istanbul) was not favorable but as the weeks passed (their stay lasted nearly seven)[18] he became extremely fond of the city and its life. They engaged a room in the European quarter of Pera, just across the Horn, from "a splendid chap" who obligingly whitewashed everything before they moved in—but failed to exterminate the bedbugs. The room was on the fourth floor, with three large windows overlooking the Golden Horn and the mosques of Stamboul, the ancient and historic (now Turkish) quarter of the town (to parents, July 22). He began a schedule of writing in the morning and, after the noonday meal, wandering (Baedeker in hand) through the streets and surrounding countryside. He enjoyed Pera almost more than Stamboul (Ritter, n.d.). Klipstein, meanwhile, was continuing research for his doctoral dissertation, the subject being Byzantine influences on the paintings of El Greco.

From the pictorial documentation of his sojourn, Jeanneret's interest in architecture is again confirmed, this in contrast to the impression given at Vienna. Images of the great mosques abound, but what is exceptional, yet not entirely unexpected after the Balkans, is his fascination with common, everyday, vernacular buildings, usually houses, that are too unpretentious to catch the average eye. These he often recorded in perspective, looking down the street, rather than as elevations. Several occur in his sketchbooks, others are on larger sheets—watercolor sometimes highlighting the design. The upper storeys, usually built of wood, or wood and roughcast combined, frequently extend over the street and are supported by angular brackets. Often the roof pitch is too slight to be observed from below, and windows so closely placed as to create a horizontal band. However plans and interiors are absent—unlike in the friendly, rural Balkans—because Jeanneret lacked access to these city dwellings (fig. 190).

Among the great mosques sketched and photographed, that of Sultan Süleyman (built 1550–57 by Sinan) was most frequently depicted (fig. 191). Another favorite was Hagia Sophia, the domed Christian basilica, built and rebuilt between the fourth and sixth centuries, a design that became seminal for the majority of Constantinople's future mosques. In Jeanneret's time it actually was a mosque, before becoming a museum in 1935. Three years previously, in Paris, he had sketched its plan and section while reading Corroyer's *L'Architecture romane*, and now, while in situ, he prepared sketches (Carnet 1, p. 78, and Carnet 2, pp. 116–18) to study its geometric composition and analyze its scale (fig. 192). His thoughts are well expressed in words: "An elementary geometry

18. "Nous sommes ici pour un mois" he wrote Ritter on July 6, yet they left on August 22 after having arrived on July 5. On each leg of their trip they fell further behind. At Vienna, for instance, Jeanneret wrote that he would be at Bucharest until June 10 but he didn't leave until June 22—twelve days behind schedule. At Mount Athos they planned to stay one week and remained more than two. By the time they reached Athens they were running well over six weeks late!

**Fig. 192.** Constantinople, Hagia Sophia (above) and Galata Tower, Pera (below), along with notations concerning scale and proportions. Pencil sketchs in Carnet 1, pp. 78–79, 1911.

disciplines the masses: the square, the cube, the sphere" (*Voyage,* p. 78). Such remarks carry overtones of what he had learned in Germany; their lesson is sinking in.[19] Likewise the effect of light, in aiding to define form and determine scale (chiefly on interiors), is another recurring theme. Occasionally he concealed himself within a mosque at prayer time, an experience that left him much moved. The combination of light and scale and

19. Whereas Cézanne, one of Jeanneret's favorites, often emphasized geometric forms with curved surfaces (cylinder, sphere, cone), Jeanneret underscored those with right angles and flat surfaces (the cube and square).

**Fig. 193.** Constantinople, Cemetery at Eyüp. The "windows" cut into these Turkish cemetery walls, as well as the outer walls at the Chartreuse d'Ema, would serve as precedent for those at the Jeanneret house near Vevey (1924) and the Villa Savoye at Poissy (1929). Pencil on paper. 12 × 19.5 cm. (FLC 6086)

open space would become almost overwhelming. However, rarely did he manifest much interest in the details of mosques, as he did with domestic buildings.

Notable exceptions were shapes and forms in the buttressing system at Hagia Sophia. He imagined them as almost sphinx-like,[20] and whereas his photos seem of minimal interest (see fig. 355, Chapter 10) they held for him a deeper meaning because five years later their details would appear in La Scala cinema at La Chaux-de-Fonds.

Other mosques were sketched or discussed, including those of Ahmed (the Blue Mosque), Bayezid, Nuru Osmaniye, Selim, and Yeni. Fountains, whether of the wall-niche variety or water temples, likewise caught his fancy as did the Galata Tower built by Genoese traders in 1349 (fig. 192).

Concerning the ornament in mosques Jeanneret had nothing but disdain: "all the Turkish mosques, except that at Bursa which was saved by Loti, have suffered the ignominy of ignoble, repugnant, revolting painted ornamentation" (*Voyage,* p. 77). This aversion may help explain the near absence of visits to museums or, with one or two exceptions, sketches of Turkish ornament (other than that on tombstones). His love for the decorative arts, meanwhile, was fulfilled at the Great Bazaar, where purchases included Persian miniatures, carpets (some at 150 francs), and a great deal of Bukhara embroidery (one piece at 400 francs!). Several of these items, however, were procured on consignment for L'Eplattenier and Perrin.

Cemeteries continued their attraction and consumed disproportionate amounts of time and film. That at Scutari (Üsküdar) on the Asian shore of the Bosporus, with its toppled tombstones strewn among rigid cypress trees, was repeatedly photographed; that at Eyüp, north of Constantinople and near the tip of the Golden Horn, Jeanneret pronounced "a dream" (L'Eplattenier, July 18; fig. 193).

On July 23 Constantinople yielded to one of its periodic fires, an event of great interest to Jeanneret who lavishly recorded its aftermath on film. It spurred him to write "Le Désastre de Stamboul" on "ce lundi 24 juillet 1911," the only *Voyage d'Orient* chapter written concurrent with the event it describes and the only chapter about Constantinople completed on Turkish soil. The date almost coincided with, at home, publication (on July 20) of the first of his articles, an incident which caused a contretemps between father and son when papa not only offered Edouard advice about his writing (see note 11) but slightly edited the manuscript prior to its publication. Jeanneret was furious, but his annoyance was quickly mitigated upon learning that Albert had also contributed to the revision process (Albert, after all, could do no wrong).[21]

20. See drawing illustrated in *L'Art décoratif d'aujourd'hui* p. 215.

21. Upon learning that publication of his articles was suspended (between September 13 and October 13), Edouard reluctantly admitted that the early ones were not much good: "C'est dommage pour moi [the suspension], car les derniers étaient bons; les premiers du fumier" (to parents, October 15).

For his parents, the summer of 1911 differed somewhat from previous years. No excursion to the mountains was planned and as compensation the family rented what they described as ideal accommodations near town in an area known as Les Foulets.[22] The Chalet de la Forêt, as the house was called, was handsomely appointed, had plenty of space, and from its high location enjoyed splendid views across La Chaux-de-Fonds toward Les Bulles. As a result they did considerable entertaining between July 1 and September 15. Throughout this period, and beyond, Albert was at home and this gave his parents great pleasure. He had now received his teaching certificate from Jaques-Dalcroze's eurythmics institute at Hellerau and also obtained a teaching post there for the following year, but, as Jeanneret senior wrote Edouard on June 27, the remuneration was so low that Albert must find additional work to do on the side—perhaps teaching violin.

The father was also concerned about Edouard who showed so little interest in matters architectural. On September 14 he wrote his youngest son: "One thing that surprises me in these articles is that you are everything except an architect: painter, colorist, poet, sensitive to the beauties of Nature, of the landscape, swooning before ceramics and pots of all kinds, yet thus far one has difficulty finding two or three allusions to buildings in the many cities that you have already visited."

Tragedy struck the family on October 4 when fire destroyed the building at 6, rue de la Loge where for twenty-five years papa had had his atelier and Pauline, his sister, her apartment. Both quickly found new quarters although his was some walk from home and quite expensive; it did, however, resolve one question: their future "petite maison" should house his workshop. Two days after the fire, amongst all the confusion, Albert left for Dresden. Meanwhile Edouard, upon learning of the catastrophe, shot off a letter from Rome (where he had belatedly arrived) offering to catch the first train home to assist with his father's relocation. Generous acts for those in need was one of Edouard's traits; loyalty was another.

Meanwhile, in Constantinople, toward mid-July, Auguste Perret arrived from Paris, coming to oversee work on the French legation. Jeanneret spent most of an afternoon and evening with him, gleaning news of musicians, poets, and painters in the Parisian capital. This made him feel like a typical provincial. Moreover Perret was speaking enthusiastically of his new commission to design the Théâtre des Champs-Élysées in Paris with Antoine Bourdelle as sculptor and Maurice Denis executing interior paintings.[23] Perret therefore needed to expand his staff and offered Jeanneret a job. He would

22. The address was Les Foulets no. 3 but the Chalet de la Forêt was later demolished when a larger house was built on the site. I am indebted to Mlle Augsberger and Mlle Sémon for helping me locate this spot.

23. The role of Perret vs. van de Velde in the design of the theater has long been debated, therefore I quote Perret's version as reported by Jeanneret to L'Eplattenier on August 4, 1911: "Le théâtre c'est celui qu'il [Perret] a volé à Van de Velde qui été mis à la porte." Incidently, Bourdelle's sculptural panels for the

have welcomed this opportunity to learn ("une telle occasion d'apprendre") but, as he wrote L'Eplattenier on August 4, the time had come when he should return home, not to mention the fact that he had committed himself to doing so. Writing of the Perret visit to William Ritter, however, was a tactical error; it rekindled an already delicate debate.[24]

Long before leaving Constantinople the youths made a quick trip to Bursa in Asia Minor, taking the traditional route by sea to Mudanya, then overland to the ancient Ottoman capital. Although they stayed little more than a day, Jeanneret filled many pages of Carnet 3 (pp. 5–33) with notes and sketches. These included the Great Mosque (Ulu Cami) of 1421 which, with its twenty domes, reminded him of the Eski Djami at Adrianople, six pages of drawings of the Green Mosque (Yesil Cami) also of 1421 (fig. 194), and the nearby Green Mausoleum (Yesil Türbe) of which Jeanneret did a watercolor in his sketchbook. Also sketched were Roman ruins, baths, and shipboard scenes. He actually made more use of his sketchbook in Bursa than in Constantinople, to which they returned on Friday, August 8, with the hope of departing for Mount Athos by Tuesday the twenty-second. The Bursa trip, for some reason, is not included in *Voyage d'Orient*.

Prior to departing, Jeanneret's acquisitions had to be packed and shipped, their purchase price greatly worrying the frugal father as to the sanity of his son. In a card (addressed to the atelier rather than the home) Edouard says: "My dear papa. You have good reason to be astonished. The 1,600 frs. are gone, and here is how." There then follows a list of all the reasons for buying at this time, including the suggestion that a profit would be realized from any potential sale. We also learn that Jeanneret is living on 3 or 4 francs a day, including room, so his purchases were equivalent to about one year's living expenses; no wonder his father was concerned![25]

Jeanneret expected to spend a week at Mount Athos en route to Athens, yet the trip took three—thanks to ship schedules, quarantines, and the travelers' propensity to tarry.

---

theater undoubtedly inspired Jeanneret to commission Léon Perrin to execute reliefs for the Villa Schwob in 1916.

24. Having mentioned Perret to Ritter in an undated card from Constantinople, Jeanneret then found it necessary to defend himself on September 10: "Mais je me sens heureux aussi d'aller retrouver L'Eplattenier, car je lui dois tout et c'est mon grand ami. Je me suis aperçu particulièrement pendant ce grand voyage de ce que sont les vraies amitiés. On est comme un pupitre qui porte beaucoup sur sa tête et ses pieds trouvent ici un appui, là un autre et plus il y a d'appuis plus il y a de stabilité, de sécurité, de sérénité. Je sens l'immensité de l'Europe et combien un homme est perdu là-dessus. Mais je me sens quelques points fixes qui m'honorent, m'élèvent, m'exaltent et me disent de voir haut. Et c'est une bienfaisante chose."

25. His total expenses were recorded in Carnet 2, p. 82, covering the period May 25 to August 23, 1911. They were: "Cost of trip including postage and photographic supplies 595 [Swiss] francs; at Bazaar and works of art 1,200 francs; owed by Klip 50 francs; on hand 55 francs; [total] = 1,900 f." The source of these funds is listed as: "Letter of credit 1,600 [the amount papa knew of]; L'Eplattenier 200; Perrin 100 = 1,900f."

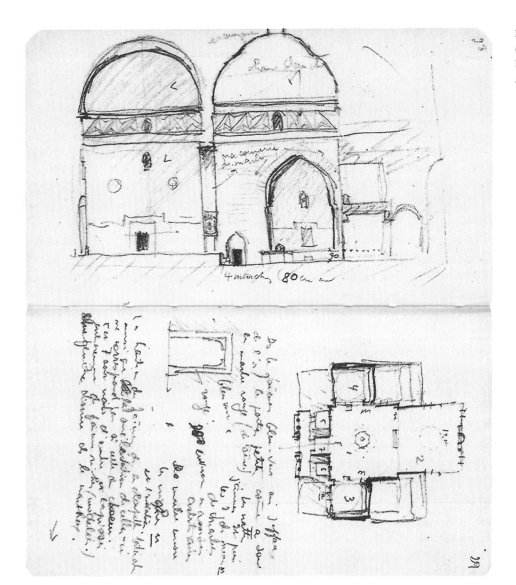

**Fig. 194.** Bursa, Green Mosque (Yesil Cami), longitudinal section. Pencil sketch in Carnet 3, pp. 28–29, August 1911.

The quarantines resulted from a major cholera epidemic then raging in southeastern Europe; it kept the parents worried but not the youths. The day they embarked, the ship—for some ill-explained reason—was kept in quarantine which allowed Jeanneret to make several sketches looking toward the shore (fig. 195). His initial preconception of Constantinople had been largely formed by Paul Signac's painting of this view (to L'Eplattenier July 18), though subsequently he found the city quite different (to K. E. Osthaus, July 28). Because of Signac he believed the city would be luminous and white, yet found it a dirty gray. So, like Signac, he portrayed the mosques as white. And in homage to Signac he sketched sailboats scampering on the Sea of Marmara with the Seraglio perched behind. Later, working from this annotated sketch, he executed two

**Fig. 195.** View of Constantinople from aboard ship during Jeanneret's departure, ca. August 21–22, 1911. Pencil sketch, Carnet 3, p. 37.

watercolors of this scene using brush strokes like those of Signac. One of these was included in his Langage de Pierre exhibit (fig. 196).

The "pyramid" of Athos, as Jeanneret called it with his new propensity for seeing geometry almost everywhere,[26] rose 6,670 feet (2,033 m) from the Aegean Sea and was visible for hours before the ship, on whose deck they had spent the night, passed close by and entered the little port of Daphni. A ride by mule in the deepening dusk brought them up the slope to Kariaí (Karyaes), the only town on the peninsula, where they stayed the night. Thereafter they ate and slept at monasteries along their route (figs. 197, 198).[27] Meals were spare yet wine was always plentiful. And by week's end (August 30 or 31), Jeanneret contracted a severe, persistent case of diarrhea that left him weak and miserable.

From Mount Athos he wrote neither to his parents nor L'Eplattenier. The only contemporary account is his letter to William Ritter of September 10: "In truth, Athos is only the ghost of what it was. Of frescoes: [no] more, with the exception of one or two; of miniatures, nothing outstanding. The Bibliothèque Nationale offers a hundred-

26. The pyramid description first appears in a letter to Ritter of September 10, then reappears several times in the "Athos" chapter of *Voyage* where, in a related context, he says (p. 127): "Et j'aimerais les rapports géométriques, le carré, le cercle, et les proportions d'un rapport simple et caractérisé." He has therefore completed his turnabout since earlier in the year when, in Behrens' office, he discovered with consternation that geometry was the friend and not (à la Sitte) the enemy of the designer.

27. How many of the twenty monasteries they visited is unclear. Sketches in Carnet 3, pp. 43–91, suggest they saw at least six, the best-represented being the Great Laura (founded 963 A.D.), Iviron, and Philothéou. He had postcards of eight yet these required no visit. His photographs are few and most often of the monks.

**Fig. 196.** Sailboats, Sea of Marmara with Constantinople in background. Ink and watercolor. 23 × 29 cm. (FLC 1939)

fold more. Athos is not beautiful, but it is interesting. And at the end of 15 days one has had enough of it, whereas after 7 weeks in Stamboul you have planted roots that must be uprooted painfully."

The lengthly "L'Athos" chapter in *Voyage d'Orient* was not written until 1914; therefore it contains few details. Essentially it is a series of images usually too abstract or symbolic to be easily understood.[28] Certain affinities exist with his paintings of ca. 1913–14. One of these, entitled "Vin d'Athos" and dated February 1913, shows a female nude flailing her arms while astride a half-seated mule with a small pyramid (Mount Athos) in the background (fig. 295 in Chapter 9 below). The sharp, diagonal lines of the pyramid are duplicated in both human and animal forms that owe much to German expressionism and perhaps specifically to Franz Marc, yet without his more sensuous, curvilinear rhythms.

The word "vin" (wine) probably refers to the artist's state of mind. Throughout the "L'Athos" chapter there are references to abundant wine and also to strange visions occurring in half-sleep or in hallucinations resulting from extreme fatigue. We therefore

28. The symbolic "open hand," so important in Le Corbusier's later years, finds early expression here where the "main ouverte" is likened to a tree (p. 139).

**Fig. 197.** Mount Athos, Agiou Dionysiou Monastery. Pencil sketch, Carnet 3, p. 47, August 1911.

assume that the imagery of these paintings results from the artists real or imagined semidelirious state, during which his travels are running through his mind.

And while speaking of pyramids (or ziggurats), there is a sketch among the Mount Athos drawings where the notation reads: "August speaks of an observation tower made like this. It's really a monumental thing. It must be in Germany" (fig. 199).[29] One is struck by the similarities between this sketch and Le Corbusier's proposed 1928 design for the Musée mondial which was part of the Mundaneum project in Geneva. Surely this is no coincidence.

Egyptian pyramids were also on his mind. He intended to visit Cairo, and perhaps Jerusalem as well. He planned to leave from Athens, despite his delayed schedule. The trip was canceled, however, because of diarrhea, this he announced to Ritter on September 10 and to his brother on the twenty-seventh. A month later, from Florence, he wrote Klipstein: "My next trip will be to Egypt returning via Athens."

The sea voyage to Athens included two nights under the stars.[30] But rather than debarking at Piraeus, Athens passengers were put ashore (under a cholera flag) on the tiny quarantine island of St. George, there to remain a miserable four days. While there,

29. On the facing page is sketched the Galerius mausoleum at Mount Athos which consists of three concentric drums of diminishing size. This building must have reminded Klipstein of the circular observation tower.

30. Apparently they left Mount Athos September 6, having arrived August 24. Jeanneret rarely gives exact dates, so approximations are determined by addition and subtraction, a method complicated by whether one counts days or nights. The trip from Athos took two nights, but how many full or partial days? The quarantine lasted four days, but included how many nights?

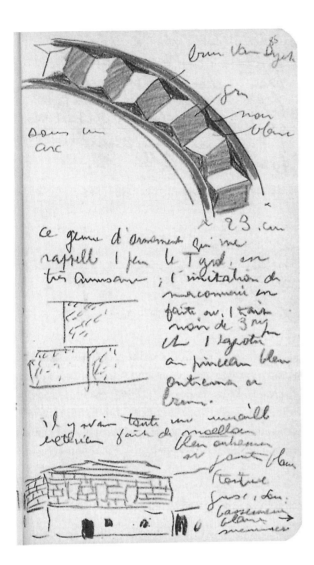

**Fig. 198.** Mount Athos. Typical sketchbook page with detail of architectural ornament and description of imitation masonry on exterior of Great Laura Monastery. Lead pencil and brown pencil, Carnet 3, p. 85, August 1911.

and within sight of Eleusis across the bay, Jeanneret penned his long letter to Ritter and may have worked on his articles, but could do little else.

Transferred to Athens the morning of September twelfth,[31] Jeanneret picked up his mail, read it while sipping coffee in a café, then intentionally awaited the romantic hour of sunset to first visit the Acropolis (figs. 200–203).

For three weeks he remained in Greece, and over the years frequently wrote of his impressions. However, *no contemporary account exists.* He wrote neither to his parents nor

31. Three items support a September 12 date, the day count (see previous note), Klipstein's "Orient Reise" that mentions being in Athens on the twelfth, and Jeanneret's laundry list (Carnet 3, page 182) which is dated "Athènes, le 13 sept."

**Fig. 199.** "Auguste parle d'une tour belvédere ainsi faite." Sketch, made while at Mount Athos, of a building described by Klipstein. Perhaps this provided Le Corbusier with the idea for his "World Museum" project at the Mundaneum in 1928, which he published in the thirties. Moreover, this circular museum project may have encouraged Frank Lloyd Wright to use circular forms for the Guggenheim Museum. Carnet 3, p. 86.

to L'Eplattenier, and postcards to Albert and Ritter concerned other things. Nor did he maintain his journal because he had no intention of writing about his post-Constantinople trip.

Three years passed before he recorded his impressions of Greece. The first occasion was when writing "Le Parthenon" chapter in 1914 while unsuccessfully trying to get the articles published as a book. The essay is a lovely song of praise, unquestionably the best-written chapter of the intended book. Finally he had developed a smooth, praiseworthy style which achieved the descriptive power and rhythmic flow he seemed to be seeking from the start. Pleasant image-provoking metaphors replace his hitherto excessive use of adjectives. By 1914, of course, he enjoyed the advantage of leisure time and the critical advise of William Ritter. But how much his ideas about Greece had changed during these three years, we do not know.

The Acropolis apparently surpassed Jeanneret's highest expectations. "It harbors the essence of artistic thought" (*Voyage,* p. 158). For two weeks he visited little else. The Parthenon—and the Propylaea—represented a perfection that he dared not believe could exist. Here—though in dramatic ruin—stood the proof, the answer to a question that had bothered him for years. This one building, on its immortal site, achieved the Ideal: the absolute perfection of an idea. And this, he perceived, was the natural response to fundamental laws, the actual embodiment of universal rules. His nomenclature underwent a change; he saw measure and mathematics, not just the interaction of geometric shapes, as holding the key to this perfection. This intensified his interest in numbers, eventually leading to the Modulor. But, whereas he admired the technical skills demonstrated in the construction, these never offered the slightest personal challenge.

**Fig. 200.** Athens, view of the Acropolis, September 1911. Pencil sketch, Carnet 3, p. 123.

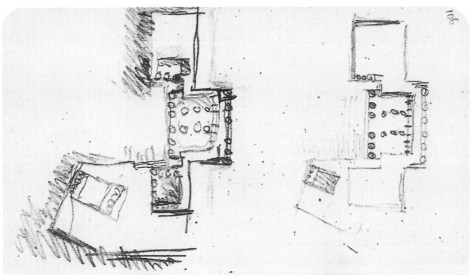

**Fig. 201.** Athens, Propylaea. Plans and elevation on facing pages of Carnet 3, pp. 106–107, September 1911.

His reaction to the Parthenon was intensified, perhaps molded, by his purchase and reading of *Prière sur l'Acropole,* a twelve-page pamphlet by Ernest Renan, whose *Vie de Jésus* he had read in Paris. Both works use a litany of similar words such as laws, rules, mathematics, measure, and pure art that had not been part of Jeanneret's vocabulary in the past. And when Renan declared the Parthenon "the ideal crystallized in pentalic marble" (p. 1) Jeanneret was certainly in accord; his early reading of Provensal now acquired greater relevance than before.

His Acropolis encounter, however, did nothing to diminish his idealized belief in peasant art. Actually, it reinforced it. It confirmed in his mind the idea that universal laws were at work, whether in the most sophisticated structures erected by man or in

**Fig. 202.** Athens, view of Parthenon as observed through the screen of columns of the Propylaea. Pencil sketch in Carnet 3, p. 115, September 1911.

**Fig. 203.** Ch.-E. Jeanneret standing in the Parthenon, September 1911. (BV)

the humblest Serbian pot. The same abstract principles were at work in each, with the peasant intuitively responding to laws and rules similar to those that produced the Parthenon.

Sketches by Jeanneret of Greek architecture are fewer than one might expect, perhaps because he saw these buildings as less "useful" to his future work. His drawings, but not his photographs and paintings, emphasized the Propylaea, and general views of the Acropolis, where the attraction was apparently the spatial juxtaposition between masses of different size, height, and transparency and how, overall, this achieved a balanced asymmetry. Details were not recorded, only the relation of part-to-part. Irregularity, not regularity, caught his eye.

Three larger pen and ink drawings, one each of the Propylaea, Parthenon, and Erechtheum, show what is special about that particular building. The cross section of the propylaea shows the height and degree of transparency of its interrelated structures (including the Temple of Athena Nike); of the Erechtheum a plan and section of the differing floor levels because these are unique among Greek temples; and at the Parthenon, "the non-alignment of columns at the corner with those of the second range" (fig. 204).[32]

As for his watercolors, they are so sketchy as to appear unfinished, their brush strokes imitating the soft pencil lines characteristic of his drawing style; what he illustrates is merely the lower part of column shafts where they make contact with the temple floor

---

32. The full caption reads: "Parthénon. non-coïncidence des colonnes d'angle avec celles de la seconde enceinte. Les platonnets ne s'occupent en rien de la situation des colonnes: le caissonnage m par ex est typique. *Partout règne une asymétrie déconcertante*" (emphasis mine).

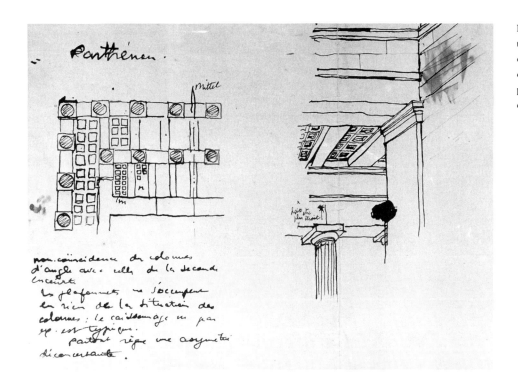

**Fig. 204.** Athens, detail of the Parthenon showing "the non-alignment of columns at the corner with those of the second range." Pen and ink on paper, September 1911. 22.5 × 36 cm. (FLC 1786)

(fig. 205). Three of these expressionistic works he included in the Langage de Pierre exhibit.[33]

Unanticipated, however, was his keen interest in the decorative arts, especially jewelry (fig. 206).[34] Perhaps he recalled Paris where he copied vase designs, small terra cottas, and other ornament. Classical sculpture caught his attention as witnessed by his photographs, taken mostly in the Acropolis and National Museums. Meanwhile his most striking architectural photographs show the fallen Parthenon columns, their drums strewn along the ground.

Klipstein left for home on September 27, due perhaps to the approaching academic year. He had been an excellent companion, respectful of Jeanneret's interests and idio-

33. The few watercolors that Jeanneret executed during 1911 show a rapid evolution of style, yet underlying each of them is the vigorous pencil technique he used in sketching. He might imitate this in his brush stroke, or the pencil (or pen and ink) lines may read through the superimposed watercolor wash, or color may be used merely as a highlight. One is tempted to give the three above-mentioned paintings a post-Athens date, yet on the matting of one of them Jeanneret wrote: "Ces 3 aquarelles du Parthénon furent faites sur L'Acropole en sept. 1911." Jeanneret thereby identifies our illustration as the Parthenon, yet more likely it is the Propylaea, thus bringing into question the accuracy of his remarks.

34. See Claude Malécot, "La sculpture et les arts décoratif grecs," *Le Corbusier: le passé à réaction poétique* (Paris: Caisse nationale des Monuments historiques et des Sites, 1988), pp. 144–52, for many sketches made by Jeanneret of the decorative arts in Paris and Athens.

**Fig. 205.** Athens. Watercolor showing lower part of columns at the Propylaea. Observe how closely Jeanneret's watercolor technique coincides with his drawing style; compare with figure 202. This painting was included in his Langage de Pierre exhibit. 17 × 26.3 cm. (FLC 2849)

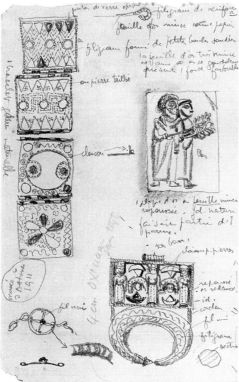

**Fig. 206.** Ornaments sketched at the National Museum, Athens, September 1911. The ornament at lower right was illustrated by Le Corbusier in *L'Art décoratif d'aujourd'hui*, p. 207. Pencil on detached sketchbook sheet, 21.6 × 13 cm. (FLC 1901)

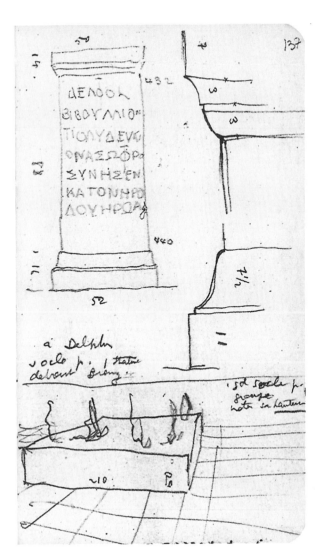

**Fig. 207.** Delphi, detail of pedestals. Pencil sketch in Carnet 3, p. 137, ca. October 1, 1911.

syncrasies as well as his particular need for quiet time (see *Voyage,* pp. 113–15, 161). Their artistic concerns also had much in common.

After Klipstein's departure Jeanneret visited two other classical sites before he himself left Greece. The first was Eleusis, which he had viewed from afar while in quarantine. Now, with Baedeker in hand, he went to study its ruins. The opening carnet account, however, is autobiographical: "I am drunk as a cow," and then he vividly describes the various phases of his long-lasting diarrhea that he hopes to cure by getting stinking drunk on mastic.[35] He did have the strength to sketch the ruins of the Temple of De-

35. Mastic is an alcoholic liquor flavored with resin mastic and aniseed. On occasion Jeanneret liked

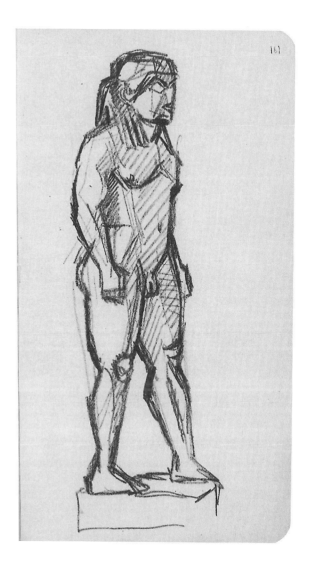

**Fig. 208.** Delphi, statue of Biton, ca. 600 B.C., in Delphi Museum. Pencil sketch, Carnet 3, p. 161, ca. October 1, 1911.

meter in his sketchbook as well as on the pages of his guidebook. He also made two landscape studies in watercolor, complete with verbal notations, intending to create finished paintings at a later date (Carnet 3, pp. 133, 135).

At Delphi he showed greater concern for details (of buildings, steps, seats, pedestals, etc.) than previously and made two sketches of Biton, the archaic free-standing sculpture (ca. 600 B.C.) in the Delphi Museum (figs. 207–9). He also sketched the landscape.

The next two drawings illustrate the small steamship that carried him to Italy (one

strong drinks like absinthe, mastic, and pastis. See, for example, Jerzy Soltan, "Working with Le Corbusier," in *Le Corbusier,* H. Allen Brooks, ed. (Princeton: Princeton University Press, 1987), p. 16.

**Fig. 209.** View from Delphi. Pencil sketch, Carnet 3, p. 167, ca. October 1, 1911.

**Fig. 210.** Near Petras, Jeanneret's point of departure from Greece. Pencil sketch, Carnet 3, p. 163, of ca. October 4, 1911.

view looks aft, the other toward the bow), but his route between Delphi and Patras (Pátria) is unknown; he sailed, it seems, on October 4 (fig. 210).[36]

His father's letter of September 14 was the last received in Greece; it contained forbidding news. A debate was raging whether or not to create three new teaching

36. A note in Carnet 3 says "de Patras Brindisi mercredi Vendredi," days that fall on October 4 and 6. As Jeanneret wrote and mailed a card to his parents from Naples on Saturday, October 7, saying he had just spent two days at sea, the October 4 departure from Greece seems correct.

posts at the Ecole d'art and, as Jeanneret senior wrote, "your 'friends' at the *Sentinelle* are still not mature enough for questions of aesthetics. In any case they have declared themselves inflexible adversaries of L'Eplattenier as a person, and have used means that are not to their honor; these will be turbulent times. . . ." He therefore warns his son to be prepared to prove himself, yet fortunately "the 'bourgeois' at the *National* firmly support you, and that's a point."[37] It took three years, but finally the socialists at *La Sentinelle* won the day, forcing the closure of L'Eplattenier's Nouvelle Section at the Ecole d'Art and causing Jeanneret to resign.

The more immediate and personal debate was that of Ritter vs. L'Eplattenier. As Edouard wrote his brother (letter received September 27) "Ritter sent me a parsimonious letter, threatening me and accusing me. He wants me to dance to his tune." So Jeanneret replied to Ritter: "One cannot have two popes, it's contrary to definition," and then restated much of what he said two weeks before (see note 24 above): "But would you demand that I leave him [L'Eplattenier] all alone, this pope, my most devoted friend? After all that he has done for me I must return, even though my faith has flagged because I know that a successful result is impossible." And then "I see my route. I would have preferred to go to Paris chez Perret to build his new theater. But first I will go and test my wings at home. Nothing imprisons me there, but everything holds me there." And again, as in his September 10 letter, Jeanneret expressed feelings of his own inadequacy for the job before him: "Me, I have never been up to the level of my task. Since the age of 14 I have felt as tight as a spring. . . . And my tyrant was neither a driving father nor a prodding teacher; it was me. I have been battered only by myself, because people have always praised me, encouraged me. But adulatory praise has always done me harm, and immediately plunged me into anxiety. . . . It is necessary that I achieve something, that I try, and that there be results. There will be. You laugh, my confessor!"[38]

Jeanneret arrived in Italy on his twenty-fourth birthday, October 6th. Six weeks had passed since he left Turkey and his need to complete the articles was quite obvious. Thus he worked on "Constantinople" while on the ship to Brindisi, "Elles et Eux" on

37. La Chaux-de-Fonds had more than its share of newspapers. *Le National Suisse,* in which Jeanneret senior had advised Edouard to publish his articles, was to the political right; it was the oldest paper, being in its fifty-sixth year. The *Feuille d'Avis de La Chaux-de-Fonds* (eighteenth year) and *L'Impartial* (thirty-first year) were both politically neutral. All three were dailies, except for Sunday. *La Sentinelle* (twenty-seventh year) was, in 1911, a weekly with the subtitle *Organe des socialistes du Jura.* It was, as noted earlier, the paper of Edouard's choice.

38. These penetrating insights, written just prior to Jeanneret's twenty-fourth birthday, are on two (he ran out of space) undated postcards mailed from Athens about September 25, 1911.

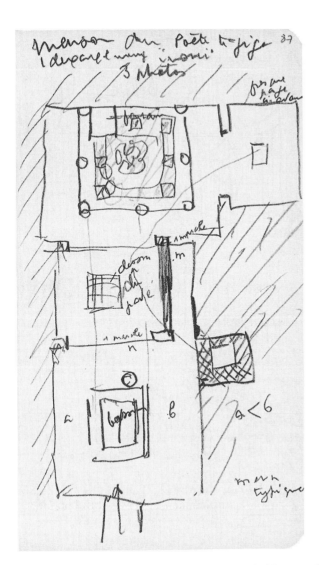

**Fig. 211.** Pompeii, House of the Tragic Poet, plan. Pencil and green pencil, Carnet 4, p. 87, October 1911.

the train to Naples, "Deux Féeries, Une Réalité" in Naples on Sunday evening October 8, and "En Occident" while at Pompeii and/or Naples "ce 10 oct."[39]

In Naples he received no mail but wrote his parents on October 7, observing how strange it seemed to see trees and green grass again, yet complaining that his diarrhea still persisted. And that morning he shipped home a Romanian carpet, bought at Mount Athos, but the terra cottas purchased in Athens could not be legally exported. As for his writing, he said it was progressing well, yet he wished that his parents' friend, Georges Dubois, would publish the articles more quickly, and certainly before month's end.

39. The manuscript for "En Occident" is in Carnet 4 nestled among Pompeii drawings on pp. 67–70 where it is dated "ce 10 oct." Nearly half the text was eliminated prior to publication.

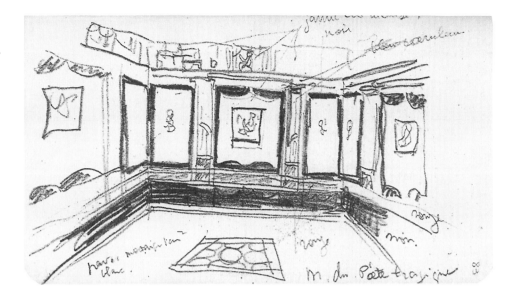

**Fig. 212.** Pompeii, room decorations in House of the Tragic Poet. Pencil sketch, Carnet 4, p. 83, October 1911.

Following a brief stay in Naples, where he both sketched and photographed the unusual facade treatment of the Gesù Nuovo church with its rustication composed of little pyramids, he moved to Pompeii where he spent five captivating days. His Baedeker (*Italie des Alpes à Naples* [Paris, 1909]) has annotations and arrows that supplement his drawings and bear witness to what he saw. And as in Constantinople, his interest focused on two building types: houses and religious structures, including their related precincts (the relation between temple and forum, for example). Axes and spatial sequences were often spoken of and drawn, and, as in Greece, it was the little asymmetries, and slight deviations of axes, that he believed gave life and vitality to the design. Later, when discussing a plan he had sketched at Pompeii (figs. 211–13), he said: "And here in the House of the Tragic Poet we have the subtleties of a consummate art. Everything is on an axis, but it would be difficult to apply a true line anywhere. The axis is in the intention, and the display afforded by the axis extends to the humbler things which it treats most skillfully by optical illusions. The axis here is not an arid thing of theory."[40]

Similar asymmetries, and the nonadherence to any strict, clearly defined bilateral axial symmetry—such as Beaux-Arts teaching would require—he observed at the forum in Pompeii, and his sketch thereof he repeatedly published in later years (fig. 214).[41] Another favorite was looking down the axis from the Temple of Jupiter, the columns of which he "restored" in order to give a better sense of space (Carnet 4, p. 103). Of

40. Le Corbusier, *Towards a New Architecture,* translated by Frederick Etchells (London, 1927), p. 175.

41. This sketch he published in *L'Esprit Nouveau, Vers une architecture, L'Oeuvre complète, La Ville Radieuse,* and *Creation Is a Patient Search.* Of it he said "The plan of the Forum contains a number of axes, but it would never obtain even a bronze medal at the Beaux Arts; it would be refused." (ibid, p. 175).

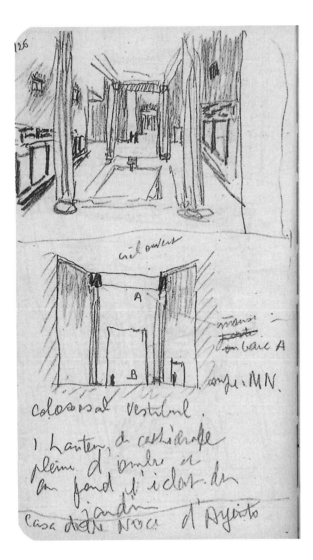

**Fig. 213.** Pompeii, Silver Wedding House showing axial view through house toward garden; and below, the vestibule. Pencil sketch, Carnet 4, p. 126, October 1911.

this subject he made a watercolor for inclusion in the Langage de Pierre exhibit (FLC 2859). He also made numerous photographs, as well as drawings, not only of the forum but of houses, sepulchers, and streets (fig. 215).[42]

Decoration and decorative motifs continued to attract considerable attention, whether wall frescoes (see fig. 212), floor mosaics, or items of furniture. Absent, however, are studies of the classical orders, the sole exception being the diverse variations found in the curve and size of the echinus of a Doric capital; this would be one of the few classical motifs he subsequently employed. Free-standing figurative sculpture

42. This severe Arch of Drusus, deprived of its ornament and standing beside the ruined Temple of Jupiter, reappears as the axial entryway for his "City for Three Million People" of 1925.

**Fig. 214.** Pompeii, plan of Forum. Le Corbusier frequently reproduced this drawing in his books. Pencil sketch, Carnet 4, p. 47, October 1911.

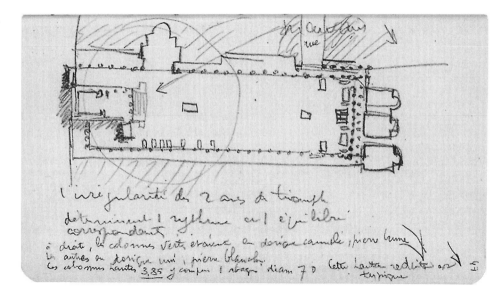

**Fig. 215.** Pompeii, Temple of Jupiter with its flanking arches at the Forum. Lead pencil on paper. Portion of 29.6 × 24.5 cm. sheet. (FLC 1937)

(National Museum, Naples) remained an attraction. Nowhere, however, does Jeanneret show the slightest interest in methods of construction, except insofar as surface materials may serve as decoration.

In view of Jeanneret's intense fascination with decoration and interior design, we should note how he misrepresented these attitudes of 1911 when writing about the

Voyage d'Orient at the height of his rebellion against decoration in 1925: "After such a trip the allure of decoration, for me, was gone for good."[43]

On Saturday 14, Jeanneret arrived in Rome. There mail informed him of the October 4 fire that consumed his father's workplace and his aunt's apartment. Straightaway he wrote a letter and a card (his first letter and only eighth card since leaving Germany in late May) offering to return home immediately if he could assist in establishing a new atelier. Parenthetically he bemoaned the presumed loss by fire of the encyclopedia and *La Patrie Suisse,* both of which he often used and needed.

Soon thereafter a long letter arrived from papa (and a card from "Mutti") saying there was no need to rush home; meanwhile both urged Edouard to prepare his articles with greater care. Father penned another in-depth analysis of his son's writing style, simultaneously regretting Edouard's interdiction against editing and saying that Dubois was continuing publication only as a personal favor.[44]

Reading the parent's correspondence is a joy. The father always concerned about his son—about his health, that he take care if having sex, that he not hurt himself while boarding trains, that he not buy unnecessary things (like pots!), that he not stay too long in Constantinople (but be sure to go to Athos), that he pay more attention to his writing skills, and that he write home more often.

Mother's style is much looser and more flowing. She discusses people, events, and her visual surroundings. From her we learn who has come to call, who is getting married, what concerts they attend, who played what and how well, and how the Chalet de la Forêt is furnished and what one sees from the various windows. And what both parents appreciate most of all is the expression of affection from their sons—and the sons in turn from them. The love and respect between the brothers also runs very deep. Obviously the family is a very happy one, in spite of the father's incessant worries.

To L'Eplattenier and Ritter he sent off cards from Rome, asking the latter whether Cingria-Vaneyre might still be in Florence; if so, could he please send the address. Unfortunately this correspondence provides minimal help in reconstructing Jeanneret's movements or impressions while in Rome. For this we must rely on his sketchbooks. Already his sojourn had been cut from several months to a few short weeks, and now he reduced it still further until both Rome and Tivoli together were compressed into a brief ten days, about two-thirds of which was spent in Rome.

Carnets 4 and 5 demonstrate that Jeanneret visited the usual Roman sites including St. Peter's, the Sistine Chapel, Hadrian's Tomb, the Pantheon, Piazza Navona, Capitoline, Forum, Arch of Constantine, Colosseum, and in Carnet 5 the Basilica of Santa Maria Maggiore, Santa Maria in Cosmedin, Atrium of the Vestals, Villa Farnesina, Villa

43. "Confession" in *L'Art décoratif d'aujourd'hui* (Paris, 1925), p. 211.

44. The father reported: "Franchement, Mr. Dubois te trouve trop prolixe, trop spécial, pas assez à la portée des lecteurs et j'ai l'impression qu'il redoute de voir tant de place consacrée à tes causeries."

Lante, and the Baths of Caracalla (fig. 216). He rarely recorded seventeenth-century Baroque designs. Baedeker remained his faithful guide.

A new element now appears among his drawings. He starts to analyze buildings, and their visual composition, in terms of basic geometric elements such as horizontals and verticals, or as square, cube, cylinder, cone, sphere, and pyramid. On some drawings he jots these words over the building represented (fig. 217), and on somewhat more carefully finished drawings we see that the whole composition is an abstract arrangement of basic geometric shapes (fig. 218); in the latter case they read (left to right) as vertical, cube, horizontal, square; this is not my interpretation but Jeanneret's as given on the following sketchbook page. The resulting arrangement, pictorially speaking, creates a unified and harmonious whole, well balanced yet asymmetrical.

Translating these silhouettes and solids into nonclassical components, we realize that this constitutes a lesson in the fundamentals of basic design. Jeanneret, apparently, was endeavoring to devise a method of teaching architectural composition, a course he must soon teach, and teaching is itself an educational experience. Quite soon these pure geometric shapes would appear in projects submitted to Jeanneret by his students. For him this became an elemental creed, with few of his drawings being more frequently reproduced than this, which he called The Lesson of Rome (fig. 219).

Among Renaissance masters, Michelangelo received the most attention. Two of his Last Judgment figures were sketched, the Capitoline was both sketched and photographed, and the apse of St. Peter's recorded in numerous photographs. Years later he

**Fig. 217.** Rome. "To compose a city landscape" with its various vertical and horizontal elements is how Jeanneret labels this pencil sketch in Carnet 4, p. 140, of October 1911.

**Fig. 218.** Rome, Forum with Arch of Septimus Severus as "Composed" by Jeanneret to emphasize its geometric components. Pencil sketch, Carnet 4, p. 179, mid–October 1911.

returned to these themes, juxtaposing Michelangelo's St. Peter's with the elevation of the Colosseum (fig. 220).

Perhaps the building most influential for Jeanneret's future was by the Mannerist artist Giulio Romano whose Villa Lante on the Janiculum was recorded in sketches, photographs, and a larger drawing (fig. 221).[45] Jeanneret's annotations in Carnet 5 speak

45. Obviously it was not his 1909 Baedeker that drew Jeanneret's attention to the Ville Lante because the only mention is: "La route passe plus loin devant la villa Lante (à dr.) et l'église St-Onuphre pour . . ." (p. 338).

**Fig. 219.** "The Lesson of Rome." This page was published in *L'Esprit Nouveau,* no. 1 (1920), but when reprinted in *L'Esprit Nouveau,* no. 14 (1922) and in *Vers une architecture* (1923) the lower portion, showing the decorated cylindrical forms, was omitted. See next chapter for how these forms reappear in work by Jeanneret's students at the Ecole d'art.

« Tout est sphères et cylindres. »

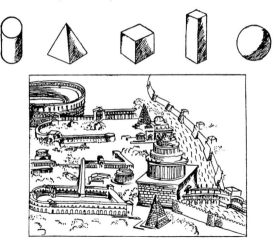

Il y a des formes simples déclancheuses de sensations constantes.

Des modifications interviennent, dérivées, et conduisent la sensation première (de l'ordre majeur au mineur), avec toute la gamme intermédiaire des combinaisons. Exemples :

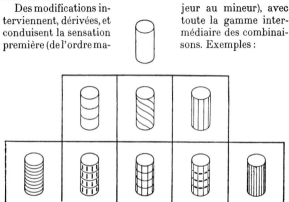

of it as the affirmation of the cube, and aspects of its design would soon appear at La Chaux-de-Fonds and in his earliest work in France.

From Rome Jeanneret went to Tivoli where he spent less time than at Pompeii. Hadrian's villa was the main attraction although at least twice he visited the Villa d'Este (mid-sixteenth century) where the spatial sequence of the gardens fascinated him; he acquired ten postcards in addition to his sketches and photographs.

At the Villa Adriana (Hadrian's villa) he filled forty pages with sketches and plans, focusing attention on the Poikile, the Library and its many-columned courtyard (fig. 222), the Piazza d'Oro with its adjacent temples, and especially the apse end of the Canopus with its great exedra wherein formerly stood the statue of Serapis (fig. 223). No less than seven pages were devoted to this one design which later (1948) inspired his project for the underground basilica of Sainte-Baume and soon thereafter the

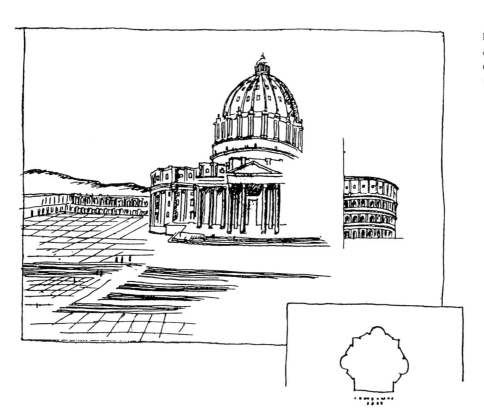

Fig. 220. Rome, Michelangelo's design for St. Peter's compared to the Colosseum. (*Vers une architecture,* p. 137)

Fig. 221. Rome, Villa Lante, Giulio Romano, architect. Pencil and green pencil on paper, mid-October 1911. 13 × 18 cm. (FLC 6110)

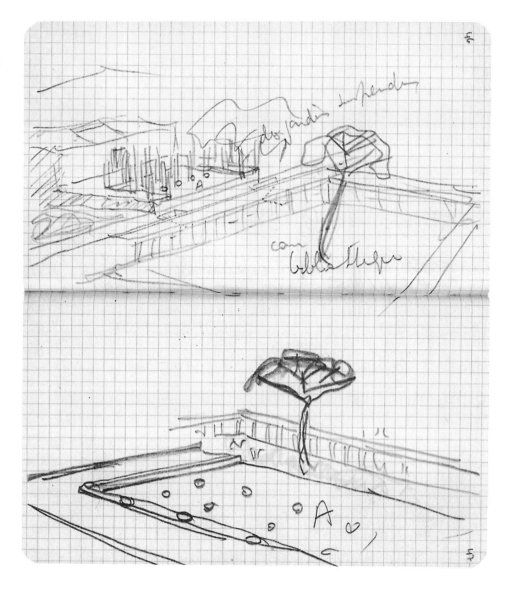

periscope-like light shafts above the secondary altars at the pilgrimage chapel of Ronchamp (1950–55). At this later stage of life Le Corbusier was no longer sensitive about revealing his sources of inspiration and therefore, after first redrawing them, he published the sketches from pages 68, 69, and 71 of Carnet 5 in *Oeuvre Complète,* volume 5, along with his designs for Ronchamp.[46]

A conclusion we can draw from Jeanneret's visits to Rome and Tivoli is that from the entire Renaissance period, the fifteenth to eighteenth centuries, what appealed to

46. Most architects are more impressed by the so-called Marine Theater (Natatorium), Hadrian's circular island hideaway, yet Jeanneret devoted only a single page to this highly complex structure.

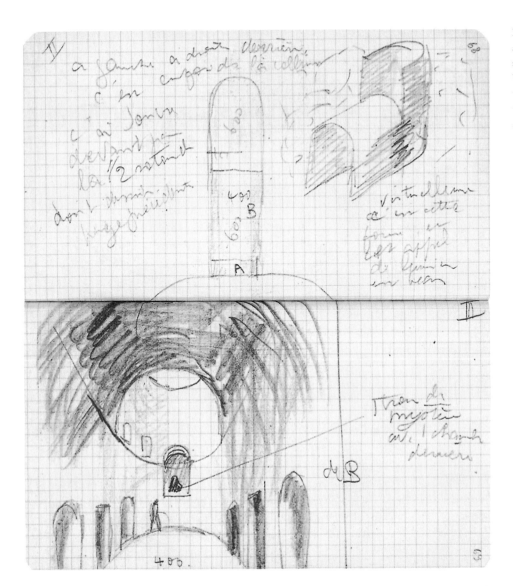

**Fig. 223.** Tivoli, Hadrian's Villa, apse end of the Canopus. Pencil sketch in Carnet 5, pp. 68–69, October 1911. Le Corbusier later redrew these sketches and published them as the idea-source for the chapel towers at Ronchamp.

him most was the sixteenth century, that is, the Mannerist years following the High Renaissance and preceding the Baroque.

Precisely when he left Rome, or arrived in Florence, is not known (probably October 25) but when writing Klipstein he said: "You will note that I bypassed Assisi, Orvieto, Sienna [and apparently also Perugia and Arezzo] because I am momentarily incapable of admiring eclectic things." He was also propelled by a desire to get home, as suggested by his letters. Therefore he remained only two or three days in Florence, then one or two in Pisa (and perhaps Carrara), before setting out for Lucerne, Switzerland, in order to visit Hermann Jeanneret, whom he called Hagen and described as one of his closest friends.

**Fig. 224.** Florence, Chartreuse d'Ema, "promenade architecturale" and courtyard of one of the monk's cells. Pencil sketch, Carnet 6, p. 13, October, 1911.

From the same letter to Klipstein, begun in Florence and finished on the train Monday evening October 30, we learn that he would like "to erect an altar to Michelangelo and to Rembrandt. But also an altar to our own generation."[47] He then singled out the Last Judgment and Medici Chapel for special praise. Most Italian painting, however, he maligned, especially the things which, in 1907, he had admired. Nevertheless he listed three exclusions: "Memmi aux Espagnols is an exception, Orcagna at Pisa, Ucello at the Uffizi." As for architecture, he still praised Giotto's Campanile (because now he saw in it a cube) and "the Baptistery I adore."

Pisa, not Florence, had been, and remained, his first love.[48] The Camposanto (cemeteries again!) and its frescoes (especially those then attributed to Orcagna) were constantly on his mind and often mentioned in his letters; also the triumvirate of baptistery, cathedral, and leaning tower. But most of his sketches, as expected, were of the Chartreuse d'Ema (Galluzo) that had so inspired him in 1907 when he wrote his parents: "I would like to live all my life in what they call their cells. It is the [perfect] solution to the working man's house, type unique or rather an earthly paradise."[49] Thus Jeanneret

47. He expressed similar thoughts to Ritter on November 1: "Il faut dresser deux autels à Michel Ange et à Rembrandt. Tous les autres des histoire de l'art sont du fumier. Piero della Francesca est un poète. Cimabue est un peintre. Et Giotto, un décadent." What a reversal from his Ruskinian views of 1907!

48. "Pisa fut ma première admiration et reste la dernière" (to L'Eplattenier, October 29, 1911), while of Florence he commented in Carnet 6, page 5, "J'étais tout à fait désolé de tout, Florence laid, et Fiesole banal. . . ." To L'Eplattenier he also remarked: "L'Italie me fait regarder l'orient. L'Italie est encore et aussi un mythe."

49. Written to his parents September 15, 1907. For a discussion thereof, including the influence of the Chartreuse on his later work, see Le Corbusier, *Précisions sur un état présent de l'architecture et de l'urbanisme* (Paris, 1930; reissued 1960), p. 91.

**Fig. 225.** Pisa, sketch of baptistry and cathedral with wall of campo-santo at right, October 1911. (Le Corbusier, *Creation Is a Patient Search*, p. 41)

fulfilled his vow of four years before: to revisit the Chartreuse d'Ema at the conclusion of his years of travel and apprenticeships (figs. 224, 225).

In anticipation of his arrival home, he asked L'Eplattenier if he might stay with him while seeking lodgings of his own (he wanted something similar to the old farmhouse at Mount Cornu). He had no wish to spend a single night at his parents because he wanted independence and solitude. This recalls his previous request of 1909 upon his return from Paris.[50]

A long letter to Ritter, written from Lucerne, exemplifies Jeanneret's state of mind during one of his periodic "highs." It is like a stream of consciousness that, for the most part, says little which is meaningful while giving the impression that the writer is in a dream.[51] One is tempted to attribute it to having boozed it up with Hagen, yet a previous card to Ritter from Florence was written in a similar vein. Perhaps he was just rejoicing at not losing Ritter's friendship over the L'Eplattenier affair, or was excited about getting home with its new challenges and the chance to see old friends.

50. "Je ne logerai pas chez mes parents par force majeure et aussi il est mieux et nécessaire que je sois libre. Et toujours par force majeure je ne pourrai passer même les premiers jours chez eux" (to L'Eplattenier, October 29, 1911). Finally, however, he did stay with his parents in their tiny apartment where, we should recall, he had no room of his own, whereas the L'Eplattenier house was quite commodious.

51. Such visions, however, must not be dismissed too lightly as they sometimes foretell design ideas he will later endeavor to realize. When reading the following lines from his October 31–November 1, 1911, letter to Ritter, think, for example, of Le Corbusier's plan for Rio de Janeiro of 1929 or the Plan Obus of 1932–33 for Algiers: "Les rues droites avec des fenêtres en damier aux façades. Pas d'ornement. Une seule

In any case, we read in the father's Journal: "Edouard arrived the evening of November 1st in good health after a trip of 7 months [since leaving Behrens' office]. He has the intention of establishing his career here as an architect."

---

couleur, un seul matériau dans toute la ville. Des autos déferlant, des aéroplanes passent sans plus qu'on les regarde. Il y aurait de vos rues sur les toits, au milieu des fleurs et des arbres. On y monterait par de vastes escaliers et on passerait sur des ponts. Puis on descendrait."

# III

EARLY PROFESSIONAL CAREER

*1912–1916*

# 9

## THE VILLAS JEANNERET-PERRET AND FAVRE-JACOT, AND JEANNERET'S ROLE AS TEACHER

### *1912–1914*

Upon his return to La Chaux-de-Fonds on November 1, 1911, Jeanneret launched into a prodigious work schedule that was sufficient to exhaust the average man yet one he maintained for the remainder of his life.

Immediately, he started designing his parents' house while simultaneously writing, and within three months completing, his first published book, *Etude sur le mouvement d'art décoratif en Allemagne* (discussed in Chapter 7). Likewise he continued writing and editing his Voyage d'Orient articles hoping to publish them as a book, especially as the unfinished series, after a long hiatus, was again appearing in the hometown press. Other articles, reports, and pamphlets soon followed. Meanwhile, in January, his teaching commenced which required twelve classroom hours per week, and the following month he started designing a large villa for the founder of the Zenith Watch Company at Le Locle. And before year's end he entered the field of interior decoration which soon became his major preoccupation. This necessitated selecting and buying fabrics, furniture, light fixtures, wallpaper, etc. for his clients, thereby requiring trips to Paris and in Switzerland—sometimes accompanied by his clients. Soon, however, he began designing furniture on his own. He thoroughly enjoyed this role as decorator, except when dealing with certain of his clients.

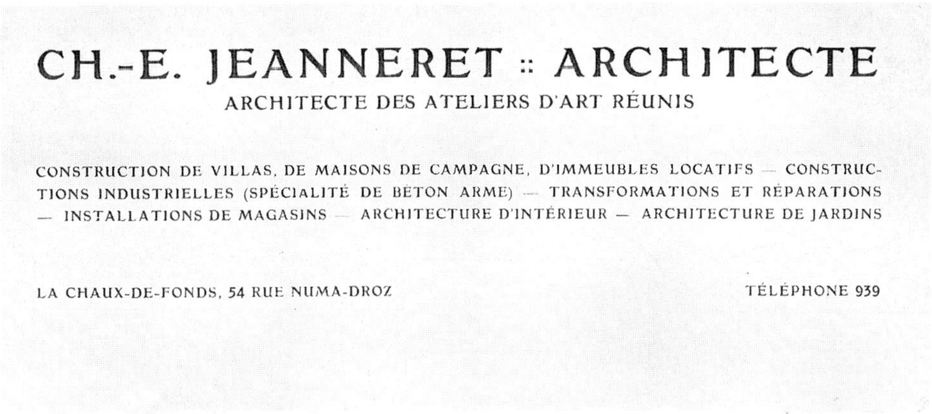

**Fig. 226.** Letterhead designed by Jeanneret in 1912.

# CH.-E. JEANNERET :: ARCHITECTE
## ARCHITECTE DES ATELIERS D'ART RÉUNIS

CONSTRUCTION DE VILLAS, DE MAISONS DE CAMPAGNE, D'IMMEUBLES LOCATIFS — CONSTRUCTIONS INDUSTRIELLES (SPÉCIALITÉ DE BÉTON ARMÉ) — TRANSFORMATIONS ET RÉPARATIONS — INSTALLATIONS DE MAGASINS — ARCHITECTURE D'INTÉRIEUR — ARCHITECTURE DE JARDINS

LA CHAUX-DE-FONDS, 54 RUE NUMA-DROZ                    TÉLÉPHONE 939

He relished organizing things and soon joined several committees involved with publications and the arts. He helped found the Ateliers d'art réunis in 1910 and now became its energetic secretary; they rented space in the old hospital at 54, rue Numa-Droz where Jeanneret installed his office and where the Nouvelle Section of the Ecole d'art occupied the upper floor. His father (Journal, November 20, 1911) regretted his son's business association with old school friends; he felt that Edouard should strike out independently on his own. Yet Edouard was too fond of being a big fish in a small pond to heed such advice. His stationary clearly emphasized his choice: "Ch.-E. Jeanneret Architecte: Architecte des Ateliers d'art réunis" (fig. 226). Les Ateliers had, as discussed in Chapter 6, decorated the main hall of the new post office (1910), the crematorium (1909–12), the Hirsch Pavilion at the observatory in Neuchâtel (1910–11), and the living room and exterior entryway at 30 bis, rue Grenier, the home of Emile and Hélène Moser (1910).

Jeanneret also shared living accommodations with his friends. Prior to returning home he arranged to spend a few days with L'Eplattenier but eventually stayed four weeks! Octave Matthey and Eric de Coulon were then living in an old farmhouse called "Le Couvent"; this filled Jeanneret with envy.[1] He therefore rented the upper floor and remodelled it, installing a beamed ceiling, plaster walls that he painted white, and cutting through the outer wall to install a large window; later he even brought in a piano (figs. 227, 228). However the coke-burning stove provided insufficient heat during the depths of winter. Meals he took at home, which was only a five-minute walk away. He remained at Le Couvent for nearly a year, until his parents' new home was finished; therein he provided a room for himself and his brother as well as a commodious drafting room. Matthey and de Coulon, meanwhile, had left the farmhouse with the onslaught of winter.

1. Why it is called Le Couvent is uncertain; it never served that purpose. But apparently a Neuchâtel monastery once used it as a tithe barn for storing grain, thus its name. The present address is 28, rue du Couvent.

**Fig. 227.** "Le Couvent," with Jeanneret posed in front of the large second-floor window that he had had cut through the farmhouse wall. Summer 1912 (BV)

**Fig. 228.** Albert, at piano, Edouard, wearing fool's cap, and their parents in the apartment that Edouard designed for himself in "Le Couvent." 1912 (FLC)

"La petite maison" was often mentioned in correspondence during the previous year and on December 18 Jeanneret wrote Ritter, "at the time of my departure in 1907 I proposed to my parents a nice little lodging—not even a room for their sons." Yet once he started developing his ideas "la petite maison" became a very substantial villa. Nonetheless its design and construction were completed within the year he returned to La Chaux-de-Fonds (see color plate V).

Work on the design commenced in November and was well along by early February when he received an important commission from the industrialist Georges Favre-Jacot at Le Locle. Thereafter he worked on both projects simultaneously hoping to start construction immediately after the spring thaw, about April 1. The building of "la maison blanche," as he ultimately called his father's house, actually began April 15 but it was not until the following month that the Villa Favre-Jacot got underway.

The father's journal keeps us posted:

*April 30, 1912:* The house comes out of the ground; the foundations advance.

*May 21:* The house advances, the basement is finished, the ground floor partly. We go there every evening. Edouard manages the affair very well. He is also much occupied at Le Locle and with other projects. He has received from notables in various countries congratulations for the great value of his report on Germany.

*June 25:* The house is under roof since several days; we celebrated the "raising" Thursday the 21st, in the house itself, with thirty workers and friends; collation: sausage and cheese, wine, beer, rhubarb tarts, cigars . . . cost 103 frs. This is a nice gesture but *too grand* for our family, and most regrettable when we have not established an estimate for the cost of construction.

*July 2:* Work on the interior, but there are delays . . . installation of water, electricity.

*July 17:* Masons on strike this past week, stopping their work on our house; it advances slowly; tomorrow "éternite" [an asbestos type of shingle] will be installed on the roof; it seems that the budget will be surpassed—and by a considerable sum.

*August 1:* The building advances *very slowly,* it is enormous this thing that [Edouard] has made—interior, exterior, terraces which will cost us dearly.

*August 10:* The house advances steadily; they are installing the windows, the wood blinds, the plaster of Paris; there is still much to do.

*October 10:* The house is nearly finished, we will move in toward the end of the month!!!

[Winter then caused a six-month hiatus in outside work]

*May 13, 1913:* This week some ten masons and terrace builders arrived to do exterior construction—terraces, walls, etc.

**Fig. 229.** Romanian house sketched by Jeanneret during Voyage d'Orient. Carnet 1, p. 65. 1911 (FLC)

*June 25, 1913:* Much work has been done around the house, terraces, sustaining walls, painting woodwork, all of which considerably augments the initial cost which will now certainly reach 50,000 frs. What a sum!

On February tenth Edouard wrote Ritter that he regretted painting the upstairs windows and columns black (he had admired black at Behrens' crematorium) and intended to repaint them white like the rest of the house, thus emphasizing the wall as surface and the sense of the house as a cube. This, of course, was another expense.

Aside from wanting the house to appear as a cube, there is only one written reference to his source for the design. It appears in a letter to Klipstein of December 18, 1911: "Send me, *as fast as possible,* either the negatives or the bromide prints of the *Balkans,* Kuajewatz, Radejevatz, the monasteries at Bucharest, Kasanlik and above all the *terrace of the Skite Sainte-Anna.* I need them for the villa that I'm designing at this moment."

Other factors confirm that Balkan architecture influenced his design. Not only do sketchbook drawings of a Romanian house (Carnet 1, pp. 62–65) have similarities with the villa but the same carnet contains Jeanneret's earliest known drawing for the villa, thereby confirming that he was studying Balkan architecture while designing the family home (fig. 229).

He also praises, in his sketchbooks, what he calls the Balkan "chambre d'été," a terraced, often trellised, private courtyard that forms an extension of the house. This term, with reference to its Eastern origin, he used to describe the enclosed and trellised terrace at the side of his parents' house. Finally, in the *Voyage d'Orient,* he applauds the Balkan custom of employing blue for trim around doors and windows. This regional hallmark, unknown in central Europe, appears around the door of the Jeanneret house;

it is also the dominant color of the entrance hall where even the floor is of tiles that are blue and white.[2] And, as a final observation, when that aficionado of southeastern Europe, William Ritter, visited the house in 1915 his thank-you note to Mme. Jeanneret (October 2) spoke of her "white and grey house transplanted from The Bosphorus."[3]

In another *Voyage* sketchbook (Carnet 5, pp. 17–19), as well as in a drawing at larger scale, Jeanneret sketched the Villa Lante on the Janiculum in Rome. He showed it in a worm's-eye view, just as one sees the Villa Jeanneret-Perret, and its cubic mass is often referred to in his notes, clearly emphasizing what attracted him to this design (fig. 221 in chap. 8 above).

In spite of its references to Italy and Eastern Europe, the Villa Jeanneret-Perret would not be out of place in any of the fashionable new suburbs around Berlin. With numerous examples to choose from, I illustrate one from Charlottenburg of 1909 (fig. 230). This house, and others like it, might be cited as a source for Jeanneret's design what with its cubic form, hipped roof, central dormer, wide roof overhang, continuous row of second storey windows, high string course coinciding with window sills, and curved projection in the middle of the facade—not to mention the exterior finish of stucco or cement plaster.

**Fig. 230.** Villa in Charlottenburg, Germany. Wolfg. Siemering and J. Habicht, architects. (*Architektur des XX Jahrhunderts,* 9 [1909], plate 57)

Other Germanic references may derive from Josef Hoffmann and his Villa Hochstätter, drawings of which appeared in *Deutsche Kunst und Dekoration* (19, 1906, pp. 39–41) with photographs of the completed house in volume 24, 1909, p. 202. The thin slab of the entrance veranda roof, hipped roof of the house, high string course, and glazed, semicircular projecting room are all features found in Jeanneret's design. Meanwhile the curve-sided dormer window at the Villa Jeanneret recalls that of Wolf Dohrn's villa at Hellerau designed by Theodor Fischer (1909–10) and published in *Deutsche Kunst und Dekoration* in 1911 (volume 27, p. 446), a villa Jeanneret knew from his visits to Hellerau. Yet the German architect whose design sensibility was the closest of all to Jeanneret's was that of his former teacher, Peter Behrens, whose work was obviously well known.

This litany of possible sources for the Villa Jeanneret-Perret demonstrates the futility of trying to isolate a single dominant source for a design by Jeanneret, even at this early stage of his career.[4] It fails to account for his extraordinary power of synthesis. It is far

2. The original blue door trim and floor tiles are still in situ although the entry walls were repainted red by later occupants because they sought a warmer color.

3. The rectangular oriel window of the antechamber on the northeast side of the villa may also derive from the Turkish house.

4. Paul Venable Turner ("Frank Lloyd Wright and the Young Le Corbusier," *Journal of the Society of Architectural Historians,* 42, no. 4 [1983], pp. 350–59), maintains, and is supported by other writers, that the predominant influence on both the design and the plan of the Villa Jeanneret was Frank Lloyd Wright's architecture as known to Jeanneret through the *Schweizerische Bauzeitung* issue of September 1912. (He uses 1913 for the design of the villa.) He also contends that the Dom-ino projects, the Villa Schwob, and, to

**Fig. 231.** Villa Jeanneret-Perret. Preliminary sketch, ca. December 1911. Carnet 1, p. 121.

more reasonable to acknowledge the rich variety of visual experiences available to him and then indicate how he wove these ideas into the final fabric.

Few preliminary sketches for the villa exist. Perhaps the earliest, judging by its discrepancy with the final design, is, as previously mentioned, found in the same sketchbook as a Romanian house (fig. 231). All the elements of the final design are present except that the horizontal band of windows and arched front door appear on the same, rather than opposite, sides of the house. This suggests that Jeanneret initially considered placing the entrance at the basement level, and therefore closer to the street.

Another small sketch, subsequently sent to Ritter, shows the definitive cubic massing but with a circular window in the living room and a row of niches (or are these windows?) in the terrace wall (fig. 232). Meanwhile three pages of crude pencil sketches in the Carnet Bleu (Sketchbook T 71) show fenestration closer to the executed design while, of the several plans, that at the upper right most closely resembles the final scheme (fig. 233).[5]

Perhaps the last perspective to be drawn by Jeanneret carries the number 21 at the upper left (FLC 30266); therefore it belongs to the series of twenty blueprints prepared for the construction of the house (fig. 234). Because numbers 17 and 18 (pertaining to the structure) are signed and dated April 26 and 27 respectively, construction commenced before the last drawings were complete.

varying degrees, four of Le Corbusier's "Five Points" of architecture were influenced by Wright. In short, without Wright, Le Corbusier's architecture would have been quite different. I disagree.

5. The worm's-eye perspective on this particular sheet indicates little about the roof except its overhang. The elevation, drawn on the previous page, shows that the roof was to be hipped.

**Fig. 232.** Villa Jeanneret-Perret. Preliminary study, ca. January 1912. 14.6 × 18 cm. (BV)

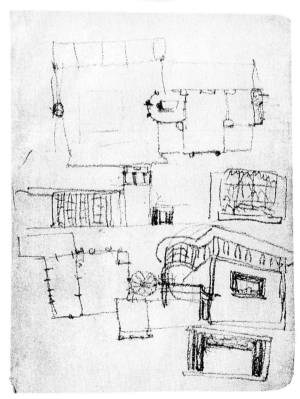

**Fig. 233.** Villa Jeanneret-Perret. Studies for elevation, plans, and windows. Sketchbook T 71, p. 3. (FLC)

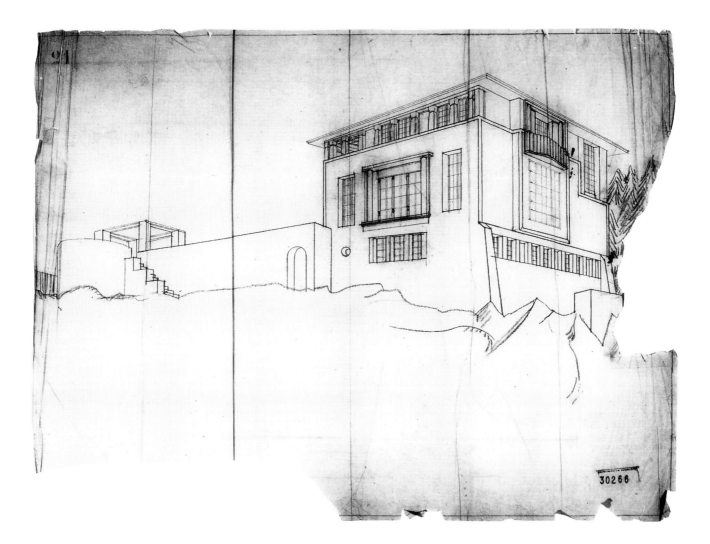

**Fig. 234.** Villa Jeanneret-Perret. Perspective study. Of the eight spaces between piers (upper level, front) two are without glazing and open onto a porch and two others (third and sixth) are blind. Pencil and charcoal on tracing paper. 58 × 80 cm. (FLC 30266)

The fenestration was constantly undergoing change; the four elevation drawings (nos. 5–8) do not correspond to perspective no. 21 and the latter fails to correspond to the finished building (figs. 235, 236). Also, the large third-floor dormer window (the sons' room) does not appear in any of the designs. Notwithstanding these minor variations, however, it is remarkable how relatively close all the sketches are to the basic massing of the finished building. Therefore Jeanneret's ideas were substantially fixed before he committed himself to paper.

Figure 237 shows the house soon after completion and before the black areas were repainted white. Note here the dormer that is missing in the drawings, and the band of eight windows with two more around the corner. These corner openings originally were not glazed because this was a small porch. The rather squat, flat-sided columns dividing the openings have their origin in the Jura; their shape comes from sixteenth-

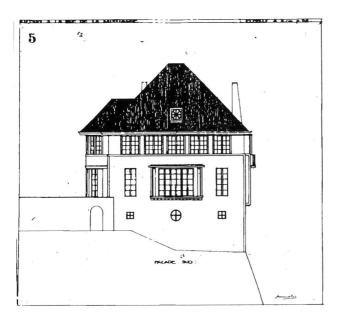
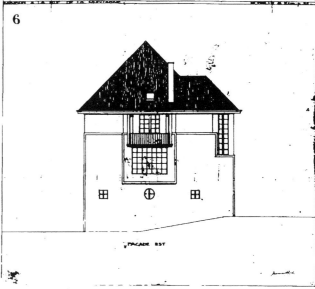

to early nineteenth-century columns that might support the fireplace hood in a Jura farmhouse.[6]

Solar heat in summer proved excessive within the house, and awnings were soon installed at both the living room and "petit salon" windows, and when subsequent owners moved in they closed the third and the sixth openings of the second floor for the same reason. These two windows are actually shown as closed in Jeanneret's drawing 21, our figure 234.

The plan deserves our special attention. It is remarkable for its openness and almost bilateral symmetry (figs. 243, 244). The central area forms a T, the short stem being the living room (its axis running from fireplace to great window) with the long arms being an antichamber and dining room respectively, each aligned on the same axis and extending beyond the cubic confines of the house. Both, however, terminate in different geometric shapes and both are generously glazed. Between these rooms a modicum of privacy and thermal control is gained from thinly mullioned French doors that can be folded back upon themselves (figs. 245–48). One Victorian characteristic remains, and that is the placement of heavy drapes at every opening.

To square off the T and emphasize the cube, Jeanneret introduced secondary rooms (approximately nine feet square) below the arms of the T that he called "petit-salon" and "bibliothèque." The bilateral symmetry and strong axial organization of these five rooms (the two smaller ones being basically unnecessary) demonstrate a lingering influence on him of certain principles of Beaux-Arts planning.

Fig. 235. Villa Jeanneret-Perret. Original blueprints (here with color reversed) of front (southeast) and side (northeast) elevations as drawn by Jeanneret. Modifications, however, occurred during execution. 1912. (BV)

6. Such columns may conveniently be seen in the restaurant La Cheminée, at 91 Charrière, only a few paces from the cemetery and crematorium at La Chaux-de-Fonds.

**Fig. 236.** Villa Jeanneret-Perret. Cross section (approximately south–north) through staircase. (Original blueprints redrawn for clarity by Etienne Chavanne and Michel Laville)

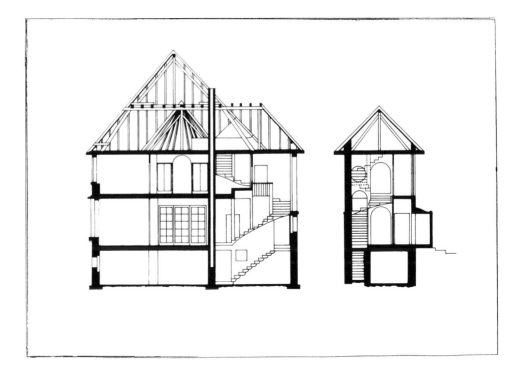

**Fig. 237.** Villa Jeanneret-Perret. Photographed by Jeanneret during the winter of 1912–13 before he had the black window casements repainted white and had completed the terrace. (BV)

**Fig. 238.** Villa Jeanneret-Perret. Photograph by Jeanneret showing completed terrace and addition of awning over the living room window, ca. 1915. (BV)

**Fig. 239.** Villa Jeanneret-Perret. West facade prior to completing the "chambre d'été," summer 1913. The opening in the pavement, lower right, is a stairway leading up from the street, while the front door is approached under the covered portico at extreme left. The opened storm windows of the ground storey give the appearance of shutters. (BV)

**Fig. 240.** Villa Jeanneret-Perret. Detail of south corner showing surface texture of roughcast and the lower part of second-storey piers. (Photo by author)

**Fig. 241.** Villa Jeanneret-Perret seen from the west after completion of the "chambre d'été," ca. 1915. The terraced hillside setting is quite evident. (BV)

**Fig. 242.** The "chambre d'été" at the Villa Jeanneret-Perret near completion, ca. 1916. (FLC)

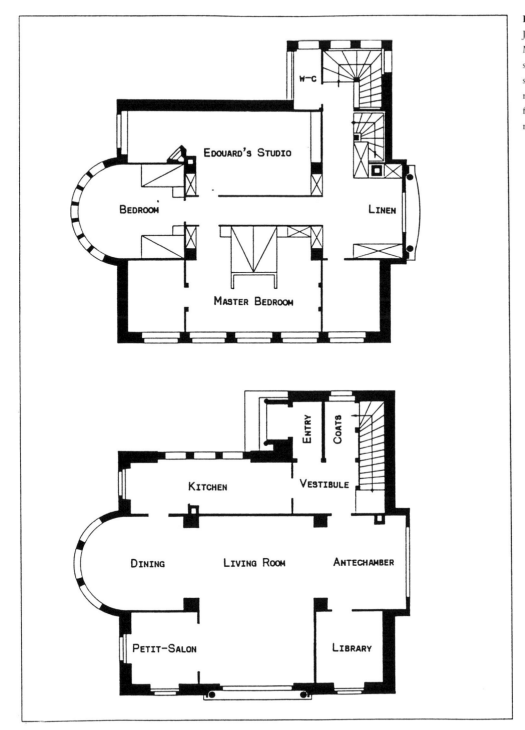

**Fig. 243.** Villa Jeanneret-Perret. Jeanneret's plans, redrawn for clarity. Modifications occurred during construction, especially to the second-storey fenestration and the small rooms beside the master bedroom. A fireplace was also added in the living room.

W-C

EDOUARD'S STUDIO

BEDROOM

LINEN

MASTER BEDROOM

ENTRY

COATS

KITCHEN

VESTIBULE

DINING          LIVING ROOM          ANTECHAMBER

PETIT-SALON          LIBRARY

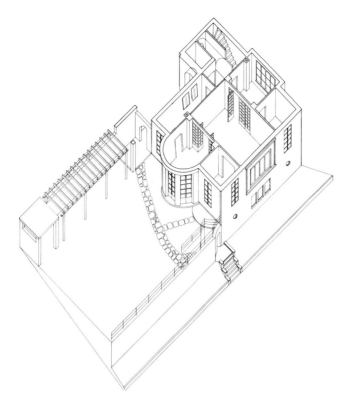

**Fig. 244.** Villa Jeanneret-Perret. Cut-away axonometric seen from the southwest. (*Le Corbusier,* Academy Editions, [London, New York: St. Martin's Press, 1987], p. 81)

**Fig. 245.** Villa Jeanneret-Perret. Living room looking toward dining room. Lack of wall space makes furniture arrangement difficult, thus the grand piano is in the middle of the room and the desk against the draperies of the "petit-salon." Ca. 1915. (FLC)

**Fig. 246.** Desk, designed by Jeanneret, in living room at Villa Jeanneret-Perret, ca. 1915. (FLC)

**Fig. 247.** Living room (east wall), Villa Jeanneret-Perret. Sofa designed by Jeanneret; note his selection of wallpaper. Piano is visible at left and drapes close off the antechamber. (FLC)

**Fig. 248.** Detail of fireplace with portion of Jeanneret's painted frieze that is signed and dated "1913 Ch. E. Jt." (Photo by author)

On visiting the house, my reaction is always the same; the principal rooms seem more American, due to their openness, brightness, and lack of compartmentalization, than any comparable European houses that I know; only Perret's 25 bis, rue Franklin apartments have an analogous sense of continuing space. By American I refer especially to Queen Anne and Shingle Style planning of about the 1880s which, however, would be less uniformly axial than Jeanneret's plan.[7]

The approach to the house is circuitous. From the street one climbs several steps, then mounts a steep slope before reaching the level of the basement where one turns left and ascends a steep, narrow staircase to the terrace which then must be crossed before arriving at a pergola where one turns right and finally faces the front door. To follow this route in bad weather when carrying packages must be a daunting task.

The front door, trimmed in blue and of heavy fireproof construction, has the shape of a ship's bulkhead, yet the non-nautical door handle has the form of a lizard, similar to that of the lizards at the Villa Fallet. Inside, the vestibule and the barrel-vaulted coatroom are illuminated by a porthole-type window; a staircase, the square balusters of which are set at 45°, rises to the right (fig. 249). The coatroom, antechamber, and

7. This openness, however, is not at all similar to that of the far more sophisticated and complex spatial constructions of Frank Lloyd Wright. For an analysis thereof, see my *Writings on Wright* (Cambridge: MIT Press, 1981), pp. 175–88, "Wright and the Destruction of the Box."

library doors are carefully aligned on axis. The kitchen is off the vestibule, providing easy access to the front door.

The "lingerie" or linen room is at the top of the stairs and, by its size, large window, and little balcony, serves as an upstairs sitting or sewing room. On axis, down the corridor, is the guest room with its semicircular bay window.[8] To the left of this corridor lies the master bedroom with its auxiliary spaces (fig. 250) while to the right is Edou-

8. Initially Edouard slept here (to Ritter November 17, 1912). It was painted yellow, with his parents' room being white.

**Fig. 250.** Edouard's parents in master bedroom, showing continuous row of windows, separated by exterior columns. Tall chest of draws cum desk is ca. 1800 (note pots from Jeanneret's collection on top) while the vernacular chair in foreground is also early; both were perhaps purchased by Jeanneret. These, and the living room desk, are today in the house at Vevey. (FLC )

ard's splendid workspace, consisting of two areas opening into one another; one is adjacent to the window and contains a fireplace while the larger space behind is evenly lit (even in the darkest weather) by a large skylight (fig. 251). On the third floor, under the roof, the boys' room is laid out like a European train compartment with its narrow table set perpendicular to the window with benches and beds on either side. The basement, meanwhile, contains the father's workshop as well as a laundry room, heating plant, and coal bin. As city water was unavailable, rain was collected on the roof and stored in an attic cistern and in an even larger reservoir in the basement; the system was so efficient that in the 1990s it was still in use, decades after public water mains reached that part of town.

The terrace, or "chambre d'été," was completed over a period of several years. The trellised walk walled off the woods on the uphill side while the downhill side was entirely open. Subsequently, when the original wooden trellis rotted, it was replaced with concrete of the same dimensions.

The villa was built on an ancient quarry, so extensive excavations were unnecessary. Construction of its exterior load-bearing masonry walls was quite traditional (fig. 252),

**Fig. 251.** Edouard's studio, Villa Jeanneret-Perret, including Amédée Ozenfant, Albert, and Edouard, who is clowning with his favorite Serbian pot, August 1919. Overhead illumination is provided by a skylight. (BV)

yet the interior support system was far less orthodox. Four massive (50 × 60 cm.) masonry piers, clearly visible on the plan (where the dining room and antechamber abut the living room), not only carry much of the roof's weight but also eliminate the need for *interior* load-bearing walls. Iron beams, supported by these piers, carry the timber floor joists. Therefore only lightweight partitions were required on the interior, and these could be rearranged at will because they were independent of the structure. Two years later this idea was incorporated into Jeanneret's Dom-ino system of construction.

Concrete played a negligible role and apparently was used only for the decorative columns and lintels separating the second-storey windows. Although Jeanneret long had been convinced that concrete was the material of the future, he was still incapable of designing it and therefore wrote to Max Du Bois in Paris explaining his needs and asking Du Bois to send the proper specifications.

The exterior is of roughcast, its roughness being more typical of English or Scottish usage than that of central Europe (see fig. 240). The color is white except for brownish-tan in the recess around the picture window and in certain "blind" windows at the rear.[9] Both the surface and the paint are original although the éternite roof and dormer

9. A later owner subsequently installed mosaics around the front window. However the original tan color, never restored, is still visible in the "blind" rear windows of the house. The house, being occupied by members of the same caring family for almost seventy years, has remained in virtually mint condition.

window were soon replaced. Inside, the linoleum floors remain in situ except in the master bedroom, the colors being grayish-green or natural wood. The tile floors, except where replaced to change the color, are still in place. The staircase is of unpainted wood. The living room was originally wallpapered, the entrance hall painted blue, the guest room yellow, and most of the remaining rooms were white.

The furniture, when of Edouard's choice, was either of his own design (see desk and sofa in figures 246 and 247), of Louis XVI or Directoire style (original or revival), or simple, unsophisticated vernacular wooden chairs and tables.[10] Of this, more will be said later.

In 1919, after only seven years, the Jeanneret were obliged to sell. The war had ruined the watch industry, and arthritis combined with premature aging made Mr. Jeanneret an old man at sixty-four. He needed a climate that was less severe and humid, and the financial burden of the villa was far beyond his means. Meanwhile its cost consumed funds intended for his pension.

10. After the sale of the house Jeanneret wrote the new owner, Mr. Jeker, an *eleven*-page letter (September 11, 1919) counseling him on how to respect the house. He should keep the canapé, of Jeanneret's design, in the Grand Salon, buy a Morris chair, buy a purist painting and an antique round table in the Louis XVI or Directoire style for the dining room, and buy a certain table lamp from Léon Perrin (three days thereafter Jeanneret wrote Perrin asking for his share of the price); Jeanneret stressed the need for simplicity and severity in all things so that they would complement, not destroy, the architecture.

Too late did Edouard realize his selfishness in building a villa much larger than his parents' needs, and well beyond their financial means. In a long letter to Ritter (May 9, 1913) he made a confession and asked his mentor what to do. He observed that his return home had been motivated by a sense of duty to L'Eplattenier, but now he had taken upon himself a more important duty to his parents—and this precluded leaving La Chaux-de-Fonds as he eventually wished to do. He said:

> Duty: I have a father and mother of modest origins who with great labor have attained average circumstances that I have carelessly and thoughtlessly almost totally ploughed into the construction of a house. My father, highly intelligent and of very refined taste, has for 40 years practiced a foul and loathsome trade: the making of watch dials. . . . My mother has an interesting ancestry: $\frac{1}{2}$ Belgium—remotely Spanish, $\frac{1}{2}$ Rochefort! Teaches piano. . . .
>
> The utter blunder of building this house, done apparently as a necessary and instinctive reconciliation between 3 beings . . . was a stupid mistake. It is evident that I cannot leave my father and mother here, far from town and from any neighbors, to go to Adrianople, Paris, or Chicago.
>
> This town, I hate it. The people also, a priori. . . .
>
> What then is my duty? To abandon one's father and mother in this situation to let them wither away from anxiety and isolation?—and go elsewhere to build cities, mansions, or palaces? Or must one remain and demean oneself and lose everything—enthusiasm, drive, the value of preparatory studies and even one's soul as an artist? . . .
>
> Here I am useful to my parents: even necessary.
>
> Thus, dear sir, I seek your counsel.

We lack, however, Ritter's reply.

Prior to the villa's sale Edouard prepared a six-page document to inform the real estate agent about the house, its setting, and its monetary value. From this we glean bits of information about the construction, the fact that 130 people were easily accommodated during musical auditions, and the care with which room proportions were determined by the architect.[11]

Two entire pages discuss the villa's monetary value, based on construction costs, and therefore estimated by Jeanneret at 115,000 Swiss francs after considering the 100 percent inflation rate since 1912, plus the augmented cost of labor and materials and the architect's fee. Edouard had charged his father 6 percent (vs. his usual 10 percent fee)

11. ". . . les proportions de toutes les pièces ont été étudiées de très près et que certaines des pièces obéissent même, par leur proportion, à certaines lois de l'architecture complètement perdues aujourd'hui et qui ont été employées autrefois dans les grandes époques d'art de l'antiquité (rapport numérique, largeur, profondeur, hauteur)." ("Note Relative à la Vent de la Propriété de la Rue de la Montagne 30 B," dated "Paris le 21 janvier 1919," p. 3; BV.)

based on construction costs of 41,864.23 (plus his 2,511.84 fee for a subtotal of 44,376.07, plus the cost of land, etc.).[12] Mr. Jeanneret, we will recall, said that costs were approaching 50,000 prior to completion of work and this may not include his son's fee.

However, if Edouard expected the real estate agent to set the asking price at 115,000 he was quite mistaken. The house was offered at 65,000 and actually sold for 60,000. If Edouard's 100 percent inflation figure is correct, his parents took a terrible loss, realizing only about 30,000 in 1912 francs on their 50,000 franc investment. Yet that was only the beginning because the purchaser defaulted on his payments, the house was repossessed and resold, with the Jeannerets sustaining a further loss in excess of 25,000 on the original sale price of the villa—in addition to what they had lost through inflation. Therefore the saga of the Villa Jeanneret-Perret virtually wiped out the parents' frugal lifetime savings.

The Villa Jeanneret-Perret was the pure expression of Edouard's ideas unrestricted by the conflicting wishes of a client; this makes it very special. At Le Locle he also found a sympathetic client, although one who did set a few requirements. This was Georges Favre, the sixty-nine-year-old semiretired entrepreneur who had founded the Zenith Watch Company.[13] The site, near the Zenith factory and overlooking the town, was along a precipitous hillside on a long, narrow terrace, supported by a retaining wall, and upon which stood a chalet and nearby coach house. The approach was at grade level along the terrace, the address being 6, Côte des Billodes. These physical restrictions, plus the retention of the old coach house, established special conditions for the architect (see color plate VI).

Jeanneret received the commission in mid-February 1912, having been chosen, apparently, over two other architects who were considered. The design evolved rapidly during the following month and the final working drawings were completed between March 30 and April 21, 1912.[14] Construction commenced in late April or early May, interiors were underway by November, but the final touches were not completed until September 1913 at which time Jeanneret conducted parties of approving visitors through the house (to Ritter, September 27, 1913).

The few preliminary sketches still extant approximate the final design except for changes in fenestration. A bird's-eye perspective dated March 1912 is perhaps the earliest since it shows no dormers and the windows of the second storey are not a continu-

12. Regarding the fee, see "Note d'Honoraires" dated October 14, 1914, in Edouard's Copie de lettres, p. 106 (BV).

13. Jeanneret's relations with Favre were very amicable, except for minor disagreements, and on December 26, 1913, he sent Favre a photo album of the house as a Christmas gift, along with a very appreciative letter (Copie de lettres, pp. 28–29; BV).

14. As with the Villa Jeanneret, the last numbered blueprint registered with the Commune is 20, yet numbers 10 through 15 are missing and therefore were presumably details.

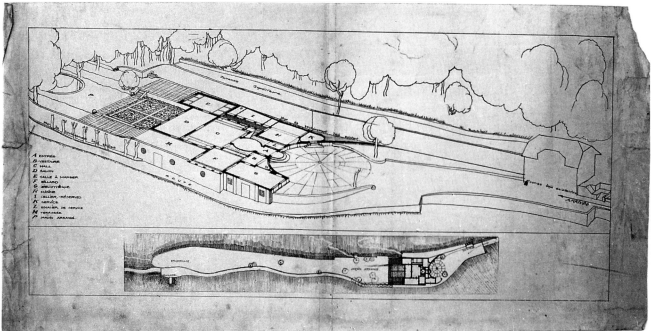

ous band. Except for this the design seems almost complete (note the existing coach house at far right; figs. 253, 254). A still more conceptual series of sketches appear in figure 255 where the architect is studying both the design and placement (at garden's end) of a drive-through garage (a town ordinance required that the passage below the retaining wall be kept open). Meanwhile a pen and ink sketch of the south elevation is very close to the final design and the first to show dormer windows (fig. 256).[15]

15. A quick, worm's-eye view of the house from the southwest exists in Carnet 1, p. 6, among notes

**Fig. 253.** Villa Favre-Jacot, Le Locle. Preliminary sketch, signed and dated March 1912. Pencil on tracing paper. 22 × 71 cm. (FLC 30277)

**Fig. 254.** Plan and site plan of Villa Favre-Jacot, Le Locle. 1912. Print made on heavy paper. 38 × 80 cm. (FLC 30278)

**Fig. 255.** Villa Favre-Jacot. Sketch of garage, garden, and house from west side including various studies for the garage that was not built. 1912. Pencil on tracing paper. 46.6 × 47.5 cm. (BV)

**Fig. 256.** Villa Favre-Jacot. This is the earliest study to indicate dormer windows. Pen and ink on tracing paper. 31.8 × 72 cm. (BV)

made in Germany. The real significance of this drawing is its proof that Jeanneret was studying his German sketchbooks while preparing the Favre-Jacot design.

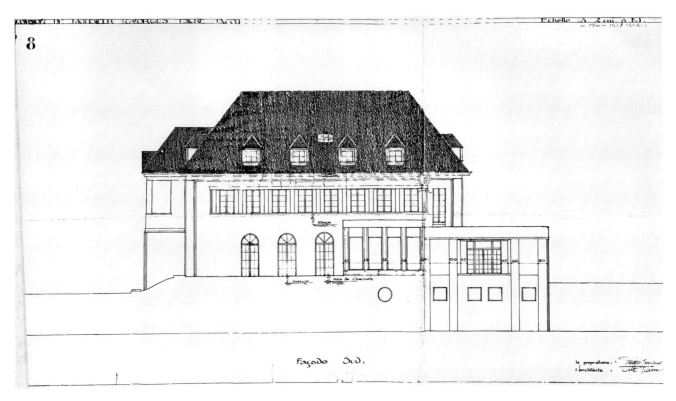

Façade Sud.

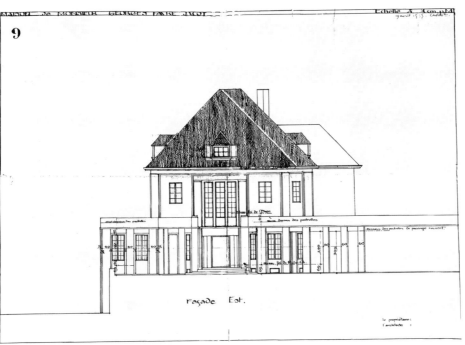

Façade Est.

**Fig. 257.** Villa Favre-Jacot, Le Locle. South elevation drawn by Jeanneret and showing original dormer windows (the blueprint's colors are here reversed). Signed and dated April 15, 1912. (Hôtel de Ville, Le Locle)

**Fig. 258.** Villa Favre-Jacot, east, or entrance, elevation. Signed and dated April 19, 1912. (Hôtel de Ville, Le Locle)

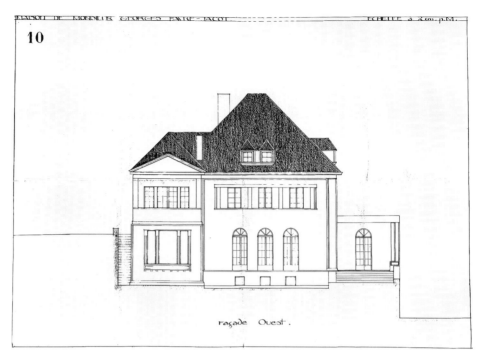

Fig. 259. Villa Favre-Jacot, west, or garden, elevation as drawn by Jeanneret. (Hôtel de Ville, Le Locle)

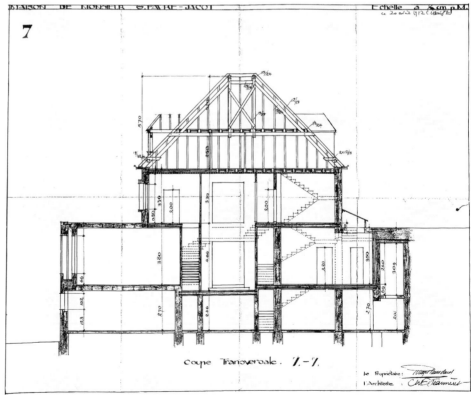

Fig. 260. Villa Favre-Jacot, section (north/south) through circular vestibule. Signed and dated April 20, 1912. (Hôtel de Ville, Le Locle)

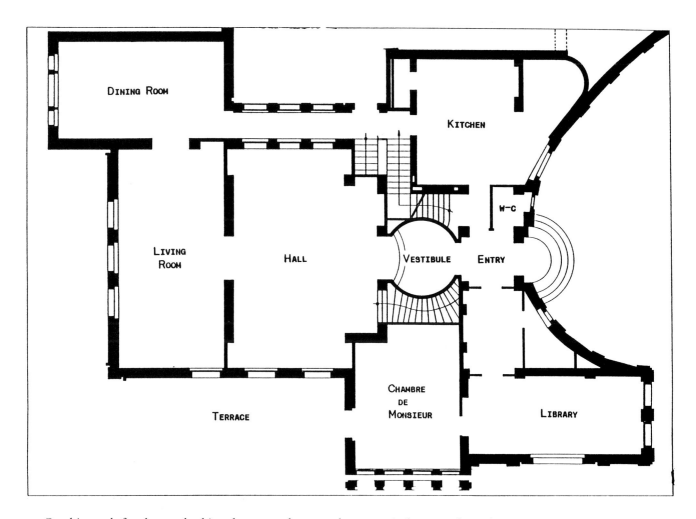

On this south facade, overlooking the town, the second-storey windows are framed by an unusual motif consisting of columns and lintels that are differentiated from the surface of the wall by their color and their slight projection. And because the windows are broadly spaced, rather than contiguous, a section of wall divides them. Columns are placed at the center of each wall segment, yet to prevent the column from being imbedded in the wall a niche is carved into this wall to accommodate it; here, again, is a premonition of the Dom-ino system which clearly separates wall and support (pilotis). The capitals atop these cylindrical columns are stylized Jura spruce trees or cones (fig. 262).

On the west, or garden facade, the dining room at left projects forward and is topped by a small porch. My photograph (1978) intentionally shrouds the roof to hide the remodelled dormer windows (fig. 263). The capitals, differing in design at each location, were sculpted by Léon Perrin, with whom I visited the house and who told me

**Fig. 261.** Villa Favre-Jacot, Jeanneret's plan, redrawn for clarity. Some modifications occurred during construction.

**Fig. 262.** Detail of second storey, south facade. (Photo by author)

**Fig. 263.** Villa Favre-Jacot, garden facade (south facade is at right) with rebuilt roof dormers (by others) shrouded by leaves. (Photo by author)

**Fig. 264.** Villa Favre-Jacot, entrance, or east, facade as approached from driveway. At left is Georges Favre's suite, to the right the service entrance and kitchen. (Photo by author)

**Fig. 265.** Entrance, with three contiguous cylinders (rather than columns) on either side and mosaic design on stoop. The monogram GFJ appears in the iron railing overhead. (Photo by author)

that the formal gardens and their plantings were carefully designed by Jeanneret, and of them he was most proud.

Upon approaching the house one senses a certain tension between balance and imbalance, symmetry and asymmetry. The concrete circle of the forecourt, its radii strongly marked, is not on axis with the entry, nor do the lateral wings of the villa align with the circumference of this disk. Furthermore the two-storey portion of the house, which gives the impression of symmetry, is not symmetrical, as can be seen in the lines of the roof (fig. 264). Only the entrance and the window above are truly symmetrical, and they establish a strong axis that runs through the interior of the house (the entry, vestibule, hall, and salon are all on axis).

The vestibule is the pièce de résistance of the plan. Three semicircular steps lead to the stoop which is given privacy and protection by three contiguous cylinders on either side. These are pure cylinders, not columns, as there is no entasis, fluting, capital, or base, thereby reminding us of Jeanneret's praise of such geometric shapes while in Rome (fig. 265).

Passing through the metal door, one stands in a square entry with lateral access to coatroom and W.C., while straight ahead is the vestibule in the shape of a hollow cylinder (diameter 3 m 40 cm.). Around the outside of this well-like space winds a staircase with its half-landing in front of the great window; from the second floor one looks down into this well of space (its upper rim being visible through the outside window in figure 264).

The walls of this cylinder are painted in vertical strips that are alternately blue and white and imitate the French Directoire wallpaper of which Jeanneret was so fond. Verticality is thereby emphasized (fig. 266). On the floor an elaborate mosaic is divided by six radii that correspond to the six wood columns placed on the upper rim of this well-like space. The six pie-shaped segments thus formed contain abstract floral motifs consisting of intersecting arcs, their lines being black, the flowers yellow, gray, and black, while the background tone is cream.

Next after the vestibule is the hall which, like the salon beyond it, is broad rather than long (fig. 267). The dining room is off the salon, against the hillside, and close to the kitchen and service area.

Georges Favre's suite, which consists of his room and a library, is located on the ground floor but is virtually independent of the house itself; it is accessed through the entry at the front door. When seen from the exterior, the "chambre de Monsieur" is the dominant feature of the south facade, especially as seen from below (fig. 268). It projects forward and stands proudly on its acropolis, somewhat recalling the Temple of Athena Nike in Athens which Jeanneret had often sketched. The five carefully detailed piers, their corners inverted, stand free of the window-wall which is set well back. Meanwhile a round-arched doorway at the west end of the suite picks up the rhythm established by the windows of the salon and becomes the focal point of a long axis that

**Fig. 266.** Looking up from the vestibule one sees the circular balcony, with columns, at the second-floor level as well as the original blue and white striped walls. (Photo by author)

**Fig. 267.** Villa Favre-Jacot, the "Hall," looking toward the terrace and, at right, the living room. Wallpaper, drapes, and chandelier were apparently selected by Jeanneret. (FLC)

**Fig. 268.** The "Chambre de Monsieur" as it projects out from the retaining wall and assumes a dominant position on the south facade. (Photo by author)

runs across the raised terrace, down the monumental stairs, and along the promenade beside the garden (fig. 269). The library, by comparison, assumes a subsidiary visual role because it is lower, set further back, and uses pilasters instead of free-standing piers.

For the construction of the villa, Jeanneret was asked to use bricks because his client had vast quantities of them on hand. These he covered with roughcast, but not quite so heavily textured and rough as at the Villa Jeanneret. The principal points of support (black squares on the plan) were emphasized, yet apparently these were not of concrete since there is no mention of them in his May 27 letter to Du Bois wherein the only reinforced concrete calculations requested seem to be (as at the Villa Jeanneret-Perret) for the lintels and colonnettes (the carved capitals were of soapstone). He also sought help in framing the roof, i.e., the question of beam design and whether iron tie-rods were necessary. Iron I beams ("fer à I") were extensively used under the floors.

The Villa Favre-Jacot, unlike Jeanneret's earlier essays in residential design, embraces much from the classical tradition yet simultaneously subverts many of classicism's fundamental principles. A complete break exists with accepted classical morphology and syn-

tax; for example, columns and piers adhere to no known order. Such an arbitrary and often inventive interpretation of classicism has parallels in his famous predecessor, Claude-Nicolas Ledoux, whose Royal Saltworks of the late eighteenth century at Arc-et-Senans in France is not distant, geographically speaking, from La Chaux-de-Fonds (the train to Paris passes within sight of it), though no evidence exists, in letters or sketchbooks, that Jeanneret ever visited it. Clarity, sobriety, and pleasing proportions characterize the villa design and although the perception of symmetry is present, it is not; balance, instead, prevails. In Le Locle this villa was a maverick; in Neuchâtel it would, stylistically, have been more at home.

Whereas the neoclassicism of the Villa Favre-Jacot has little affinity with the architectural scene in Le Locle or La Chaux-de-Fonds, it perhaps reflects Jeanneret's wish to express the Latin or Mediterranean values advocated by Alexandre Cingria-Vaneyre in *Les Entretiens de la villa du Rouet* (discussed in Chapter 7). Yet his sources are often elusive and always diverse, as one expects from Jeanneret.

One antecedent for the forecourt could be the Villa Madama in Rome, designed by Raphael in 1518, continued by Giulio Romano, yet never finished. Fondness for such spaces likewise owes something to Michelangelo's Capitoline Hill which Jeanneret repeatedly sketched a few months earlier while in Rome.

He may also have seen the recently republished (1909) *Plans, coupes, élévations des plus belles maisons et des hôtels construits à Paris et dans les environs de 1771 à 1802,* by Johann

**Fig. 270.** The base of the southwest corner pier, Villa Favre-Jacot. (Photo by author)

Karl Krafft, wherein the demolished (1826) Maison de Beaumarchais, built in 1788, was illustrated. The plan, like that of the Villa Madama, has a circular courtyard embraced by semicircular wings but, in addition, this eighteenth-century example has a circular vestibule with, around its circumference, a circular stairway. The combination of these three elements—circular courtyard embraced by contiguous wings, circular vestibule, stairs encircling the vestibule—makes this plan, particularly due to its 1909 publication date, among the plausible sources for the Villa Favre-Jacot forecourt and entry (fig. 271).

Nevertheless, the most pervasive influence on the Villa Favre-Jacot was the work of Peter Behrens. His Villa Cuno (1909–10) at Hagen-Eppenhausen has been cited as a model, not for the forecourt, but for the curved entry stoop combined with a circular staircase in the open vestibule.[16] Likewise his sharply incised, round-headed French doors and windows at the Villa Goedecke (1911–12) and Catholic Workingman's Union (1908–10) are repeated at the Villa Favre-Jacot. Also, Behrens' predilection for geometric shapes had preconditioned Jeanneret for their "discovery" while in Rome; Behrens, in 1906, had already substituted cylinders for columns in the Binnenhof at the Dresden exhibition.

Yet Behrens' influence was not limited to individual features or motifs; it was an aesthetic that favored severity and the relative absence of molded surface detail. Jeanneret's adherence to such an aesthetic is mentioned in his remark to Du Bois (May 27, 1912), to wit, that the Villa Favre-Jacot has a "south facade devoid of all that is unnecessary (only the carcass remains)."

Restraint and severity also characterized the architecture of Karl Friedrich Schinkel. His early-nineteenth-century designs influenced not only Behrens but Jeanneret as witnessed by the inset piers at the corners of the Villa Favre-Jacot which occupy a space bounded by masonry frames that define the plane of the two adjoining walls (see fig. 270). This detail is seen at the rear of Schinkel's Altes Museum in Berlin (1824–28), a feature that also caught the eye of Mies van der Rohe.

One could expand this list of possible sources for features found at the Villa Favre-Jacot yet here, as in the Villa Jeanneret-Perret, the essential fact is that Jeanneret has absorbed ideas from a vast spectrum of history and, through synthesis, created something refreshing and new.[17]

16. Jacques Gubler (*Le Corbusier, une encyclopédie*, p. 228) notes that the two-storey oval entry at the Villa Karma at Clarens, Switzerland (which, however, lacks an encircling staircase) might have prompted Jeanneret's well-like space, although that villa was only just completed in 1912.

17. Could the rhythm of certain Baroque church facades, such as Bernini's San Andrea al Quirinale, have enhanced his interest in columned, semicircular entrance stoops, or was the axial sequence of interior space a partial response to the Casa del Noce at Pompeii concerning which he wrote (*Vers une architecture*, p. 169): "Again a little vestibule which frees your mind from the street. And then you are in the Atrium; four columns in the middle (four *cylinders*) shoot up toward the roof" (emphasis in the original).

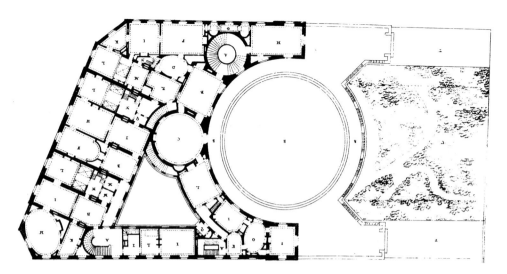

**Fig. 271.** Maison de Beaumarchais, 1788: Plan. Published (1802–1803?) in *Plans, coupes, élévations des plus belles maisons et des hôtels construits à Paris et dans les environs de 1771 à 1802* (plate 23) by Johann Karl Krafft, reprinted 1909.

Occurring simultaneously with Jeanneret's work on the Villa Favre-Jacot was the demolition of an old, seventeenth-century farmhouse owned by Georges Favre and situated across the valley from his new home. The location was not far from Les Jeanneret whence Edouard's ancestors had come. Known as "La maison hantée," Jeanneret visited it after the roof and wooden superstructure were removed and only the masonry walls remained. These walls captured his imagination; he sketched how they might be reused to create a modern villa. The flat roof was trellised to become a roof garden and exterior stairs (such as seen in Bernese farmhouses) were added at the side. Clear, rectangular form is emphasized. Here perhaps lie the seeds of Le Corbusier's Maison Citrohan of 1920 (figs. 272, 273, and 436).[18]

During this same month of March 1912, Le Locle announced a competition for its new town hall. Jeanneret collected the necessary documentation on April 10 and, concurrent with work on the two villas, prepared his entry (of reinforced concrete) which was not among the four winners in spite of the fact that the competition rules seemed to coincide with his aesthetic solution.[19] He was tremendously proud of his proposal which later (on moving to Paris) he entrusted to Léon Perrin, who subsequently lost the drawings. I therefore asked Perrin (June 30, 1974) to sketch from mem-

18. See Fritz Jung, "Le Corbusier et la 'Maison du Diable,'" *L'Impartial* (January 28, 1966), p. 15, and Patricia Sekler in *The Open Hand,* p. 53.

19. ". . . le règlement de concours pose les conditions suivantes: 'Le caractère principal des façades doit être d'une grande simplicité. L'effet d'ensemble doit être obtenu par l'harmonie des lignes et non par une décoration coûteuse ou peu en rapport avec le climat du Locle'" (M. W. Baillod, *Étude historique sur les Hôtels de Ville du Locle* [Lausanne, 1919], p. 66). There were 83 competitors, the winners being announced on July 5. Construction began in September 1913 but due to the war was not completed until October 1918. The design can hardly be described as exhibiting "great simplicity"; its rusticated masonry is rather Romanesque in character and the exterior stair tower and complex roof structure further complicate the scheme.

**Fig. 272.** The "Haunted House," near Le Locle, seventeenth (?) century. Postcard. Envision the masonry walls, once wooden superstructure and roof were removed, then compare with Jeanneret's adaptation. Note also the typical Swiss-Jura wood chimney, or tué, with its single shutter on top; this we discussed in Chapter 6.

**Fig. 273.** Jeanneret's proposed adaptation of the partially demolished "Haunted House" that belonged to Georges Favre; 1912. (BV)

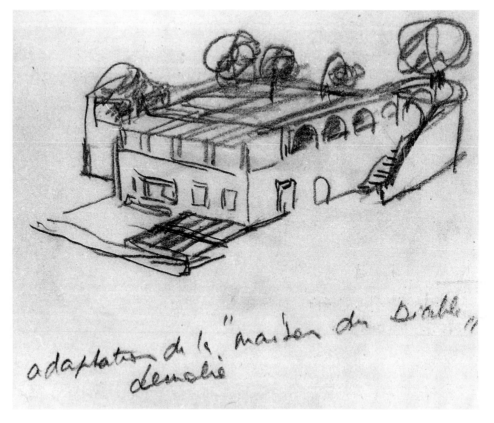

Concours pour:
un Hôtel de ville du Locle d-ch Ed Jeanneret

Vague
Souvenir de Léon Perrin.

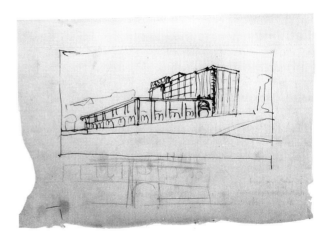

ory the general character of the design (fig. 274). It has certain stylistic affinities with an unidentified Jeanneret project (that might also be the Movado factory) wherein the two-storey annex is labeled "garage d'auto" on a related drawing (fig. 275). The flat roof was fast becoming part of his design vocabulary.

Jeanneret's activity as architect for the Ateliers d'art réunis (of which he also served as secretary) proved insignificant, and except for one commission in 1912 he merely oversaw the organization's gradual demise.[20] That one commission was to redecorate and equip the Buvette (also called Foyer) du Thêatre at the Salle de Musique. Negotiations began in July and work was completed in December. Jeanneret designed the refreshment counter, radiator covers, and wood-and-plaster work throughout the room, but only the latter perhaps exists today. Perrin executed several panels in metal repoussé.[21] The total bill, including work subcontracted to others, was 8,403 Swiss francs.

In December 1912, having completed the installation of the Buvette du Thêatre and while taking a short leave from the Ecole d'art, Jeanneret visited Paris for the first time in three years. And what a change three years had wrought! The Middle Ages were now forgotten and his time was spent studying furnishings and interior decoration from

**Fig. 274.** Léon Perrin's sketch, made from memory on June 30, 1974, of Jeanneret's competition design of April/May 1912 for the Town Hall at Le Locle. (Brooks collection)

**Fig. 275.** Unidentified project by Jeanneret. Because the multistorey portion has similarities with Léon Perrin's sketch, this is perhaps a study by Jeanneret for the Le Locle Town Hall. Ink and pencil on tracing paper. 19.5 × 31 cm. (BV)

20. Les Ateliers d'art réunis was dissolved in financial insolvency on February 15, 1916. Its viability ended with the resignation (1914) of L'Eplattenier and Jeanneret from the Ecole d'art and the closing of the Nouvelle Section. Also, potential clients sought out Jeanneret, not Les Ateliers, to design interior decoration. The achievements of the Ateliers were discussed in Chapter 8.

21. I visited the room with Léon Perrin on June 30, 1974. He identified the two large repoussé panels of masks (Comedy and Tragedy) as his work but could not be sure whether the four panels showing fruit were his or not. He doubted whether the wood pilasters and casements were those designed by Jeanneret, but I tend to disagree. The bar itself, and the curtains, have long since disappeared. No old photos exist but a dossier of thirty items concerning the project is at BV (Reserve MS 158).

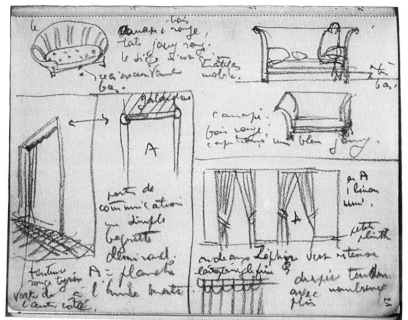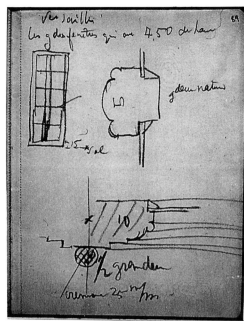

**Fig. 276.** Sketches of furniture and furnishings made while in Paris, December 1912. Carnet Bleu (T 71), p. 21. (FLC)

**Fig. 277.** Versailles, profile of moldings on French door at Versailles. Sketched by Jeanneret, December 1912. Carnet Bleu (T 71), p. 89. (FLC)

the era of Louis XIV–Louis XVI; buildings per se were virtually ignored. As often before, he behaved like an interior designer, not an architect. He filled nearly an entire sketchbook with studies of furniture from the Pavillon de Marsan at the Louvre and of doorways, window casements, etc. at Versailles (fig. 276, 277).[22] He also purchased postcards of these furnishings and on the photographs noted pertinent measurements and, on the back side, added sketches, details, and comments (fig. 278). On two large sheets he made detail studies of a Louis XIV armchair and a Louis XV commode, these in pen, pencil, and watercolor (fig. 279).[23]

22. The first 105 pages of this Carnet Bleu, or T 71 (FLC), concern the December 1912 trip and include, in addition to furniture and details of architecture, sixteen sketches of a nude model. The remaining pages span an extended period including a trip to Ornans on August 6–7, 1913, and one to Frochaux in May 1914. At Versailles he painted watercolors of the orangerie.

23. Few problems of dating have proved more difficult than these furniture postcards and watercolors due to the fact that Jeanneret's visits to the Pavillon de Marsan spanned the long period from 1908 to 1915. Once assembled, however, the documentation nicely confirms the year as 1912. The 1908–9 date is excluded because several of these items were not yet acquired or exhibited that year. Also the two watercolors (FLC 1780, 2238) are painted on the back of blueprints of the Legation de France à Cettigné which was underway in 1912, and one of Jeanneret's postcards is of the identical chair. His three weeks in Paris also provided ample time unlike his shorter and highly charged visits in 1913; the Carnet Bleu (1912+) and Paris Automne 1913 sketchbooks support this conclusion. And by the date of his 1915 Paris trip there is no hard evidence that he was still studying antique furniture. My thanks to Mlle Yvonne Brunhammer, Musée des Arts Décoratifs, for research and assistance on this problem.

The trip, as we learn from the Ritter correspondence of December 3 and January 14–16, began on Sunday December 8, 1912, and lasted three weeks.[24] His visits to Versailles are repeatedly mentioned and special attention was given to the orangerie and its staircase: "j'étais devant un dieu." In Paris he did see some "peinture moderne très belle" but is not specific about where he went and who he saw.[25]

One objective of the trip was to retrieve the watercolors sent to the Salon d'automne (October 1–November 8) but never returned.[26] To Ritter (October 15, 1912) he had reported that Maurice Denis "les trouva bien" which perhaps explains his purchase in November of Denis' *Théories 1890–1910: Du symbolisme et de Gauguin vers un nouvel ordre classique* (deuxième édition, Paris, 1912). Jeanneret did receive an offer to buy his watercolors but refused to sell, saying they were a much too personal souvenir.

His next major trip began June 24, 1913, and had several objectives. First he went to Leipzig to visit the Internationale Baufach-Ausstellung and while there wrote a "Lettre de voyage" concerning "Le monument à la bataille des peuples" describing the soon to be dedicated Völkerschlachtsdenkmal. The latter graced the same park as the building trades exhibition, but of it we learn nothing.[27] Jeanneret's sketchbook (he must have carried one) has not been found and descriptive letters do not exist. The Leipzig exhibition was like a small world's fair (but more tastefully done) with buildings representing various states and industries. Works by Wilhelm Kreis, Josef Hoffmann, and Bruno Taut (his octagonal glass and metal Steelworks Federation Building) were there. The architecture (except for Taut's) was typical of the period—a stripped and often austere classicism.[28]

By month's end Jeanneret was in Hellerau, ostensibly to attend a building exhibi-

**Fig. 278.** Postcard of Louis XVI armchair on which Jeanneret has added the basic measurements. He saw the chair at the Musée des Arts Décoratifs, Louvre, Paris, during his visit of December 1912. (FLC)

24. And from the Ecole d'art records we learn that he asked for leave to visit Paris from December 9 through 24.

25. The inside front cover of his Carnet Bleu lists five names with addresses: Rupert Carabin, André Groult, Pagès, Du Bois, and Lacroix.

26. The 1912 Salon d'automne catalogue (p. 135) lists five items by Jeanneret. Nos. 823–26 are identified only as "Langage de pierres (aquarelle)" and no. 827 as "Intérieur (aquarelle)." A Ritter letter identifies one of the former as "Frankfort." On a cardboard mat (FLC 2849) Jeanneret later wrote: "Langage de Pierre . . . à Paris 1913 [sic] Salon d'automne 13 [sic] pièces dans l'axe d'une des 2 grandes salles au haut des escalier—sous van Dongen." The incorrect date (he did not exhibit in 1913) has led historians astray.

27. His June 28 "Lettre de voyage," written in a flamboyant and rather pompous style, was published in *Feuille d'avis* on July 1. The following day a letter to the editor entitled "Un mot à M. Ch.-E. Jeanneret" concluded with the remark, "je connais des personnes qui ont le cerveau gonflé de la supériorité de leur race. . . ." By contrast, Ritter admiringly republished an entire paragraph from the article as the leading theme in his "Le Mouvement artistique à l'étranger" in *L'Art et les Artistes* 18 (November 1913), p. 98, an act that pleased Jeanneret greatly.

28. For illustrations see "Die Architektur der Internationalen Baufach-Ausstellung Leipzig 1913," *Dekorative Kunst* 16 (July 10, 1913), pp. 441–55. The following month (pp. 536–44) there was an article on "Die Architektur der Jahrhundert-Ausstellung in Breslau" at which Max Berg's tour de force in reinforced concrete, the Festhalle, was the feature attraction, but there is no indication that Jeanneret was present.

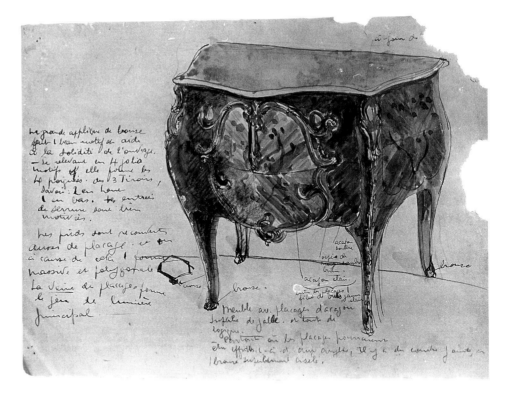

**Fig. 279.** Watercolor by Jeanneret of eighteenth-century commode in the Musée des Arts Décoratifs, Paris, of December 1912. Still on exhibit, its label reads: "Commode/Bois de Rose et de Violette/Att. à J. Dubois, Me. en 1745/ Don Perrin 1909/ #16395." The painting is on the verso of a blueprint captioned "Legation de France a Cettigné" for which the Perret Brothers were the general contractor. 26.5 × 37.5 cm. (FLC 2238)

tion[29] but actually to participate, along with his brother, in the festivities marking the dedication of Heinrich Tessenow's Festival Theater for the institute of Jaques-Dalcroze. This event was what determined the timing of his trip. To justify his presence there he wrote a second "Lettre de voyage," "Hellerau" (dated July 1, published July 4), discussing the architecture and planning of this utopian garden city for which he had much praise. Tessenow's theater was lauded for its utilitarian character rather than for striving self-consciously to be a work of art.

By July 6 the brothers were back home (Albert for his summer vacation) after stopping in Munich en route to visit William Ritter who by now had become not just Jeanneret's mentor and confidant but, by his own admission, virtually a father.[30]

Earlier in 1913 Jeanneret submitted sketches and models to Georges Ditisheim who proposed constructing the Paul Ditisheim watch factory at 120 Boulevard Léopold-

29. The minutes of the commission of the Ecole d'art for June 26, 1913, state: "M. Jeanneret demande par lettre 3 jours [*sic*] de congé du 30 juin au 2 juillet afin de pouvoir assister à l'exposition du bâtiment à Dresde. Accordé. M. L'Eplattenier fait remarque que M. Jeanneret est déjà loin." L'Eplattenier, obviously, was no longer covering up for Jeanneret.

30. "Quoique je vous aie une confiance illimité, d'enfant. Pourquoi? Tant vous fûtes un père et tant je sens votre présence fréquente. Vous le confierai-je? plus que celle de qui que ce soit. Au reste vous êtes un confesseur à pouvoir absorbant. Voilà pourquoi vous êtes le seul à qui j'*écrive*. Ce que signifie: se déshabiller ou à peu près" (to Ritter, January 14, 1913).

**Fig. 280.** Preliminary project for the Paul Ditisheim Buildings, La Chaux-de-Fonds, 1913. Pencil and ink on tracing paper. 33.2 × 53 cm. (BV)

Robert.[31] The existing drawings show only the facade, making it uncertain whether the ground floor would be office or retail space. Meanwhile the upper storeys are heavily glazed to enhance interior lighting.

The initial project envisioned a building four bays wide wherein there was a serious lack of resolution between vertical and horizontal elements in the design (fig. 280). The definitive scheme, three bays wide, resolves this problem by creating a nice interplay between the vertical and horizontal components (fig. 281). The cube-like massing recalls a Renaissance palazzo, yet the general scheme (parti) is that of Louis Sullivan of Chicago who originated the three-part vertical division of office building facades in which the first two floors are clearly separated from those above, the middle floors all have identical fenestration, and a strong cornice terminates the upward thrust of the pilasters that rise above the second storey. The building, as we learn in a letter to Auguste Perret asking for a letter of recommendation, was intended to be of concrete construction.

Paul, Georges, and Jules Ditisheim all lived in an undistinguished mid-nineteenth-century apartment building at 11, rue de la Paix (just down the street from no. 27 where

31. See letters to Georges Ditisheim of December 15(?), 1913, and March 2 and 23, 1914, in Jeanneret's Copie de lettres. Other factory projects undertaken by Jeanneret included 25,000 francs' worth of remodeling work at Jules Perrenoud et Cie at Cernier and a feasibility study for a hydroelectric plant on land owned by Max Du Bois' parents along the river Doubs. The latter, Du Bois told me, was done to prevent the government from requisitioning the land; the family had no intention to build.

**Fig. 281.** Definitive project for the Paul Ditisheim Building to be located at 120 Boulevard Léopold-Robert, La Chaux-de-Fonds: 1913. Pen and ink and soft pencil on tracing paper. 36.8 × 55 cm. (BV)

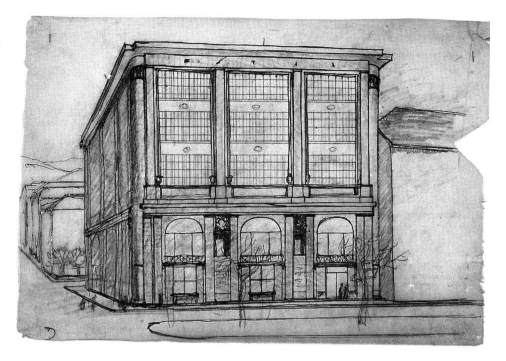

Blaise Cendrars was born the same year as Jeanneret). In 1913 Jeanneret redesigned the entrances on all three floors, the entrance from the street, and made modifications within the apartment of Jules Ditisheim on the third floor (2ième étage). The four designs are all related, yet distinctively different. All are elegant and refined and clearly in the spirit of eighteenth-century and early nineteenth-century French design (fig. 282).[32]

The zeal with which Jeanneret entered into each of his decorating commissions is quite remarkable, and the time and energy he devoted to every aspect of the design, acquisition of materials, and supervision of execution is truly amazing. He spared no effort in finding precisely the right fabric, piece of furniture, or light fixture, and showed an alacrity for interior decoration equal to that of any undertaking of his subsequent years. And the quality of what he achieved was beyond compare. His clients were full of praise; his taste was impeccable. But the hours he lavished on each project cost

32. A partial source for these doorway designs may be found in the Carnet Bleu, December 1912, p. 95, which Jeanneret identifies as "Versailles vestibule de la gds. galerie." His bill indicates that work for Georges Ditisheim cost 7,093 francs, that for "Paix 11" (presumably the entrance from the street) 4,421, the two totalling 11,514 with the architect's 10 percent honorarium equalling 1,151 francs. Jeanneret noted that the project required 135 visits and conferences on his part. He also researched and designed a "jardinière, un socle, 1 aquarium" (42 hours of work) but Georges Ditisheim refused to pay. A dispute also arose with Jules Ditisheim, who accused Jeanneret of overestimating his artistic value, having a swollen head, and overcharging. See Copie de lettres, pp. 1–4, 114–15, 207–9, 214–17.

dearly and some clients balked at the bill. His charge was 10 percent (others charged 5 percent) of the cost of construction or purchase of items, and in addition he secretly demanded from merchants a kickback of 10 percent on whatever they might provide. His correspondence is ladened with such claims. He was almost neurotic on matters of payment, even billing his mother for a piano case he designed for her (but he later relented).

He never underestimated his artistic ability. His correspondence makes that clear. And long letters are filled with self-righteous indignation if someone questioned his bill. He did have a swelled head, though not without reason, and he enjoyed his role as local mentor of taste, a role he realized he could never play in a metropolis like Paris where he would be lost in the crowd. He did not like La Chaux-de-Fonds, but it did have advantages.

Initially he purchased—mostly in Paris—furniture needed by his clients. By 1915, however, he designed most of it himself, employing a local (though trained in Paris) cabinetmaker, Jean Egger, to do the work.

Two members of the Schwob family, Salomon and Anatole, both living at 73 Léopold-Robert, were among his first clients and for each he served as interior decorator ("architecte conseil") for their respective apartments. For Anatole he initially decorated a "fumoir" (smoking room), later designed some furniture, and finally built the now famous villa in 1916. The "fumoir" included the installation of electric lighting and the selection and purchase of furniture, wall hangings, wallpaper, curtains, and light fixtures for the sum of 4,837.60 Swiss francs plus 10 percent architect's fee (bill dated June 11, 1914).

For Salomon Schwob he designed and furnished several rooms, the furniture being purchased rather than custom-built. This required several trips to Paris, Zurich, and elsewhere, those to Paris being in the second week of October, 1913, for five days, then again for four days from October 29 to November 1, and a third time, for three days, over Christmas. During the second trip Jeanneret spent several hours each day conferring with Salomon Schwob and showing him things in various shops that the architect had previously reconnoitered. This was time-consuming (although Jeanneret was also learning) and not overly productive, as we learn in a December 7 letter wherein Jeanneret offered to resign since his taste proved so different from that of his client. Ultimately, however, the commission was completed and Jeanneret's bill, dated July 17, 1914, informs us that 21,750 was spent on remodelling and furnishings (including two chandeliers) plus his honorarium of 2,175 Swiss francs, an amount, therefore, equal to approximately half of what the Villa Jeanneret-Perret had cost. Nothing now remains of this undertaking, nor of the apartment of Anatole Schwob.

From the Paris Automne 1913 sketchbook we learn more about these trips. For the second one, that of late October, he lists the four days of appointments including his daily rendezvous with Salomon Schwob. The schedule is most enlightening, including visits to such shops and department stores as Baguès, Gagneau, Kohn, Innovation, Sala-guad, and perhaps more significantly the names of Groult, Iribe, and La Maison Martine.

André Groult, whose name and address is also listed in the Carnet Bleu of 1912, was a furniture designer who owned two stores, an antique shop and one devoted to contemporary design. He exhibited, annually, furnished rooms at the Salon d'Automne. His brother-in-law was the famous couturier Paul Poiret, who founded the fashionable Maison Martine where furniture as well as robes could be seen. The graphic and furniture designer Paul Iribe was among his protégés. All these men admired the relatively light, elegant, neoclassicism of circa 1800 of which Jeanneret was so fond; in such work, as well as his own designs, he sought the seeds for a renewal of the decorative arts in France such as he had called for in his *Etude*.[33]

This same notebook was his constant companion in December while at the Salon d'Automne where he went to study the decorative arts (no mention of painting) with an attentive eye to the needs of his clients. One is especially struck by the lavish six-page spread devoted to two rooms designed by his near-contemporary Robert Mallet-

33. For an excellent survey, focusing on the French side of the question, see Nancy J. Troy, *Modernism and the Decorative Arts in France* (New Haven & London: Yale University Press, 1991), especially the chapter "The *Coloristes* and Charles-Edouard Jeanneret."

Stevens. Both rooms are sketched in plan with detailed descriptions of the decor, light fixtures, and various pieces of furniture. Mallet-Stevens' hall has strong British over-tones and emphasizes the right angle, whereas his music room has softer, less rigid forms including four pairs of cylinder-like columns at the corners that caught Jeanneret's attention. Yet the straight-legged furniture lacked the elegant taper favored by Jeanneret.

Near the end of the sketchbook, among a list of reminders, he wrote "Choisy Histoire de l'architecture" and sure enough Jeanneret's own copy is signed and dated "Paris Noël 1913." Since Auguste Choisy followed the rationalist approach espoused by Viollet-le-Duc this purchase would have been more appropriate in 1908–9, an observation confirmed by the fact that Jeanneret left many pages uncut and limited his marginal notes to the sections dealing with laws, proportions, and harmony, sections that he later reread while researching *The Modulor*. Choisy's axonometric drawings, however, were frequently reproduced in Le Corbusier's books.[34]

These trips are also documented in two long, revealing, and often introspective letters to William Ritter, each commenced prior to arriving in Paris and concluded during the train trip home. Concerning interior design he was decidedly upbeat, saying that the fourteen interiors seen at the Salon, which was the purpose of his trip, filled him with joy and confirmed for him that "The triumph of modern ideas is no longer a myth." He took heart in the fact that even the general visitors were enchanted by what they saw. Then, in what seems a contradiction, he says in the same paragraph "My admiration, without reserve, goes to the engineers who create amazing bridges, who work for utility, the strong and the sound. I wish that in art we wanted to do like them. . . ." And, a few paragraphs later, "Cingria-Vaneyre, read in 1909 [1910 actually], remains always present in my mind; he expressed much of what I felt too clearly for his memory not to be present at this moment"—which to us is rather ambiguous (but probably not to Ritter) since the use of a past tense ("je sentais") may possibly imply that Jeanneret has begun to question Cingria's ideas.

Concerning painting, Jeanneret was shocked by the cubists (specifically mentioning Metzinger and Picasso) for what he called their brazen violations of the right to paint.[35] Cézanne, Matisse, and Hodler remained his favorites, yet quite unexpectedly his previous letter had lavished praise on Tiepolo for the quality of his light and the way he

34. Other than Choisy and Denis, Jeanneret's reading included Paul Claudel, *Connaissance de l'Est* (Paris, 1907), Gabriele d'Annunzio, *Le martyre de Saint-Sébastien* (Paris, 1911), and Ritter's *Edmond de Pury* (Geneva, 1913). Also purchased at this time were Stéphane Mallarmé, *Vers et prose* (Paris, 1912), *Jahrbuch des deutschen Werkbundes: 1913* (Jena, 1913), and *Les chefs-d'oeuvre d'Ingres* (Paris, n.d., but inscribed 1914).

35. "J'y [Paris] voyais le salon d'automne et, triomphe! j'y blasphémais les cubistes, Metzinger, et Picasso, me révoltant devant leurs hardies violations du droit de peindre. Et souffrant de tant de médiocrité masquée sous les appâtes d'un technique cézannienne ou matissienne; je parle comme un bourgeois, n'est-ce pas?" (December 23, 1913). Jeanneret's vehemence may in part have been intended to patronize Ritter, who disliked modern art.

respected the surface of a stucco wall. Palladio was also mentioned *en passant* as was the Villa Rotonda.

The Perret brothers, who epitomized for Jeanneret the Parisian avant-garde, were visited in October (as well as Max Du Bois and Eugène Grasset) and presumably through them he was introduced to the writer-poet Charles Vildrac (a fellow member of the Artistes de Passy) whom Jeanneret saw both in October and December. Vildrac, in turn, advised meeting Francis Jourdain (son of Frantz Jourdain) whose exhibits at the Salon (his ultrasevere dining room was certainly influenced by the American Arts and Crafts movement) Jeanneret much admired. Jeanneret, however, did not look up Jourdain until later but did send him an ingratiating letter saying that he was bothered by problems of interior decoration and seeking direction; he also discussed the writings of Adolf Loos.[36]

Apparently Auguste Perret introduced his protégé to the writings of Adolf Loos since Jeanneret thanked him for the Loos articles in a letter of November 27, from which we also glean that it was Perret who guided his erstwhile pupil toward an appreciation of Jourdain's work. *Les Cahiers d'aujourd'hui,* with which Vildrac was directly involved, had published, in French translation, Loos' "Ornement et crime" in June and his "Architecture et le style moderne" the previous December (1912). The impact of these essays on Jeanneret would prove profound and durable and do much to wean him away from his obsession with historic furniture and point him toward new, less style-conscious routes in the future.

A more personal and private aspect of Jeanneret's life also finds expression in these autumn letters to William Ritter. It concerns marriage and a parental attitude that he cannot abide. "I have horror of marriage" he begins in one letter,[37] and in the next expresses his annoyance at repeated parental suggestions about marriage and children and especially their outrageous assumption that if he goes out in the evening and returns late (after a lengthy discussion of Cézanne, Hodler, Titian, and Tintoreto with friends), that the house is closed and his parents suppose he has been out whoring.[38]

36. "Loos a éclairé un grand bout de la route avec son 'ornement et crime'; il a cristallisé en matière invulnérable, des impressions vagues, des sentiments naissants ou déjà bien développés mais n'osaient point trop s'avouer à cette heure ou la furie de l'art décoratif, la folie du *Beau* anéantit et stupéfie, le simple, l'instinctif, le nécessaire, et l'unique vrai Sentiment de *Bon*—le Bon ou *Bien* étant Beau par essence même" (to Francis Jourdain, December 21, 1913). Other items mentioned to Ritter on November 3, 1913, include: *Les Cahiers d'aujourd'hui, L'Occident, La Nouvelle Revue Française,* and Jacques Copeau's recently inaugurated Théâtre du Vieux-Colombier.

37. ". . . j'ai horreur du mariage, le considérant trop comme un gouffre où toute rencontre est possible, la mauvaise avant la bonne" (November 3, 1913).

38. "Figurez-vous: il m'arrive d'aller le soir avec des amis, chez eux, à quoi faire: à nous raconter toujours les mêmes histoires: Cézanne, Hodler, Titien, Tintoret. Je rentre passé minuit, la maison étant close. Et on s'imagine chez moi que je me putinise, que je vois des ou une garce." And after certain comments about how marriage and raising a family presumably establishes one in a specific social milieu, he says: "J'aimerais

Of family affairs, the father's journal keeps us posted. The most traumatic event during 1913 was the departure in March of Annie, their maid, after five and a half years of faithful service. Household routine was thrown into chaos. Her replacement quit on April 15 and another was fired in May. For five weeks thereafter the family took meals, *en pension,* at the Stotzer's. May marked their thirtieth wedding anniversary but nothing special was planned, nor did anyone take a vacation that summer. Albert, as usual, returned home, departing September 23 after ten weeks but returning again for Christmas, when the four stayed quietly at home together. New Year's (1914) occasioned a family reunion at their new house with the Henri Jeannerets coming from Soleure.

August witnessed the outbreak of war and, although Switzerland remained neutral and both sons were exempt from military service for reasons of health, gloom descended due to a severe depression in the watch industry. In September Mr. Jeanneret reported making only 5 francs per week (and he had just built a house costing 50,000 francs!). Thereafter, for nearly a year, he had no work at all. They did, however, visit the Swiss National Exposition at Bern in October for two days ("une merveille"), and he relates the amusing story of elephants delivering, in September, their winter supply of coke.[39]

Edouard, during 1913, had been active in founding the Swiss Romande equivalent of the German Werkbund, called L'Oeuvre. In May an organizational meeting was held in Lausanne where he was appointed one of the eleven commission members. They, in turn, sent out a call (September 21) for members and then convened a general assembly for November 9 at Yverdon where L'Oeuvre: Association Suisse Romande de l'Art et de l'Industrie came into being. And, in conjunction with the Swiss Federation of Architects, they began publishing a *Bulletin Bimensuel* and *L'Oeuvre,* a monthly review to which Jeanneret contributed "Le Renouveau dans l'architecture" in the second issue.

He was also appointed to two subcommissions of L'Oeuvre, one to judge a design competition for youngsters roughly between the ages of seven and eighteen (1,450 drawings were received) and the other to assess the different methods of teaching design. Jeanneret actually wrote both reports. The first, *Un Concours de dessins: Rapport du Jury,* was dated April 20, 1914, and was published twice.[40] The second, a hefty thirty-

mieux chaque fois m'adresser à mon radiateur, parce qu'il garderait un silence utile et fécond pour moi" (to Ritter, December 23, 1913).

39. The circus elephants were trapped in Switzerland by the outbreak of war so they were put to work hauling heavy loads. Photographs of the Villa Jeanneret-Perret showing elephants therefore date from September 1914.

40. The full subtitle of the eleven-page booklet is *Rapport du Jury sur l'Examen des 1450 Dessins du Concours organisé par les "Etrennes Helvétiques" sous le Patronnage de l'"Oeuvre" Association Suisse Romande de l'Art et de l'Industrie* (La Chaux-de-Fonds: chez Georges Dubois, n.d.). The five jurors are listed and after Jeanneret's name he later added, in longhand, "rapporteur" and after the title on the front cover he wrote "par Corbu" (FLC). The report was also published in the *Bulletin Bimensuel* of L'Oeuvre on June 19 and July 10, 1914 (nos. 5 and 6, pp. 17–22).

seven-page typescript, was written late in 1914 and published in France after the war, but never in Switzerland. It carried the unassuming title: *Rapport de la sous-commission de l'enseignement de l'Oeuvre.*

Georges Dubois, editor of both *Feuille d'Avis* (which published Jeanneret's Voyage articles)[41] and the annual *Etrennes Helvétiques* which had organized, and published, *Un Concours de dessins,* asked Jeanneret for a popular essay on "La Maison suisse" for his 1914 issue of the illustrated almanac. Jeanneret agreed, and provided a light, readable piece that was heavily indebted to Alexandre Cingria-Vaneyre for its dialogue form of presentation as well as the concept that rural Swiss Romande architecture had classic origins—"Je me sens ici comme en terre classique."[42] These words were written late in the summer of 1913, prior to his seeking certain illustrations from Ritter in October, and prior to his three trips to Paris.

His next article, a short one intended for the professional audience of *L'Oeuvre* and written during the early weeks of 1914, was entitled "Le Renouveau dans l'architecture."[43] Here his ideas are somewhat confused and not entirely resolved. Initially he asks two questions: (1) Why are people opposed when "new" architecture creates a certain dissonance with the buildings surrounding them, and, (2) Does the architect have the possibility of avoiding this by creating a regional architecture? The first question leads to a discussion of how historical styles have successfully managed to live together, and how each, like "new" architecture, used, in its time, the latest in construction techniques. Yet Jeanneret never describes or defines what "new" architecture is.

Perhaps his illustrations suggest an answer. Juxtaposed are two plans, that of Mansart's ca. 1700 dome of Les Invalides and Perret's Théâtre des Champs Elysées, both in Paris.

41. Jeanneret, as noted in Chapter 8, worked intermittently from 1911 until at least 1914 on his Voyage d'Orient articles concerning which he had a real hang-up. He repeatedly sent them back and forth to Ritter whose advice he sought. In October 1912, for example, he asked whether the Constantinople series was better than the Balkan group; then on rereading them himself, he found the articles less good than he had originally thought. By November he promised to write about Adrianople and the Acropolis; fifteen months later (February 1914) he has sent Ritter the Acropolis article, then in June says he is working on Mount Athos.

42. "La Maison suisse," *Etrennes Helvétiques, Almanach Illustré* (Paris, Dijon, La Chaux-de-Fonds, 1914), pp. 33–39. A drawing from Jeanneret's favorite illustrator, Rodolphe Töpffer (*Voyage en Zigzag*) leads off the text.

43. "Le Renouveau dans l'architecture," *L'Oeuvre,* 1e année, 2 (1914), pp. 33–37. Its publication began serially in the *Bulletin Bimensuel,* 1e année, 3 (April 3, 1914), pp. 9–10, which made Jeanneret furious since he wrote it specifically for the monthly review. So off went a flurry of letters prohibiting its continued publication except in a single issue of *L'Oeuvre.* The title, incidently, recalls L'Eplattenier's earlier "Renouveau d'Art," *L'Abeille: Supplément du National Suisse,* 2 (February 20, 1910), p. 1. Stanislaus von Moos, in *L'Esprit Nouveau: Le Corbusier et l'industrie* (Zurich/Strasbourg, 1987), pp. 128–29, has identified the quotation with which Jeanneret concludes his article as being from Adolf Loos, "L'Architecture et le style moderne," thereby confirming that Jeanneret, while writing the article, had Loos on his mind.

The former requires massive amounts of masonry for structural support while the modern work, using new techniques, needs only eight concrete piers. The contrast is striking and makes its point, but Jeanneret avoids the question of why both buildings are clothed in classical forms. The remaining three illustrations are exterior views of Curjel and Moser's University of Zurich, a freely conceived, severe, stripped classical building, yet these views were not, as Jeanneret complained to Perret in a letter of June 11, those which he intended. However it seems safe to conclude that the stripped classicism represented by the Théâtre des Champs Elysées, Villa Favre-Jacot, and Villa Brakl (admired in Munich in 1910) represent his ideal of "new" architecture and that this ideal had not substantially changed for him during the previous few years.

The second question posed in Jeanneret's article concerns regional architecture, the topic of his previous essay. He says that "I do not think that one can bring about, a priori, a regional architecture" (p. 36). Therefore he is rejecting L'Eplattenier's erstwhile call for an art based on the natural forms of the Jura. But this is nothing new; by 1914 regional manifestations of Art Nouveau were a thing of the past. However Jeanneret takes this argument one step further by insisting that no architect could comply if asked by a client to design a Swiss house or a Neuchâtel or La Chaux-de-Fonds house. And once having made this point he seems to contradict himself by saying, at the end of the article, that an architect who is sensitive to his surroundings will gradually reveal its influence in his work and that this is generally a good thing.[44]

Jeanneret seemed more in his element when writing *Un Concours de Dessins: Rapport du Jury* at the end of April, 1914. Its first pages list conditions, categories, and prize winners followed by a "Commentaires du Jury" that is incisive and highly critical of all levels of teaching design. His major criticism is leveled at the instruction, or lack thereof, offered to young apprentices, this being particularly apparent among those who were studying architecture, the group submitting the greatest number of designs.[45]

Obviously this question of teaching needed investigation, and as luck would have it the Swiss National Exhibition (held in Bern May 15–October 15, 1914) had arranged a major design exhibition organized among both primary schools and professional schools of arts and crafts. L'Oeuvre's subcommission on teaching leapt at this opportunity and Jeanneret, acting much like a one-man committee, wrote the thirty-seven-page typed report that reflected his views and attitudes in every line. Perhaps this, combined with the negative findings and highly critical conclusion, explains why the

44. "Mais, j'aurais pourtant l'espoir qu'avec le temps, un travail sincère m'apportât sa leçon; que la nature environnante, la vie du milieu que je fréquente, m'imprègnent petit à petit et que mon travail en trahisse l'influence. L'esprit local ne s'acquiert pas par un acte de volonté; ce doit être une emprise lente, une intuition" (p. 37). Does this, therefore, preclude an architect building outside his or her own locality?

45."Il y a, parmi les . . . concurrents architectes, une grosse proportion de futurs enlaidisseurs" (p. 10), and further on, "Ces remarques pessimistes montrant la situation précaire des apprentis du bâtiment et des métiers faisant usage du dessin . . ." (p. 11).

text never appeared in *L'Oeuvre* and then waited out the war before being published in Paris in *Les Arts Français* in 1918–19.[46]

This *Rapport de la sous-commission de l'enseignement de l'Oeuvre* holds few surprises. Jeanneret's stance against ornament is gradually formulating, reinforced by his reading of Loos. He continues to advocate the study of the history of art, insisting that this is the best way to develop taste, because taste is dependent upon intuition and cannot be taught. He also maintains that the surest signs of a modern style are to be found in contemporary dress, weapons of war, means of transport, and machines.

While Jeanneret was preparing these various articles and reports for the Swiss Romande's counterpart of the German Werkbund, the Parisian periodical *L'Art de France,* under the title "En Allemagne," reprinted virtually his entire *Etude sur le mouvement d'art décoratif en Allemagne* in two consecutive issues during April/May 1914.[47] This certainly pleased him, but it fell far short of what he had been seeking, for more than a year, which was the republication of the entire book in France; that would have given him a status in the French capital which the newly founded, small-circulation *L'Art de France* could not.[48]

Education and teaching were among Jeanneret's paramount concerns, and to them he gave generously of his time. The last publication dating from this hectic spring of 1914 (which witnessed five new articles or reports plus two reprints) was a booklet bearing the title *Un Mouvement d'Art à la Chaux-de-Fonds, à propos de la Nouvelle Section de l'Ecole d'art.* The booklet was dated April 2, 1914, and the opening sentence read: "The objective of this booklet is to make known an institution created in our town along with the alleged pretext given for its destruction." Here the reference is to L'Eplattenier's Nouvelle Section at the Ecole d'art which had been the chief reason for Jeanneret's return to La Chaux-de-Fonds in November 1911, and to this earlier date we must return in order to place the 1914 booklet in proper perspective.

46. *Les Arts Français: Bulletin du Comité Central Technique des Arts Appliqués et des Comités Régionaux,* 24 (1918), pp. 87–92; 25 (1919), pp. 1–8; 26 (1919), pp. 9–12; 27 (1919), pp. 13–14. The typescript is at FLC.

47. "En Allemagne," *L'Art de France,* première année, 9, 10 (April, May 1914), pp. 347–95, 457–73. Only the first fourteen pages of Jeanneret's seventy-four-page booklet were not reprinted. Thus most of chapter 1, "Considérations générales: Le Renouveau," was excised, this section being Jeanneret's personal version of history and the relation between the arts in France and Germany. His specially prepared autobiographical note was characteristically boastful, dropping names all over the place and claiming he was "engagé à Vienne, en 1908, par Joseph Hoffmann" (p. 347). The title "En Allemagne," however, should not be confused with "France ou Allemagne," which was the title Jeanneret proposed for a book based on his *Etude* but consisting mainly of juxtaposed illustrations. He worked on and off on this project between 1915 and 1917 but never found an interested publisher. See sketchbook A2/1915 p. 99, etc.

48. With Emmanuel de Thubert, editor of *L'Art de France,* Jeanneret developed a cordial correspondence and at one point mentioned "Les Allemands sont plus forts que nous [the French] parce qu'ils savent *unir* les forces au lieu de les opposer" (April 30, 1914); de Thubert soon thereafter commissioned Jeanneret to review the forthcoming German Werkbund exhibition at Cologne, but the war intervened.

Why Jeanneret returned to La Chaux-de-Fonds has always baffled historians, but when everything is taken into account it was probably his most reasonable course of action. First of all, as discussed in the previous chapter, he felt a strong sense of loyalty, and this he translated into duty, to the patron who had made everything possible for him in life. L'Eplattenier had rescued him from the dreary, dead-end career of engraving watchcases, steered him into architecture (which necessitated formulating a program in architecture at the Ecole d'art), then coaxed him to study urbanism (in both these professions he would become the most influential practitioner of the century), managed his early training, then provided financial livelihood by way of several architectural commissions, a travel grant, and finally a salaried appointment at his alma mater. Could Jeanneret possibly be so false to his benefactor as to withhold his support and participation in L'Eplattenier's great new dream—to create a school of applied arts embodying the ideals and principles which Jeanneret had studied during his year in Germany? Obviously he could not.

This decision was governed by other factors as well. We must not forget his strong sense of mission and his reading of such authors as Nietzsche and Schuré—*Zarathustra, Les Grands initiés*—which instilled in him the significance of the prophet/teacher who sought truth in order to impart it to mankind. The architect, the artistic genius, must be the standard-bearer who educates and leads the uninitiated on the path to a better life.

Finally, we repeatedly noted Jeanneret's unwarranted lack of self-confidence, his feeling of being ill-prepared for the ultimate task confronting him. This sometimes made him cautious, or perhaps prudent is a better word. He required time to organize and synthesize his thoughts, and he welcomed an opportunity to put his ideas on teaching into practice. He was not ready—not yet—to compete in the big leagues. Recall what he wrote Ritter from Athens: "I would have preferred to go to Paris chez Perret to build his new theater. But first I will go and test my wings [passer mes ruades de poulain] at home. Nothing imprisons me there, but everything holds me there" (September [25?], 1911).[49]

This choice was entirely rational. In Paris he would have been nobody, one employee among many in an office, and one among thousands in the city who were trying to reach the top. In La Chaux-de-Fonds he already had a reputation, would be his own boss, had a commission awaiting him (his parents' villa), and in the small town he would soon be at the top. From such a vantage point he could more easily assail Paris—and that is exactly what he did. One negative factor, nevertheless, must be contended with: for several years he must live in a provincial small town dealing with people he would just as soon avoid, in contrast to being among the Parisian avant-garde and enjoying the cultural advantages of the capital.

49. When Perret met Jeanneret in Constantinople and offered him work in Paris, the Ecole d'art appointment was not ratified and therefore Jeanneret was not officially bound to return home.

The Nouvelle Section was an outgrowth of the Cours Supérieur that L'Eplattenier had established in 1905 and in which Jeanneret was in the inaugural class. The Cours Supérieur had known only one instructor, L'Eplattenier, its enrollment was limited to the most promising students, and the instruction prepared them for a broad range of professions related to the industrial and commercial arts, rather than training craftsmen specifically for the watchmaking industry. Yet administratively it was under the jurisdiction of the director of the Ecole d'Art.

The Nouvelle Section, by contrast, had its own director, L'Eplattenier, and was entirely independent of (what came to be called) the Ancienne Section of the Ecole d'art. There were two levels (degrés), the first taught exclusively by L'Eplattenier and the second by three of his former students—Jeanneret, Perrin, and Aubert. This resulted in a homogeneity in teaching but led to cries of nepotism from the Ancienne Section where, incidently, there was no uniform pedagogical approach, each instructor going his own way (I say "his" because no women taught at the school). Admittance was by examination and open to a similar age group (post-primary school) as the Ancienne Section. Instruction, as in the Cours Supérieur, was both theoretical and practical with the ultimate objective supposedly being "an efficacious collaboration of art and industry"—yet no instruction in the use of the machine or how to design for it was offered. In fact, the word "machine" never appears, only "industry." The emphasis, therefore, was on the artisan and the unique one-of-a-kind object rather than on mass production. Thus the philosophical approach was closer to that of Ruskin/Morris than that of most of the applied-art schools in Germany. Les Ateliers d'art réunis were presumably concerned with production, yet they produced only one-of-a-kind.

The budget for the Nouvelle Section is revealing. L'Eplattenier taught sixteen hours per week for an annual salary of 4,000 francs, Jeanneret twelve hours for 1,320 francs, Georges Aubert ten hours for 1,100 francs, and Perrin six hours for 660 francs. The total budget was 7,080 francs whereas that of the Ancienne Section (fifteen instructors) was 70,000 francs.[50]

Jeanneret's course description reads as follows:

Geometric elements, their character, their relative value decorative and monumental.

Divers applications to architecture, furniture, and various objects (working drawings, plans, sections, perspectives, etc.).

50. The source here, and for much of the above, is *Un Mouvement d'Art à la Chaux-de-Fonds à propos de la Nouvelle Section de l'Ecole d'Art* (n.p., n.d. [1914]). The other important sources are: *"Nouvelle Section" de l'Ecole d'Art: Prospectus* (La Chaux-de-Fonds, 1912); the *Rapport de la Commission, Ecole d'Art de La Chaux-de-Fonds,* published at the end of each school year; the longhand (unpublished) minutes of the commission of the Ecole d'Art; and the *Procès-Verbaux du Conseil Général de La Chaux-de-Fonds,* volume 8, pp. 583–89, for June 8, 1914 (BV).

Practical application of architectural works, interior decoration, and divers objects.[51]

The phrase "geometric elements" recalls sketches made by Jeanneret a few months earlier while in Rome (which he labeled horizontal, vertical, cube, sphere, etc.), but how he translated this into a pedagogical method can be gleaned only by photographs of student work exhibited in June 1913.

One panel is captioned "Study of different characteristics of architecture" with the projects at the right identified as "in height" and at lower left "in length" (fig. 283). Both utilize the forms of simplified classicism and show concern for their landscape setting. That at the right seems indebted to Tessenow's design for Jaques-Dalcroze's institute at Hellerau while the "Maison locative" at upper left is a somewhat simplified and classicized version of Perret's 25 bis, rue Franklin in Paris.

Another panel is captioned "Projects for architecture" and, except for the "Grand Magazin" at top center, all are signed by Paul J. Grandjean, Jeanneret's most outstanding pupil (fig. 284).[52] Meanwhile on the abutting wall are drawings of historic structures, mostly Italian. These remind us of Jeanneret's travels as well as his emphasis, when writing his L'Oeuvre reports, on the need to study the history of architecture.

Finally, a panel of eight sheets captioned "Comparative study of volumes and their decorative and architectural application" recall imaginative studies for piers and columns made by Jeanneret in 1905–7. At that time his motifs derived from the Jura but by 1912–13 he was instructing his student (Mlle Richard, who planned to become a teacher) to rely on abstract geometric shapes (fig. 285). Thus some of her designs approach the level of abstraction found in Le Corbusier's cylinder drawings later published as "The Lesson of Rome" (fig. 219).[53]

Jeanneret, obviously, had abandoned neither decoration nor Jura motifs upon his return to La Chaux-de-Fonds. We already observed the mosaics and decorative capitals he and Perrin created for the Villa Favre-Jacot, and at his parents' home he painted a pair of birds, cornucopia, and flowers on the glazed tiles over the living room fireplace, signed and dated 1913. He also prepared designs for the cover of the Prospectus of the

51. *Prospectus*, p. 7. L'Eplattenier's course description reads (p. 6): "Etudes dessinées, modelées et peints d'après nature. Figure humaine, animaux, paysages. Application de ces études à la composition décorative. Peinture murale, affiches, vitraux, sculpture décorative et monumentale, médaille, etc." Equally revealing is the description proposed by L'Eplattenier (at the commission meeting of June 12, 1911) for Jeanneret's course: "composition décorative appliquée à l'architecture jusqu'aux plus petits objets."

52. Patricia Sekler has proposed that two of Grandjean's studies, that at lower right and center left, are indebted to Emil Hoppe and Josef Hoffmann respectively, via drawings published in Vienna. See *La Chaux-de-Fonds et Jeanneret* (Musée des Beaux-Arts et Musée d'Histoire de La Chaux-de-Fonds, Niederteufen, 1983), pp. 52–54.

53. Another section of Jeanneret's students' work was devoted to "Eléments floraux et géometriques utilisés pour l'architecture et décor d'objets."

Nouvelle Section which were based on Jura motifs (fig. 286). Other drawings for ornament are postdated to this period. One pencil and watercolor study (FLC 1764) carries the statement: "La Chaux-de-Fonds ornement avec forêt de Sapin 1911" and on another (FLC 1763) "La Chaux-de-Fonds, Sapin en hiver 1911." It is clear, therefore, that he continued to use nature's forms for decoration well after 1911, and not just during his student days.

The major change that characterizes these later drawings is the existence of an under-

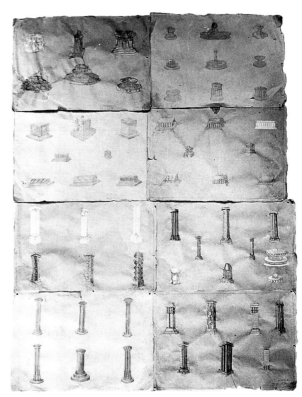

lying grid or unit system. This derives from at least two sources. One is evident at the bottom of "Sapin en hiver" (FLC 1763, fig. 287) where a repetitive pattern is drawn; it is upon this pattern that Jeanneret's decorative scheme (the watercolor at center left) is based. This pattern, I submit, is taken directly from Eugène Grasset, *Méthode de composition ornementale,* volume 1, page 216, figure 35A (fig. 288).

The second source is revealed in sketches at the right of this same sheet, or even more clearly in FLC 2515 where the identical theme is treated and where one sees in the background, and at the right, a series of parallel pencil lines, both diagonal and vertical, that establish the regulating lines upon which the decorative "sapin" pattern is based (fig. 289). Such lines were in common use among architects in central Europe, including Peter Behrens' office, although H. P. Berlage's use thereof at the Amsterdam Stock Exchange (1897–1903) is the example most often published. These lines are an early example of Jeanneret's *tracés régulateurs,* an idea not nearly as original as he wanted us to believe.

These two drawings (FLC 1763 and 2515) are being discussed simultaneously because I wish to demonstrate that both were of the same circa 1911–12 date, thereby resolving a problem (long on my mind) of finding evidence that 2515 was not a drawing

**Fig. 284.** Designs executed by Jeanneret's student Paul J. Grandjean and exhibited in June 1913. To the left are drawings of historic buildings. (BV)

**Fig. 285.** "Comparative study of volumes and their decorative and architectural application" as prepared by Jeanneret's student Mlle Richard and exhibited in June 1913. (BV)

**Fig. 286.** One of Janneret's several studies for the cover design of the booklet *Ecole d'Art/Nouvelle Section/Prospectus*. Note his combination of a unit system (contiguous circles) with the Jura motif of the "sapin." Ink on tracing paper. 20 × 15 cm. (FLC 2012)

from Jeanneret's student days (as he later indicated) but rather one from his career as teacher, a conclusion that separates it by some six years from such "sapin" drawings as FLC 2520 (fig. 53).[54]

Other studies for decorative designs, such as nos. 2230 and 2231, certainly date from this same period(figs. 290, 291). The latter, although drawn on graph paper, is governed by a series of contiguous circles scribed with a compass, the resulting curvilinear rhythms once again suggesting familiarity with Grasset's *Méthode de composition ornemental* as, for example, figure 26 on page 373 of volume 1. A different arrangement of contiguous circles were noted in FLC 2012; figure 286.

By 1911–13, therefore, Jeanneret's stance on regionalism was ambiguous. He largely rejected L'Eplattenier's idea of creating a Jura style based on natural forms but he himself persisted in the use of Jura motifs, rather than other sources, for his decorative designs. Nevertheless, the regionalist concepts of Cingria-Vaneyre he continued to support, but these were not based on nature. Such inconsistencies created the difficulties he experienced while writing his articles during the winter of 1913–14.

The long-presaged break with L'Eplattenier, based mostly on ideological and theoretical grounds, occurred in mid-1912. Unfortunately it was not restricted to professional matters alone.[55] So for months thereafter L'Eplattenier refused to communicate with, or even acknowledge, Jeanneret. Precisely what event, or series thereof, precipitated the rupture is unknown, but presumably it related to the basis of their teaching in the Nouvelle Section. Jeanneret was grievously wounded by L'Eplattenier's reaction and tried to restore the relationship; this partially occurred, especially after Jeanneret's defense of L'Eplattenier and the Nouvelle Section during the crisis of March–April 1914.

Once before Jeanneret "broke" with his mentor on the matter of teaching (as recorded in his famous Paris letter of November 22–25, 1908) at which time some of the same issues were at stake. Yet then their friendship was not in jeopardy as L'Eplattenier did not feel threatened or betrayed.

Of Jeanneret's students (in total perhaps fewer than twenty) I located but one, Paulo Röthlisberger, a Neuchâtel sculptor who enrolled in the Nouvelle Section in 1912 and left within a few months, after finding the school lacking in spirit and L'Eplattenier present only in the evenings. Of Jeanneret as teacher, he said he was Cartesian, with

54. Le Corbusier, therefore, improperly dated FLC 2515 (fig. 289) as 1904 when he published it in *L'Architecture d'aujourd'hui,* 19e année (April 1948), p. 82.

55. "C'est fini entre L'Eplattenier et moi! . . . Des ans ont échafaudé une amitié basée sur l'intérêt. . . . Des concepts d'art trop divers, trop opposés ont peu à peu congelé toute sympathie. Il ne reste plus entre nous que la *masque*" (to Klipstein, August 20, 1912). And on September 4 he wrote Ritter, expressing the deep hurt he felt by this development.

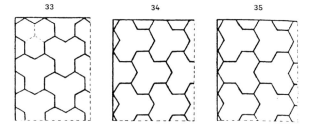

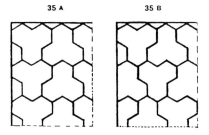

services, puisqu'il présente à lui seul huit variantes, et qu'il se compense parfaitement.

En voilà assez pour montrer la variété des réseaux construits avec une seule et même figure et dont la nomenclature un peu sèche sera excusée

33    34    35

par le lecteur. Les simples tracés qui précèdent peuvent être considérés comme étant des dessins en eux-mêmes et non pas seulement des constructions dont on utilise surtout les *places* fournies par les *angles*

35 A    35 B

des figures. Dans le premier cas il suffira d'appliquer à ces réseaux les développements que nous venons d'employer pour les figures composant les bordures, doublements, effets alternés clairs et foncés, etc.

clarity of thought and with disciplined and organized thinking—yet simultaneously showing great warmth and enthusiasm.[56]

None of these young instructors (Aubert, Jeanneret, or Perrin) had any credentials as teachers and this was immediately cited by critics of L'Eplattenier's Nouvelle Section. Therefore the commission, on February 13, 1913, asked each to obtain his "Brevet de Capacité," which Jeanneret secured on October 6.[57]

Even before students enrolled in the Nouvelle Section the antagonists were seeking its suppression. The initial salvos were fired in the local press during August 1911. The criticisms were often unfounded and easily refuted but they kept the supporters on the

**Fig. 287.** Study for decorative designs. Postdated "La Chaux-de-Fonds/Sapin en hiver/1911." Observe, at bottom, the unit system upon which the repetitive decorative pattern is based. Also compare the conventionalized "sapin," at right, with our figure 289, FLC 2515. Pencil and watercolor on paper. 27.5 × 21.5 cm. (FLC 1763)

**Fig. 288.** Eugène Grasset, *Méthode de composition ornementale* (Paris, 1905), p. 216. Much admired by Jeanneret, Grasset was surely the source for Jeanneret's repetitive unit system; compare Grasset's diagram 35A with Jeanneret's "Sapin en hiver."

56. Jeanneret mentions Röthlisberger to Ritter on May 13, 1912, while seeking some work for him. His name also appears in the 1912 (but not 1913) list of students published in *Un Mouvement d'Art à la Chaux-de-Fonds,* p. 45.

57. "Le Conseil d'état de la République et Canton de Neuchâtel . . . délivre le Brevet de Capacité pour l'enseigement du dessin artistique dans les Écoles secondaires au citoyen Charles-Edouard Jeanneret, originaire du Locle (Suisse). Donné . . . le six octobre 1913." Document at FLC.

**Fig. 289.** Decorative pattern of "sapin" as structured by Jeanneret on a series of diagonal and vertical regulating lines that may be seen faintly in the background. Pencil and ink on heavy sketchbook paper. Detail of 13 × 31.5 cm. sheet. (FLC 2515)

defensive, including Henri Bopp-Boillot, president of the commission of the Ecole d'art, and William Aubert, director of the Ancienne Section, both of whom were sympathetic to L'Eplattenier but both of whom resigned during 1912–13.

After the resignation of an interim president, the commission's chair passed to Jean Hirschy, who often sided with E.-Paul Graber, the secretary, who initially had spearheaded the attacks on the Nouvelle Section. Animosity, we already noted, existed between teachers at the Ecole and L'Eplattenier, especially after the founding of the Cours Supérieur in 1905, and this enmity intensified with the creation of the Nouvelle Section in 1911. Politics were also involved. The socialists, who had won the recent elections, and their newspaper, *La Sentinelle,* were persistent opponents of L'Eplattenier, in part for personal reasons, and partly because they considered his ideas elitist and catering to the few.

The most prominent of the adversaries was Paul Graber who, in addition to being a member of the commission, was a councilman in the commune, and subsequently (1915–19) editor of *La Sentinelle;* thereafter he became the secretary of the socialist party in Switzerland. No one played a more active role in the destruction of the Nouvelle Section than he, yet history, and especially Le Corbusier, have probably overemphasized the part played by the socialists, who would never have succeeded but for the internal weakness of the Ecole which lacked sufficient unity and direction to properly defend itself. Not only were there divisions among the staff but there was no uniform pedagogical approach (such as existed in the Nouvelle Section), and the administration,

which seemed unable to communicate with the general public, saw the problem merely as one resulting from the separation of the school into two self-governing units. The situation was truly comic, except for its tragic ending.

Throughout this tragedy Jeanneret excelled in his defense of the Nouvelle Section and in attempting to resolve its problems. It became a cause célèbre in spite of his differences with L'Eplattenier. He employed the power of the pen and almost single-handedly (notwithstanding the signatures of all four members of the Nouvelle Section) prepared the forty-five-page booklet *Un Mouvement d'Art à la Chaux-de-Fonds à propos de la Nouvelle Section de l'École d'art*. This devastating document presented the situation with such clarity as to virtually destroy the opposition, yet events had moved too rapidly to be reversed. L'Eplattenier's resignation was submitted March 18, Aubert junior's on April 8, and although Jeanneret's resignation and booklet both date from mid-month the effective date for his resignation was set for April 30. Meanwhile he labored to reconstitute the Nouvelle Section under the aegis of the Ecole (which L'Eplattenier

**Fig. 290.** Stylized pattern of snow-covered "sapin" (and faces?). 1911–12. Acrylic on coarse paper. 21 × 17 cm. (FLC 2230)

**Fig. 291.** Decorative design based on underlying unit system of contiguous circles apparently inspired by Eugène Grasset. Compare with figure 286. Pencil and watercolor on graph paper. 1911–12. 22.5 × 17 cm. (FLC 2231)

opposed) yet by May 28 he finally abandoned the effort and reaffirmed his earlier resignation. Perrin alone had not resigned, I assume because of concern for his financial future.[58] The value of the Nouvelle Section was belatedly recognized, producing calls for a new Cours Supérieur, but without the driving force of L'Eplattenier or Jeanneret the matter was effectively dead.

Jeanneret's booklet makes persuasive reading. The initial twenty-two pages trace the history of the school, the founding of the Nouvelle Section—its program, organization, and achievements—and chronicle the steps taken by the opposition, its methods and results. The pièce de résistance, however, is Chapter 8, fourteen pages in length, wherein Jeanneret brilliantly elicits an international panel of experts to judge the Nouvelle Section—its teaching, the quality of student work, and the potential value to local industry. Such testimonials, from Europe's great centers of artistic achievement, had a profound effect.

What Jeanneret did, concealed under the signature of five prominent local citizens, was write an identical letter to Eugène Grasset and Rupert Carabin in Paris, Karl-Ernst Osthaus in Hagen, Peter Behrens in Berlin, Theodor Fischer in Munich, and Alf. Roller in Vienna—all, except perhaps the last, being personal acquaintances (I wonder why Josef Hoffmann was absent from the list?). The letter, dated March 6 and listing all six of those approached, set forth the history and objectives of the school, the Cours Supérieur, and the Nouvelle Section. Enclosed were photographs of the June 1913 exhibition of student work (cf. figs. 283–85), as well as the 1912 *Prospectus* with its nine pages of illustrations, thus enabling the correspondents to judge the qualitative value of the Nouvelle Section. Responses were received from all but Roller, who was out of town, and there was an additional one from Hector Guimard, designer of the famous métro stations of Paris, who probably had been solicited by Léon Perrin, his former apprentice. All were effusive in their praise. But these replies, dated March 10 to 28, overlapped L'Eplattenier's resignation (March 18) and arrived too late to effect the fast-moving course of events.

Throughout this period of Jeanneret's involvement with the Nouvelle Section his other activities proceeded unabated. We discussed his two reports on the teaching of design prepared for L'Oeuvre, and "Le Renouveau dans l'architecture" published in its journal. And work continued on his travelogue, specifically the Athens and Athos chapters, during this first half of 1914.

As architect, planner, and interior designer he was equally active but with less result. During January and February he labored intently on a competition design for the Banque Cantonale de Neuchâtel but his entry, one among seventy-two, was eliminated in the very first round. Instead of being disheartened, however, he interpreted the event as an educational experience that proved how much he still must learn about architec-

58. Perrin was evasive and somewhat embarrassed by my questions on this subject, therefore my assumption.

ture; he also acknowledged that the winning plans had real merit.[59] His competition designs, like those for the earlier Le Locle town hall, have not survived.

In May another great opportunity came his way. Arnold Beck, a real estate developer, had acquired a large tract of sloping land on the south side of town near Beau-Site. He asked Jeanneret to prepare the street layout, presumably because of a talk he had given the previous winter.[60] His plan closely followed the contour of the land while using curving streets of different widths with closed vistas at the ends, all of which conformed to the donkey-path concept he had advocated in 1910 while writing "La Construction des Villes." What was different, however, is that he located the houses only on the up-hill side of the streets, thus providing each with long views across the town to the Pouillerel mountains beyond. Might this reflect John Wood's planning at Bath, England, where the Royal Crescent occupied but one side of its sloping site and, if so, did this constitute an early instance of Jeanneret's attraction to eighteenth-century planning ideals which by the following summer (1915) would play such a paramount role in his studies and in his thinking?

A long (five-page) contract between Jeanneret and Beck was prepared in June which is remarkable for offering the architect virtually complete control over every aspect of this "Cité Jardin," from establishing the plan and parceling up the land to being the exclusive architect for all 120 houses—including perpetual authority over subsequent major changes. One clause even specified the use of the most modern construction techniques, thereby perhaps foretelling the architect's often disastrous experiments with new methods during the late teens and twenties. His commission was to be 5 percent of the selling price (not construction cost) of each house, exclusive of the land.

The validity of the contract, however, was dependent upon receiving a variance from the commune for the use of curved streets, a use that violated the official grid plan. As late as October Jeanneret hoped to obtain this variance and get the contract signed, but with the war raging and an acute depression in the watchmaking industry it was no time for speculative building.

Although Jeanneret failed to design a single house for Arnold Beck, his intentions

59. In a postcard to Ritter dated February 23, 1914, Jeanneret announced that his entry was "à l'instant" completed, and on March 24 a long discussion of the competition commenced with the following: "J'ai mesuré à un récent concours pour la Banque Cantonale de Neuchâtel combien l'architecture m'est encore inconnue, combien je suis un gamin et j'ai reconnu l'impossibilité de bluffer et de tout de même affirmer une chose que j'ignore. Le problème était dur et long, et de haute envergure. Un travail de deux mois m'a amené à un résultat nul. Je fus écarté au premier tour. Il y avait 72 projets. Et les primés, certes ont de réels mérites de plans pratiques." Jeanneret, at this time, was in one of his upbeat moods and elsewhere in this letter said of his mental state: "Je suis loin d'être malheureux."

60. This talk is known from his August 20, 1912, letter to Klipstein: "Puis je reprendrai mon travail sur les villes pour en faire des conférances cet hiver. L'idée m'en est venue ainsi: Un client m'a donné à faire le parcellement de son terrain . . . [etc.]," thereby providing the theme for his slide lecture. Jeanneret's correspondence with Beck is recorded in Copie de lettres and the unsigned contract is at BV.

are revealed in a bird's-eye view of the proposed development (figs. 292, 293). The homes appear quite conservative with their steep roofs and varied massing yet close examination indicates a similarity to several at Hellerau, especially those designed by Riemerschmid, Tessenow, and Baillie Scott; Le Corbusier, in fact, later illustrated one of the Tessenow houses in *L'Esprit Nouveau,* no. 27. The buildings, which often are contiguous and curve in conformity with the street, are also, in their layout, characteristic of certain English garden cities sketched by Jeanneret where a continuous wall connects each house along the principal street (as here along the rue de la République). But neither of these influences should surprise us.

During this same month of June, Jeanneret entered into one of the entrepreneurial projects that fascinated him over the next few years, although none would prove a financial success. This early venture was called Lumière and the letterhead of its stationary identified it as a "Société Pour La Fabrication De Lustrerie D'Art." The association included a merchant and a banker with Jeanneret serving as consulting architect for the design and manufacture of electric light fixtures for which, judging by his sketchbooks, he possessed a very special interest.[61]

Jeanneret's correspondence during these months shows him to be in a cheerful, upbeat mood, full of spirit. "I am far from being unhappy" he wrote Ritter (March 24, 1914), and well he might. He had his thumb in many pies, and was developing more than a local reputation. This led him to be somewhat boastful, and one name he frequently dropped was *L'Art de France,* not just because it republished his *Etude* in April–May, but because (on his suggestion) its editor asked him to report on the Werkbund congress in Cologne—which Jeanneret gleefully interpreted as giving him the status of a foreign correspondent.

His trip to Cologne, and its dates, can be reconstructed from correspondence.[62] His sketchbook—he must have carried one—has not been found, and presumably because of the war his article was never written. Thus we know less about this important trip than we might wish.

> *June 27, 1914:* Left La Chaux-de-Fonds. First stop Colmar to see Grünewald's early sixteenth-century Isenheim Altarpiece in the Musée d'Unterlinden which he tremendously admired.[63] Second stop Strasbourg, where he spent one

61. What little is known of Lumière is recorded in a letter to Max Du Bois of June 24, 1914, and its undated sequel, as well as one of October 9 to "Maison Daum frères" in Nancy which says "la société "Lumière" qui cherche précisément à grouper les quelques artisans des goûts de notre région. . . ."

62. To Ritter, June 17: "Je pars dans 10 jours pour *Cologne,* par *Colmar* (Grünewald) et *Nancy,* je suis invité au congrès du werkbund 3, 4, 5 juillet. Je dois être le 7 à Genève pour les représentations du centenaire, puis à *Lyon* de suite après."

63. "Tout seul, Grünewald, pour tout le nord, pour donner des amplitudes du dômes, aux valets peints d'un retable. Je voudrais ce Grünewald, dans une ferme du Jura, en pleine montagne, seul" (to Ritter, June 28, 1914).

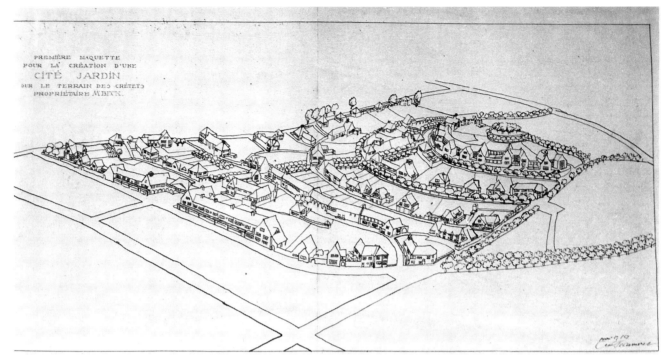

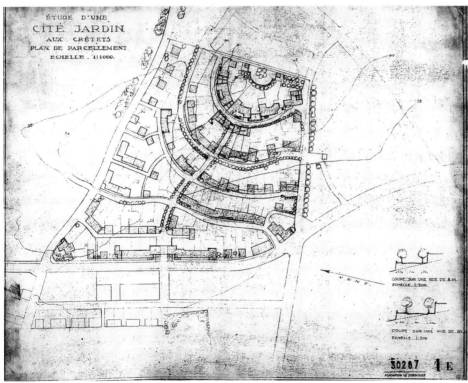

**Fig. 292.** Garden suburb project for Arnold Beck, La Chaux-de-Fonds. Signed and dated May 1914. Pen and ink on heavy paper. 55 × 108 cm. (FLC 30268)

**Fig. 293.** Plan of proposed subdivision for Arnold Beck. Pen and ink on heavy paper. 59 × 63 cm. (FLC 30267)

hour enraptured by the interior of the cathedral which he called "la plus belle que je connaisse" and which revitalized his admiration for the Gothic. Then on to Nancy for the night.

*June 28:* Nancy. Spent hours walking up and down, back and forth, through Place Stanislas, Place de la Carrière, and Hemicycle, marveling at the plan and the palaces. No mention of the famous Art Nouveau buildings. That evening, still in Nancy, penned a long letter to Ritter and on the envelope added "Cologne post restante jusque dimanche [July 5] matin 9 heurs. Genève poste restante le 8 et 9 juillet." However, the letter was not mailed until July 1 at Cologne.

*June 29–30:* There is no record of his whereabouts although he did make an unscheduled trip, either at this time or while en route from Cologne to Geneva, to see Felix and Editha Klipstein in Laubach, Germany, which resulted in his being asked to design their house.

*July 1–5:* In Cologne to attend the Werkbund congress and the Werkbund Exhibition where the architecture left him entirely unimpressed and buildings by such architects as Walter Gropius or Bruno Taut were never mentioned. Only van de Velde's theater was singled out for discussion, in order to denounce it as a sad setback to the cause of architecture by a man of high reputation and acknowledged artistic taste, all this being expressed in a long letter, significantly, to Auguste Perret on July 1.[64]

*ca. July 6–9:* Geneva. Centenary celebrations at which Jaques-Dalcroze's group, including Albert Jeanneret, participated. Parents in attendance on fifth and sixth (father's journal).

*ca. July 9–12:* To Lyon with return home via Beaune in order to see Rogier van der Weyden's *Last Judgment* altarpiece (ca. 1450) at the Hôtel-Dieu.[65] The objective of his Lyon trip, though not mentioned in correspondence, was obviously to visit the International Town Planning Exhibition (Exposition internationale urbaine: "La Cité moderne") that took place in the still uncompleted buildings of the cattle market and abattoir "La Mouche," of which Tony Garnier was the architect. Perforce, therefore, Jeanneret experienced some of Garnier's industrial work and undoubtedly saw designs by Garnier that were on exhibit, such as the Gerland Stadium begun the previous year (but for which only the racetracks, not the triumphal entryways, had been completed) and drawings for the Grange-Blanche hospital. Garnier's own house at Saint-Rambert, completed in

64. And three months later he wrote to Ritter: "Et mon enthousiasme n'allant point de tout à la Werkbundausstellung, mais à certains indices de celle de Lyon" (October 9, 1914).

65. "J'ai vu à Beaune le retable de van der Weyden. C'est moins imposant que celui de Grünewald. Au reste c'est une autre race. Van der Weyden est beaucoup plus austère, plus chaste, moins passionné" (to August Klipstein, July 21, 1914).

1912, was probably not visited and there is no indication that Jeanneret met Garnier at this time. However, what Jeanneret wrote most enthusiastically about at Lyon was neither architecture nor urbanism but what he described as a "superb" exhibition of modern painting and sculpture.[66]

Jeanneret's wish to see paintings was certainly instigated by his growing activity as an artist. Prior to 1912 his hundreds of watercolors were mainly of buildings, architectural details, and decoration, along with an occasional landscape or cityscape. They served as an aid to memory; creating the work fixed the image in his mind and simultaneously preserved it for future reference. Color was of capital importance as witnessed by his paintings, notes, and letters. He discovered white in 1910, yet never lost interest in color. Therefore the fauve painters of France held special appeal since his paintings often contained unnatural colors (see color plate VIII).

A major change occurred upon his return to La Chaux-de-Fonds late in 1911. His paintings suddenly assumed the role of pictures in their own right. This is not to say that during the previous decade he had not made charming watercolors but rarely were they intentionally created as works of art. His attitude now changed, and this affected his feeling toward his earlier work; he became anxious to exhibit it. He assembled various watercolors ranging from views of Fiesole and Sienna of October 1907, Potsdam of November 1910, and the remainder from 1911—a view of medieval Frankfort, the church at Gabrovo, Constantinople, seen from the sea (as inspired by Signac), three pictures of columns standing on their stylobates at the Acropolis in Athens (rendered in unnatural colors),[67] and the forum at Pompeii. This group he entitled "Langage de Pierre" and exhibited part or all of them at Neuchâtel (IVe Exposition de la Section neuchâteloise de la Société des peintres, sculpteurs et architectes suisse), April 13–May 20, 1912; the Salon d'Automne, Grand Palais, Paris, October 1–November 8, also in 1912; and at the Kunsthaus, Zurich, March 30–April 27, 1913—thus three times within a twelve-month period. His next group show was in 1916 at Zurich, by which time he had very different works to include.[68]

66. "A Lyon se tenait une superbe exposition de peinture. Tous les modernes, sauf une salle avec Bonnats et consorts. Ils avaient triste figure. Beaucoup de Redon, des Rodin admirables, Renoir, Bourdelle, Denis, Bonnard etc. etc.—toute la sainte kyrielle" (to August Klipstein, July 21, 1914). And to Du Bois (n.d.) he merely said "Je reviens de Cologne et Lyon à voir ce que font un peu partout les Modernes. . . . Je me sens les forces pour être une fois quelqu'un."

67. "J'ai fait un Parthénon avec du vert émeraude et du vermillon. Un autre avec du vermillon et du noir. Et l'autre jour le temple de Jupiter avec du noir, du vert et du rose-caleçon. Je perds la tête, ça me dégoûte ce que je fais, je bâcle en 10 minutes et cependant je ne répudie pas" (to Ritter from Florence, October 15, 1911).

68. A letter from Albert to his parents of April 24, 1913, remarked: "Quel plaisir qu'Ed. fasse de la peinture et qu'il y mette rancoeur, violence, émois, colères, sensualités, comme cela s'exprime bien en couleurs."

**Fig. 294.** *Persistantes souvenances du Bosphore.* 1913. Charcoal, ink, and gouache on drawing paper. 55.5 × 57.5 cm. (FLC 4099)

**Fig. 295.** *Vin d'Athos.* Dated February 1913. Pencil and aquarelle on drawing paper. 42.5 × 45 cm. (FLC 4098)

His letters, both before and after returning home, referred to artists he admired and these we occasionally noted. Hodler, the Swiss, was repeatedly cited, as were Cézanne, Signac (in 1911), Maillol, and Matisse—who by 1912 was a great favorite. So was Kees Van Dongen, although also named were Van Gogh, Gauguin, Bonnard, and Denis, to speak of but a few. The twentieth-century German Expressionists were rarely if ever mentioned; expressionism, for him, was epitomized by such Renaissance masters as Grünewald, whose masterpiece he traveled to Colmar to see.

His subject matter also underwent a change, proceeding from the real world to an imaginary one. This is evident in the titles of his paintings: *Vin d'Athos, Hellade* (i.e. Greece), *Persistantes souvenances du Bosphore,* and *Souvenir turc: Marmara.* Indeed, this latter title recalls Matisse: *The Blue Nude—Souvenir of Biskra* (1907).

Symbolism has merged into fantasy, as the surrealists later were wont to do, and the forms may be full, rounded, and voluptuous or else angular and emphasizing straight lines. *Persistantes souvenances du Bosphore,* dated 1913, represents the latter, with its abstract, geometric forms and only the head, hands, and feet of a female figure discernible, while above are sea, mountains, and a yellow sky; the shape at the upper left perhaps defies description unless it represents some part of a pier or ship (fig. 294, and color plate VII). This painting is truly an "Homage à l'angle droit."

*Vin d'Athos* (fig. 295) was discussed while mentioning Jeanneret's inebriated condition while on Mont Athos and the hallucinatory state it left him in. The thought of a female nude astride a mule was wishful thinking in that land where women were forbidden, yet only the distant sea and mountains (lower left) provide any hint of the location.

**Fig. 296.** *Female Nudes on a Beach* 1912–13. Charcoal and watercolor on paper. 19 × 29 cm. (Private collection)

**Fig. 297.** *Nude on the Beach* ca. 1914–15. Lead pencil and watercolor on paper. 31.8 × 42 cm. (FLC 4083)

Here the sharp, angular forms, crowding the limits of the painted surface, are more typical of German expressionism and possibly certain characteristics of Franz Marc's work than anything concerning the shapes, colors, or subject matter of French fauvism. Nevertheless Jeanneret's paintings do not embrace the often emotional subject matter, or social criticism, found in German expressionism; he rejected these deeper meanings as did the painters in France.

*Female Nudes on a Beach* (1912–13; fig. 296), of which he painted two versions, relies heavily on color rather than perspective to differentiate between the two nudes. The figure in front is shaded in blue with white paper providing the highlights, while that at the left is sketched in red, thus reversing the normal arrangement of placing cooler colors in the background. Again the figures are distorted to fit the strictures of the paper and the small "signature motif" of sea, mountains, and yellow sky occupies an insignificant part of the picture. The theme of two nudes soon became prevalent in his paintings, often as two lesbians making love. Jeanneret described this painting in his letter to Ritter of April 6, 1913.[69]

Matisse's *The Blue Nude—Souvenir of Biskra* foretells how Jeanneret would draw in color (colors often rich, unreal, and vibrant as we saw in his Acropolis paintings), while exaggerating the human figure and subordinating the landscape setting. Perhaps closest to Matisse are Jeanneret's *Nude on the Beach* (FLC 4083; fig. 297) or *Three Bathers* (FLC 4078) of ca. 1914–15, the latter also embodying certain qualities of Cézanne.

Meanwhile two pots that Jeanneret bought in the Balkans dominate a still life dated 1914 (fig. 298). Their full, placid, almost classic forms recall his earlier references to "Ma Maillol" and his contemporary comment to Ritter: "un Maillol, ô mon Dieu si tranquille, serein, benêt dans ses pommiers en fruits et son verge, et modelant les cylindres des cuisses et les vases des ventres" (March 24, 1914). The monumental, abstract

---

69. Due to its relevance, the entire section is quoted here:

> L'obsession. "L'Obsédance" que me paraît plus fort. De souvenirs dressés comme des juges; de figures attirantes, séductions décrépitantes et intenses, motrices, m'intimant d'oeuvres. La sève de vie, et cette présence peut-être morbide des choses aimées, s'imposent sous forme de femmes à peindre; nues ou vêtues, onanisme de célibataire. J'ai déshabillé l'Ariane endormie des jardins de Versailles, et l'ai peinte comme une grande fraise opulente, sur un fond de vert intense. Et l'horizon d'Andrinople me fait esquisser une femme blanche et voilée au regard horizontal et permanent, la pénétration; une femme accroupie, nue et rouge avec la tête droite et le corps dans le même axe; une femme écarlate vêtue et le menton haut; le ciel et la terre s'équivalent en jaune citron.
>
> Je ferai brune, la vallée de la Maritza, brune la tiare de la Coupole et des minarets. Le ciel citron toujours. Le citron c'est l'Asie. . . .
>
> L'homme nu est pour celui qui s'est surmonté et a satisfait son corps. C'est un complexe aux plans fermes et rectangular. L'homme nu est pour moi l'architecture. Quand je ne fais plus d'architecture, je vois tout en femmes.

**Fig. 298.** *Still Life with Pots.* Dated 1914. Lead pencil and gouache on drawing paper. 47.5 × 63 cm. (FLC 4500)

geometry of Maillol's figural volumes certainly appealed to Jeanneret even though specific sculptures, such as *Mediterranean* (ca. 1901), are never mentioned by name.

His letters, especially those to Ritter, are filled with poetic word-pictures. These include mixed images and references to color regardless of whether paintings are being described or not. They sometimes portray a subconscious dream world, partly nostalgic, seldom real, as was noted in his November 1, 1911, letter from Lucerne (p. 302 in chap. 8).

Landscapes were always important among his paintings and drawings, whether his earliest watercolor of October 1902 or his works from later travels to many lands. Stylistically they cover the gamut from realism to fauvism, to impressionism, to virtual abstraction, depending on what he hoped to achieve.[70] Upon Ritter's return to Switzerland, forced by the war, they often painted together, and landscapes, during 1915 and 1916, were virtually the only paintings Jeanneret did. It was not until 1917, and his move to Paris, that he more or less picked up from where he left off in 1912–14. And throughout all these years pencil, ink, watercolor, and gouache would remain his media. Not until 1918 and his friendship with Amédée Ozenfant did he seriously turn to oils.

70. Three of these ca. 1913–16 landscapes are illustrated in Le Corbusier's *Creation Is a Patient Search,* pp. 42–43. That atop p. 42 (FLC 4089) was, I believe, painted from an upper window at the Villa Jeanneret-Perret. He dates all three "before 1914" but that on p. 43 is stylistically close to FLC 4072 which is signed and dated "ChEJt/1916."

In point of fact, many of the most fascinating and original paintings he ever did are from the period 1912–17, and of this more will be said later on.[71]

Immediately after his Cologne/Lyon trip, which included Laubach, he dispatched a letter (July 15, 1914) to Felix Klipstein enclosing 14 watercolors, 8 larger sheets, 175 drawings, and 4 sketchbooks from his Voyage d'Orient trip, and from these Felix was requested to seek ideas for his house and sketch what he particularly liked (remember, Felix was an artist) and send these to Jeanneret. The design process is interesting, and closely recalls what Jeanneret had done while designing his parents' home—first reviewing what he admired in both historic and contemporary architecture and then assimilating the chosen components into something new. And he emphasized, as is true of any creative process, that time for reflection was necessary before committing oneself to the actual design. He admitted, nevertheless, to already having certain ideas in mind, and by bombarding Klipstein with visual material from the Mediterranean world he makes it clear that (à la Cingria-Vaneyre) the house was to have a southern personality rather than being reminiscent of central Germany where it would be built (this despite the regionalism he espoused in his recent articles).

Any drawings Felix prepared no longer exist, but during the autumn Jeanneret presented his corresponding ideas in a series of eight perspectives rendered in ink on tracing paper which he mailed on November 6.[72] These are our only record of the project because the tentative plans and sections dispatched on January 4, 1915 (from which contractors were to prepare approximate bids) have not survived. In February a bid of 30,000 marks was received, but this was more than Felix could afford. What amazed Jeanneret (and me too) was that at the height of World War I both labor and materials were available in Germany to build a private house. Jeanneret stressed that the materials and exterior finish would be exactly the same as those used in his parents' house and that these were the least expensive possible. Then, much later, Jeanneret again wrote (June 28, 1915) to say he had completed his most pressing jobs and was free to resume work on the Klipstein project. However, he received no go-ahead from Felix and after the war Klipstein's finances were depleted by inflation.[73]

The proposed site was a west-sloping orchard terminating at a small brook, the access

71. Only one publication has treated Jeanneret's pre-1918 painting seriously and that is the catalogue accompanying the 1987 exhibition held at the Musée des Beaux-Arts, La Chaux-de-Fonds, prepared by Edmond Charrière and Danielle Perret, *Le Corbusier: Peintre avant le purisme* (La Chaux-de-Fonds, 1987). My thanks also to Susan Nasgaard who, in 1976, wrote for me a splendid paper on this topic.

72. The original pencil sketches (BV) are on tracing paper. These, in turn, were traced in ink and this set, also on tracing paper, was sent to Klipstein. Some were also reproduced as blueprints. Felix was thirty-four (born December 21, 1880) and that year had an operation on his foot, factors that perhaps explain his temporary exemption from military service.

73. My thanks to Frl. Christiane Klipstein and her brother Felix for their timely assistance during my 1978 visit to Laubach. For memoirs of the events, see Editha Klipstein, *Gestern und heute* (Schloss Laupheim: Ulrich Steiner Verlag, 1948), especially pp. 107–8.

Fig. 299. Project: Felix Klipstein house, Laubach, Germany, November 1914. Ink on tracing paper. 15.5 × 20 cm. (Private collection)

Fig. 300. Project: Felix Klipstein house, Laubach, Germany, 1914. Pencil on tracing paper. 20 × 28 cm. (BV)

**Fig. 301.** Study: Hallway for Felix Klipstein house, 1914. Front entrance is at the left, living room behind the wall at the right. Ink on tracing paper. 23.5 × 16 cm. (Private collection)

**Fig. 302.** Study: Living room for Felix Klipstein house, November 1914. Both doors lead into the hallway. Ink on tracing paper. 10 × 28 cm. (Private collection)

road (Andrée Allee) being above and therefore out of sight; Felix–Klipstein–Weg, across the brook, is a modern incursion. The house was to be situated parallel to the brook and orchard and near the top of the slope (figs. 299, 300). Despite its L-shaped massing, the impression is of a rectangle when seen from below. The courtyard facing the street was nearly square and would be dominated by two tall poplars that Jeanneret urged Felix to plant immediately so they might grow. A larger, private courtyard, with rose garden and pool, extended to the south; on the view side it was open except for a view-framing trellis that was topped by a walkway connecting the house to the two-storey studio at garden's end. This "chambre d'été" recalls the one at his parents' home, an idea he imported from the Balkans and later implanted on terraced rooftops designed in Paris in the 1920s.

One entered from the poplar courtyard into a well-lighted, beamed-ceiling hallway (recall the ceiling at Le Couvent) furnished with antiques and a small fountain splashing near the door. Parallel to this corridor (which led to the bedroom wing and the staircase to the guest rooms above) was the living room, its long side facing the western view and having a fireplace at one end (figs. 301, 302).[74] Jeanneret had mentioned his wish to create the ambience of a farmhouse, and this seems evident here.

In this connection a postcard illustrating an old farmhouse near Sarliac in the Dordogne, France, that Jeanneret sent his parents takes on special interest (fig. 303). His message begins: "This is the region where they make real architecture, good houses in which to live." Perhaps this, or a similar building, provided the theme for the Klipstein design.[75]

74. Jeanneret describes the plan in his November 6 letter to Felix. A rough sketch of it appears on the back of an accounting sheet concerning *L'Esprit Nouveau* (FLC Box A2 [15]).

75. Actually, this card probably postdates the Klipstein design. Jeanneret dated it "Toulouse vendredi" and the postmark is illegible. Nevertheless it is a traditional type that dates back to the Roman Empire as James S. Ackerman points out: "the early villas [of Palladio] are bound unconsciously to an ancient tradition that . . . had survived without a break from the Roman Empire . . . a three-bay loggia flanked by two projecting tower-like blocks" (*Palladio* [Harmondsworth: Penguin Books, 1966], p. 43).

4019. - LES CHAUZES, près Sarliac (Dordogne)

Fig. 303. Farmhouse near Sarliac in the Dordogne, France. This postcard Jeanneret mailed to his parents; compare with Klipstein project. (BV)

# 10

## DOM-INO, LA SCALA, THE VILLA SCHWOB, AND FURNITURE DESIGN
### *1914–1916*

The war that enveloped Europe in August 1914 had surprisingly little impact on Jeanneret's private life. Obviously it curtailed new commissions, and thwarted his chance of building the Villa Klipstein. Yet he was free from military service due to the eyesight problem which, in 1905, resulted in his transfer from the study of watchcase engraving to studying architecture. And as a citizen of neutral Switzerland he was free to travel either in France or Germany as he might wish. Actually Albert, also deferred from military service (general frailty), spent the autumn of 1914 in Germany where he studied the fugue at Freiburg im Breisgau (just across the Rhine from Colmar, France) although this did raise eyebrows in La Chaux-de-Fonds where sympathies, unlike those in Germanic Switzerland, lay solidly on the side of France.

The war, and Jeanneret's withdrawal from the Ecole d'art, provided time for other pursuits. He enjoyed a sojourn in Paris (summer of 1915), carried on his painting, frequently visited William Ritter who had fled Germany for his native Switzerland, began designing (rather than buying) furniture for his clients, and, as a reaction to the war's dramatic destruction of housing, devised (in consort with Max Du Bois and Juste Schneider) a system for rapid, low-cost construction of extensible housing in reinforced concrete ("Constructions économiques extensibles en béton armé") that he called Dom-ino. Finally, in 1916, he obtained major commissions—the Villa Schwob and La Scala cinema—but by then his dream of moving to Paris was so near reality that, with

**Fig. 304.** Project: Pont Butin over the river Rhône near Geneva, February 1915. Jeanneret's perspective, along with Du Bois and Schneider's detailed construction drawings, were entered in this competition. Charcoal. 0.64 × 1.22 cm. (FLC 30279)

the war in a dangerous deadlock prior to the intervention of the United States, Jeanneret, in January 1917, moved definitively to Paris where he resided for the remainder of his life.

The war's devastation stirred Jeanneret profoundly, less for its human loss than its destruction of buildings (by contrast his father's journal is obsessed with the human suffering). The laying waste of Reims Cathedral was for him a nightmare, especially so soon after his emotional experience at Strasbourg; he believed that Reims should not be rebuilt but remain as a reminder. The ruin of so many workers' and farmers' homes in Belgium he viewed as a great opportunity. Already he had been discussing monolith ("Monolythe") reinforced concrete housing with Max Du Bois, and the Belgium situation turned his mind toward reconstruction.

Another opportunity, nevertheless, distracted him. In December 1914 a competition was announced to design the Pont Butin over the Rhône River near Geneva. Jeanneret entered with alacrity. Masonry construction was prescribed (thus precluding concrete, iron, or steel) with special attention given to its ornamental qualities. The bridge should carry two parallel railroad lines and, at an upper level, a highway twenty meters wide.[1] These prerequisites suggested Roman forms and Jeanneret immediately asked Du Bois to research aqueducts and other viable solutions. Later he acknowledged that the vaulting of Roman baths had been a major inspiration. Yet the question of how many arches the bridge should have remained unanswered until the last moment since this depended upon engineering as well as aesthetic considerations.

Without any engineering background, Jeanneret was wholly dependent upon others for assistance. Therefore he turned to Max Du Bois who, while trained as an engineer, was primarily an administrator and thus deferred most questions to his colleague Juste Schneider. Jeanneret dispatched ten letters to Du Bois in forty-four days anticipating, by return mail, solutions to all the engineering problems as well as expecting Du Bois

1. See *L'Oeuvre,* 1e année, Bulletin 7 (January 1915), pp. 25–26, for the requirements of this competition which was restricted to Swiss nationals.

to write the specifications and furnish the detailed construction drawings (Jeanneret only prepared a perspective, fig. 304). His letters were often demanding, sometimes to the point of rudeness. He requested Du Bois to do lengthy research in libraries, make telephone calls, contact merchants and—most of all—to provide, gratis, an incredible amount of engineering expertise for which he would never be given credit. Why Du Bois was so obliging I cannot imagine, except that he was a very mild-mannered man who took things easily in his stride.[2]

As the deadline approached, Jeanneret became increasingly frantic. All the calculations were being made in Paris with Jeanneret directing the operation by wartime mail from Switzerland. He insisted he would come to Paris but never did, and the timetable for getting documents to Jeanneret for delivery to Geneva was repeatedly advanced.

Du Bois described to me (April 10, 1976) the saga of the final hours. Submissions were due by noon on February 22. The previous night Du Bois took the train from Paris that went via Lausanne to Geneva, where it might arrive a few minutes too late. Therefore he left the train and, taking a shortcut by taxi, delivered "Jeanneret's" submission at Geneva shortly before the deadline.[3]

Le Corbusier was especially proud of the Pont Butin design and included it as one of the three from his youth that he published in *Oeuvre Complète*.[4] Another was Dom-ino. For both he took full credit without ever mentioning Schneider or Du Bois,

2. My source for both the Pont Butin and Dom-ino discussions are Jeanneret's letters to Du Bois found in Copie de lettres through October 8, 1915 (BV) and thereafter the somewhat abridged transcripts made by Du Bois (FLC). All these letters I reviewed with Max Du Bois during 1976 and 1977 and I am much indebted for his help.

Max Du Bois (1884–1989) lived at 15, Avenue du Trocadéro (subsequently renamed President Wilson) in the fifth-floor walkup apartment he first occupied in 1912. Its furnishings remained unchanged from those sketched by Jeanneret in 1915. His chief concern in business was the generation and transmission of electricity in the region south and east of Paris. He was also involved with others in organizing a series of interrelated holding companies including S.A.B.A. (Société d'Applications du Béton Armé) and S.E.I.E. (Société d'Entreprises Industrielle et d'Études). The latter (S.E.I.E.) was founded largely on Du Bois' initiative (and finances) as an umbrella for establishing Jeanneret in Paris ("bureau d'architecte") and for founding the brickworks (briqueterie) at Alfortville of which Jeanneret was put in charge (and oversaw its demise in bankruptcy; see next chapter). During the war Du Bois helped the Swiss government, initially in screening and transporting people who sought refuge in Switzerland, and later he was in charge of transporting wheat from the Atlantic ports to Switzerland; he held a diplomatic passport. Through his business and diplomatic activities he made numerous influential friends, several of whom he introduced to Jeanneret. Raoul La Roche was one of these and in 1923–25 Jeanneret built the La Roche villa (now part of the FLC) and helped the owner assemble his fine collection of modern art.

3. The Pont Butin dossier, like Jeanneret's earlier competition entries at Le Locle and Neuchâtel, has vanished. He received no prize. The winning entry was also modeled on Roman aqueducts, yet the design is rather stiff and rigid, lacking the smooth, more monumental rhythms of Jeanneret's submission.

4. On April 25 Jeanneret sent Ritter a copy of his drawing saying: "Ce pont est beau. Il est romain, et c'est, de moi, la première oeuvre faite avec enthousiasme et dont il me semble pouvoir être satisfait. Il y a vie et organisme [?], et plasticité."

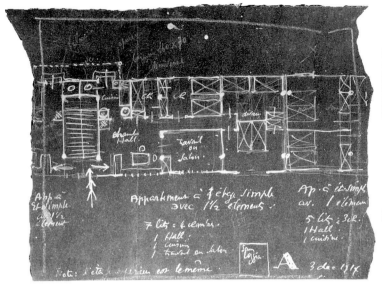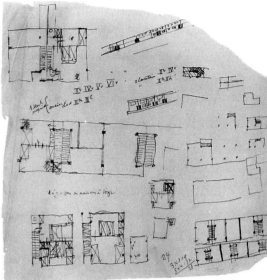

names, in fact, that never appear in his extensive writings. This, however, was character-istic.[5]

With the Pont Butin competition completed, Jeanneret again focused on his Mono-lith (i.e., Dom-ino) project with its salient traits of, first, substituting free-standing con-crete piers in place of load-bearing walls and, second, constructing the reinforced con-crete floor and ceiling slabs without the use of traditional wood formwork which required support from below, and, third, doing all this in such a manner that the slabs were flat and smooth on both sides *and* joined to the supporting piers at right angles. The second idea, compounded by adding the third to it, proved very difficult from an engineering standpoint and for more than a year Jeanneret pestered Du Bois and Schneider to find a solution.[6]

December 3, 1914, is the earliest extant date on Dom-ino drawings and although these are plans rather than construction details we see that the piers are set back from

**Fig. 305.** Dom-ino. Study for Type A housing unit, dated Decem-ber 3, 1914. Note that the piers or columns coincide with interior parti-tion walls but not with the exterior walls. (FLC)

**Fig. 306.** Studies for Dom-ino plans, 1915. India ink. 35 × 35 cm. (FLC 19140)

5. One thinks not only of all the influential names and experiences he never mentioned from his year in Germany, but of *Vers une architecture,* which initially appeared as a series of articles coauthored by Jeanneret and Amédée Ozenfant. However, when Jeanneret subsequently published the essays verbatim as a book he deleted the coauthor's name, thus making Ozenfant furious and contributing to the breakup of their friendship.

6. For primary sources regarding Dom-ino see note 2, Sketchbook A2, pp. 78–84, 93–94, 109–12, 115–24, 146–50, and the numerous drawings at FLC that are more readily available in H. Allen Brooks, ed., *The Le Corbusier Archive,* vol. 1 (New York: Garland Publishing, 1982), pp. 19–77. The best secondary sources are Brian Brace Taylor's exhibition booklet *Le Corbusier at Pessac* (Harvard University and FLC, 1972), and Eleanor Gregh, "The Dom-ino Idea," *Oppositions,* 15/16 (Winter/Spring 1979), pp. 61–87.

the outer, but not the inner, walls (figs. 305, 306). This concept of using piers rather than load-bearing walls for support had already been explored by Jeanneret at his parents' villa in 1912 where four symmetrically placed *masonry* piers freed the interior (but not exterior) walls of their load-bearing function. In the Dom-ino system, however, the piers carry the entire upper floor so that none of the walls, interior or exterior, are needed for support. These floor slabs and piers, prior to the addition of walls, resemble a domino number four or six—thus providing the name. This analogy is heightened as dominos are placed end to end, thereby creating the "extensible" arrangement of modules that Jeanneret sought.

The idea of separating wall and support was not new. In rudimentary form it exists in Gothic cathedrals where colonnettes are set against piers or walls; there the objective was visual rationalization rather than a structural system. Materials new to the nineteenth century resolved this problem, and in the great reading room (1862–68) of the Bibliothèque Nationale (where Jeanneret spent so many hours) Henri Labrouste placed his iron columns just inside the outer walls. Another Parisian example is Victor Baltard's Church of Saint-Augustin (1860–67), located not far from the office of Max Du Bois.

The Dom-ino floor slab idea presented major problems, not because concrete slabs were difficult to construct but because Jeanneret sought to invent, and patent, a new method of constructing them. His objective was on-site mass production to be achieved by eliminating the labor-intensive process of constructing temporary wooden forms upon which the concrete could be poured. He also imposed certain aesthetic ideals that inevitably made the process more difficult and expensive. The first was that the underside of the completed slab must be flush and smooth. This required incorporating hollow tiles (which, though hollow, added weight and expense) in the slab rather than employing recessed coffers with reusable molds. Such a system, however, could never produce a truly smooth undersurface due to small ridges developing where ever tiles and concrete met.

The second concept Jeanneret wished to achieve was to have the horizontal slab meet the vertical piers at right angles. This precluded creating Y-shaped or mushroom tops on the piers to help support the slab.

Nevertheless, the major problem he created was designing forms that required no support from below, that is to say no temporary structural underpinning of wood that necessitated employment of skilled labor. To this end he proposed using metal I-beams to carry the ends of the hollow blocks while leaving sufficient space between each row for the iron rods and concrete that would create flat arches of reinforced concrete. Secondary I-beams would be laid crosswise to support the primary beams that were serving as the surface against which the concrete was poured. These secondary beams, in turn, would be temporarily secured to the side of the vertical piers by a bracket or

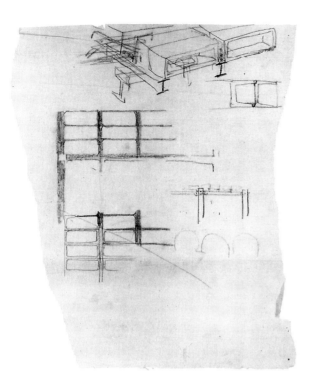

**Fig. 307.** Study showing how I-beams would support both hollow tiles and reinforcing rods prior to the pouring of concrete in Dom-ino construction and, below, a plan indicating the location of a pier (unshaded square at far left) and the concrete joists supporting rows of hollow tiles, 1915. Pencil. 30 × 35 cm. (FLC 19136)

collar ("collier") supported by a steel pin incorporated in the pier at the time the pier itself was cast.[7] Therefore piers and slabs could not be poured simultaneously. And the I-beams could not be placed on top of the piers because this is where the slab itself must rest. All this is illustrated in figures 307–9.

Aside from these technical difficulties, the weight of the I-beams, combined with that of the slab, required strong concrete piers that were well cured. And contrary to Jeanneret's initial wish, this ruled out the use of unskilled labor at this basic stage of construction. Therefore he belatedly realized that the frame must be built by professionals, not laymen, and then sold to clients who, with or without recourse to skilled labor, could put walls, doors, and windows where they wished in order to have a completed house (but how could they install plumbing and a chimney through the completed slab?). For each skeletal frame ("ossature") sold, Jeanneret would receive a royalty on his patent.

Smooth bottom slabs, rather than those with open coffers, were not new to the industry, their construction being show in figure 201 on page 219 of Mörsch's *Le Béton*

7. Reference to such pins and brackets to support the I-beams is minimal. Figure 307, at lower right, shows the piers, pins, and the brackets or collars under the I-beams. A larger sketch appears in Sketchbook A2, page 117, showing a peg near the top of a square pier with the words "1 fer rond engagé sert à fixer le collier embrasse recevant le fer I." It seems that a more definitive solution was awaited from Juste Schneider in Paris.

**Fig. 308.** Cross section of Dom-ino. Pencil and India ink. 46 × 92 cm. (FLC 19204)

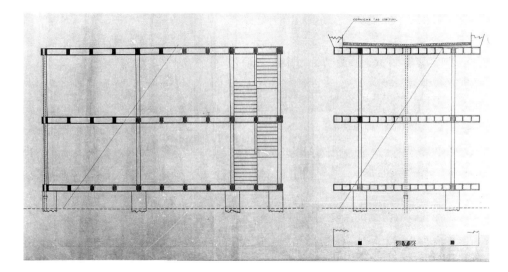

**Fig. 309.** Perspective of a Dom-ino module, 1915. "Monolithe—ossature de béton armé coulée sans coffrage. . . ." India ink and pencil. 47 × 57 cm. (FLC 19209)

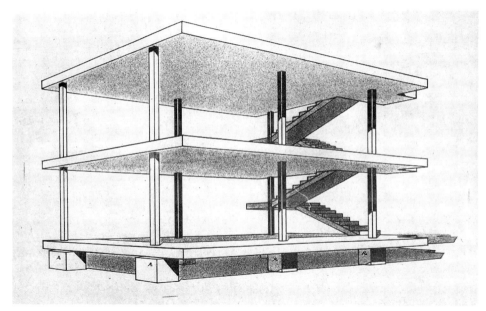

*Armé* translated by Max Du Bois in 1909 and well known to Jeanneret (see Chapter 6). The system is also illustrated in Maurice M. Sloan *The Concrete House and Its Construction* published by the Association of American Portland Cement Manufacturers, Philadelphia, 1912, a book which Jeanneret owned (although its date of acquisition is unknown).

Jeanneret's patent application was submitted on his behalf by Max Du Bois (who performed the same task for the Pont Butin competition) on January 29, 1916; Du Bois also paid the 100-franc registration fee (the Bulletin de Versement, signed by Du Bois,

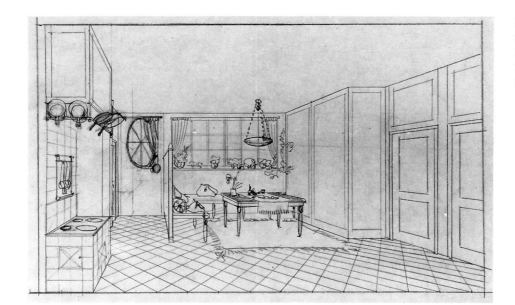

**Fig. 310.** View of entry, kitchen, and dining area of Dom-ino Type B house, 1915. Hanging lamp is probably one that Jeanneret designed for Lumière. (FLC)

is at the Fondation Le Corbusier). The dossier consisted of a cover sheet (Demande d'un brevet d'invention) signed and dated by Jeanneret on January 11, 1916, a three-page "Mémoire descriptif," and four sheets of "Dessin." There was also a longhand note, signed and dated January 15, 1916, authorizing Max Du Bois to deposit the Brevet d'invention on behalf of Jeanneret (also at the Fondation).

The three-page "Brevet d'invention concernant les constructions économiques extensibles en béton armé" was written by Jeanneret; it discusses the purposes and advantages of the "invention" but not the technical aspects of construction.[8] The essential four sheets of designs showing the construction of the "ossatures monolithiques en béton armé" are missing, possibly because copies were never sent to Jeanneret in La Chaux-de-Fonds; they were prepared by Juste Schneider in Paris and may not have been seen by Jeanneret. In any event, no patent was ever issued.

Max Du Bois, in various conversations with the author, insisted that Dom-ino was of no significance in and of itself but that, in his mind, the objective of the exercise was

8. The text of the "Brevet d'Invention" begins: "La présente invention a pour objet la construction de maisons en béton armé sur la séparation des deux fonctions 'ossature rigide supportant les efforts' et 'cloisons légères' formant les parois intérieures et extérieures, amovibles à volonté sans modification de l'ossature rigide.

"Les ossatures monolithiques en béton armé comprenant le plancher et les piliers de support sont étudiées pour former des éléments juxtaposables et superposables selon un . . . module dont les multiples et sous-multiples autorisent un mode de coffrage automatique et extensible indéfiniment" (FLC). Notes for writing this brief exist in Sketchbook A2, p. 120.

to establish precedence for future on-site prefabrication in reinforced concrete. He also felt that such a patent, if issued, could not be defended against infringement and that his main reason for helping Jeanneret was merely to humor him. The validity of Du Bois' negative assessment of Dom-ino seems confirmed by Jeanneret himself, who never once used the system in his own work, preferring to employ more traditional methods of concrete construction.

In November, Jeanneret suddenly became apprehensive that Du Bois might secretly patent Dom-ino in his own name since Du Bois, not Jeanneret, possessed all the essential material. Therefore he wrote Du Bois a conciliatory letter (November 17, 1915) acknowledging Du Bois' great contribution and insisting that he intended to include Du Bois' name along with his own on the patent application. Jeanneret had needlessly worried, however, because, as noted, Du Bois' low estimation of the project left him uninterested in sharing credit for any possible patent.

Jeanneret's most intensive work on Dom-ino occurred between August and December 1915 although he had envisioned the concept late the previous year. Two events (see below) of that summer spurred him to greater action, the first being his visit with Auguste Perret, who thought the proposal "très bien" but that it needed major refinement, and the other being his six-week sojourn with Du Bois in Paris where the matter could be discussed at ease.

During the autumn Jeanneret spent much time preparing a promotional brochure (never published) since he expected to earn a great deal of money from his Dom-ino patent. Several finished drawings (typical plans, perspectives, and interior views [fig. 310], as well as notes on what the text should say, exist but not much more. Meanwhile he constantly urged Du Bois to complete the patent documents. On page 87 of Sketchbook A2 he carefully outlined his future schedule: Du Bois to file patent application in September, Jeanneret to prepare drawings for brochure September/October, brochure to be printed November/December, Jeanneret to move to Paris January 1916. This sequence of events implies that Jeanneret expected Dom-ino to launch his career in France. Yet without the patent he stayed at home.

Jeanneret needed to establish a typical size or module for Dom-ino that conformed to affordable limits for workers' housing. Therefore he read (see Sketchbook A2, pp. 81–82) Alfred de Foville's two-volume *Enquête sur les conditions de l'habitation en France: les maisons-types* (Paris: E. Leroux, 1894–99) and Charles Janet's *Les habitations à bon marché dans les villes de moyenne importance* (Brussels: Mayez, 1897). From these he learned standards for peasant houses including their usual size, the number and types of rooms, and the maximum costs—in other words the norms for minimal housing in France. Keeping this in mind he established the optimum size for a Dom-ino module and then divided up the space into rooms according to how large or small each unit was to be. The different-size plans he designated as Maison-Type A, Maison-Type B, etc., having

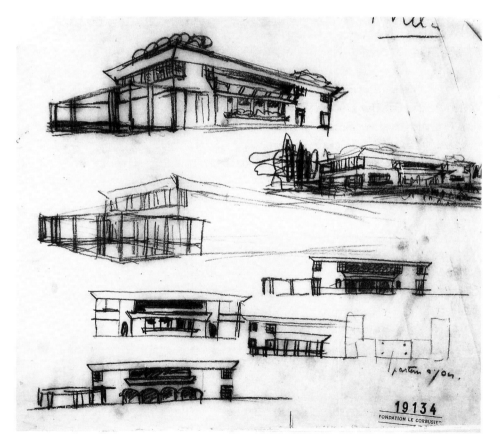

**Fig. 311.** Type B Dom-ino villa, 1915. Charcoal, black ink, and pencil. 35 × 85 cm. (FLC 30291)

**Fig. 312.** Studies for Dom-ino villas, 1915. Pencil. 35 × 41 cm. (FLC 19134)

**Fig. 313.** Extensible Dom-ino housing, 1915. This drawing Le Cor-busier published in *Oeuvre Complète*. India ink on paper. 30 × 79 cm. (FLC 19132)

**Fig. 314.** Extensible Dom-ino housing, 1915 or 1916. Published in *Oeuvre Complète*. India ink on paper. 37 × 104 cm. (FLC 19131)

borrowed this term from Foville. Much effort went into perfecting these plan-types and several of them were carefully drawn to scale, probably for inclusion in Jeanneret's proposed brochure.

The exteriors are far more interesting. They fall into two distinct categories: the single Dom-ino module for one or two families, and the "extensibles" of linked modules creating two-storey apartment buildings that extend across the landscape, often forming a large U (figs. 311–14). The extendibles predominate among Jeanneret's drawings, as witnessed by *Oeuvre Complète* where their presence may be a response to Tony Garnier's work.

Jeanneret's chief concern, aside from fenestration, was the treatment of the cornice; many pages of Sketchbook A2 are devoted to this problem. For his extensible housing he terminated the roof with a projecting horizontal slab, but for single houses he sought something more imposing. This often consisted of a heavy cornice flared out at nearly 45° and containing a trough-like planter box, the plants therein serving to soften the otherwise rigid silhouette of the flat-roofed building; this solution he soon would use at the Villa Schwob. Meanwhile the massing and fenestration for Dom-ino designs, whether single or multiple units, was inevitably symmetrical, thus emphasizing classical tendencies without resort to classical forms.

Coinciding almost precisely with his work on Dom-ino (and Pont Butin) Jeanneret experienced the most active phase of his life as furniture designer and interior decorator (for which he preferred the term "architecte conseil"). It was also the only time when he alone prepared designs rather than, as with the more famous tubular furniture of the 1920s and 1930s, in collaboration with Charlotte Perriand or others. From the very beginning he occasionally designed furniture (Villas Fallet and Stotzer) and in 1913 he actively began remodelling and decorating various apartments, including those for the Paul Ditisheims at 11, rue de la Paix and for Anatole and Salomon Schwob. For the latter he purchased ready-made pieces, thus needing to make several trips to Paris, Zurich, and elsewhere in the autumn of 1913. The following year, however, he designed virtually all the furniture needed by his clients, much of which was for another branch of the Ditisheim family, the brothers Herman and Ernest-Albert, who were building their two-family house at 119, rue du Temple-Allemand, designed by the fashionable architect Léon Boillot.

For the Ditisheim brothers he created over thirty pieces of furniture and also designed their apartment entrances (oak doors, iron staircase railings, flooring, and ceiling lights) as well as the "salons" or living rooms, including their marble fireplaces, cove ceilings, choice of wallpapers and window drapes and, in Herman's salon, virtually all the furniture (figs. 315–18). These pieces, some twelve in number, are now in the collection of the local Musée des Beaux-Arts (neither fireplace was saved). Meanwhile for Ernest-Albert (who used existing furniture in his salon) Jeanneret designed items for the bedrooms as well as various tables and chairs (figs. 319–22).

The correspondence and time sheets for the latter job were graciously retrieved for me by Maurice Ditisheim, Ernest-Albert's son (and are now deposited at the Bibliothèque de la Ville). These time sheets, seven pages, cover the period from December 19, 1914, to February 3, 1916, and account for every hour spent by Jeanneret on the job—whether in conference with the client, on correspondence, designing, or site inspection—for a total of well over six hundred hours. This clearly demonstrates the care and minute attention lavished on furniture design. His hourly charge of two francs fifty covered everything except conferences with the client ($15\frac{1}{3}$ hours) for which the established rate was four francs an hour. Most of the designing was completed during January–March, 1915, with the cabinetmaking done primarily by Jean Egger of La Chaux-de-Fonds who had been trained in Paris.

The designs are conservative rather than innovative and their ultimate source is often French late eighteenth century or its subsequent revivals. It seems that Jeanneret more or less backed his way into Louis XVI and Directoire classicism as a result of his exposure, during 1910–11, to the classical revival in Germany. The German work, as highlighted at the Brussels Arts and Crafts Exhibition of 1910 and in all the art and architecture magazines, was, strictly speaking, a revival of German Biedermeier, which was a

**Fig. 315.** Hallway at Villa Ditisheim 119, rue du Temple-Allemand, La Chaux-de-Fonds, 1915. Door and iron railing designed by Jeanneret. (Photo by author)

**Fig. 316.** Living room in apartment of Herman Ditisheim, 1915. The room, fireplace, and furniture were all designed by Jeanneret. (FLC)

**Fig. 317.** Herman Ditisheim furniture, 1915. Armchair and stool are recovered. Collection Musée des Beaux-Arts, La Chaux-de-Fonds. (Photo by author)

Fig. 318.    Desk chair and sideboard of Herman Ditisheim, 1915. Collection Musée des Beaux-Arts. (Photo by author)

Fig. 319.    Ernest-Albert Ditisheim furniture for his daughter's bedroom, 1915. (Photo by author)

Fig. 320.    Ernest-Albert Ditisheim furniture seen in the Ditisheim villa. (Photo by author)

**Fig. 321.** Table and chairs (reupholstered) for E.-A. Ditisheim, 1915. (Photo by author)

**Fig. 322.** Armoire for bedroom of E.-A. Ditisheim's son Maurice, designed March 1915. Fabric and paint original. Except for the basketweave capitals at corners, the furniture for the two sons has a more modern, less historic, air. (Photo by author)

**Fig. 323.** Sofa (and two similar arm chairs) were designed for Anatole Schwob, ca. 1914. Original fabric was dark gray. (Photo by author)

national style that developed after the Napoleonic Wars but had its origins in circa 1800 France (Directoire and Empire). Indeed the closest parallels to several of Jeanneret's pieces exist in German early twentieth-century work while others depend more directly on French precedent. Characteristically, however, Jeanneret remained silent about his German sources (just as he did concerning German architecture) while lavishing praise on the earlier French examples.

Jeanneret's designs have the same clear articulation of parts (i.e., the way legs join the seat rather than flowing into one another) found in the Louis XVI, Directoire, or Empire styles, yet the wooden members are simplified by being largely stripped of their historic moldings so as to emphasize smooth surface (see figs. 316–22). These surfaces are lighter in tone than their early counterparts, thereby revealing the grain; only on children's furniture did he specify paint. The lozenger-shaped basketweave motif, so characteristic of both Directoire and German early twentieth-century design, was a favorite of Jeanneret's and for both upholstery and wall coverings he selected broad, vertical strips typical of Directoire, often using yellow and green which was occasionally defined by black (see figs. 316, 318).[9] No longer is there any hint of Jura regionalism or Swiss vernacular which typified Jeanneret's furniture seven years before.

**Fig. 324.** Sewing table designed for Mme Anatole Schwob. (Photo by author)

9. Jeanneret's extensive postcard collection of furniture and interior decoration is chronologically more limited than his collection of architecture. Except for the few cards, previously discussed, of Louis XIV and Louis XV pieces in the collection of the Pavillon de Marsan, the vast majority represent the epoch of Napoleon and especially the furniture associated with Empress Josephine in the various châteaux redecorated during the Napoleonic era. Jeanneret's great favorite was clearly Malmaison, but he also showed interest in the refurnished rooms at Compiègne, Versailles, the Grand Trianon, and Rambouillet.

**Fig. 325.** Two chairs (one with arms) from set designed for Anatole Schwob (reupholstered). In background a divan designed for Moïse Schwob with fabric of Jeanneret's choosing. (Photo by author)

Other commissions, smaller and less well documented than those of the Ditisheims, added to Jeanneret's activity, and with the exception of some interior decorating done for his cousin Marguerite Jeanneret of Soleure prior to her wedding in 1915, for which his bill was 524 francs, all his work was commissioned by the Jewish community of La Chaux-de-Fonds; they alone were the ones responsive to the character and the quality of his work. In addition to the five Ditisheim families, these included Anatole Schwob, his brother-in-law Marcel Levaillant, Moïse Schwob, Raphaël Schwob, Solomon Schwob, and the Israelite club called Nouvelle Circle.

The Schwob pieces are quite close to Directoire (and especially the work of Georges Jacob) and therefore somewhat less personal than the Ditisheim examples. For Anatole, Jeanneret designed two upholstered arm chairs and a matching sofa (the original fabric was a dark gray), a sewing table, and a set of wood chairs (with and without arms) that incorporate basketweave motifs in their backs (figs. 323–25). For Moïse his designs included a divan, piano stool, upholstered armchair (fabrics originally a goldenrod yellow that Jeanneret, according to Lucien Schwob, soon replaced with the present silvery greenish-gray material), and a writing desk for Madame that, in its flowing curves, is unique in being Art Nouveau in inspiration (à la van de Velde) yet lacking any inlaid decoration to detract from the fine quality of the natural wood (figs. 326, 327).

Jeanneret's furniture has survived the years in a way that his interior decoration has not. One room only remains pristine and that is due to the long life of the original owner. Looking at early photographs we see that nothing has changed, been repainted, or even moved in the library of Mme Raphy (Raphaël) Schwob, 121, rue du Temple-

**Fig. 326.** Armchair and piano stool for Moïse Schwob. Jeanneret chose the present silvery greenish-gray fabric after being discontented with his original choice of yellow. (Photo by author)

Allemand, next door to the Ditisheim villa (figs. 328, 329). Jeanneret designed none of the furniture (although the shaggy fabric lamp shade is in the style of which he approved) and the wall paintings just below the ceiling are by his friend Charles Humbert and dated 1916. The woodwork (painted a light grayish-green) is inspired by Directoire, and the smooth, unadorned curved surfaces, basketweave motif, and simplified classical elements all recall Jeanneret's furniture of this period. He actually wrote (December 14, 1913) to Léon Boillot, architect of the villa, hoping to establish a cooperative arrangement that would permit him to design interiors for this highly successful architect, yet his direct appeal to Mme Schwob obviously had better results (yet for the smallest room in the house).

Many architects endeavor to join clubs in search of clients, and Jeanneret was no exception. On September 17, 1914, he applied for membership in the Nouveau Circle, a prestigious, wealthy men's club founded by the local Jewish community.[10] One of its members, however, accused him of being anti-Semitic, but after providing a written defense of his position he was admitted on November 23. As a result he did redecorate several rooms at the club but nothing remains today except a photo of one of the four-

**Fig. 327.** Desk for Mme Moïse Schwob with chair made for Anatole Schwob. (Photo by author)

10. "Le Nouveau Circle est de fondation israélite, n'ayant pas de caractère exclusif. Il admettra des adhérents de toute les confessions. . . . Elle a pour but de favoriser le développement intellectuel de ses membres. . . ." (*Status et Règlement,* 1913).

Fig. 328. Library for Mme Raphy Schwob, ca. 1915. 1974 photo. (Photo by author)

Fig. 329. Library for Mme Raphy Schwob as seen in circa 1916 photograph. (FLC)

branch light sconces that he designed but that were modeled by Léon Perrin (Perrin was my source).

Another cooperative venture with Perrin was a pair of terra-cotta table lamps designed and painted (blue and white) by Jeanneret and modeled by Perrin, who also informed the author that Jeanneret's inspiration was Turkish folk art. The lamp shade is typical of several designed by Jeanneret; it is also characteristic of German work of ca. 1910. Drawings of this and similar lamps are found in Sketchbook A1, pages 25–26, where the idea of removable conical cups set in the base is first explored (fig. 330).

The final item to be considered is a desk designed by Jeanneret for his mother. Among all his pieces this is the most original; it synthesizes various ideas from different countries (England, France, Germany) and from different times (fig. 331). It cannot be called Sheraton, Directoire, or Biedermeier although it contains elements of all three. Nor is its asymmetry to be expected; meanwhile its simplicity of form clashes with the exceptionally rich graining of the wood. The inverted obelisk (the fourth leg) pivots forward, providing for deep storage or waste.

Jeanneret's approval rating among his clients (except where personality conflicts got involved) was extremely high and, on certain occasions, perhaps too high for his own good. Take, for example, the encounter he had with a potential client the afternoon of November 1, 1915, as reported in a letter to William Ritter:

> I, a large merchant, will build my 200,000 franc villa and will not give you the commission, dear Mr. Jeanneret, although for four years I have had the opportunity of watching you at work. During these four years you have employed us to execute your commissions and, consequently, I have had the opportunity to judge—and this has happened often—that you fiercely uphold the interests of your clients, and that you are their tireless trustee dedicated to the triumph of "quality." . . . You have created an awakening in our population, in our clientele . . . you have awakened taste, and we [my company] are the victims. . . .
>
> I will not give you my villa to design because, as I know you, you will see to its execution with all the care that your reputation will once again affirm . . . and that will be injurious to [the financial future of] my furniture store.[11]

Another provider who voiced a flattering appraisal was Jean Egger, Jeanneret's principal furniture-maker, who wrote: "it is rare to find a man like you who truly appreciates the difficulty an artisan goes through in pursuit of his work."[12]

Although Jeanneret derived great pleasure from his work as decorator and furniture designer, it was certainly disheartening to spend three years without a viable architectural commission. His parents urged him toward Belgium due to the lack of work at home (letter to Du Bois, March 9, 1915). Throughout the latter part of 1915 he implored Du Bois to establish him in Paris with an office, telephone, secretary, typewriter, etc. (see Sketchbook A2, p. 86), and once these were provided (along with potential architectural commissions from Du Bois' various companies), Jeanneret was prepared to move. These demands were great but characteristically Du Bois eventually came through. Meanwhile Jeanneret continued in La Chaux-de-Fonds and occasionally made trips in Switzerland or to France.

His greatest pleasure derived from Ritter's presence nearby—not far as the crow flies but often two to three hours by train, tram, and then bike or on foot. He frequently

**Fig. 330.** Table lamp designed and painted by Jeanneret and modeled in terra cotta by Léon Perrin, ca. 1915. (Photo by author)

11. Quoted in a letter to Ritter of November 1–2, 1915. I suspect the encounter was with the manager of Progrès, the large La Chaux-de-Fonds furniture store where Jeanneret ordered fabrics and furnishings for his clients. Only a portion of this episode is quoted here.

12. This was in a thank-you note dated January 14, 1918, written in response to a postcard sent by Jeanneret (FLC). Arthur Rüegg, "Charles-Edouard Jeanneret, architecte-conseil pour toutes les questions de décoration intérieure" (*Archithese* 2–83 [March/April 1983], pp. 39–43), also discusses Jeanneret's early clients and the furniture he designed for them.

**Fig. 331.** Desk for Mme Jeanneret-Perret, ca. 1915–16. (Photo by author)

made the trip. In good weather they convened at some predetermined spot and painted watercolors of the landscape; otherwise they took long walks. Jeanneret often spent the night. He regularly planned excursions for Ritter to La Chaux-de-Fonds but no real evidence exists, except once about October 1, 1915, that he ever came.

Ritter, who left Munich at the outbreak of war, first settled in Monruz and by year's end moved to nearby Le Landeron overlooking Lake Biel to the northeast of Neuchâtel. This was the period of Jeanneret's closest attachment to Ritter, following the break with L'Eplattenier and prior to his friendship with Ozenfant. Their voluminous correspondence (now addressed "Bien cher Monsieur" but never using a first name) continued unabated in spite of their frequent visits. As Jeanneret noted: "I think of you many times each day" (February 8, 1915; underlined in original).

The completeness of L'Eplattenier's break with Jeanneret was evident in December 1914 when L'Eplattenier held an exhibition of pastels to which M. et Mme Jeanneret-Perret were invited but not their son. Edouard nevertheless attended and twice L'Eplattenier turned his back on him after which the former student said, "My apologies for coming without being invited," to which L'Eplattenier made no reply but seemed to derived a certain satisfaction from giving the offense (to Ritter December 22, 1914).

Earlier that autumn Jeanneret spent three exhilarating days at the Swiss National Exhibition in Bern, an event that filled him with enthusiasm and pride. It also provided an opportunity to visit August Klipstein, newly wed and now living in the capital (to Ritter October 9, 1914). Otherwise the winter was uneventful, relieved only by occasional trips to Geneva and elsewhere including, of course, his regular visits with Ritter.

Ritter introduced him to Fritz Zbinden, who planned to build near Erlauh, and although Jeanneret prepared two sheets of rough sketches nothing came of this affair (fig. 332). The drawings, all perspectives, are for a similar design as seen from different angles. They show a two-storey, nearly square, central block topped by a low hipped roof (cf. Villa Jeanneret-Perret). There is a one-storey, arcaded extension at one side and a trellised (or, alternately, hipped roofed) terrace/porch on the other.

Only with summer did Jeanneret spread his wings. In May he obtained an invitation from Auguste Perret to visit at Théo van Rysselberghe's villa near Hyères (Var) on the Côte d'Azur. He accepted with alacrity and departed May 27 (with return June 5), passing through Geneva, Lyon (where he hardly left the station), and Marseilles, which thrilled him because of its vitality. This we learn from one of Jeanneret's writing exercises, a travel essay that he submitted to Ritter (June 9, 1915) for comment and correction. Its rich descriptive prose, embedded in extended sentences, endeavors to emulate Ritter's style which he so admired.

To Du Bois (June 15) he wrote that Perret "finds *very good*" the preliminary idea for Dom-ino and suggests that it might be equally appropriate for factories, schools, and public buildings. Perret's approval rekindles Jeanneret's enthusiasm, and he likewise observes that "The moment seems judicious to me to publish my study, which is already [*sic*] written, on "La Construction des Villes." I could come to Paris immediately to find a publisher." And this is what he does.

On Monday, July 26, 1915, he picked up his passport at Bern, went to Ritter's for the night, returned to La Chaux-de-Fonds on Tuesday "and probably to Paris Wednesday evening [July 28] where I go to work at the Bibliothèque Nationale to complete the documentation for my book" (to Ritter, July 25). He intended to remain three weeks but stayed seven. Repeatedly he postponed his return home which eventually occurred on September 14. Throughout his sojourn he was the guest of Max Du Bois which provided ample opportunity to discuss Dom-ino as well as his wish to move to Paris.

However, once he began library research he realized that "La Construction des Villes" was far from finished and once he started studying eighteenth-century principles of urban design his thinking underwent a radical change. This motivated his rejection of Camille Sitte's romantic ideas in favor of classical values such as he had already accepted in architecture and furniture design but had continued to reject (witness the project for Arnold Beck of June 1914) in town planning.

His Ritter correspondence flagged (three postcards) during his Paris stay and any to his parents I have not found. This lessens our knowledge of his day-to-day activities, as well as whom and what he saw. He did, however, visit Aristide Maillol at his home in Marly-le-Roy on August 2–3, an event that moved him greatly. He was absolutely ecstatic at spending the night under the same roof as this artist whom he so revered! And he wrote at great length of the experience.[13]

His Paris sketchbook, A2, provides surprisingly little information about his Paris stay; its first twenty-two pages relate to "La Construction des Villes" but eighteen of these are merely headings such as "Le sens républicain," "Venise/Louis XIV/Athènes," or "Bruges" under which nothing at all is written. Then follows the section on Dom-ino, already discussed, and the sketch of a head from the Reims exhibition held at the Pavillon de Marsan that is dated September 13, 1915, the day before he left Paris.

13. On August 4 he penned the experience as a writing exercise for William Ritter yet did not send it until January 13, 1917. Entitled "Grandeur et Servitude . . . Un jour et une nuit dans la maison d'Aristide Maillol, à Marly-le-Roy," it is nine typed pages long and makes rather dull reading due to the excessive reverence accorded to his host.

Subsequent pages contain a mélange of things up to 1918 but nothing to chronicle his daily activities.[14] The war apparently had little or no impact on his life or routine.

The largest cache of material from Paris is found in a box at the Fondation Le Corbusier marked "Bibliothèque Nationale." This contains several sheets of bibliography, many Bibliothèque Nationale and Département des Estampes call slips (listing 15, Av. de Trocadéro—Max Du Bois' apartment—as his address), scores of small blue cards that index the drawings, somewhat larger yellow ones that include both notes and drawings, and—most important of all—some one hundred and fifty sketches and tracings made on relatively small pieces of architect's yellow tracing paper; the latter also include those made during the summer of 1910. The method of filing is ingenious. Each sheet was interleaved between pages of his 1914 copy of *Schweizerisches Bau-Adressbuch* with page numbers noted on the drawing itself—thus the fragile sheets of tracing paper could be indexed, filed, and refiled with relative ease.

From these we learn that Jeanneret was undergoing a conversion to classical ideals of urban design. Many of his notes, bibliographic references, and drawings follow the same themes as did his research in 1910—plans of cathedral squares at Strasbourg and Rouen, views of Mont-Saint-Michel and medieval Nuremberg, and repeated references to the works and writings of those involved in the Garden City movement in England.[15] Likewise, from contemporary times, Eugene Hénard received repeated mention; his 1903–9 plans for the transformation of Paris had a very profound impact on Jeanneret/Le Corbusier's thinking.

What is strikingly different, however, is the sudden interest in classical examples ranging from Roman antiquity to the present yet emphasizing the eighteenth century (cf. his furniture designs). Places seen during his previous travels particularly attracted him and these he traced or sketched from books. Michelangelo's redesign of the Capitoline Hill had intrigued him while in Rome and more recently he had marveled at the eighteenth-century plan of Nancy (figs. 333, 334). The latter he both sketched and traced from Pierre Patte, *Monuments érigés en France à la Gloire de Louis XV* (Paris, 1765, plate 24) and from the same source sketched a view looking west from the Tuileries that he subsequently published in *Urbanisme* (fig. 335). He also studied books of engravings by Du Cerceau, Callot (from whom he copied the formal parterre at Nancy),

14. Interspersed among the Dom-ino pages in A2 are indications of his growing awareness that "the buildings of every great period of architecture conform to an elementary geometric 'module' with every part submitting to its multiples and submultiples" (p. 112).

15. Two factors permit us to distinguish between the 1910 and the 1915 drawings. First of all, the use of a rubber stamp in the form of a hollow square; a note by Jeanneret expresses his intention to buy such a stamp in order to identify drawings made at the Bibliothèque Nationale. Second, he often wrote on these drawings the call number of the book from which it came.

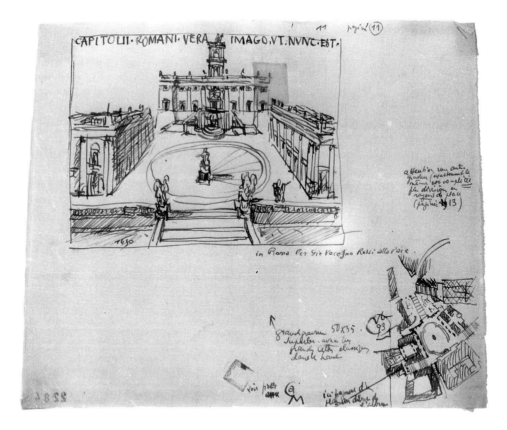

Piranesi, and others. In addition, names like J.-F. Blondel, Laugier, De l'Orme, and Le Pautre often appear in his bibliography.

Meanwhile the text of "La Construction des Villes" received scant attention (research, after all, is more fun than writing). Before leaving home Jeanneret scribbled across the section called "Thèse," "Probablement inutile, 23 juin 1915," thus confirming that following his mid-June decision to visit Paris he reread the manuscript and wisely decided to omit this overly general statement. The only writing dating from 1915 seems to be a new "Avertissement" wherein the mention of rebuilding Flanders and the 1914 exhibition at Lyon clearly establish its post-1910 date. Conceived more as an outline than a foreword, its brief listing of topics offers minimal insight into Jeanneret's position pro or con. What we do learn, however, is that the intended format remained unchanged and that chapters on streets, squares, and enclosing walls would, as before, be followed by sections on bridges, trees, parks, and garden cities.

Upon his mid-September return to La Chaux-de-Fonds Jeanneret found things pretty much the same. His father still had almost no work and it would be another year (October 1916) before plentiful orders came in; by then, however, the inflation-augmented cost of materials kept his earnings down. Inflation also hit food and fuel and

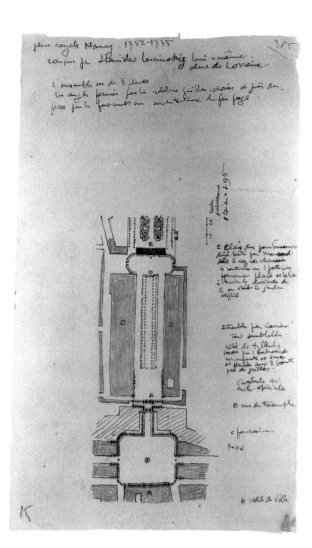

**Fig. 334.** Nancy, plan (bottom to top) of the Place Royale, Place de la Carrière, and Hemicycle as copied by Jeanneret from Pierre Patte, *Monuments érigés en France à la Gloire de Louis XV* (Paris, 1765, plate 24). Pen and ink. (FLC)

the father's journal chronicles their steady rise. It was Marie's earnings that sustained the family, including mortgage payments. However Albert, now teaching rhythmics and occasionally playing in concerts, was no longer a drain on their finances. Edouard, as we have seen, was without architectural commissions; he only had some minor, though time-consuming, activities as interior decorator.

Both boys continued to live at home where work on the terrace and gardens advanced and produced a profusion of color in spite of unseasonably cold weather. Temperatures repeatedly plunged into the lower 40s (7°C) which required activating the central heating in July and again in August, and this with the price of coke rising almost daily. However the family suffered no severe hardships. Summer holidays, nevertheless, were canceled, yet short trips such as New Year's with the Jeannerets at Soleure re-

**Fig. 335.** Tuileries, Paris, looking west. Copied at Bibliothèque Nationale in 1915 from Pierre Patte and later published by Le Corbusier in *Urbanisme* (1925). Pen and ink on tracing paper. (FLC)

mained a cherished tradition. Marguerite Jeanneret, Edouard's first cousin, was married August 24, he alone among the family missing the ceremony.

Visits to Ritter resumed upon Jeanneret's return from Paris. Plans for a Ritter visit to La Chaux-de-Fonds were often prepared but, as previously noted, only once, in early October, do we know that Ritter actually came. In November an overnight was planned to coincide with an exhibition of L'Eplattenier's paintings and to include a visit to the Villa Favre-Jacot in Le Locle—but Ritter could not be enticed to come.

In October Jeanneret prepared an intriguing drawing showing a house that faced a trellised peristyle with a fountain at its center. The client, if one existed, is unknown and there are no other sketches or views except this single two-dimensional facade. The perspective was executed first as a pencil drawing, then as a watercolor that was signed "pour Le Moulinet/oct 1915/Ch.E. Jt." (which serves as our only identification), and finally as a photogravure (fig. 336); each of these was a nearly exact copy of its predecessor. The fact that Jeanneret carried this drawing through three successive stages proves how pleased he was with the design, as well he might since it contains precedents for his next two buildings, both designed the following year. However, his source for the design is unclear.

Columns tapering downward (thus similar to chair and table legs) are combined with a low-pitched pediment, the marquee thus formed recalling that at La Scala of the

following year. And variations of the heavy, corbelled cornice, large central window, and panels intended for decoration are all to be found at the Villa Schwob.

These decorative panels are of particular interest since they provide clues as to Jeanneret's original intention for the facade of the Villa Schwob that remained blank at the time he was discharged as architect, and prior to the completion of the house. At Le Moulinet ("the little mill") four such panels exist and their sketchily rendered decoration seems to consist of numerous right angles, an early "homage à l'angle droit" that creates more of a texture than an image. This, apparently, was his intention. Indeed, several Dom-ino designs show right-angle motifs on their walls (fig. 337).

In addition, a means of creating this ornament is demonstrated in Sketchbook A2 (p. 112) where one sketch shows a wall covered with such decoration while another has a single ornamented concrete block followed by these words: "80 × 80. A square of cement with molded design forming a tapestry of thin moldings (whitened later with whitewash) would give a dignified decorative appearance" (fig. 338). Therefore thin cement blocks, 80 cm. square, containing a precast abstract ornament, would be set against the walls. This system recalls Frank Lloyd Wright's textile blocks used at Midway Gardens (1914) and later in his California houses.

A final significant event of 1915 was receipt of a letter from Tony Garnier dated December 13 in reply to one by Jeanneret written *seventeen* months before, that is, in July 1914 following his visit to the town planning exhibition at Lyon. From the response we learn that Jeanneret had requested photos of Garnier's work to include in a publica-

**Fig. 337.** Project: facade for a Dom-ino house, ca. 1915 (Detail). Charcoal. Full sheet 35 × 82 cm. (FLC 30293)

tion; Garnier sent none but expressed a willingness to do so. Nevertheless the real significance of this letter lies in the proof that the two men had never met, as well as the fact that Jeanneret initially became an admirer of Garnier's work during his visit to Lyon in 1914.[16] Actually, there is no firm evidence that they met prior to 1919 in spite of the fact that Jeanneret's 1916–22 sketchbook has a page of small sketches of Garnier's house at Saint Rambert near Lyon that show two views from the street and a sketchy plan that is labeled "inexacte." Written across the page is "Maison de Tony Garni [*sic*], Lyon. 8 nov 1916" yet nothing implies that the men met or that Jeanneret saw other Garnier buildings at this time.

Five years elapsed prior to Jeanneret's second known letter to Garnier. Dated May 14, 1919, it begins: "I saw this morning, for the first time, your book 'La [Une] Cité Industrielle'" and after praising Garnier profusely he brags effusively (for nearly three typed pages) of his own activities and accomplishments, particularly his involvement with the design of slaughterhouses (abattoirs). Nothing in the letter indicates that the men had met. Yet within eight weeks, on July 8, 1919, he wrote his parents that he had visited Lyon, interviewed Edouard Herriot (the strong-willed mayor who backed Tony Garnier) and had seen Garnier several times.[17] Thereafter Garnier wrote Jeanneret on November 16, the latter replying on November 21, 1919, and again December 9, 1920. Jeanneret also telegraphed Garnier March 18, 1920, saying he would be in Lyon on the morrow and desired a meeting. It is clear, therefore, that Jeanneret's really intense interest in Garnier's work centered around 1919–20 rather than much earlier as previously had been thought.

The final year of Jeanneret's residency in Switzerland, 1916, opened uneventfully and closed with great activity. Indeed, after the family's annual New Year's gathering at Soleure, little of significance occurred during the next six months. True, January had seen Du Bois file the patent application for Dom-ino, and prior to the Paris opening of La Cité Reconstituée exhibition in May Jeanneret thought seriously of building a Dom-ino model on the grounds, near the Jeu de Paume, but Auguste Perret dissuaded him and Du Bois' organization failed to offer funds.

Throughout these months Jeanneret sporadically worked on yet another book, "France ou Allemagne," which he envisioned as his passport to Paris. Its theme would be the dominance of French art and architecture over that of the Germans. Auguste

16. In *Oeuvre Complète,* page 9, Le Corbusier says "J'ai recontré Tony Garnier à Lyon vers 1907." This statement has led many scholars astray.

17. "En route depuis 5 jours, à Lyon et Auvergne, pour des abattoirs! . . . Hier une heure de puisant et violent entretien avec Herriot, le tribun de romaine puissance. Vu plusieurs fois Tony Garnier qui fait pour Herriot des travaux formidables" (to parents, dated "Clermont Ferrand, ce 8 juillet 1919"). These visits were apparently made in the company of Thomson MacLeod of Glasgow to whom Jeanneret wrote September 9, 1919.

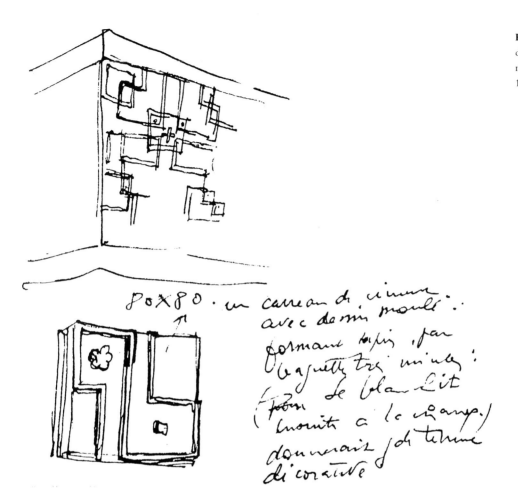

**Fig. 338.** Procedure for making decorative concrete blocks as ornamentation for a building facade, 1915. (Sketchbook A2, p. 112, FLC)

Perret's assistance was sought at many levels. First, on December 14, 1915, Jeanneret admitted knowing less about French architecture than German (that's significant!) and asked Perret for a list of buildings and for help in finding photographs. A list was sent on January 17, 1916, which included all the well-known metal and glass structures beginning with Labrouste's Bibliothèque Nationale reading room and Baltard's Halles Centrales.

A week later Jeanneret announced that his research was almost finished (shades of "La Construction des Villes") and that the book would include works from 1870 to 1914. Yet as the months dragged by, his periodic progress reports proved overly optimistic and he never had anything ready for Perret to see. The book's thrust was visual rather than verbal, using juxtaposed photographs of French and German work to demonstrate the superiority of the French designs; a minimum of text would be included. Therefore he sometimes referred to it as an album. By early autumn some page layouts were sent to Perret accompanied by the request that Perret assist in finding a publisher. None, however, was forthcoming, nor was the book ever finished.[18]

With the arrival of spring Jeanneret spent several days bicycling around Lake Neuchâtel with a group of friends while carrying Sketchbook A1 in hand. At Morat he sketched the interior of La Croix Blanche with its horizontal band of windows and secondary room set a half level above the ground floor (shades of both "la fenêtre en longueur" and also the Pavillon de L'Esprit Nouveau). At Avenches, the Roman city founded by Augustus, he drew the amphitheater and at medieval Estavayer recorded a Pietà perched in a niche at the corner of a building. Finally, rounding the lake on May 1, he sketched at Concise an imposing structure with double stairway and wrought-iron railing that he labeled "Louis XVI." Whereas their circuit took them within range of William Ritter's, Jeanneret recalled his mentor's interdiction against unannounced visits, so they dispatched a postcard instead.

Also in May Jeanneret met one of his idols, Alexandre Cingria-Vaneyre, author of *Les Entretiens de la villa du Rouet*. This took place in Geneva and a few weeks later the author visited Jeanneret at La Chaux-de-Fonds to learn something about reinforced concrete, all this being detailed in letters to Auguste Perret (May 19 and June 14, 1916).

With the arrival of summer Jeanneret's fortunes underwent a dramatic change. The first indication is revealed by a single plan on heavy paper labeled simply "Projet F" and, elsewhere, "immeuble locatif" with the date "4 juillet 1916" (fig. 339). It is unsigned; there are no ground-floor plans, elevations, or preparatory sketches. It is for a deluxe, free-standing apartment building which is uncommon in La Chaux-de-Fonds. And why called Project F rather than by a client's name? Without corroborating evidence we might question whether this was by Jeanneret's hand.

All evidence, however, points directly to Jeanneret, including a possible eighteen-century source for the plan. The initial proof is certain interior sketches signed and dated "22 juin 1916" that correspond precisely with the plan (fig. 340). Note the sequence of three rooms, from salon to dining room, with a bow window at the end. The furnishings, incidently, show he continues to favor prominent, blotchy wallpaper, pictures of varying shapes and sizes, and a sofa that recalls those designed for his parents and the Ditisheims.

Additional confirmation is found in the interrogatories of the lawsuit filed by Jeanneret against Anatole Schwob in July 1918. In explaining the background of the Schwob commission, he states: "In April 1916 C.-E. Jeanneret undertook the study of a large apartment house for the account of a group of people who would themselves

18. Sources for "France ou Allemagne" are letters to Auguste Perret of December 14, 1915, January 26, March 29, an undated letter, and June 14, 1916, at the Fonds Perret, Institut Français d'Architecture, Paris, and to Ritter of October 2, 1916. In Sketchbook A2, p. 99, he reminds himself to "Make a book 'Where does French art stand [where does] German art [stand].'"

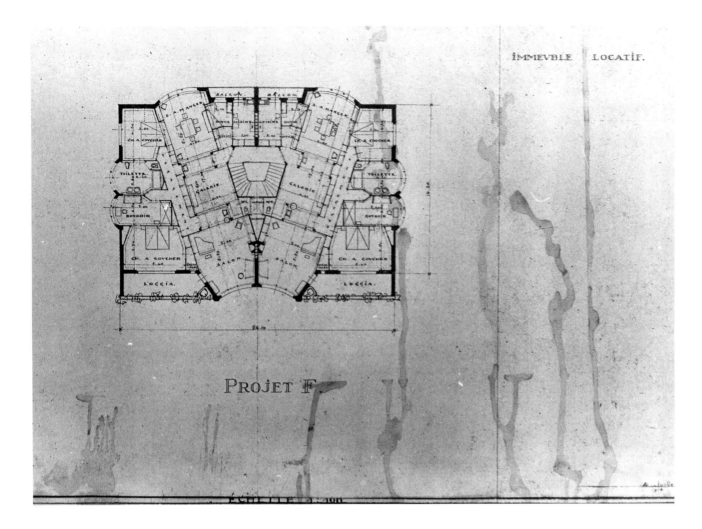

IMMEVBLE | LOCATIF.

PROJET F

Fig. 339. Project F, dated July 4, 1916. Plan for an upper floor in an apartment building. Ink on heavy paper. 62 × 80 cm. (FLC 30276)

form a Société anonyme [limited-liability company] in the event that construction would be decided upon. A. Schwob would have been one of the shareholders of the Société, and at the same time one of the principal tenants. Subsequently he gave up this project judging the [financial] conditions not particularly favorable" (Dossier 5, question 81). This explanation reveals why no complete set of plans exists and why no specific client is named.

A possible eighteenth-century source for Project F also points a finger at Jeanneret, this being Germain Boffrand's second project for the Palais de la Malgrange at Nancy of 1712. When published in his *Livre d'architecture* (Paris, 1745, plate 19) the oversize plan opens out as two folded sheets on either side of the spine; if only one foldout is opened, revealing only half the cross-shaped plan, its configuration has striking similarities to Project F (fig. 341). Jeanneret merely needed to enclose the two arms of the V

**Fig. 340.**   Project F, view of salon looking toward gallery and dining room, signed and dated June 22, 1916. Photogravure. 42 × 64 cm. (FLC 30084)

**Fig. 341.**   Germain Boffrand, Palais de la Malgrange, Nancy, second project, plan, 1712 (detail).

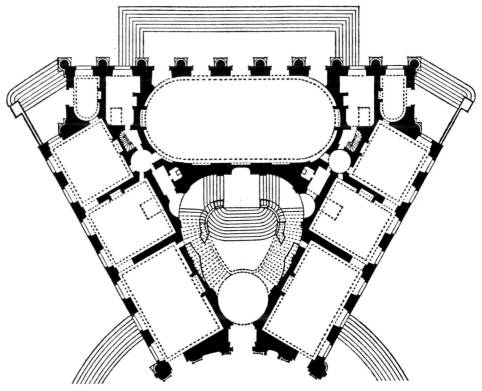

**Dom-ino, La Scala, and the Villa Schwob   413**

(each having three rooms en suite and connected by a central stairway) within a rectangle to create a more traditional exterior form. He undoubtedly studied Boffrand's work at the Bibliothèque Nationale in 1915, and the originality of this plan may have caught his eye.

Jeanneret's V-shaped plan is actually encased in a rectangle 24.10 meters by 14.20. Two apartments share each floor. The skylight-lit staircase and other services (kitchens and W.C.) lie within the V, each arm containing a suite of three rooms—salon, gallery, and dining room—with the gallery serving as both entrance and reception area. Jeanneret's sketch shows a view through these rooms. Along side this suite, and contiguous with its outer wall, a passageway connects three bedrooms and a bath; off the master bedroom, yet accessible from the salon, is a spacious loggia.

That this highly inventive plan is indeed by Jeanneret is now confirmed by a newly surfaced letter in the Fonds Perret at the Institut Français d'Architecture, Paris, of July 21, 1916, wherein Jeanneret includes a small sketch of Project F along with its description.

The circumstances surrounding Jeanneret's next commission are extremely complex and have created much misunderstanding and confusion, some of which may never be resolved. Also certain actions by the client, and especially Jeanneret, bring the professional ethics of both men into question. The story begins in June 1916, when Edmond Meyer asked René Chapallaz to design a combination cinema and variety theater called La Scala. Between the tenth and thirtieth of June Chapallaz prepared a complete set of plans, some seventeen in number, including all the necessary floor and plot plans, sections, elevations, sight-line diagrams, and street facades.

Jeanneret would have liked this commission and it seems that he contacted Meyer, rather than vice versa, about being appointed architect in place of Chapallaz. The first hint of Jeanneret's involvement occurred ten days after Chapallaz's earliest scale drawings were prepared on June 10. This is recorded in a letter to Auguste Perret of June 20 in which Jeanneret announced that that very afternoon he had been asked to design a theater. He seeks Perret's advice on several technical matters and makes two sketches, one a longitudinal section of the theater, the other a floor plan.[19]

These two sketches by Jeanneret leave no room for doubt: they reproduce Chapallaz's drawings nos. 2121 and 2119 of June 19. Not only are the designs similar but so are the critical dimensions such as seven meters for the cantilever of the reinforced concrete balcony and sixteen meters for the width of the auditorium. There is no way

19. This letter, and one of July 21 that discusses the Hetzer structural system and contains a diagram, are at the Fonds Perret, Institut Français d'Architecture, Paris. The letter of the twenty-first also includes a sketch of the Villa Schwob, as built, and the Project F plan. René Chapallaz, with whom I discussed La Scala on February 18, 1974, said that Jeanneret apparently convinced Meyer that he could build the theater more quickly and cheaply than Chapallaz, and that was a major reason why the client changed architects. I failed to ask whether Chapallaz received any compensation.

Jeanneret could have arrived at these crucial dimensions on a moment's notice; Meyer had obviously shown Jeanneret the Chapallaz scale drawings and Jeanneret ran with the ball from there. However, another two weeks passed before he had the commission firmly in hand.

Meanwhile Chapallaz, unaware, continued work on his design, finishing the two facades on June 22 and the final plan on June 30. The previous day, June 29, *La Feuille d'Avis* announced a competition for La Scala's facade design that was open to all past and present students of the Ecole d'art; the closing date was set for July 15. This was obviously a publicity stunt organized by Meyer to put La Scala in the public eye; it also recalled earlier competitions within the school itself. On July 18 the verdict of the jury, which no longer included Chapallaz's name, declared none of the twelve entries completely satisfactory, so no first prize was given. The designs were then exhibited.

Concurrent with these events Jeanneret wrote Ritter on July 4 that he anticipated constructing La Scala.[20] The earliest date on his working drawings (no preliminary studies exist) is July 12. Two days later, on July 14, construction commenced without either the plans or technical calculations complete. The contractor was Alfred Riva and the client insisted on completion within four months; actually the inauguration took place on December 1. The floor plans that Chapallaz had perfected through three successive stages were dated June 10, 19, and 30. We noted that Jeanneret's June 20 sketch had been based on Chapallaz's of June 19. In like manner his final plan of August 3 was derived from Chapallaz's definitive plan of June 30, with only minor modifications (figs. 342, 343).

Jeanneret registered his set of blueprints with the commune on August 19. All, except for the two street facades, are closely related to those of Chapallaz. So is the structural system: reinforced concrete for the broad balcony that has no view-obstructing piers underneath, and five laminated wood arches to span the ceiling and support the roof, these being a patented technique designed by Hetzer of Zurich whose blueprints are dated July 24 (fig. 344).

Chapallaz subsequently accused Jeanneret of stealing his design. There seems little doubt that, except for one or perhaps both facades, the plans, the sections, and the structural system represent Chapallaz's "intellectual property."

The question of attribution did not arise until the decade of Le Corbusier's death. This is because none of his La Chaux-de-Fonds buildings, other than the Villa Schwob, had ever been published, amazing though that may seem. In 1960 *Perspecta 6: The Yale Architectural Journal* was the first to print photos of La Scala and of the villas Favre-Jacob and Jeanneret-Perret, the latter two being so recently discovered as to be called the

20. "Je suis servi à souhait: je construis la 'Scala.' Cinéma variété! Et dans quelles conditions. Le client une hyène; pas d'argent, des délais et des amends à faire frémir et un tas de saletés autour de ça" (to Ritter, July 4, 1916). This seems to imply that the commission was already in hand but that construction might never take place.

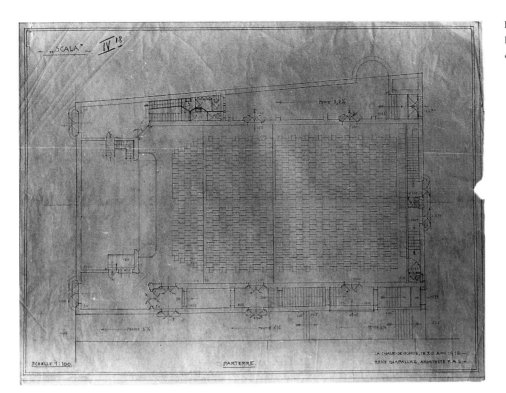

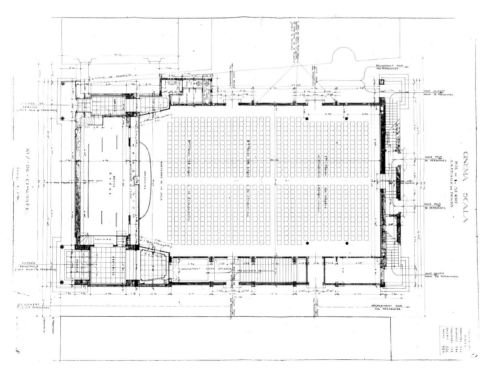

**Fig. 344.** La Scala, construction photo showing Hetzer laminated wood beams in place. (BV)

villas Fauvre and Cornu and erroneously dated 1905 and 1911 respectively; at that time, 1960, the villas Fallet, Stotzer, and Jaquemet were still unknown. *Perspecta*'s caption for La Scala read: "The attribution of this building to Le Corbusier is largely by the citizens of La Chaux-de-Fonds. The date probably falls in the period from 1912–1916." The initiatives of Professor Henry-Russell Hitchcock had led students to this research.

Almost simultaneously two students of Professor Alfred Roth at the Eidgenössische Technische Hochschule (E. T. H.) in Zurich, Etienne Chavanne and Michel Laville, undertook more detailed research that was published in *Werk 12* in December 1963. This included all the La Chaux-de-Fonds and Le Locle buildings *except* La Scala. They omitted La Scala, as we learn from their thesis (Zurich, 1962), because when interviewing Chapallaz he claimed the plans were his and that only the rear elevation facing the rue du Parc was entirely Jeanneret's (this led a whole generation of architects and historians to publish only the rear of La Scala, falsely assuming it to be the main facade because it faced on a street; obviously they had never been to La Chaux-de-Fonds). Meanwhile Chavanne and Laville also prepared simplified tracings from the blueprints of all the buildings, including La Scala, that were found in the archives of the respective communes.

Le Corbusier died in 1965. Articles appearing in the local press listed La Scala as one of his works. Chapallaz's response was immediate. He wrote both the editor and the writers and followed up by having his lawyer file a certified statement with the newspaper. Therefore when Jean Petit published *Le Corbusier lui-même* in 1970 (a book begun with Le Corbusier's assistance and cooperation) he illustrated (without acknowledgment) Chavanne and Laville's *rear elevation* as "Cinéma La Scala à La Chaux-de-Fonds" (pp. 47, 202). This encouraged other biographers, relying only on secondary information, to proclaim that the back of the building was actually the main facade. My article and paper of 1982 rectified this mistake.[21]

The site of La Scala is a slightly sloping rhomboid plot between rue de la Serre and rue du Parc, the latter street being both higher and further from town. The seating, therefore, follows the natural slope, although this reversed the normal circulation pattern since attendees must walk the theater's length to reach the rear seats or the balcony. This required isolating a supplemental access route alongside the auditorium.[22] Exiting was done though outside passageways beside the auditorium or by the front and rear doors; balcony spectators had the additional choice of exterior stairs. These stairs are

21. H. Allen Brooks, "Le Corbusier's Formative Years at La Chaux-de-Fonds," *The Le Corbusier Archive,* vol. 1, H. Allen Brooks, ed. (New York, London, Paris, Garland Publishing, 1982), pp. xv–xxxiii, and in a paper given that same year before the annual meeting of the Society of Architectural Historians, "Charles-Edouard Jeanneret's La Scala Cinéma (1916): Attribution and Sources."

22. This seemingly awkward arrangement has precedence in the earlier (1912) Royal cinema at Tavannes, a nearby town where Chapallaz previously had his office. However, at Tavannes the ground did not slope toward the street.

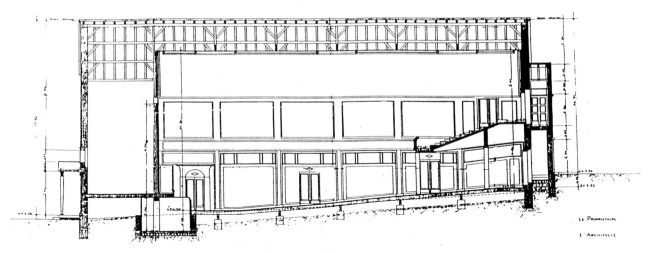

CINEMA SCALA.
RUE DE LA SERRE
LA CHAUX DE FONDS.

COVPE LONGITVDINALE.

ECHELLE.1:50.

Le Propriétaire

L'Architecte

3 Août 1916.

**Fig. 345.** La Scala. Longitudinal section. Blueprint (with color reversed) dated August 3, 1916. Note tapered column at entrance porch, cantilevered reinforced concrete balcony, and unexcavated sloping ground upon which the theater was built. (BV)

**Fig. 346.** La Scala. View from stage toward balcony. Drawing published in the official program of December 7, 1916. (BV)

one of the few variations from Chapallaz's scheme; Chapallaz had placed them within the building rather than on the outside wall.

Unfortunately no photographs of the interior exist. We know it from Jeanneret's longitudinal section and a crude drawing published during the inauguration (figs. 345, 346). These fail to correspond since the drawing shows classical pilasters between each panel on the walls while Jeanneret's elevation lacks this enrichment. Newspaper reports merely praise the design's simplicity as being in good taste. Could this simplicity be partly inspired by Francis Jourdain's remodeled Théâtre du Vieux Colombier in Paris, a design admired by Jeanneret?[23]

La Scala's facade design, dated July 25, is rigorously symmetrical and features a great semicircle that is lightly incised into the smooth wall under the gable roof (figs. 347–50). To either side are narrower bays, slightly recessed, topped by a broken pediment, their dignity being enhanced by simplified pilasters that, however, fail to correspond to the richer Corinthian order specified on the blueprints. Two pedimented porches, supported by downward tapering columns like those intended for Le Moulinet, mark the lateral doors; these porches are connected by a flat roof protecting the area reserved for posters. Above the marquee are a series of crisply cut square windows.[24]

The symmetry of the rear elevation, facing rue du Parc, is deceptive because the bay to the right is a false front; nothing lies behind it, as one can see from the plan and perhaps in the photograph (figs. 351, 352). Symmetrical exterior stairs lead from the balcony down to the street and between these there is a small projection booth, subsequently (1930) enlarged. Simplified pilasters also articulate the rear facade.

Although construction of La Scala commenced on July 14, with Alfred Riva as contractor, the work was complete in four and a half months with the opening taking place December 1.[25]

The story, however, does not end here. Central heating caused snow to melt near the top of the low-pitched roof with an ice dam developing closer to the eaves. Water

23. Of the Vieux Colombier, Jeanneret wrote to Ritter (November 3, 1913) that it had "un mode de décor auquel je souscris enfin . . . pour la première fois." The wall pilasters at Pompeii may also have served as inspiration (see Carnet 4 of 1911, p. 41).

24. Three noteworthy changes differentiate Jeanneret's blueprint from the executed facade: (1) the Corinthian pilasters were simplified into unfluted Doric, (2) the pediments over the lateral bays were raised higher than the principal gable roof, and (3) the decorative cartouche and word "Scala" above the arch were omitted. Meanwhile, thoughts passing through Jeanneret's mind during the creative process can be observed in the poster designs he scribbled on the facade. One shows an airplane, another three Corinthian columns, and a third a classical temple. Unfortunately the Scala facade burned on December 26, 1970, and another design was substituted in its place.

25. Jeanneret senior, always quick to acknowledge Albert's achievements, never mentioned Edouard's La Scala or Villa Schwob except on December 7, 1916, when he praised the recently inaugurated movie theater.

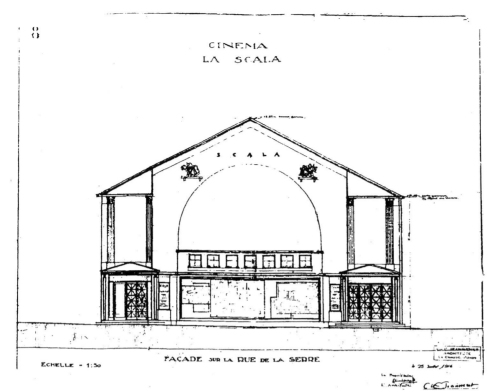

**Fig. 347.** La Scala. Blueprint of facade with color reversed. Signed and dated July 25, 1916. (BV)

**Fig. 348.** La Scala. Front elevation. Blueprint as retraced by Etienne Chavanne and Michel Laville. (BV)

**Fig. 349.** La Scala. Photograph by René Chapallaz, ca. 1917. (BV)

**Fig. 350.** La Scala. Photograph by Etienne Chavanne, ca. 1962. (Courtesy of Etienne Chavanne)

backed up and found its way inside. Photos of December 20 record this problem. Meyer, the owner, sued Jeanneret, Jeanneret sued both Meyer and Riva, Riva sued Meyer, and the lawyers had a field day. Jeanneret claimed that Riva failed to follow building codes and sought 10,000 francs in damages, Meyer sued Jeanneret for 4,000, and Jeanneret sued Meyer but soon withdrew the case. To make matters worse, Jeanneret was suing Anatole Schwob and Schwob was suing Jeanneret. To help cover expenses Jeanneret borrowed 6,000 francs from E. L. Bornard, his associate in Paris, due November 30, 1917, which he was unable to repay. Therefore Bornard sued Jeanneret in 1919 for principal plus interest, and because the Villa Jeanneret-Perret had just been sold Edouard borrowed the money from his father. Most of these lawsuits where settled out of court, so their final resolution is unknown.

More fascinating, concerning La Scala, is its main facade and possible sources of design. Although it was a highly original work, visual ideas existed in Jeanneret's mind. Foremost, of course, were the conditions set by the use of Chapallaz's plan and the knowledge of Chapallaz's June 22 facade design. The latter displayed many features recalled in Jeanneret's solution, including the overall symmetry of the design, the lateral doorways, each protected by a marquee, the long billboard between these doors, the series of square windows (yet grouped in pairs) over the billboard, and a whole sequence of arches (rather than just one) in the pediment of the roof (fig. 353). Jeanneret, however, omits the cornice below the pediment and delimits the area above the doorways as separate bays; this provides his facade with totally different proportions, visually speaking, even though the height and width are almost identical to those of Chapallaz's design. Also, there is Chapallaz's assertion (to the author, February 18, 1974) that he originally proposed using *semicircular* Hetzer arches at La Scala with the semicircle being expressed in his preliminary sketches for the facade. Therefore various features extant

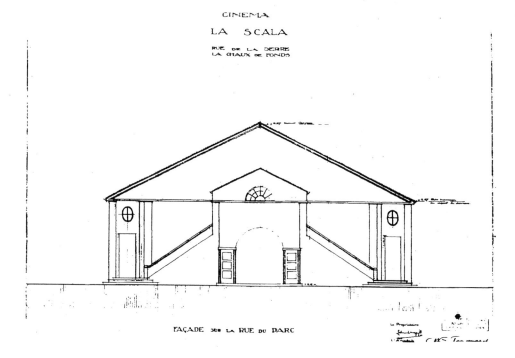

**Fig. 352.** La Scala. Rear facade showing projection booth (behind the word "Scala") and twin exit stairs leading down from the balcony. At the right observe the free-standing spur wall, with its doorway to no-where, that was built for the sake of symmetry. René Chapallaz photo, after 1917.

Fig. 353. René Chapallaz's design
for the front facade of La Scala, dated
June 22, 1916. Pencil on heavy paper. (BV)

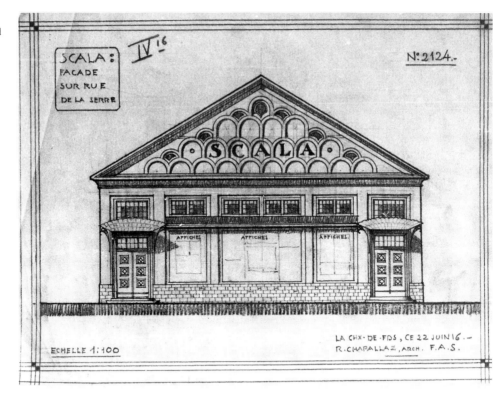

in Jeanneret's facade design have their origin in Chapallaz's work and these help substantiate Chapallaz's claim that only the rear facade of La Scala is entirely Jeanneret's
own idea.

A more distant stimulus for the facade perhaps endured since childhood. That is
Jeanneret's auditorium study of ca. 1905 (Chapter 2, fig.38). Sketched during his brief
Art Nouveau period, this project included a large, curved (but not quite semicircular)
central window set against a gable roof.

Much closer to La Scala is Louis Sullivan's bank at Owatonna, known to Jeanneret,
who greatly admired Sullivan's work, through its publication in *Schweizerische Bauzeitung* (60, no. 11 [September 14, 1912], p. 150) wherein P. H. Berlage wrote: "In my
opinion Sullivan's masterwork is a bank which he has recently completed in the small
American town of Owatonna, Minnesota. A great mind always creates new surprises,
and so does Sullivan's. . . . There is, as far as I know, nothing comparable to it anywhere
in Europe." The facade of that bank is characterized by a large semicircular window cut
into the wall with two decorative cartouches placed at either side; under the great arch
is a row of deeply cut square windows (fig. 354). All of these features reappear at La
Scala. In addition we already noted parallels between the flaring, corbeled-out cornice
of this bank and those proposed by Jeanneret for Le Moulinet and his Dom-ino designs.

Actually the most common use of semicircular arches under a gable roof are those

found at railroad stations, as at the Gare de l'Est in Paris. Therefore Jeanneret certainly had a wide choice for inspiration. Yet one could argue that all of the above were glazed rather than being "blind." However it is precisely such a blind arch that Jeanneret took pains to photograph at Hagia Sophia in Turkey five years earlier and that is perhaps a direct source for the arch he used at La Scala (fig. 355). Four familiar elements appear in this Hagia Sophia photo: (1) a recessed, blind, slightly more than semicircular arch directly under the central gable roof, (2) what appears, due to the angle of the photograph, to be a broken gable (but which actually is the shed roof of a massive buttressing pier), (3) the relatively thin cornice on the roof, and (4) the little square windows located under the blind arch. However, since Jeanneret took several photos of these buttresses we must assume that their massive, majestic forms, rather than the blind arch, was what initially attracted him.

The Mannerist, broken gable at La Scala may also have Italian origins. Giacomo della Porta's Villa Aldobrandini at Frascati (1598–1603) is perhaps too remote; Palladio would be a better choice. Yet Jeanneret's fascination with interior decoration may point to a more appropriate broken-gable source in eighteenth-century, especially English, designs for highboys, doorways, and overmantels.

Concerning the rear facade at La Scala there is ample precedent for a symmetrical pair of exterior stairs. These include Michelangelo's Capitol in Rome, Theodor Fischer's Gustav-Siegle Haus in Stuttgart (1907–12), and the medieval town hall in Bern (1416), all well known to Jeanneret. Ultimately, however, the most significant thing is the synthesis going on in Jeanneret's mind.

Concurrent with La Scala, Jeanneret commenced what was unquestionably the most significant commission of his early career, one that dramatically bridged the gap between his years at La Chaux-de-Fonds and Paris. This was the Villa Schwob (color plates IX, X), the one and only hometown work that he ever published, restricted in time though that acknowledgment was. This he did in *L'Esprit Nouveau*, nos. 5 and 6

**Fig. 354.** Louis H. Sullivan. National Farmer's Bank, Owatonna, Minnesota, U.S.A., known to Jeanneret through its publication in *Schweizerische Bauzeitung*, 60 (1912), plate 33.

**Fig. 355.** Hagia Sophia, Constantinople, Turkey. Jeanneret's photo of heavily buttressed west wall with its blind arch. 9 × 12 cm glass-plate negative. (BV)

(1921)[26] and *Vers une architecture* (1923), but by 1929 his attitude had changed and he chose to exclude it from his *Oeuvre Complète*.

Certain questions concerning the design's development will always remain unclear, although many have been answered by documents that my research unearthed during the early 1970s including all the blueprints for the construction of the villa as well as the voluminous court records relating to Jeanneret's lawsuit against Anatole Schwob for not paying the architect's fee. Filed at the Tribunal Civil in La Chaux-de-Fonds on July 5, 1918, these written interrogatories of Schwob, Jeanneret, Jeanneret's three draftsmen, the contractor, various townspeople, and a panel of experts, comprise some 200 typed pages of invaluable information.[27]

The court records establish the chronology of the Schwob commission. Anatole Schwob (1874–1932), executive of Schwob Frères & Co. S.A. and the Tavannes Watch Company, commissioned Jeanneret in 1914 to redecorate the smoking room of his apartment at 73, rue Léopold-Robert (1/1).[28] Desiring more spacious quarters, however (5/82), he and others proposed forming a limited partnership and in April 1916 asked Jeanneret to prepare a feasibility study for a rental building that they might share (i.e., Project F). The resulting design was considered too costly and the idea was dropped (5/81).

About this same time Mme Raphy [Raphaël] Schwob, the cultural and social leader of the community, along with Mme Paul Ditisheim, visited the Villa Jeanneret-Perret and were "enchanted." The former declared, "Build such a house for my cousin Ana-

26. The article, "Une Villa de Le Corbusier 1916" (pp. 679–704), was signed by Julien Caron, that being one of the pseudonyms of Amédée Ozenfant. Parts of the article, and possibly its theme (that architects should serve as the bridge between engineer and artist), were certainly by Le Corbusier. Little is actually said of the villa. The published plans are modified from the September 1916 working drawings while the elevations, which demonstrate the use of "tracés régulateurs," had already been published in *L'Esprit Nouveau*, no. 5. An excellent translation appears in *Oppositions*, 15/16 (1979), pp. 187–97.

27. I discovered these records at the courthouse in October 1973. But in order to remove them to have them photocopied, I was requested to seek a local attorney. Maurice Favre graciously assisted me, then immediately published their contents without my knowledge or consent. See Maurice Favre, "Le Corbusier à travers un dossier inédit et un roman peu connu," *Musée Neuchâtelois*, no. 2 (1974), pp. 49–59, which was reprinted in English in *The Open Hand*, Russell Walden, ed. (Cambridge and London: MIT Press, 1977), pp. 97–113.

I also located and interviewed Jeanneret's chief draftsman, Marcel Montandon, as well as Lucien Schwob, Anatole's nephew (son of Anatole's brother Moïse), who, after his uncle's death, married his aunt and lived in the Villa Schwob. Both men subsequently placed their Villa Schwob documents in the Bibliothèque de la Ville. Likewise I found the contractor who built the villa and had retained every blueprint used in its construction, but in this instance I was unable to persuade Emile Biéri to transfer his archive to the BV.

28. Numbers in parentheses refer to the dossier and item number in the "Demande pour Charles-Edouard Jeanneret contre Anatole Schwob; En paiement Frs. 483.75 et 33,792.10," filed July 5, 1918, but withdrawn, after an out-of-court settlement, on June 25, 1920.

tole," and asserted that she would induce him to do so (5/3). As a result, early in July, Anatole contacted the architect, who presented several sketches. Anatole was so enthusiastic that, while still in Jeanneret's presence, he telephoned Mme Raphy Schwob to say he would follow her advice and build (5/85).

The first dated plan (a main floor and garden plan that is now lost but was listed among the lawsuit exhibits), as well as a perspective study, were both dated July 14 (76/1). (Nevertheless an earlier plan and elevation, for a much smaller house, do exist but are not mentioned in the proceedings.) After July 14, except for preparing a now lost basement and a second-floor plan dated July 24 (76/1), matters moved more slowly. On August 7 Jeanneret agreed (based on his cost estimate of 110,000 to 115,000 francs) to a fixed commission of 8,000 francs; this proved to be his undoing. He confirmed the arrangement by letter the following day (5/48–49) and that same day Anatole visited the Villa Jeanneret-Perret (3/9). The next day, August 9, is the date recorded on three elevations (north, south, and east facades) which were submitted to the tribunal but are also now lost (76/1). On August 11 a contract with the builder Hans Biéri (older brother of Emile) was signed by Schwob, Jeanneret, and Biéri and on August 22 one between Jeanneret and Schwob.[29] At some uncertain, yet crucial, date during August, Schwob authorized Jeanneret to augment the size (cubage) of the house by a whopping 46.7 percent (144/7), or according to Jeanneret's calculations 47.5 percent (1/20).

Between September 7 and 22 the definitive plans ("Plans de sanction") were completed; they are identical to those deposited with the commune. These include the well-known south and north elevations which are dated September 13 and 22 respectively. During October and November specific activities are not recorded but construction continued. A drawing of December 16 relocates the kitchen from the basement to a side pavilion, although this was previewed in the "Plan de sanction" of September 8. As late as May 11, 1917, plans were prepared for an underground garage on the rue du Temple Allemand, opposite the Villa Raphaël Schwob, but this was never built.

Construction began soon after the signing of contracts, and perhaps as early as September 4 (see letter to Du Bois of September 8), yet long before the final plans were drawn, every effort being made to enclose the building before winter. Hans Biéri subsequently testified that the concrete frame was completed early in December, the roof in January, and the brick facing in March or April (100/2).[30]

29. The one-page "Convention" states, in part, "Ces travaux sont remis par M. Anatole Schwob à M. Ch.E. Jeanneret architecte. L'exécution de l'immeuble est basée sur le plan daté du 14 juillet 1916 et sur les esquisses l'accompagnant—plans d'étage, de combles, de sous-sol, et croquis de façades. . . . Le montant des honoraires a été fixé à Francs 8,000 (Huit Milles) en bloc selon la lettre du 8 août 1916 adressée par M. Jeanneret à M. Schwob. . . . Le montant de ces honoraires implique tous les travaux d'architecture, ainsi que la décoration intérieure et éventuellement l'installation." The contract with Biéri is in Biéri's files.

30. Construction photos at FLC show the completed concrete frame, which Jeanneret dated December 4, 1916. However, comparison with other photos taken at different times may invalidate some of his datings

The structural engineers for the reinforced concrete were Terner and Chopard of Zurich. Their drawings are dated September 30 and October 14. They show the floor slabs as 6 cm thick and joists or edge beams 22 cm, for a total of 28 cm. These concrete joists are 10 cm broad and spaced 55 cm on center. Jeanneret, in *L'Esprit Nouveau*, p. 687, gives 20 cm per side as the breadth of the four central interior piers that support these slabs; there were eighteen or so piers in all. Their positioning carefully conforms to the building's plan; they are not independent thereof as he advocated for Dom-ino. Therefore none of the construction ideas promulgated for Dom-ino were incorporated in the structural system at the Villa Schwob.

Hans Biéri alerted Schwob to what the client should have realized—that costs were mounting steadily, toward 300,000 francs. Schwob demanded new estimates. After some delay Jeanneret provided these from Paris where he was now living. Dated January 23, the amount was 303,400 Swiss francs—almost three times the original estimate (1/26). Schwob was dumbfounded and accused Jeanneret of deceit (3/58). He had, he said, asked for a house in the price range of the Villa Jeanneret-Perret. Immediate economies were ordered, especially on the unfinished exterior but also the grounds—eliminating a leveled terrace and garden, a fountain, two lanterns, a garden pavilion, and two relief sculptures intended for over the twin front doors (3/60, 62, 63).[31]

Jeanneret's direction over the construction was now suspended although he continued as aesthetic adviser. Schwob assumed authority over the builders (3/58, 59, 61) and Marcel Montandon, Jeanneret's chief draftsman, was hired on the side as supervising architect (although he actually continued in Jeanneret's employ).[32] Therefore Jeanneret was unable to bring his work to a final conclusion. He was also denied further payments.

Consequently, on July 5, 1918, Jeanneret filed suit against Schwob for 19,275.85 francs. This included a 6.5 percent fee on the definitive 276,802 franc cost of the villa and its gardens (17,992), plus 800 for additional work done, minus 5,000 already paid in honorarium, plus 5,000 in compensation for damages done to Jeanneret's reputation.

---

when judged by the amount of brickwork completed. One photo, that of the basement showing the underside of the ground floor, is dated September 4, 1916, which must be wrong.

31. In a letter of April 24, 1917, Jeanneret discussed his intended economies with Schwob who now held the architect in "l'attitude du plus complet mépris" (BV).

32. Jeanneret, whose office was in the old hospital (ground floor, east end), employed three draftsmen. Marcel Montandon was on the payroll from September 1916 through September 1917 at 270 francs per month (6/35) and Alfred Robert and Pierre Varenchon (at 200 francs) for shorter periods. Montandon, whom I interviewed on February 21, 1974, said he was engaged to draw up the Schwob plans, that Robert worked primarily on interior details, while Varenchon handled La Scala. Montandon mentioned that he never saw Jeanneret at the drafting boards; Jeanneret had the ideas but did none of the basic drafting. Montandon also said that the "blank" square on the facade of the Villa Schwob was intended to contain a mosaic or perhaps a painting.

In addition to this there remained the unpaid balance of 483.75 (10 percent of 4,837.50) for redecorating Schwob's smoking room in 1914. The net amount was therefore 19,275 francs (18,792 + 483).[33]

Jeanneret, in his written interrogatories, endeavored to demonstrate that Schwob was responsible for generating the increased costs by augmenting the size of the building by 46.7 percent, as well as by adding bathrooms, wash basins, closets, etc. and by demanding the highest quality of materials. Schwob, on his part, insisted the cubage increase preceded the date of their contract (3/18, 20), that the interior amenities were largely envisioned from the start, that Jeanneret was guilty of expensive taste, and that the concrete frame was an unnecessary extra expense of 20,000 francs.[34] Schwob also accused Jeanneret of requesting and receiving kickbacks from suppliers, yet nothing was ever proved.

To help resolve these questions the court appointed two architects from Neuchâtel and Basel as experts. They visited the villas Schwob and Jeanneret-Perret in September 1919. Their cost figures generally corroborated those already known but they were unable to resolve disputes over who authorized what or at what date the augmented expenses had been authorized. They faulted Jeanneret for calculating his initial estimate of 115,000 francs on the cubage of the building rather than on a list of materials and labor costs. They agreed with him that the preliminary project of 1916 was based on the Villa Jeanneret-Perret, yet was greatly developed.[35] They mildly chided Schwob for saying the materials and appointments in his villa were no more costly than those at the Villa Jeanneret. They also noted such costly extras as a heating system that was concealed within the walls and floors (144/16). Likewise they noted the cost of inflation,

33. The breakdown of the total 276,000 cost was (exclusive of land): building 230,000, garden 38,000, architect's honorarium 8,000 (3/64 and 144/12). The cost of the garden had been reduced from 53,000 by the following economies: elimination of one pavilion, of a stairway down to the street at the south, of a cover over the courtyard (la couverture du préau), of contouring and grading the garden to a single level, of a fountain, and of two lanterns (3/63). After visiting La Chaux-de-Fonds on September 30, 1917, Jeanneret wrote Mme Schwob of his extreme distress over the symmetrical planting of trees in the garden: "La maison est toute symétrique, le jardin est au cordeau. Si vous ne coupez pas une asymétrie indispensable ce sera créer une lassitude réelle, et rétrécir tout le monumental de la façade" (BV). He included a sketch showing the proper asymmetry.

34. The experts concurred that the reinforced concrete frame cost an added 20,000 francs but denied that it had no technical or aesthetic benefits (144/17, 18). Furthermore they insisted that it was not, as Jeanneret claimed, the concrete frame that permitted construction to continue throughout the winter (144/16). Concerning the kitchen, moved at Schwob's request, they agreed that this cost an additional 15,000 francs (5/90).

35. Jeanneret asked the experts: "Le projet de villa de juillet 1916 . . . n'est-il pas dans son ensemble avec quelques modifications celui de la maison Jeanneret-Perret, rue de la Montagne? *Réponse.* Le principe de la villa Jeanneret a été effectivement adapté à la villa prévue par l'avant-projet de juillet 1916, mais considérablement développé" (144 p. 18, #1).

which in the home building industry had risen some 66 percent during the period of construction (144 II/11).

Inevitably Schwob launched a countersuit against Jeanneret for 20,000 francs, seeking damages for inadequate estimates and certain technical oversights in the design. The result, as might be expected, was that on June 25, 1920, after two years of costly litigation, Jeanneret's lawyer notified the court that the parties, "following a transaction," had withdrawn their lawsuits (Dossier #147). The transaction apparently amounted to Schwob paying the 483.75 francs owed for redecorating and furnishing his smoking room in 1914 and the unpaid balance on the 8,000 franc honorarium agreed to in August 1916. Therefore Jeanneret received no fee on the difference between his preliminary estimate of 115,000 and the final cost of 276,000. Moreover his name was severely tarnished in the eyes of precisely those townspeople who were his potential clients. Fortunately for him, however, he had already moved to Paris where he was busily engaged in painting, journalism, entrepreneurship, and, occasionally, the practice of architecture.

In conclusion, therefore, Jeanneret neglected his moral duty to his client but legally had done nothing wrong. As he himself admitted to Schwob, "My fault was of not notifying you in writing of the exact amounts exceeding the original idea of a modest home. I accept this wrong" (April 24, 1917). His other error was, contrary to conventional practice, agreeing to a fixed honorarium that did not provide for an additional fee (at 6.5 percent) in the event the client aggrandized the initial concept. Schwob, meanwhile, in consultation with the architect, was perfectly free—according to their contract—to modify the scope of the project. As a result, Schwob could look forward to obtaining a nice house at a more modest price; Jeanneret, on the other hand, was anxious to build a villa that would enhance his reputation.

However false it may be, the premise still persists that the initial design for the Villa Schwob is what we see today. Jeanneret's sketches, and the interrogatories, completely refute this myth, including the fable that he forgot to include a kitchen.

In actual fact, Jeanneret prepared three sets of designs for the Villa Schwob. The first was for a bilaterally symmetrical building of two storeys (figs. 356, 357). The second, dated July 14, added a third floor accessed by a three-storey stair tower placed against the street facade; meanwhile the original two-storey design underwent no apparent change (figs. 359–61). The third resulted from Anatole Schwob's August request for a still larger house. This third enhancement added an impressive 46.7 percent to the volume. However, the increase is scarcely noticeable because, except for moving the kitchen, it involved no add-ons and was achieved by ballooning the entire design; everything was simply made larger. The cube of the house was enlarged, the radius of the bays increased, the stair tower expanded, and the ceiling height raised. It is this design that was finally built (figs. 379–83).

The original concept, in early July, envisioned a two-storey building. We know of

**Fig. 356.** Villa Schwob. First project. Early July 1916. Soft pencil on tracing paper. 18.9 × 28.2 cm. (BV)

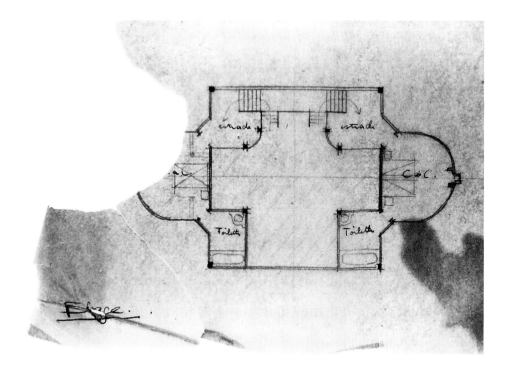

**Fig. 357.** Villa Schwob. Earliest plan, of which we have only the second, or bedroom, floor. Pencil and ink on tracing paper. 22 × 30 cm. (FLC 31827)

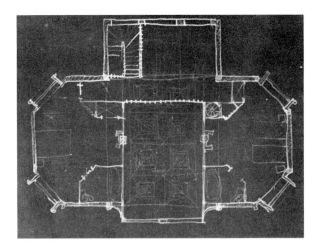

**Fig. 358.** Project: "Maison bouteille," 1909. Plan of second floor. Blueprint. 16 × 20.5 cm. (FLC)

the design and plan from two quick drawings that convey an extraordinary amount of fundamental information. They disclose everything except Jeanneret's initial intention for the street facade which, in all probability, would have imitated certain motifs seen on the garden side (fig. 356).[36] The flat roof with sharply flaring cornices (intended for planter boxes) was in the tradition of Dom-ino, while the cubic form and curved bays remind us of the Villa Jeanneret, and the two-storey glazed living room window recall the "Maison bouteille" project of 1909. In fact, we discern a gradual evolution from the villas Stotzer, Jaquemet, and Jeanneret as the forms become increasingly geometric and purified while at the same time the secondary cross axis is developed more fully both as an exterior expression and significant interior space.

Corresponding (but not exactly) to this perspective is a somewhat more carefully drawn, but water-stained and torn, plan for a second, or bedroom, floor (fig. 357). It has a striking resemblance to that of the 1909 "Maison bouteille," thus corroborating Le Corbusier's statement that Schwob, on chancing across this project in his portfolio, said "Make me something similar to this" (fig. 358).[37] Both show a void of space over the living room with identical bedrooms placed laterally in the half-octagons or half-circles at either side. Even the bathrooms share the exact same position in both plans with only the location of the bathtub and washbasins reversed. The corridor connecting

36. This drawing apparently survived by being sent to Ritter and later given by Josef Ritter-Tcherv to the BV.

37. "En 1916 un client de Le Corbusier feuilletant un portefeuille dans son atelier tombe en arrêt devant le dessin [of Maison bouteille] et dit: 'faites-moi quelque chose de semblable'" (Le Corbusier, *L'Esprit Noveau*, no. 6 [1921], p. 704). Likewise in a letter to Auguste Perret of July 21, 1916, he specifies that the plan of the Villa Schwob was based on "Maison bouteille" and gives its date as 1909. The design was discussed and illustrated in Chapter 5 (figs. 129–33).

**Fig. 359.** Villa Schwob. Perspective view of the second project as seen from the garden. Signed and dated July 14, 1916. Photogravure. 50 × 103 cm. (FLC 30077)

the bedrooms overlooks the living room in all the plans although in the earliest scheme for Schwob this is merely a landing partway up the stairs. No third floor was intended (there are no stairs) and the disposition of ground-floor rooms can be inferred from the second-floor plan as well as the perspective. This initial scheme has many similarities to the villa as built. However it is not mentioned in the lawsuit.

Note that the plan, minus the bays, is a perfect square and the diameter of the semicircular bays is one-half the width of the walls. Therein Jeanneret demonstrates his concern for proportions as well as geometric shapes. Note also his intention to use concrete piers, as indicated on the plan.

A careful reading of the plan provides useful information about the street facade. First of all it was symmetrical. Second, the stair landing, which is less than half-way up to the second floor, negates the possibility of a central entrance door. Therefore the door must be near the corner under the "estrades," but because the design is symmetrical there are undoubtedly doors under each of the two "estrade." What, then, would we find over the stair landing itself? Light is needed so there could be a large window, yet this would reduce privacy because of the buildings across the street. Therefore corner windows at the level of the "estrade" might be more appropriate. In that event the exterior wall over the stair landing needs some kind of architectural definition or decoration, and for this purpose perhaps a framed decorative panel, such as exists in the executed design, was intended; this might logically echo the glazed panel of the garden facade.

Presumably it was this two-storey design that Jeanneret presented to Anatole Schwob at their meeting in early July. Everything that Schwob, Jeanneret, and Mme

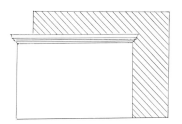

**Fig. 360.** Schematic drawing showing how the enlargement of the villa, requested by Anatole Schwob in mid-July, was wrapped over the earlier design. (Drawing by author)

Raphy Schwob had in mind is incorporated in this design. Almost immediately, however, Anatole's idea of the house began to expand. By contrast—and this is significant—Jeanneret's vision of the design did not. He never lost sight of the original concept; he could have redesigned the villa from scratch, but he did not.

Figure 359 shows Jeanneret's new design of July 14. The first two storeys remain unchanged. But to gain additional space, as requested by Schwob, a third floor is planted upon the roof and, although not visible, a large stair tower (cage d'escalier) is affixed along the street. Actually all he did was clamp an inverted L-shaped mass over the old design (fig. 360). The perspective also reveals Jeanneret's landscape design. Unfortunately, however, the intended leveling of the site, the terrace that mirrored the great glazed window and was to be flanked by lamp standards and a fountain, the asymmetrical planting of two trees, not to mention the various pavilions, all were sacrificed when economies were suddenly ordered in 1917.

Except on the street facade, Jeanneret held his new third floor back from the sides of the building. He then covered its walls with latticework, thus giving the appearance of a penthouse (as one might see in Paris, including Perret's penthouse apartment at 25 bis, rue Franklin). This was an ingenious solution on Jeanneret's part; he thereby preserved, on three sides, the appearance of his original two-storey design while likewise retaining the character of a single-family dwelling which otherwise might have been lost. All this, of course, was made possible by his use of flat roofs.

The plans for this second design, dated July 14, no longer exist. They were returned to their owners following the lawsuit and have since disappeared. It seems certain, however, that, except for the street facade and kitchen, their layout was virtually identical to the third and final design, called "Plans de sanction," of September. This we learn from the dimensions supplied by the legal proceedings wherein the size of the Villa Jeanneret-Perret is compared (for comparative cost reasons) to the July 14 plans *and* to the "Plans de sanction" from which the house was built. The experts testified that the volume of the Villa Jeanneret was 1,848 cubic meters, the July 14 plans for Schwob 2,085 cubic meters, and the "Plans de sanction" 2,979 m³.[38] The latter represents a 46.7

38. I quote the cubic measure and costs for the villas Schwob and Jeanneret as listed in the experts' report of April 1, 1920, response #2. The Schwob figures are those of the July 14 project, for which the plans are lost, rather than those of the executed design.

*Evaluation de l'architecte du 14 juillet 1916: Villa Schwob*

| | | | |
|---|---|---|---|
| sous-sol | 440 m³ à 13 | = | Fr. 5,720 |
| Rez-de-chaussée | 660 " à 40 | = | " 26,400 |
| ler étage | 660 " à 40 | = | " 26,400 |
| combles | 325 " à 25 | = | " 8,125 |
| | 2085 m³ | = | Fr 66,645 |
| | le mètre cube = Fr. 31.96 | | |

*Evaluations pour la maison Jeanneret-Perret du 6 septembre 1913* [i.e., date when fire insurance calculations

percent augmentation in volume since July 14 and includes the newly annexed kitchen, greenhouse, and pavilion (144/3, 5, 8).

This augmentation was also specified in specific dimensions: the ceiling height of the ground floor was raised from 3 m to 3 m 25 (i.e., by 25 cm), the radius of the bays from 2.70 to 2.90, the breadth and width of the house from 11 to 11.80 (vs. 12 m. at the Villa Jeanneret) and the footprint of the stair tower from 8.20 × 2.90 to 9.45 × 3.60 or an increase of 1 m 25 by 0 m 70 (approx. 4′ 1″ × 2′ 4″) (144/6). The last group of figures is especially significant because it is the sole proof we have (1) that the stair tower is coincident with the July 14 perspective, and (2) that this tower subsequently underwent a major increase in size. These facts, and certain commonalities of rendering style, allow us to associate an undated drawing of the street facade (FLC 32109) closely in time with the July 14 perspective—and to some extent with the lost plans.[39]

Figure 361 (FLC 32109) is the rendering in question. It represents Jeanneret's initial intention for the three-storey street facade. Evidently it was drawn just prior to preparing the to-scale plans of July 14, now lost. On July 14, the lawsuit informs us, the breadth of the tower was 8 m. 20 versus 11 m. for the house itself. This left only 1 m. 40 at either side of the tower for the windows, and that was not enough. Jeanneret's perspective, therefore, is out of scale. It does not correspond to the above dimensions since it indicates the stair tower as being much narrower than the expanse of wall behind it.

Nevertheless it shows us his original idea, even though this idea could not be realizable in terms of space. He intended that this opaque panel, with its symmetrically placed windows at either side, should create a visual dialogue with the glazed panel and symmetrically placed windows of the garden facade. This perhaps recalls certain aspects of the earlier, two-storey facade design.

---

were prepared]

|  |  |  |  |
|---|---|---|---|
| citerne intérieure | 38.500 à 12 | = | 462 |
| sous-sol | 385.644 à 17 | = | 6,556 |
| Rez-de-Ch et 1er ét | 857.355 à 25 | = | 21,434 |
| comble | 567.000 à 18 | = | 10,206 |
| plus value pour avant-*corps ouest* | | = | 1,600 |
| | 1848.499 | | 40,258 |

le mètre cube = 21.78

39. The rendering, actually a type of photogravure, exists both as a single sheet, FLC 32109, and as a facsimile affixed to a larger sheet, FLC 30083 (several such three-image groups exist; see Brooks, ed., *The Le Corbusier Archive,* pp. 121–23). These duplicate renderings equate closely in style and reproductive technique with FLC 30082 and 32111 from which the more meticulously drawn perspective of the garden facade (FLC 30077), signed and dated (July 14), was cloned. These early drawings of the two facades may easily be compared in Petit, *Le Corbusier lui-même,* p. 50. Another small (1 × 1½ inch) sketch of the garden facade survives on a postcard to Ritter dated July 30, 1916, and in a letter to Perret of July 21, 1916.

Uncertain, however, is exactly how he wished to redesign the north elevation once he realized his proportions were all wrong. Figure 362 probably provides the answer. The tall, narrow window, two storeys in height, continues to dominate the tower's end wall except that now it is moved back flush with the body of the house. Whether this is significant in terms of interior planning we do not know. What is important, however, is the dramatic reduction in wall space on either side of the tower, leaving no room for windows. The 1 m. 40 of exposed wall on either side of the tower, mentioned in the lawsuit, looks about right, but the 1 m 18 in the ballooned version of September is so nearly similar as to provide no proof-positive in determining the date of these sketches.

The decoration shown in the central panel at upper left is important to note; it is similar to what Jeanneret intended for various Dom-ino projects as well as for Le Moulinet in 1915. Other creative ideas include interrupting the second-storey cornice before it abuts the tower, and adding little niches to the plain brick walls flanking the central panel. These niches eventually evolved into elliptical windows and the brick walls were modified to contain recessed panels.

One of the happiest aspects of this early design was the tall, narrow windows at each end. They emphasized verticality in contrast to the more static street facade, and their scale was in keeping with the frontispiece itself. They neatly separated the tower's mass from the two-storey elevation behind it. It was a "clean" solution compared to the awkward one eventually adopted. Nevertheless, this idea for the illumination of a two-storey stair hall was not wasted; Jeanneret reused it for his very next villa, that at Vaucresson, France, for Georges Besnus, in 1923.

Other studies for joining the stair tower to the house are closer to the final design (fig. 363). The architect is still undecided (sketch at left) how and where to terminate the heavy second-storey cornice. The center sketch shows a bowed-out protrusion

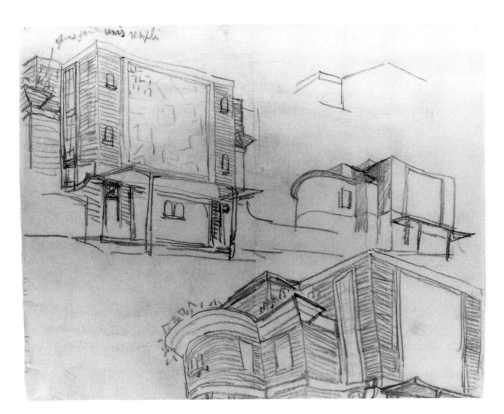

**Fig. 362.** Villa Schwob. Early studies for stair tower. Note how ornament, similar to that proposed both for Dom-ino and for the facade of Le Moulinet in 1915, is shown as decorating the central panel. Pencil on tracing paper. 21.3 × 27.2 cm. (BV)

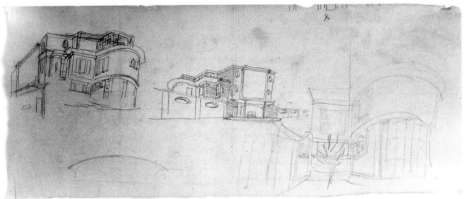

**Fig. 363.** Villa Schwob. Study sketches for enlarging the street facade. Pencil on tracing paper. 18.2 × 49.5 cm. (BV)

where the two masses meet; this element resembles the definitive design except for the relatively large amount of wall space at its left. Meanwhile the faint sketch at lower right shows the west elevation of the original two-storey villa; no penthouse is indicated here nor stair tower against the street (at left). Therefore these studies could be of either mid-July or August. Their evolution is apparently right, left, center.

Figure 364 is still closer to the final solution; it lacks, on the tower facade, only the projecting cornice and the recessed panel enclosing the oval windows (fig. 365).

**Fig. 364.** Villa Schwob. This sketch is close to the definitive solution for joining the three-storey tower to the two-storey design. However the facade design of the tower is not fully resolved. Pencil on tracing paper. 20 × 60 cm. (BV)

**Fig. 365.** Villa Schwob. Detail of northeast corner. Compare this with the previous sketch. (Photo by author)

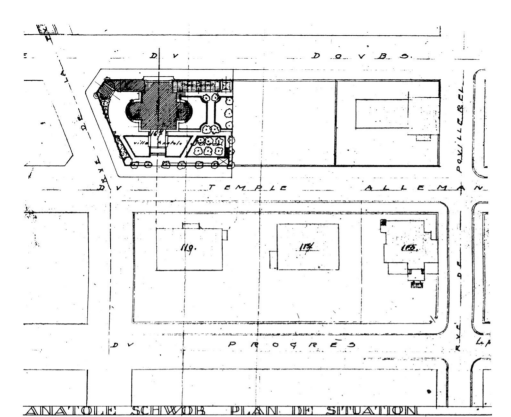

**Fig. 366.** Villa Schwob. Jeanneret's original plot plan. Detail. (BV)

Jeanneret is here struggling with the 46.7 percent increase in size authorized by Anatole Schwob in August. The swelling protrusion that replaces the tall, narrow window fails to correspond to the geometric shapes that characterize the remainder of the design. Therefore it calls attention to itself as a somewhat awkward, unhappy compromise which, however, foretells Le Corbusier's subsequent willingness to place unrelated shapes in collision. Its thin, delicate cornice does not relate to the other cornices and, horizontally, it picks up no responsive cords. Its purpose, apparently, is simply to gain 67.5 cm (26 1/2 inches) greater interior breadth to make possible a newly proposed maid's room and, on the opposite end, an additional toilet. However more is lost than is gained, because this second-floor stairway and hall are now virtually devoid of natural light (fig. 368).

Once the problem of joining the enlarged stair tower to the enlarged house was resolved, the design of the third and final version of the Villa Schwob was complete. Photographs, blueprints (the so-called "Plans de sanction" of September 7–22, 1916), and the building itself, indicate Jeanneret's intentions although numerous modifications took place during construction. These were of two types: first, internal changes in the plan, especially on the second level (compare the blueprint dated September 9, fig. 369, with Jeanneret's post-facto plan of 1921, fig. 368, taking note of how virtually everything surrounding the void over the living room has been reorganized, including the shape of the open space itself); second, the changes instigated for the sake of economy, some of which involved using less expensive materials, others involved either omitting or redesigning significant parts of the intended building.

The most serious exterior modifications occurred in the great framed areas on the two principal facades. These, unlike the villa's basic form and finish, were not yet executed when drastic economies were suddenly ordered in 1917. Concerning the two-storey glazed window overlooking the garden, it was designed to be constructed of metal mullions and large sheets of plate glass.[40] Now wood mullions and regular panes of glass were substituted. This dramatically effected the appearance of this glazed wall (cf. 371, 381, 389). The new window is more fussy and active; worse still, few of the horizontals line up properly with other horizontals in the facade design. And the new door is particularly awkward; its casement does not align with either the horizontal or vertical mullions—Jeanneret is just making the best of a bad situation. Compare this with the well-integrated scheme illustrated in the blueprint.

Meanwhile on the north, or street, facade the panel was already weathertight so it could be left in its unfinished state (fig. 379 and color plate IX). Discussion of the intended decoration will follow shortly. Other economies included eliminating the bas-reliefs (by Léon Perrin) over the two front doors, a roof over the east terrace, a sun room and other amenities on the third floor, a greenhouse, several pavilions, and much of the landscaping.

Throughout Jeanneret's process of design an overriding concern was his predilection for simplicity, clarity, symmetry, and geometric forms. He himself confirmed this in one of the interrogatories: isn't it true "that Mr. Jeanneret, architect, has for several years executed both interior and exterior construction in which he has, without exception, always striven for a simplification of forms and a simplicity of materials that was a genuine innovation in our region and that this manner of building initially aroused, among both workers and contractors, amazement and a certain opposition?" (108/ contre-question 1). Simplicity, in refined detailing, does not come cheaply (cf. the work of Mies van der Rohe) and this is what Schwob failed to comprehend.

Symmetry was equally important in Jeanneret's mind. It controlled not only the interior disposition of rooms but also the building's form. Blank, false windows were added to the east and west facades in order to create an illusion of symmetry where it did not exist (figs. 374, 382), while on the street facade a duplicate front door was designed for similar reasons. None of his previous houses took symmetry to such extremes.

His emphasis on clarity, order, and symmetry is, of course, characteristic of classicism, but the Villa Schwob is virtually devoid of traditional classical forms. Its crispness may

40. Concerning Jeanneret's intention to construct the window using a metal frame, see lawsuit interrogatories 3/28, 100/8, 144/9, and 31.

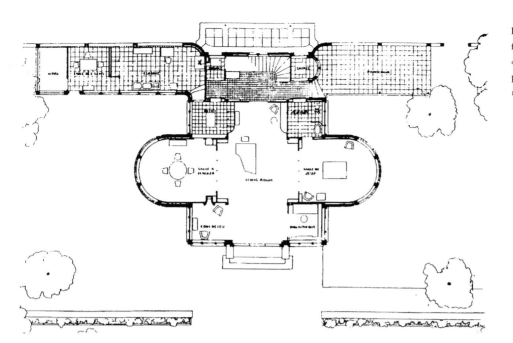

**Fig. 367.** Villa Schwob. Ground-floor plan as modified by Jeanneret to conform with the house as built, and published by him in *L'Esprit Nouveau,* no. 6 (1921).

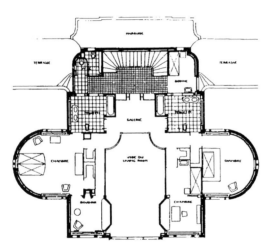

**Fig. 368.** Second-floor plan as published in *L'Esprit Nouveau,* no. 6 (1921).

**Fig. 369.** Villa Schwob. Blueprint (with color reversed) of Jeanneret's second-floor plan ("Plan de sanction") that is signed and dated September 9, 1916. The gallery and bathroom plans were subsequently modified. (BV)

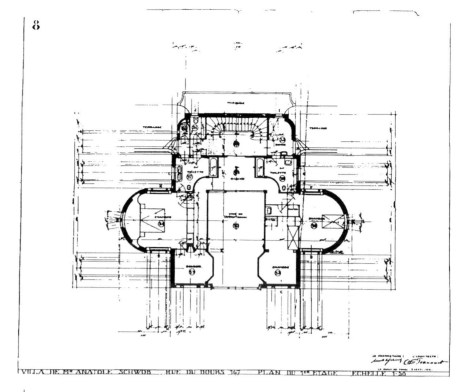

**Fig. 370.** Third (penthouse) floor plan. Blueprint signed and dated September 9, 1916. (BV)

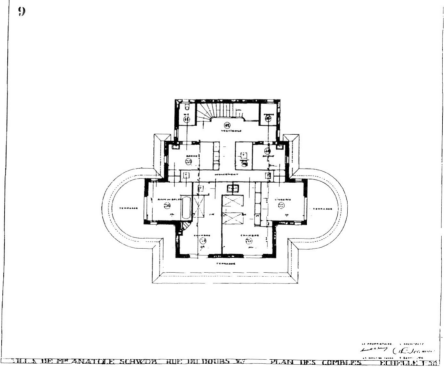

VILLA DE Mᵣ ANATOLE SCHWOB RUE DU DOUBS 167          FAÇADE SUD          ECHELLE 1:50

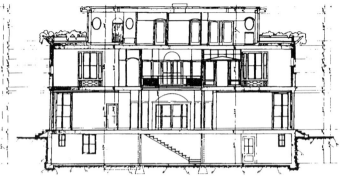

**Fig. 371.** Garden (south) elevation. Blueprint (color reversed) signed and dated September 13, 1916. (BV)

**Fig. 372.** Cross section through dining, living, and game rooms. Blueprint (color reversed) signed and dated September 18, 1916. (BV)

18

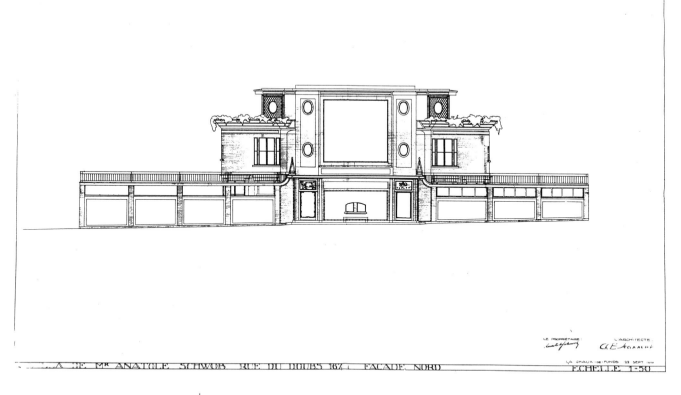

VILLA DE Mr ANATOLE SCHWOB RUE DU DOUBS 167. FACADE NORD   ECHELLE 1-50

**Fig. 373.** Street (north) elevation. Blueprint (color reversed) signed and dated September 22, 1916. (BV)

**Fig. 374.** East elevation. Blueprint (color reversed) signed and dated September 15, 1916. (BV)

recall early nineteenth-century neoclassicism, such as seen in Munich, yet Jeanneret always tended to be more sculptural and the few pilasters, columns, and capitals he did use eschew the semblance of "correctness."

Having said this, we must view the villa while approaching it along the street (fig. 380, color plate IX). From this typical angle (the street corner) the side of the villa disintegrates into an unresolved mess, if we judge it by Jeanneret's own criteria. Nor did it help matters to wall up the lower half of the large bathroom window or add a chimney stack along the side. Everything that Jeanneret sought to achieve eludes him at this point. He simply failed to wed the two- and three-storey elements into a unified design.

Hand in hand with Jeanneret's concern for clarity and symmetry was his search for pleasing proportions. Those at the Villa Schwob he considered under the rubric *tracés régulateurs*—regulating lines—and from these early beginnings emerged, during the 1940s and 1950s, his much heralded books on *The Modulor* and *Modulor 2*. Nevertheless our knowledge of their use at the Villa Schwob derives from post-facto published sources rather than contemporary documentation.

"The tracé régulateur is an assurance against the arbitrary; it provides gratification for the spirit" he wrote in his earliest pronouncement on the subject in *L'Esprit Nouveau,* no. 5 of 1921 (p. 563), soon republished as a chapter in *Vers une architecture.* Therein he mixed truth and conjecture by tracing, chronologically throughout history, various systems of regulating geometric systems, from those used by primitive man on through Persia, Greece, the Middle Ages and the Renaissance. His most poignant example demonstrated that the principal elements (divisions of the facade, inclination of the stairs, height of the piano nobile) of Michelangelo's Capitol in Rome all could be determined or verified by positioning a right-angle triangle at a crucial location in the design such that the lines emanating therefrom would terminate at other essential points.

Jeanneret's own system, however, less often depended on sloping lines emanating from an inverted right angle (although he did utilize them on the street elevation of the Villa Schwob) than on a related acute angle that frequently approached 60°, 59° being the slope of a diagonal drawn through a rectangle constructed from the golden mean (1:1.618). Parallel and perpendicular to this primary slope (which usually established the width or height of the facade) he drew shorter lines that often determined the size (and in certain cases the placement) of doors and windows. It is these subsidiary parallels and perpendiculars that Le Corbusier apparently claimed as his own invention.[41]

Figure 375 illustrates the facades of the Villa Schwob as published by Le Corbusier in 1921. The slope of angle A on the garden side determines the width in relation to

41. P. H. Berlage refuted this claim in a letter to Le Corbusier (FLC) dated December 30, 1923, in which he asserted that in Holland a similar system was in use since the 1890s.

the height of the facade while on the street side angle A determines its height. However, the architect took great liberty in choosing where to place his angle and where to terminate his lines—all done with the intent of proving that the system actually works. On the garden facade angle A is situated *above* the narrow rectangular panels that are below the cornice, while the slope of the diagonal, in order to achieve the desired width for the facade, terminates below the floor level and within the foundation wall. The exact opposite is true on the street elevation where angle A is set at floor level, rather than below it, and the diagonal terminates *below,* rather than above, the narrow panel that is under the cornice. The system, therefore, depends on decisions that are often entirely arbitrary. Nevertheless, the architect would probably call them poetic considerations, or the expression of artistic license.[42] It was, after all, a corrective measure and not a creative force.

My own drawing provides additional insight into the proportional system at the Villa Schwob (fig. 376). I have retained Jeanneret's angle A as well as the exact points at which his sloping tracé begins and ends (A and H). If we use this tracé as the hypotenuse of a right-angled triangle, one side has the length AD. With AD we can create the square ABCD. And by dividing the square in half, EF, and using the diagonal FB as the radius of a circle, its arc will intersect point H. The rectangle thereby established, AGHD, is a golden section. Therefore the facade conforms to a golden section although Jeanneret did not admit it (perhaps because he thought this would diminish his claim to originality);[43] we already noted that the distance separating the base line, DH, and top line, AG, was "adjusted" in order for these lines to be the proper distance apart. In addition (and likewise not demonstrated in Jeanneret's diagram) the arc of the circle (derived from the square ABCD) when continued as a semicircle to its intersection with the extension of HD at I, establishes the distance that the bays project beyond the main house.

Also, by placing a right-angled triangle so that its hypotenuse coincides with the base line HI and the sides are of equal length, then the right angle occurs at L, which falls at the top edge of the cornice, thereby establishing its height. According to Jeanneret (*L'Esprit Nouveau,* p. 568) this system of combining a semicircle and pyramid to determine roof heights was used by the Greeks for the facade of the Arsenal at

42. Such arbitrary decisions are evident wherever he claimed to use regulating lines. This is glaringly apparent at the Ozenfant house and Villa Stein where he found it necessary to create an imaginary base line above the actual ground line. To compensate for this at Garche he placed a mound of earth at the foot of the staircase leading to the garden because the slope of these stairs (as determined by the tracé régulateur whose base line was above ground level) prevented the stairs from reaching the ground.

43. His description of the system at the Villa Schwob merely states: "Le bloc général des façades, tant antérieure que postérieure, est réglé sur le même angle A qui détermine une diagonale dont de multiples parallèles et leurs perpendiculaires fourniront les mesures correctives des éléments secondaires, portes, fenêtres, panneaux, etc., jusque dans les moindres détails" (*L'Esprit Nouveau,* no. 5 [1921], p. 570). Nowhere is there any mention of golden sections, right-angle triangles, circles, etc.

**Fig. 375.** Drawings by Jeanneret showing *Tracés Régulateurs* as applied to the Villa Schwob. These were published in *L'Esprit Nouveau,* no. 5 (1921), p. 572. (BV)

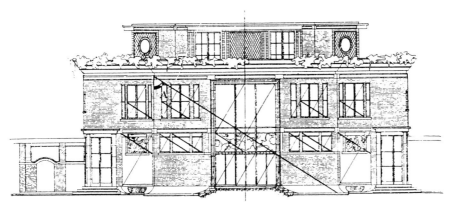

*CONSTRUCTION RÉCENTE D'UNE VILLA*

Le bloc général des façades, tant antérieure que postérieure, est réglé sur le même angle A qui détermine une diagonale dont de multiples parallèles et leurs perpendiculaires fourniront les mesures correctives des éléments secondaires, portes, fenêtres, panneaux, etc., jusque dans les moindres détails.

Cette villa de petites dimensions apparaît au milieu des autres constructions édifiées sans règle, comme plus monumentale, d'un autre ordre (1).

LE CORBUSIER-SAUGNIER.

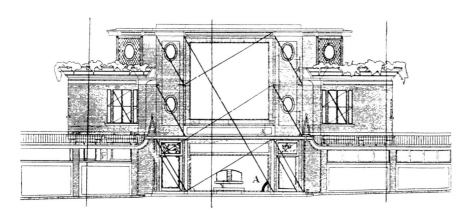

Piraeus.[44] And this may be why he chose to exclude this diagram from his Schwob drawing. It is evident, therefore, that Jeanneret's tracés régulateurs actually included several different systems, including the golden section, right-angled triangles, and arcs of circles, in addition to regulating lines.

44. Jeanneret's diagram of the Arsenal at Piraeus, which appears on page 568 of *L'Esprit Nouveau,* is identical, except for the lettering, to that on page 389 of Auguste Choisy, *Histoire de l'architecture* (Paris, 1899).

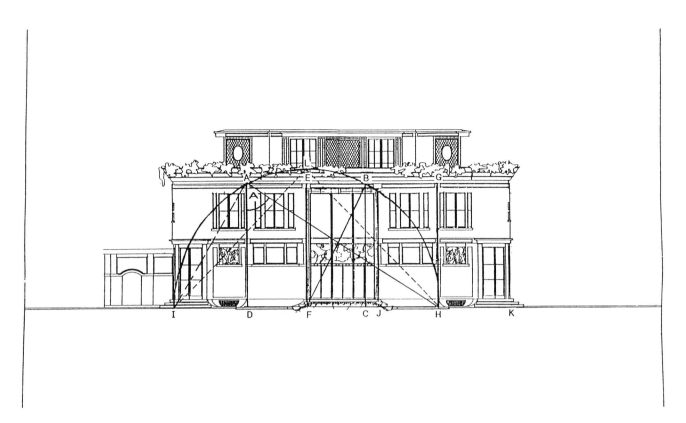

**Fig. 376.** Drawing by author to demonstrate how Jeanneret used, in addition to regulating lines, (1) the golden section to determine the height and width of the facade, (2) the arc of the golden section to establish the projection of the lateral bays, and (3) a right-angle triangle with equal sides to define the height of the cornice.

Just when and how Jeanneret became interested in proportional systems is not known; undoubtedly, since childhood, there was a growing concern that began with his study of nature. His year in Germany (1910–11) certainly introduced him to the proportional theories of August Thiersch, not necessarily through Theodor Fischer or the school at Munich where Thiersch had taught, but from Peter Behrens in whose office Thiersch's son, Paul, had earlier worked. The same source may also have introduced him to Heinrich Wölfflin's reflex-diagonals.[45] Later, in Greece, Jeanneret became anxious to discover the "laws" that governed perfection (yet the tracé régulateur was no law) and in Rome he learned to admire pure geometric shapes. The catalyst, he suggests in *The Modulor* (1948, p. 27), was his reading of Auguste Choisy's *L'Histoire de l'architecture* which he purchased in 1913 and wherein regulating lines are discussed.

The earliest evidence we have of what he learned from Choisy is recorded on page

45. Actually the closest to Jeanneret's system was that of Heinrich Wölfflin, who extended August Thiersch's theory of proportions to include perpendiculars drawn through the diagonals that, as Wölfflin demonstrated with the Cancelleria Palace in Rome, establish the proportions of doors and windows. See Wölfflin, *Renaissance und Barock* (Munich, 1888), or English translation, *Renaissance and Baroque* [Ithaca: Cornell University Press, 1966], p. 66. J. L. M. Lauweriks was a name also known to Jeanneret and he too was concerned with systems of proportion. For a discussion of Thiersch, Wölfflin, etc. see Jacques Paul, "Neo-Classicism and the Modern Movement," *Architectural Review,* 152, no. 907 [September 1972], pp. 176–80.

Fig. 377. Construction photo looking from the east-southeast. This and the following photo were labeled by Jeanneret "Construction Schwob 4 décembre 1916" but the different amount of brickwork that is shown completed in the two photos calls into question these dates, as does the contractor's testimony in the lawsuit. (FLC)

Fig. 378. Construction photo looking east from master bedroom across the void over the two-storey living room. Note that the Dom-ino system of reinforced concrete construction is not being used. (FLC)

112 of Sketchbook A2 (1915). He lists "The vaulted Achemenid monuments/the Porte-Saint-Denis/the Piraeus Arsenal/the façade of Notre-Dame/ . . ." all of which he illustrated and discussed in his 1921 article on "Les Tracés Régulateurs." And on the next two pages, captioned "modulor lines [tracé modulaire]/of Achemenid vaults/ Dieulafoy," he roughly sketched the diagrams that appear on page 569 of his article.

These, in turn, are derived from page 28, volume 4, of Marcel Dieulafoy's five-volume *L'Art antique de la Perse* (Paris, 1884–89) in the section entitled "Les Monuments voutés achéménides." By using a somewhat similar system of squares and circles Jeanneret then demonstrated, on another page of his article, that the main horizontal elements on the facade of Notre-Dame, Paris, can be ascertained by similar means. All these examples seem to legitimize Jeanneret's own quest for "an assurance against the arbitrary." Geometry and mathematics have now replaced nature as an ordering element in his work.

Converting the Schwob plans and blueprints into a finished building was considered while discussing the interrogatories of the lawsuit. This included the pros and cons of Jeanneret's use of reinforced concrete for which Terner and Chopard of Zurich served as engineers. Figure 377 shows the structural framework already in situ and the first of the brickwork in place. Figure 378 shows the interior looking across the open void over the living room from the master bedroom; much more of the brickwork is complete. Concerning the structural system, note that the ceiling has open coffering with supporting beams perpendicular thereto, and that there are a great number of vertical piers; none of these elements relate to Jeanneret's Dom-ino method of construction.

Close-up photographs show the high quality of exterior brickwork (see fig. 365). The bricks are from Lausen near Basel and are a rich, warm yellowish-orange in sunlight but more tan or camel's hair when seen in shadow; their overall tonality is quite light. They are juxtaposed against the natural color of poured concrete, itself lightly tooled to create a consistent surface and remove any minor imperfections caused by formwork. The narrow panels cast in concrete below the second-storey cornice recall the similar motif found in the living room under the gallery—as well as in late eighteenth-century furniture design. Stone, where used around windows and for relief sculpture, has a similar tone (see color plates IX, X).

Brick is rare as a building material in La Chaux-de-Fonds and this made the Villa Schwob rather special. Nevertheless brick was quite popular among the Parisian architects admired by Jeanneret including Henri Sauvage (whose Habitation Hygiénique à Bon Marché at 7, rue de Trétaigne of 1903–4, employed a similar light-tan brick), Anatole de Baudot (at St. Jean-de-Montmartre of 1894–97 where concrete and brick were also juxtaposed), and Louis Süe's rue Cassini studio-apartments where, however, the brick color was quite different. Light yellowish-tan brick was also used by Walter Gropius and Adolf Meyer at the Fagus Factory, Alfeld-an-der-Leine (1911) and at Gropius' administration building for the Werkbund Exposition, Cologne (1914). Therefore Jeanneret had ample precedent for the use of this material as well as this particular color.

Turning next to the interior, we know of its original appearance from Jeanneret's preconstruction sketches, photographs taken in 1920, and by the now modified interior itself. Jeanneret's sketches—signed, labeled, and dated July 24, 1916—show the front hall and upstairs rooms. They are virtually identical to the villa as built, thus confirming

**Fig. 379.** Villa Schwob. North (entrance) facade. 1975 photo. (Photo by author)

**Fig. 380.** Villa Schwob. Viewed from northwest. 1975 photo. (Photo by author)

**Fig. 381.** Villa Schwob. Garden facade, facing southeast. 1920 photograph. (BV)

**Fig. 382.** Villa Schwob, seen from the east. 1920 photograph. (FLC)

**Fig. 383.** Detail of doorway from living room to terrace. Note the double glazing and, between the layers of glass, the heating pipes that warm this space in winter. 1975 photo. (Photo by author)

that his concept of the interior was largely complete by that date. The photographs, taken professionally in 1920, indicate that certain changes, albeit minor, occurred after the "Plans de sanction" of September were complete.[46]

The house is entered by the door at the left. One is in a small vestibule. The coat room is opposite and, to the right, a hallway with its staircase against the outside wall. Facing these stairs, French doors admit a thin shaft of light; they lead to the living room. Jeanneret's July 24 sketch (fig. 384) illustrates this hall virtually as built (compare to photo in *L'Esprit Nouveau,* no. 6, p. 693).

A photograph shows the far end of this hall (fig. 385). Its detailing is thin and seem-

46. Jeanneret wrote to Léon Perrin on June 12, 1920, thanking him for sending the nine Groepler photographs that he had requested. On October 6 he again wrote, this time requesting interior photos and enclosing sketches of exactly which views he wanted; Perrin sent these in early November. Meanwhile on October 9 he wrote Madame Schwob (with whom he remained on good terms) instructing her how the furniture should be arranged. He also informed her that the Société des Editions de l'Esprit Nouveau intended to publish a high-quality, large-format monograph on the house after first publishing an illustrated article in *L'Esprit Nouveau.* The article appeared in March 1921 with fourteen photographs but soon thereafter Le Corbusier's interest in the villa waned, apparently due to a change in his aesthetic criteria, and the monograph was never published (copies of Jeanneret's letters are at FLC).

PALIER AU 1ER ETAGE

**Fig. 384.** Villa Schwob. Jeanneret's sketch of proposed front hall. Signed and dated July 24, 1916. Photogravure. Detail of 100 × 45 cm. print. (FLC 30081)

**Fig. 385.** Villa Schwob. Detail of front hall showing the door that leads to the terrace. To the right is the coatroom. 1920 photograph. (FLC)

ingly weightless, monochrome in color, and thereby forecasting his designs of the 1920s. It also reveals the architect's evolution since designing the library for Raphy Schwob which had more components (moldings, basket-weave capitals, etc.), was two-tone in color (in addition to the murals by Charles Humbert) and, in sum, was less simple (cf figs. 328, 329). Note the curved corner pilasters where Jeanneret comes closest to a classical form. Meanwhile the oval mirror, facing the front door, echoes the oval windows outside. The door itself, leading not to the street but to a side terrace, is of glass with a metal frame. Within its sidelights, and suspended there by little metal balls, are secondary metal frames with their appropriate glazing.

Upon stepping from this dimly lit hall though double doors and into the living room, one is struck by the change of scale and by the flood of light from the two-storey, wall-to-wall, southeast window that overlooks the town and the mountains beyond. Deep hemicycles on either side enclose a dining room (cf. Villa Jeanneret) and game or music room. Further on, and facing one another across the living room, are (as at the Villa Jeanneret) two small rooms, one a library and the other an inglenook (coin de feu), the latter having a miniature fireplace such as would soon become a hallmark in Le Corbusier's residential work.

**Fig. 386.** Living room. 1920 photograph of which Jeanneret disapproved because of the wall hangings and furnishings. The chandelier, which he designed, is in the form of the original house plan. (FLC)

A photograph of this living room, looking back toward the French doors, so displeased Jeanneret that he never published it. This was because he disliked the heavy drapes that closed off the rooms at either side; he also objected to the amount of furniture, often of mediocre quality (fig. 386).[47] Nevertheless the two chairs at the left are of his design as well as the chandelier resembling the initial plan of the house.

On the second floor the hallway has a similar configuration to that below but only a single glazed door leads into the gallery that overlooks the living room; this gallery provides access to the bedroom suites at either side (fig. 387). The casement around

47. Jeanneret's relations with Mme Schwob, née Camille Levaillant, remained cordial and she sneaked Amédée Ozenfant and Jeanneret into the house in 1919. In his thank-you letter (BV) of September 8, 1919, Jeanneret, who had not previously seen the completed building, was very happy except with the living room: "Je dois le dire sans modestie j'ai été véritablement surpris de la tenue architecturale de cette maison, de sa force, de sa certitude. . . .

"Le Hall [living room] est la seule pièce qui ne soit pas encore au point. La raison capitale en est l'affreux et immense tapis qui enlève toute tranquillité, toute grandeur et détruit l'esprit de cette architecture. L'encombrement de meubles d'un dessin peu sûr en est cause aussi; il faudrait épurer beaucoup, comme vous avez si bien su le faire dans les autres pièces. . . .

"Dans une architecture aussi impérieuse que celle-là, toute la grande tâche consiste à épurer, à éliminer le superflu, à ne conserver que l'utile, le fort, le calme."

Jeanneret's taste, and terminology, have undergone a change. The Villa Jeanneret-Perret always had heavy drapes against the walls but in this post-Purist year of 1919 he now seeks to purify (épurer) the interior.

**Fig. 387.** Entrance into the gallery that overlooks the living room. The bookshelf, at left, like the chandelier, shows the original plan of the villa. 1920 photograph. (FLC)

the doorway is quite unusual (the sides perhaps recall the metal door in the hall below or the deep niches beside the fireplace at the Villa Jeanneret). Still more novel is the bookshelf that takes the shape of the villa's early plan, the top tier perhaps indicating how the house was originally intended to front on the street.

A view in the opposite direction, over the living room, is illustrated by a sketch of July 24 (fig. 388). Above, at the far end of the living room, are paired projections that remind me of those alongside a freight train's caboose, what with their little windows looking out the side (fig. 389). Such sculptural elements provide interest and gain space for the rooms inside, the one at the right being a "boudoir" (fig. 390) and at the left "chambre jeune garçon." The latter adjoins the "chambre de la jeune fille" (fig. 391; and plan, fig. 368). These drawings keep us abreast of Jeanneret's taste in interior decoration, whether for wallpaper or furniture design.

The bathroom off the master bedroom is very revealing since it shows the growth pains through which the house had passed. The earliest plan designates this area "estrade" or open platform; it overlooked the living room from atop the stairs. Later the "estrade" became a bathroom; this necessitated walling up half the window over the washbasins and closing off a door that then becomes a full-length mirror. The arch over the bathtub is perhaps a modified remnant of the archway once connecting the gallery with the master bedroom (fig. 392).

Fig. 388. Gallery, with view overlooking the two-storey living room. Sketch dated July 24, 1916. Photogravure on heavy paper. 22 × 29 cm. (FLC 30082 and 32106)

PLATE-FORME SUPÉRIEURE DU HALL.

Fig. 389. Schwob living room as seen from the balcony. (Photo: Antonia Mulus)

**Fig. 390.** Boudoir that overlooks living room from second floor. Note Jeanneret's taste in wallpaper and furnishings. Signed and dated July 24, 1916. (FLC 30082)

**Fig. 391.** Chambre de la jeune fille (east bedroom). Signed and dated July 24, 1916. Photogravure on heavy paper. Detail of 89 × 44 cm. print. (FLC 30083)

**Fig. 392.** Bathroom off of the master bedroom. 1920 photograph. (FLC)

Concerning the third floor we know nothing of its original appearance, only the plan. Neither sketches nor photographs exist. And the plan underwent modifications when the economies ordered in January took place. The "Plan de sanction" of September 9 shows six rooms, two for guests, two for maids, a sun room, a linen room, and an open terrace that encompassed three sides of the second-storey roof (see figure 370).

The sharply flaring cornice served two purposes: it contained planter boxes and kept people some distance from the edge.

The question of sources for the Villa Schwob has attracted almost as much attention from researchers as the building itself. Usually writers have concentrated on distant and occasionally exotic influences. Yet instinct leads me to seek examples associated with Jeanneret's own immediate experience.

Jeanneret, in his July 21, 1916, letter to Auguste Perret, and also in *L'Esprit Nouveau*, no. 6 (1921), p. 704, states that "Maison bouteille" was the original source for the Villa Schwob. The similarities of plan, already discussed, and the two-storey living room with glazed facade overlooked by a second-floor gallery, the high square windows on either side, and the shape and disposition of rooms on the second floor, clearly substantiate his claim (see figs. 358 and 129–33).[48] Add to this certain modifications suggested by the Villa Jeanneret-Perret including the strong cross-axis with small square rooms under the arm of the "T," as well as the projecting hemicycle, and you pretty well have the completed concept for the initial Schwob design.

Further refinement of Jeanneret's ideas was occasioned by his vivid memory of Theodore van Rysselberghe's studio which he visited at Auguste Perret's invitation in May 1915 and of which he included a sketch when writing Perret in late March 1916, only three months prior to receiving the Schwob commission (fig. 393). This interior enlarges on, and perfects, his thoughts on how to treat the Schwob living room, and at this point we almost have the final design.

This being said, I give no credibility whatsoever to the widely held belief that Jeanneret's ideas for the symmetrical plan, the two-storey living room with overlooking balcony and glazed end wall, as well as the twin entrance doors on the street, all derive from the work of Frank Lloyd Wright and specifically from his Thomas Hardy house, Racine, Wisconsin, of 1905. True, all these features exist at the Hardy house, but what all claimants have totally failed to consider is the fact that they themselves have had access to drawings and photos that Jeanneret did not.[49]

48. The true significance of "Maison bouteille" could not be properly appreciated from the single elevation published along with Le Corbusier's statement in *L'Esprit Nouveau* (see fig. 130). However, once I successfully identified an unclassified cache of blueprints at the FLC as being "Maison bouteille," their relevance immediately became apparent.

49. Jeanneret, of course, knew of Berlage's 1912 article where a perspective drawing of the Hardy house, seen from the lake, shows its central window—yet there are no plans, interiors, or street elevations. The same is true of Wright's 1908 *Architectural Forum* article which, in any event, Jeanneret probably never saw. As for the large, rare, two-volume folio issued by Wasmuth in 1910, which did include plans but no street views, we have no indication that this expensive publication was known to him, only the smaller 1911 Wasmuth that he may have owned in the 1920s but which, in any case, did not illustrate the Hardy house. The only instance when the street facade of the Hardy house was published prior to 1916, and this was

**Fig. 393.** Jeanneret's sketch of Theodore van Rysselberghe's studio on the Côte d'Azur that was included as part of his letter to Auguste Perret of March 29, 1916. (Fonds Perret, Institut Français d'Architecture, Paris)

As for those twin doors at the Villa Schwob, the true source is certainly not the unknown Hardy house but the more obvious precedent of Jeanneret's own youthful designs (see fig. 34) and especially Auguste Perret's 25 bis, rue Franklin, where Jeanneret once worked. Perret and Jeanneret's two doors even serve identical functions, that at the left leading to the living quarters, and that on the right to the work space.

Still more important, however, are questions posed by the blank panel on the street facade. Was it intended to remain forever blank? And why a framed panel in the first place?

Although writers universally believe that this panel was intended to remain forever blank, I would dispute this "fact." The first clue is the panel itself which in photographs (and in situ) has a blemished (i.e., unfinished) surface that is at odds with the high quality of workmanship throughout the villa. Therefore I sought advice from those present in 1916. Marcel Montandon, Jeanneret's chief draftsman for the Schwob commission, told me unequivocally that Jeanneret intended the panel to be decorated with either a mosaic or perhaps a painting (February 21, 1974). He said Jeanneret discussed the matter with him because of indecision as to which medium was best to use.

I repeatedly posed the same question to Léon Perrin over a six-year period (1973–78). Each time he insisted the panel was to be decorated with either a mosaic or fresco painting; he recalled Jeanneret having several times debated the question with him. Of Lucien Schwob, artist, nephew of Anatole, and close friend of Jeanneret's, I asked this question three times between 1973 and 1979. On each occasion he confirmed that the panel was to be decorated, remembering that he had heard it directly from the architect. Thus the verdict is unanimous, the "blank" panel on the facade of the Villa Schwob was created for the purpose of containing ornament.

Ample precedent exists for decorating such a panel. In Jeanneret's own work he used sgraffito or fresco on the facades of the villas Fallet, Stotzer, and Jaquemet. A more abstract decoration was intended for his Dom-ino designs and Le Moulinet in 1915. Similar designs are shown in one of the drawings for the Schwob facade (fig. 362). Perhaps this decoration would have looked like the abstract patterns he created a few years before (figs. 289, 290).

Elsewhere, at the crematorium in La Chaux-de-Fonds, panels were specifically designed for mosaics (fig. 150). Jeanneret also purchased postcards of two Munich buildings with large framed panels containing paintings. One was the Villa Stuck (1897–98)

a perspective drawing, was in a three-page article by C. E. Percival in *The House Beautiful* issue of June 1906 (20, no. 1) entitled "A House on a Bluff." The two doorways, which incidently lead to courtyards and not into the house itself, are partly visible here. However the chances are about zero that Jeanneret knew of this ten-year-old popular magazine article, and even if he did, why would he have chosen it over the precedent set by his own work? Nevertheless, Colin Rowe still publishes post-1916 photographs of the Hardy house street facade in connection with the Schwob design ("The Provocative Facade," *Le Corbusier, Architect of the Century* [Arts Council of Great Britain, 1987], p. 25).

**Fig. 394.** Jeanneret's annotated postcard of the Neuere Pinakothek, Munich, with its decorated facade panels. Detail. (BV)

visited in April 1911 and owned by the painter Franz von Stuck, and the other was the Neuere Pinakothek (August von Voit, architect, 1846–53; fig. 394). The framed paintings on both these buildings give a good idea of what Jeanneret perhaps had in mind.

Why a framed panel in the first place?

Jeanneret's decision to place a staircase against the center of the street facade required that something be done to articulate the wall. This need has already been discussed. And the concept of a framed panel was not new to him. Even his early studies of Gothic cathedrals were sufficiently present in his mind to include a rose window, enclosed in its frame, from Notre-Dame, Paris, in *Oeuvre Complète* (fig. 395).

A more immediate and obvious example is Perret's Garage Ponthieu with its huge glazed window and decorative mullions radiating from its central core (fig. 396). Here the square has its own built-in structural decoration, in some respects recalling the structural requirements of a rose window. That Jeanneret was thinking of the Garage Ponthieu we know from his drawing of it in Sketchbook A2 (p. 150).

His favorite modern building, the Théâtre des Champs-Elysées, may also have played a role. Presumably more important than the executed building, however, were certain preliminary drawings and models probably familiar to him from his numerous visits to Perret's office. Paul Jamot, Perret's biographer, informs us that after Auguste Perret and Henry van de Velde presented, in May 1911, their respective ideas for the facade, that Perret, in June, submitted a model concerning which "The building committee . . .

**Fig. 395.** South transept rose window at Notre-Dame, Paris, studied by Jeanneret in 1908, and published by him in *Oeuvre Complète,* vol. 1.

**Fig. 396.** Auguste Perret, Garage Ponthieu, Paris, 1907. (Paul Jamot, *A. & G. Perret,* Paris, 1927)

asks for modification of the center which, in this early project, was blind [aveugle];" elsewhere he notes that Perret "initially designed a blind facade, without windows, with only bare space."[50]

Unfortunately this earliest project is unknown, yet a slightly later scheme may be Perret's response to this criticism (fig. 397).[51] One can easily imagine this area as being blank, whether with or without the bas-reliefs above. Also important, from Jeanneret's standpoint, would be the incised vertical panels at either side; they recall those at the Villa Schwob prior to Jeanneret's addition of elliptical windows. Compare also the marquee, the strong horizontal cornice, and the curved bay at one side; square windows above a marquee were also present at La Scala. Significantly, the Théâtre des Champs-Elysées, at the time of its dedication in 1913, was criticized as being much too austere and Teutonic and not sufficiently in the French tradition.

A Teutonic work well known to Jeanneret was, of course, the Elektra Boathouse in Berlin that Jeanneret assisted with while in Peter Behrens' office (fig. 398). The central rectangle is distinct (here infilled with windows) and it is flanked by vertical panels at either side. This symmetrical scheme, beginning one storey above the ground, is topped by a horizontal cornice. This general arrangement, including some of its features, is seen at both Perret's Théâtre des Champs-Elysées and at Jeanneret's Villa Schwob.

These contemporary designs, well known and liked by Jeanneret, would, in addition to the great glazed window of the garden facade of the Villa Schwob and the decorated panels on certain German buildings, provide more than ample inspiration for him to create such a rectangular panel on the street facade of the Villa Schwob (the panel is actually slightly wider than it is tall). However, a considerable community of thought, inspired by the writings of Colin Rowe, believes that concerning "the blank panel—one remains compelled to cite the highly obvious precedents of the so-called 'Casa di Palladio' in Vicenza and of Federico Zuccheri's studio in Florence."[52] But Rowe fails to document that Jeanneret knew, and was interested in, these two buildings; they are not mentioned in his writings, nor did he visit Vicenza.

Sources for other, less commanding, features of the Schwob design also deserve mention. The most striking is the heavy cornice under the flat roof. As early as 1907 Jeanneret was fascinated with heavy cornices while in Florence and Siena. At Or San Michele, in addition to drawing the building itself, he recorded no less than two sepa-

50. Paul Jamot, *A.-G. Perret* (Paris and Brussels, 1927, pp. 13, 17. Although Perret was not permitted to use, at the theater, a blank panel for the facade, he revived the idea at the Ecole Normale de Musique, Paris, which he built in 1928.

51. My thanks to Henri Poupée of the Conservatoire National des Arts et Métiers for locating this early Perret drawing.

52. Colin Rowe, "The Provocative Facade: Frontality and Contraposto," *Le Corbusier, Architect of the Century* (Arts Council of Great Britain, 1987), p. 26. This is an enhanced restatement of Rowe's 1950 "Mannerism and Modern Architecture" article first published in *Architectural Review.*

**Fig. 397.** Auguste Perret, early project for the Théâtre des Champs-Elysées, Paris, 1911. (Conservatoire National des Arts et Métiers)

rate details of the cornice and noted that "The top is crowned by a magnificent cornice" (FLC 2082). Of more recent origin is the broad, striated cornice used by Peter Behrens at the Cuno house or, as Brian Taylor first observed, the rue Vavin apartments by Henri Sauvage in Paris. In Jeanneret's work such cornices first appear in certain Dom-ino designs and in the Le Moulinet project of 1915.

Nevertheless the Schwob cornice is unique in its long horizontal ridges that divide broader, somewhat concave bands that gradually flare out from the facade at nearly 45°. Failing to be corbelled in the usual way, these suggest that Jeanneret was probably influenced by a vernacular Swiss method of wood construction used for creating wide eaves as protection against the weather (figs. 399, 400). Such eaves are usually concave with horizontal battens running along the joints between the boards. It seems likely that Jeanneret translated this method of wood construction into concrete for his design at the Villa Schwob.

The idea of bas-relief panels (by Léon Perrin) on the garden facade was probably inspired by those of Antoine Bourdelle at the Théâtre des Champs-Elysées, Paris, Bourdelle being an artist much admired by Jeanneret and often mentioned in his letters. Such relief sculpture is also seen at Vaudijon, the neoclassical villa near Neuchâtel, although the Parisian example is more relevant.

Another decorative device, the engaged columns and capitals between the doors of

**Fig. 398.** Peter Behrens, Elektra Boathouse, Berlin, 1910–11. Entrance facade. (Hans-Joachim Kadatz, *Peter Behrens* [Leipzig, 1977], p. 76)

the hemicycles, was inspired by illustrations on page 83, volume 2, of Dieulafoy's *L'Art Antique de la Perse* that Jeanneret transcribed on page 108 of his A2 sketchbook.

One final word concerning sources. Locally the Villa Schwob is called the Villa Turque. This has encouraged writers to seek Turkish origins. Yet I suspect the real source for this nickname lies in French slang where the word "turque" carries the meaning exotic, queer, strange, or unconventional. Surely this is what the inhabitants of La Chaux-de-Fonds had in mind.

During the latter part of 1916 Jeanneret's architectural practice kept him exceedingly busy; this in sharp contrast to the previous three years when no building construction was underway. He constantly complained to Du Bois (on September 8, October 5, December 9) that he had no time to visit Paris, yet he did, in fact, spend two weeks there (October 27–November 9), returning via Lyon where on November 8 he sketched Tony Garnier's house but apparently, as previously noted, failed to meet the architect.

His activities in Paris and Lyon are poorly documented. A letter to Ritter of October 31 speaks extensively and glowingly of Auguste Perret with whom he passed the day.

They must have discussed "France ou Allemagne," Jeanneret having finally sent Perret a mock-up several weeks before (to Ritter, October 2). Nevertheless neither man was able to find a publisher.[53]

Jeanneret marvelled at Perret's 25 bis, rue Franklin roof-top garden suspended nine storeys above the street with its panoramic view of Paris. He sketched it on the page next to Tony Garnier's house and later would imitate it on the roofs of all of his Parisian villas. He was in a very upbeat mood. He enthused over Paris as the eternal city, its qualities always present, even in wartime with so many men away. But of those other than Perret he made no mention.

His father's journal of November 10 remarked: "Edouard returned yesterday evening from Paris where he said he made excellent arrangements from the standpoint of his future." Presumably that, and "France ou Allemagne," were what the trip was all about.

Jeanneret briefly became an art critic. In *Feuille d'Avis* he reviewed Marie-Louise Goering's silk screens on November 25 and the painting exhibition "Woog, [Lucien] Schwob, Zysset, Humbert" on December 2 and 4. As a reviewer he proved kind and encouraging to his hometown friends. Earlier, in August, he installed the Oeuvre-sponsored traveling exhibit "Arts du Feu" (porcelain, pottery, enamel, glass, mosaics) in the great hall of the post office, for which he received generous praise (*Feuille d'Avis,* August 16).[54]

He himself exhibited ten watercolors at the Kunsthaus, Zurich, October 1–29, 1916. On this occasion, unlike in his most recent group shows (Zurich 1913, Paris and Neuchâtel 1912), he omitted his architectural series, "Langage de Pierres," including only landscapes, some buildings, still lifes, and a memory image of Turkey. For the first time, therefore, he was exhibiting as a painter—as an artist—rather than as an architectural student displaying his travel drawings.

Actually his concurrent activity as watercolorist underwent a hiatus at this time, both in number of works produced and their originality. Visual reality, rather than fantasy, once again prevailed. Landscapes predominate rather than the symbolic memory images that were so prevalent in 1912–14. This, however, was followed by a new burst of activity in 1917 (after his arrival in Paris) when imagery, although often inspired by reality, was profoundly transmuted by his mind. This would undergo further modification in 1918 after his meeting with Amédée Ozenfant.

Ritter's impact on this change is obvious. His residency in Switzerland facilitated frequent meetings when they drew and painted together, sessions at which Ritter's conservative taste prevailed. Several of the India ink and charcoal landscapes, dated

53. As for his own reading, Jeanneret acquired from the estate of his cousin Jeanne Soutter, whose funeral he attended, Goethe, *Faust;* Michelet, *Jeanne d'Arc;* Musset, *Poésies;* Plutarch, *Manuel moral;* Poe, *Eureka;* Wordsworth, *Grèce,* all of which he inscribed in September, 1916.

54. Two sketches studying the proposed entrance to the exhibition appear on pages 30 and 33 of Sketchbook A1.

**Fig. 401.** *Landscape,* signed and dated "Ch E Jt 1916." 32 × 48 cm. Gouache on paper. (FLC 4072)

January 23 and 24, 1916, are seen on the first pages of Sketchbook A1.[55] In black and white they reproduce well, but Jeanneret's watercolors and gouaches, due to their emphasis on color rather than form, often look smudgy and murky by comparison. Figure 401, signed and dated 1916, is a case in point; the building in the foreground merges with the forest as well as the hills beyond while the clouds are dense despite generous amounts of white paper showing through. *La Tène,* one of the watercolors exhibited in Zurich in October 1916, is somewhat brighter thanks to the cloudless sky being reflected in the water, yet none of these painted landscapes merit much praise as pictorial compositions (fig. 402).

Often his pencil or charcoal renderings are more sensitive to the shape of the page, such as the portrait of Ritter dated "Landeron, 23 janvier 1916" (fig. 403). Where outline is equally important as color, as in *Nude on the Beach* (postdated 1915, see figure 297, Chapter 9), which is a painting previously discussed in connection with Matisse, Jeanneret's watercolors can be "read" with greater ease. But because Ritter was no friend of contemporary art, we can conclude that he vigorously disapproved of these

55. I would propose that this region, especially the landscape shown on page 5 and dated January 23, 1916, is the basis for one of Jeanneret's most beautiful purist pictures which, contrary to typical purist subject matter, is a penciled landscape with a lake in the foreground and, I believe, the same mountain chain behind (see fig. 431). This is probably the region recorded on page 213 of Sketchbook A3 which covers, in spite of its cover dating, the period 1917–23. Incidently, the room interior on page 12 of A1, following these landscapes, is probably Ritter's library.

**Fig. 402.** *La Tène.* Postdated "1915 ou 16?" Exhibited at Kunsthaus, Zurich, October 1–29, 1916. Pencil and watercolor on paper. 35.5 × 42.5 cm. (FLC 4088)

fauvist or expressionistic works and probably this explains their reduced number among Jeanneret's paintings during 1915–16.

In Jeanneret's unpublished sketchbook, called "1916–22," there are numerous pencil sketches from this period.[56] One, on page 15, shows a *Nude Kneeling on the Beach while Kindling a Fire.* This is surely the source for the previously mentioned watercolor, while page 17—*Three Nudes on the Beach Around a Fire*—corresponds to yet another watercolor (FLC 4078). In all probability the first twenty-one drawings in this sketchbook represent a single outing since all scenes are interrelated, including those of sailboats and ferry docks (fig. 404); presumably it was Jeanneret's choice to depict all figures in the nude.

The next several pages emphasize vernacular structures, especially those with stairs set against their outside walls. A similar building is recorded in Sketchbook A1 (p. 37) and dated 1916. These are the obvious source, along with Jeanneret's adaptation of the so-called Haunted House at Le Locle (see fig. 273), for Jeanneret's exterior stairs at his

56. This sketchbook, as previously mentioned, was not included by the FLC in the publication *Le Corbusier Sketchbooks* (New York: Architecture History Foundation, 1981). Its sole internal date is November 1916, i.e., for the drawing of Tony Garnier's house. My pagination is that of Jeanneret, not the renumbering done by the FLC.

**Fig. 403.** *Portrait of William Ritter,* dated "Landeron, 23 janvier 1916." Pencil on heavy paper. 27.5 × 41 cm. (FLC 3783)

**Fig. 404.** *Ferry Dock,* ca. 1916. Observe the vigor and confidence with which this quick sketch is made as well as the care given to its composition. Lead pencil in Sketchbook 1916–22, p. 33. 23.3 × 15.5 cm. (FLC)

Citrohan houses of the early 1920s (fig. 436). Next is the only dated drawing in Sketchbook "1916–22," Tony Garnier's home (November 8, 1916), followed by Perret's Paris penthouse, several purist sketches and, after a break in chronology, Jeanneret's trip to Venice. Though little known, this sketchbook is of great importance.

By 1917 Jeanneret had largely achieved his objectives in La Chaux-de-Fonds. Ritter, at the time of the Voyage d'Orient, had urged him to renounce his provincial home and move directly to Paris. Jeanneret, however, felt it necessary to stretch his wings and prove himself before moving to the metropolis. He succeeded. The Villa Schwob gave him both the confidence and the credentials that he needed. Moreover he had proven himself as a furniture designer, published his first book, honed his writing skills, and with increasing seriousness turned to the art of painting. Likewise he had fulfilled his obligation to L'Eplattenier, in spite of its unexpected consequences. Thus he could leave La Chaux-de-Fonds with a clear conscience, and from a position of strength.

# IV

## POSTSCRIPT

# THE TRANSITIONAL YEARS

*Jeanneret's Move to Paris*

*1917–1920*

T his postscript will endeavor to bridge the gap between Jeanneret's departure from La Chaux-de-Fonds in January 1917 and the time when, nearly four years later, he assumed the pseudonym Le Corbusier at the age of thirty-three.

I call it a postscript rather than a chapter for various reasons, the most obvious being that it postdates Jeanneret's formative years in La Chaux-de-Fonds which are the stated concern of this book. Equally important is the fact that the years 1917–20 are so complex and the documentation so rich that a truly comprehensive discussion would result in this being the longest chapter of the book—almost a book in and of itself. And because these years are relatively unknown—with the exception of events surrounding the creation of purism in painting late in 1918—it would be unfortunate to leave the reader without a rather detailed survey that unites the La Chaux-de-Fonds years with the date when Le Corbusier and so many of his biographers have chosen to begin their discussion of his career. The *Oeuvre Complète* lists his earliest built works as the villa at Vaucresson and the Ozenfant studio-house in Paris, both of 1922–23, thereby surreptitiously excising the first seventeen years of his architectural career. In similar fashion he feigned to have begun painting only in 1918 which, of course, is not true.

The real unsung hero in Jeanneret's career was Max Du Bois. Without Du Bois Jeanneret's biography would read quite differently than it does today. For one thing, he probably would not have moved to Paris in 1917; this might have precluded his partici-

**Fig. 405.** Ch. E. Jeanneret, self-portrait, summer 1917. Page 31 in Cahier 10. Lead pencil and watercolor wash. 33.5 × 26.5 cm. (FLC 5131)

pation in purist painting. And upon arriving in Paris he definitely would not have had an office, a secretary, and architectural commissions awaiting him. Neither would he have been given directorship of a manufacturing plant producing building materials. Nor would he have met the bankers and men of business who were Du Bois' friends—men such as Raoul La Roche for whom Jeanneret built the famous villa in Paris (1923–24) and advised on the purchase of contemporary paintings (a collection now in the Basel museum), and from whose largess he benefited on several occasions (such as financial backing for *L'Esprit Nouveau*).

However, one searches in vain for Du Bois' name among Le Corbusier's voluminous writings. Nowhere can it be found. It has been excised with the same assiduous care as his early years as architect and painter. Why? Apparently for the same reason, that of creating the image of a precocious, self-made man. Jeanneret owed far too much to Max Du Bois to let it become public knowledge. L'Eplattenier, in certain respects, served a similar role but it is one thing to acknowledge one's teacher and quite another to admit dependence on one's own more proficient contemporary.[1]

1. Another factor may have been Jeanneret's financial indebtedness to Du Bois. This I have not researched but know through conversations with Du Bois, who maintained that Jeanneret owed him a good

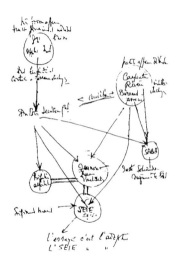

**Fig. 406.** Sketch by Max Du Bois showing how Jeanneret related to the various interlocking holding companies which he served. His architectural office is at lower center and the Briqueterie d'Alfortville, which he administered, is at left, both being within the umbrella group Société d'entreprises industrielles et d'études (SEIE) at bottom center. The Société d'application industriel is listed above and SABA (Société d'applications du béton armé) to the right. (Brooks collection)

Du Bois was an excellent organization man. He was quick to see opportunities and seize upon them, and skilled at creating interlocking corporate entities. When explaining to me how he created a place for Jeanneret in the overall scheme of his organizations, he made the sketch in figure 406. Du Bois is at center left, Edgar Louis Bornand at center right, the former concerned with developing a network for the production and distribution of electricity, the latter with electrical installations. The "bureau d'architecte" was established to provide a place, and a job, for Jeanneret (lower center) to whom certain construction projects would be funneled. Jeanneret reported to the Société d'entreprises industrielles et d'études (SEIE, bottom center) which Du Bois established as an umbrella organization to include Jeanneret, the concrete block factory at Alfortville (to the left of Jeanneret on the organizational chart), and other undertakings.

SABA (Société d'applications du béton armé; far right), administered by Bornand, constructed buildings, factories, dams, and also the concrete poles used for electric transmission lines. However, the Alfortville operation was not part of SABA (although they bought many of the blocks) even though Jeanneret's "bureau d'architecte" directly served SABA when architectural (aesthetic) matters were involved or when supervision of construction was needed. Otherwise SABA depended on its own engineer, Juste Schneider, who, via Du Bois, had done all the concrete calculations for Jeanneret's Pont Butin, Dom-ino, as well as some for the Villa Favre-Jacob. Du Bois' principal concern was with another interrelated holding company, Société d'applications industrielles, whose generating plant at Alfortville provided the raw material for the brick factory.

The Briqueterie d'Alfortville (near the confluence of the Seine and Marne southeast of Paris) was the brainchild of Du Bois. The coal-burning generators of his Société d'applications industrielles left a residue of cinders and clinkers that had to be hauled away at some expense. Therefore Du Bois decided to recycle this free material by adding cement to the cinders and pressing them into solid blocks.[2] The umbrella group plus local bankers provided the initial capital (Jeanneret later invested considerable sums) and Jeanneret, long interested in business ventures related to the building trades, was put in charge of the brickworks (administrateur délégué). He envisioned making a fortune and then retiring in order to paint. However this, and all his other business ventures, failed, leaving him in financial straits.

Jeanneret's new duties, finalized during his October 1916 trip to Paris, were assumed in January 1917, although for the next nine months he maintained an office in La Chaux-de-Fonds while completing work on the Villa Schwob. Thus he commuted

deal of money (I failed to record the amount) from ca. 1920 but which was never repaid. Du Bois eventually brought suit in Geneva, Switzerland (as both men were Swiss), and the court ruled in his favor; but Jeanneret pleaded bankruptcy and did not pay.

2. An interesting account of the history and methods of fabricating concrete block will be found in H. H. Rice and W. M. Torrance, *The Manufacture of Concrete Blocks and Their Use in Building Construction* (New York: The Engineering News Publishing Co., 1906). The process obviously was not new.

between two offices, initially going to La Chaux-de-Fonds at least once a month but thereafter going with decreasing frequency until October 4.[3]

His initial business trip to France, of about ten days, began at Imphy near Nevers in central France where in Sketchbook 1916–22 (p. 73) there are sketches of the "type of workers' houses built at Imphy, staircase of wood." His interest in exterior staircases was first noted in 1912 (The Haunted House near Le Locle) and they often reappear, as at Saintes (1917) and in his 1920s projects (such as Citrohan) and buildings (Villa Stein). His real mission at Imphy, however, concerned a plan by SABA, yet a month later he was still awaiting a follow-up from his visit.[4] Jeanneret frequently made trips to various parts of France for SABA but these seldom were to supervise construction of his own designs.

In Paris he quickly located an apartment in the Latin Quarter at 20, rue Jacob which was in the former eighteenth-century town-house of Adrienne Lecouvreur, a fact that he delighted in and often mentioned. From the erstwhile servants' quarters on the top floor he looked out on trees and garden while on the inside he painted his "salon" white and his "chambre" black, carefully selecting furniture for both. When Albert moved to Paris in October 1918, Edouard relinquished this space to his brother and moved to the floor below. In any case his address remained the same until he occupied an apartment building of his own design at 24, rue Nungesser-et-Coli in 1933 in the more fashionable Boulogne district of Paris.

His office was located at 13, rue de Belzunce (a location he disliked) until October 1917, when SABA moved into a remodeled building at 29 bis, rue d'Astorg (near Place St. Augustin) where he rented a spacious 150 square meters on the fourth floor, for which he paid a tidy 3,500 francs per month. His telegraph address was JEANARCH.

All in all, this brief January trip to Paris was quite successful, and after only two weeks at home he was again in France where 1917 proved to be, architecturally speaking, his busiest and most fruitful year prior to the 1920s. It was also the only year during a five-year period when anything of his got built, minor though these projects were.

The first was a water tower at Podensac (Gironde) southeast of Bordeaux (figs. 407, 408). The commission was apparently SABA's due both to its nature and because Jeanneret used the SABA letterhead rather than his own. Monsieur Thévenot of the Château de Chavat was Jeanneret's contact, rather than a corporation, which perhaps

3. By letter of September 26, 1917, Jeanneret informed his Swiss clients that his La Chaux-de-Fonds office was now closed and that enquiries should henceforth be sent to Paris. Gautier, *Le Corbusier,* p. 37, reports that Jeanneret initially intended to move to Frankfurt, not Paris, but on the spur of the moment decided on France. The facts set out in the last three chapters completely refute this claim.

4. "J'ai reçu aujourd'hui de SABA le plan d'Imphy. Je ferai une étude préliminaire et irai de suite à Paris-Imphy" (to Du Bois, December 9, 1916). The lack of any follow-up is mentioned to his parents on February 14, 1917.

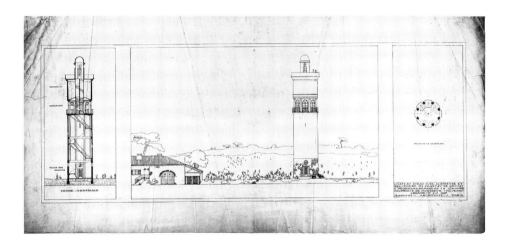

explains the "extras" in an otherwise utilitarian design; aesthetics was a real concern.

Most striking is the tower's cylindrical form, lacking the bulbous head usually associated with such designs. It is crowned by what looks like a simplified Doric capital, and the cylindrical shape of the tower is echoed in the engaged columns of the gloriette (a secluded belvedere designed to catch the view and summer breeze). The design of this tower, with its open arcade topped by a circular drum (containing the water reservoir), recalls the Galata Tower sketched by Jeanneret while in Turkey (fig. 192 in Chapter 8). At Podensac, however, he chose classical elements in a chaste manner that almost belies the ruggedness of the reinforced concrete frame; an interior staircase winds up the inside wall.

In a letter to his parents of February 14, 1917, he announced the completion of several "seductive" sketches for the château d'eau. Our illustration is probably one of these (fig. 409). It differs from the finished work in the absence of the circular staircase at the center; when I climbed the tower in 1974 I found only a ladder thrust through the circular hole that leads to the deck above.

Edgar Louis Bornand, "administrateur délégué" of SABA, provided Jeanneret with a letter (April 7, 1917) as a laissez-passer while traveling in wartime France. It clarifies certain of his activities. "This will certify that Mr. Ch.E. Jeanneret, Architect attached to our Company, supervises for our Company construction work for the power-station at Saintes and the hydroelectric works at L'Isle Jourdain (Vienne). He is also responsible, from an architectural standpoint, for the construction of buildings that we are executing at the arsenal at Toulouse. All these works are directly concerned with the national defense."

The hydroelectric plant and dam at L'Isle Jourdain on the Vienne were under construction between 1917 and 1921. Jeanneret obviously saw the intended design and apparently utilized it as inspiration for his own perspective which, aesthetically speaking,

**Fig. 409.** Château d'eau, interior view of the "gloriette" in sketch by Jeanneret, February 1917. India ink on paper. 34 × 55 cm. (FLC 22407)

is certainly superior. Both schemes have a similar division of windows separated by giant-order pilasters, yet Jeanneret's has an assertiveness of massing as well as clarity that is absent in the executed design (fig. 410).

In April 1917, the director of a large company (not specified) asked Jeanneret for a study of workers' housing appropriate for three electric power station sites located at Saintes (Charente-Maritime), L'Isle Jourdain, and La Rochelle. Two small buildings were specified, one containing an administrative office on the ground floor with an apartment for the foreman above, and the other, of three storeys (combined with a garage and forge) for the families of two watchmen.[5] In style these somewhat recall his Dom-ino units what with their slightly projecting slab roofs and occasional strip windows, but the system of construction is entirely different due to the proposed load-bearing walls (figs. 411, 412).

The plan of the three-storey unit is unusual in that the ground level is reserved for garage, forge, and storage with the living accommodations above, an idea that may have derived from Auguste Perret.[6] The room layout foretells the Type C plan at Saint-Nicolas-d'Allliermont later that same year. Note the exterior staircase.[7]

5. This description is contained in a letter of August 16, 1917, to Auguste Perret.

6. See Le Corbusier-Saugnier (i.e., Ozenfant), "Maisons en Série," *L'Esprit Nouveau,* no. 13 (December 1921), pp. 1525–42, where Perret's workers' housing has an above-ground basement as well as exterior stairways. Jeanneret's Saintes perspective is also published therein with the caption "Construites comme des bâtiments d'usine, ces maisons bénéficient de l'esthétique de l'usine" (p. 1530). A study sketch for this housing exists in Cahier 10, FLC 5114.

7. Concerning Saintes and the subsequent architectural projects leading up to the designs for Pessac, see the exhibition catalogue by Brian Bruce Taylor, *Le Corbusier at Pessac: The Search for Systems and Standards in Design of Low Cost Housing* (Cambridge: Harvard University, 1972).

**Fig. 410.** Project for hydroelectric plant and dam, L'Isle Jourdain, France, 1917. Photograph of lost drawing. 30 × 45 cm. (FLC 31455)

**Fig. 411.** Project: Administration offices and workers' housing for Saintes, France. Signed and dated Paris, April 1917. India ink on paper. 37 × 55 cm. (FLC 19314)

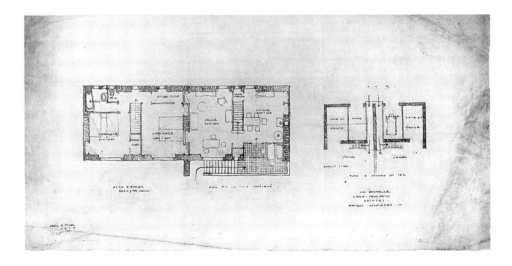

**Fig. 412.** Project: Plan for workers' housing at Saintes, L'Isle Jourdain, and La Rochelle, France. The living quarters are raised and the ground level used for storage. Signed and dated Paris, April 25, 1917. India ink on paper. 37 × 74 cm. (FLC 19315)

Painting, during 1917, was of extreme importance to Jeanneret, and as the year progressed he recognized it as the central objective of his life. All other activities—architecture, entrepreneurship, writing—helped provide financial support for painting but he often resented their intrusion on his time. Frequently he surreptitiously left his office in the afternoon in order to paint; likewise he painted evenings until midnight as well as weekends. He became obsessed by this desire.

However, despite his commitment to painting, no substantial body of works from 1917 exists. Were they destroyed? Apparently so. On October 31, 1917, for example,

**Fig. 413.** Chartres cathedral. Presumably sketched on April 30, 1917. Lead pencil and watercolor wash on paper. 26.2 × 33.6 cm. (FLC 5118)

**Fig. 414.** *Nude with Tulips,* postdated 1917. Lead pencil and gouache on paper. 35.5 × 51 cm. (FLC 4504)

he wrote that he was working on his fifth oil and that he was no longer disconcerted by the process.[8] Yet the first existing oil dates from more than a year thereafter.

Concerning watercolors, the major cache is in Cahier 10, a sketchbook with perforated pages (33.5 × 26.5 cm.) that are still in place. Therein are 66 designs, including ten made while at Chartres during an April 29–30 weekend there (fig. 413).[9] These, however, are basically sketches rather than finished paintings.

A gouache, twice the size of those in Cahier 10, is *Nude with Tulips;* it embodies many characteristics typical of Jeanneret's 1917 work (fig. 414). The figure, her body flattened and distorted and lacking any sensuality, sits at a table with various objects about. Her face, and especially the purplish-gray shading around her eyes, implies the artist is an admirer of Kees Van Dongen. Meanwhile the everyday items in the foreground anticipate the subject matter of purism, as does the manner in which they are rendered; bottle and glass are in perspective yet simultaneously their rims are seen from above. The dish is also observed from above. At the left is the architect's drafting table while at the right a vase of contorted red tulips; a red and yellow tulip is held between the woman's fingers. The heavy application of gouache suggests that oils might have been a more congenial medium.

Jeanneret's still lifes, using the more traditional subject matter of fruit, flowers, and vase arranged in a Cézanne-like manner, also suffer, as in previous years, from excessive impasto. This results in a loss of clarity that detracts from their tactile, geometric forms (fig. 415).

When using the instruments familiar to an architect—pen and ink and watercolor wash—his results were inevitably superior than when employing gouache. The shorthand method of the architect retains the immediacy and spontaneity of the moment and therefore had been used by Jeanneret during most of his European travels. Compare *Two Lesbians,* a subject matter of which he was particularly fond (fig. 416), with the works in gouache where the message tends to be blurred and largely lost. His enthusiasm for Matisse probably encouraged a more linear technique. And as for the theme, the Ritter correspondence (February 19, 1917) perhaps implies that he visited a local brothel.

In 1913–14 his memory and fantasy pictures had featured Greece and Turkey, but

8. On October 31, 1917, he wrote in his personal journal: "J'ai peint d'après Roger v. d. Weyden, une Déposition de Croix, avec mes couleurs. C'est ma cinquième huile; le procédé ne me déconcerte plus." What happened to this and his other oils? Ozenfant had destroyed his early paintings, and perhaps Jeanneret followed suit.

9. Jeanneret made lithographs (an unusual medium for him) of six different views of Chartres. These were pulled in five numbered, signed and dated (1917) copies plus one proof. In September 1919, he sent one, or possibly more, sets to August Klipstein to sell at the best possible price. The FLC still retains two or three prints of each view. Obviously quite proud of them, Le Corbusier published two in *Creation Is a Patient Search* (1960), pp. 46, 47, and on p. 44 *Le Pont Neuf,* which is another lithograph prepared at the same date. The latter, however, exists in two states of five numbered copies each.

those of 1917 dwell on Italy. These include a homage to Michelangelo as well as Masaccio, a *Birth of Venus,* and recollections of Venice ("Je vais peindre des souvenirs de Venice . . . à la lampe, comme toujours" to parents, November 12, 1917). Also there are fantastic cityscapes including Paris filled with palm trees painted while he was suffering from the winter cold (color plate XI). Tulips often adorn these paintings yet their symbolism is not explained; in all likelihood they symbolize Turkey and the Orient since "tulip" stems from the Turkish word for turban.

Occasionally a tulip is the subject of a painting. In figure 417, which is from Cahier 10, a giant tulip rises through billowing clouds while the broken Venetian campanile topples in the background. Overhead a weird dragon looks back upon the scene.

*L'Italienne,* which is equal in size to *Nude with Tulips,* differs stylistically from the latter and thus is probably a later work (fig. 418, color plate XII). Postdated 1917, it more likely is from the first eight months of 1918, a period from which no dated works survive. The colors are unnatural, the large, simplified face being blue-gray, chocolate brown, and white with deep blue-purple around the eyes. Similar colors exist throughout except for highlights in yellow and the red and yellow tulip at the bottom right. Fragments of Italian cities, primarily Florence, whirl in the background. The forms are now more distinct than before; this is due to the painted lines and edges as well as to broad areas of a single color.

Jeanneret was always a colorist at heart, and although his correspondence still speaks of "my colors," his once bold, symbolic use of lemon yellow is now much restricted and his rich, vibrant fauve colors appear far less often (one exception being his post–April 30 memory image of Chartres cathedral [FLC 5126]). Thus, by 1917 his colors are more muted.

**Fig. 415.** *Still Life with Fruit and Flowers.* Page 41 in Cahier 10 and therefore later than August 1917. Lead pencil with gouache and watercolor. 33.5 × 26.5 cm. (FLC 5141)

**Fig. 416.** *Two Lesbians.* Page 63 in Cahier 10. Pen and ink with watercolor wash. 33.5 × 26.5 cm. (FLC 5163)

**Fig. 417.** *A Dream.* Page 60 of Cahier 10. Watercolor. 33.5 × 26.5 cm. (FLC 5160)

**Fig. 418.** *L'Italienne.* Postdated 1917 but more likely early 1918. Pencil and gouache on paper. 35.5 × 51 cm. (FLC 4504)

During the last week of April 1917 Jeanneret had visited Chartres and sketched his proposals for buildings at Saintes. By early May he was in Normandy surveying the site at Saint-Nicholas-d'Aliermont, near Dieppe, for workers' housing for the clock-makers Duverdrey and Bloquel (subsequently Réveils Bayard). This was Jeanneret's own commission, not SABA's, and apparently came to him through contacts at La Chaux-de-Fonds or Monsieur Thévenot of Podensac, who was an official in the company.

The decision to respect regional architectural styles was certainly the client's choice. As a result Jeanneret spent time sketching vernacular buildings near the site, studying their massing, roof shapes, fenestration, and materials. These he recorded in Sketchbook A3, one sketch being dated May 9. Thus we can identify many features, in Jeanneret's design, that come from local buildings.

One of his sketches shows the highway site, opposite to which a subsidiary road enters at the left (fig. 419). The problem is how to enter the deep, narrow plot of land—should the entrance occur at the junction of two roads or along the communal route? Arrows indicated the choices, accompanied by the words "entrée ou"—enter here or here. Ultimately he utilized both options, thereby creating a small community plaza not unlike the English examples he had studied when researching "La Construction des Villes."

His several plot plans differ in layout, and in accordance with the amount of land acquired. The number of housing units varies from 26 to 46. Dated between May 15 and June 20, 1917, all plans have basic features in common. None have meandering streets like Jeanneret proposed for Arnold Beck in 1914. All have a single axial street, almost like a miniature Champs-Elysées, running through the trapezium plot. A playground (Place de Jeux) terminates this axis and one building is set at right angles in

**Fig. 419.** Saint-Nicholas-d'Aliermont, France. The junction of rue Vaillancourt and rue Robert Le Franc to the right of which Jeanneret proposed his layout for workers' housing. Pencil drawing in Sketchbook A3, p. 158, May 9, 1917. 13 × 20.8 cm.

order to close the view. A small service road leads to the street behind (figs. 420, 421).[10]

Jeanneret designed several house types which he designated type A (fig. 422), B, and C (fig. 423). Each went through various stages of development, primarily in the evolution of their plans. His previous reading of Foville and Janet held him in good stead in this regard, including their advocacy of adhering to regional architectural styles. Each house type referred to size, not to style; they might be one-and-a-half or two storeys high and the number of rooms varied with each type.

Jeanneret did not propose the Dom-ino system of concrete construction. Instead he urged his client, M. Duverdrey, to acquire two machines from Pasquier, Kiefer, and Bizot, engineers and contractors in Lausanne, Switzerland, plus five workers to operate them, to manufacture hollow concrete blocks on the site. However the client did not approve. Traditional bricks were used instead.

Type C, the smallest among the duplexes, was the only type built. Similar to Type A (see figure 422) in being one-and-a-half storeys high, it contains two rather than three rooms on both floors. Figure 423 shows the plan of the residence to the left in my photo (fig. 424). The careful alignment of the deep-set doors and windows, the string course above, and the dentils under the cornice, give both unity and dignity to this small yet well-proportioned design. Its symmetry, with carefully balanced parts and emphasis on the center rather than the flanks, imbues the design with a certain classical sensibility.

10. See Brooks, ed., *The Le Corbusier Archive,* vol. I, pp. 159–91, where forty-four of Jeanneret's plans, perspectives, and working drawings for Saint-Nicholas are illustrated.

**Fig. 420.** Saint-Nicholas-d'Aliermont. Final plot plan dated June 20, 1917, showing forty-three housing units. Gelatin print and pencil. 60 × 105 cm. (FLC 22376)

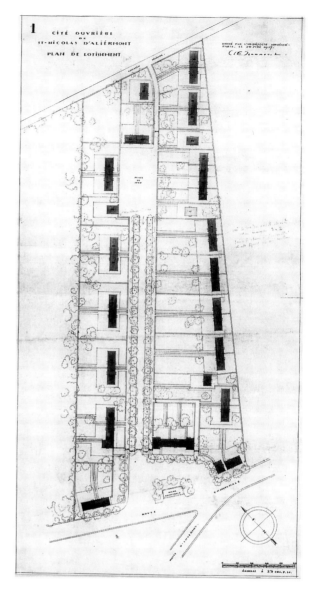

The efficient plan, with its central stairway, will remind Americans of the Cape Cod cottage. An unusual feature, however, is the penetration of the top stairs into the floorspace of the upstairs landing, thereby providing the hall with a sense of openness belying its actual size. An ingenious convoluted railing protects the open stairwell from the sides. Minimal sanitary arrangements are shown but these were augmented in the final design.

Figure 425 illustrates the intended interior of a foreman's house: Type B. The exaggerated perspective makes this very small room look large. Note the exposed beam

**Fig. 421.** Saint-Nicholas-d'Aliermont. Perspective studies of plot plan. Pen and ink. 21 × 27 cm. (FLC 19328)

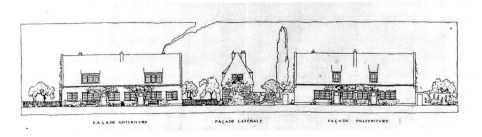

**Fig. 422.** Saint-Nicholas d'Aliermont. Front, side, and rear elevations of proposed Type A double house. June 20, 1917. India ink. 80 × 25 cm. (FLC 22405)

ceiling, a feature Jeanneret used in remodeling his own rented farmhouse in 1912 and also proposed for Felix Klipstein in 1914. In fact, all but one of his housing projects during 1917–1920 specify the use of exposed beam ceilings.

Following completion of the first unit at Saint-Nicholas, the project was abandoned because of rising costs and other difficulties. His final construction drawings were dated October 15, 1917. To reduce expenses he had already consented to accept a flat fee of 9,000 francs rather than 5 percent as envisioned in the original contract.

Jeanneret had previously met Georges Benoit-Levy, the prolific French writer and founder of the French Garden City Association. The latter obligingly wrote two similar but often inaccurate articles concerning the plan and designs for Saint-Nicholas-d'Aliermont. Entitled "A French Garden-Hamlet," one was published in America in

**Fig. 423.** Saint-Nicholas-d'Aliermont. Plan of Type C house dated July 23, 1917. India ink and pencil. 26 × 50 cm. (FLC 19326)

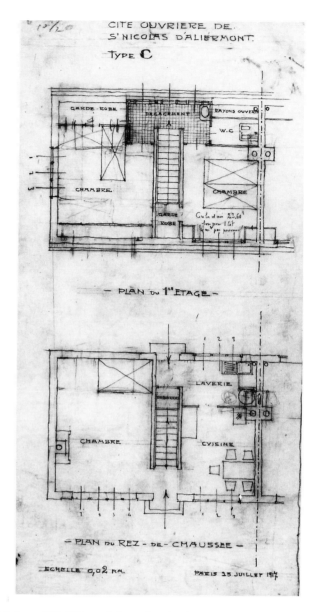

*The Survey* for February 2, 1918 (pp. 488–89), and the other in the British *Town Planning Review* (vol. 7, nos. 3 and 4, April 1918, pp. 251–52), but this publicity apparently had no fruitful results.

In November 1917, assisted by the Danish engineer J. Reeh, Jeanneret agreed to design an abattoir (slaughterhouse) in association with a small group of investors known as Société nouvelle du froid industriel and headed by Louis Berthier. They were in competition against two other consortiums and the client was the military, through the appropriate French ministry. The deadline was set for Christmas Day.

**Fig. 424.** Saint-Nicholas-d'Aliermont. Workers' housing (double house). This is the only building built by Jeanneret at Saint-Nicholas. The construction is of brick. 1974 photo. (Photo by author)

**Fig. 425.** Saint-Nicholas-d'Aliermont. Living room of proposed Type B house. Dated June 20, 1917. Gelatin print. 40 × 60 cm. (FLC 22378)

After inspecting the site at Challuy near Nevers,[11] Jeanneret wrote his parents on November 22: "At the moment I am in a competition involving three parties for the military engineers for a large American abattoir. . . . The solution is the opposite of European methods, and it is surprisingly simple and logical. Truly we [Europeans] have our eyes in the back of our heads." Then he went on to say: "My life is a paradox; exhausting. By day I am an American (as this designation seems timely) [and] read Taylor and practice Taylorism."

11. "Sur le terrain à Nevers, j'avais eu l'idée d'ensemble, je l'avais exprimée en un croquis au wagon restaurant. C'était une bonne idée. Plus le projet avance, tout s'éclaircit, s'ordonne, s'organise" (Jeanneret's personal journal, December 29, 1917, wherein he devotes several pages to discussing the history of the project).

Jeanneret, of course, was referring to the American mechanical engineer Frederick Winslow Taylor whose *Principles of Scientific Organization of Factories* had been published in France in 1912. Jeanneret, like many Europeans at the time, was fascinated with the new ideas of mass production (cf. Dom-ino) which included the efficiency of conveyor belts, a device that totally controlled his slaughterhouse designs. Likewise he ascribed his architectural forms to America, saying: "It is an architecture coming from America and Chicago."[12]

The abattoir for Challuy was designed as three separate buildings interconnected by bridges and conveyor belts. The first unit contained cattle stalls, the next the slaughterhouse, and the third the refrigeration plant. Each structure had its own distinctive fenestration (fig. 426). Although rational, this arrangement was not compact.

Within days Jeanneret was designing yet another abattoir, this one for Garchizy, also in central France (figs. 427, 428). Here the three basic functions were combined under a single roof, each differentiated by its wall treatment and fenestration. Thus the lowest level of animal stalls had a staccato rhythm of post and beam construction combined with small, high windows. The slaughterhouse, above, was distinguished by its horizontal ribbon windows and unbroken strips of walls, these emphasizing the continuity and flow of the conveyor belts inside. To the right, the windowless box is the refrigeration plant, its severity somewhat relieved by engaged piers rising to the roof. Uniting these two blocks is a narrower unit with high strip windows; it contains staircases and an elevator.

This design was of capital significance for Le Corbusier's future, especially in the years after World War II. For here lie the seeds of his famous Unité d'Habitation, the first being built at Marseilles in 1947–52. Others soon followed in France as well as Germany. Like suburban villages, these structures served interrelated functions—housing for people (rather than pigs and cows), places of work, shops, recreational areas, schools, etc., and as at Garchizy each of these functions had a different expression on the exterior of the building. Indeed, the bird's-eye view of Garchizy (see figure 428) could easily be mistaken for a Unité d'Habitation.

Jeanneret maintained a lively interest in abattoir design for several years. On November 15, 1918, he erased and redated the Garchizy plans and substituted the name "Abattoir Frigorifique de Bordeaux," although nothing is known of the circumstances surrounding either of these identical designs. The unsigned copy of a contract dated May 1, 1918, established the Compagnie industrielle du froid (CIF) with Louis Berthier as chief executive. The partnership comprised three companies, one for refrigeration, one

12. The full paragraph reads: "J'étudie en ce moment un grand abattoir. Aurais-je deviné que ce problème est magnifique et promoteur de véritable architecture? C'est une architecture venue d'Amérique et Chicago et ses boîtes de conserve me permettront de créer un château de la Loire" (personal journal, November 18, 1917).

**Fig. 426.** Project: Abattoir at Challuy. Side elevation. Signed and dated December 25, 1917. India ink and pencil. 49 × 159 cm. (FLC 22352)

for mechanical equipment, and SABA for construction. A receipt dated June 27, 1918, acknowledges Jeanneret's payment of 1,250 francs as his first-quarter remittance for ten shares at 500 francs each. The two other stockholders from SABA, Edgar Bornand and Max Du Bois, also owned ten shares each.

A year thereafter Jeanneret was still actively researching abattoirs. This we learn from a card to his parents of July 8, 1919: "Been traveling for 5 days, to Lyon and Auvergne, concerning abattoirs! . . . Saw Tony Garnier several times. . . ." Yet in spite of all this effort, nothing was ever built. Finally, in April 1925, the CIF was liquidated. Although the business venture proved abortive, the germinal idea of these designs lingered with Jeanneret throughout his life.

When Le Corbusier published the first volume of *Oeuvre Complète* in 1930, he devoted two full pages to his abattoir designs. In later editions, however, these pages were omitted—the *only* pre-1920 pages to be altered or omitted in this seminal work. Why? As a person who frequently covered his own tracks, was he concealing the source of his Unité d'Habitation design, even though it derived from his own early work?

While considering the interlocking corporate structures created by Du Bois and his colleagues, wherein a "bureau d'architecte" was established to provide work for Jeanneret in Paris, we discussed the origins of the Briqueterie d'Alfortville (fig. 429).[13] This factory, intended to manufacture concrete blocks from the by-product of Du Bois' coal-burning generators, was under the aegis of the Société d'entreprises industrielles et d'études (SEIE), and while it was the first corporate body Jeanneret presided over as

13. The letterhead for their invoice provides much useful data:

Société d'Entreprises Industrielles et d'Études
Section: Briqueterie d'Alfortville
et Matériaux de Constructions

Société anonyme au capital de 250,000 francs.

Siège Social
Paris 29 bis, rue d'Astorg
Adr. Télégr. JEANARCH-PARIS
Usine d'Alfortville 15, rue des Peupliers

The machines used at Alfortville presumably were those proposed for Saint-Nicholas; Max Du Bois informed me (April 3, 1978) that the presses did indeed come from Switzerland. Jeanneret's earliest blocks were apparently solid but later he produced hollow blocks as well. The main disadvantage of all these unfired bricks was their capillary transmission of moisture.

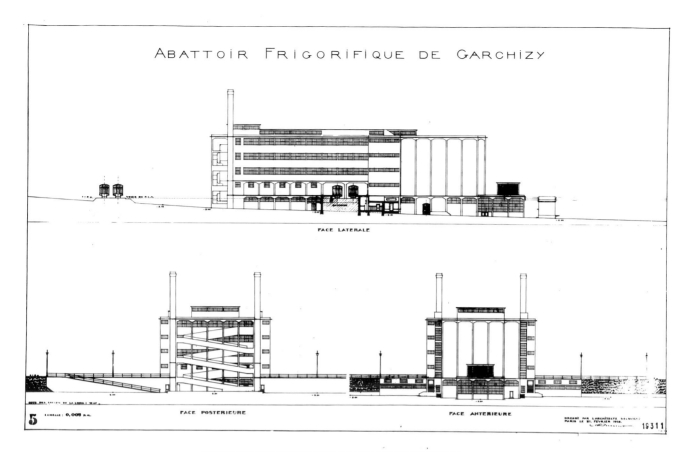

ABATTOIR FRIGORIFIQUE DE GARCHIZY

FACE LATERALE

FACE POSTERIEURE

FACE ANTERIEURE

**Fig. 427.** Project: Abattoir at Garchizy. Signed and dated February 21, 1918. India ink and pencil. 67 × 101 cm. (FLC 19311)

**Fig. 428.** Project: Abattoir at Garchizy. Bird's-eye view. Signed and dated January 15, 1918. India ink and pencil. 67 × 94 cm. (FLC 19309)

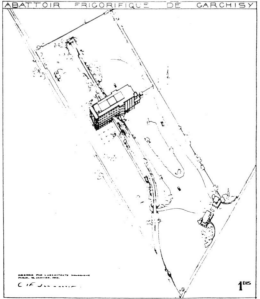

ABATTOIR FRIGORIFIQUE DE GARCHISY

administrateur délégué it was certainly not the last. Indeed, within just over a year he became chief executive of SEIE itself.

Jeanneret launched into the business world with great enthusiasm, optimism, and a romantic vision. He enjoyed the idea of being a capitalist and of wheeling and dealing in money.[14] He looked forward to quickly amassing a fortune and being able to retire and paint. He regaled in the beauty of machines, the smooth, cylindrical form of smokestacks, the engines of transport for rail, road, and river, as well as the physiques of brawny men at work.[15]

But the realities of business soon destroyed his romantic image. The Briquetterie d'Alfortville is a case in point. It began production in December 1917 after long delays. By April he had invested 50,000 francs yet had 30,000 francs in unsold merchandise. In May he enjoyed major sales but by July he was forced to borrow 35,000 francs, due August 15, which he paid off by canvassing the local Swiss community. By September he had four million blocks on hand yet bought new machinery for 70,000 francs that would produce twenty thousand blocks per day. His debts now exceeded 100,000 francs. And so the story goes—through 1919, 1920, and the first half of 1921. On July 31, 1921, he finally closed the plant, releasing his remaining ten employees and, with the collapse of his other enterprises, was left with virtually no money to his name.[16]

Everite was another building material much on Jeanneret's mind. Everite is a mixture of asbestos fibers and Portland cement rolled into sheets, usually 5 or 8 mm. thick, or molded into various shapes. Jeanneret had used it to roof his father's house in 1912. From 1918 to 1920 he devoted much energy to devising, and endeavoring to patent, new uses for Everite such as facing for doors with internal frames of wood (similar to the hollow plywood doors of today) or designing pre-formed coffers for use in pouring concrete floors. In August 1918, to his great satisfaction (personal journal, September 2, 1918), he was named "administrateur délégué" of the Société des applications de l'Everite (Eternite), yet this was a negative blessing because he spent the next eighteen months trying to regulate their affairs and finally was forced to liquidate the whole operation.

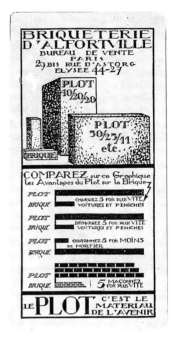

**Fig. 429.** Briqueterie d'Alfortville. Advertisement that compares the labor-saving advantages of large concrete blocks over traditional bricks. These blocks are solid, not hollow as is characteristic today.

14. Max Du Bois informed me that Jeanneret was a "bolshevik" when he moved to Paris in 1917. There is a certain contradiction here, especially as Jeanneret was usually an apolitical opportunist.

15. "Alfortville me sera peut-être une grande joie: je me sens vivre en moderne, au milieu de ce labeur des bras et des machines, dans ce concours de fleuve qui roule" (personal journal, December 2, 1917). For more on Jeanneret's idealistic fantasies concerning the business world, see his Ritter letter of October 17, 1917, as well as his personal journal for December 2, 1917, and June 13, 1918.

16. See Jeanneret's personal journal for April 4, May 6, July 9 and 26, September 2, 1918, and July 21, 1921. Although he failed in business he was businesslike in his office affairs. He conscientiously followed matters up and, once he moved to Paris and had a secretary, he left a paper trail of his every action. This included summarizing, by letter, important telephone conversations and sending, by letter, the wording of telegrams dispatched. These typed carbons are all in the FLC archives.

Whereas his interest in new materials and methods inevitably proved financially disastrous (not only for himself but also for his clients, cf. Pessac), it did strengthen his belief that modern materials called for new architectural forms, and therefore he quite self-consciously set out to lead such a movement. Unlike the French rationalists, however, he did not, at least initially, believe structural expression of new materials in and of itself was the important thing but rather the evolution of a new formal expression based on the industrial and mechanical forms that these new materials made possible. At heart, his concern was with formal, aesthetic qualities rather than any rational expression of structure.

In hindsight the most significant event of the winter of 1917–18 was not Jeanneret's activity as an architect, manufacturer, or painter, but his introduction to Amédée Ozenfant (1886–1966), who for the next seven years would become his closest friend, adviser, teacher, and collaborator.[17]

Although only a year older than Jeanneret, Ozenfant was many years ahead of him in sophistication and worldliness; he was well educated, especially in the classics but also in painting, and he had founded, in 1915, the magazine *L'Elan* which numbered among its contributors Guillaume Apollinaire, Derain, Gleizes, de la Fresnaye, Matisse, and Picasso—thus he was thoroughly immersed in the Parisian art world, which Jeanneret certainly was not.

Jeanneret was well aware of his own provincialism, and for more than a year his letters reiterate again and again his reverence for Ozenfant, in comparison to whom he felt so inadequate yet simultaneously so indebted for the privilege of being taken under his wing.[18] "In Ozenfant I have finally found a real friend" are words he repeats over and over again.

Auguste Perret, who had often mentioned Ozenfant in his letters, made the introduction at an Art et Liberté luncheon. This, apparently, was during the last weeks of 1917 because by January 23, 1918, the two were lunching together, usually at Le Mauroy, 32, rue Godot-de-Mauroy, IX arrondissement (Ozenfant lived at No. 35), a small café that existed until the late 1970s and is probably the source for the interior balcony design at the Pavillon de L'Esprit Nouveau (1925) as well as the various Unité d'Habitation.[19]

17. The most up to date scholarship on Ozenfant will be found in the exhibition catalogue by Françoise Ducros, *Amédée Ozenfant* (Saint-Quentin: Debrez, 1985). See also Susan L. Ball, *Ozenfant and Purism* (Ann Arbor: UMI Research Institute, 1981), and John Golding, *Ozenfant* (New York: Knoedler, 1973), and the previously mentioned writings of Susan Nasgaard and of Paul V. Turner (especially his excellent analysis of *Après le Cubisme,* pp. 144–55).

18. "J'ai trouvé en Ozenfant comme non révélateur. . . . Il fait plus clair en moi; je vois devant moi; j'ai traversé beaucoup d'années de confusion" (personal journal, October 21, 1918). Jeanneret records numerous such remarks in his journal.

19. Jeanneret, in his personal journal of November 6, 1917, devoted a long paragraph to the Art et

**Fig. 430.** *Still Life with Bottle, Glass, and Shell.* Summer, 1918. Pencil on paper. 26.5 × 21 cm. Undetached page 20 from Cahier 3. (FLC 4721)

Tutored by Ozenfant, Jeanneret began to think positively about Picasso and cubism although it was Matisse he admired the most. He moved his easel into Ozenfant's studio so they could paint together but, as already noted, few if any of his paintings and drawings from this period survive. His deference toward his new mentor was unbounded, at times tiresome, yet he never neglected his other Parisian friends, notably Rupert Carabin and Charles Vildrac, with whom he enjoyed discussing art, and during the summer he met Emmanuel Gondouin, whose studio he visited quite often.[20]

The war touched Jeanneret not at all, except for interfering with his visits home.

---

Liberté luncheon of November 4. He mentioned by name or occupation a half dozen of those he met and Ozenfant is not included. Therefore I assume the two met at a subsequent gathering yet well before January 23 (see personal journal, January 24, 1918). The exact date is inconsequential except for allowing us to state the precise year when they met.

20. On the domestic scene we find him reading Balzac, "Otherwise [I] eat a great deal, drink bottles of good wine and a great deal of cognac and get drunk if I feel I'm catching cold. I spend 12 francs for cognac per week (1 bottle). Moreover I smoke my pipe" (to parents, November 18, 1918; in part, I expect this represents his annoyance at his parents who worry whether their son is taking care of himself). It would be on July 1, 1920, that he took delivery of his first automobile.

Ozenfant was doing volunteer work (his health prevented military service), Du Bois was arranging transport for foodstuffs to Switzerland, and Jean-Pierre de Montmollin,[21] though Swiss, joined the French Foreign Legion in order to serve at the front, yet Jeanneret (as in World War II) did nothing to serve the cause. Only when Big Bertha started shelling Paris, in March and April, did he take note and not out of concern for his safety but rather out of amazement at the fear the shelling instilled in others. He acknowledged that he was a fatalist, in life and in business, but believed that he was born under a lucky star.[22]

Ozenfant, like many of his countrymen, fled Paris late in March, going with the family of the couturier Germaine (Poiret) Bongard to Bordeaux. Jeanneret, now on his own, continued to sketch and paint, and in a significant letter to Ritter of August 2, 1918, he summed up his activities: "I draw bottles of Médoc, coffee pots and pipes, and do this with a pencil as sharp as a needle and with the intention to create form, thence volume. And my palette is reduced to 4 colors, red-ocher and yellow, ultramarine blue and black. . . . Soon I will start working in oils and in 3 or 4 years I will be able to exhibit something."

This description perfectly fits our figure 430. A sharp lead pencil now replaces the soft lead pencil characteristic of his travel sketches, and the subject matter is reduced to a minimum. Yet the objects are still represented in real space unlike what soon occurred under purism. Compare *Nude with Tulips* (figure 414) where still-life items exist in a very different setting and with minimal concern for clarity or volume. In Ozenfant's paintings, meanwhile, bottles and books occasionally appeared by 1916, but the choice of common, everyday household objects as the subject for purist paintings seems to be Jeanneret's contribution.

A stunning exception to typical purist subject matter is represented in figure 431. This records a natural phenomenon witnessed by Jeanneret on January 24, 1916, while out painting with William Ritter near Le Landeron. Suddenly the atmosphere became virtually transparent and details were visible in the faraway Alps. Jeanneret sketched the

21. Jean-Pierre de Montmollin became Jeanneret's most intimate and trusted life-long friend, as well as banker, yet he always remained very much in the background. Although I interviewed him, he was so discreet as to offer very little useful information.

22. Comments at this time shed light on Jeanneret's personality. I quote a few. "Je le répète il y a chez moi l'inconscience du danger delà dans tout, dans les affaires aussi; je ferais un fort bon troupier. La mort ne m'effraye pas, la mienne ou celle des autres." "Il y a deux manières de regarder la vie: EN AVANT. Le reste, c'est EN ARRIÈRE" (to parents, March 16, 1918). "Et je conçois que dans la vie il est deux sortes d'hommes: les dominateurs, les toujours plus forts que tout, et les autres" (personal journal, August 22, 1918). ". . . je suis à la conquête de l'argent . . . mes instincts sont la non-sensation de la valeur de l'argent" (to Ritter, March 23, 1918). "Je suis bien trop ambitieux . . ." (to parents, March 19, 1920). And Jeanneret senior commented in his Journal: "il aime avoir des adversaires, c'est dans son tempérament" (February 4, 1921), and "C'est un bûcher formidable et qui reste sur ses positions sans concessions" (January 3, 1923).

**Fig. 431.** *Landscape.* Purist drawing signed and dated "Jeanneret 1918." Pencil on heavy paper. 29.5 × 40 cm. (FLC 2354)

scene, with lake in the foreground, in Sketchbook A1 (pp. 3–7) and two days later described his sensations, accompanied by a similar sketch, in a letter to Auguste Perret. This visual phenomenon so profoundly engraved itself on his mind that it reappears in A3, p. 213, during the summer (June?) of 1918 and then as the calm, serene, spellbinding sharp-pencil drawing seen in our illustration. Could this be the "Paysage" listed as No. 30 in the purist exhibition catalogue of November 15?

The final sentence in the previous quotation deserves our attention. When Jeanneret says he "will start working in oils" we should recall that on October 31, 1917, he said he was painting his fifth oil; therefore his more recent comment presumably refers only to his immediate campaign of painting. Thus when Ozenfant, in August, invited him to Bordeaux in order to teach him the painting of oils (personal journal, September 2, 1918), Jeanneret accepted with alacrity even though he had just spent his vacation in Brittany, including a visit to Angers. Ozenfant, in this same letter, also invited Jeanneret to exhibit with him, which soon the two would do—well short of the three or four years that Jeanneret anticipated would elapse before he was ready to show.

On September 6 Jeanneret entrained for Bordeaux, spending two weeks with Ozenfant at the coastal town of Andernos.[23] There they drew, painted, and began discussing

23. Mme Guillain-Bongard, daughter of Mme Bongard, informed me (February 25, 1976) that Ozenfant rented two rooms in the house next to theirs at Andernos where Jeanneret also stayed. The two often

the contents of a manifesto they proposed to write on art after cubism—*Après le Cubisme*. Ozenfant had already coined the word purism two years earlier in *L'Elan* (No. 10, December 1916) and he, unlike Jeanneret,[24] was quite skilled at getting things published. So, after his return to Paris in October, the two worked feverishly to complete the manuscript before the scheduled exhibition opening on November 15.[25] Jeanneret, with characteristic over-optimism, stated on October 21 that the text would be completed the following day, yet as late as November 11 they were still re-editing and polishing chapter 3. By the twentieth it was actually in press.

Jeanneret, meanwhile, had great trouble creating anything worth exhibiting, and on October 1 wrote Ritter that he had no paintings and only one drawing ready. He also confessed that "with his 33 years, Ozenfant is already 10 years ahead of me." As late as November 10 he noted (personal journal) "This week I made my first oil painting—and it will be in the exhibition." Presumably this was *La Cheminée*, of which he also exhibited an identical pencil drawing (fig. 432).

Jeanneret, like the Germans, was spared by the Armistice; the postwar celebrations provided an excuse to postpone the opening for thirty-eight days. But the catalogue, *Exposition Ozenfant & Jeanneret,* was already printed and dated November 15, so new invitations were dispatched for December 22. The catalogue, incidentally, made no mention of purism; that was the purpose of *Après le Cubisme*. The latter was announced as the first volume in a new series, "Commentaires sur l'Art et la Vie moderne" with the second volume, *Vers une Architecture,* already at the printers (but not published until 1923).[26]

Although ten works by Jeanneret were listed in the catalogue (vs. twenty by Ozenfant) only two (*La Cheminée* and *Le Livre*) were oils; the rest were either earlier works dated 1917 or drawings. In fact both artists exhibited mostly drawings, including those which were identical to their oils, thereby giving the impression that this was their

---

had meals chez Bongard where they were very much "en famille." In response to my questions she said the two were both technicians; theirs was an intellectual approach to artistic problems rather than an emotional one and this was their common bond.

24. In April 1918 Jeanneret finally announced that he had a publisher for "France ou Allemagne" as well as "La Construction des Villes." However, neither ever saw the light of day. Throughout these years, and into the twenties, he was still endeavoring to complete his "Voyage d'Orient" manuscript; this we also learn from the Ritter correspondence.

25. Ozenfant arranged the exhibition with Germaine Bongard with whom he was associated; therefore it took place in her couturier establishment at 5, rue de Penthière which was a private town house where the family lived on the upper floors. During the war, with business slack and artists in need, she often provided space for various gatherings; for the purism exhibition the space was baptized Galerie Thomas (information from Mme Guillain-Bongard).

26. Six other titles were also announced including "L'Art décoratif actuel," which Le Corbusier published in 1925 as *L'Art décoratif d'aujourd'hui,* and "Le Nombre et la Plastique," which appeared as *Le Modulor* in 1948.

**Fig. 432.** *La Cheminée* (The Mantelpiece). November 1918. Jeanneret erroneously claimed this to be his first painting; in truth it was the first *oil* painting he did not destroy. Oil on canvas. 60 × 75 cm. (FLC painting #134)

chosen medium. However, none of the illustrated works has the characteristic layered composition and flattened space normally associated with purist paintings of the early 1920s—as would be seen in the next purist exhibition held at Galerie Druet in January 1921.

Purist is a term sometimes applied to Le Corbusier's architecture of the 1920s, and while there is a certain justification for this we must remember that many of his Domino and later architectural projects (including Saintes of 1917) exhibit a number of these purist characteristics. Moreover his 1910 project for the Ateliers d'Art (see fig. 152 in Chapter 6) is closer to the objectives of purism than anything he later designed, with its emphasis on clarity and a "retour à l'ordre" based on geometric forms. One could, as Le Corbusier demonstrated by his choice of illustrations in *Oeuvre Complète*, assert that purism in architecture began in 1910 and therefore was in no way dependent upon purist painting.

The above, however, does not invalidate his statement that "The secret of my quest must be sought in my painting" (*Modulor 2*, pp. 296–97) since here he is describing the search to achieve the "poetic moment" in the evolution of a given design. No small part of this purification actually derives from classicism, as we noted at the Villa Schwob

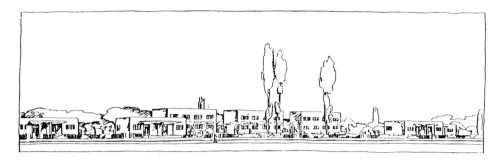

**Fig. 433.** Project: Workers' housing for J. Jourdain & Co. at Troyes. October 1, 1919. (*Oeuvre Complète,* vol. 1)

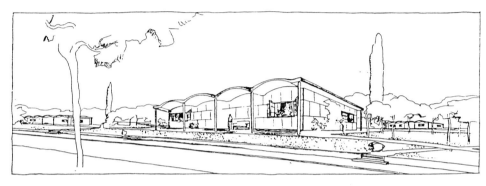

**Fig. 434.** Project: Monol houses. 1919. (*Oeuvre Complète,* vol. 1)

where he also used the golden section, regulating lines, and triangles as advocated in *Après le Cubisme* and demonstrated in his 1919 purist paintings.

His architectural projects of the next few years (he built no new buildings between 1917 and 1923) progressed in a similar vein and, with but one exception, all were for workers' housing. The first was for Jourdain & Co. at Troyes (Aube) and dated October 1, 1919 (fig. 433). This was done under the aegis of the Société d'entreprises industriel-les et d'études (SEIE) of which Jeanneret was now (since January 7, 1919) the "administrateur délégué." These are the most severe and block-like of Jeanneret's workers' houses and it is no coincidence that during the previous months he first saw Tony Garnier's *Une Cité industrielle* and met with Garnier both in Lyon and in Paris. They are his earliest designs to completely eliminate the cornice, à la Garnier, and point the way to the famous Citrohan project of 1921 (see fig. 436) as well as the corniceless houses of the 1920s. Quite surprisingly, however, the building material is listed as rough concrete rather than cement blocks such as those manufactured at Alfortville.

That same year, 1919, Jeanneret created and patented his Monol design which, like Dom-ino before it, was intended to be built "en série"—in series (fig. 434). Form, rather than structural method, was apparently the determining factor with, as Brian Taylor observed, the shallow barrel-vaulted roofs recalling Perret's work at Casablanca a few years earlier. Such roofs, however, enjoy an ancient source as can be seen at Koum, illustrated as plate 1 in Dieulafoy, *L'Art antique de la Perse* (Deuxième Partie,

**Fig. 435.** Project: Workers' housing for the Aciérie de Grand-Couronne. August/September 1920. (*Oeuvre Complète,* vol. 1)

Paris, 1884), which we previously noted was carefully studied by Jeanneret. Thereafter shallow vaults appear sporadically in his work, as at Pessac (1925), the weekend house at La Celle-Saint-Cloud (1935), and the Jaoul houses, Neuilly (1953). Oddly enough, however, he did not specify Monol when his current clients sought low-cost workers' housing.

For the glass manufacturer Saint Gobain at Thourotte (Oise), Jeanneret hoped to design 250 units of workers' housing early in 1920. His various plans restudy earlier ideas (Type E recalls Type C at Saint-Nicholas) while the double house Type B is similar to the one-storey duplexes in the Troyes perspective. Letters (FLC) reveal that he submitted these designs to a builder (J. Verdin) for pricing and learned that they were way over the client's budget.

Jeanneret fared no better with the Aciérier (steel-works) de Grand-Couronne (Seine-Maritime). His designs, dated August/September 1920, were for minimal one-storey, three-room attached houses which recall, more than anything else, his Domino serial housing of 1915 except for the absence of the second storey (fig. 435; cf. fig. 313 in Chapter 10).

His next potential commission came in October 1920 in the town of Écouen (Seine-et-Oise) where, perhaps sensing the need to make stylistic concessions, his larger, one-storey detached houses were designed with low-pitched gable roofs. Once again, however, nothing was ever built.

October 1920 also witnessed the origin of the pseudonym "Le Corbusier," which occurred in the inaugural issue of *L'Esprit Nouveau.*[27] Ozenfant, Jeanneret, and Paul Dermée (as director) founded this lively "Revue internationale d'esthétique" that, among other things, forcefully launched Jeanneret's architectural career in France.[28]

27. Concerning the origin of the pseudonym, see chapter 1, note 11. When writing on aesthetics and painting, and when painting, Jeanneret retained his own name, but in the role of architect he henceforth became Le Corbusier.

28. In 1968 I arranged for the reprinting of *L'Esprit Nouveau* through Da Capo Press in New York, which published the twenty-eight issues in eight bound volumes, thereby making this rare periodical quite widely available. That same year I also induced Da Capo to reprint Jeanneret's first book, *Etude sur le mouvement d'art décoratif en Allemagne* of 1912.

**Fig. 436.** Project: Maison "Citro-han." 1921. (*Oeuvre Complète,* vol. 1)

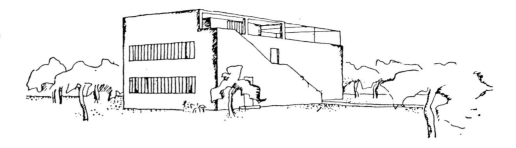

In issue no. 13 (December 1921) it published "Maison en série" illustrating many of Jeanneret's unbuilt 1914–21 housing schemes. These conclude with Maison "Citro-han," a design that many people, due to what Le Corbusier and other writers have written, assume marks the beginning of his architectural career (fig. 436).

Maison "Citrohan," with its severe rectangular form, exterior staircase, flat roof accommodating a terrace and pergola, and its whitewashed walls, reminds us, by no coincidence, of Jeanneret's sketch of the Haunted House of 1912 (fig. 273). An undeniable continuity runs through all his drawings and projects forward from 1912 to his more heralded work of the 1920s. It was also Maison "Citrohan" that led Le Corbusier to coin his famous saying, "a house is a machine for living in"(*L'Esprit Nouveau,* p. 1538), a catch phrase not necessarily aimed at minimal housing since this home boasts a maid's room and three W.C.'s.

Our discussion of Jeanneret's pre-1921 architecture would be incomplete, however, without mention of a project named for Paul Poiret (brother of Germaine Bongard). Dated 1916 in *Oeuvre Complète,* it is therein accorded a generous six drawings. Yet to properly argue the pros and cons of client, date, and locale would require several pages, so a briefer report must follow here.

Suffice to say, the project was not commissioned by Paul Poiret and may not date from 1916. Poiret was in military service during the war and his couturier business was closed. Therefore he had neither time nor money to build a palatial country house, and not until 1923–24 did his financial situation revive.[29] Also, the design is entitled "Villa

29. Mme Paul Poiret and her daughter, Mme F. de Wilde, accorded me a lengthy interview on February 24, 1976. They detailed for me the war and postwar family situation. Due to friction between Paul and his sister (who, he felt, had privately marketed some of his designs), Mme Germaine Bongard and her friends were ostracized, and this included Ozenfant. The name Edouard Jeanneret, or Le Corbusier, was unknown to Mme Poiret but she remarked that he would not have been welcome due to his friendship with Ozenfant and Bongard; nevertheless she did know and respect the name of Albert Jeanneret as a teacher of rhythmic dancing.

Being friends of the Perrets, the Poirets asked Claude Perret to design their country house at Mézy, but Paul was not pleased with the design, so he turned to Mallet-Stevens. Construction began in 1924 but work was ultimately abandoned and the property sold because of the concurrent financial strain of building a pavilion for the exhibition of 1925.

au bord de la mer 1916,"[30] yet the villa that Poiret commenced in 1924 was at Mézy near Meulan on the Seine and certainly not by the sea. For whom the villa was intended remains a mystery, but Jeanneret, never averse to wooing potential clients with seductive drawings, may have offered this as his calling card in seeking a commission, or merely wished to identify the design with a famous personality.[31]

Our dialogue on painting and architecture may have convinced the reader that such activities dominated Jeanneret's existence—yet nothing could be further from the truth. By paraphrasing a typical letter (to his parents, January 24/29, 1920) we may provide a more balanced picture of a week in the life of Ch. E. Jeanneret: It's Saturday, I'm back from Lapalisse, Bordeaux, and Toulouse where I was trying to negotiate a deal worth sixteen million francs. Sunday night I'll leave for the Dordogne to study a lignite stratum, the exploitation of which would require establishing a company backed by five million. It's the weekend now so I'll spend these days painting. Architecture is slowly reviving; I have a command to study a housing development of 250 units for Saint Gobain. By contrast Everite is in great difficulty and Alfortville is a constant worry—and to make matters worse the factory was inundated by the floods at New Year's. Pierre Jeanneret has arrived to study at the Ecole des Beaux Arts.[32] The Ballets Russes, which is sensational, played last night and Albert enjoyed his first opportunity to fully appreciate the mastery of Stravinsky.[33] Albert, Ozenfant, and I usually dine together each evening. My health is excellent; I'm thriving.

Turning back a year, to January 1919, we find Jeanneret entering this most hectic phase of his business career. He was appointed managing director of the Société d'entreprises industrielles et d'études (SEIE) on January 7, 1919, with its provisional capital-

30. In *Vers une architecture* (1923) and *Creation Is a Patient Search* (1960) Le Corbusier dates the villa 1921. I think 1921–22 would be a safe bet. The only evidence in favor of 1916 are two letters to Du Bois, one undated (but written during the construction of La Scala in 1916): "on m'annonce une construction au bord de la mer" and one dated July 28, 1916, speaking of his work: "En plus une villa au bord de la mer dans les Maures."

31. The only drawing at the FLC perhaps created with Poiret in mind is FLC 31441 because the building is situated on a river. This, however, is a different building than that shown in "Villa au bord de la mer" drawing nos. 30280, 30281, and 14711.

32. Jeanneret's initial impression of his cousin and future partner was less than favorable: "Pierre Jeanneret est arrivé, pour entrer aux Beaux Arts comme architecte! . . . Je demeure stupéfait de l'apathie de ce garçon de 23 ans, d'une nature réfléchie bien entendu, mais si peu personnel. . . . Lui commence ses études et ne sait pas quelle direction leur donner." Following his academic studies and a two-year apprenticeship under the brothers Perret, he became Edouard's partner for eighteen years.

33. Jeanneret was most enthusiastic about the music of Stravinsky, who was only five years his senior yet already of great renown. He had attended the Ballets Russes production of *The Fire Bird* in May 1917 and the same autumn wrote Igor Stravinsky asking for the score of his latest work. The postcard reply, dated Morges, October 8, 1917 (FLC), makes excuses; Jeanneret, apparently, was helping to organize some type of benefit concert.

ization of 250,000 francs. Under its aegis he founded subsidiaries such as Industries de l'alimentation that concerned refrigeration. "My position as administrateur délégué completely transforms my career" he wrote to his parents on May 9, 1919, adding that "I soon hope to have all [the money] that is necessary to totally liberate me from the material worries of life." Thereafter he intended to paint.

Throughout this time Max Du Bois remained Jeanneret's loyal and supportive friend. Regularly they lunched together, discussing affairs of business. Once, learning of Ritter's financial problems, he generously dispatched a thousand Swiss francs, saying only that he wished to buy a few watercolors—a magnanimous gesture that touched Jeanneret very deeply. "Du Bois is for me a very devoted and charming friend, one passionately fond of numbers and consequently an admirable guide for me; I owe him a votive candle as my patron saint" (to parents, January 9, 1919).

This same letter mentions Renaissance des Cités, an organization with which Jeanneret was involved and currently was sitting on its "Commission technique." Whether because of this, or his ongoing concern for abattoirs, he arranged to interview (July 7, 1919) Edouard Herriot, the great mayor (1905–55) of Lyon, whom he described as the most magnificent personage he had ever met, "a tribune of truly Roman magnitude." During the same trip he saw Tony Garnier several times (to parents, July 8, 1919).

When his uncle, Henri Jeanneret, himself a highly successful industrialist, came to Paris in May, he reported that his nephew, though in fine health, had undertaken far more work than he could properly handle (father's journal, May 20, 1919), an assessment apparently borne out by Edouard's ensuing financial collapse.

Edouard stated that one consequence of his busy schedule was abandoning, in January 1919, the writing of his personal journal which he sent to William Ritter for editorial comment. Indeed, life had become more hectic, yet this discontinuance occurred so soon after publication of *Après le Cubisme* that I suspect the real reason is that Jeanneret was changing writing masters. The long, flowing sentences advocated by Ritter had now been rejected, just as Ritter's watercolor technique had been replaced by Ozenfant's oils. Jeanneret had a new mentor.

Another major worry for Jeanneret was the future of his parent's home. What with Albert's move to Paris in October 1918 and his father's failing eyesight (at age 63, in December 1918 he could no longer read or work and was forced to close his shop)— not to mention the faulty and expensive central heating system in the house—moving into smaller, warmer quarters became essential.

Edouard was convinced, as I stated in Chapter 9, that the villa was worth over 100,000 Swiss francs plus 30,000 for the forest behind, not to mention the value of the furnishings. Yet without consulting him further, his father listed the house (June 25, 1919) and sold it for 60,000 under conditions that were risky to say the least. Even prior to the October transfer date the new owner defaulted on his initial payment (and the Jeannerets, not the bank, held the 6 percent mortgage) and that was only the beginning. By August 1921 their loss stood at 34,047, and finally the banks, also holding huge bad loans, attached the house for 270,000 francs! The Jeannerets finally repossessed and resold (December 8, 1922) with their total loss in excess of 25,000 on the original sale price. Meanwhile they lived frugally in a small, four-room rented house at Châbles-sur-Blonay near Vevey where they enjoyed a superb view of Lake Geneva and the mountains, and thrived in the warmer, sunny climate.

The villa's sale brought Edouard and his revered friend to La Chaux-de-Fonds for their August holidays. They stayed twelve days (August 23–September 4, 1919) but Jeanneret never found time to visit William Ritter who was at Les Brenets a few kilometers away. Ritter, understandably, was deeply wounded by this offense especially since Jeanneret had plenty of time to spend with Ozenfant, whom he escorted all around. They stayed at the Villa Jeanneret-Perret (see fig. 251 in Chapter 9) and also visited the Villa Schwob, concerning which Ozenfant soon wrote his article, under the pseudonym Julien Caron, for *L'Esprit Nouveau* (no. 6, pp. 679–704). They also traveled to Châbles to check out the parents' future home, and were favorably impressed. Ozenfant was tremendously popular with Edouard's parents, and with Edouard and Albert he returned the following summer (1920) when all three stayed in the little house at Châbles.[34]

That autumn Edouard's business prospects rapidly deteriorated, and his father observed (September 25, 1920) that for the first time since his son moved to Paris he seemed depressed. Gradually the postwar economic crisis deepened. "I await my destiny which depends not upon me, but on fate" he wrote December 15, a remark that left his mother in tears.

Two weeks later he answered his parents' frantic questions. "I'm losing a great deal of money, that's true. But my life has never been more replete than now. You know I'm not the type to lie down and quit. If a storm today sweeps my business away it destroys money and nothing more. I feel pity for those who are attached to money! This crisis may actually improve life for me by allowing me to undertake activities more appropriate to my skills, and which are the result of my own initiatives."[35]

As the months passed, Edouard liquidated his failing commercial and industrial affairs. In July, as previously noted, the Briqueterie d'Alfortville was finally closed. Dur-

---

34. After these two visits Jeanneret senior noted of his son: "notre fils est un homme de grande volonté, d'un optimisme tenace." (September 4, 1919), and "Il est toujours plein d'énergie et d'optimisme, mais il se fatigue à cette vie, son oeil ne s'améliore pas." (August 24, 1920). The eye problem, which in 1905 led him to abandon engraving in favor of architecture, was also reported the previous year: He is "en bonne santé sauf l'oeil gauche qui est endommagé et pour lequel il est en traitement" (August 24, 1919).

35. Jeanneret senior commented, after receiving this letter of December 29, 1920, "une lettre d'Edouard qui annonce de grosses pertes d'argent—ce qui ne paraît pas l'affliger autrement (un drôle de garçon) et se dit plein de courage pour suivre une autre destinée: les arts, la peinture et *l'Esprit Nouveau*" (January 5, 1921).

ing the previous four years only his architectural office, which sometimes employed ten men, had registered a reasonable profit, but this he had reinvested in his other affairs. *L'Esprit Nouveau* was his current enthusiasm, at least once the requisite paintings were finished and installed at the Galerie Druet for the second purism exhibition that he shared with Ozenfant from January 22 to February 5, 1921.

Actually, his financial collapse merely meant continuing with what had fascinated him since childhood: the visual arts of painting and architecture combined with writing. Therefore the transition was hardly worth noting. He simply gave up entrepreneurship and abandoned the idea of being a millionaire living off a steady income. Instead, architecture must provide the wherewithal to paint. Therefore one of his first acts, once he acquired his freedom, was to take his long-postponed trip to Rome (August 1921).

Upon returning to France in September he obtained his initial architectural commission in Paris—restoring and remodeling the house and gardens at the Villa Berque in Auteuil. Soon thereafter Albert would write his parents: "Edouard is fine, he is working with Pierre [Jeanneret] on the villa Bercq [*sic*] which they are restoring; it is the first architectural work by Le Corbusier."[36]

One episode still needs to be concluded: on December 17, 1924, Ritter wrote Jeanneret: "Concerning your recent rupture with Ozenfant, I cannot say I'm sorry. Initially I was very jealous—for you. One should never collaborate." Nevertheless, Jeanneret's break with Ozenfant, after seven years of inseparable friendship, did not result in his reestablishing the once intimate relationship with William Ritter. At the age of thirty-seven, Jeanneret, who outwardly was such a tower of strength yet inwardly was so insecure, finally felt able to stand alone.

36. Albert to parents, March 26, 1922. Pierre Jeanneret was now working part time for Le Corbusier.

# JEANNERET'S PUBLICATIONS

## *1910–1919*

1910  Jeanneret, Ch.-E., "Art et Utilité publique," *L'Abeille: Supplément du National suisse,* no. 14, May 15, 1910, p. 1.

1911  "En Orient," *La Feuille d'Avis de La Chaux-de-Fonds.* Between July 20 and November 25, 1911, *Feuille d'Avis* serially printed approximately the first half of the articles that subsequently (1966) were published as the book *Voyage d'Orient.*

1912  *Etude sur le mouvement d'art décoratif en Allemagne,* La Chaux-de-Fonds, 1912. Reprinted by Da Capo Press, New York, 1968.

1912  *"Nouvelle Section" de l'Ecole d'Art: Prospectus,* La Chaux-de-Fonds, 1912.

1913  "Le monument à la bataille des peuples," *La Feuille d'Avis,* July 1, 1913.

1913  "Hellerau," *La Feuille d'Avis,* July 4, 1913.

1914  "La Maison suisse," *Etrennes helvétiques: Almanach illustré,* Paris, Dijon, La Chaux-de-Fonds, 1914, pp. 33–39.

1914  *Un Mouvement d'Art à La Chaux-de-Fonds à propos de la Nouvelle Section de l'Ecole d'Art,* La Chaux-de-Fonds, n.d. [1914].

1914  *Un Concours de dessins: Rapport du Jury sur l'examen des 1450 dessins,* La Chaux-de-Fonds, n.d. [1914]. Also published in the *Bulletin Bimensuel* of L'Oeuvre, nos. 5, 6 (June 19 and July 10), 1914, pp. 17–22.

1914　"En Allemagne," *L'Art de France,* première année, nos. 9–10, April-May 1914, pp. 347–95, 457–73. This was a reprint of all but the first 14 pages of his 1912 book *Etude sur le mouvement d'art décoratif en Allemagne.*

1914　"Le Renouveau dans l'architecture," *L'Oeuvre,* première année, no. 2, 1914, pp. 33–37. The first part of this article was previously published in L'Oeuvre's *Bulletin Bimensuel,* première année, no. 3, April 3, 1914, pp. 9–10.

1915　"L'exposition Léon Perrin," *Le National suisse,* December 9, 1915. The article is signed "D'un collaborateur."

1916　"L'exposition de Mlle Goering," *La Feuille d'Avis,* November 25, 1916.

1916　"L'exposition Woog, Schwob, Zysset, Humbert," *La Feuille d'Avis,* December 2–4, 1916.

1917　"Une idée française, une réalisation allemande," *Le Petit messager des arts et des artistes et des industries d'art,* Paris, 1917.

1918　*Après le cubisme* (co-authored with Amédée Ozenfant), Paris, 1918.

1918　"Rapport de la sous-commission de l'enseignement [de L'Oeuvre]," *Les Arts*
–19　*français: Bulletin du Comité Central Technique des Arts Appliqués et des Comités Régionaux,* no. 24, 1918, pp. 87–92; no. 25, 1919, pp. 1–8; no. 26, 1919, pp. 9–12; no. 27, 1919, pp. 13–14.

# INDEX

All references, except for color plates, are to pages; boldface indicates principal entries. The letter *n* after a number indicates a footnote, the letter *f* a figure. Buildings are listed by architect and by city; those by Jeanneret are also listed by name.

71, 86–87, 192–97, 359; Nouvelle Section, 31, 357, 359–67. *See also* Ecole d'art, Jeanneret at; Ecole d'Art, work of L'Eplattenier's students

Ecole d'art, Jeanneret at: admitted, 15, 25–26; contract signed, 24, **26;** first year (1902–3), 28–31; second year (1903–4), 32–36; third year (1904–5), 36–39, 42; fourth year (1905–6), 43–87; fifth year (1906–7), 87–90. *See also* Cours Supérieur

Ecole d'art, work of L'Eplattenier's students: Chapelle Indépendante (Cernier-Fontainemelon), 72, **87–90,** 88f; Crematorium, 87, **193,** 194f; Hirsch Pavilion, observatory at Neuchâtel, 87, 90, 193; Matthey-Doret music room, 86–87, 86f; Moser living room, 30 bis rue Grenier, 195; Post Office (great hall), 87, 90, **195;** Salle de Musique, Buvette (Foyer), 344; Schwob veranda design, 87n, 193; Union Chrétienne de Jeunes Gens (Beau Site), 45–51, 46f–51f; Villa Sandoz, interior, 87, 193

Ecole du Jura, 90

Ecouen housing project, 498

Eleusis, 286–87

Ema, Chartreuse du Val d.', **105–7,** 106f, 107f, 197, 264, 301–2, 301f

Endroits, Les, 41

Eppenhausen: Cuno house (Behrens), 240–41; Schröder house (Behrens), 241

*Esprit Nouveau, L',* founding of, 498

éternite (everite), 310, 326, **490,** 500

*Etude sur le mouvement d'art décoratif en Allemagne,* 25, 223, 244, 247, **250–51,** 357

Evard, André, 31, 45n, 72, 87

## F

Fallet, Louis, 37, **71,** 126

Fallet, Villa, color plate I, 27, 45, 50, 52f, 55, 56f, 63, **71-85** 73f, 87, 113, 144n

farmhouses, **5–6,** 183, 185–89, 186f–89f, **227–28,** 228f, 462, 463f, 466, 481

Farrère, Claude, 257

Favre-Jacot, Villa, color plate VI, 87, 310, 329–41, 330f–41f; construction, 339; interior, 337, 338f; plan, 337, 330f–34f; sources of design, 331n, 340–41, 342f

Firminy, chapel, 5, 190, 191f

Fischer, Theodor, 211, 213–14, 213f, 312, 367

Florence, **99–110,** 300; Duomo, 109–10; Or San Michele, color plate II, 99, 101–3, 103f–4f, 461–62; Palazzo Vecchio, 99, 100f, 101

Foville, Alfred de, 389–91, 482

"France ou Allemagne," 357n, 409–11, 464, 495n

Fribourg, 91, 463f

## G

Gallé, Emile, 68n

Gallet, Louis, 72

Galluzzo, Chartreuse de. *See* Ema

Garchizy, abattoir project, 487, 489f

Garnier, Tony, 149n, 371–72, 391, 408–**9,** 497; Garnier house, Saint Rambert, 409, 463

Gaudí, Antonio, 27, 48

Gauthier, Maximilien, 5n, 83n

Gigy, René, 26, 45n

Gobineau, Comte de, 238, 244, 251

Gondouin, Emmanuel, 492

*Grammar of Ornament. See* Jones, Owen

Grand-Couronne, workers housing project, 498, 498f

Grasset, Eugène, 67n, 68, **158**–59, 255, 353, **362, 363,** 364f, 367

Gropius, Walter, 239, 371, 449

Grünewald, Matthias, 369–71

Guinand, Sully and Elisa, 8, 15, 40, 185

## H

Hadrian's villa. *See* Tivoli

Harder, 193n

"Haunted House" (old farmhouse), 342, 343f, 466, 499

Heaton, Clément II, 25

Hellerau, 235, 245, 346–47, 369; Deutsche Vereinigte Werkstätten factory, 235

Hénard, Eugène, 404

Hoffmann, Josef, 118–20, 122, 148, 242, 251n, 260, 312; Cabaret Fledermaus 118, 120, **148,** 149f; Purkersdorf Convalescent Home, 118, 120; Wiener Werkstätte sales room, 118, 259–60, 261f

Houriet, Louis, 72, 83f, 87, 193n, 195

Humbert, Charles, 398, 453

# I

Imphy, 474

# J

Janet, Charles, 389, 482

Janson, Hermann, 220, 229n

Jaquemet, Villa, color plate IV, 126–30, 135, **138–44,** 139f–46f

Jaques-Dalcroze, Emile, 225, 235, 371

Jeanneret, Albert (brother), 7n, **9–16,** 36n, 41–43, 91, 125, 152, 177, **180,** 182, 228, 235, 245, 274, 326f, 354, **381,** 474, 500

**Jeanneret, Charles-Edouard:** ancestors, 8; as architect (*see* Jeanneret, Charles-Edouard, buildings and projects *and individual entries*); birth, 9; childhood, 3 and passim; as entrepreneur, 488–90, 500–502; eyesight defect, **36,** 42, 43, 502n; folk art, 255, 264f, 282–83; ideal, the search for an, 151–53, 159, 171, 172, 173, 179, 192, 238, 252, 256, 281; Langage de Pierre exhibit, 97, 107, 248, 266, 268f, 277, 278f, 284, 285f, 292, 346n, 372, 464; laws (that aid design), 68n, 69, 147, 202, 206, 255, 281–82, 352; letter to L'Eplattenier of November 22, 1908, 153–54, 192, 238; lithographs by, 479n; module/modulor, 70, 101, 444; parents, **7** and passim, 10f, 11f, 18f, 39–43, 180–82, 225, 227, 245n, 274, 405–7 (*see also* Jeanneret-Gris, Georges Edouard; Jeanneret-Perret, Marie); personality, 13, 42, 96n, 153–54, **172–74, 218, 233–34,** 239, 289, 353, 493, 502; photographs/drawings of, 10f, 83f, 91f, 155f, 181f, 225f, 236f, 283f, 309f, 326f, 472f (*see also frontispiece*); piano lessons, 12; publications (*see* Jeanneret, Charles-Edouard, publications *and individual entries*); religious training, 20, **41;** socialist and syndicalist views, 215; watchcase (design of), 64–67, 66f, 83; as teacher (at Ecole d'art), 359–64, 361f–62f; tracés régulateurs, 70, 362, 444–49, 446f–47f, 497; unit system, 63, 64, 362, 366f

—addresses at which he lived: 38 rue de la Serre, 10, 10f; 17 rue Fritz-Courvoisier, 10; 46 rue Leopold-Robert, 10, 11f, 40; 8 rue Jacob-Brandt, 7, 16n, 40; Le Couvent, 28 rue de Couvent, 308, 309f; 30B rue de la Montagne (Villa Jeanneret-Perret), 308; 20 rue Jacob, Paris, 474

—furniture design studied: at Ecole, 36; in Germany, 222, 241–42; in Paris, 345, 345f–47f, 351, 392–96

—furniture designed: for Villa Fallet, 79, 81f; for Paul, Georges and Jules Ditisheim, 348–49, 350f; for Herman and Ernest-Albert Ditisheim, 392–96, 392f–95f; for Anatole Schwob, 350–51, 396f–98f; for Moïse Schwob, 397, 397f–98f; for Salomon Schwob, 351–52; for Villa Jeanneret-Perret, 322f, 399–400, 401f

—as painter (vs. architectural drawings): in 1911, 284n; in 1912–14, **372–77,** 373f–76f; in 1914–16, 464–67, 465f–67f; in 1917–18, **472–80,** 478f–81f; in 1918, **493–96,** 492f–96f

—schooling: Froebel kindergarten, 10, 20; primary school, 20; secondary school, 13, 20–21; Ecole d'art (*see* Ecole d'art, Jeanneret at)

**Jeanneret, Charles-Edouard, buildings and projects.** *See* Banque Cantonale de Neuchâtel; Beck, Arnold; Challuy; Château d'eau; "Citrohan" house project; Ditisheim, Paul; Dom-ino; Ecouen housing project; Fallet, Villa; Favre-Jacot, Villa; Garchizy; Grand-Couronne; Jaquemet, Villa; Jeanneret-Perret, Villa; Jourdain & Co.; Klipstein, Villa; Le Couvent; Le Moulinet; L'Isle Jourdain; "Maison bouteille"; "Monol" project; Moser living room; Pont Butin; "Project F"; Saintes; Saint Gobain; Saint-Nicholas-d'Alicrmont; Scala, La; Schwob, Anatole, Villa; Schwob, Anatole, fumoir; Schwob, Raphy; Stotzer, Villa; Union Chrétienne de Jeunes Gens; Zbinden

**Jeanneret, Charles-Edouard, publications.** See *Après le Cubisme;* "Art et Utilité publique"; *Concours de dessins;* "Construction des Villes"; *Esprit Nouveau; Etude sur le mouvement d'art décoratif en Allemagne;* "France ou Allemagne"; "Maison suisse"; *Mouvement d'Art à la Chaux-de-Fonds; Nouvelle Section de l'Ecole d'Art;* "Rapport de la sous-commission de l'enseignement de l'Oeuvre"; "Renouveau dans l'architecture"; *Urbanisme; Voyage d'Orient*

Jeanneret-Gris, Georges Edouard (father), **7** and passim, 9, 10f, 18f, 15–19, 36, 39–43, 91, 245n, 294, 354, 405–6

Jeanneret-Gris, origin of family name, 7–8

Pont Butin (competition design), **382–83,** 382f

Post Office (competition design), 31n, 44, 54f, 55

Potsdam: Sansouci, 222–23, 236

"Project F," 411–14, 412f–13f

Provensal, Henry, 27, 58–58, **60–71,** 172, 197, 255, 282

purism, 20n, 479, 493, 495, 496, 503; in architecture, 496

Puvis de Chavannes, Pierre, *176,* 245

# R

"Rapport de la sous-commission de l'enseignement de l'Oeuvre," 355, 357

Ravenna, 110–12, 111f

Rembrandt van Rijn, 301

Renan, Ernest, **172–74, 282**

"Renouveau dans l'architecture, Le," 355–56

Richard, Daniel Jean, 16

Riemerschmid, Richard, 235, 369

Ritter, William, **217,** 228, 258n, 259, 263, 289, 302, 347, 376, 400–**401,** 407, 464–66, 467f, 501, 502, 503

Rodin, Auguste, 113, 114n, 115

Rome, **294–95,** 295f–98f, 503; Baths of Caracalla, 295f; Villa Lante (Giulio Romano), 296, 298f; St. Peter's, 295–96

Rowe, Colin, 459n, 461

Rüegg, Arthur, 400n

Ruskin, John, 63, 68–**69,** 72, 98, 101, **104,** 108, 114, 123, 179n

# S

Saint Gobain, housing project, 498

Saintes, project for worker's housing, 475, 476, 477f

Saint-Nicholas-d'Aliermont, worker's housing, **481–85,** 482f–86f

Salbris, La Saulot (Perret), 161–65, 161f–63f

Sauvage, Henri, 51n, 158, 449, 462

Scala, La, cinema, 55, 414–24, 416f–22f; sources for design, 421–24, 423f–24f

Schaltenbrand, Eugene, 30–31

Schinkel, Karl Friedrich, 240, 244, **341**

Schneider, Charles, 155, 219

Schneider, Juste, **382–84, 388,** 473

Schuré, Edouard, 70, 114, 123, 358

Schwob, Anatole, 350–51, 397, 412, **425**

Schwob, Anatole, fumoir, 350–51, 397, 396f–98f, 425, 429

Schwob, Anatole, Villa, color plates IX, X, 50, 408, **424–63,** 502; construction, 426–28, 448f, 449; contract, 426; design, scheme I, 429–33, 430f; design, scheme II, 433–36, 432f–36f; design, scheme III, 429, 433–38, 437f, 442f–43f; facade panel, 427n, 459; floor plan, 426, 431–32, 440f–41f; interior 449–57, 453f–57f; lawsuit, 425–29, 433–34; modifications of 1917, 439; proportional systems, 444–46, 446f–47f; sources for design, 428, 458–63, 459f–63f

Schwob, Camille (Mme Anatole Schwob), 452, 454

Schwob, Raphy, library, **397–98,** 399f, 425

Schwob, Salomon, 351–52

Schwob, Moïse, 397, 397f–98f

Segantini, 35–36

Seidl, Emanuel von: Brakl house, 226, 227f, **231–** 32, 233f; International Exhibition, Brussels, 235n

Sekler, Patricia, 28n, 63n, 65n, 114

Siena, 107–8, 108f–9f

Signac, Paul, 276–77

Sitte, Camillo, **200–**206, 213–14, 216, 219, 238n, 403

slaughterhouse. *See* abattoir

Société d'applications du beton armé (SABA), **473–**74

Société d'applications industrielles, 473

Société d'entreprises industrielles et d'études (SEIE), 473, 488, 497, 500–501

Société nouvelle du froid industriel, 485

Soutter, Louis, 8n

Stemolak, Karl, **121,** 128, 150, 261

Stotzer, Villa, color plate III, 73f, 79, **126–37,** 132f–37f

Stravinsky, Igor, 500n

Stück, Franz von, 115, 459–60

Sullivan, Louis, 348, 423, 424f

# T

Taine, Hippolyte, 98, 257

Tavannes: Chapallaz studio, 85, 85f; Villa Sandoz, 87, 193